What people are saying about
WHAT DOES IT MEAN TO BE WHITE IN AMERICA?

"These deeply honest personal stories examine the effect and affect of being white–which for so many years has meant ignorance or denial of how racism benefits and forges our own Caucasian identity. Reading this important collection, I am reminded of how processing whiteness is a journey–although we may all be at different points of discourse, it is still critical to enter the conversation. May this book get people talking."

—Jodi Picoult, *New York Times* bestselling author of
LEAVING TIME and SMALL GREAT THINGS

"The conversations about race in the U.S. have been unnecessarily one-sided and unfairly the burden of people of color. Without the white perspective, indeed white engagement, the struggle for change or even dialogue becomes even more challenging. WHAT DOES IT MEAN TO BE WHITE IN AMERICA? offers a long-overdue response that aims to complete the politicized discourse with this varied collection of exploratory essays that moves beyond expressions of guilt and admissions of privilege. The tones range from moving to provocative, from emotional to intellectual, but their common mission is to break away from apathetic silence and to help examine one the most charged issues affecting this country today. This is a timely and vital anthology."

—Rigoberto González, writer, book critic, award-winning poet and
the author of OUR LADY OF THE CROSSWORD and MARIPOSA U

"WHAT DOES IT MEAN TO BE WHITE IN AMERICA? captures the expression of a wide spectrum of voices and locations along the path toward greater white awareness and racial justice. The collection speaks to the varied tapestry of white experience and the ties of deep structural privilege. It promises to move each reader further down the path."

—Jacqueline Battalora, professor of sociology and
criminal justice and author of BIRTH OF A WHITE NATION

"WHAT DOES IT MEAN TO BE WHITE IN AMERICA? is a must read by all. This collection of personal narratives provides varied perspectives about being white, white privilege and other counter points that need to be said and read. We tend to see and hear only one side of the discussion about white folks, now it's their turn to make their voices heard. After reading these personal narratives, I believe this book is on track to become a best seller, but more importantly, it will generate discussions and a much needed dialogue about race, and a catalyst for positive change in this country. This may be hopeful thinking, but hope is always a good thing."

—Andrew P. Jackson (Sekou Molefi Baako)
Activist Librarian and Adjunct Lecturer

WHAT DOES IT MEAN TO BE WHITE IN AMERICA?

WHAT DOES IT MEAN TO BE WHITE IN AMERICA?
BREAKING THE WHITE CODE OF SILENCE
A COLLECTION OF PERSONAL NARRATIVES

EDITED BY
GABRIELLE DAVID AND SEAN FREDERICK FORBES

INTRODUCTION BY DEBBY IRVING
WITH AN AFTERWORD BY TARA BETTS

2LP EXPLORATIONS IN DIVERSITY

NEW YORK
www.2leafpress.org

P.O. Box 4378
Grand Central Station
New York, New York 10163-4378
editor@2leafpress.org
www.2leafpress.org

2LEAF PRESS
is an imprint of the
Intercultural Alliance of Artists & Scholars, Inc. (IAAS),
a NY-based nonprofit 501(c)(3) organization that promotes
multicultural literature and literacy.
www.theiaas.org

Edited by: Gabrielle David and Sean Frederick Forbes
Copy edited by: Carolina Fung Feng, Adam Wier, Erick Piller and Deborah Mashibini-Prior

Cover art, book design and layout: Gabrielle David

FOR MORE INFORMATION ABOUT THIS BOOK,
VISIT WWW.WHITEINAMERICA.ORG

2LP EXPLORATIONS IN DIVERSITY
Series Editor: Sean Frederick Forbes

Library of Congress Control Number: 2015913482
ISBN-13: 978-1-940939-48-3 (Paperback)
ISBN-13: 978-1-940939-49-0 (eBook)

10   9   8   7   6   5   4   3   2   1

Published in the United States of America

First Edition | First Printing

The publisher wishes to thank its editorial team, Carolina Fung Feng, Adam Wier, Erick Piller and Deborah Mashibini-Prior; and Rachel Hobble for handling social media marketing for the book.

2LEAF PRESS books are available for sale on most online retailers in the U.S., U.K., Canada and Australia. Books are also available to the trade through distributors Ingram and YBP Library Services. For more information, contact sales@2leafpress.org.

DEDICATION

This book is dedicated to all of those who fight for social justice, civil rights and humanity, and who dare to engage in honest conversations.

And to James Baldwin, who envisioned it.

"It bears terrifying witness to what happened to everyone who got here, and paid the price of the ticket. The price was to become "white." No one was white before he/she came to America. It took generations and a vast amount of coercion, before this became a white country."

—James Baldwin, "On Being White and Other Lies"
Essence Magazine, April 1984

CONTENTS

■ ■ ■

"I know that people can be better than they are. We are capable of bearing a great burden, once we discover that the burden is reality and arrive where reality is."

—James Baldwin, *The Fire Next Time* (1963)

■ ■ ■

Gabrielle David and
Sean Frederick Forbes

The Making of "What Does it Mean to Be White in America?"

WHAT DOES IT MEAN TO BE WHITE IN AMERICA? was a moment of creative insight due to the escalating racial tensions we've experienced lately that has collided with the constant stream of ideas that flow in one's unconscious mind. It's not really so much an original concept, but it's a question that's been around for hundreds of years waiting to be asked and answered honestly. In fact, until recently, it was a question primarily addressed by race scholars and anti-racist activists until Barack Obama became president, and then the term "post-racial" came along and changed everything.

As it turns out, post-racial America was nothing more than a myth. Such wishful thinking led to a denial of what race relations in America has been all along, it has not gone away, but merely "festered like a sore." When people say racism has gotten worse during the Obama presidency (alluding that somehow it is the president's fault), what's not readily admitted is that a whole lot of people were incensed when an African American man became president of a white majority led country. No surprise, really. It simply proves that our racial biases are not only deeply ingrained into our nation's history, but also into the fabric of ourselves.

"I think about being black every single day, prepared to defend myself from some form of microaggression. If a day goes by when I don't think about being black (which by the way is exhausting in itself) and just think of myself as a human being, there will always be that one person who will kill my glee and go out of their way to remind me that I am just that. Black. African American. Minority. Different. Ethnic. Or something less than that. And because I 'speak well' or appear 'informed or educated' I am suspect, because I don't fit into that person's idea of how a person with dark skin should be. When this happens, after I kick myself for letting my guard down, I have to decide whether to defend myself, or pretend it doesn't bother me and move on."

— Gabrielle

"I grew up in a predominantly African American community in which I was coined 'the light-skin kid with good hair.' I was often asked 'What are you?' as in what is my racial and/or ethnic makeup. I'd respond by saying that I was mixed, which was what my grandparents and mother told me, but they were never specific about this mixture. As a teenager, I began to say that I was black. I am often mistaken as being biracial, white and black specifically. In my first few years in college, I began to tell people that I was Latino, Colombian in particular. Later on, I began to say that I was Afro-Caribbean. Then I had those snarky moments when I would tell people that I was simply racially ambiguous. I am often mistaken for Egyptian, Israeli, or Dominican. My full name, at times, is equally confounding since it doesn't sound Spanish like my parents' names (Hermes Delano, Teresa Mercedes). I now identify as a gay American man of color, specifically Afro-Latino, but the truth of the matter is that all I have experienced is evidence of my diasporic family history. My racial and ethnic background is complex, layered and vast and cannot be categorized neatly into any one box."

— Sean

A big part of the problem is that discussions on race usually appear as a somewhat one-sided concern from people of color, especially black people, because white people rarely think about race, unless it directly affects them. As a result, their perception of race is somewhat unrealistic. We're not referring to extreme white racists who unabashedly express their feelings about race and white supremacy, but rather, white people who are our neighbors, friends, and colleagues who frequently avoid meaningful discussions about race for fear of making a comment that might be interpreted as inappropriate or racist, or dismiss the conversation altogether because in their minds, racism no longer exists. This constant avoidance creates a debilitating silence that hinders one from engaging directly with pervasive issues of race.

This year alone, racism and intolerance have become huge topics of debate among people of all hues. The Whiteness Project[1] and *The New York Times*' "A Conversation on Race"[2] are just two examples of how people are tackling this difficult and uncomfortable topic. As writers, editors, and lovers of literature who publish multicultural works by diverse writers, we wanted to contribute to this engagement by publishing this book, a collection of narratives from white people who are willing to break this silence. Why? Because sharing stories is an endeavor that often builds empathy and leads to changed attitudes and actions. We felt that if white people shared their stories, then readers of all ethnicities would listen carefully about how they are unpacking whiteness, as James Baldwin and many others did before him, as a means of trying to understand what others feel and experience to help us understand ourselves. This is this book. Indeed, before we advertised the call for personal narratives, we were reminded of Audre Lorde's statement, "Your silence will not protect you,"[3] and that became the guiding mantra for *What Does It Mean to Be White in America?* What follows is our story about this book, how we feel about ourselves and about race, and why we think this book is an important contribution towards our country's discourse on race.

---

1   The Whiteness Project, produced in association with American Documentary, POV and Two Tone Productions, 2014. http://www.whitenessproject.org.

2   *The New York Times:* Op-Docs, "A Conversation on Race." Op-Docs is a forum for short, opinionated documentaries, produced with creative latitude by independent filmmakers and artists. http://www.nytimes.com/interactive/projects/your-stories/conversations-on-race.

3   Audre Lorde, "The Transformation of Silence into Language and Action." *Sister Outsider: Essays and Speeches by Audre Lorde* (Berkeley CA: Crossing Press, 1984), 40-44.

The Story Behind the Book

RACE HAS BECOME A GROWING frustration among black and white Americans, as well as Asian Americans, Native Americans, Latinos, Arab Americans, and other people of color. Blacks seem to have grown weary of explaining why they feel the way they do, and of being told that their feelings are not currently relevant in regard to racial issues and tensions. Whites seem to feel that they are being ostracized about a history that does not concern or affect them personally and hate being loaded down with guilt. This is when we both came to the conclusion that in order for us to move forward, there needs to be an open and honest conversation from white people about race. If white people told us how they really feel about race, how they feel about themselves in a racial context, and how they feel about people of color, this engagement could help create the type of coalition building that will once and for all eradicate racism.

"I was actually doing some research for another book on the Internet and landed on Quora.com, a question and answer website. I was browsing the site when I ran across this question, 'Why do white people think they understand how it feels to be racially profiled?' and was amazed by the honest responses. My wheels began to turn and as I dug in deeper, checking out variations on this question, I quickly realized that while African Americans, Latinos, Native Americans, and Asian Americans have shared their feelings of being 'other' – people of color – there's never really been a collection of personal narratives about how white folks feel about race. It seemed to me that in order to have a real discussion white folks need to talk openly about race, and we, people of color, need to listen because the 'listening' can help further along our cause. Once I was able to wrap the idea around my head, I contacted Sean and said, 'We've got a book to do!'"

—*Gabrielle*

"When Gabrielle first mentioned this book idea to me, I thought it was compelling and controversial. A few weeks later, I had a discussion with my partner and two close friends of ours—all three are white—about race in American society. Throughout the conversation, which soon turned into a heated argument between my partner and me, I realized that I

wasn't allowing him the opportunity to voice his thoughts and concerns. I kept silencing him whenever I felt he wasn't acknowledging his white male privilege. He made a statement that was pivotal in my thinking about this topic: 'You've never asked me how I feel about being white.' It was a turning point for me, and as many of the contributors in this collection often voiced to us, they too were never asked what it means for them to be white in America."

—*Sean*

We wanted a white racial justice educator to write the introduction to the book and help guide us with the process. After narrowing down the list to three people, Debby Irving really stood out. We liked her book, *Waking Up White, and Finding Myself in the Story of Race* (2014), because of the raw honesty and vulnerability we found in her personal narrative, which was very much aligned with what we wanted to achieve in *What Does It Mean to Be White in America?*

Once Debby agreed to become a part of this project, we had some immediate concerns to address, from developing submission guidelines, to how to get the word out, all the while pondering how much hate mail we would receive. We were not looking for neat and tidy politically correct stories nor did we expect or want white people to shy away from controversial topics or ideas in deference to our blackness. We both agreed that if a potential contributor submitted an honest, well-written narrative that answered the title's question, we would accept it, whether we agreed with their answer or not. We both had certain expectations as editors in terms of wanting to read narratives from whites who weren't necessarily race scholars or academics.

"Initially, I expected we'd receive a lot of hate mail, but we only got two snarky emails from white men in response to the call for submissions. The first email was on September 15, 2015. It read: 'I say this as a middle-aged white guy: this is easily the stupidest damned idea anyone has come up with this year. Are you sponsored by the Klan or the American Nazi Party?' The other email was on October 19, 2015, in which the gentleman made it clear that he doesn't do submissions and he writes: 'I would not write on a subject like this, as placing people in some group based on skin tone or where there [sic]ancestors came from is sooooooo

[emphasis his] 20th Century! Has the 21st Century happened for you yet? Does the term DNA mean anything to you?' Both emails display explicitly strong acts of avoidance in regard to discussions about race. The assertions by both are projections and assumptions about the editors and the project as a whole. In the first email, he is assuming, most likely on the title question, that this must be the inner-sanctum of one of those white supremacist groups because the call specifically addresses white Americans. In the second email, the assertion is predicated upon the belief that one can wish away the problem of race by not talking about it anymore since it was a major concern of only the twentieth century, which ignores the fact that race has been a prevalent factor in American society, culture, and democracy before and since its inception. The statements presented in these emails reflect that we're not living in a 'post-racial' society as many are led to believe, and provided the necessary fodder that Gabrielle and I needed to continue to shape the collection during the call for submissions."

—Sean

In the first set of submissions we received, people sent us academic essays and poetry (which we did not ask for) written in the third person that merely poked at the question. We finally asked Debby her thoughts on this and she sighed, "I'm not surprised. Most white people don't know how to talk about race." Debby suggested we rewrite the submission guidelines to include prompts and suggestions to help facilitate the writing process. Between that and the updates we posted on our website to let people know of our progress including the problems we were having with the submissions, the quality of the submissions improved immensely.

While we did not know exactly what to expect when we undertook this project, the comments and opinions by people from both sides of the fence were telling, indeed. When word got out that the editors of this collection are African American, some people made incorrect assumptions. To be honest, we never got that from the people who submitted their work to us, or from the contributors we eventually selected for inclusion in this project. However, we did receive a piqued yet muted interest from some of our African American, Latino, and Asian American colleagues. Many had doubts as to whether or not we could actually get white people to talk openly about race. Others felt that black voices should be included in this project and were chagrined when we said no, simply because we felt that would be a different kind of book. Others felt white narratives had already been represented for centuries and therefore didn't need to be highlighted yet again. We were very specific in that this book should only address the question, what does it mean to be white in America?

"I personally invited many of my white friends and colleagues, many of whom are writers, to consider submitting personal narratives for this collection. Often I was told that the title question left a bad taste in their mouths and that they wouldn't ever write about such a topic. As more and more of the submissions kept coming in, I noticed that many white people mentioned how daring and bold this collection was and that they were challenged to think about their race and more specifically about the ways in which race has or has not affected them."

—Sean

Debby shared with us that the #BlackLivesMatter movement has made her more aware than ever how important it is that space for black leadership be created. "I'm not sure I would have signed up for this project if it had been white led," she said, which we thought was interesting. During our discussions with Debby, she explained that there was a complexity to the project that intrigued her based on us initiating, leading and shaping the body of work. We were not sure if we unconsciously knew our blackness would play a vital role in the formation of this book, but we did think it was interesting that there exists a kind of built-in expectation based on who is leading discussions about race.

What we also found interesting is that while we did not ask people to write about racism and white privilege, hundreds of personal narratives did just that. Surprisingly, the submissions went straight to addressing black and white relationships in America, with very few addressing Asian Americans, Native Americans, Arabs, Latinos and other groups in this country. This black/white binary paradigm, as it is commonly referred to, conceptualizes blacks and whites as the two dominant races, and conceives all racism according to anti-black racism.

Unfortunately, one of the damaging effects of this paradigm is that it renders invisible the experience of Asian Americans, Native Americans, Arabs and Latinos eliminating the possibility of transformative collaboration among people of color, and between whites and people of color. While we were profoundly disappointed, we realized that the black/white binary paradigm, while a one-sided representation of race in America, is one that needs to be addressed before moving forward in dealing with people of color as a whole.

Despite our decision to only feature narratives by white people in this book, along the way we developed a sea change and felt the need to have a black person write an afterword who would offer an assessment of the book that also spoke directly to people of color. We also received a personal narrative from a black man who is often visibly labeled as white by many in public and private settings, and at first we did not know what to make of his submission.

"We asked several highly recognizable black women to write this afterword, and they declined, some due to time constraints (we were moving rather quickly with the book), and some simply did not wish to associate their names with this project. We were running out of time. And then, my good friend, colleague and supporter, Tara Betts, dropped me an email about getting involved with the book, and the light bulb went on."

— *Gabrielle*

"Prior to asking Tara Betts to write the afterword, we received a narrative titled 'How I Became White' by Benjamin V. Marshall. The title caught our attention and I didn't know what to expect. A colleague of mine who is a Russian Jew mentioned to me that when she and her parents emigrated to the United States her father stated: 'Now we will be white in America.' Initially, I didn't know Marshall was black. Based on the title alone, I thought his narrative was writing about not being categorized as white in his country of birth but upon emigrating to the U.S. he was then labeled as such. I was surprised to learn that he's a black man who is often perceived by others as white, and while he never passes for white, depending upon particular situations, others actively categorize him as white. His narrative made me take pause because this is an anthology by white Americans, so would including his narrative cause an issue

for readers? Gabrielle, Debby and I came to the agreement that this is a narrative that addresses specifically how skin color value works in the American framework. When I was working on the order the narratives would follow, I kept thinking about the ways in which these narratives are engaged in different types of conversations, and Marshall's offers an intriguing vantage point about the title question of the anthology. It seemed fitting to make his narrative the last in the collection as a way to think critically and question the social construct of race in American society."

— Sean

The History and Politics of White Privilege

IN DISCUSSING RACE, racism and white privilege, we thought it prudent to cover a few points. First, the actual meaning of racism has gotten mixed up with other aspects of racism, such as prejudice, bigotry, stereotypes, and ignorance, so we have included a glossary that covers some of the terms used in this book, as well as a bibliography of books that go into greater detail about some of these topics. But for all intents and purposes of this preface, we thought it would be best served if we focused on addressing white, whiteness and white privilege, since many of our contributors used these terms consistently throughout this volume.

"When I began thinking and reading about this concept of whiteness for the book, I quickly learned that I was entering as a layman into conversations that had been going on for decades in academia, and that the answer to the question 'What does it mean to be white in America' is actually a lot more complex than I realized. I learned that many scholars and historians have argued for a non-traditional definition of 'whiteness,' one where 'whiteness' is understood to be a social construct that had changed over time. While new to me, this understanding actually made a lot of sense when applied to the broader conversation about race relationships in the U.S. and my own experiences as an African American, which in effect guided me as I worked on this book."

— Gabrielle

It has been our experience that when people of color refer to "white people" it is a shorthand reference to "whiteness" that is often defined as the privileges and power that people who appear "white" receive, and how they are not subjected to the types of racism people of color often face. The knowledge, ideologies, norms, and practices of whiteness affect how we think about race, what we see when we look at certain physical features, how we build our own racial identities, how we operate in the world, and what we know about our place in it. Whiteness is shaped and maintained by a full array of social institutions—legal, economic, political, educational, religious, and cultural.

Remarkably, when we think about race, we are inclined to look to the black construct for ideas and solutions, but we rarely consider examining whiteness as a social construct, which indelibly can offer us far more answers about race. The problem is, we really do not know what white identity is, and as you investigate American history, it is pretty difficult to pinpoint it as a social construct. Look at it this way: While we can easily recognize the evolution of "slave" to "nigger" to "negro" to "colored" to "black" to "Afro-American" to "African American," we draw a blank when we try to identify and track whiteness, because no evident labels exist. However, while the white social construct is not as glaringly obvious as its black counterpart, it does exist, and in fact has a rich history of multiplicity that has changed, shifted and evolved in response to the social, economic and political needs of the day.

Actually, whiteness did not exist when Europeans first came to North America. Prior to that time, although Europeans recognized differences in human skin color, they did not categorize themselves as white, simply as a European from a specific country. "Whiteness" was initially developed as a socially constructed reality that was explicitly tied to white skin color. It grew into a social status with benefits conferred upon poor white-skinned people by rich white-skinned people that eventually became what we know today as class warfare. This invention and use of whiteness was used to divide, exploit and conquer people by preventing poor, indentured and enslaved white people from commingling with people of color by pitting them against each other along the color line. To this end, the white elite would occasionally elevate the poor whites just enough to make them think they were participants and beneficiaries in a system of European power instead of victims of it. While the benefits of whiteness were conferred upon people of color from time to time who obeyed the systems of power and adhered to certain values, this was the exception rather than the rule.

Over time though, the white elite needed a way to stave off slave and proletariat rebellions, so they invented this common "race" for some Europeans as laid out in Nell Irvin Painter's *The History of White People*,[4] which at first consisted of wealthy men from Northwestern Europe. Eventually, the knowledge, ideologies, norms, and practices of whiteness and the accompanying "white race" became part of a system of racial oppression designed to solve a particular problem in colonial Virginia – slavery. By the Jacksonian era of the first half of the nineteenth century, citizenship criteria migrated from wealth to race, although in time they really became one and the same. You could say that the value of both assets, money and whiteness came from our nation's faith in them. Few examples demonstrate this reality more starkly than when the country went to war with itself. While the Civil War is known for freeing the slaves, when studied and analyzed, the bottom line is that one side attempted to steal wealth and whiteness from the other. It means that when examined closely, race is also a form of currency – and at one time, even property – as expressed in the majority opinion ruling of *Plessy v. Ferguson* in 1896 at the conclusion of the Civil War:

> "If he be a white man and assigned to a colored coach, he may have his action for damages against the company for being deprived of his so-called property. Upon the other hand, if he be a colored man and be so assigned, he has been deprived of no property, since he is not lawfully entitled to the reputation of being a white man."[5]

In the early twentieth century, different groups of immigrants such as the Irish and Jews, and Southern Europeans such as the Italians, Spanish and Greeks, were considered outsiders. Prompted by Israel Zangwill's idea of *The Melting Pot* (1908), immigrants began to shed their heritage, language and customs in order to assimilate and become white.

4   Nell Irvin Painter, *The History of White People* (NY: W. W. Norton & Company, 2011).

5   *Plessy v. Ferguson,* 163 U.S. 537 (1896).

By World War II, politics and the mobilization of Americans opened up "Americanness" to people who had been considered alien races. Although the melting pot was a notion that was extended to white immigrants, that pot never included people of color. As Eduardo Bonilla-Silva stated, "Blacks, Chinese, Puerto Ricans, etcetera, could not melt into the pot. They could be used as wood to produce the fire for the pot, but they could not be used as material to be melted into the pot."[6] As new immigrants assimilated into whiteness, its trajectory was once again redefined.

The war economy and labor needs expanded opportunities for both blacks and whites that substantially reduced economic disparities, but by the end of the war, the white elite decided to elevate the status of poor whites in small economic and social ways. For example, while the GI bill provided returning veterans with money for college, businesses and home mortgages, people of color did not benefit nearly as much as whites. Although the GI bill itself was not discriminatory, it was enacted to accommodate segregation and Jim Crow and as a result, discriminatory practices (redlining and discrimination in sales, financing and homeowners insurance, with educational gains limited to a small segment of black America) contributed to the wealth gap between whites and people of color that exists today.

W. E. B. Du Bois called such benefits the "psychological wages of whiteness" because they were benefits or "wages" that were "paid" to poor white people just for being white-skinned. While in some cases these "wages" did little to change the economic situation of many poor whites, they had a great effect on personal treatment and deference shown to them.[7] Over time, the benefits of whiteness have become automatic for those that are obedient to the right power structures and adhere to the right values. Interestingly, the economic benefits of the GI bill created a newly affluent but uneasy white middle-class that by the 1950s, adopted conservative social values due to real or imagined threats

---

6   Eduardo Bonilla-Silva, "RACE: The Power of an Illusion," California Newsreel/Independent Television Service (ITVS), 2003.

7   W. E. B. Du Bois, *Black Reconstruction in America, 1860-1880* (Herndon, VA: Transaction Publishers, 1998).

to their status quo. While it continues to exist, whiteness as a distinct social status is no longer talked about or named because it has become an invisible reality that has succeeded in impacting race relationships in the United States and elsewhere.

The civil rights movement represented one of those rare moments in American history where many whites and blacks were able to come together as Americans and not clash as racial antagonists. What most people don't realize is that during the civil rights movement, a white pan-ethnicity emerged as a dominant paradigm, with white ethnics asserting that they too suffered, and should be the recipients of social programs to address inequality in the United States. Unhappy with their socio-economic position in America, they accepted the civil rights demand for outlawing discrimination because they believed that everyone, including blacks, should be allowed to carve out their own rightful place in society. The irony here is that while antipoverty and civil rights programs and policies have been portrayed as benefitting blacks and Latinos exclusively, many white ethnics, particularly women, also benefited from these programs.[8] The idea and concept of whiteness would again change as some whites began to denounce affirmative action and other civil rights initiatives.

It took several decades for the legacy of the Civil Rights Act of 1964 to be fully felt. By the 1980s, affirmative action, which was created in 1961 and expanded to include sex in 1967, came under attack by conservative activists who alleged that colleges and corporations used illegal quotas to increase the number of minorities at white people's expense, which is why many whites are against affirmative action. What's fascinating is that the wealthiest sector and dominant cultural force of American society has embraced a status of victimhood, persecution and oppression in the form of reverse discrimination and racism. While the principle of fairness may be a driving concern in white people's attitudes towards policies such as affirmative action, social welfare and fair housing, the malleability towards creating a level playing field is anything but fair.

During the 1990s, we saw civil rights issues once again bubble to the surface as race riots erupted in Los Angeles over the Rodney King

---

8   Melanie E. L. Bush, *Everyday Forms of Whiteness: Understanding Race in a 'Post-Racial' World* (New York: Rowman & Littlefield Publishers, 2011), 25-26.

incident in which white police officers were acquitted after being videotaped beating a black man. As the thirty year anniversary of the 1964 Civil Rights Act approached, a Gallup/CNN/USA Today Poll in 1993[9] found that 65 percent believed the civil rights movement had had a significant impact on American society. And then, after the turn of the century, we elected a black president but the notion that America is now "post-racial" and free from racial preference, discrimination, and prejudice, is a concept that is as misguided as it is delusional.

We acknowledge that there have been some major improvements. Black people can be found in positions and places that were inconceivable fifty years ago. The fact that slavery, segregation, Jim Crow and lynchings are no longer legally sanctioned in this country does not mean that racism has disappeared entirely. What has happened is that they have morphed into something else: prisoners are used as cheap labor for major corporations, public schools are being closed down or sold to corporations, Jim Crow has been replaced with James Crow, Esq., and bullets have replaced rope for lynchings. Some equality has trickled down to a few, but not nearly enough, and in this tug of war between the government and the capitalists, white people have been caught in the middle. And racism has never gone away, it's where it's always been, bubbling beneath the surface.

Although many Americans find themselves struggling economically these days, middle-class whites in particular have correctly perceived that their economic fortunes have deteriorated over the past fifty years, with poor whites finding themselves further down the rabbit hole. Instead of looking at how capitalists have done everything possible to deny Americans economic advantages, from anti-union and anti-government positions, to deregulation and outsourcing jobs overseas, an entire idealized empire of politicians, corporations and a very loud right-wing noise machine emerged to convince folks that the reason behind their downward trajectory is because people of color are sucking up all the government benefits. They then pitch a return to a more idyllic time in America, like the 1950s, of small town living and a simpler lifestyle,

---

9   Lydia Saad, "Thirty Years Later, Americans Still Believe Watergate Was Serious Matter." (Gallup, Inc., 2002) http://www.gallup.com/poll/6208/thirty-years-later-americans-still-believe-watergate-serious-matter.aspx.

when in actuality, it was the racist-sexist-repressed-homophobic-red-scare-good-old-days. They dangle race in front of white people like a carrot, and then hijack them emotionally, politically and economically, right before their very eyes. No wonder they are angry and pissed off!

The irony here is that many white Americans have a lot more in common with their counterparts in the black and Latino communities than the rich whites they listen to that promote this bunk. It just shows how powerfully pervasive race has become in America where you can convince a group of people to vote against their own self-interests simply because they distrust or dislike people of color. As a result, the policies in the United States, whether advanced by Republicans or Democrats, have by and large created, reinforced and entrenched white privilege in a system that has choked all of us socially as well as economically. Why? Because by concealing the true nature of their politics, they've succeeded in undermining all efforts to build economic populism or socialism, or any other form of class-based political movements in America.

But why do a lot of white people buy into this? It's because, as far as many of them are concerned, the vision of healing and reconciliation conjured up so eloquently by Martin Luther King Jr. more than fifty years ago has now been fulfilled. We now have a two-term African American president. Many believe that the federal government has given away lots of free stuff to black people who don't work or pay taxes, all the while grinding down the white man, "so black people need to stop complaining and get over it." Some actually believe that poor blacks and Latinos stubbornly persist in being poor, living in disadvantaged circumstances, getting shot by the police for no apparent reason, and are going to prison in large numbers because they are all criminals.

These ideas are not held by just Republican/Tea Party hardcore ideologues, who have built their power and influence on thinly-veiled racism, there is a much larger population of white Americans who are deeply entrenched in this ideology, but we believe there is an even larger group of white people out there who can counter this. Troubled by what has been happening, many have been afraid or unwilling to engage, but the tide has been changing. Think about it, not only black people put Obama into office – twice – there are a lot of other people, including white people who voted for him as well, a fact that is commonly overlooked by the pundits and politicians. However, whether people like it or not, we are now entering into a new phase that has purported a new idea: You no longer need to be white to be considered American. In the era of Obama, our once-narrow concept of whiteness and Americanness has become at once far broader and less important than ever before, but many of the natives still cling dearly to the past.

The most insidious power of white privilege is the way it renders itself invisible and unconscious, because it appears as the norm. That's probably the reason why so many white Americans believe that racism is a suggested factor, and that white privilege does not exist, especially for poor white people. Many misinterpret the term "privilege" for *monetary status*, when in fact the context in which it is used is about *skin color value*. It is about receiving the benefit of doubt in a number of situations, simply because one is white. Certainly a poor white person's experience with race is not the same as a rich white person's experience. Clearly, a rich white person and a rich black person have more in common than their poor counterparts. This is not to say that poor white Americans do not experience some of the same injustices that many people of color have had to encounter (police brutality, lack of education, unemployment, etc.), but again not nearly on the same scale. White privilege is a built-in social advantage that most white people often cannot perceive or are reluctant to acknowledge. Think of it this way: black people cannot enslave, colonize, marginalize, imperialize nor politically and economically disenfranchise white people. We simply do not have access to the systems and resources to do so. But no matter what we say or do, there will always be those white people who will never see in a concrete way how their own race has positively affected them. For them, their ignorance is blindness they mistake for bliss.

In just a few decades, people of color will collectively account for a majority of America's population. What it doesn't take into account is what Michael Lind has described as the "beiging" of America, that is, the many interracial children who may or may not chose to self-identify as being white. As Americans see themselves less uniformly white, the country will continue to change culturally. What will it mean to be white after "whiteness" no longer defines the mainstream? We'd both love to live long enough to witness that shift in perspective.[10]

In the meantime, while we agree that some white people have a particular tendency to bury their heads in the sand on issues of race, we also realize there are many more out there willing to play an important role in acting out on behalf of racial and social justice, and look forward to a less racialized America. Thus, the purpose of this book is twofold: to provide a bully pulpit for those white Americans who are brave enough to take a stand as they encourage others to fully participate in meaningful conversations about race.

What We Hope *What Does It Mean to Be White In America?* Will Achieve

THE NARRATIVES INCLUDED IN *What Does It Mean to Be White in America?* highlight a diversity of white perspectives that range from age to gender to ethnicity to socio-economic status. Some of the narratives capture conversations that the contributors have had with relatives, co-workers, neighbors, and even strangers about race relations in the United States. Others tackle their conflicted feelings toward their whiteness in which they view it as "racist hatred" more than anything else. We were surprised to see how some of the contributors perceived their white identity as a state of "racelessness" and "culturelessness" with a detachment to their European ancestry. Some contributors mentioned resenting being identified as "white," which to them has come to represent a very negative connotation. Other narratives from people of Jewish ancestry, including a prominent rabbi, directly address the ways in which Jews became white in America, or how someone once mentioned to them that they wouldn't be considered white in a given regional context due to their Jewish ancestry.

Working on this collection, we both observed that older white people who experienced segregation and Jim Crow firsthand have been extremely forthcoming about their experiences as it pertains to whiteness and racism. Some of their stories are told very matter-of-factly, with a

---

10   Hua Hsu, "The End of White America?" *The Atlantic*, January/February 2009 Issue. http://www.theatlantic.com/magazine/archive/2009/01/the-end-of-white-america/307208/.

finely gauged forlornness of what could or should have been if the situation had been different. Of the white people aged fifty-years-old and younger, we found some of them grappled racism in an assortment of ways, from those who acknowledge their white privileged existence, to those who felt that their childhood and adult experiences weren't white privileged existences, to those who are working to break free from white privilege by becoming either active in social and racial justice circles, or by simply changing their perspectives on race.

As one reads these eighty-two narratives, one will find that the overall sentiment found in this book is acknowledgment. Sprinkled throughout this collection are short, almost filmic, vignettes that capture a specific moment in which a contributor recognized their whiteness in ways they never had to before. Some of the contributors go further by accepting they can no longer remain as silent onlookers, and understand that white people need to stand up and say that they will no longer allow politicians, pundits and corporations to hijack American culture, or to conduct racist politics in their name.

This collection brings together varied dialogues about race in American society, and given the current political, social and cultural climate in which misunderstandings about race abound, it's pertinent to recognize that racial problems do exist in America, which is an important first step towards moving our country forward. We had no expectations from the contributors to provide a prescription about America's race problem, in fact many of them, in their narratives, actually ask the questions, "How do we evoke change? What do we do next?" However, it is in the telling of these stories that we ask people, both white people and people of color, to listen and not judge, to think and reflect, and perhaps use some of these stories to find insightful ways to make a concerted effort in their lives to help build bridges.

In the end, with all the socio-economic and political information we have shared with you about this book, this is not that book. It is not an academic treatise. It is not even a book about whiteness. It is a book about a group of courageous people who have opened up and honestly shared their feelings with you, dear readers, about a very sensitive subject: race. The question is: Are you willing to join in the conversation? ∎

ACKNOWLEDGMENTS

■ ■ ■

A S THE CO-EDITORS OF THIS PROJECT, we are providing our acknowledgment in three different sections: a joint acknowledgment and our own personal acknowledgments.

We would like to jointly thank the following folks for their help and support:

With gratitude, we thank the Intercultural Alliance of Artists & Scholars, Inc. (IAAS), the parent organization of 2Leaf Press, and board members Andrew P. Jackson (Sekou Molefi Baako) and Stephanie Ann Agosto for their help and support in this project. Special thanks to 2Leaf Press' editors, Carolina Fung Feng and Adam Wier for endless hours of copy editing, with additional help from Erick Piller and Deborah Mashibini-Prior, whose assistance was invaluable.

A big thank you to Debby Irving, who became a vital part of this project from its inception, and whose guidance and support has been greatly appreciated; and to poet, activist and scholar Tara Betts, who stepped-in at the last minute to write a much-needed and informative afterword to this book.

We greatly appreciate our intern turned social media marketing specialist, Rachel Hobble, for all of her good work in helping to promote this book.

Producing this anthology, without question, has been challenging. Since most white people feel uncomfortable talking about race, we wish to thank all of the people who willingly submitted work for consideration. Lastly, we wish to thank our contributors for providing informative and transformative stories for which this book would not be. We feel privileged for being entrusted with providing a platform and a safe space for them to freely articulate their feelings about race. We hope that those who read *What Does It Mean to Be White in America?* will be prompted to engage in frank conversations about race.

From Gabrielle David

THANKS TO ALL OF THE PEOPLE I've met in my travels over the years – some of whom I kept in touch with, some of whom I've recently met and others who have profoundly changed the trajectory of my life. Without you, I would not be where I am today.

I am especially grateful to Sean Frederick Forbes. This book would not be this book without him and I am eternally thankful for everything he has done, under a grueling and somewhat challenging schedule. I would also like to extend my thanks to Debby Irving and the help she provided us as we worked to put the pieces together during the formation of this book. Many thanks to Tara Betts, a good friend who took on an unwieldly project at such a late date.

I would like to acknowledge with great affection, Abiodun Oyewole, Shirley Bradley LeFlore, Lyah Beth LeFlore, Bob Holman, David Henderson, Tonya Foster, Ammiel Alcalay, David Cruz, Myrna Nieves and Vagabond Beaumont for their continued support.

In loving memory of Carmen Pietri Diaz, who supported and saw the vision of 2Leaf Press, and Judy Stafford who believed in me and it.

With love and gratitude, I would like to also acknowledge my family members. In particular, I wish to thank my parents, Radcliffe and Delores David, and my godparents, Eugene and Yvonne Aiken, who kept the faith when they walked upon this earth and continue to do so now that they are in heaven. Love to my godmother, Donna Aiken.

From Sean Frederick Forbes

I AM INDEBTED TO MY PARENTS, Hermes Delano Forbes and Teresa Mercedes Shah; my stepmother Luisa Elberg-Urbina; to my grandmother Aillen Robinson whose beauty, strength and self-determination I admire greatly; to my sister and brother-in-law, Rose Marie and Naji Kharma; to my aunts and uncle, Lucia Désir, Ofelia Robinson, and Norberto and Maria Robinson. To my dear friends, colleagues and editors: Cathy Schlund-Vials, V. Penelope Pelizzon, Ellen Litman, Robert Hasenfratz, Gina Barreca, Dwight Codr, Jason Courtmanche, Amy Nocton, Lynn Z. Bloom, Kerry Carnahan, Justine Cozell, R. Joseph Rodríguez, Cedric Ellis, Rigoberto González, Martha Collins, Jacob Easley II, Jarred Wiehe, Laurencia Ciprus and Miller Oberman. Special thanks to my partner Peter C. MacKay for the frequent debates and discussions about race in America. To my good friends Yariel Diaz, Kendra Hill, Dinamary and John Horvath, Marie Le Claire, and Sue and Randy LaCoille who offer guidance, love, and support. To John M. Ryan for the pep talks, words of wisdom, for pointing out keen insights and observations that I rarely see, and for listening intently each and every time, *Sláinte!* To Debby Irving, a newfound friend. To Tara Betts for joining us on this journey. And, of course, to Gabrielle David for telling me, "We've got a book to do!" ∎

—February 2016

"To act is to be committed, and to be committed is to be in danger. In this case, the danger, in the minds of most white Americans, is the loss of their identity."

— James Baldwin, "My Dungeon Shook,"
The Fire Next Time (1963)

INTRODUCTION

■ ■ ■

Debby Irving

Breaking the Code of White Silence

N 2009, WHEN I BEGAN TELLING white friends, family, and perfect strangers that I planned to deepen my understanding of racism,
and shared with them the questions that filled my mind, something
remarkable happened. Far from the silence and shunning I anticipated,
most leaned closer, lowered their voices, and said something like, "Me
too. I've wondered that too." Often the comment would be followed
by a story of an unresolved upset or confusion. Everyone, it seemed,
had a story. Most also had questions.

I am especially grateful for the way this collection reveals a range of
white experiences and cultural differences; each narrative adds nuance
to what it means to be white in the United States of America. While the
use of the n-word is commonplace in some white worlds, many others
teach racism less directly by speaking in code about the "inner city,"
automatically locking car doors in "those" neighborhoods, and being
taught to "stick to your own kind." I learned that the Connecticut town
my own husband grew up in let stand the removal of the letter "D" from
its "Welcome to Darien" sign. When I read this, I remembered with a
thud in my gut that I had heard about this sign as a teenager, and that
I had laughed at the cleverness of the person who removed the "D."
It sickens me to realize how easy it can be for a white child to accept
as normal, or even humorous, what we can later see as unforgivable.

For me, the most poignant stories in this anthology are the ones in which we witness the unwitting complicity of children and young people in buying into and perpetrating racial oppression. Be it laughing at a public sign about white supremacy, donning blackface and KKK costumes, rejecting a young suitor because of his skin color, passing along a racial myth to a brother, or calling a housekeeper the n-word, young white people are alarmingly able to be both ignorant of their own racial history and reproduce it as if following a blueprint. Roger Barbee's essay, "Useless," epitomizes the way a mean-spirited act of racism can be normalized in white boyhood circles, setting into motion a lifetime of anguish for both bully and target. In Beth Lyon Barnett's essay, "Liza Pearl," my heart ached at a cross-racial childhood connection destroyed in a single moment, and still very much alive and festering in Beth's eighty-something year-old soul. It seems there is no shortage of white childhood regrets reverberating, unresolved and unhealed that perpetuates shame and an unfulfilled yearning for repair.

It's no wonder that lifetimes of racially charged moments remain alive in white America's collective hearts and minds. Unspoken shame and injury combined with unprocessed memories and confusions create a toxic mix of anxiety and discord. Speaking and processing all of that seems to me like the obvious antidote, but how do we move forward in a culture in which talking about racism is considered taboo; where white silence is an entrenched cultural norm and merely saying the word "racism" can get you called racist.

Members of America's dominant white culture, caught in a vicious cycle of racial oppression maintained by silence and compliance, have a fundamental choice to make: uphold or break the code of white silence. Breaking the silence not only means disrupting a social norm, but also dredging up painful memories, encountering shocking new truths, acknowledging ignorance, and tolerating the stomach-clenching fear of saying (or writing) something problematic. Amidst the silence, white people remain trapped in ignorance, paralyzed by underdeveloped emotional stamina and conversational skill, while black and brown Americans bear the burden of that incompetence.

The collection offers readers a chance to explore how white silence—and attempts to break it—show up across ethnic, religious, geographic, era, and class lines. We see racial dynamics in the workplace, in the classroom, at the kitchen table, and on the ball field. We see white people using their words, their actions, and their art to shake awake white family, friends, and audiences. Better understanding of how whiteness, complicity, and efforts to expose it manifest in a range of contexts offers us all an opportunity to raise awareness. By all I mean the wide range of white Americans and the wide range of Americans of color who navigate whiteness everyday.

Stories of identity contortion reveal the cost/benefit calculations of whiteness. In Perry Brass's essay, "Whiteness is Only Sin Deep," the costs of navigating a Jewish identity that's white but not really white; where being Jewish is acceptable only behind closed doors is palpable. Stories about whitening an "ethnic" name are counter-balanced by stories of distancing oneself from whiteness by trying to appear more Hispanic, more middle-eastern, more anything but white. Efforts to distance oneself from whiteness, interestingly, are limited to a desire for social acceptance. In contrast, Benjamin V. Marshall's essay, "How I Became White," reminds us that when it comes to accessing life-sustaining resources such as financial loans, the material benefits of whiteness are irrefutable.

The essays contained in this anthology span not only a range of identities and contexts, but also a continuum of understanding. Some contributors have studied and deeply understand white supremacy, and their role in it as historical and systemic. Other contributors, likely more representative of the average white person, understand racism only at the interpersonal level. Of all the differences that can divide us, this "gets it"/doesn't "get it" divide is the one that I witness white people struggle with the most. Let us use this difference, as we can with all difference, to increase our curiosity and understanding in order to decrease judgment and misunderstanding. Sam Tanner's essay, "White People are Crazy," offers words apt on this point: "We have the luxury of this time together, [the] only rule is that we cannot knock down each other's card houses. It is in our shared interest to learn to build together."

I am still learning that just when I think I "get it," I learn the limitations of my understanding. The weight of an inherited history and identity I didn't ask for, yet so effortless to reproduce, can drain me at times. It is a weight that need not be borne alone. Though all of these essays made me feel less alone in my ongoing journey to wake up to my whiteness, Wendy Zagray Warren's essay, "Choosing to See," had particular impact on me. The vulnerability in her story of showing up as a Montana Writing Project Summer Institute co-director, located on the Blackfeet Nation, with her "carefully worked up" agenda in hand, reminded me of my own misplaced good intentions. A willingness to share the implications of unexamined white ways and blind spots allows all of us to examine them together as we each search for our own. May every reader find multiple stories in this collection that carry particular resonance.

What Gabrielle and Sean's anthology offers white Americans is an opportunity to break the code of silence, to begin to process long held thoughts, emotions, stories, confusion, shame, and tension. Despite being socialized to fear the perceived racial other, this collection reveals the kind of longing that fuels connection and inspires hope. I hear in these stories a desire to understand, to be seen and heard, to see and hear, to connect, to learn, to be brave, to own up to ancestral investments in whiteness as well as to everyday collusion. In Carole Gozansky Garrison's essay, "The Kindness of Strangers," I glimpse a vision of what could be, a day when biases are managed quietly and maturely in our minds so that we can get to the business of trusting one another enough to build something new, together.

Thank you to Gabrielle, Sean, and all who contributed to this project. May the risk you all have taken be rewarded with a breaking down of the real and imagined barriers that keep us from one another. ■

"To be black was to confront, and to be forced to alter, a condition forged in history. To be white was to be forced to digest a delusion called white supremacy. Indeed, without confronting the history that has either given white people an identity or divested them of it, it is hardly possible for anyone who thinks of himself as white to know what a black person is talking about at all."

—James Baldwin, "Dark Days"
James Baldwin: Collected Essays by Toni Morrison (1998)

Sean Conroy

What Does Race
Have to Do with It?

I JUST DON'T SEE WHY she always has to point out that there was a non-white person there. I think it is a generational thing, she is fifty. My sister and I strolled down the dirt road leading back to her farm in the middle of nowhere Nebraska. It's always, "there was a black guy there, and he said..., or there was a Mexican at our table at the reception..." As we continued I thought about our upbringing in southwest Nebraska. I recalled certain phrases my father used without a second thought that I will never repeat, not even here, and others that I don't know whether they are safe or not. "My cotton pickin' truck won't start" he might say. Not knowing the origin of the phrase, but knowing how his brain has worked before, I dare not have a "cotton pickin'"anything. I thought back to the fact there was never an African American family in town, until one moved here when I was in high school. The only African Americans I recalled meeting up to that point in our town were adopted children of white families. I feel like we grew up to be accepting enlightened individuals despite the odds. "Maybe it is because around here, at least when they were growing up it was rare to run into a black person." "Maybe, but now days I just don't get it, why can't it just be 'There was this guy and he said, there was this guy at our table, whatever!" I considered this, and nodded in agreement, "It would be nice, I see your point, but humans are programmed to see differences in each other, it goes back to nomadic days when you watched out for the 'other tribes' that might mean you harm. Now days we are told to ignore this instinct to notice differences. We ignore that we noticed. I think older people might be more prone to ignoring this social rule, to ignore the differences." "I guess, but it just makes me upset she has to be like that." I considered how wonderful the world according to her thought process would be. Yet how impossible it is in our country; a country with a history of slavery and a civil rights movement still younger than some of its citizens. The social stains of inequality have not yet been washed from memory, and new ones are still appearing. As we walked farther down the road it dawned on me, the other side of the situation, "There is the other problem though, younger people ignore race almost to a fault, sometimes coming full circle and dancing around the issue so much it becomes an issue again. Take for example, if you needed to let someone know who Gary is, and Gary is a black guy. Your friend approaches you and asks which gentleman in the next room is Gary. If he is the only black guy it would be easy to say that, and you are done, but instead we dance around it 'he has a short haircut,' 'but they all do,' 'he has, you know, brown pants on.' 'Three of them do...' 'Ummm well, he has glasses...' 'Sean...is it the black guy? Just say Gary is the black guy and we can be done.'" "Yeah I can see how sometimes it would be easier just to acknowledge that he is the only black guy, but that is my point, why does he have to be the 'black guy?!'" "Because he is, and it is silly to ignore that fact. I see patients all the time, and the fact remains that African Americans have a higher risk for hypertension and diabetes. If I do not acknowledge their race, and treat them medically based upon it, I am performing a disservice." "Still, in the real world it seems stupid." "Not really. I can guarantee you that given identical circumstances, identical roads, and the same officer, if you and an African American were pulled over, and had to tell the story later on, you would have drastically different views on the situation. If we do not realize a person's race, we cannot empathize with their world versus ours. At times, I would say to ignore race, even in the real world, is to not fully appreciate another person's existence. If you were with that other person in the car when you got pulled over, you need to understand the fear in their eyes, and their sudden silence." "I guess I can see how you have to admit race sometimes, you just have to, but you shouldn't just out of convenience." "Steph, what if going back to pointing out Gary it was the other way around, what if Gary was the only white guy in the room, would it be okay to say 'Gary is in there, he is the white guy?'" "Of course it would!" "It would?" "Well yeah, because he is the same as you!" "Are you telling me it is an 'our word' type of thing! That is ridiculous! What if Gary is in a wheelchair, can I say that?" "Well yeah that is fine." "So disabilities are fine, but race is not, what if he has crutches due to cerebral palsy, that seems a bit touchier. What if he has one leg and is on a crutch?" "I don't know, now it is getting delicate." As we arrived back at her yard I pulled out the trump card, "Okay, what if he is an African American with vitiligo? Can you say he is the splotchy guy? Leaving race out of it? Of course not, because you are talking about the double-edged sword of race and medical condition. Albinism isn't so disabling, how about that? What if he is an albino African American? I met one once; that is a very distinguishing factor, you will not mistake Gary if you mention that." "Yeah, and then he is the not-black black guy and that sounds absolutely dreadful… it is all just so confusing." As the back door closed behind us, I wrapped it up the best I could, "It is certainly a lot of gray areas, we talk about black and white, but it is anything but that." ■

Patrik McDade

Give Me Some Skin:
How I Became White

DIDN'T ASK TO BE BORN WHITE. It just happened that way. And for most of my life, I didn't even know I was White. I knew other people were Black, though. And I knew there weren't many Black people in my neighborhood. But if you're Black you knew it.

What did I know about myself? I knew I was born in Sacramento, California to an Air Force dad and a mom who was a waitress. We were in Tucson because there was an Air Force base there, but by the time I was four, my mom and dad were divorced, and my mom remarried soon after, a carpenter. We were all White, and none of us knew it. Why didn't they tell us?

I knew I was Polish, though. I knew that because it was weird. My mom told me my family had a lot of Polish, and I told someone, and pretty soon, that's what I was. When you're in school, whatever makes you weird is what you are. But I was a shy, smart boy who liked to hang out with the girls, and so I was a little bit proud that I was weird, because I didn't really like the people who weren't weird. This was in the 1970s, so if you're reading this and can relate to what I'm saying, you can probably see that much hasn't changed. But even though I was a weird "Polack" who hung around with girls and used big words, I didn't know I was a White Polack.

I have a White friend who said to me one time: "How often do you think about your race?"

I told her, maybe three or four times a week. I thought I was being honest with myself, admitting that I sometimes think about race, but

I am generally pretty non-racist because I don't think about race or skin color very much.

Then she said—"See that Black guy over there? How often do you think he thinks about race?"

And then it happened. I turned White.

Actually, that story isn't exactly true. I wish it were. The process of discovering my Whiteness, and how deep it goes, and how unconscious it is, has been much longer and more meandering. The story I just told came from a friend, and she was asking another White person the question "How often do you think of race?"

I thought that was a pretty good way to realize that everyone's reality is not the same. That it's not a level playing field. But it didn't really change him. In fact, he went away thinking that Black people were more racist, because they are just locked into their own way of thinking about themselves as disadvantaged.

Actually, I'm not sure if he went away thinking that. But because I talk about this all the time, I know that White people will often say that. Actually, it's not just White people who will say that, people from all backgrounds will say that. And maybe it's even true in a way. But this is also a way of blaming people for something that happened to them. Because, racism isn't like it was—for the most part, it's not about the active hating and violence, the lynching, the slavery. It's about the assumption that White is normal. It's about the deck being stacked.

Something I've learned about my Whiteness is that it's slippery. And that's how it is with all privilege—one of the ways you know you have it is if you don't think you have it. If you don't believe me, try calling everyone by their race—not just Asians, Blacks or Mexicans—but call all white people "White," too.

One of the things that will happen is that a lot of White people will call you racist. What's really going on is that they want you to protect them from never having to think about race. That's protecting their privilege—the privilege to walk through life whistling and not having to think about it.

So, I'm trying to stop using the word racism. People get confused about racism. We think that all there is to say is:

"I'm not racist, I think everyone's equal."

Or,

"I'm White, but I never owned any slaves – that Black guy hates me because I'm White. That's racist."

Or,

"Why should I say hello to the only Black student in my class – if I say hello to her, but I don't say hello to everyone else, isn't that racist because I noticed that she's Black?"

The "Big Problem" is not the feeling of hatred, because most people don't think that's normal anymore, but we have forgotten to fix the things that make our society treat White as normal, and everything else as weird. Those things that make it so that white skin is beautiful, but Black skin is not. That Black men are dangerous, but White men are just white men, some good; some bad. That Mexicans are hard workers who love God and family. That Asians are really smart and quiet. That Indians are drunks.

Instead of racism, I say white superiority these days. This is *the assumption that being white is normal and everything else is unusual.* It's different than white supremacy, which is active hatred. Most white people are no longer white supremacists, but still believe they are "superior." In order to not be white superior, you have to recognize there is an assumption that Whiteness is normal – and you have to commit to ending it, not just pretend it isn't there.

I'm still discovering my Whiteness, every single day. Sometimes I hate thinking about race, ethnicity, and skin color. I think about it more than I used to, and I see more of my biases – but even more, I see biases all around me.

White people need to start seeing White people. Instead of just seeing who isn't white. And as those of us who benefit from Whiteness start to get tired of reminding ourselves of our race all the time, we'll get tired of reminding everyone else of their race as well. Maybe then we can move from "Black" and "White" to "black" and "white." ∎

Martha Collins

A Blinding Whiteness

THERE'S SNOW IN SANTA FE, in the air, on the ground, on every horizontal surface. It's a wet snow, so the smaller branches are hidden in whiteness; only the larger branches reveal their underlying gray.

Of course the whiteness of snow has nothing in chromatic common with my own "whiteness": if I put my arm against the window, it's almost as different from the snow as it is from the big branches. But the fact that some people have called themselves "white" for several hundred years is perhaps reason enough to ponder the metaphorical significance of today's weather. Cold, the snow, and covering things over. Not rooted, but nonetheless dominant, leaving little untouched by its presence.

As we should all know by now, though I did not know it in my childhood, the roots of white people are not deep: we are migrants whose ancestors went north from Africa, whose skin faded to allow the weaker sun to reach us with its necessary vitamin D. And we in the United States are of course doubly migrants, a people who first defined themselves as white in relation to the original inhabitants of a land we immediately began to cover as incessantly and thoroughly as today's snow. In this place I am visiting for a few weeks, it is impossible not to be conscious of indigenous people, whose faces and names and diminished ancestral homelands are prominent enough to remind me of my own outsider status in the history of what I so casually call "my country."

My own immediate ancestors were not settlers who, having begun to conquer the original inhabitants through war and disease, became importers and enslavers of their distant African ancestors and thus participated in our second great national sin of racism; my people came late from northern Europe and thus were not, as far as I know, direct perpetrators of those great national crimes. Nor have I lived in places where slavery has been the defining fact of history: there were no slaves in Iowa, where I grew up, and slavery had been abolished early on in Massachusetts, where I live now.

But the very absence of immediate historical connection, and the resulting dominance of "my" people in the places where I live and have lived, may have given me a greater degree of white privilege – psychologically, at least – than I would have experienced elsewhere. If I had lived in the South, where descendants of slaves are everywhere, it might have taken some repressive effort to avoid thinking about my connection to a slave-holding past. But in a place where there are few people of color and where research is necessary to uncover the history of institutional racism, it may be easier to exempt oneself from ancestral guilt.

The population of Iowa was over 99 percent white when I was growing up. With 25 percent of the nation's grade-A soil, the state was primarily agricultural from the beginning, which meant that there wasn't much incentive for black people to go there during the Great Migration. So even though I lived in Iowa's largest city, no segregation laws were necessary to keep my middle-class family's life almost completely white. There was, I knew, an unofficial "colored section of town," and we saw some of the people who lived there (or, I later learned, in "mixed" neighborhoods) when we went downtown during those pre-mall days. But everyone in my grade school was white, everyone in my church was white, everyone I ice-skated with, swam with, and ate in restaurants with was white. In school, we learned about slavery, but it had nothing to do with us: it had occurred in the South.

Only recently have I realized that aside from those downtown glimpses – through the snow, as it were – my first encounters with non-white people had some connection to our country's racist history after all. The first black person I met in my hometown had come from the South to continue serving as a full-time maid to a family who had recently moved from Mississippi. About the same time (I must have been five), I became aware of the live-in couple who worked for my well-to-do aunt and uncle in Southern Illinois. And then there was

Beloved Belindy, a brown-skinned doll with a bandana and painted-on grin who was the "mammy" of my Raggedy Ann and Andy.

Later, when I was in junior high, my parents replaced our white "cleaning lady" with a light-skinned African American woman whose unrealized dream had been to attend Fisk University. My school was not, by then, an altogether white affair: there was a Japanese American girl in my junior high class, and one African American in the class below mine—and so it was in my high school: always, as I've written elsewhere, only one. Finally, when I was working with an interurban church group during my senior year, I met a black girl who was planning to attend Earlham College in the fall: not quite a friend, but at least a peer.

In my own college years, I continued to live in a kind of white oblivion at my west coast university, where there were only a few Asian Americans (one of whom I knew) and one black person in my class. It wasn't until I went to Boston to teach in an urban commuter university that people of color became part of my daily life. Although Boston is, as metropolitan areas go, not particularly diverse, the streets where I walked and the neighborhood where I lived were no longer exclusively white. More importantly, I had a number of students and a few English department colleagues who were not white either, and who became, in effect, my mentors. Increasingly, the literature I read and the literature I taught became what we would now call diverse; eventually (before gender issues came to my serious attention), I created and taught an American literature course called "The Red Man, the White Man, the Black Man and the Land."

And so I lived for some time in the relative comfort of being a northern person who has gradually become aware that her world is more diverse than she once would have dreamed: the snow, so to speak, was melting. But what needs saying is that it was a comfortable melt: I could enjoy my new knowledge, my new interactions, and, increasingly, my new activism. Rather than acknowledging my own complicity in my country's racist past and present, I could—silently, half-consciously—applaud myself for helping to correct it.

And then I saw an exhibit of lynching postcards and discovered that the hanging my father told me he'd seen as a child in Southern

Illinois was actually a lynching, its primary victim (predictably) an African American. I don't know how many times I've written some version of that sentence in the last fifteen years – partly because I ended up writing a book that focused on the lynching, but also because it was a defining moment for me. I have a number of friends who have discovered, acknowledged, and dealt with the fact that their ancestors held slaves. But until I saw those postcards and realized my own legacy of racism, I could unconsciously distinguish myself from them. Now I recognized ancestral complicity, which invited me to think more deeply about ways in which I was a direct as well as an indirect beneficiary of our racist past.

And so I began to read – not just literature, but history. It was true that Iowa had been on the underground railroad, and had been the fourth state to pass civil rights legislation after the Civil War. But it was also true that black people were required to pay $500 to move to the state, and that even then they were not allowed to vote or attend white schools: it wasn't just the relative lack of manufacturing that had given me an almost exclusively white childhood. And if Massachusetts had abolished slavery early on and had been home to important abolitionists, it was also true that the Commonwealth's early professionals had owned slaves, and that its economy – banking, shipbuilding, textile manufacturing – had benefited greatly from the slave trade. Nor was it an accident that, despite the large population of Asian Americans in California, there were only a few in my university: discrimination and legislation against Chinese and Japanese laborers had begun before Japanese internment in World War II.

Recounted in writing, these revelations may seem like mere facts, and familiar ones at that. But for me they became almost physical, giving roots to the snowy-white privilege I had experienced since my childhood on a daily basis. Before I researched the lynching my father witnessed, I thought very little about my own race: as others have noted, white was default; race was what other people had. If I had once considered whiteness a given, or hadn't considered it much at all, I now have to consider it a *taken:* all of the benefits of my life – educational, material, intellectual – have been at the expense of others. As Eula Biss[1] wrote in a recent article in the *The New York Times Sunday Magazine*, I am indebted – in debt – to the people of color whose diminishment and exclusion have allowed me to move smoothly through good (almost-white) schools, a good (almost-white) university, and, without a racial thought or glitch, into the work and life I have enjoyed in the decades since.

I will not attempt to recount here the ways in which I have experienced and continue to experience white privilege in my immediate life – not the least of which, we all must realize by now, is the freedom to drive down the street with a broken tail-light or an expired license without danger to my life. What seems important to say is that, like the one-time worker in the slave trade who wrote the great hymn, "I once was blind, but now I see" – not well, not completely, but at least a little better than I did. The seeing has affected how I live and how I interact, what I do as an activist and what I write as a writer. I am still, so to speak, "covered" by whiteness: I can neither escape white privilege nor be aware of every aspect of it at any given moment. But I keep trying.

The snow is melting outside now: the roofs are still covered, but the trees are their usual wintry bare selves. That I can't think for long about trees without thinking of lynchings is perhaps a disturbing thing, but it's a good thing too. An important thing. And it's about time. ▪

---

1   Eula Biss is an award-winning American non-fiction writer.

Jan Priddy

White Noise

SKIM MILK AND NEW SNOW, Americans' teeth, the inside of most apples, stratus clouds, locker room towels, fleet trucks, bathtubs, coconut flesh, porcelain, chalk, sugar, bleached flour, drawing paper, Jockey shorts, daisy petals – loves me or loves me not? – picket fences, the whites of their eyes, the fog line beside the highway, and the sign that warns "Do Not Pass."

I am granted the option, but I do not decline to acknowledge my race on the forms. I check the box Non-Hispanic Surname Caucasian, though All of the Above is closer to the truth. My great grandmother on one side was from Mexico, and on the other was perhaps Blackfoot. I was never made to suffer for their color or languages. I am white. My relatives spoke English before I was born. My mother's skin was pinkish, her eyes were blue, her hair was pale. All my dolls had pinkish skin, blue eyes and blond curly hair. They did not resemble me in any detail. I dismantled them, pulled apart their arms and legs and removed their heads, studied their soft plastic joints, reassembled them in different order, used nail polish remover to wipe away their red lips and their dimpled pink cheeks, filled their bodies with dirt, left them out in the rain in the backyard. My childhood fury is what I conjure to remind myself what it means to stand before the master narrative and find myself excluded. No president has been a woman. It is not true that the masculine implies the feminine, as I was taught in school.

The White House, white nights, doves, frosting, feathers, pinprick stars, white chocolate, white out.

In the Western world, white is the color of innocence and brides, and what we name white diamonds in her ring is a colorless stone, clear like the raw white of a fresh egg. In the East, white is the mourning hue, not unblemished but the unadorned and empty void. In most Asian nations, brides traditionally wear saffron or red.

In light, white is all colors, in pigment it is the absence of color. White is a matter of perspective. White opals are valued for the color sparking their interior. A white paper is the concise and authoritative guide to solving a problem. Black Friday is the biggest shopping day of the year—the day retail goes solidly into the black and makes a profit. White imperialism, black power. Black heart, white swan. How we are named and what we are called.

Sun-bleached shells are white. In death, barnacles leave behind a white anchor and sand dollars I find on the shore are never white until they have passed dying and been thoroughly scoured by sea and light. The perched bald eagle I stood below this morning on my walk has white feathers on her head and also on her tail, but her heart and wings are clothed in brown.

Colors show on white. The pale page reveals the dark text, like the stripes make the zebra. It is the words that register, not the paper.

The leader of a workshop on teaching about race assured her audience that race did not exist. Scientifically, we accepted she was correct, but she was speaking to public school teachers. She compared distinguishing features between black and white to believing Asian people could be recognized by country of origin. She said that Japanese, Korean and Chinese people look alike. You know she was white. I told her: You grew up in the Dakotas; I grew up in Seattle. It would be unwise to tell a Korean American she looks Japanese. Not being able to see the difference between Italian and Swedish, or Indian and Chinese heritages shows you have not been paying attention. Physical anthropology aside, telling my students that race does not exist is unhelpful. Race exists in my country. It is a social and political reality. Yes, we invented it, but it will not go away because we pretend it does not exist. Race and gender are the first things we notice about a person. This is my country. This is where I live.

Dress shirts, bleached cotton, froth on the leading edge of every wave, white supremacists, white lies, fresh bandages.

I do not decline to answer because that seems a shameful way of pretending that, all things being equal (they never are), being white is something or anything other than an advantage in my country. I am fortunate, I am privileged, I am white. I cannot deny this.

Most pearls are not true white, but tinged cream or pink. The most valuable pearls are those with color: the South Sea pearls in aubergine, amber, and smoky gray. My mother's skin was not white and neither is mine. We are white but not white. The white ermine turns to a brown stoat in response to longer hours of daylight. A white elephant is the gift you have no use for. Polar bears show yellow shadows, a white Russian is only white on top, a great white shark is only white underneath, we tell white lies to avoid getting into trouble, and white water is the dangerous but thrilling stretch of rough river where we want to almost drown. White names are the ones discarded by slaves when they took back their freedom to identify themselves. That is not my people, they are my people. On white nights the sun never goes down. In a white out, your life is at risk from cold and confusion.

Race should not stand between people, should not make us suspicious of motive and genuine affection. But it does. Race matters. Sometimes the white fog between people bars friendship because the advantaged (me) and the other (them) cannot see past it. White means I might be asked where my people are from, and I can respond with the names of countries people have learned about in school, not a continent or region they cannot identify on a map. White means I glow in the dark. If I were a white male, white people would assume I earned my job and forget that my father might have friends, HR was hiring someone who looked like him, or I worked for bigots. If I were a black woman, I would not be allowed to speak at all.

Hospital sheets are not all white anymore. White chicken meat is not white and the dark is not so very dark. Pork is the other white meat and it is not white either. White is bleached, white is dead, white is blinding bright. Some Arabian horses are born dark chestnut or black and silver with age to gray and sometimes appear pure white, but these horses all have black skin underneath.

All skin is colored except for the albino pink skin that reveals the blood flowing inside us all.

Lives matter. I do not need to say that. Black lives matter. That needs to be said out loud.

My president is not white. He is a person of color, the child of a broken home but also fortunate to have grandparents who paid for private schools. His culture is mainstream, not ghetto, not poor. He did not wait on the porch on paydays for groceries to enter his kitchen. He did not walk to school in flip-flops because he had no other shoes. Advantage is a relative thing. When they were in high school, my sons walked into department stores and they were not automatically followed by Security, but I would bet money that both Barack and Michelle Obama had that experience as teenagers.

The steady hum of white noise puts us to sleep.

I do not decline to answer. I am answerable. I have no answers; I listen. Times change but not fast enough. We are a nation of many skin colors.

We are all shades of human. ▪

The Nothing

PBS IS HELPING ADOPTED CHILDREN "connect with their culture." The children who need to discover their roots are, of course, non-white. I skim the article with a fury I know is un-PC. I've tip-toed around this problem, afraid to say anything loud enough that anybody might hear, to say, *I have no culture, and I'm sick of people pretending I do.*

It's not that I think children adopted into U.S. households from Korea and China don't deserve to know about where they come from. But it's problematic that the only children anyone thinks need a cultural identity and history are non-white children. I don't believe Britain is exporting their children to the States, but if they did, would people see a need to connect those children to their roots? Would a typical middle-class American family understand there is a difference between the English, Irish, Scots, and Welsh? Would they take it one step further and understand there are distinct cultures within those distinct countries? The dividing line between Irish Catholic and Irish Protestant? Between Hackney and Greenwich? Or would they raise these children with American accents and slap braces on their teeth, and say, good enough? As if "white culture" is a monolith. As if you could swap out someone from Boston to Edinburgh, or Little Rock to New York, and nothing would be lost in translation. As if I've never felt an ache for a "culture" that wasn't plain old capitalism.

Maybe if my hair or eyes were dark, or if I had a bump in my nose, I could pretend I had some heritage worth discovering. I have light hair and blue eyes and my nose is small and unremarkable except that it has a mole on the tip. I am pale with freckles. I am probably part Irish, but who knows? I don't know. The thought of maybe being Irish does not make me feel found, like I could say "my people" the way so many around me casually throw out that phrase. If I ever uttered the words, "my people," others would find those two words laced with bigotry. I am white. I am part of the problem, all of the problems, generations, decades, centuries of problems, from my race, *my people*.

Irish. What would that mean? I think of leprechauns and cloudy skies and men hunched over pints of warm beer – that awkward dance where the top half of a body stays completely still while legs kick in frantic patterns. The superficial evidence – my appearance, my father's last name – points towards Ireland. Why would I bother to see if that's true? As if I could find out and say, *Ah yes, the Irish, my people.*

I would like to belong somewhere. I have no culture, no known ethnicity, nothing but pale freckled skin to label me white. I do not have a beach house in the Hamptons or wear designer clothes, so my culture isn't that sort of white. I am not interested in NASCAR and was never into *Hee-Haw,* so I guess I'm not that sort of white. I did not live in the suburbs or shop at The Gap while in high school – my family was poor – so I am not that sort of white. What sort of white am I? What stereotype fits best? Where is this culture everyone seems entitled to?

There are rumors of Native American blood on both sides of my family – as I assume there are in many white, history-less American households, as there are in so many black diaspora households. I wish I had the sort of shamelessness that would allow me to hear such a thing and declare it true, drop everything, embrace the Earth Mother and say, *Ah yes, it makes sense, my people.* I could fashion myself a headdress, beat a drum, dance, and scream out the connection I've been looking for that I cannot find.

I've toyed with the idea of being Greek. I like olive oil and yogurt. In high school, I bought a picture book, *Cats in the Sun,* on a whim. It shows feral cats running and lounging about Greece. I suppose adults are supposed to call such artifacts coffee table books. I would probably remember that better if I was that sort of white person.

My mother's father's grandmother was 100 percent Greek, fresh off the boat. That makes me 1/16th. Am I Greek?

I doubt it. What customs were ever taught to me, what rituals performed? What secret language spoken in soft voices just within earshot?

I'm not anything.

If I ever had a culture, it was Christianity. That's the closest I came. But I hate Christianity, hate organized religion. I am not interested in stories of mythical men in the sky who say you can sell your daughters into slavery if you need some extra cash, and if your wife or concubine pisses you off, feel free to cut off her ears and nose.

I'm sick of pretending I think there is such a thing as a "good Christian." I think any thoughtful person who still calls himself a Christian is deficient in reasoning, intentionally blind, digging a few sparkling bits out of the steaming piles of evil in centuries old texts for no reason other than his fear of his own mortality.

I don't mean it when I tell someone I think they are a "good" or "okay" Christian any more than the people who have told me I am a "good" or "okay" white person have said it with conviction, without a little shudder that betrays the belief in their bones that I am implicitly related to all the not-so-good and outright evil white people.

Fair enough.

Maybe I should believe in the mystical man in the sky. I could convince myself that I chose this life, chose this body, said, *Ah yes, those two idiot teenagers, I'd like for them to be my parents. They seem stable, both coming from single, alcoholic mothers with their histories of being shipped back and forth across the country, their GEDs obtained from alternative schools. Those are the ones, Almighty White Man in the Sky, that's where I want to be!*

Given a choice to be born into a series of different hypothetical worlds, where lots will be determined at random, most people will not choose the world where everyone is equal, has the same amount of stuff, is comfortable. Few choose the world where a handful are at the very top and most are at the bottom (though some do, and I assume those are libertarians who believe they can beat the experiment one bootstrap at a time). Most people pick the world where some have a fair bit more and most have a little less. They'd risk having less than the Joneses' for the chance to have more. For most people, an un-ideal world would be one in which everyone has what they need and no one has more or goes without.

To the best of my knowledge, they've only run this test on Americans. Depending on culture, results may vary.

That's my culture: capitalism, apple pie, baseball, imperialism, reality TV, oppression, brute force.

No one is going to adopt me. They tolerate me. I amuse them and probably piss them off more than they let on with my constant ignorance, my incessant questions, my endless epiphanies about what it might be like to not be white.

I was bonding with Alice Walker over *Anything We Love Can Be Saved*. I was envying her easy love, thinking of how to try it on. I was amen-ing her thoughts on being a woman, on religion, on mother-daughter relationships. I was crying in recognition and hope, but the whole time, I felt her arm stretched out from the pages of that book, her warm, worn hand planted firmly on my chest. *That's close enough, white girl.*

I wanted a way in. I wanted to tear the pages from their binding, scrape the glue with my nails.

I must be a brazen asshole.

All the privilege seeping from my pores, and I want to complain that I have no culture, that people look at me and see the evil in the world, that they want to distance themselves from me, that they call me "other." It's my own fault. My people called them "other," still call them "other." My people did this. My people created the chasm with boats and suburbs and fast food and entitled penises. *My people.*

I flinch every time someone says "my people." It reminds me who my people are, that I have no right to use that phrase, that generations of assholes sunning themselves in the Hamptons and dumping oil into the oceans and killing brown people for sport and profit have left me a legacy where I have no culture, and I do not belong. I am like a child brought about by rape or incest: people feel bad about not wanting me around, but they don't want me around. They know it's not my fault, but they can't help the way their skin crawls, the way they sometimes think they see my father's wicked eyes peering out from my face.

No one can tell me what white is, only what it is not. It is never Hispanic. I know from the countless affirmative action forms I filled out while trying to gain meaningful employment. The top box was always WHITE with a tag to specify "non-Hispanic." I'd read over the forms, looking for some other box to pick, something that seemed to maybe almost define me as a person. I'd yell at the forms, Race doesn't exist! But I know it does. Biologically no, but socially yes, so I'd read the forms carefully, look for a loophole, puzzle over people whose "race" was one thing on one form, something else on the next.

Each time, I'd cave. I'd check the box next to WHITE with a shaking hand. I'd swear I'd do better next time, but I never did. Once, in frustration, I read a sheet, and read it again. I couldn't make sense of it. The lights in my room became too bright, my furniture sped out away from my body and I scrawled THESE CATEGORIES MAKE NO SENSE. I DO NOT KNOW WHAT YOU'RE TALKING ABOUT across the form.

There is no victory in denying my whiteness. Those forms are not for me, which is why they put my box at the top, expecting me to put in a neat little check mark or X and forget about it. Those forms are supposed to be a safety net or at least an accounting, a record of prejudice and bigotry overcome or not. Denying my whiteness would only slant the figures, would only make me that much more wrong.

My people, my people, my people, my people, my people.

What's weird about my dawning realizations of my own possible Irishness is that two of the best friends I've had were obsessed with their Irishness. They know how to stand on their toes and lift their knees, the top halves of their bodies perfectly still. They do not think of leprechauns. The men with pints of warm beer are men to be embraced. I never understood their obsessions, never imagined that I too could be Irish. The dancing and music and stories never had anything to do with me.

Dyeing my blond hair red made me look more Irish. I should have gone dark brown, the hair I've always wanted, the hair I've envied on the dainty quiet girls and the self-assured badass women with dark eyeliner, bright lips, and straight across bangs. Maybe with dark hair I'd feel more Greek, but Greek or Irish, it's all the same. None of it has anything to do with me.

My hair is red like my rage, my endless rage about everything I and everyone else have to endure. Told to pick an element to represent me during a writing exercise, I chose fire in the nanosecond it took the words to leave the professor's mouth. I was surprised most people did not choose fire. They were wispy air, go-along water, sturdy rocks.

I forget other people are not like me.

I forget that so many of my people, who also do not have houses in the Hamptons or watch NASCAR, can walk through the world unaware that the majority of people on the globe do not like them, do not trust them, have a special face they put on when whitey is in the room. I know about the mask or second face. Or really, I should say I know of it since I will never experience it myself, never really know. Most of my people can walk through life oblivious, both to the suffering of others and their own bizarre privilege, can think all that matters is that they try to be a good person.

That is not enough.

The problem is, there is no answer, nothing I can do, no way I could get people who are important to me to show me their real faces. I've come so close with one of my oldest friends and mentor, but even she cannot show me her true face, would not begin to know how. When I was babysitting her toddler daughter, an old episode of *Sesame Street* came on, and some black woman was acting the fool. I can't even remember exactly how because it meant nothing to me. My beautiful, wonderful, perfect mentor blushed, turned away, said "I am *so embarrassed.*"

I know how to feel sorry for myself, how to take on burdens that aren't mine, but I cannot imagine living every moment of my life as a representative of *my people,* of having to constantly turn away from Fox News or MTV or the speeches of politicians and CEOs and say, *I am so embarrassed.*

Because I have no culture, I do not have to be a representative. It is the dominance of my people, the economic and legislated and military dominance that keeps me above scrutiny, beyond blame, and completely without trust. How could I understand what it is to be co-opted, demeaned, deprived? How can you trust someone with no soul, no ancestors, no heritage or history? Someone who came wriggling and screaming into the world with pale skin, white hair, and blue eyes? My color is the absence of color. My culture is the absence of culture. My identity is comprised mostly by what it is not.

I am a product of my culture, raised on Kraft singles and *90210*, living without extended family, an island of school and work, the only traditions national holidays, served with a hodgepodge of store-bought nothingness. No one in my family liked cranberry sauce, so we stopped having it for Thanksgiving. Since we had no traditions, we made everything up as we went.

One of my moronic epiphanies involved a good friend telling me he was in college before he read a book whose protagonist was *like him* (Asian). It changed his life, discovering that there were books by and about people like him. A new universe of possibilities opened in that instant when he discovered everything didn't have to be white all the time.

I have no idea what that is like. I cannot imagine from a young age only seeing faces on the television that never resembled my own, and if one vaguely like mine snuck in, it was some horrible, grinning caricature of a human being who was ridiculed and humiliated by hordes of white people. I do not know what that's like, what it does to you, how it starts to create your second face.

There are thousands of stories of white "everymen" with their mundane lives and families and monetary concerns, and bosses and mothers and breakups. I have rarely cared or been invested in such tales. Occasionally a good essayist can move me, but in fiction, the plight of your average white cultureless, ungrounded, American-dreaming protagonist leaves me cold. Their lives are devoid of meaning and import in a way that mirrors my own nothingness. *The Neverending Story* nailed it: "A hole, that would be something, but no, this was *nothing*." I think of that line when I try to figure out my culture, American culture in general, white American culture, the culture of *my people* in specific.

Yes, I am properly ashamed of my romanticization of indigenous cultures, my secret longings to be native, to be "other," to be anything not white. I desperately want to belong, but not to "The White Man," please. Just, please.

[handwritten margin note:] Disagree — sounds like internalized shame to me

I once dreamt I was confronted with a faceless donkey. Inside the donkey was the nothing, it must have been, because what I saw there was devoid of anything. I drew a picture of its head with pastels, wearing the black stick down to a nub. After years of being chased by that vision, I had one of my obvious epiphanies. I was sitting at my desk, pissed off and paralyzed, when I realized:

That faceless donkey is me.

A lot of people think they know me. They think that because I'm loud and say things others wouldn't, that they always know where I stand, what I think. They imagine they can see my face when all they can see is fire. The closest I come to showing my face is in my essays, but even then, it's hard to make out. You have to get past the fire and confront the nothing. Most people cannot confront the nothing, it consumes them or they flee.

But I like to think I have a true face, that just for a minute, Alice Walker reached through my mask and caressed my true cheek with gentle fingers before pushing me back to a safe distance. I like to imagine my true face looks something like sunshine on a clear day, that it has room for birds and lush grass, that somewhere, under the fire, under the nothing, exists a soul of love, that loves and is loved, that might someday push through the nothing, extinguish the flames and say, *look at me, I'm right here.*

My secret hope is that we could start making our own cultures, our own traditions. That I could look around and say, *this feels right,* and not worry that I'm appropriating someone else's heritage, their ancestors, their culture that includes so many plus signs while mine has never been anything but the nothing. I dream of a world where I could say, *my ancestors are black,* and not have people hate me. Because they are, and we all know this fundamental fact, but we do not want to say it out loud. We are all children of Africa, however far and wide our ancestors ranged, no matter the sunlight that fell or didn't fall on their faces, creating the spectrum of melanin we find now. My appearance is the simple mathematics of vitamin D absorption into the skin, what worked best for my recent ancestors who rarely saw the sun.

We know the superficial differences between us are not so vast as the similarities, the sinews and sweat and bones and blood of our relatedness. We know the entire world has been constructed by those who wish to maintain order, keep what is unfairly theirs from the rest of us. They created borders and race and poverty. It is nothing we chose. Nothing I chose.

I forget other people are not like me.

Given a chance to play the game, in the nanosecond after the experimenter read the rules, I would laugh and cry out, *the perfect world!* The one where no one wants, where everyone can be happy together. The world where we all support and love each other, where everyone's needs are met, where we aren't born powerful or weak because of our bodies, be they soaked in melanin or bereft, whether our genitalia is internal or external or both. A beautiful world where we could all walk around, proudly displaying our faces that look like a sunny day or the soft snowfall of winter or a gust of autumn leaves. We could hold each other's faces in our warm hands, look into those portals, cry at the beauty, whisper, *I see you.* ▪

Lynn Z. Bloom

Locating Whiteness

L IKE SNOWSHOE HARES, where we are – in the bright snow, the brown woods – determines how we look, how we see ourselves, and how we are understood.

Durham, New Hampshire, 1940s. As a child growing up in the postcard pretty college town of Durham, New Hampshire I am unaware of being white except when I turn lobster red from a cherished day at the beach. As if rendered by Norman Rockwell, the town – not far from the White Mountains – is enveloped in whiteness: pristine winter snowfalls, the white congregational church, white houses, and the all white local schools, from pre-kindergarten through college. White teachers, white students, white staff, including maintenance workers. Color creeps into our consciousness with glimpses of Jamaican migrant apple pickers, largely out of sight in the orchards. Yet sinister submarine shapes – real and imaginary – menace the Portsmouth Naval Shipyard where the Piscataqua River feeds into the Atlantic. They might be Japanese, a manifestation of the yellow peril we're taught to fear from the *March of Time* movies we watch in school assemblies, made by Louis de Rochemont, a famous filmmaker who actually lives here. But in fact they are Nazi U-2 boats, which from my second grader's perspective seem somehow less threatening because my family – a proud clan of Zimmermans – is German, right down to my kindly grandfather's menacing name, "Oswald Adolf."

Fifteen years later I leave that town for good to marry Martin, in exile in England, startled by my father's curse, "As Martin's wife you'll be the victim of anti-Semitism for the rest of your life. If you marry him, we will have nothing to do with you, or him, or any children you may have" — a claim my parents fulfill over the decades of our marriage. I don't argue. I understand that evidence will not change bigots' minds or melt their hearts. But I do resolve never to be prejudiced against anyone, ever, on the basis of race, religion, ethnicity, class (soon I add gender, much later, disability). Over time, I realize how complex this simple assertion can become, because there are so many ways in which prejudice can be manifested, often subtly and below the radar. So this vow has numerous iterations, powerfully influenced by where I live.

Cleveland and Cleveland Heights, Ohio, 1960s. With a new Michigan PhD, two new babies, and a first book in progress, a biography of world-famous pediatrician Benjamin Spock, come new experiences related to race. I am startled when I respond to an ad for a housekeeper and a child answers my "May I please speak to..." with "Mama, there's a white lady on the phone!" Never, in all the linguistics I've studied, has race ever been associated with accent. I hire black (the PC term *du jour*) women with children of their own to clean my house and babysit two days a week so I can teach part-time and write. I invite them to come in through the front door; I prepare the lunch we eat together. They tell me that these courtesies are unusual. They accept my higher pay scale, which I think is only fair; as parents, we're in the same boat.

My research on Dr. Spock involves visits to the Case Western Reserve Family Clinic, where medical students are assigned to work with the same family throughout their four years in school. The students are white, the families are black and poor. Spock stretches his 6'4" frame to sit on the floor to hold the children on his lap, beaming as they treat him like a jungle gym. Because my own children are the same ages as these, I can soon ascertain a major difference between what I privately call "black" medicine and "white," although it actually reflects socio-economic status rather than race. At the clinic, black babies receive massive single-shot doses of medicine on site, or hospitalization, for the same ailments that my children, as a physician's private patients, are treated for at home with small doses of medicine spread over ten days. "Why the difference?" I ask Spock. "We can't count on clinic parents to obey the instructions or to follow through by giving medicine over time, so we put the children in the hospital to make sure they get the right treatment."

With my children in a stroller, I join Spock, ever relaxed even during the time of the race riots in Cleveland's Hough district, and a multiracial assortment of activists (aka hippies) on marches – against nuclear testing, for racial equality, against the Vietnam War. These Cleveland marches are so good-natured that I am oblivious to the scrutiny of a former student turned ratfink for the FBI; from then on we answer the phone to clicks and heavy breathing, "Hello, spies." The marches in New York, led by Dr. Spock and Dr. Martin Luther King Jr. are on a different order of magnitude (est. 500,000), tension (no babies here), and level of danger. When from the front row I see that Dr. King is surrounded by a flying wedge of black-suited black bodyguards, I understand that I too am in the line of fire, but there is no turning back.

Albuquerque, New Mexico, mid-1970s. For three exhilarating years I commute two thousand miles a week, between St. Louis, where we live, and Albuquerque, where I direct the writing program at the University of New Mexico. There, where hot air balloons sail over campus toward the Sandias, I teach the widest range of students that I'll ever encounter in a long career. In this Land of Enchantment, Anglos are a minority in a culture dominated by Hispanics, Latinos, and Native Americans (with accents of black, Asian, and Pacific Islanders). The University, with a largely white faculty, Latino and Indian staff, is racing to accommodate this expansive mixture. Although I remain baffled by Navajo sheep jokes and the gesture language of shrugs and tics that evokes roars of laughter from other Indians, I am always learning from the students – ranchers and bikers, activists and artists from the rez, skiers and hikers and rodeo riders. They teach me how to survive in extreme mountain climate ("always drive with water, blankets, sand, and a shovel, even in summer"); how to eat fry bread and blue corn tortillas and (essential for this effete Easterner) to avoid any chilis hotter than *anchos;* how to flat out have fun in fiesta, but duck the rifle shots on Cinco de Mayo. l learn, too, to listen to the lilting lingua franca of flutes, guitars, and the throbbing drums carried high on the western wind that never stops, heartbeats of the mesa. As a writer, I feel most at home living on the edge of so many vibrant cultures; we'd move there in a heartbeat if my husband could find a job there. But he can't, so we move to an entirely different colonial society.

Williamsburg and Richmond, Virginia, late 1970-80s. The blackest society we've ever lived in, and the most complicated because of the cultural ropes and pulleys that extend from colonial times to the present. First, I teach at the College of William and Mary, a state university that flaunts private privilege while fitfully endeavoring to overcome two centuries of white domination. My office is down the hall from the Center for Adult Literacy, and after a couple weeks of directing older blacks who arrive in my office by mistake, I realize they can't read. Deprived of schooling during the years when public schools became private rather than desegregate, now embarrassed and proud, they are eager to change their lives. I learn to lead them to the right office, rather than point to the signs. When I see them later in the grocery store, puzzled by the prices on packages of chicken backs and necks, "I forgot my glasses," they say, I explain that because drumsticks are on sale this week, they're the better buy.

At the other end of the educational spectrum is the first black faculty woman the College has ever hired, upbeat, energetic, and supersmart. We become very good friends, although not until researching this essay do I learn that her father, a cotton farmer, was jailed for a year, accused of stealing a bale of hay; or that as a Stillman College student how different her participation in civil rights demonstrations was from mine, for in Tuscaloosa blacks were routinely gassed, beaten, and jailed – experiences that undergird her distinguished scholarship on the complexities of blacks in the South. When offered a better job (both of us on a fast track to endowed chairs), she asks my advice. "Take it," I say, affirming the obvious, "You deserve it." I too, move on, to Virginia Commonwealth University, the blackest white school in the state, close enough in ambience to New Mexico to feel like home. Then on to the University of Connecticut in Storrs, as white in the 1980s as Durham, New Hampshire was in the 1940s, and a quarter-century away from incorporating the colors – and the snowshoe hares – of this iridescent world. ■

Adam Wier

Translating Whiteness

'VE BEEN TOLD ONCE THAT TRANSLATION is one of the few professions where you cannot be racist or a bigot. This is only partially true. It's a profession that, by definition, requires you to be in contact with people of another culture, and not merely to be in contact with them, but to speak for them, to share their ideas and point of view, retelling them as sincerely and earnestly as if they were your own. This, however, doesn't exempt a translator or interpreter from being racist. It just makes blatant racism difficult. What we are waking up to today is the fact that racism doesn't normally look like shouting a slur or an act of violence, but it's the participation, often unknowingly, in social constructs that have been set in place long before you and I were born.

Growing up white in America, these constructs are normally completely invisible. We get the luxury of not having to think about them or notice them because they don't affect us, or if they do affect us, they affect us positively. It's completely possible that a white person in America can live out his or her life without asking once, "What does it mean to be white in America?" It's not until he or she has significant contact with people of another race that the question even has any hope of forming. Culture can never be understood directly. It has to be compared to another to uncover its invisible-like-air characteristics. For me, translation has helped me begin asking that question.

I first began to notice my whiteness, and therefore set on the road to asking "What does it mean to be white in America?" when I was in college studying translation. In my courses for Spanish literature, language, and translation, there was a noticeable divide between the native and second language speakers. To a degree, this is to be expected:

The two groups have very different approaches to the language and are learning in distinct ways. However, it was this separation that planted the seed of the question.

The divide became more noticeable when, a few semesters later, I enrolled in a course on translation from English to Spanish. Translation is traditionally done to your native language, and therefore the class, unlike the others, who were split pretty equally, had predominantly native speakers. I can still remember the woman behind me who would say under her breath but still loud enough that I could hear: "No...., no...., uhn huh..." every time I suggested an improvement during class exercises. Of course, my answer was not always the best choice, but it used to drive me crazy how she would say it with a particular tone in her voice, as if I were a silly child who just couldn't figure it out. The tone of superiority drove me nuts. It was clear that I was out of my element, that I had crossed into foreign territory. The seed began to sprout.

Years later after graduation when I would go on to work with writers and poets to help translate their works, I experienced the same kind of reaction. Though now my language and translation skills had vastly improved, I was still often met with a lot of resistance when I would suggest changes and improvements to translations. I would try to ask questions to probe at what the source of their dissatisfaction was with my suggestions, but even my questions were met with resistance. At first I chalked it up to nothing more than artists being artists. Creative types often do live up to their reputation of being difficult to work with, especially in art forms such as writing, where collaboration isn't a necessary part of the creative process. However, when emails would come back to me bilingually, first in Spanish and then translated into English, it dawned on me: They didn't believe that I was actually able to comprehend Spanish. They didn't believe it because my name was Adam Wier, and I was clearly not Hispanic. I was a *gringo*.

You see, I, like most, never thought about my culture or race until I was "othered." When you're the majority, there's no reason and there's no method to do so. But when you grow up not white in America, you're "othered" from the moment you're born. The question is one that has been asked before your birth, and to a greater or lesser degree, you inherit the question and, hopefully, all the work that's gone into solving it before you, to which you will also contribute. When you are white, there is often no such inheritance. You have to figure it out on your own, if you're going to even attempt to figure it out at all. "What does being white in America mean?" It means, in part, being absolutely clueless.

For example, many people in America would be surprised to know that though their ancestors are considered white today, they weren't always. We ask each other, "What is your heritage?" And in the Midwest especially, we rattle off a list of countries our ancestors are from, but we never say "white" and leave it at that. To a degree, this is not inaccurate. For example, in my own family, the most recent immigrants are Italian, with my great-grandfather being the one to across the ocean and come to America. While I don't know if you could really call our family Italian, you can still see vestiges and roots of it in our food, in our family relations, in the few curse words my family still remembers in Italian, but really, we are no longer Italian. Why is this? Italians were once subject to racism, just like other "white" nationalities, such as the Irish. The difference between them and other minorities is that they looked, to a greater or lesser degree like the majority, and instead, they exchanged a question for a statement: "We are white too," though no one really knew what that actually meant. This, over time, changed the definition of what is white. Once Italian and Irish were not considered white. Now they are. "What does being white in America mean?" It means you're with us or against us. And herein lies the major problem.

Up until now, this has been the mentality: "You are with us or against us." This kind of thinking is simplistic and, of course, not very conducive for questioning. However, many do not have the option to join up. Their only option is to keep on with the question. As the cultural landscape of America changes to include more and more people without the option or desire to whitewash themselves the question of "What does it mean to be white in America?" becomes all the more relevant. Slowly but surely, the "with us or against us" mentality is fading to sincerely ask the question, but to do so, it is necessary to make contact with other cultures and ways of thinking.

Our social groups are becoming less and less insular, though they still have a long way to go. I was lucky in that I had an aptitude and love of languages that lead me to become a translator. I've had the privilege of working with different cultures and using that to help ask myself the question. I've traveled abroad and lived in countries where my foreignness was obvious at first glance. In life I've continually sought out these experiences and reflected on them. Because therein lies the rub: Finding the answer to the question "What does it mean to be white in America?" isn't in facing it head on. When we do that, we just invent our own narrative. It's in examining the border of whiteness with blackness, of whiteness with Chineseness, of whiteness with anything else. We can't see ourselves without a mirror, and for white people in America, these mirrors are scarce.

So what does it mean to be white in America? It means to be born completely unconscious of your race, live your life completely unconscious of your race, and to never examine the question until you are blind-sided by it. But not for long. Finally, we've begun to answer the question that others have been facing for generations before. Slowly but surely. And when we've found the answer, it's my hope that we'll let go of this confrontational mentality that's been our bane. Only then can the U.S. be the tapestry of cultures and races it is meant to be. ■

Christina Berchini

How to Be White:
A Primer

THERE IS A SERIES OF RULES GOVERNING being white in America. The inculcation into *How to Be White* begins at an early age, and with the most committed of educators—usually one's family. But first, a primer of lazy platitudes—a series of unfortunate tropes that highlight some of the most common stereotypes about what it means to be white in America:

"Racism is over–we have a black president!"

To be white, for some, is to believe that we live in a post-racial society—that racism is, indeed, "over" by virtue of electing a black president into office for the first time in this nation's history. According to the primer of *How to Be White*, a good white will equate Barack Obama's presidential victories with the dissolution of racism; they will then proceed to dismantle affirmative action policies, support tough voting restrictions and suppression, and instigate heated discussions about theories of self-reliance involving bootstraps and the American dream—with or without an audience.

"You know what? I was discriminated against too. I experienced "reverse racism," so don't talk to me about racism."

To be white is to believe in the myth of reverse racism—as though whites actually experience institutionalized racism because of one or two individualized experiences during which they felt personally slighted or even "oppressed." The most devout whites are prepared to pull the reverse racism card for any and all instances in which what they wanted did not come as easily or as quickly as they are accustomed to (e.g., success, opportunity, admiration, or even that order of fried cheese curds they've been waiting for, for fifteen entire goddamned minutes). Indeed, chapter three of the primer on *How to Be White* very thoroughly explains that all people – regardless of social positioning – begin in the exact same place with the exact same access to all that life has to offer.

"A mosque should not be anywhere near the World Trade Center site!"

To be white is to have no idea whatsoever that many of Middle Eastern descent considered themselves "white" until society after 9/11 told them that they were not. The very best of whites associate a legitimate place of worship with terrorism while excluding churches from this same classification, despite observable evidence to the contrary.

"I didn't own slaves, so racism isn't my problem."

To be a good white is to dissociate from the problem of racism simply because one was not born in the eighteenth or nineteenth century; as though racism – both institutionalized and individualized – has not since persisted as a metastatic cancer in the vessels, cells, veins, organs, bones, and muscles that keep society "functioning." Indeed, very good whites maintain that racism "isn't a problem" for as long as slavery remains outlawed and for as long as whites continue to benefit from racist institutions (e.g., educational, legal, entertainment, etc.) in tangible and symbolic ways. The most devout whites will watch Viola Davis make history as the first African American to win an Emmy Award for best actress in a drama and wonder what the hell she was being so goddamned "militant"[1] about.

"See? They're all evil. Just look at the Boston marathon bombers!"

To be white is to condemn an entire group and culture when individuals from an unfamiliar ethnic background commit a heinous crime.

---

1   Clover Hope, "Viola Davis Explains the 'Militant' Harriet Tubman Quote From Her Emmy's Speech," *Jezebel.com*, September 30, 2015, http://jezebel.com/viola-davis-explains-the-militant-harriet-tubman-quote-1733762557. See Hope's discussion of Viola Davis' historical Emmy's acceptance speech, in which Davis invoked the words of Harriet Tubman to discuss the racialized state of the entertainment industry as black women have come to experience it.

To be white is to not ever have said or believed, "See? They're *all* evil. Just look at Timothy McVeigh!" in response to the bombing of Oklahoma City's Murrah Building in 1995. To be white is to be exempt from the same group-condemnation in which they participate willingly. The primer is quite clear about this point: When a white commits a crime (such a person is considered a bad white, to be sure), *good* whites divert our attention toward the "individual" with "mental health problems," as with when James Holmes shot up a movie theater in Colorado, or more recently, when Dylann Storm Roof went on a murderous rampage in a historically black church in South Carolina. To be a white murderer is to be a lone individual in need of psychiatric care; it is to never, ever be a member of a larger contemptible social group. I believe Oxford is in the process of updating their dictionary in this regard (see "Caucasian" and "unearned privilege"), so sit tight.

"But, but, but, what about black-on-black gun violence, huh?! What do you have to say about that?!"

To be white is to sputter and deflect from the reality that most mass shootings in this nation's history have been committed by white men.[2] To be white is to invoke nonsensical arguments about people of color in order to close down any discussion about the ways by which whiteness and racism intersect with violence; to be a good white is to avoid any idea that perhaps, just perhaps, whites—as a group—have proven themselves astonishingly capable of incredible acts of violence and terrorism.

"I'm not racist, but..."

To be white is to be unafraid to speak the word "but" in a sentence beginning with "I'm not racist..." To be white is to believe that you are not "actually" racist, even if you use the word "but" to rationalize racial epithets, racist generalizations, and the racist views to which you espouse.

---

2   Mark Follman, Gavin Aronsen, and Deanna Pan, "A Guide to Mass Shootings in America," *Mother Jones* October 2, 2015, http://www.motherjones.com/politics/2012/07/mass-shootings-map. This article exposes how more than half of mass shootings in America have been committed by young white men.

"I'm not racist – I have a black friend!"

To be white is to believe that knowing the name of a person of color renders one exempt from acknowledging their own social location in a racialized society. To be white is to eschew all responsibility for learning about present-day forms of racialized oppression from which many whites benefit directly. A black friend gives whites a pass – all good whites know that having black friends makes all forms of institutionalized racism and oppression that much easier to tolerate, and perhaps even enjoyable.

"Black lives matter, you say? How about this – All lives matter. Ah-hyuck, hyuck, hyuck, hyuck…"

To be white is to take the issue of systemic violence committed by the police force against people of color and smugly turn it into some sort of competition with rhetorically powerful – yet hopelessly ignorant – phrases such as "all lives matter." To be white is to derail important conversations about why whites will never be racially profiled or violently targeted by authorities and institutions in the United States strictly because of the color of their skin – despite what so many young white men in particular have proven capable of. To be white is to ignore how some lives seem to matter more than others if we allow the evidence to speak for itself. The very best whites update their Facebook and Twitter feeds with #colorblind in order to remind everyone of how good they are.

"The way you talk about white people makes you racist!"

I can't even… I just can't even.

In short, these oft-used platitudes might signify that to be white is to derail; it is to dissociate from the responsibility of working toward a more socially just society; it is to believe that the statements and arguments put forth above are legitimate and informed statements and arguments. And finally, to be white is to never be called to task by other whites for any of these harmful and distracting ideas.

When I received the call to contribute to a volume on whiteness, my internal responses ran the gamut. I was mostly excited by the opportunity, but I was also nervous. What sort of entries would the editors receive? What sort of entries would they *accept?* If my entry were accepted, what sort of stories, anecdotes, and arguments would my words live amongst and between? There is not any shortage of whites who are afraid to cry "reverse racism!," "I'm not racist, *but…*" or "All lives matter" (or, worse yet, "*Blue* lives matter!") when invited to do so. As such, with whom and in what ways might I be considered guilty by association? To discuss what it means to be white is, potentially, a perilous thing. Like a petulant toddler or a Republican official with far too much disposable income, you never quite know the trouble that the "words of whites" are going to cause.

As a whiteness scholar, I share my interpretations and stories with a bit of trepidation. My livelihood rests on my contributions to my field of study: the study of whiteness, specifically as it plays out in education (e.g. schools, teaching, and curriculum). To share my stories is risky – if I tell them in the "wrong" way, I risk condemnation from my field and professional community, which expects me to know how to talk about these things. If I tell my stories in the "right" way, I risk my (white) family noticing and becoming, well, pretty damned angry. If I choose not to share my stories about my own education into whiteness, my own "primer," I have no one but myself to blame. All of these fears and concerns have ultimately conspired to dictate my decision to contribute to the discussion about what it means to be white in America. I am telling my stories because, while the statements and pronouncements with which I open this essay are upsettingly common and normal (and hyperbolized for my own amusement), we need more stories. We need other stories. To be white is to be a bit more than a walking series of quick platitudes, wielded and adapted at our convenience. To be white is more than participating in a vicious forum on CNN. There is much more to the story than this, and my guess is that we'd all be hard-pressed to locate a white person who cannot attest, on some level, to the emotional and physical toll associated with being white.

Besides, not all whites abide by the "primer" with which I opened this essay. Many of us are well aware of our social location and struggle with what this means in our daily lives – those of us who are a bit more aware are working with a different sort of primer: One which allows us to understand, truly, why the platitudes I described above are so infuriating and even hopeless. Moreover, my musings are not to suggest that the toll associated with being white even comes close to the experiences of people of color, or the stories they might tell. This essay is also not to compare the two; it's not a competition. It intends to show how, for many, what it means to be white in America is to constantly walk a tightrope between one's home community and a larger world aching to become more socially just.

Now that we have our primer on what it means to be a good white in America, let's talk about some of the rules.

■ ■ ■

The first rule of being white: *Interracial marriage is "trouble."*

"It's not that we're racist. But if you marry a black man, you're asking for trouble. Just look at your cousin."

I could not have been more than nine or ten years old when my mom "educated" me about the dangers of entering an interracial relationship. Nor was I even remotely thinking of marriage and future prospects. Before this discussion with my mother, the only thing I knew was that I liked my cousin Maggie and her husband, Sabri. They were kind to my sister and me; as children, that was all that mattered to us. They had a daughter around my age, and a son a bit older. My cousins and I would see each other often and got along well when we did. I never thought about Sabri's race, or even noticed that his children had a bit of a darker complexion than my sister and me.

Before my mom's "warning," I never would have guessed that my cousins were shunned at best and brutally harassed at worst because of their biracial family. The 1980s were not kind to these sorts of dynamics, not even in New York City–the place we called home, and the place that seemed like such a far cry from the kinds of bucolic, less-evolved parts of the country; those parts of America where it might seem that racism, intolerance, hate crimes, and violence are explicitly built into state constitutions as characteristics, behaviors, and outcomes to be revered.

Perhaps my mom was just acting racist disguised as "concerned" for her daughter's future, or maybe her goal really *was* my "safety" and protection from social disapproval and rejection at best, and retaliation at worst. I did not respond, or pay much mind to my mother's attempt to instill this first rule of being white; as a child, I did not think much about her dedication to educating me out of any idea that interracial relationships were an option for my own future relationships.

Besides, I was not raised to be racist in any explicit sort of way. So I didn't think twice about my parents' attempts to laugh off my maternal grandfather's horrifically racist views and his frequent threats to disown me if I even *thought* about marrying a black man. I ignored him when he said disgusting things about people of color by invoking racial stereotypes that were common in his day (e.g., his frequent references to "Sambo"). A lot of this idiocy fell on my young, deaf ears. My grandfather was who he was; he also lived across the country, so we were not exposed all that much to his unevolved ways of thinking. Here again, I was not explicitly raised to be racist, and for me, that was all that mattered.

And then I became a teenager.

■ ■ ■

THE SECOND RULE OF BEING WHITE: *"Stick to your own kind."*

Mike was tall and muscular with thick, curly dark hair, and eyelashes that grown women envied. He inherited his mom's light blue eyes and his dad's chocolate skin—a fortuitous accident of genetics that did not go unnoticed by other girls my age. Mike admired his grandfather and loved his baby brother; he often teased his little sister, as older brothers are wont to do. I was as smitten as a sixteen-year-old girl could manage to be. And this beautiful young man liked me right back.

I suppose I should have predicted that the color of Mike's skin would lead to more trouble; more rules from my family, governing how to be white. But I did not predict this continued education. Instead, and like many blissfully oblivious teenagers who find love, I had stomach butterflies to think about and phone calls to anticipate.

"Stick to your own kind," my grandmother admonished, after she saw Mike and me together.

I was dumbfounded. My grandmother did not often take a harsh or critical tone with me. Indeed, I'd never really given her a reason to. She was not an educated or accomplished woman, but she loved me fiercely and had only ever been proud of me, her firstborn granddaughter. That is, until she took notice of my love interest. That's when the gloves came off.

She must have noticed my stunned expression, because her voice softened, but only somewhat. "Whites need to stick to their own. That's just the way it is," she said.

I had no idea, at the time, what my grandmother had seen in her nearly six decades on the planet. And I didn't ask. I didn't want to know. I was a curious kid, but I also burrowed into the bubble of ignorance that tends to encapsulate one's youth, as frequently as I could get away with. So I didn't ask. Besides, adults are always right, right? And children should be seen and not heard, right?

My grandmother's words and tone seemed markedly different from my mother's; my mother's rule of being white seemed to come from a place of misguided concern. My grandmother's rule of being white seemed to come from a place of unchecked disdain.

What I would find out nearly two decades later was that my grandmother was a product of rape. Allegedly, the rapist happened to be a person of color. While my knowledge of this event certainly does not excuse her poisonous perspective, it does explain, on some level, why she said what she said. I'll never know which rule of being white might have been passed down to me had my great-grandmother's rapist been a white guy.

But I do know this: That summer, my feelings for Mike would be the thing to chip away at my relationship with my grandmother. So I found a way to tell Mike that I couldn't see him anymore. It seemed that my relationship with my grandmother depended on it. I've never quite been able to forget how my attraction to a young man of color threatened my relationship with a woman I loved deeply. Unfortunately, the second rule of being white lowered over my relationship with my grandmother like a pall for the next ten years, which happened to be her last ten years on earth. Deviating from the rules of being white—in particular, the expectation that young white women should "stick with their own kind" – is an act of defiance that can divide families and destroy relationships.

The ways by which whiteness has the power to change relationships is a lesson I continue to learn the hard way when whiteness became my life's work – and especially when I began to talk about it publicly.

■ ■ ■

THE THIRD RULE OF BEING WHITE: *"Don't talk about being white."*

As a whiteness scholar, one of my goals is to make my work with whiteness accessible to a more mainstream audience; to make my work "readable" to those beyond the academy, my colleagues, and peers. As a result, when I write for more mainstream venues, I often enter the rink with the entire Internet – a bottomless pit of morbidity and doom consisting of mainly anonymous pathogens who are averse to any talk of what it means to recognize how whiteness and racism play out in institutions, society, and personal relationships. For this faceless audience, there is only one rule of being white: Don't talk about being white, under any circumstances.

To openly struggle with whiteness and white roots is a no-no; the black-hole-of-doom (i.e., the Internet) idly sits by, waiting for the first opportunity to pounce like vermin on those who reject this rule. One such example is when I decided to write about a conversation with my mother, when she commented on the possibility of a mosque being erected in her New York City neighborhood:

"We got dressed to go to the gym, but decided to put our house on the market instead," my mother casually delivered this news to me on the phone and across the 1,100 miles that now separate us. She was in the middle of preparing dinner; I was in the middle of a power-walk.

I always talk to my mother in transit. It is my way of multitasking, and she despises it. I think taking care of my phone calls with my mom while power walking is also my way of physically relieving the stress that I know is bound to arise from a conversation with her.

"Uh…what?" Her news threw me off. She and my stepfather bought this home eight years ago. It was their first home. Have they even broken it in yet?

"What happened?" I was genuinely curious about how one leaps from going to the gym to listing their home on the market. But, I have not yet learned that simple questions like "what happened?" are dangerous questions. And not only are they dangerous questions, but they are also painful reminders of how my relationship with my mother has changed over the last six years.

"The neighbors' backyard smells like dog shit and it's wafting over into our yard and I am sick of it. And there's another Mosque going up and I'm sorry, but I associate mosques with terrorism."

Interesting, I thought. My view of churches might be chalked up similarly. I no longer say these things aloud, though. My relationship with my mother depends on it.

I am no longer shocked to hear about my parents' ignorant and hateful views toward cultures and people about whom they know nothing other than some observable semblance of "difference." I am no longer shocked when the words they spew mirror that of a Fox News feed. The only thing that continues to shock me (and I think it always will) is the ease with which they say these things to me.

I study race in education. I study racism. I study what it means to be a white person with white privilege in a society that prizes whiteness over all else. I work toward anti-racism in education, as a teacher educator. This is my life's work. My students' efficacy, as future teachers, depends on my capacity to engage these issues with them in meaningful ways.

My students depend on my capacity to prepare them to enter schools with the understanding that they are responsible for knowing how racism manifests in schools and society.

The work is exciting, but it is inherently painful and difficult. This work is made harder when you are forced to face family members who think nothing of their harmful/hateful views, and who, moreover, think nothing of publicizing them.

It hasn't always been this way. I was not taught to be hateful or intolerant toward racial or ethnic diversity. I grew up in Brooklyn, New York. I went to extremely diverse schools. I had a wonderfully diverse group of close friends. I am grateful for these experiences. I have had many colleagues who grew up in the suburbs and attended schools in segregated communities.

I am grateful for being unable to imagine a life that does not reflect the realities of an increasingly diverse society.

Something happened to my mom in recent years. I'm not sure what it is. I've noticed that she's become incredibly fearful of the world around her. Her fears are manifested in our conversations in a range of ways; for example, there is not a conversation that goes by where she is not warning me about some imagined danger or another (i.e., "lock your windows," "be careful walking to work when it's still dark out," etc.). And I know that our conversation about her home also emerges from a place of fear, as with all forms of racism, intolerance, and exclusion.

It's strange. She raised me as a single parent. That takes an incredible amount of fearlessness. I have become an adult who admires and respects all that my mom sacrificed to raise my sister and me.

She has since remarried, became an empty-nester, and retired (in that order). And somewhere along the way, she forgot how to live.

I do not make any excuses for her or anyone else who feels or says the things she feels or says. There are no excuses.

What I need to study more about is how to respond to these things because silence is not working for me. Silence makes me complicit in (her) racism and intolerance. Silence makes me a hypocrite. But attempting to dismantle my parents' views will leave me without a mom. Of this I am sure. And I have not yet figured out how to walk this line, toward productive ends.

In the meantime, I hyperventilate when I see my mother pop up on my cell phone once a week. Just don't tell her. It would break her heart.

I never share my writing with my mother; our relationship depends on her not knowing that I struggle with her views, views that are new and surprising to me. Complicating my relationship with my mother is one main point that I cannot seem to emphasize enough: I was not raised around the same kind of blatant racism that she freely displays now. If I did challenge her, she'd likely chalk up my point of view to the fact that I am now twelve years removed from city-living, and that I "have no idea what it's like" to "live around" diverse people, cultures, and ways of being. She might also reduce my views to some sort of unchecked elitism, because of my education, life experiences, and overall refusal to accept most anything at face-value (including my family's brand of Catholicism with which I now refuse to identify). For my family, there is only one "right" way—a way that does not challenge everything they know to be normal, justified, and true.

More to the point, however, is how the public responded to my post, a post that was featured and main-paged on a popular blogging site for millions of viewers to consume (and as reality would have it, spit out). The following response is representative of the many I received on my post and other writings about my experiences with whiteness and racism:

> "This woman is so selfish; I don't even know where to begin. She claims her mother is ignorant and racist because her mothers [sic] fears mosques. In the same breath, she claims she has the same feelings about churches. Seems like you're your mothers [sic] daughter, sweetheart. The rest of the article was hard to read. She is a despicable daughter and should be ashamed of herself."

I've come to expect such personal reactions to the issues I write about. This particular response, however, left me irrationally worried that my mother might somehow locate my pseudonymous musings; that someone, somewhere, might be able to identify who I am and then brazenly send my mother this piece out of some sort of act of revenge against me, the white traitor who dared to say a critical word about her personal experiences with whiteness and racism. I knew one thing for sure – my mother would agree with every poorly punctuated sentiment this woman shared in her response to my post. And that was a chance I was not willing to take at the time.

So worried, I asked the website to remove the post. They surprisingly obliged. The lesson was clear: The third rule of being white is that you don't talk about being white under any circumstances. Not if you want your closest relationships to remain intact.

■ ■ ■

I AM FORTUNATE. I was not raised in a world surrounded (only) by white people. In fact, my childhood and much of my adulthood resembles quite the opposite. I attended wonderfully diverse schools, and had friends from all corners, backgrounds, colors, and languages. I have no idea what it means to grow up and experience life surrounded by predominantly white populations, and I bring my experiences to my classrooms and students. At times, I was the only white kid at the lunch table; my childhood experiences are a reflection of the diverse world in which we actually live in, and not the segregated, white, gated communities that work to vociferously shield themselves from the world and those in it. For all of this, I am grateful beyond words.

And yet, there is a common thread running through the stories I share. Deviating from white norms (e.g., entering interracial relationships) and expectations for silence can have devastating consequences for personal relationships with white family members. I have to wonder about the extent to which white children eventually become adults who resent their upbringings in white communities; following this, I have to wonder about the extent to which whites deny (or defend) their racialized privileges and racist perspectives as a way of coping with what their families demanded of them; with what their families have done to them. This is precisely why we need more stories. Whites are not only or always "just" racist, or "just" colorblind; they were taught (by other whites) to be this way, and I can only imagine the stories of abuse, threats, alienation, and untethered conditioning that might emerge if the opportunity presented itself.

In sharing my personal stories, I realized: Nothing about institutionalized racism and oppression changes just because a random white woman recognizes how fucked up whiteness is. Even as someone who has made this her life's work, I haven't quite been able to wrap my head around how to inspire institutional and systemic change in a way that truly achieves socially just ends. For now, though, the point is to offer a more nuanced view of whiteness. A view that goes further than the shamefully common platitudes with which I open this essay. All of us—whether we are white or not—are educated into whiteness; we all have a primer and rules from which we operate. Whether or not we do so consciously is another story altogether. ■

Sam Tanner
_____

White People Are Crazy

SMARTER PEOPLE THAN ME have worried that white people are crazy.

Incidentally, I do not capitalize the word white in this piece because it was never meant to describe an intentional community grouping. I do not want to give the label any more credibility than it already has.

Anyway, comedian Paul Mooney has a stand-up routine about analyzing white people on a psychologist's couch. In fact, much of his catalogue contains tragically hilarious, accurate accounts of ways in which white people are, in fact, crazy.

More serious people have shared Mooney's concern. Author Toni Morrison told Charlie Rose in a 1998 interview that she worries that white people in America suffer from a "profound neurosis" that has a "deleterious effect" on white people. Morrison positioned whiteness as a worrisome condition. Furthermore, The Reverend Dr. Thandeka – a race scholar – described white identity in her 1999 book, _Learning to Be White,_ as a conceptually failed self that struggles to relate intimately with others. Toni Morrison also wrote about the craziness of whiteness in her 1992 book, _Playing in the Darkness._ Morrison went so far as to claim that "an internal devastation is linked with a socially governed relationship with race" (p. ix).

Incidentally, all of the people that I have mentioned thus far in this piece are people of color. I am not. I am just a crazy white guy. Moreover, I have been a high school teacher for a decade and am now a college professor and a white scholar. My whiteness has always mattered (in confounding, troubling, and confusing ways) to me. It has been a problem. But I am trying to learn how to get better. Another person of color helped me think more about my condition in a college class.

The scholar Mahmoud El Kati visited a class I was taking about this history of race in America in the fall of 2013. I was working on my doctorate at the time and El Kati came to speak about his scholarship, which, broadly, is about black liberation movements.

It was a cold night in autumn. I was sitting in a small graduate course at the University of Minnesota. Eight people were gathered around a table. I was the only one who was white. Students were pestering him with questions. I recorded the audio of our discussion on my laptop because I was enamored by El Kati's eloquence. I described my interest in understanding whiteness to him. He responded by sharing a story about being a little boy.

El Kati grew up in the segregated south. He described himself as a southern born black guy. There was only one white-owned shop on the main street in his hometown in Georgia. The white-owned shop was a bakery. One morning, when he was eight, El Kati walked up to the window. The scent of fresh glazed donuts drew him near. What child would not want to gawk at fresh donuts? As El Kati was standing at the window, the white baker calmly put down what he was doing. He walked out to where El Kati was standing and kicked him in the butt as hard as he could. The white baker then calmly returned to what he had been doing without saying a word. El Kati did not tell anyone about the experience. But it stayed with him and came out in our talk nearly sixty years later.

Years later, El Kati said that reading Richard Wright's *Black Boy* helped him to better understand this story from his childhood. *Black Boy* is a memoir of growing up black in the south. In it, Wright wrote a story about a black elevator driver who let a white man kick him everyday for fifty cents. El Kati used this moment from *Black Boy* to interpret his childhood memory. Here is a transcript detailing what El Kati said:

> "It is just something that stuck with me. You know, kick me, why'd he kick me? *(laughs)* And I was able to answer it years later. Richard Wright helped me understand it.

Somewhere in his *Black Boy* he described, you know that man, when that elevator driver guy, had the guy kick him everyday, and I thought about that, before I was able to figure out the compulsiveness, what blacks do to people's senses, you know, you know, it's not, nobody I know, nobody's born that way, you know, it's a release, it becomes a part of people's emotional life. It is a part of emotional life, you know, emotional lives are warped and they don't even know that they are that way. This is what black people should say more of. You know, there is another kind of, another kind of vocabulary we need to develop, you know, you know its not just protest, you know, you see the old people used to say that white people are like little bad children because of the way they behave towards them you know like children could be very kind and mean at the same time, that's like white grown people, they're children, you know what I mean?" (El Kati).

El Kati's interpretation of his story is profound and the way he makes sense of the kick the white baker gave him is disconcerting. According to El Kati, the white baker reacted to his blackness out of compulsion. The baker had an almost emotional response to his presence outside of his bakery. El Kati credited this to the baker's warped emotional life that stemmed from his whiteness. According to El Kati, this neurosis is what caused the baker to lash out at him. Furthermore, El Kati described the baker as a mean child. He concluded that this was symptomatic of the baker's whiteness.

I walked away from class that night with a serious question: Are white people really this crazy?

El Kati's story stayed with me just as the actions of the baker stayed with him. His telling suggested to me that white people are stunted in their emotional development. Indeed, what more evidence do we need of this condition than American's ongoing struggle with a condition of white supremacy? Surely there is a problem in this country when we consider the continuing violence in the aftermath of Ferguson and the subsequent response of the #BlackLivesMatter movement. *All of us should be worried about the childish, violent potential of white people to lash out and commit violence.*

■ ■ ■

SO YES, I HAVE WHITE PRIVILEGE. But I also have a white problem. So where did this condition come from? How did it begin?

My great-grandmother used to deal in guilt trips.

"Sammy," she would tell me. "Don't you think you should call your Gammy more often?"

My mom was unable to say "grandma" when she was a little girl. She said "Gammy." So the name stuck.

Mom was spoiled. Her parents *privileged* her with anything she wanted. This was because they had grown up poor and wanted to spare their daughter from that same fate, to the degree that they could.

Gammy's real name was Dorothy Truman. Her father was a Norwegian immigrant and labor activist at the turn of the century in Truman, Minnesota. This is all I know about him. Gammy ran away when she was sixteen. She played piano at nightclubs in St. Paul and attached herself to whatever man would pay the bills. Gammy was poor. By the time I met her, she was an old, wrinkled, white face.

By then, her white face was the only thing I had to understand where I had come from on my mom's side.

"Sammy," she would tell me as a child, taking a plate of food away from me, "you don't want to end up being a fat, Russian Jew boy like your dad, do you?"

Dad was the son of poor Jewish immigrants from Russia. Mom married Dad, developed serious alcoholism, and spent the rest of her life in continual, self-sustained crisis.

One thing I learned from Gammy was that her guilt trips did not work. I resented the way she skirted topics, imposed her ideas on me, and tried to manipulate my identity. It seemed juvenile to me at the time even though I was a child and she was an adult. She accused me of the crime of being a fat, Russian Jew boy. As a child, I did not understand why somebody might think this was a bad thing.

She demanded that I be contrite to her idea of normal without being explicit about what she meant.

Years later, being "taught" about the white scholar Peggy Macintosh's work on white privilege in a workshop as a white, high school teacher felt a great deal like being talked at by my grandmother. The white workshop facilitators wanted my contrition. It was as though I was supposed to admit that the achievement gap in K-12 American schools was my fault because I was a white teacher. These facilitators, also white teachers in my school district, seemed to think everything would be fixed if I admitted my racism. They wanted a particular performance from me that would do nothing other than to make sure people knew that I knew I was racist. They wanted this without any mention of our nation's explicit history of white supremacy or my deeply complicated ethnic background, my family history.

This confused me. I was told to be quiet when I tried to bring up my confusion. The facilitator pointed her white finger at me.

"That is your privilege talking, Sam," she told me.

The facilitator was cruel in her accusation. Even as the facilitator was trying to implicate me in acts of oppression, her close-minded teaching was enacting a violence that kept us from discussing race sincerely. Ultimately, their obsession with pointing out white privilege kept more generative conversations about whiteness from happening. It concealed white supremacy.

White supremacy provides a great deal of possible material privilege for those of us who are white. It is predicated on a European colonialism that exploited and decimated nonwhite cultures and ways of being for nearly five hundred years. This material atrocity cannot be denied or avoided. However, making all white descendants of this insidious history admit they enjoy the same blanket list of privileges without understanding how whiteness is made will not undermine white supremacy as an organizing principle of American reality.

"Sammy," I pictured Gammy saying, "don't you think that you should feel bad about all of this history?"

I did feel bad about this history. But simply admitting privilege is not going to accomplish the complex task of understanding my own white identity and systems of white supremacy. It was not teaching me anything and I was not *learning* from it.

My mother listened closely to Gammy all of her life. So she wallowed in her own guilt for nearly sixty years. She felt bad about abandoning me when I was seven, terrible about how her alcoholism broke up our family, and she was so sorry that she took pain pills to escape from reality.

But she never changed anything about herself even though her actions and habits were materially destroying her. She never *learned* anything. Her problems were too deeply rooted in her psyche and nobody ever *taught* her another way to be.

It is not enough for white folks to identify and admit the privileges they get from being white. White people need to understand the damage that participating in white supremacy is doing to them.

Yes, my grandmother on my Dad's side was a Jewish immigrant who was chased out of the Ukraine by Cossacks during the Russian Revolution. Her husband, also a Jewish immigrant, changed his name from "Tankenov" to "Tanner" in order to Americanize it, to whiten it. Gammy was the daughter of Norwegian labor activists. Both of these women grew up in poverty in St. Paul. Dad was a manic-depressive. He was a Jew-for-Jesus-Freak, life insurance agent, and far more interested in smoking pot than raising me. Mom was a narcissist. So they did not teach me the white, middle-class values that folks often assume I possess when they see the color of my skin.

Still, I figured out how to survive despite my caretakers. This survival entailed picking up the mannerisms of whiteness. Dad made a fortune selling life insurance and bought a house in an affluent, white neighborhood in the suburbs. I learned to be white from watching my teachers and friends. This complicated history informs the way I carry myself in the world.

And it informs how I carry myself as a teacher.

■ ■ ■

I HAVE ALWAYS TRIED to mentor my students regardless of what they bring to the table. This has been true of white students or students of color. It has been true of children, teenagers, and adults. I work with people so they can see that their actions have consequences, consider their empathetic connection to others around them, and understand how they have been positioned in the world.

All of my formal classrooms begin with a story I tell. I do not share a story about a baker. Instead, I share a story about my first year teaching high school. I tell my students about card houses.

I watched a ninth grade girl build a house of cards on her desk during a study hall during my first year as a teacher. The girl meticulously added card after card until she had built a tower on her desk. I was mostly unsuccessful as a first-year teacher so I remember thinking about how profound that girl's act of creation was. She built something remarkable in a chaotic, classroom space.

After the girl finished, a group of boys across the room noticed what she had made. One of the boys threw something at the card house and destroyed it without stopping to think. His act was compulsive. Then the boys started to build their own house of cards. The girl spent twenty minutes trying to knock down their card house. The bell rang, the students left, and cards were everywhere.

I was devastated.

Why in the world did the boys feel the need to destroy the girl's work? Why did she need to knock back? I spent some time thinking about this story. I came to understand it as a microcosm in the way that my students interacted with each other and with me. All too often we spent our time destroying each other's individual work. We caused each other harm rather than working together to make something. My pedagogy was transformed. I have shared this story with every class I have since taught. I have a simple message.

"We have the luxury of this time together," I tell my students on the first day, "my only rule is that we cannot knock down each other's card houses. It is in our shared interest to learn to build together."

This story has been the organizing logic of my teaching. It works because it demands that students understand how their individual acts might harm the collective effort of a class. It necessitates either constructive or passive participation in the teaching and learning that happens in a space. If anyone is destructive or harmful (including the teacher), it is both our job as a group of people and my job as a facilitator to acknowledge the harm and adjust the situation so it does not happen again. This needs to happen regardless of the destructive compulsion to destroy things that is rooted in our psyches as evidenced by the story about card houses. This is true regardless of different, oftentimes competing backgrounds, interpretations, and purposes. I see the classroom as a space to dialogue with and figure out participation in generative ways.

I thought about the boys who had destroyed the girl's card house as El Kati shared his story on that night in the fall of 2013 about the baker with me. I had spent years teaching high school students to overcome their compulsion to destroy each other's card houses. Could the same pedagogical logic transfer to my work as an anti-racist, white educator? I was coming to form a question. Could I help teach white people to understand their racial compulsions? Was it possible for them to overcome the distortion of their emotional life, their psyche, in order to overcome what El Kati described as their stunted development? Could I help them learn to grow up?

Growing up is a different sort of learning objective than traditional education privileges. There is no clear, measurable outcome of acquiring a critical perspective and wisdom. It does not afford the simple answers to simple questions traditional schooling fosters.

My teaching (and my learning) values wisdom that comes from asking questions instead of arriving at simple answers. Anti-racist pedagogy should not admonish and advise in isolation. Instead of the watered down multiculturalism that undergirds so much of our contemporary pedagogical practices of anti-racist work with white people, we need critical practices of coming to a deeper, more nuanced understanding of traditions that crystallize in order to produce our contemporary, oppressive racial realities. Our educators need to practice a teaching that locates, engages, and expands our understanding of concepts. Using what El Kati, Thandeka, and Morrison show us about the white psyche, it becomes possible to imagine how we might locate and engage whiteness in localized contexts in order to expand beyond contemporary, neo-liberal or even explicit practices of white supremacy. Indeed, I have spent years coming to articulate this kind of anti-racist teaching.

I spent four years of my teaching career working at a large, urban high school in the Midwest. I taught English and drama. That was my first job as a teacher. It was also the first time that I stood in front of a room of mostly black students and realized that my whiteness had serious pedagogical and ethical implications. I spent four years learning how to navigate my whiteness and the way it obstructed my ability to connect with my students. This experience forced me to reflect on the racial norms that had been inscribed on me by my own high school experience in an affluent, white suburban high school. It also troubled my undergraduate work at the University of Minnesota where I had been surrounded by white people and white systems.

One of my ninth graders shared something that stuck with me at the end of my fourth year teaching in this school. It happened during a discussion of the use of the n-word in *To Kill A Mockingbird* in ninth grade English. I always chose to read this word aloud when I taught the book in order to honor the author's choice to include it. It always made me uncomfortable to read this word because I was white. I told my students this.

"It is okay if you say the word, Mr. Tanner," Chris told me, "you are one of *us*."

Chris was black. In that moment, he recognized a racial solidarity in our work in the classroom. I do not know what this meant to him. It meant a great deal to me. This was not permission for me to use the word – something I did not feel comfortable doing. It *was* a moment where Chris saw that the work he and I were engaged in disrupted traditional racial boundaries. We were building metaphorical card houses together despite our racial positioning. I had spent four years learning to identify with my black students. Chris publicly acknowledged that he saw that in class.

The next year I took a job at a different high school. This high school was a first-ring suburban school in the same city. Though the student population was becoming more racially diverse, it felt more like the mostly white school I attended as a high school student. So I returned to a white space. The honest discussions about race that I experienced in my first classroom were replaced by anxiety, silence, and seemingly preprogrammed responses. Again, I felt surrounded by a neurosis.

"It is better now, Mr. Tanner," was a typical response from my mostly white, eleventh grade students when we worked through *Black Boy* by Richard Wright in American literature together. "We don't need to talk about this anymore."

The bell would ring after the class would agree that racism was pretty much solved. White students would congregate near the music and art rooms. Some of them would hang out in my classroom, the drama room. I would overhear disparaging comments about "Compton Corner," the student moniker given to the space near the administrative offices where the black students hung out. Or I would hear a joke about "Hmong Mountain," the area at the top of the stairs, near the media center where the Asian students hung out.

It was as though the white students were unable or unwilling to see how discourses of white supremacy were reproducing themselves in their social and schooling contexts. A cloaking of white supremacy was playing out on the microcosmic level in the school. I understand schools as microcosms of their social context. I also understand them as sites of transformation.

The realization that whiteness was a disguised problem for *everybody* who lives in America became the inspiration for my academic research and teaching. I wanted to build critical interventions for my students who participated complicity in white supremacy. Could I help white people become aware of their own whiteness? Could I help them see how accepting the mythology of race both privileged and harmed them? Could I help them, as El Kati put it, grow up?

■ ■ ■

I HAVE NOW SPENT YEARS trying to identify whiteness with white people in high school English and drama classes, college courses on race, and even through collaborative, original theatre projects about white identity and white supremacy. It has been unpleasant work. I have few conclusions other than I am not sure how we fix racism in America. I do know that it is more fruitful to have frank, honest discussions with white people than to set-up situations where white people are accusing other white people of having privilege and silencing deeper discussions about white supremacy.

I worry that white privilege training often becomes an excuse for crazy white people to act out. Certainly, Paul Mooney comes to mind when I think about all the white people I have met who so badly want to prove they are not racist. The Reverend Dr. Thandeka's words about a failed self return to me. Toni Morrison's courageous work to expose whiteness as a neurosis comes to mind. The fall evening I shared with Mahmoud El Kati continues to haunt me.

I wonder if white people in America can accept the diagnosis of these intelligent people and begin to work on getting healthy? This makes me think about my students. I think about my family.

The first of my two sons was born two years ago. I now have two little boys who could grow up to be white. I do not want this to happen to them. I do not want them to suffer the neurosis of whiteness.

I am like any parent—I want my children to be *healthy*. ▪

Notes

1. Mahmoud El Kati, Personal interview, 2013.

2. Interview by Charlie Rose and Toni Morrison. n.d.: n. pag. Web. <https://www.youtube.com/watch?v=6S7zGgL6Suw>.

3. Toni Morrison, *Playing in the Dark: Whiteness and the Literary Imagination* (New York, Vintage, 1992). Hereafter cited in text as PD (1992).

4. Thandeka, *Learning to be white: Money, race, and God in America* (Continuum International Publishing Group, 1999).

Darci Halstead Garcia

What It Means to Be White

I GREW UP IN THE 1970S and came of age in the 1980s. I lived in a small city in New England. My parents were quite liberal and race was never discussed, good or bad. Certainly, I never heard them make any kind of derogatory remarks. In school, we had an array of multi-racial students, although to be fair, not many. There was never a sense of color, or of any differences. It was almost an afterthought. The distinction did not really exist, at least not then, or maybe not to the extent that I would be aware of it. We all went to school together, ate lunch together, went to dances together and in general, we did what kids do.

In the early 1990s, as a result of a divorce, I found myself making a huge leap and moved to Florida. I was a single mother with no resources, and only a high school education. It was terrifying, but I had always been a rebel, and moving 1,500 miles away, with no family or friends, was vintage for me. I settled in a beautiful area by the water and began my new life. It was difficult finding a job, but I was lucky enough to get one as a secretary in a medical practice. Actually, secretary was a step up. In reality, I was a medical records clerk making a whopping $6.00 an hour. Poverty level, in fact.

I worked with seven other women, three of whom were black. They all seemed very welcoming, however, with my black coworkers, our relationship did not extend beyond work. There, they were courteous, helpful and relatively talkative. However, there was a most distinct wall between them and me. I was never invited out after work, never invited to their birthday celebrations and noticed that often, even though they never said it, felt they would have preferred to be sitting together on their own at lunch. When I did join them, it seemed strained, almost awkward. My white coworkers, on the other hand, embraced me fully, inviting both myself as well as my daughter into their lives, both at work and our personal time. It seemed whether I liked it or not, an invisible line of demarcation existed between my black coworkers and me.

I gradually became an office manager and landed a job with a large multi-physician practice. It was more responsibility than I had ever had and more money. It also put me in the unique position of being the boss to predominately black employees. Most were women although I had a few male medical assistants on staff as well. My first day on the job I held a meeting to introduce myself to everyone and went over how I liked to run things. I was met with blank stares as well as an utter lack of enthusiasm. After the meeting I went back to my office, feeling pretty beat up with no idea why. Not for the first time I wondered if maybe it was just me. Maybe I was not likable, or had a mean resting face or came on too strong. I truly wrestled with all of these feelings and made a conscious decision to really pay attention to my mannerisms and speech. I did this and sadly, nothing changed. I began to wonder if I should change my major. During this time I had started college with a major in health service administration. As time went on I came to accept that there was just some intangible force that existed and I simply did not know how to push past it. Frankly, I just did not understand it.

The answer became clear, however, when I needed to have surgery and a replacement was called in to cover me for the next eight weeks. She was a wonderful woman, the wife of a local pastor and as white as the driven snow. When I returned to work, we had a sit down, and she was in tears. She felt she had failed at every turn with the staff who she described as "hostile" and "mean-spirited." Now, if this woman, who was an absolute angel, could evoke that kind of response then I felt safe in assuming, finally, that the issue was not me. It was the color of my skin, as I had feared, but could not seem to wrap my mind around. What had I ever done to them? Who cared what color our skin was? Clearly though, they did.

For thirteen years I ran this practice, continued on with my education and during that time only befriended three black women who remain in my close circle today. I learned much from them about how African Americans feel towards white people, and while they did not claim to represent all black people, they certainly had their finger on the pulse. In truth, I had not had this experience with any other culture despite having worked with many varied ethnicities. I found myself defending, for the first time in my life, my whiteness. I became angry at black people, for no other reason than they were mad at me. I was not the sum total of the sins of my fathers or grandfathers or great grandfathers and frankly, where the hell was history in all of this? Didn't African Americans know that it was their own Kings and Queens in Africa that gladly sold them off? That black slaves were initially owned by *other* black people? Why was I, as a white person, being blamed anyway?

This anger rooted itself where none ever existed. I became sensitive to black-white issues, especially since this seemed to be the uppermost agenda in the minds of Americans. As a result, I began speaking out loudly against the divisive nature of our politics and what it was inherently doing to propel issues of race into the forefront, but not in a good way. It had changed me, how I felt about the world and about humanity and how we interacted together as a whole and invariably, it caused me to study the subject extensively. I laughed out loud at the concept of white privilege. It was a ridiculous notion at best. No such thing exists. Maybe once upon a time, but not now. Not even close. Must I then apologize for my education because it allows me to be upper middle-class, drive a nice car and live in a nice house? Is it fair then to say I am the reason that African Americans, Asian Americans or Muslim Americans cannot do the same? I cannot recall where my white privilege was when I was unable to afford more than a bag of potatoes to eat for a week and borrowed money to buy milk for my child.

I believe being white in America today is rife with the potential, at any given moment, to insult the sensibilities of not only the black population, but any non-white culture. White Americans have been called on the proverbial carpet, so to speak, with the responsibility of giving retribution for years of slavery, segregation, Jim Crow, atomic bombs and a host of atrocities over our almost 240 year history. It matters not that I personally had nothing to do with the above, I must now make it right. Except, I cannot. White Americans cannot. No one can. The past must be relegated to the past. We should learn from it, however, to revisit it and remain in it will only continue to perpetuate this attitude of entitlement. This belief that the color of your skin is a reason to remain uneducated and in poverty is, in fact, merely a smokescreen to hide a complete lack of ambition with little to no work ethic. I have sat in classrooms with many men and women of non-white ethnicities who were there after working full-time jobs and taking care of their children. They went on to graduate and are now physicians, nurses, lawyers and entrepreneurs.

This applies to any person, of any culture. My whiteness does not, nor has it ever, defined me. My whiteness did not take me out of poverty. I had to do that myself. My skin color merely came along because I had no choice. Had I waited for my whiteness alone to save me, assuredly, I would still be in poverty, and my life story would be much different. I do not apologize for anyone, past, present or future nor do I feel in any way obligated to anyone of any culture. Bias exists everywhere and no one, not even white people, get a free pass. If we are not judged by the color of our skin, then it's on the size of our homes, the cars we drive, the clothes we wear and how much we weigh. This is not a utopia. This is the world we live in, at once blessedly kind and incredibly cruel.

If I could, I would sit across from any non-white person, reach across the anger and hurt that has been forged in half-truths, ignorance and myths and ask them this question: Please tell me, what am I doing to stop you from achieving your dream? Has the color of my skin, my white American skin have that much power over you? Over your life? It does not. Today, being white in America has become a cause for shame, a reason to apologize, and that, I will not do. Not today, not tomorrow, not ever. ∎

Lauren Kinnard

What Does It Mean to Be White in America?

A S I READ THIS QUESTION, many images pop into my mind, along with songs, phrases, memories, and people. I've stewed over this question for a few months now, unable to get past initial brainstorming that included stories wrapped in cynical judgment of coworkers I deemed ignorant, self-pitying thoughts about how difficult it is to be an "aware white person," and instances of ally-ship to justify myself worthy of addressing this topic.

All of this initial thinking took me further from any answer I had hoped to find. As a private-school-educated, middle-class white woman, I was trained my entire life to search for research-validated, socially-acceptable, and middle-of-the-road explanations to all questions. As a student of equity and an aspiring ally in the fight for racial justice, I have learned the importance of personal stories of lived realities, a willingness to embrace vulnerability, and the realization that the most widely accepted answer is often wrapped in the ugliness of society.

Thus, my only hope in attempting to answer this question was to share my lived experience as a white American. In learning to see the reality of racism in our country, I'm learning to lose my attachment to being right, agreed with, or accepted.

So what did it mean for me to grow up white in America? What has it meant as an adult? What will it mean for me in the future?

Initially, being white in America meant assurance. Being white in America meant self-assurance, assurance of opportunity, assurance of security, assurance of morality, assurance of belonging and assurance of humanity. Since the inception of our country, whites have had these assurances. Rather, whites have taken these assurances from other groups to create them for ourselves.

Growing up white brought me these assurances. Sure I had insecurities, fears, and questions (mostly tied to my womanhood and religion), but my existence was always validated, celebrated and cherished. I never questioned my right to exist, my safety in public spaces, my ability to earn what I believe I deserved, or the ease with which others' perspectives were dismissed. The narratives I heard about our nation aligned with whom and what I saw in my community. They assured me that reality was as I knew it. They gave me assurances that I was good, those around me were good, and this nation was just.

Until they didn't. Until I sat in a women's studies class as a twenty two year old and heard stories about the sexism and racism embedded in our welfare system. Until I stood in front of a group of black high school students in metro Atlanta, having never thought of myself as being a racialized being. Until I heard the story of my Teach for America mentor being held at gunpoint by police as a teenage black boy. Until I realized the "Dixie Girl" shirt I wore at ten years old was not an innocent style choice. Until I recognized that the token black ball player at my high school was accepted because he fulfilled an acceptable role.

So what does it mean to be white in America? It means fear. It means insecurity. It means shame. It means a queasy feeling in my stomach when asked to represent my heritage on a cultural day at school. It means attempting to rid myself of any connection to racism by distancing myself from loved ones I deem ignorant or close-minded. It means encroaching on the space of people of color in an attempt to gain a sense of solidarity. It means realizing that self-judgment is the source of my contempt for others that look like me.

I have spent my time surrounding myself with people of color, saying intellectual things about white supremacy, joking about my people's inability to dance (while pointing out the times POC have complemented my rhythm), priding myself on living in Atlanta, reading W. E. B. Du Bois, and comforting myself with India Arie. Yet, despite all these efforts to convince others and myself that I'm one of the good white folks, I still feel scared and ashamed of my whiteness.

I have lived in this space for a few years now – learning to understand racism and my whiteness intellectually, but refusing to truly engage with my own identity – letting fear, shame, and insecurity guide my actions. It was not until recently that I began to truly acknowledge my whiteness and its effects on me, and allow myself to grieve the legacy of my people. This acknowledgment has given me hope for a new definition of what it means, and will mean, for me to be white in America.

I am learning to see my whiteness as an opportunity, and an invitation to engage more deeply in society. It's an opportunity to become part of the healing process, and perhaps most importantly, an opportunity to acknowledge my own humanity. Growing up white taught me to view the world as black and white, literally and figuratively, as good and bad, with anything labeled bad as something to eliminate or overcome. Becoming conscious of my whiteness is teaching me to accept that there are parts of me, parts of my society, and parts of my world that I will never be rid of. There are parts of me that will never be pretty, perfect, acceptable, or just. I will never be rid of the racism that has shaped my culture and my people. I can never undo the years I spent cashing out my white privilege. I will always belong to a group whose legacy has meant oppression.

But this reality does not have to defeat me, nor does it have to be the end of my story or the story of my people. Racism, oppression, and injustice will continue to define whiteness until we begin to acknowledge them as an integral part of the fabric of whiteness. Until we are willing to face our whiteness and all its ugly implications, we will continue to live in a place of fear, insecurity, and shame. It was only recently that my strategy for dealing with difficulty had been avoidance. When I was growing up, my mother (who serves as an example of individuality within this culture) always told me to "just walk straight through it, Lauren. You'll spend much more time and cause yourself more agony if you try to walk around it." Well, white folks, it's time for us to walk straight up to and through our whiteness. Sure, it will be a hell of an ordeal to get through, but healing will come much more quickly if we use our whiteness as an opportunity to engage in creating a more equitable reality for all people, including a more authentic reality for ourselves. A reality where fear and insecurity don't reign. Where we can accept and appreciate differences and conflicts. Where our acceptance of others stems from an acceptance of ourselves – the good and the bad, the beautiful and the ugly, the just and the unjust. ■

Sidney Kidd

A Cracker's Ladder to Success

A PERSONAL NARRATIVE ON THE allure of special privileges from a cracker's perspective sounds…risqué, surreptitious, alienating, divisive, klannish, incestuous and kind of fucked up—are you folks over at 2Leaf Press sure y'all want to be involved in all of this? Have you lost your damn minds? Y'all might better roll up those 2 leafs afore we begin; this is bound to get messy.

But, perhaps, it is less universal, more confined, and not nearly as provocative so we won't piss off quite so many. In fact, I've found white privilege to be much more selective and refined than the stereotypical, "All you whiteys got it made in the shade" cop out. Still, we do love the juicy gossip, and what ifs that come with it; as if, being honky is akin to some type of racial mistress. It's one of those things which causes us to cringe when it is mentioned in "mixed" company. We tilt our heads and hold our breath listening intently from the bathroom stalls. We scream foul when we see it benefitting others but become totally oblivious when it opens the doors that we never deserved to enter.

Privilege is one of those concepts that we can't quite come to terms with; somehow it seems shady and yet we each partake to various extents—very much like a secret society to which we vow allegiance. Ah, come on, you know of those jobs that suddenly appear for certain folk, those odd raises and mysterious bankers' hours for that one person that everyone at work wonders, "How did that fuck up get this job?" Usually, we advertise the white perspective—the "shades of pale" as it were, from another skin tone's eye, but what about "my" real world experiences here in "God Bless My White Ass America"?

Don't get me wrong, I've seen special privilege. I've experienced and witnessed those selective nods in my lifetime, but perhaps not from the perspective that others may assume. White privilege exists along with all the other pigments, but, it is highly selective. We all have "an angle" – a stereotypical view of a person's connections. In an essay of this sort, the author can only describe his experiences growing up and functioning in this silent "no see'um" caste system we each perpetuate in America. Perhaps the editor will find that epiphany from the many conflicting views – reality is relative to the observer.

My mama never knew my daddy and it followed that neither did I. My childhood was spent surviving in a procession of three room shotgun shacks spaced ten feet apart fronting the old Atlantic Coast Line Railroad tracks. Tobacco markets framed the dirt poor area of town known as Chinch Row – a title awarded by the farmers who came during the summer months to sell their harvested and cured tobacco from North Carolina, South Carolina, and Georgia. You see, while the Farmer Johns awaited their tobacco to be auctioned to the tobacco companies, apart from their families, they passed the time drinking and carousing. In the process, they became the livelihood of not only the whores but also the very same bed bugs our beds and lives were infested with. Chinch Row became synonymous with the lowest rung of a complicated, intricate Bible Belt sanctioned caste system. Seriously, what better way to gauge your ascension to heaven than to create others to look down on?

Our society had three distinct school systems: one for the blacks, one for the upper- and middle-class whites, and the other, which defined my privilege, was the one designed to package the dirty whites and the local American Indians that fell beneath the tribe of Lumbee. The three social groups would cross paths at times away from school – usually, a series of snickers or wide eyed stares. I lived near the black section of town affectionately known as New Town. We worked together in the cotton fields, the tobacco fields and the cucumber fields, working from sunup to sunset for 50 cents an hour, noted in a white farmer's logbook who realized we were too young to question his math. Besides, if we did … what was our recourse? We were in survival mode, eating bad produce and meat from the dumpsters behind the A&P. Still, I marveled at the black folk's homes which had proper roofs, solid floors, doors that offered security and porches upon which no mail man was afraid to step upon. I stared at their clothes which fit and were not thread bare, shoes that secured their feet safely away from the hard, sharp world.

The blacks looked down on us, making fun of our plight in a society that supposedly benefited folks of our "white ass" kind. The blacks ate from the farmer's store, sustaining a running credit, while we went all day without food. We drank pump water from the cups of our tobacco stained palms that were never very white. Nearly, all my classmates and friends became extremely anti-social and took the easy route of three squares and a cot to reform school and later to prison. It was a society that touted self-fulfilling prophecies to buttress an innate superiority.

My three best friends each took their turn and committed suicide before achieving our American dream, which we all dreamt of as we stared into the darkness. Anger filled my existence for years as I hated them for taking the easy road and leaving me here to face society alone. I attended their services at funeral homes; there was no church service as none of us belonged to a church. Each was buried in the pauper's field behind the local chain gang camp, locked behind a fence so that no family or friends were allowed to visit – banished punishment for not paying their financial burdens of being dead. We committed no more, nor any greater crimes than the favored sons. Looking back we were actually better humans and citizens than the main stream. But, justice and desserts have nothing to do with life; I allowed such grand vapors of equality and merits to ascend and pollute the heavens above.

I don't want my entire life to come across as one of contempt and blame. I enjoyed my childhood immensely. I saw things that many in our society refuses to see, and felt things others tug their insulated collars upward to shield themselves from. Once, my best friend, Randolph and I were caught stealing from the very same A&P from which we depended upon for its discarded goods. I stood and marveled, memorizing my friend as he went into his theatrical presentation of instant, immaculate rehabilitation. Like a whore on Sunday, he'd seen the light and began talking in tongues with his face turned upwards to the heavens.

A convincing salvation with genuine tears and all the glory. Sleeping Jesus – the local black officer, stood wide-eyed and stared, patiently allowing Randolph to finish. A small group of shoppers assembled about, taking in the rehearsed scene as Randolph played his part to their approval. Later, as Sleeping Jesus walked us through town to the jail, he laughed along with us and said, "You white boys really think I buy all that shit? Y'all gonna be reformed when they bury your white asses behind the chain gang camp like all the rest." Congealed grits and wet toast is good food for a hungry person.

One of our partners in survival, caved to the system and grassed us out. On the verge of "being sent off to reform school" but mostly from his betrayal, my crowd decided the only option was to kill ol' Sammy. I, patiently, allowed them to each add to the details of their perfect crime. Once they all had their say, I smiled and added, "That's a good plan for sure. Bound to end that little problem, while creating a bigger one for us all." They all frowned, feeling I'd somehow belittled their solution. Later that night we picked up Sammy, walked him to the old abandoned grave yard near the swamp, tied him up in a seated position upon a grave, propped against Buford Miles' head stone. "Sammy, a fellow can do a lot of thinking, sitting upon a grave alone. You just relax and think about things and in the morning you tell us how you intend to become a person who is more like the living than the dead." Sammy immediately recanted his attack upon our spotless characters and told Snuffy Sanders he was simply having a little laugh on his part, "You know those guys ain't got sense enough to pull off nothing like what I told you." From then on Sammy became "Near Death" and was a loyal friend until his death in prison.

Later when the public schools were forced to desegregate, I was thrown into the top section of the new segregation of races by classroom. For some reason, which I never understood, my test scores kept me with the town's elite. Perhaps I was simply a token but there I remained throughout middle and high schools.

In high school, I charmed the old black lunch ladies who gave me the leftovers after everyone had eaten. I ate till I was full and then took what I could home to share. Eventually, the principal discovered and stopped these charitable donations. It was a time of plenty while it lasted and no one was fired, so I didn't complain.

White privilege came my way when one of my teachers submitted my name for consideration to our state's Palmetto Boys State. A select few from each high school were interviewed and if selected, spent a week in the summer touring our state capital and legislature as the Stars and Bars of "Heritage, not Hate" fluttered overhead. The interview was held in the commons area of our high school by three prominent white leaders of our community. The elaborate, in-depth selection process consisted of one question, asked by one of my fellow classmate's father, "I don't know you. Who is your daddy?" I replied, "I have no idea. My mama has no idea. It could be anyone – even one of you." The interview ended as I anticipated inquiries into my knowledge and curiosity of how our state makes laws and the legislative processes, the civil responsibilities of citizens and the stirring of the melting pot. But, of course, such things were not needed in the selection process – a list of awarded selections had already been submitted long before this charade of interviews was ever arranged. By the way, I also remembered these three leaders from the days of my youth when I hid in the shadows of the bonfires while they dictated the values and morals of our local society, and lit the kerosene soaked crosses for the local Klan meetings.

Later after graduating from high school, I began applying for work at the local yarn mills and amazingly as I handed in my written work application, I was asked by the receptionists who read my name from the roll up yonder, "I don't believe I know your daddy." I'd stand and think of a proper reply to get a favorable result, but I never discovered one.

Still, I persisted and eventually hit the lottery. I worked seventy hours a week at a yarn mill, to pay for an education in the local university. Upon graduating I took a higher paying job as a car mechanic at a local dealership. With a degree in biology, I decided to apply to our state's medical university. Oh, in all honesty, I wanted the salary and wealth not the cockle warming benefits of helping those less fortunate – get real, there were none. A large part of the application process was the formal interviews with staff from the university. The day's applicants met in an expensive wooden paneled room, adorned with ornately framed, distinguished alumni surrounding an expensive wooden table. I listened intently as my fellow applicants nervously chatted about their MCAT scores and was shocked to realize my own scores were much higher, and my GPA was right there as well. They spoke of their expensive coaching in preparation to assure the world they possessed "the state or quality of being apt."

The president of the college entered and began chit chatting with everyone, in turn. Oddly, it became apparent he knew each applicant's name but also their respective families and histories. He began inquiring, "John, is your mother still teaching next door in our pharmacy college? She is so excited that you are going to be a doctor. Mary, is your father still practicing in Spartanburg? Samantha I understand your father is now practicing in Philadelphia." This continued as I sat with my mouth agape, and my eyes bulging out of my sockets. He personally knew each applicant. Well, until he came to me. He saved me for last, changing his expression into a furrowed brow. I fully expected him to ask who my daddy was but instead I received an, "I'm not acquainted with you. Perhaps you should introduce yourself." I did so and mentioned the city I was from and the college from which I graduated. There was something about me that he recognized, and for the oddest reason asked, "What type of work do you do?" I replied that I worked as a car mechanic; there were audible gasps from the applicants, and the president simply stared as a slow purposeful smirk contorted his face. He shook his head in a knowing, "I thought so affirmation" and said, "You should consider staying at that job; they make good money." He turned from me, put his hand upon the shoulder of the applicant to his right, leaned in and asked how his sister was getting along with her residency in Charlotte.

In theme with this essay, not all of these applicants were white; some were black, some Hispanic, others Asian, but all fit the mold of privilege, of never being hungry for food or social promotion. I marveled at their resources to "fly in" from distant states as I drove there in a twelve year old Tercel with a slipping clutch and a hunger for oil. Need I add that I was not invited to attend medical school? I'm guessing that you guys already got the gist of that.

History boasts of our nation's founding as a melting pot society that ventured forth to escape religious, class and economic persecution but immediately began persecuting the native inhabitants as well as the different ethnic and diverse nationalities that immigrated here with us – in the name of God, of course. Mostly, we hear the clamor of equality from the lowest groups of society – a universal right which somehow changes as our dirty flat feet climb a rung or two of the ladder. Very few actually ascend to be equal, we lust for superiority and legitimize ourselves with insane notions of genetics or being the children of one of our "Capitalistic Gods." We forge our gods into the image in the mirror and loan shark salvation with high starched family loans.

We have accepted racism, bigotry and discrimination into nearly all aspects of our everyday lives. But, oddly, each racial and ethnic group clings intimately to its very own prejudicial systems and stereotypes of the human ingredients that make up our stew. The whites elevate themselves by who their daddy was and their history of wealth. The blacks that I grew up with, had a system based upon their varying skin tones and the thickness of their lips – blue black, blue gum, high yeller, caramel, passing. The Lumbee Indians are a mixed race group that bases their prejudices upon the straightness of hair among other features. Of course, the higher social standing is awarded to the ones with the most Caucasian European characteristics, including stereotyping one another according to their generalized surnames such as Locklear, Hunt, Oxendine, Chavis, Sweat, Owens; with the lowest members of the caste being the ones of predominately African American characteristics. The Lumbees that I grew up with, and worked with, referred to the lowest rung of "their type" as kinky headed. Then, below the Indians were me and my type – white trash that gave the aristocracy a bad name. We had no one literally or figuratively to look down on, so we mostly stared upwards hoping the upwardly mobile wore skirts and had firm round bottoms.

I worked with a Chinese immigrant who informed me out of the blue, that Southern Chinese were similar to Southern White Americans – smarter and better people than those from Northern China. He said Northern Chinese were like the blacks. But, from another perspective, I asked my black neighbor the other day why my white neighbors didn't like me but invited him over to eat dinner. He frowned and hesitated thinking of how to phrase his synopsis.

"Sidney, they hate you niggers. You see, I tell them I hate niggers too, and they worship me. They even cut my grass for free while my naked black ass is laying up watching porn. See, I'm a lot like that Ben Carson guy. I give them legitimacy and a black friend to bring up at the Klan meetings down at the hunting club."

I responded, "But Charles, they used to be my Sunday school teachers at First Baptist."

"Sidney, you miss the point; the church hates you too."

"Well, yeah, but..."

"Didn't they say something to you like...they felt you'd be more comfortable around your own kind?"

"Well, yeah..."

"And, then you said some stupid shit about Jesus never hanging out with his own kind."

"Well, he didn't..."

"Ran your white ass off though, didn't they? You can't depend on ideals, especially around church folk. Just like me and my lady, we only go to church to watch the preacher do his shuck and jive bullshit, like a monkey dancing for an organ grinder. It's a social club for Sunday after doing the other clubs on Saturday."

Reality, sank in once again for me as I still don't feel equal, much less better than anyone. But, maybe I've gone on long enough with my experiences. The subject of this essay was meant to be what it means to be white in America. As in most things, none of us can speak universally. I can only say that I've not received those awarded privileges that I hear are so prevalent for my race and gender. I have seen many more examples where special privilege was garnished upon the wealthy of all races. Sadly, wealth seems to have its own judicial system as well as tickets to heaven up yonder.

I'm not sure that any of this is of value to your purpose or your readers. My attempt was to present a realistic take on the subject from a very personable perspective – perhaps a bit too out of the stereotypical mainstream of white America for most white tastes but, also, taking away some thunder from the other abused and held down racial groups. I stayed away from a dry scholarly recitation and hope, if published, others who remember their own past will smile and chuckle in fond remembrance of those "good ol' days" preached from the pulpits of Conservative America. Don't get me started on churches—I was asked to leave two Southern Baptist churches here in my hometown as three different Sunday school teachers informed me, "We don't like Dimmercrats in our church." But, you know the ol' tongue in cheek adage, "God Bless America." ■

Carole Gozansky Garrison

The Kindness of Strangers

SOME YEARS AGO, 1979 to be exact, I lived in a small predominantly white upper middle-class New Jersey community bordering the then prestigious Bell Laboratories, New Providence. I taught public administration and criminal justice at Kean College. My teenage daughter, Debra, was attending boarding school in Vermont, and coming home by train for the Thanksgiving holiday, and I was picking her up at the station in downtown Newark, New Jersey. With my nine-year-old daughter, Samantha, securely fastened to my hand, we climbed the stairs to the platform to await the train. Newark at the time was a city with a reputation for crime and violence, and I felt uncomfortable, if not afraid, among the throngs of train station denizens and the large number of African Americans departing and arriving. I clutched my daughter tightly and waited as the train pulled into the station.

Debra arrived dragging what looked like a dozen large duffel bags. I could only imagine she brought home everyone's laundry or every item she owned for the weekend! I couldn't imagine how I was going to get off the platform and downstairs to a trolley while securing my nine-year-old, my purse, my teenager and her mountain of duffel bags.

Just then a large, neatly dressed, African American man came over and asked if I needed help. Holding my hand up as if to stop him, I said, "No thanks, we can manage." I pulled both my daughters and my purse closer to me. But as I looked around it was obvious that I couldn't manage and I turned back to the man and said, "Please, yes, I do need some help." Wordlessly, he proceeded to sweep up Samantha, most of the duffel bags and headed down the stairs—Debra and I closely on his heels, dragging the rest of her belongings.

As we came down the stairs a woman and three children were looking up smiling and waving in our direction. The man helping me was grinning back, unable to wave given all he was carrying. Our small band of *informal porters* reached the trolleys at the bottom of the stairs. He quickly unloaded his bundles and Samantha only to be crushed by his own family as they rushed to greet him. I called to him before he got away, "I don't know how to thank you."

He turned momentarily from his reunion and said "Don't thank me, just pass it on."

Shame and guilt mingled together in a stew of remorse. This wasn't the first time I felt fear among people of color—made wrong assumptions, and it wasn't the first time I was found lacking.

What really angered me was how hard it was to learn the lesson—goodness wasn't the province of white people. ■

Janie Starr

What's a White Girl to Do? White Privilege from the Inside Out

THE PROBLEM WITH MOST DISCOURSE on white privilege is that it leads to blame, guilt, punch, counter-punch. I have been reading, writing, and speaking about white privilege off-and-on for much of a lifetime, but then I lapsed. That's one of the perks of privilege: I can choose to hit the off-switch whenever I become too overwhelmed by racist rantings or simply too preoccupied with other life matters that assail me. My friends-and-colleagues-of color cannot. It is the water they swim in and, at times, drown in, whereas I am free to dip my toe in or not, at my pleasure.

I cannot help that I was born white in a society where white is might, is right. It is not my fault that I grew up in Nashville, Tennessee, during segregation and lunch counter sit-ins, too young to realize what was going on across town from my cozy childhood home. I woke up slowly to race-awareness in my teens. I began to see the disparities around me and to speak out tentatively about social injustice. I cringed when my dad referred to black men as boys, and when my mom described our maid as childlike and uneducated. Yes, we had a maid. Her name was Laura.

In 1967, I attended Vanderbilt University, the same year that Perry Wallace did. His entry was momentous because he was breaking the color barrier in the basketball southeastern conference. As he has said numerous times since, he did not set out to be a pioneer, but the fact was, if he wanted to play, he had no choice. While a white player focused on perfecting his jump shot, with no thought to representing his race, a student athlete-of-color was both an anomaly and a lightening rod for attack. Wallace had to do that shuck n' jive thing off the court, while leading his team to victory under the hoop.

When my father complained about black players being the ruination of his beloved college basketball team, I knew I was done whispering. My attempts to argue with him were futile, however. He was a formidable opponent. In his presence, I stumbled and mumbled my words. He would not bend. I was afraid of breaking. I married and moved away to the Pacific Northwest.

In the early 1990s, I joined forces with an African American teacher at my sons' school in Tacoma, Washington. Together Stan and I began to preach and teach, and lead trainings with whomever would listen on the subject of racism, sexism, and white privilege. We were relentless, and then we weren't. He supported the U.S. invasion of Afghanistan after 9/11. I did not. I began to witness and protest against that war, as I had done against previous wars. Stan continued to teach high school, to coach girls' basketball, to fulfill his military commitments in the reserves. We lost touch. I moved again.

I never forsook my fire-in-the belly for racial justice, but I allowed the embers to die down and stoked them less frequently. I thought about Stan often, along with the stories he told of integrating an all-white school in Louisiana, joining the military because it was the safest place to be a black man married to a white woman, raising mixed-race sons, driving while black, shopping while black, *being* black.

I have continued to work for economic, racial and social justice: to take up the torch on behalf of the environment and climate, women and girls, domestic violence survivors, and people-of-all-colors suffering from hunger and food insecurity. I have attempted to advocate for Latinos, the major minority where I live, but I had allowed myself to forget the role of privilege in the perpetuation of these wrongs.

I did not sleep through the news in recent years as stories of police brutality escalated. I grumbled at the so-called liberal voices on NPR, yelled at the voices of vitriol and hatred on Fox News, bemoaned voices of cocooned white people like myself. I whined with those friends who agreed with me, and I did not act. I did not organize. I did not speak out in public. I did not read the articles I chose to "like" on Facebook. I did not "comment." It was *just too much.*

Then one day, a young white man walked into the Emanuel AME Church in Charleston, South Carolina, where the predominantly African American congregation welcomed him with open arms. After berating them, he opened fire and gunned down nine people, including the senior pastor, and I woke up.

I have been reading, and "commenting" ever since, but only on the small stage, the small screen. President Obama's stirring eulogy of Pastor Clementa Pinckney, pushed me right out of my safety zone onto the page:

> "Once the eulogies have been delivered, once the TV cameras move on, to go back to business as usual – that's what we so often do to avoid uncomfortable truths about the prejudice that still infects our society. To settle for symbolic gestures without following up with the hard work of more lasting change – that's how we lose our way again."[1]

I was tired of holding myself back with endless self-doubt. What the hell did I have to offer as a sixty-seven-year-old white woman? What could I say that hadn't been said already? What useful role was left for me? The president called me to action and I am responding. I finally realize that it doesn't matter if I have anything new or unique to offer. What matters is that I no longer remain silent. What matters is that I make my own noise, and that I add *my* voice to the crescendo of all people demanding justice to work together to seek solutions for all people. I really do mean all people, not as a whitewash, but in recognition that black lives have not mattered very much in this racist world of ours.

A black friend and entrepreneurial colleague, with whom I have been collaborating, suggested recently that we make allyship a growth industry. We haven't worked out the details, but I am game. Allies are supporters. They have your back. Allies interrupt racist (sexist,

---

1   "Remarks by the President in Eulogy for the Honorable Reverend Clementa Pinckney," College of Charleston, Charleston, South Carolina, June 26, 2015.

homophobic, etc.) jokes and slurs wherever they hear them. They engage their own race and gender in conversations about privilege and action. Allies step out of their comfort zone and take some risks. They do not merely tsk-tsk in the safety of their homes. They advocate and gesticulate and offer support when needed. Allies stick their necks out. They do not take over, speak over, run over the very people they seek to empower. They listen.

While reading *The Guardian*, I came to understand that I am called to do more. Feminista Jones, a thirty-six-year-old social worker and writer, enlightened me further. According to her, "The definition of ally-ship is to mutually benefit and support.... We are not working together on a mutual goal. My goal is to live. You don't have that same goal."[2]

Jones was, by no means, suggesting we white folk move out of the way. She was exhorting us to engage further: "What I need is for people to come and work with us in the trenches and be there alongside us. It's not about being on the outside and saying 'yes, I support you!' It's about '...I am here with you. I am rolling up my sleeves. What do I need to do?'"

She is prodding us to notch it up and to become co-conspirators, in solidarity with black, and I would add, brown and native activists, who risk their lives daily, because they have no other choice.

I am heartened by the fact that more and more white people are moving away from their screens, NPR stations, and *The New York Times* editorials, and are taking up their own placards and home-made signs, hitting their own streets, and street corners, witnessing and speaking out. I am heartened by the response I have received to my own rants on the subject.

We are not all demonstrators and agitators, stump speakers and sign wavers; some of us are too old to hit the streets; some of us too young. Still, whatever our shtick, our life circumstances, I believe we have something to offer: we are singers and songwriters, visual artists, dancers, musicians, and mimes.

I am not intimating that all white people lead charmed lives. While our white skin gives us an advantage, it does not guarantee our success.

---

2   Rose Hackman. "'We need co-conspirators, not allies': how white Americans can fight racism," *The Guardian*, June 26, 2015.

Some of us are struggling just to get by, holding down two jobs, raising our kids alone, out of work, underpaid, and without much hope of our own betterment.

In the main, however, we do not fear for our lives, our families, our homes, and jobs, and future, for no other reason than our skin color. We get a pass. So I am suggesting, no, urging, goading, and inciting my fellow white ones, to move beyond guilt, self-justification, fear, or blame, and to take up the banner, in whatever way makes meaning and is possible for you. Somewhere, there is a role for you to play: housing segregation, school-to-prison pipeline, police brutality, and racial profiling all demand our attention.

Choose your heart cause, your area of expertise, seek new knowledge, apply a new skill. Tweet, chat, stand in silence, speak at your place of worship and work, chat with your workout buddy, your childcare provider, involve your friends and coworkers in conversation. Share information, and, by all means, tell your own story as well. Keep on keeping on, no matter what. And please, include your kids. Find out what they think, what they see and participate in at school. Let them help you if they ask. Mostly, let them be reassured by your own action.

During the 1980s, I gave presentations on children's fears about war in the nuclear age. Researchers had learned that children whose parents were working to prevent such a disaster, instead of wringing their hands in despair or locking down in denial, felt more optimistic about their future and were less likely to participate in self-destructive behaviors.

I think kids are scared to death right now and don't know where to turn. When they witness their parents bitching and moaning but essentially doing nothing, acting defensive about their privilege, acting as if working hard and raising a family is enough, ignoring the fate of people of color despite the evidence of a building shit storm, well, those kids are left without allies, mentors, or guides for their own participation. I believe many white young people want to care, do care, and don't know what to do. Our example might just make a world of difference.

There is so much to do that it is easy to become overwhelmed. I have been there; I am committing to not go back there again. We need to save the Earth, stop climate change, feed our families, and find work, pay our mortgage, take care of our aging parents, procure health care. Still, I implore you: Do not allow yourself to become overwhelmed, to take a pass even though you can.

Being pro-black or pro-brown does not require us to be anti-white. It requires us to act. As members of the dominant culture, whether or not we feel dominant, we have the opportunity, as well as the responsibility, to change that culture, from the inside out. It's on us. If we do not embrace all of us, and teach our children by our words and deeds, then really, what are we striving for?

From my privileged perch, I look down into the dark and dangerous waters and understand that I get to choose. For me being a restrained ally is no longer enough. The time has come for me to make noise, to co-conspire, in heart and deed. I urge each of you to join me. Think of the splash we'll make if we dive in together. So, what's this white girl to do? Show up. Take a leap. Swim like my heart and soul depend on it, because, in fact, they do. ■

Abe Lateiner

The Risk of Greater Privileges

Any real change implies the breakup of the world as one has always known it, the loss of all that gave one an identity, the end of safety. And at such a moment, unable to see and not daring to imagine what the future will now bring forth, one clings to what one knew, or dreamed that one possessed. Yet, it is only when a man is able, without bitterness or self-pity, to surrender a dream he has long cherished or a privilege he has long possessed that he is set free–he has set himself free–for higher dreams, for greater privileges.

– James Baldwin

IN A SOCIETY WHERE MATERIAL COMFORT is presented to us as the best we can hope for, can we even imagine Baldwin's concept of "greater privileges" beyond those that come with whiteness?

The Charnel House

TODAY THERE IS BLOOD EVERYWHERE. Mixed in with my food. Stained dark and deep into my clothes. Soaked into this computer keyboard. Flowing through the middle of the sweetest moments with my family. Everything I would experience as beautiful, and all my memories of beauty, now sit in a soaking rain of blood.

My toddler learns to take her first steps, and shrieks with absolute joy. Her eyes twinkling, she totters towards me. Her seven little white teeth shine through her grin and her little pink shoes splash puddles of gore with each awkward step forward.

At the movies with my wife, on a rare date night, our two young children are at home with a babysitter. The film is beautiful, illuminating a core part of our shared humanity. Blood oozes from the walls of the theater, throwing dripping shadows across the ceiling and pooling on the floor down by the screen. By the end of the movie, the first three rows of seats are islands in an impassable, stinking ochre lake.

I go to a bar to see a show for the first time in ages. I forgot how much fun it is to have a few beers and listen to loud music. At the end of the night I walk out into the clear, warm night, burp, and enjoy being tipsy under the summer stars. The gutters run red with silent torrents of gore, clogging the storm drains and overflowing onto the sidewalks.

All the wealth and material resources that have been accumulated in the United States rest on a foundation of land theft from Native Americans, theft of labor from enslaved Africans under torturous conditions, and ongoing exploitation of mostly brown-skinned people across the world.

So as one of America's most cherished, protected children, my entire material existence is saturated with the blood of both the ancients and those who still die today in my name.

As my white comfort is uncovered to reveal the black death beneath, my instinct is to scream. I was raised to believe that I always have the right to speak my mind. For the first time, though, I find myself mute, choking on mouthfuls of blood.

When an old acquaintance asks what I've been "up to," or a stranger asks what I "do," or a family member asks what I'm "working on," instead of confidently speaking my truth, I hesitate, wincing slightly, as I work to cobble together an answer that will honor myself while not alarming their unstated expectations of my answer.

"I'm an organizer."

"I do social justice work."

And if I'm having a particularly confident day, "I work for racial justice."

The power of whiteness is in its silence. Our bloodbath has been made to be weightless, transparent, silent, and thus nearly invisible to those of us who are comfortable in it.

So to name whiteness is to give that term shape, weight, form, color, and sound. To shape reality by uttering a word is to play God, and such play has never gone unpunished.

■ ■ ■

The First Victims of Racism

THE REVEREND DR. THANDEKA, IN HER BOOK, *Learning to be White,* says that white people are the first victims of racism. She argues that white supremacist culture begins with the violent policing of white children's racial behavior by their parents and caregivers, which creates white people who are shamed into violently policing the behavior of people of color.

For people who are skeptical as to how powerful white culture's stranglehold is on us, Rev. Dr. Thandeka challenges us to play "the race game."

> "The Race Game, [as described to a white colleague], has only one rule. For the next seven days, she must use the ascriptive term "white" whenever she mentioned the name of one of her Euro-American cohorts. She must say, for instance, 'my white husband, Phil', or 'my white friend Julie', or 'my lovely white child Jackie' . . . I guaranteed her that if she did this for a week and then met me for lunch, I could answer her question [what it felt like to be Black] using terms she would understand. We never had lunch again. Apparently my suggestion had made her uncomfortable."

Even if we as individual white people can overcome our personal fear of confronting our own whiteness, that doesn't change the fact that most of the other white people around us are still unlikely to be willing to confront it with us.

This makes sense. It is terrifying to confront whiteness because it means we'll have to start seeing a living nightmare. We bathe our white children in hot blood every day and teach them so thoroughly to not talk about it that soon they learn to truly believe they can't see it, let alone talk about it.

But those of us who have been taught to see again, and to develop a resistance to unseeing, embark on what may be a lonely journey. We find that many of our closest loved ones are not on the journey with us. Many are in fact invested in never even seeing that the journey is possible. And so silence descends.

■ ■ ■

The Dream

But what is that?

Is that the society we dream of, that our ancestors fought for?

A society in which we can't speak our truths to those who love us?

In which we fear to convey the paradoxical sense of joy that comes with being able to finally see the truth, even though that truth is a nightmare?

Please assume: yes, I want to talk about the blood.

I have to talk about it. Now.

I can't unsee it.

No, it can't wait. The bath is rising.

If we're having a conversation and it doesn't come up,

I am drowning.

Silenced for the first time, I hear, from faraway halls, the voices of movement ancestors: Ella, Anne, Fannie Lou, Marlon, Yuri, Grace, Toni, Maya, Malcolm, Rosa, Martin, Lillian, Sitting Bull, Frederick, Bell, Angela, César, James, Stokely, and thousands more whose names and faces I'll never know, whose words I'll never hear with my ears.

These voices tell me, above all, to remember.

They say remember that I will always have to fight to stay awake. I live in a society that offers me so many sedatives, soft beds, fresh linens, warmth. To not fall asleep is an act of constant effort, and I'll never be done waking up.

They say remember to stay humble. White supremacy is baked into my being and is always, always maneuvering just outside of my peripheral vision. The day I think I'm done fighting it is the day I stop being useful to the rebellion.

They say remember that I'm not the first white person to do this, and I'm not alone today. There have always been white people who have rejected white supremacy, and have refused to succumb to the death culture that offers them material comfort while destroying their souls. Today, in the time of #BlackLivesMatter, there are tens of thousands of other white people alongside me who are waking up to our racial reality, and who are showing up with their bodies and hearts in the fight to end white supremacy.

Above all, they say remember to love, even in rage, and to remember that such love is the only way towards the new world we are fighting for.

■ ■ ■

The World of "Greater Privileges"

As I commit to the deliberate practice of remembering these commitments, the shape of a world of "greater privileges" begins to take form, though it remains so dimly lit as to be nearly indescribable. But it is illuminated, piece by piece, as I work with others like me to try to learn how to live it into existence.

In the world of "greater privileges..."

■ Instead of choking on blood, I'll spit it out like prophecy, painting impromptu pictures all around me. As a white person, my only hope for healing lies in first learning to see and claim ownership of my bloodiest works. This is how my white racial healing begins, and as I heal, I help to create space for the billions of people who aren't considered white to figure out their own healing as they toil under the global system of white supremacy.

- I will be able to be trustworthy... no longer an unknowing agent of COINTELPRO. No longer a walking time bomb of fragility for people of color, for women, for queer people, for everyone who doesn't share my velvet-lined identity as one of society's most protected children.

- I will live without the laughably delusional idea that I am well positioned as a moral, intellectual, and spiritual authority simply because I was born into this particular body and context.

- I will get to reclaim my own humanity, stripped away by our delusional, racist society with the allure of shiny, material, soulless rewards.

■ ■ ■

Know this:
every second I am not working to create this new world,
the corners of my diseased eyes are blooming with cataracts,
gently spidering out at the edges of my vision,
velvet white fog,
(gently, gently)
and behind the murk
gears straining and servos whirring,
sweaty, trembling,
malnourished
hands pull levers and shovel coal
inside a groaning machine,
wheeling
maneuvering
recalibrating
recalculating
pivoting to
silently,
lovingly,
gas me back to my cloudy sleep. ■

Notes

James Baldwin, "Faulkner and Desegregation," *Partisan Review* (Fall 1956); republished in *Nobody Knows My Name: More Notes of a Native Son* (1961).

Thandeka, *Learning to Be White: Money, Race and God in America,* (New York: Bloomsbury Academic, 2000).

Lorraine Saint Pierre

Looking for Trouble, Surely

'VE LANDED AN APARTMENT IN HARLEM, on Manhattan Avenue, near the train station at 125th Street that serves me with two local, and two express lines traveling downtown. It cuts my travel time to most venues by forty minutes.

The neighborhood is in a state of transition, the majority of its inhabitants are working class blacks, but whites are moving in. They buy the brownstones and refurbish them to their former elegance. Some buildings on the street look great while others are in the hands of slum-lords. Suffice it to say, when I first go to check out the apartment, I know immediately without looking at street numbers, which is the correct building. The apartment is in similar condition, its backyard a jungle.

The garden apartment, which encompasses the whole of the ground floor brownstone, has a serious bedroom, a small open kitchen, a large living area with one brick wall and more than enough room to accommodate a dining area, a living room and office; there are five double door closets, and a terrace out front with a gate on which, with the landlord's permission, I hang my counseling sign and card holder.

While waiting for the agent to arrive, I stop at the McDonald's joint to get myself a coffee. Everyone turns to look... a *white person*. At the gate outside the apartment drinking my coffee, the next door neighbor comes out from his garden apartment to put trash bags on the sidewalk, a very white man, blond. After he deposits the trash, he goes up the stoop to the other level – *he owns the building*. There's another man down the street, same situation. So the neighborhood is a mix.

The agent, who is the landlord's niece, demands $1,650 in cash, for herself or she will not let me have the apartment. I pay it. The rental is not without its problems, the last tenant departed in a hurry leaving his furnishings and clothing behind, but for the price, I can't complain.

After the deal is settled, I stop at the neighborhood bar taking no heed upon entering that I am the only white woman there. My mind is spinning with the implications of my decision, both major and minor. *Where am I going to shop?* The music is loud rock, but good. *And my address, she didn't give me the zip code.*

"Excuse me, bartender, do you know the zip code for this area?"

He doesn't know, but asks the guy sitting next to me. That man won't tell me, *Gee, that doesn't feel good.*

After the bartender walks away, Kirk turns around and gives me the zip code and introduces himself. He just wanted to be macho. It had nothing to do with my race.

When settling my bill, the bartender discovers I am French. Andre is Haitian. He introduces me to other Haitians and word travels down the bar, everyone shakes my hand, *Enchanté de faire votre connaissance.*

I have stumbled into a French world. *Enchantée!*

Had I more money, I would be tempted to look for another place, but that many moves in such a short period of time is psychologically unhealthy. You might say my lack of funds prevents me from running away from the situation.

■ ■ ■

ON A VISIT TO MY OLD NEIGHBORHOOD in Chinatown, I note the activity on the street. Asians, in an ethnic neighborhood like my present Harlem, venture forth in all directions. They are carpenters, mechanics, they cut glass, make signs, design websites, perform acupuncture, own restaurants, cleaning establishments, sweat shops. One can get the freshest vegetables and fish at their outdoor stalls for a fraction of what is charged midtown. It's a far cry from what I see happening in Harlem. The very opposite is true; I pay $5 more for a bag of cat food on 125th Street than I would midtown.

Asians are industrious. What's more, they're smarter than whites. A noted scientist, Charles Murray, was forced to resign his post because he wrote, in *The Bell Curve* that blacks are not as intelligent as other groups. Turns out, he's right. Recent research has confirmed it. What's more, whites are not as intelligent as Asians. What does it mean? The intelligence tests, I've studied a few in psych courses at the university, have little to do with "native intelligence" which includes wisdom as one of its scales. What the tests focus on is "normal," "average," "median." The more one fits into the prevailing groove, the more likely one is to make intelligent and balanced decisions that accord with the consensus.

Tests measure how well one fits into the society one lives in. Working Emergency Services for people in crisis, whether for a hospital or a mental health center, I've concluded that some people are not fitted for the prevailing culture. They cannot function in it. Are they crazy? The problem is not resolved by stating that they are not behaving, are not following the rules, speaking inappropriately, behaving shamefully, are schizophrenic, neurotic, psychotic. They have a rhythm that society has no use for. It does not de-legitimize them. The field of psychology functions as a societal and governmental restraint on inutile behavior. Breaking the law is deemed "mental illness." *Do not deviate from the norm, is psychology's motto.* According to this criteria society's most gifted should be classed as lunatic. One need only spend an evening watching television fare to confirm that it is society that is deranged.

Living among blacks, one is exposed to a more social, courtlier culture. Then again, there is anger, great anger. Some of it directed at me. At the laundromat on Frederick Douglass Boulevard, I am treated so rudely I vow not to return. Another laundromat on Adam Clayton Powell Boulevard: I enter, remove my laundry bag from its dolly and deposit it on the floor next to the scale to be weighed. Two women at the counter size me up.

The big one has a hissy fit about my rudeness, how I dumped the bag, blah, blah, blah. Her friend seethes at me. What's to be done? I am traveling further and further afield to get my clothes washed.

The story told by a black woman who moved to France comes to mind. She tried cutting to the front of the line at a Paris movie theatre and was overwhelmingly cussed out by the French women and directed to the end of the line. The black woman recounted how she easily got away with such behavior with American white women because of their guilt feelings. It described my response to the laundry worker. What had I done to offend her?

I would not have allowed a white woman to disrespect me in such a manner. With these exchanges under my belt, I am ready for whatever unfolds at the Harlem bookstore when I read from my memoir. Not only am I ready, but see it as an opportunity to steel myself against reviews I will undoubtedly endure when the book gets published.

The first woman (late 40s early 50s) who gets up to read has a poem addressed to white women, *We've Got To Talk*, she says. She then lays out all of the atrocities committed against her people while white women did nothing to stop it. Then a man gets up and reads a poem attacking white men. Later, a young woman goes after southerners and their lynching proclivities.

I'm the only white person in the room, and at first am taken aback by this vitriol, but it quickly passes. I recognize that anger, have experienced the same feelings from bigotry endured back home at the hands of the dominant Anglo culture that took pleasure in humiliating and degrading my people. That anger becomes a shield, a two-way mirror where one can see out, but none see in, and natural affection is replaced by sarcasm, bitterness and passive aggressive acts.

I could explain that I too have suffered from bigotry, that French people had nothing to do with this country's slavery, but I do not. Explaining myself is futile. I know that anger, and words will not make it go away. It's a comfort to those afflicted.

In my depression, I see the fragility of the human psyche and how easily it is wounded, how years and years are spent with bad feelings trying to come to terms with them, or not. The perception of me as oppressor is faulty. Jailer shares the same prison as jailee. Both are oppressor and oppressed.

■ ■ ■

I AVOID AS MUCH OF THE ANGRY FEELINGS as possible. Discrimination is a more complicated issue than can be solved by good intentions. Two streets to the west of where I live is the white world, and Columbia University. I had avoided it, reasoning that there was no sense moving to Harlem if I was going to remain in the white world, but on the weekend I cross over to Broadway and find all the things I've been missing, good bread, coffee beans, olives at Gristede, coffee shops, bistros, outdoor cafes, interesting restaurants and stores, a salon that carries Framesi products which I use exclusively for my hair, then the public library serving a college community. I become a person who takes advantage of the rents in Harlem, but shops elsewhere. The Harlem Library branch made a mistake with a $2 fine I had paid, but was still being charged for. I spoke to the librarian and was told nothing could be done. I would have to pay it again. At the Broadway branch, after explaining the situation the fine is quickly removed.

No one is planning against me, it's that respect and trust are a rare commodity here. On Broadway, I buy the *Times,* have a hot chocolate outdoors and attend a free concert at the Presbyterian Church, a Mahler symphony, no less.

But alas, I haven't found a laundromat to have my clothes washed.

■ ■ ■

UNLIKE THE CARL SCHURZ PARK on the Upper East Side which is highly cultivated, the new Morningside Park where I now jog, is wilder with mostly trees, bushes, paths and rocks; it rests on a Manhattan schist that sprouts up way above my neighborhood, a natural barrier separating the white from the black neighborhoods. Climbing its stairs to get over to Morningside Heights and the Columbia University neighborhood, one sees a grand vista of Manhattan upon reaching the top. The schist was formed millions of years ago. This type of rock is easily recognized because it contains sparkling mica. It is the foundation of Manhattan's skyline whose tall buildings are firmly planted in this bedrock.

The human being's journey out of this world, for we are not born into the world, but out of it, (we are formed by it) is similar to the creation of land masses. From a central fiery core of passion that is the earth's gift to us, a child is born. That is the schist, the bedrock, some of it may remain underground or jut out into the world depending on prevalent conditions in one's setting.

■ ■ ■

AN EARLY APPOINTMENT DOWNTOWN on the East Side. The train pulls up just as I get to the station, and is packed with workers. One has to cram in, but the woman in front of me just stands there looking into the car. The doors will shut momentarily. I jump in pushing against her in the process. The black woman executes her victim-oppressed routine about dealing with the rapacious majority.

"JUST GET IN, AND SHUT THE FUCK UP!" I shout taken aback by my own vehemence. But as the day progresses I feel rather proud of my outburst—I don't want to be guilt-tripped. Then again another exchange at the supermarket, and good markets, like laundromats, are a rare commodity in Harlem. This one is four avenues and five blocks from my apartment. The best I can find in the neighborhood, and it's not that great. The milk isn't as fresh as is advertised on its carton, which means it's been waiting in the bay without refrigeration for a whole day before being stored. I get my order to the register and notice that I'm in the ten items or less row, but the woman in front of me has more than ten items and there's no one in line, and few people in the store.

"This is a ten-item register," says the girl. What about the woman in front of me and the lack of customers, but then a customer comes behind with a couple of items, so I let her through. Once her order is rung up, the girl will not process my groceries, and somebody else comes behind me. The bag boy gets in the act and screams, "Come on, come on," he motions to the customer in back, "She's got more then ten items. "

They are playing a game.

"You're obviously enjoying this power play," I snap at the grocery checker.

"I have no power," replies the clerk.

And that's the truth, "you have no power," I reply. Not a very nice thing to say for which I am not proud.

On the way home feeling badly about what transpired, I resolve not to go to that market anymore. I will order my food from Fresh Direct. I have my laundry delivered, my wine delivered, and now food. I'm beginning to feel like a rich lady.

On the subway going home, exhausted and feeling depressed, I see a mother smack her little boy in his stroller because he kicked up his foot and it grazed her girlfriend's coat. Then another on the train screams at her little girl, maybe three years old, "SIT DOWN!" This mother wears the latest designer ghetto clothes and is all dolled up. I hate her for mistreating her child, which she seems to feel is an inconvenience in her life. I am upset seeing children being scarred, for life. *How does one survive such harsh parents?* I note both kids ignore their mothers' ire as surely they have to in order to survive.

What is happening to me?

What is happening is that I am seeing the effects of poverty, and more importantly, the lack of hope, first-hand and a lot of it is not pretty. The anger, ignorance, the hatred, and lack of respect are part and parcel of living on the edge in America, they who work as grocery clerks, launderers, street sweepers, garbage collectors, the underground schist that supports society in fine fashion.

I do not pass judgment, but I do not want to become a part of it. All do what they have to, to survive.

On a shopping trip for garden tools, seeds and fertilizer for the new garden, I encounter the now familiar subway scene of some woman abusing her boy. This is a young woman, probably twenty-five, her son is about eight or ten. She had him young. I'm not sitting close enough to hear what transpires, except the mother is screaming at him with a look of pure hatred on her face. I look at the boy as the mother walks away from him, and sits down at the other end of the car. It's the same look I see in other neighborhood children in similar situations. How to describe it? It's not defiant, but it is also not fearful of the adult. Rather there is disrespect, an understanding that the adult is not to be counted on. These children have lost their childhood. There is no safe, protective environment to nurture them. They are small adults navigating in a treacherous world.

I awake at night from a nightmare. Heart wrenching cries from a child whose mother is abusive. Mayor Giuliani urges me to give the child my name and number so there will be someone that cares if the child needs help. I desperately look for the right piece of paper... and I awake.

I lie in bed exhausted and drained trying to figure out its significance. Rudy left much to be desired as mayor, but he does have his principles, unlike Clinton and McCain who will say and do anything to be elected, Rudy draws the line. That's probably why he didn't put his heart into the presidential run. It was becoming too costly for him ethically. What I remember about him as I lie there, is his attack on the artist Chris Ofilli who had a painting hanging in the Brooklyn Museum depicting Jesus' mother Mary surrounded by elephant dung. Rudy was furious and was looking into the possibility of cutting the museum's funding. Although I agree with him about its lack of artistic merit, I thought Rudy was wrong to try and censure the artist. I also admired him for speaking up when everybody disagreed with him. As a Catholic, he did not want to see the nurturing Mother Mary defiled.

■ ■ ■

SINCE MOVING TO HARLEM getting my clothes washed has been the bane of my life. During this time I have been angry and unforgiving of my neighbors. I've made a point not to shop in Harlem, was not going to spend money in business establishments where I was treated contemptuously.

Then again, with two weeks worth of laundry and a dwindling supply of underclothes, I have run out of ideas and places to take my laundry to. I return to the laundromat on Frederick Douglass Boulevard where I first took my clothes and washed them myself. I bring a magazine and settle in, only two other people in the place. After my laundry is washed and dried I offer the magazine to a woman. Reading material being akin to a bottle of water in the desert at a laundromat, I am gratefully blessed. I've decided to forgive and get beyond this.

Fact: I am not liked by some people in Harlem; I say, deal with it!

■ ■ ■

SOME FOLKS ARE SUING THE CITY to stop the gentrification of Harlem. What's more they are traveling downtown and joining forces with the Chinese and Latinos who are similarly being threatened with 'luxury condos.' An alliance from Brooklyn also joins in the protest. The city attaches a stipulation to builders' permits that the condos must include 20 percent affordable housing for the present residents. But even the affordable housing is not affordable to most residents, and 20 percent doesn't save the neighborhood, it tokenizes it. If the city has its way there will be no one making less than $100,000 in Manhattan. Folks are starting to wise up and join up. There is life at the lower levels of the socioeconomic ladder, the poor, the working poor, the lower middle-class and the middle middle-class, that is worth protecting, and is the life blood of the city. A Manhattan populated solely with rich people? What a pitiful place that would be, a deadly gated city.

■ ■ ■

ON 125TH STREET, A MAN CORRALS PASSERSBY to sign his petition seeking an end to the rising rents in Harlem. I stop to sign it. The man is nonplussed, a white woman signing a petition for a situation he believes I am responsible for? Yet, I do not want to see rents go up any more than he does. The forces behind the rise in rents in the West Village, the Lower East Side, Midtown, the Upper East Side, and its concomitant shift of population to the outer boroughs are not white or black—they are green. *but the developers - investors - who are they?*

Harlem congressman, Charles Rangel, it's been discovered, lives in a luxury building, Lenox Towers. He has four rent stabilized apartments (his home has appeared in the *Style* and *Grace Magazine*) for which he pays less than a thousand a month apiece. What's more, it seems governor David Paterson, his father Basil, another politician, and Percy Sutton, the former Manhattan Borough President also have rent stabilized apartments in the building. Need one mention that the owner is a big time New York developer?

"There's money to be made in Harlem" stories are coming to the surface. *New York Magazine* does a piece entitled "Whose Harlem is it?" This story is about Willie Suggs, the Queen of Harlem Real Estate.

Willie sells homes to 'whites' at unheard of prices for the area. Her last deal was for two mil and she's looking to sell another one for three mil plus. A non-stop talker, she inveighs against her fellow African Americans for criticizing her dealings. "'Black' people can be racist," she says. "We were never... never, the first owner of these houses. They were built for, and owned, by 'white people.'" Willie is accused of doing underhanded things and cheating home owners, those who want to sell, and also her agents. Lots of people are angry and say bad things, some have even taken her to court.

The Village Voice weighs in with a piece entitled, "Sugar Hill: A Sweet Spot in Harlem." Apparently Sugar Hill is enjoying a revival; they now have chain stores, banks and supermarkets. What with City College there, one resident states, "I see a lot more foreigners... I can expose my family to the wider world right here." There's money to be made in Harlem, and as the saying goes, "He who sups with the devil should have a long spoon."

Then you have the *Times* with a story about the sound of West African drums in Marcus Garvey Park. This has been going on every summer on Saturday night till 10 p.m. since 1969. Apparently, there have been complaints emanating from the luxury co-op with its million dollar apartments across the way. Seems its tenants couldn't listen to their TVs, talk on the phone or get any rest while the ruckus was going on. The *Times* chose to label its residents as "young 'white' professionals." There have also been ongoing complaints by blacks about the noise, but that's not news.

A *New York Press* newspaper that someone has left behind on a park bench shouts, "HARLEM: IT'S A HARD KNOCK LIFE." Within is a story about a Euro American woman who was knocked to the ground and had her pocketbook taken as she walked out of St. Nick's Pub, a jazz bar on Sugar Hill. She's now trash-talking the African American community. The robbery was done in full view of the people inside the bar, and her assailant didn't even bother to run away afterward. He had cheated her in the past, so she knew the score. He casually walked off turning to laugh at her. No one at the bar came to her rescue or wanted to lend her a cell phone so she could call the police, and no one had seen a thing when the police questioned them.

The woman, Susan Crain Bakos, is a sex journalist whose last *NYPress* story was entitled "A White Woman Explains Why She Prefers Black Men." Ms. Bakos goes to a bar that has a bad rep playing disrespectful sex games and expects that it will not be challenged.

"What's a woman like you doing in a dive like this?" the police ask when they get there.

Looking for trouble, surely. ■

Genna Rivieccio

"Hey Snowflake"

I T TOOK ME A LONG TIME to come to the conclusion that to be white in America is, and truthfully always has been, undesirable. While history tells otherwise, it is often those who are white that are deemed the collective enemy, the oppressor responsible for everyone else's woes. The more the shift in racism veers toward white people as a result of it being "our turn" to suffer from discrimination as recompense for all those centuries we were at the top of the racial food chain, the more we become fodder for being the butt of other ethnicities' jokes. For instance, a new show from Aziz Ansari, *Master of None,*[1] makes frequent reference to the banality and loathsome qualities of whites. Ansari's character, Dev, tells his white girlfriend that honky is "a semi-racist term for white people," but is mild in comparison to the slurs reserved for other races. Is it simply the so-called non-harsh sound of it, or because he feels white people couldn't possibly be offended by any demeaning sort of affront?

I suppose it was during my mid-twenties when I became defensive about being called "Caucasian." I grew up in a suburban setting that had a scant population of black, Asian, Hispanic or Arab inhabitants. But I never thought anything of the people with a skin color different than mine. It was fine to simply co-exist without questioning it. Then again, you figure that children possess the innocence to think in such a way. I moved to Los Angeles when I was eighteen, where, as is true to the stereotype, Hispanic culture thrives. This was the beginning of

---

1   *Master of None* is an American comedy television series, which was released for streaming on November 6, 2015 on Netflix. The series was created by Aziz Ansari and Alan Yang, and stars Ansari in the lead role of Dev, a 32-year-old actor who attempts to make his way through life in New York City.

my awakening to race—not because I suddenly developed a prejudice toward those with darker skin now that I was around them more, but because I suddenly saw how much worse their quality of life appeared to be. This began my phase of white guilt, the need to constantly apologize and self-flagellate for being born into more privileged circumstances.

This guilt quickly faded when I made the transition to New York City, where black people make up a much larger part of the population. The anger and resentment toward whites in this town cannot be over exaggerated. Walking down the street, especially if you happen to be near the projects (of which there are many peppered throughout the city), you can *feel* the animosity being directed at you simply because you are white and everything is your fault as a result of this. It seems as though the vibes of a black New York resident are far different than those of, say, a Southern one. In the South, black people still rightfully fear the wrath of racist whites. But in New York, it's the other way around. White people experience far more fear due to the intensity of black rage in this metropolis that epitomizes disparate classes and socioeconomic backgrounds. When I first moved there in 2010, I was living in Spanish Harlem. I naively thought it was close enough to the Upper East Side to be practically the same. I was highly mistaken.

I lived in a five-story walk up in between Third and Lexington on 118th. It was off the 116th Street stop on the 6 train. Every day when I would walk to and from the train, all I wanted to do was run so as to avoid the insane barrage of comments about my whiteness, as well as the requisite lecherous remarks directed toward any woman ambling down the street in this neighborhood. A mixture of Puerto Ricans and black people composed the group of sidewalk commentators tormenting my existence. I wanted to bash their heads in when they spoke to me and made me feel as though I was wrong to my very core because of my skin tone.

On one particular day while riding the subway from downtown, I took the 4 express train to 86th so I could transfer to the 6 there, but I became engrossed in reading whatever book I was poring over at the time and ended up forgetting to exit when I was supposed to. The next stop was 125th Street, or what I call "Third World" New York, a hub of the poverty-stricken and the limbless. I was still new to the area and therefore instantly horrified upon reaching the street level to apprehend my surroundings. Leering black women glared at me as though to non-verbally ask, "What the fuck are you doing here?" One woman, possibly schizophrenic, even screamed at me to get my "white pussy" away from her. It was all very unclear. Why wasn't it okay for me to be there? Why do Americans in general feel the need to separate themselves into different neighborhoods according to race? Before I could contemplate the answers, I remembered to move my body toward 118th Street.

Practically speed walking, I still couldn't avoid the ogling and the cat calls of the stoop sitters. But one epithet in particular has always stuck with me: "Hey yo snowflake, whatchu doin' here?" Snowflake. The most offensive and simultaneously humorous slur a white person could be called. Barring the pure white color of this phenomenon of nature, a snowflake is something that floats down carelessly from the sky in mass to form a giant mound of oppression on the black or brown earth. When I examined it in this way, the aspersion made sense. I was seen as a flake, and where there's one, there's sure to be many, many more. They feared me. They feared that I would bring an entire white army with me to gentrify their neighborhood, the only thing in the world they could ever lay claim to. I gleaned then that the fear among races is always mutual. And yet, the uncomfortableness I felt in not being among "my own kind" prompted me to move to another part of town, one where I didn't experience the inclination to sprint toward my apartment to avoid judgment for being white, ergo a piece of shit with Columbus-esque tendencies in terms of an area takeover.

In the end, being white in America is rather a lot like being any race in this country: you feel the need to sequester yourself within a community of others who share your skin color as a means of self-protection. ■

J. Kates

August 1965

MITCH GURFIELD AND I HAD BEEN arrested on the complaint of two eleven-year-old white boys, who testified how we had driven up to them in a station wagon in a public park in Natchez, Mississippi, jumped out, and started chasing them with knives in our hands. It was a stirring tale, and, as I listened to it unfold on the witness stand, I whispered to our defense attorney, "It sounds so believable, I'm not sure I wouldn't convict me."

"Men have been hanged on the lies of kids like these," the lawyer whispered back.

The boys were testifying because their fathers were notable figures in the local White Knights of the Ku Klux Klan[1], and because Mitch and I had been organizing black steam-laundry workers as part of our civil rights work with the Student Nonviolent Coordinating Committee (SNCC). At the very time that we were supposedly chasing little boys around the park, we were actually meeting with laundry workers – to whom we had promised confidentiality – at our Freedom House office. Had we taken the stand in our own defense, either we would have had to produce an alibi that would name courageous local people whose anonymity we had promised to protect, or we would have had to perjure ourselves. We were prepared for the latter – to say that we were in a "staff meeting" at the office.

---

[1]   Or was it the United Klans of America? During the summer of 1965, jurisdiction was being disputed by the two separate organizations, and Edward L. McDaniel, the father of one of the two boys testifying, was leading the swing away from the White Knights to the United Klans. The FBI report of the incident identifies McDaniel as UKA.

The accusation was fabricated on absurd premises. The station wagon so circumstantially described actually belonged to independent filmmakers hanging around our project (one of whom was my brother-in-law). The kids who fingered me as the driver had no way of knowing that I had no license at the time, and officially didn't know how to drive. (Well, I had driven illegally in Maine two summers before, but backwoods Maine in 1963 was not quite the same as Mississippi in 1965.) The prosecution didn't bother to establish motive. Nor was it likely a coincidence that the park where the incident supposedly occurred was itself the focus of a desegregation campaign actively opposed by the local Klanspeople.

Mitch and I had been picked up off the street, taken in, booked, held overnight at the police station, and released for trial the following week. (I remember vividly even after all these decades my rush of relief when the police car that transported us actually turned downtown, towards the jailhouse, instead of the other way, out of town.) Apparently a policeman slapped me upside the head for not calling him "sir," a detail so ordinary I forgot it for twenty years, until I read about it as part of my FBI file released under the Freedom of Information Act. What I do remember from that night in the downtown Natchez lock-up is the curious plumbing that sent a single turd floating back and forth between Mitch's cell and mine, and my neighbor on the other side, a white man jailed for threatening his girlfriend with a knife. He and I chatted enough for me to learn that fact, and also that he worked at the Armstrong Tire plant. In the morning, the authorities moved us into a single cell, hoping, I think, that he would beat me up. But it was too late. We had already established a contact of person to person that transcended our roles. He needed $26 for his bail, and our project bailed him out ahead of me, just to keep me safe. He said he'd come by the Freedom House to pay us back, but we never expected him to, and he didn't. Soon enough, Mitch and I were out on bail, too.

When we came into the courtroom for the trial, eight or ten white men subtly but visibly armed occupied the front row. Several of them, I'm sure, worked at that same Armstrong plant, which was a recruitment center for the Klans.

The judge was up for re-election. In spite of that, after listening politely to the prosecution, and before calling on any defense at all, he dismissed the charges against us, saying that the prosecution had failed to make a case. Thus he preserved us from perjury. We waited around the courtroom while two other cases were argued and decided. In one, he convicted a local black teenager of insulting a police officer by giving him the finger; in the last case, he acquitted another volunteer in our project of the crime of "kicking a car."

A couple of days later, before the Klan could act out of frustration or revenge, by the general decision of the Natchez project, Mitch and I were driven to the Jackson airport and sent into the rest of our lives.

When I got to New York, I reported to the office of the Friends of SNCC to ask how I could be useful. I suppose I felt somewhat guilty for having been run out of Mississippi. I suppose, too, I could have gone quietly to the project in another part of the state where I had worked the summer before. But maybe it was time I came closer to home, anticipating a more general movement of white volunteers the following year. As it turned out, it would be another nineteen years before I returned to Mississippi.

There was a job I could do. Friends of SNCC had organized a support rally for the corner of Lenox Avenue and 125th Street, and someone had to go uptown to make sure that everything was properly set-up, and to meet the people who were bringing a portable sound system. The Fugs—at that time a newly formed counter-cultural musical collective—were going to play music. A Democratic mayoral candidate, Congressman William Fitts Ryan, was scheduled to speak. There was to be an appearance by Ben Chaney, the twelve-year-old brother of James Chaney, who had been murdered the summer before in Philadelphia, Mississippi, and Ben was waiting in the office with his mother. She had other business, would I take Ben with me and go uptown?

I did not know Harlem. I had grown up in the suburbs, and 125th Street was usually a stop I glanced at as the train paused on its way to Grand Central Station. I had no particular fear of the neighborhood, just no reason to be there. I had read all the appropriate books. I knew about the Apollo and the Harlem Renaissance and rioting. I had read *Invisible Man*. Once, on the train, I sat with a black high school classmate of mine who got off at the 125th Street station to go to her hairdresser. That brought the location alive for me. The apartment buildings pressed up close to the railroad tracks, and sometimes I imagined the life inside those apartments, as I always like to do on a train. Over the years, I watched the windows empty out like dying stars, and the buildings themselves decay and crumble. They're all gone now. In February 1965, Malcolm X had been scheduled as the featured speaker at a civil rights conference at the University of Massachusetts. His assassination the week before the conference changed its tone, and one speaker talked about walling off Harlem to keep whites from getting in. The black woman sitting next to me said, "We'll give you a passport, and let you in."

So, more than a half-year later, with no special documentation, Ben Chaney and I got off the 3 train and blinked into the sunshine on 125th Street and Lenox Avenue. There was a drugstore on the corner. The only other people on the street were those going about their own business, and we had nothing to do but hang around, a twenty-year-old white civil rights veteran from Westchester County playing sidekick to a twelve-year-old black boy from Mississippi. I had a camera with me. I took a picture of Ben, a snapshot I still have. In it, his eyes look exactly as Paul Good describes them in his book, *The Trouble I've Seen*: "His face was locked in woebegone sadness disturbingly different from the momentary griefs of childhood... He looked at me with the young-old hopelessness of a Mississippi Negro kid who knows the score."[2]

Time passed. As usual in the movement, nobody showed up on schedule.

And then three young men came sauntering toward us down Lenox Avenue. They were all wearing bright dashikis—clothing still unfamiliar in most of the United States, and as political as it was colorful. They did not ignore us. They came right up to me and stood shoulder to shoulder in front of me, reminding me of three white men on a street in rural Mississippi the year before, who had told me to get out of

---

2 Paul Good, *The Trouble I've Seen*, (Howard University Press, 1975), 114-5. Now that I know Ben Chaney as an adult, I can see a permanent physiognomy that Good and I, each in our turn, may have romanticized.

town by sunset. One of them asked what I thought I was doing there. I explained. They would have none of it. I was white, and needed to get out of their neighborhood right away, or they would, they made perfectly clear, beat the shit out of me.

Ben, whose brother had been killed the year before in the first interracial lynching in our country's history, looked at them and at me in puzzlement.

One thing I could not do was tell war stories. I could not discourse about the White Knights of the Ku Klux Klan in Natchez, or reminisce about the three cowboys in Como the year before. I could not strip my sleeve and show my scars. Nor could I say, "Hey, guys, I'm on your side," because I wasn't, even though I thought I knew, almost literally, where they were coming from. They were closer kin to the defensive Klansmen on Natchez streets than they, or those Klansmen themselves, could imagine at the time. The fact that they didn't know where I was coming from – that I may have been a white boy from Westchester, but I wasn't *only* a white boy from Westchester, didn't matter. Race trumped politics.

Here was a moment that would have been a different crisis for many of my colleagues in the movement – those whites who so identified with the black "experience" that they thought they actually were participating in it, in one way or another. For them, there would have been no irony in this confrontation, only outrage at what they would have perceived as a misunderstanding, and then disillusioning rejection. Luckily, I had escaped that trap. If I had ever been tempted, the year before would have immunized me. During the previous winter, I had spent a lot of time in Paris with West African students, and became startled to recognize that they trusted me more than the mutual acquaintance who had introduced us to one another, a black woman working with the United States Information Service. However sympathetic Yvonne was to their aspirations after years of assignments in USIS libraries in several African countries, she worked for the United States government. However white I looked, I had taken my stand against racist politics these students identified with the established government. This distinction was definitive for the Africans. For these students, emphatically not

"African American," politics trumped race, but this was completely irrelevant to the nationalists of Lenox Avenue. They would have let Yvonne pass or stand without blinking an eye. From me, not even a passport signed by Marcus Garvey would have sufficed.

What could I do?

I did exactly what I had been trained to do, what I would have done on a street corner in Natchez, Mississippi. With Ben at my side, I retreated slowly into the drugstore, found a public telephone, reported the incident to the office downtown as if I'd been confronted by a Delta sheriff, and went back out into the street. The dashiki-wearers had disappeared, and did not return. As the years have gone by, they have turned into more of a symbol than a physical threat, as if they just had to appear at a particular moment to represent an ideology. We waited for the Fugs and William Fitts Ryan and Mrs. Chaney. Soon enough, somebody brought a bullhorn and a couple of speakers. There was nothing memorable about the rally itself. We didn't draw much of a crowd. The best I can say is that, like those drifting young men in their dashikis, we made our presence and our politics known.

And then I went home. ∎

Anne Mavor

I Am My White Ancestors: Self-Portraits Through Time

I N FALL OF 2013, I HAD JUST COMPLETED a series of paintings of ancient stone circles and mounds in Britain—my attempt to connect with the land of my ancestors. Following the exhibit of those paintings, while casting around for my next step, I came up with the idea of inviting a Native American artist to collaborate with me on a project comparing our relationships to our sacred sites. But a few days later, I realized what I was doing. Like many well-meaning white people, I had conveniently side stepped my own heritage and instead was using a person of color to legitimize my artwork. So I asked myself, "What if I turned it around completely? What if I claimed my own people instead and took responsibility for their actions? What would that look like?"

As if it was a gift from the cosmos, the answer came back immediately and fully formed, including the title, *I Am My White Ancestors*. I would research and choose twelve ancestors, six men and six women, who represented the range of oppressive actions committed throughout European and American history. I would create costumes, paint backdrops and photograph myself as those characters. The portraits would be life-size and displayed together in an installation. And the ancestors would tell their conflicting and dramatic stories through audio diaries.

Then the doubts began to crowd in. Could I really do this? What would it take? How long? How would I fund it? Create the costumes and paint the backdrops? Record audio diaries? Who am I kidding? I know little about European history. But among those thoughts was the knowledge that within European American history the seeds of racism were sown. I wanted to reveal them, whatever it took.

It helped that hanging in my hallway were portraits of Confederate ancestors who had owned slaves[1] in South Carolina. I am embarrassed that I didn't even think about that possibility until about ten years ago when I read transcripts of my grandmother's recollections. After all, she grew up in South Carolina with a Civil War cannon ball in the front yard. They were also prosperous and had been there since 1735. It stands to reason that my ancestors would be part of the slaveholder economy.

So that's where I started my project. Among the photos in my hallway are matching oval portraits of my great-great-grandmother, Eugenia Mary Felder Buchanan, and her husband John. I decided to begin with Eugenia for my first self-portrait. She was pretty and elegant with lace at her throat and wrists. John was black haired with fierce eyes. The story passed down was that they were Confederate spies. That turned out not to be exactly true, but John did have to escape to Mexico with a price on his head during General Sherman's March at the end of the Civil War. For my research I used letters, my grandmother's taped recollections, and a book about Eugenia's escapades during the war.

Later, as I sat sewing Eugenia's enormous skirt and reading her letters, I was hit with a new understanding about my family legacy. The characteristics before me were all so familiar: obedience, separation, ignorance, and quiet endurance. Following her husband all over the South to avoid the northern aggressors. Leaving her baby daughter behind in South Carolina with her sister. Watching Union soldiers burn down the family home. Not understanding why her remaining slaves didn't want to travel with her on to Chappell Hill, a bastion of South Carolina confederates in eastern Texas. Finally, joining her husband in Mexico where they spent ten years trying to start a sugar cane plantation.

After six months of full-time research, I ended up with a combination of characters covering 2000 years of European American history from 1870 back to 300 BCE. In America, the list includes two slaveholders from South Carolina and a pilgrim from Plymouth Colony who gained land and resources from the Wampanoag. Traveling back

---

1   Non-oppressive terminology: Africans held in bondage without pay.

in time to Britain, I chose a Scottish farmer who was a juror on a witch trial, an English mercenary soldier and social climber who fought to colonize Ireland, and an English noblewoman caught in the middle of the bloody War of the Roses. In the medieval era there was a Basel cheese maker who supported the execution of Jews during the Black Death, King Edward I of England who conquered Wales, invaded Scotland and expelled the Jews from England, and a Frankish countess who became a nun and benefited from the colonization of Jerusalem during the Crusades. Lastly, I found a Norman knight who helped Duke William conquer England, a female Viking who invaded Orkney, and a gold metalworker from the Celtic Iron Age who supported the warrior elite.

I am not exceptional. Similar ancestor stories are replicated throughout history. My particular family came to America from England, Scotland and Switzerland during the early development of the country with all the benefits contained therein: land, slave and indentured labor, and raw natural resources. In addition to being white, I was raised Protestant (the dominant religion), with money and resources that came directly from that early arrival. There is no question that I have profited from being European American from the day I was born. Could I use my history to model what taking responsibility might look like?

In choosing the ancestors, I looked for individuals in each century who were involved in carrying out oppressive actions against other people and who I could show were also oppressed or hurt in some way. It was important not to simplify their lives but to make them real and complex enough so that white people today, in particular, could identify with their choices. As a white person living in the twenty-first century, I still carry all those stories and beliefs in me, though they may be disguised or invisible, at least to other white people.

It has been easier for me to understand and identify with the female characters. I share the experience of being a wife and mother, steeped in sexist institutions, so feel more empathy toward them. On the other hand, Sir Nicholas Baganel is not someone I want to know. Born in Staffordshire, England in 1510, he fled to Ireland after being accused of murder in a pub brawl. Known as a ruthless warrior, he was employed by Henry VIII and Elizabeth I in their efforts to keep the Irish down.

Sir Nick eventually became the Grand Marshall of Ireland, in charge of the military. In addition to scorched earth tactics and battles, the English soldiers and their Irish collaborators rounded up the migratory Irish into plantations. He must have learned early that violence was admirable and the Irish were expendable. It reminds me of the genocidal treatment towards Native Americans one hundred years later.

My assumption when I began the research was that oppressive beliefs and behaviors like racism, colonization, and genocide had their source in Europe. We must have learned them somewhere, or at least become vulnerable to accepting them as truth. Patterns like greed, arrogance, superiority, and believing that conquering other people and their land and resources is the right thing to do, in the name of honor, religion, family, and country. I was not proven wrong. All those things are illustrated in European history over and over.

As a result of this process I now have a better sense of European history. I am impressed by the constant migrations of people, the vast trade networks, and the march of technological advancements. I expected to learn about the wars and invasions and was not disappointed. They were almost constant. The need to conquer and control land and people was endemic. I was surprised to learn about the power of the Christian church during the entire medieval period. When Pope Urban II urged Christians in western Europe to conquer the holy sites in Jerusalem and other nearby lands, it was no wonder people all over Europe embarked on crusades for the next 200 years. It helped that anyone who went on a crusade would receive forgiveness for his or her sins. For nobles and knights, it was a way to fulfill their feudal obligations and profit from the economic and political opportunities that came with any colonizing venture.

The most profound part of the project for me has been acknowledging that I came from these specific people. My body is connected to them, the color of my skin, the shape of my nose and eyes, texture of my hair, my height, my hands, all of it. That is why the act of physically embodying my ancestors has been so important. For the photo shoots I put on types of clothes they might have worn and imagine my hands fingering a sword, wielding an ax, carrying a bowl of soup, skinning a rabbit, sewing a dress, preparing for the next battle. Believing that I am right.

I truly am my white ancestors. My life is filled with decisions I make to maintain a privileged life based on the oppression of others past and present. I keep silent when I hear comments among my white friends that are subtly racist. I live off of money I inherited from my grandparents and parents. I don't have many friends who are not white. I let fear stop me from reaching out to people of color. I buy clothes made by people who are paid poorly and work in unsafe conditions. I live in a nice apartment and eat healthy food and look away from people who are homeless or poor. Mostly these are ways I stay passive and unconscious because to feel the full truth about racism and the harmful effects of capitalism would be unbearable.

I don't recount these transgressions to feel bad about myself or to make other white people feel bad. Heaven knows white people are already drenched in feeling bad. I list them to remind myself that I am no different than my ancestors except for the fact that I have the benefit of hindsight. Looking ahead, will my great-grandchildren shake their heads that we waited so long before turning global warming around?

One more story. My ancestor Desire Howland Gorham was born in 1623 in Plymouth Colony. Her husband, Captain John Gorham, fought and died in King Phillip's War, the last stand of the Narragansett Nation and their allies against the English. Following this war all captive Indian males were enslaved and sent to the West Indies and their tribal lands distributed to English soldiers, including the Gorhams. However, any Indian servants who were already employed by English settlers could remain with their employers and avoid being deported. In one of the genealogical books, I found more than one reference to an Indian servant named Tooto who worked for Desire. In his will dated December 22, 1691, Tooto asked to be "buried as near his mistress' feet as may conveniently be" and left two oxen to pay for his burial. He then gave all his possessions to Desire's children and grandchildren.

I always want to cry at this point in the story. I want to believe that Tooto was a cherished person to this family, crossing the social and ethnic barriers. Perhaps his family was gone and he didn't have anyone else to leave his possessions to. But mostly, I want to believe that given a chance, human connection always wins out.

Embracing white identity and heritage as a step towards ending racism might seem counterintuitive. But this history is living in all white people in varying ways and the more we deny it the bigger it looms. For me this process has been a way to understand and feel a part of my historical family, while at the same time taking responsibility for their actions and the privileges I inherited. ■

Project Description

I Am My White Ancestors: Self-Portraits through Time is an installation of twelve life-size photographic self-portraits that explores European-American heritage, my family history, and our role in the history of race, class, colonization, and genocide. The ancestors, mostly real and some imagined, span over 2000 years from the Celtic Iron Age to Civil War South Carolina. The 7 ft. x 5 ft. portraits, printed on fabric panels, combine photography, performance, costuming, and painting and are accompanied by short audio diaries from the perspective of each ancestor. It will premiere Fall 2016 at the Alexander Gallery, Clackamas Community College, Oregon City, Oregon. Designed as a lightweight traveling show, it will be available for touring starting January 2017.

Sara Estes

Welcome to Midnight

O N APRIL 12, 1970, RAINEY POOL, a fifty-four-year-old, one-armed sharecropper from Midnight, Mississippi, was beaten by a group of white men and dumped in the Sunflower River. That's not fiction, that's real.

I didn't know Mr. Pool and I had never heard of Midnight before, but that sentence, the one you just read, never left me after I first saw it. The sentence wasn't in the newspaper. It wasn't a book or anywhere most people would see it. I found the sentence in the basement of a performing arts center. Far underground, in a hidden windowless art museum, an artist named Jessica Ingram had taken a photograph of the river, and hung it framed and pristine on the wall, with the sentence posted next to it. I stared at the river in the photograph, overgrown and moody, and I reread the sentence, which I recognized as one of the most horrifying and beautiful sentences I had ever read. There was something about the man's name, Rainey Pool, that seemed innocent and lyrical. I thought about the way rain falls on a puddle, the concentric ripples and dots that look like they're rising from the bottom but they're not. How can such a hateful thing happen to a man with a name like such poetry. I read the sentence again.

Dumped in the Sunflower River. How can a man be dumped in the Sunflower River? A man should swim in the Sunflower River. He should bask and breathe and become holy in the Sunflower River. He should collect wildflowers and skip rocks along the Sunflower River, he should bathe with his wife in the Sunflower River, he should make love in the Sunflower River, and he should grow old in the Sunflower River and crack jokes and drink fizzy water and eat lunch next to the

Sunflower River, he should not die in the Sunflower River, he should not be dumped in the Sunflower River, he should not be left for dead in the Sunflower River. He should not be dumped. *Dumped*. A man should not be dumped. I read the sentence again.

When you live in the South, it's sentences like these that haunt you. It's hard to tell stories about past niceties and privilege and gaiety, because what starts with an innocuous elegance ends in some kind of horror, and if it doesn't end in horror then you can be sure that it began with it. The ghosts are real here, they haven't left, they aren't finished yet. We all know in our bones that there's still so much haunting left for them to do.

In the South, no matter who you are, you can't shake the ghosts. The ghosts of guilt and shame and terror and pain. The ghosts that live in our houses, in our yards, and in our heads. The stories that begin and end with hate and denial. The ghosts are there because we never dealt with them. Not to begin with and not now. So they stay. I don't despise the South but I despise the ghosts. Are they one and the same? I despise that ghosts have to exist at all. Our cities are built on graves, marked and unmarked. Beneath our feet are bones and histories that have been prematurely buried, hidden, swept below in a white-washed hush. *This is what I came from,* I say to myself. I was born of this. I was born into this hideous tale. I can do nothing to change what happened, yet I know I have agency with the future. Even if, at times, it doesn't seem that way. Most times it feels hopeless, seeing the headlines and watching the videos that show the way people who have the color of my skin treat people who do not have the color of my skin. I feel I cannot stop it all, but at the same time I know I can stop some of it – that which exists in my corner of the world, my fabric, my community. I believe that the actions of one person count. We are not no-count people, no matter what anyone tells us. None of us are no-count people. I don't know what to do about the ghosts other than to meet them. To know them. To ask for their stories, in hopes that they can finally be laid to rest. *Have a seat,* I say. *Tell me what happened.*

On a cold night in December, when the leaves had turned and were beginning to die, I drove down to Midnight. I decided to visit the bank of the Sunflower River at dusk, and to ask for its story, much like Jessica Ingram had done in her photograph. The drive was quiet and eerie, miles of bumpy roads lined with tipsy electric poles leaning to whatever side they did. Farm fields and rows of cotton gins huddled together like giant chess pieces in a game no one was winning. When I arrived in Midnight, whose population barely grazed 200, I felt haunted and weary. The town was riddled with dilapidated houses that to me all embodied, to some degree or another, the ghost of Mr. Pool. They were sharecropper homes, they were collapsing, they were holding on for dear life. I drove through Midnight to Louise and finally to the Sunflower River. All that time I thought I'd been going down there to ask Mr. Pool to tell me his story. I couldn't do much, I thought, but I could do my part. But when I got to the bank of the river, I felt something else. Something far more disconcerting. The ghost that was haunting me wasn't Mr. Pool. It was the others. The white men. *This is what I came from,* I thought with disgust. *How could you dump a man in the Sunflower River?* I asked them, tears welling up in my eyes. *You fuckers, how could you dump Mr. Pool?* I begged them to tell me their story, to give me something, anything that could remotely justify the wretchedness that destroyed such precious words. *Rainey Pool,* I cried. *Sunflower River,* I cried. *This is what I came from.*

I slept by the river that night. Waiting for something to happen, or waiting just because I didn't know what else to do. I grieved for Mr. Pool, and I grieved for the white men who lived with so much hate in their hearts. White men with skin like mine, but nothing else, not heart or soul or mind. I tell myself skin is just skin, but is that all it is? Not here, not down here. It's a history here, one you can't escape from. One you cannot outrun or ignore or exchange. It's yours. It's your story, your ghost that follows you as loyally as your shadow. It's behind you when you're standing in the sun; it's huddled beneath your feet when you look up at the stars. In the South, people never stop grieving because they can't. It's not in their cards, you see. Those with my skin color have a special weight, too. A thousand years of grief for all the wrong we did and the suffering we caused. A thousand years for our loved ones. A thousand years for each body gone silent in the cacophony of hate.

And the grief comes, and when it does we must invite it in without a fight, lest we deny it and allow it to grow stronger and more violent. Yes, it comes. If it doesn't show up at the start of our lives, it shows up at the end. It waits for us by our bedside, ready to sing us to sleep. ▥

Marla Cooper

We'll Always Have Walmart

A MAN ON TELEVISION was singing real pretty. I pointed and said, "Daddy!" With a nervous laugh, my mother pulled my hand away. Though I was only three years old, I could tell I had said something wrong.

"No, darling, that is *not* your daddy." She hustled me out of the room.

"You kids turn around and walk back to the house if they try to make you get on a bus. I will not have my children going to school with those filthy Mexicans," Daddy said. I was eight years old. Turned out it was the Mexican kids who had to ride the bus. My grade got two boys, both cute as could be and neither one of them looked dirty.

I was almost eleven when somebody blew up a church in Alabama. Four little black girls *died*. Not long after that, President Johnson signed a law that said everybody had the same rights no matter what color they were, or what religion they believed in, or whether they were a boy or a girl. They had to take down the "whites only" sign on the water fountain at the store where my Girl Scout badges were sold.

My daddy said, "Somebody ought to shoot that nigger." There he was, right on television: a black man, Rev. Martin Luther King Jr., just stirring things up. I was twelve years old. Daddy shook his head, lit another cigarette then went to the kitchen to freshen his drink.

I went back to my room in a world of confusion. Daddy did not make any beans about where he stood when it came to black people. He would tell you right out they were not as good as we were, and little white girls ought to be careful around black men because they were animals and could not be controlled.

Mom was different. She had a friend, Mrs. Washington, who came to the house now and then to pick up the clothes Mama had washed but did not have time to iron. Often, when Mrs. Washington brought the load back neatly pressed and folded, Mom would give her money then offer her a piece of cake and a cup of coffee. They would sit and visit for a while. Mrs. Washington had a laugh that filled up the whole room. I liked her, but I felt shy. She was black, like that man on television Daddy said needed shooting.

The city of Los Angeles exploded with rage the summer I was thirteen. For almost a whole week black people burned the place down and stole everything they could from the stores owned by white people.

Cassius Clay, a black man who was a really good boxer changed his name to Muhammad Ali because he wasn't a Christian anymore. He had joined the religion of Islam. Then he refused to go fight in the war. He said nobody from Vietnam ever called him a nigger, and he wasn't mad at them. The government tried to put him in jail for that.

In my American history class the instructor taught us that the Civil War had nothing to do with slavery. It was fought over states' rights and the South seceded because the Yankees were trying to tell us how to live. Also, I was taught to take pride in Manifest Destiny and to revel in the way we killed the native people who lived here before us.

I was fifteen when a man named James Earl Ray shot Martin Luther King Jr. Daddy was perfectly satisfied, but I wondered why Mr. Ray killed him. On television, all I ever heard Martin Luther King Jr. talk about was nonviolent resistance to unfair treatment. That seemed okay to me. He had not stolen anything, and he had not hurt anyone. He was not trying to get black people to go on a rampage either, but they sure did after Rev. King got shot. Riots broke out all over this country.

A friend gave me a book called *Black Like Me,* and I read it. A white man took treatments to turn his skin black, then he lived for a while like black people had to live. The things that man went through were awful!

When I was sixteen, my best friend and I drove to a town just twenty miles away to shop. A car full of black teenage boys pulled up next to us at the red light. We knew we were supposed to be afraid, so giggling like crazy, we locked our doors. They saw us doing that, and I felt ashamed.

There were 545 kids in my high school senior class. We had no blacks and only twenty-three Mexicans, making my class 96 percent white, and 4 percent Mexican.

Because of affirmative action, I was not accepted the first year I applied to an allied health program offered by my community college. I tried again and got in the next year. We had one black, two Mexicans and eight whites. The black girl was one of the smartest kids in the class, but a little stand-offish. One of the two Mexicans was fifteen minutes late almost every day. I found out the other one was from Guatemala.

In 1980 my husband and I traveled to Acapulco as representative prize-winners of the shop where he worked, because they had exceptional sales of a particular air-conditioning company. Young Mexican people put on a vibrant show of Folklorico for the group we were with. At the end of the production, the narrator exuberantly called, "¡Viva México!" and encouraged the audience to join him. Not one person said a thing. I looked into the eyes of the rednecks sitting around us, their arms planted like oak trees on the tables in front of them, their hands cradling cigarettes or drinks they were nursing. "¡Viva México!" the young man called again. I looked to my husband whose eyes were just as dead as all the others. I dared not speak. I've never been so ashamed of myself or of the people I call my own.

Later during the 1980s, the media told us to say *African American* instead of black. Also, *Hispanic* replaced Mexican, as the politically correct term.

A large number of doctors from India came to town. Eventually, they got together and built a second hospital where the majority of the physicians were Indian. A few of the people in the hospital lab where I worked were also from India. One day, I admired the necklace my friend, Ambuja, wore. She lifted it over her head and insisted I take it. I still have it and I treasure it.

My son faced an America where it seemed more advantageous to be African American, a member of any other minority, or female. Growing up, one of his best friends, Adam, was African American. My son is just American, though he could be Scot-Irish-English-Scandinavian-Spanish-Native American. He speaks only English, American English. He dare not say the n-word, but he tosses the f-word around like candy from a piñata. He says the b-word just as frequently.

The high school I graduated from so many years ago is now majority Hispanic. The city where I was born and raised is mostly Hispanic.

I'm sixty three years old, born in 1952, almost right in the middle of the Baby Boom Generation. Being white in America means I must press one for English when I phone most businesses or government offices since 17 percent of our population is now Hispanic. They don't have to learn English, but Western European immigrants did. In May we celebrate Cinco de Mayo out of regard for an 1862 Mexican victory over the French. What has that got to do with the United States? In September and October, we celebrate Hispanic Heritage Month out of regard for the 1810 declaration of Mexican Independence from Spain. Again, I ask, what has that got to do with the United States?

For me, being white in America means in January I am bombarded with advertisements for events celebrating the birth of Martin Luther King Jr. In February I am reminded that it is African American History Month. All this occurs out of respect for the citizens in our country who are of African American descent though they comprise less than 13 percent of the population.

This country has long celebrated St. Patrick's Day, but no offices or businesses close. Why doesn't the country celebrate Scottish heritage? Or Native American heritage? Or English heritage? Or Italian heritage? Or German heritage? Or Polish heritage? Or Jewish heritage? Or Russian heritage? Or French heritage? Or Scandinavian heritage? Or maybe we should not celebrate any *particular* heritage at all. Why not just celebrate being Americans?

For me, one of the 64 percent Caucasians in the country, being white in the United States of America means I feel I must first, ignore the way I was raised and second, apologize for it. Being white in America means realizing things are not the way they used to be and will never again be the way they were. That's good, but right now, *political correctness* and *affirmative action* have gone overboard in an attempt to make up for past sins. These two concepts have done more to divide us than to unite us. Reverse discrimination is still discrimination.

A couple of years ago, an African American man offered to mow my yard for a reasonable price. I hired him, and he did a terrific job. He asked if I could loan him some money. I did. Eager to show I held no bias, and probably out of white guilt, I loaned him money a second time. I have not seen a penny of payment toward either of those "loans." I felt to ask for it would be considered racist.

A week before Halloween this year, I spoke to an African American man standing in front of the scented candles, air-sprays and incense products at Walmart. "Decisions, decisions," I said as I waited for a lady with a cart to pass so I could make my way down the aisle. "Hard to make up your mind with so many options, huh?" I asked, never expecting a response.

But he did respond. "Yes, it is difficult," he said.

His accent told me he was new to this part of the country. Ignoring the burn I suffered at the hands of that African American yard man two years before, I smiled and asked, "You're not from around here, are you? Where ya from?"

He turned to look at me and said, "New York City."

"What in the world brings you to West Texas?" I asked.

"I'm just passing through. I'm on my way back to McKinney," he said. "Actually, I hate Texas, but I'm trapped here."

"Well, we do have a bad attitude, and we're damned proud of it too," I said. "But why are you trapped?"

"It's my students. And their mothers. They love me and won't let me go."

"Really?! What do you teach?"

"Tennis."

"I love tennis," I said. "Serena's my hero!"

"But she's on the way out," he said. "There are new techniques coming to tennis."

"Well, if Serena's not going to be on top, who do you see taking her place?"

His eyes lit up as he started in on one of his favorite topics. "Not so long ago a young Italian woman came out of nowhere and showed her stuff then disappeared again." He started to call her name, but I beat him to it.

"Francesca Schiavone?"

"Why, yes!" he exclaimed.

"And didn't she win the French Open a few years back?"

Oh, he was really excited this time and pointed his fist at me. "I cannot believe you know that!"

I wasn't sure what to do with that fist pointing at me, but I had seen on television folks making a fist bump. So, I folded my hand and touched it to his. When he smiled, I knew I had done the right thing.

People with carts and tag-along children were obviously inconvenienced by our conversation there in the middle of the aisle, so I scooted to a more open spot near a standing display.

He followed me fussing with his telephone and asked, "Well, how do you feel about black and white movies?" He thrust the phone in front of my face.

I recognized the female star and the movie, "Of all the gin joints…." I started in and looked up. "Isn't that Ingrid Bergman?"

"Yes!"

"*Casablanca* with Humphrey Bogart, right?"

"Yes!"

Out came the fist and this time I knew what to do. "As a matter of fact," I said, "My boyfriend and I are going this evening to a black and white film at a historic theatre downtown. We are going to see the original *Dracula* with Bela Lugosi. You have to come with us!"

"You have a boyfriend?" He seemed unhappy about it. "I don't want to be a third wheel. Don't you have a girlfriend you can call?"

I thought for a moment and said, "Yes. I know just the one."

"Call her right now," he said.

So I did, but the call went straight to her voice mail.

Again he said, "I do not want to be a third wheel. Your boyfriend is going to kill me."

"No, he will not. You will like him. He is a nice open-minded musician-type guy."

"Musician? What does he play?"

"Guitar. Lead guitar."

"No! This cannot be! *I* play lead guitar."

"Well, then, where are you on Yngwie Malmsteen?"

His eyes grew wide and he almost shouted, "No! How can you know that name?" He put his hand to his head as if someone had conked him. "Nobody knows that name!"

"Oh, you are going to get along just fine with my boyfriend."

I still had to pay for my items, so we got in line behind a young Hispanic woman. She seemed uncomfortable and made a point of ignoring him. In the confusion that is Walmart, he jostled her, then excused himself, but she continued to show no interest at all. Offended, he spoke to her in Spanish, "*¿Me escuchas?*" She spoke a little louder to her girlfriend who was ahead of her and already checking out. He upped his volume as well, "*¿Me escuchas ahora?*"

The young ladies hurried away. I believe they were frightened. And who knows? Maybe they did not understand because a lot of Hispanics in this town do not speak Spanish.

He turned my way, spread his arms wide and made a face that said, *Can you believe that?*

I shrugged and shook my head. Once we were through the line and outside, he pushed the cart to my van, mumbling the whole time about the young Latina. We loaded my stuff in the back, then, with a little hesitation, he asked, "Are you sure about this? I feel like I have been invited to be the special guest at a Ku Klux Klan meeting."

"For heavens' sakes, get in the van. You are going to be just fine." All the way home, he continued expressing his uncertainty and how he hated Texas. When we pulled into the drive at my house, my boyfriend, T. J., had just started out the front door. He did not look too happy when he saw my guest sitting in the front seat, but once inside, I made introductions and quickly explained that my new friend, Leslie, played guitar. That was all it took to melt away the concern. I added that Les was going with us to the movie.

"We do not have much time," T. J. said as he started to turn off his amplifier.

"Do you mind if I play your guitar for just a minute?" asked Les. "It has been months and I really miss it."

With no hesitation, T. J. said, "No, I don't mind a bit. I understand how it is. We have a little time. Go ahead."

He only got to play a few licks, but Leslie proved himself more than worthy of the label: guitar player. Then we loaded into my van, the men happily discussing Stevie Ray Vaughn versus Steve Vai and Clapton and Hendrix. When we got to the movie, T. J. bought the tickets and Les bought popcorn and drinks for the three of us.

When the movie was over, we took him back to Walmart where his R. V. was parked. We agreed to meet up inside when he finished with his shopping. I settled in at the Subway restaurant located at the front of the store while T. J. went in search of my new friend.

After a late supper and more conversation, I realized the time was getting on and said, "We better let him go. He has a long drive tomorrow." Reluctantly, they both agreed. They shook hands as a farewell gesture, but I grabbed Les and hugged his neck. I did not say it out loud, but I was thinking, *We'll always have Walmart.*

Look, what's done is done. Being white in America means we need to turn loose of revenge and remorse, victim-hood and sensationalism. Rodney King had it right when he asked, "Can't we all just get along?"

Yes, Rodney, I think we can, but we have to look at each other as individuals, not as examples of an entire race, religion or culture. Most importantly, *all of us,* black, white, brown, red, purple-haired people have to commit to seeing what makes us the same, not what makes us different. ■

Gil Fagiani

What Does It Mean to Be White in America: My Multi-Metamorphoses

If I am not what you say I am, then you are not who you think you are.[1]

– James Baldwin

OVER THE COURSE OF MY SEVENTY YEARS, I have experienced being white in a myriad of incarnations: from racist, civil rights movement supporter, honorary soul brother, racial disguise artist, dope fiend hipster, to revolutionary comrade, subordinate of the black vanguard, minority, loser, crime target, race-traitor, and progressive Italian American.

I grew up in a white, suburban community in Connecticut, and while attending Springdale Elementary School, I already knew that dark skin was perceived to be a sign of inferiority, and I viewed Italians – or at least some of them – as bearing that stigma, because they seemed to be the darkest, dumbest, crudest group around. Once, on my paper route, a shirtless Italian construction worker jumped off his bulldozer. "Driving all day in the sun," he said disgustedly, "made me as black as a *nigger*." And, indeed, his skin was a deep shade of brown, which, combined with his kinky hair, made him look darker than many Cubans and Puerto Ricans.

---

1   James Baldwin. "The Negro Child–His Self Image," *The Saturday Review,* December 21, 1963.

Another time, a WASPY friend's mother was driving us to the beach and my friend suddenly turned around and asked me, "What's the sound of an Italian machine gun?" When I gave him a blank look, he said, "Guinea, guinea, wop, wop, wop," as his mother hollered at him to be quiet. During that period, I didn't think of myself as white, but as Italian, a group whose racial status was murky, at best.

My exposure to black people as a child was limited. There was a black paperboy whose customers openly called "Sambo," who only lasted a few days on the job. And the black garbage men who were always fleeing the snapping jaws of neighborhood dogs. The few direct experiences I did have left me fearful of black people. Once, when I was with my mother on our way to a shoe store in downtown Stamford, I heard angry voices coming from an alleyway – a black man was punching a woman to the ground. I grew up in an Italian family where women were revered, and this image of – for me, incomprehensible violence – left me with a frightening impression of black men.

Another time, at Sherwood Island State Park, two boys jumped me, one black and the other white. They knocked me to the ground and looked through my pockets for money. The black boy made fun of my orthopedic shoes, took one off, and threw it down a wooden latrine. I was about twelve, and this incident humiliated and enraged me.

As I grew older, I engaged in a form of verbal jousting that my male peers called "ranking," which was similar to what African Americans call the "dozens." At that time, the ultimate put-down was "your mamma's name is Beulah," which was the name of the first TV sitcom to star a black actress, Ethel Waters, or "your mamma was born on Pacific Street," a run-down part of Stamford where Negroes – as they were called by polite society – lived.

I excelled in this "ranking," and embraced the notion that blacks were an inferior race – and, to my relief – a group with less status than Italians. At the time, I palled out with a boy named Roy Black, whose father was English and sold Jaguar sports cars. I tormented Roy by going to class early and inserting the word "is" between his first and last names on the blackboard. When the students arrived, they broke out laughing. I probably had more fights with Roy than any other kid in Springdale. I thought it was well worth it – the girls thought I was a riot.

While in junior high school, I had an attractive African American math teacher, whose name, coincidentally, was Beulah. My hormones had kicked into overdrive and I had sexual fantasies about all my young, female teachers. But my math teacher was off-limits, and I recall saying to myself, *What a piece of ass; too bad she's black.* Denigrating blacks and acting prideful about being white made me feel secure, since all my peers acted the same way and I wanted to be one of them.

In my final year of junior high, I was a member of the track team. During a relay race, as I went to pass my black opponent, he jabbed his elbow into my ribs. I succeeded in running by him, but I racialized the incident; that is, I saw it not as rough play but as an expression of black hostility toward white people. Being white, I surmised, could make me a target for black intimidation.

As I entered high school, the civil rights movement was exploding into public consciousness. While my father voted Republican, favoring Eisenhower and Nixon, my mother was a New Deal Democrat who strongly supported the movement. Together we watched TV news images of African Americans being attacked by southern mobs opposed to desegregation. My mother's compassion for the poor and oppressed, and her willingness to defend unpopular positions, deeply impressed me. Following her example, I refuted my earlier racist sentiments and became a white sympathizer of the civil rights movement who felt an obligation to struggle against racism.

As a teenager, I had ferocious arguments with my classmates who claimed that blacks were an inferior race, while others said that black civil rights protesters should know their place, and called me a "nigger-lover" for supporting them. I don't recall any of my peers agreeing with my views. I was an insecure, marginal student – both academically and socially – and I strongly identified with the underdog, which in this case was blacks, who were at the bottom of the social ladder.

Following high school, I attended Pennsylvania Military College (PMC), which was located in Chester, Pennsylvania, about twenty minutes south of Philadelphia. It had been a boomtown during the two world wars, but by the early 1960s, much of its heavy industry had closed down, and a palpable sense of economic doom had engulfed the city.

While I was a cadet, there were still some white, working class neighborhoods of Poles, Ukrainians, Lithuanians, and Italians. A group of children who looked Eastern European walked by my barracks on their way to school. Their hair was unkempt, their teeth rotten, and they wore raggedy clothes. In suburban Connecticut, I didn't know poor whites, and equated whiteness with being middle-class. Now social class became a factor when I thought about white identity.

A handful of blacks attended PMC, and they were harassed by some of the white cadets. Along with a few other sympathetic white cadets, I helped protect the blacks by confronting their tormentors.

By the early 1960s, there were *civil rights disturbances,* as the newspapers called them, in Chester. PMC employed local black workers for menial jobs, such as kitchen help and maintenance work. There was a groundskeeper named Eddie who talked slowly and walked with a limp. Every time he encountered a cadet, he'd smile and say, "Won't be long now!" At first, I thought he meant it wouldn't be long before semester break. As time went on, I started to wonder if there wasn't a more ominous meaning to his words, like, it won't be long before the white, middle-class cadet corps would be set upon by an angry black mob.

At PMC, I had access to several black radio stations in the Philly area, and was a loyal listener of WDAS radio DJ and civil rights activist Georgie Woods, "the Guy with the Goods." I was already a big fan of the Motown sound, when Georgie and other black DJs introduced me to a deeper shade of soul music–the Memphis Sound–that featured such artists as Wilson Pickett, Otis Redding, Carla Thomas, Sam & Dave, and Booker T. and the MGs.

This was when I entered what I think of as my "honorary soul brother phase." The civil rights movement was my religion; black authors, like Claude Brown and James Baldwin, were my prophets; black women were my lust objects, and soul music was my soundtrack.

My sense of being white changed. I saw white people as divided between a reactionary majority who were racist and an enlightened minority, which included myself, who supported the black freedom struggle. In addition, I began to feel that many aspects of black culture were superior to that of white Americans; in particular, music, dance, fashion, and the poetry of everyday speech. Playing the reverse snob, I looked down on many whites as square, uptight, and lame.

After finishing my junior year at PMC, I joined an East Harlem student project sponsored by Cornell United Religious Work and the East Harlem Tenants Council. The purpose of the project was to provide opportunities for students to learn about poverty and racism, as well as to engage in the struggle against social injustice. Along with five other students, I lived for ten weeks in the Project's East 104th Street collective.

The staff at the East Harlem Tenants Council emphasized that students were in East Harlem to learn from community people and to assist local leaders. They were told not to impose their white, middle-class ideas and values on the East Harlem residents. Earlier in 1966, Stokely Carmichael had become the new chairman of the Student Nonviolent Coordinating Committee (SNCC). He popularized the concept of "Black Power," which no longer sought racial integration but instead focused on blacks leading their own organizations. As a result, whites were told to organize in poor white communities. This paradox – white students joining the fight against racism and poverty in a neighborhood of color at a time when this strategy was being discredited – played itself out all summer long. For the first time, I felt confused, resentful, and disillusioned about how my whiteness could be used to limit my involvement in organizations ostensibly committed to social change.

My summer in East Harlem had a radical impact on my politics, cultural interests, friendships, and eventual career choices. I also met my first wife, a pretty brown-skinned Puerto Rican woman from the neighborhood.

I suffered through my senior year at PMC, flying high in my Afrocentric phase: hanging out in a honky-tonk bar in the black section of Chester, chasing after black women, digging soul music, and closely following developments in the Black Power and civil rights movements. One evening, my friend Ray and I went to a sorority mixer at Glassboro Community College. We met two black women there who invited us to a party, encouraging us to follow them to their car. We had traveled about twenty minutes in the boondocks of Southern Jersey when we were suddenly cut off by a car full of black men who jumped out and came charging at us with chains and tire irons. Ray just barely managed to maneuver his car off a soft shoulder and hightail it back to Pennsylvania. This incident hammered home to me just how dangerous being white could be in the face of black rage. It made me realize that some black people hated white people to the point of wanting to kill them.

After my final semester at PMC, I visited my friend Roger for a week at Tougaloo College, a historically black school in Jackson, Mississippi, and got my first taste of the Jim Crow South. Whites would drive around in pickup trucks with rifle racks and KKK license plates, and all the public swimming pools remained closed – in spite of torrid temperatures – rather than comply with federal law mandating them to be desegregated. Walking the narrow sidewalks, I was mortified when older black men jumped into the street to give me the right of way. At a party one evening, I met a young woman who had been crowned Miss Black Mississippi. I asked her why she didn't move to the North. "I feel more comfortable here," she said. "Things are clear; I know who my enemy is. Up North, your enemy hides behind smiling faces." As a white person struggling against racism, I began to experience whiteness as similar to original sin – that is, an innate moral stain that can never be erased.

After my trip to Mississippi, I took a job with the East Harlem Tenants Council and rented an apartment on East 121st Street. I began to spend more time hanging out with blacks and Puerto Ricans in the neighborhood. I met a friendly black marijuana dealer named Paul who had just come out of prison. He had a lot of status on the street and, as we grew closer, I was accepted by his large network of customers and friends, many of them street hustlers. With curly black hair, a mustache, chin beard, and skin that tanned, I easily passed as Puerto Rican. This was my hipster period of racial disguise, a time when I was in total rebellion against mainstream white society, and adopted black and Puerto Rican culture as my own, a posture immortalized in Norman Mailer's 1957 essay "The White Negro: Superficial Reflections on the Hipster."

Paul and I became roommates. By this time, I had been drinking heavily for a couple of years, as well as smoking marijuana. Now I started using heroin and cocaine, and lost my moorings. Being white in Harlem's drug world was uncool and dangerous. Whites looking to score drugs were routinely robbed. Once, while sitting in a park, I watched two of Paul's white customers, who resisted giving two dope-sick Puerto Rican addicts money, get savagely pistol-whipped. I sat in terror, hoping the two robbers wouldn't see through my racial disguise.

When I was strung out on heroin, I would team up with another addict and take advantage of the racial prejudices of store owners. We would enter clothing stores, and while all eyes were focused on my dark-skinned crime partner who was in the back of the store, I would be in the front, stuffing clothing into a shopping bag. When I look back on this period, I'm convinced that being white was the major factor for why I was never arrested. For example, I once initiated a drug transaction, giving two Puerto Ricans money to score dope. When a pair of undercover "narcs" blew on the scene, they searched the Puerto Ricans and arrested one of them. Then one of the narcs said to me, "Beat it and stay away from the *spics*."

Fortunately, with the help of my cousin and my girlfriend, I entered a therapeutic community for drug addicts in the Bronx called Logos. It was a rough-and-tumble program where whites were a minority and direct confrontation was used in groups to batter down the addicts' psychological defenses. Here, blacks called me racist, and at other times, whites called me a white Uncle Tom. One summer day, after a particularly grueling therapy group known as a *marathon* because it lasted more than twenty-four hours, the director brought forty of us to the Bronx Zoo. After a pleasant afternoon, the director took a shortcut back, through the Italian community of Arthur Avenue. We pranced down the neighborhood's main boulevard, arm-in-arm, men and women, white, black, and Puerto Rican, singing popular songs like *Raindrops Keep Fallin' On My Head*. It was a prototypical 1960s Utopian moment.

Suddenly, bottles started to explode on the sidewalk, and residents poured out of the stores waving bats and telling us to get the hell out of their neighborhood. James, one of my fellow black clients, tore off a car antenna and wanted to take on our attackers. After an angry exchange, I convinced him that we'd be massacred if we didn't clear out. In the end, the police rescued us and escorted us out, although they blamed us for stirring up trouble by "invading the neighborhood." Back at Logos, James cursed me out for siding with the Italians instead of fighting alongside him. To me, the incident personified America's racial insanity. Overall, Logos toughened me and helped me find a new balance. After leaving, I never used heroin again.

I began to immerse myself in left-wing politics. My sense of whiteness now became an ideological construct: black people, who suffered both class and racial oppression, would eventually lead a socialist revolution. The Black Panther Party had an exalted status and was seen as the vanguard of the revolution. As a white comrade, my role was to rally and prepare advanced elements in the white community so they would eventually ally with the broader revolutionary movement. Being white, according to this schematic, meant accepting the idea of subordination.

On the other hand, anti-white rhetoric at times reached a fever pitch. One self-described revolutionary, a Puerto Rican cocaine user with a history of mental illness, showed up at a comrade's apartment, waving a pistol and ranting that I was a police agent. Luckily, somebody tipped me off and I stayed away from him, but if circumstances had been different, I might have been killed.

In 1971, I co-founded White Lightning (WL), a Bronx-based organization that sought to radicalize white, working class people. WL's membership represented a variety of white ethnic groups. Inspired by black and Latino organizations, which used the histories of their people's resistance to oppression to fashion new and positive identities, we studied the histories of various groups of European ancestry. We learned that the Irish, Italian, Polish, and Eastern European Jewish immigrants faced discrimination upon their arrival in "the land of the free," and participated in the great battles for union recognition and social movements that led to the New Deal. We tried to show white ethnics that their history paralleled the history of poor and working class people, and how ethnic divisions, like present-day racial divisions, had destroyed political unity and discouraged social change.

This was an intense, apocalyptic period in which, for three years, I totally dedicated my life to revolutionary politics. As a result of internal divisions within the organization, burnout, and most of all, the birth of my first son, I resigned from White Lightning and took a full-time job at Bronx Psychiatric Center (BPC).

Ironically, Herman Ellis, a black friend of mine from Logos, was the director of the affirmative action program at BPC. Since his job was to recommend people of color for professional positions, he could, conversely, recommend white people for low-paying, non-professional positions. Consequently, three of his white friends, including me, ended up working as mental health therapy aides.

I worked at BPC for twelve years and was one of perhaps four white therapy aides out of a black workforce of – at its peak – several hundred. For the most part, I got along well with my coworkers, but there were times when I suspected that blacks looked out for blacks and my well-being was disregarded. I tried to overlook these feelings because they ran counter to my leftist sympathies, and because I didn't like the ugly, primitive feelings of bitterness and betrayal they stirred up. Certainly, being an extreme minority had its absurd moments.

Once, I was ordered to respond to an emergency on another ward. When I arrived, the hallway was packed with black therapy aides. A hulking black patient was standing in the doorway of his dormitory, cursing and threatening to *bust the ass* of the first person that tried to drag him into the seclusion room. Suddenly, his eyes focused on me and he yelled, "Yeah, you white niggers are the worst!" The aide assigned to that ward was a notorious drunk and, without thinking, he grabbed one of the patient's arms, which set off a melee. The patient slugged three of us. Later I reported to my West Indian nursing supervisor, along with the two coworkers who had also been hit. "You're lucky, Gil, you're white," she said, laughing. "Your injury shows."

Another time, I heard a black recreational therapist, who drove a new Lincoln and fancied himself a ladies' man, say, "If I were white, I know I'd be rich. If you're white and you're not rich, it's because you're a loser."

The living conditions in my neighborhood became unbearable. "The Bronx is burning," the media shouted, and in 1984, I was one of five white holdouts in my shabby tenement. One of the old white tenants, an Irish woman who lived with her elderly brother, was constantly spewing venom about the animals—her shorthand for blacks and Latinos—who had taken over the neighborhood. This would make me cringe, and I would plead with her to be more tolerant. Then one day I came home to find EMS workers carrying her brother to an ambulance on a stretcher. Nearby was a patrol car and two brown-skinned men in handcuffs. When the Irish woman saw me, she screamed, "Look what your monkeys did to my brother!" I felt guilty and naïve, about being white, and minimizing the dangers in my changing neighborhood.

Then the crack epidemic struck, and in less than a month, my car had been broken into twice and my battery stolen. I complained to the police, who said, "What's a guy your color doing here in Zulu-Land?"

By 1986, I moved to Astoria, Queens, to live with my girlfriend, who would become my second wife. Partly due to my relationship with her, and partly as a result of a spontaneous healing process that sought healthy and stabilizing roots, I began to reconnect with my *italianità*—my sense of being Italian American. Even though my mother and other close relatives were born in Italy, for most of my life I had rejected and felt ashamed of my Italian background. I believed that Italian Americans were always on the wrong side of the barricades politically, especially regarding the civil rights movement. Italian American politicians like Philadelphia mayor Frank Rizzo and Newark city councilman Anthony Imperiale made careers out of their virulent antagonism toward the black community. Imperiale once said, "When the Black Panther comes, the white hunter will be waiting." Later, I would learn that, historically, Italian Americans had a rich political legacy that spanned the entire political spectrum, from fascism to anarchism and socialism.

Over the years, I would go to Italy eighteen times, renew relationships with my family there, study and translate Italian and Italian dialect, and become active in several Italian American organizations. Now when I think about being white, I think first of my ethnic identity. I no longer feel saddled by a whiteness that is shameful, dishonorable, and guilt-inducing.

I still maintain my progressive stance against racism. For example, in 1992, I co-founded Italian Americans for a Multicultural US, an Italian American organization that joined blacks, Latinos, and Native Americans in protesting the Quincentennial Columbus Celebration, which included my appearing twice on *Like It Is,* a TV show dedicated to showcasing the African American experience, hosted by pioneering black reporter Gil Noble. As a result of these activities, some members of the Italian community called me a "traitor to my race."

Although I now live with a less intense feeling of whiteness, I recognize that I am less likely to be stopped by the police because I'm perceived as white, and that despite the election of a black president, the masses of black people suffer from institutional racism in housing, employment, and the criminal justice system. Thus, I believe there is still a need for an active movement to combat racism.

As a writer, however, I feel my whiteness in a very special and sad way. I have been very influenced by black and Puerto Rican writers. I write about blacks and Latinos. Four of my published collections of poetry are peopled mainly by characters who are not white – one is titled *A Blanquito in El Barrio – A White Boy in Spanish Harlem.* And while I recognize that writers tend to be a tolerant group, I still believe the whole literary enterprise – like everything else in our society – suffers from racial separateness and tokenism; a pity, since strong writing and face-to-face encounters between writers can tell the hard truths, and can go a long way toward building a foundation for trust and understanding. ■

Kurt Michael Friese

I Am The Man: Pondering My Own Privilege

AM THE MAN.

    I do not mean that in the "I'm the best, I'm the coolest" sense of the phrase.

I am The Man.

I mean that in the sense of the implication it has taken these last few decades.

I am The Man. I am The System. I am The Dominant Paradigm.

I did not build the system, did not create the dominant paradigm, but to try to claim that I am not of it – that I do not benefit from it – is to shut my eyes to self-evident truth. None of us became who we are on our own. All of us are who we are because of the words and deeds of everyone who came before us. Not just our families, but strangers too. Not just the heroes, but the villains too.

The world I inhabited was already deep in the throes of often-violent self-examination when I was born into white middle-class suburbia five decades ago. It had been over one hundred years since the end of the Civil War, but that war never really ended, it simply moved behind a curtain. Our innate human suspicion of "different" had controlled all civilization up to that point, and there was no reason to think that a few hundred thousand more dead people would change that. And it didn't.

If you were to ask me if I am racist I would say, "of course not," and look at you with self-righteous indignation that you would even suggest such a thing. This is because, like most people in my particular demographic, when I think of a racist person, I think of a southerner in a sheet, not a CEO in a suit. I am a modestly successful businessman, and while I was born to a somewhat affluent family—it all depends on who we are compared to—I still worked my way up in my industry from dishwasher to restaurateur over the course of these last thirty-five years. I worked alongside people of all races and ethnicities, and I learned from them all. I endeavored to treat everyone with the respect I expected for myself, admittedly with varying degrees of success.

From my current vantage point though, if I'm honest, I can look back at the various obstacles and turning points in my life, and I can see people who were smarter than I was, more talented than I was, harder-working than I was, who were passed over for advancement, or had additional obstacles thrown in their paths. I had access to schooling other people could not access. I was never regarded with suspicion when I walked into a bank and asked for a loan. Even now, my neighbors wave as I drive up the street. The police do not tail me when I drive home.

They have pulled me over from time to time though, usually because I tend to drive just a little too fast, and when they do, I am not scared. I speak to the officer politely and with respect. Sometimes I get a ticket, and every once in a while they let me off. This feels normal to me, so normal in fact that I find it hard to imagine such a situation developing differently for another person. That's because all my experiences with people in authority have been relatively fair. I did not grow up with family stories of persecution. I did not experience, save for a few bullies in junior high, any form of judgment for anything except the content of my character or the quality of my job performance.

There is no "stop and frisk" policy in the small, midwestern college town where I live. If a cop approached me on the street, my reaction would be "good morning, officer," not "oh shit." Nevertheless, I live in a state with the worst ratio of African American incarceration relative to population. When I look further afield, and I see the plain numbers in America's penal system, the privatization of prisons for profit, the ways the mandatory sentencing laws are plainly written to target "minorities," whether that is an intended consequence or not is immaterial. It remains a fact. To claim that I am not immune to that particular form of prejudice—in its strictest sense, "to pre-judge"—is to be intellectually dishonest or blindly stupid, or both.

This awareness on my part may still be somewhat rare but it is hardly revelatory. Though they may not talk about it, there are many middle-aged, middle-class white men who are as blithely aware of these ideas as I am. We go on about our lives, and rarely think about such things because in the backs of our minds we assume there is nothing we can do about it. We treat it like our own deaths—if it's inevitable, best not to think about it too much.

What we fail to realize though is that it is not inevitable. Just because we do not know the answer does not mean that there is no answer, nor that we shouldn't bother to look for one. I do not know the solution to the inherent inequalities in our system. I do not understand how it is that I never expect my son to be shot in the street or strangled by an officer of the law. I can't comprehend why expecting cops, or anyone in a position of power, to treat everyone fairly and equally, does not simply happen in each and every situation. I do not know what I, as one man, can possibly do about it. And that frustrates me, so I stop thinking about it.

I've lived most of my fifty years coping with my "white guilt" by invoking a line from an old favorite song: "I was just a child then, now I'm only a man."

It's helpful, consoling really, because it lets me shed any sense of responsibility. I needn't take the blame for the sins of the fathers and grandfathers and great-grandfathers who came before me. Hey, I wasn't there, right? It's not my fault.

Yet if I am willing to accept my inheritance of all the good they did, all the success they had, then I need to recognize the flip side of that coin. No one succeeds on his own. No one gains privilege without it costing someone else.

In the end though, I do not know how to shed my privilege. I do not know how to return it to the sender. So I go about my business, I try to be kind, to make things grow, and make my tiny corner of the world a little bit better than how I found it. I shake my head when I see others who don't do that, who let their fears guide their decisions—even though I know I'm guilty of that too. So I throw my hands up, because if I think about it too much, it suffocates me, and I can't breathe. ∎

Rabbi Gil Steinlauf

Are Jews White?

Adapted from a Rosh Hashanah sermon delivered at Adas Israel Congregation, Washington D.C., 2015.

THIS SUMMER I HAD A CONVERSATION with a young woman about her Jewish identity. She told me about how she grew up in a family that was very involved in her synagogue. She went to Jewish day school. She had been to Israel multiple times. Despite all this, she felt very far away from her Jewishness. Now out on her own, she didn't observe Shabbat.[1] She simply couldn't find the relevance of Judaism as she was making her way out on her own in the world. I asked her to tell me what she did feel passionate about. She told me how she has been reading and thinking a lot about racial justice in our society. What moved her was the #BlackLivesMatter movement–how, in light of Ferguson, Charleston, and seemingly endless incidents of injustice against black people in our society, she felt a pressing need to grapple with the racism that is so pervasive in this country and how it affects her identity. I asked her to explain to me more about her passion for this issue. She explained: "As a white woman, as the product of so much white privilege, it makes me all the more angry to see how other white people so blindly and carelessly feed into the racial climate of our society." "So the fact that you are white makes this issue all the more painful, all the more personal for you," I asked. "Yes," she said.

---

[1]   *Shabbat* (Hebrew: שַׁבָּת) is the seventh day of the Jewish week and is the day of rest and abstention from work as commanded by God. Shabbat involves two interrelated commandments: to remember *(zachor)* and to observe *(shamor)*.

In that moment, I certainly identified with her angst over this issue. Indeed, I find the reality of American racism, the legacy of slavery, the institutional discrimination that is so pervasive, the scourge of mass incarceration of black Americans—with its collateral damage on families; the on-going blight of housing segregation in America, and the role of law-enforcement in furthering racist systems and hierarchies—this and so much more, I, too, find unbearable. And so, I took a deep breath and asked, "Are you so sure you're white?" "Of course I'm white," she said. "I'm clearly not black, and I have had full access to all the privileges and benefits of white society."

I pointed out that she doesn't look stereotypically white: she has dark eyes and hair, and an olive complexion. She agreed that people will sometimes speak Spanish to her, assuming she was a Latina, while others have asked if she was from a Middle Eastern background, even though her family is Ashkenazi Jewish, from Eastern Europe. "But in this society," she hastened to add, "I still qualify as white." "Of course," I agreed. "But if you are regularly mistaken for a more 'brown' person," I continued, "perhaps there are some, more stereotypically white, people who don't consider you as white as you may feel that you are." She paused to consider this idea. "I suppose that's possible," she said. "Well," I continued, "in not being quite as white as you may have thought, you have found the beginning of your genuine Jewish identity."

I would like to explain more of what I meant with this young woman. You see nowadays, this woman is not alone. In our very flawed and racist society, our Jewish people are prospering, reaching the top echelons of privilege and power. With racism and injustice so pervasive and entrenched year after year, generation after generation, we Jewish people must now ask ourselves: what role do we play in that injustice now that most of us live as white people in America? This young woman is so right in questioning why her "whiteness" leads her to participate in the oppression of others. And the fact that it never occurred to her how Jewish her thirst for racial justice is—this means that we must, all of us, consider the role of race in our twenty-first century Jewish identities. Today, I will show why we all must cease to consider ourselves to be part of the social construct of being white—despite all the white privilege that America affords us – and how we must teach our children that we are, in fact, not white.

In the book of Genesis, there is a very famous story about a great tower that the early generations of human beings built after the time of Noah and the flood. The story goes that all human beings spoke one language, and in an act of extraordinary unity, they built this tower so they could reach heaven. God saw their endeavor, and realized that with only one language and one purpose, they would think that nothing, not even God and heaven, is beyond their reach. So God thwarted their plan. God confounded their speech so that one person couldn't understand the other. With their unity obliterated, they scattered to all ends of the earth, creating many peoples and many languages. And, because their speech sounded like babbling as they talked to one another, the tower came to be known as the Tower of Babel.

It's a strange story, particularly to our American ears. After all, our American motto is *E Pluribus Unum* – out of many we are one. The great blessing and promise of America to our ancestors when we came here was that it was a land of opportunity, where we are all recognized as equal, where nothing, not even the heavens, is beyond our reach. We all know that the story of the Jewish people in America is a stunning success story. Our success here is built on the efforts of the first generations of American Jews who struggled mightily to assimilate into mainstream America – to slough off the ways of the old country, to out-American the Americans. In many ways, in 2015, it's difficult for us to appreciate how remarkable this success is.

A century and a half ago, racism in America was in some ways more complex than it is today. There weren't just white people, brown people, yellow people, and black people. In those days, the white people were considered to be mostly descendants of the British and Northern Europeans. Irish people were not considered white. Neither were Italians. And of course, neither were the Jews. Well into the twentieth century, we Jews were barred from the whitest country clubs. We couldn't buy houses in the whitest neighborhoods. Some of us here today have been called anti-Semitic names, have had pennies thrown at us, or have been beaten up because we are Jewish. What some of us may not realize is that the particularly American brand of anti-Semitism has deep roots, and connections to American racism.

That young woman, and all her young adult Jewish peers today can hardly fathom being singled out, being treated as "other," because of their Jewishness. And the main reason why anti-Semitism is no longer mainstream in our society is because sometime in the last half century, we have finally convinced America that we, too, are white.

All those years of singular focus on making it in America have paid off! Our achievements in business, in medicine, in the arts, in government, in all circles of American life have resulted in something rarely known to our wandering ancestors—we are one with the power elites of our society. Look at this very synagogue—Adas Israel Congregation. I once read some papers written by the early founders of our synagogue over a century ago. They dreamt of one day building what they referred to as a "great Cathedral synagogue" standing tall and proud in our nation's capital, as powerful as the great American monuments of this city. In 1950 that great dream came true with the construction of this grand and impressive edifice. We came here to practice a Judaism that projected our American dream—complete with decorous services and royal purple-clad clergy who emulated the pomp and circumstance of the Episcopal Church.

By the end of the twentieth century, Jewish names were all over the *The New York Times* wedding section along with the rest of lily-white society weddings. The country clubs, the exclusive neighborhoods are now as Jewish as they are "waspy." Indeed, we Jewish people have been building a great, shining American tower, and we have just about reached the highest heavens.

The ancient Midrash is a collection of rabbinic legends and stories. The Midrash often fills out and expands upon stories in the Torah, giving us greater insight into their meaning. One Midrash, in *Pirkei de Rabbi Eliezar* (24:7) expands upon and clarifies the story of the Tower of Babel. Why indeed did God thwart the seemingly noble plan of the people to unite with one purpose, and build a tower heavenward? The rabbis explain that the tower eventually reached such a breathtaking height that it took a whole year to climb to the top. Each brick was baked on the ground, and had to be transported up. The higher the tower went, the more precious each brick was. Finally, the Midrash says the following: "If a person fell and died they paid no attention, but if a brick fell they sat and wept, saying, 'Woe upon us! Where will we get another to replace it?'"

It's an incredible Midrash. In a few short sentences, it conveys one of the greatest dangers of our human condition: for all our well-intended yearnings to unite, to work together to achieve collective dreams – we risk creating societies that forget our essential humanity. We risk creating societies that place ideals above human life. We risk creating totalitarian societies, fascist societies, racist societies, societies that are intolerant of difference, societies that create the conditions for discrimination, for oppression, for racial or ethnic cleansing, for genocide itself.

In our century, we are waking up to the fact that our great tower, our astounding success in America, is a pyrrhic victory. Our own children and grandchildren, raised as white American children of privilege, have completely forgotten who built the tower before them, or why their well-meaning ancestors so passionately endeavored to build it. Many no longer value their essential Jewishness in their world views or life plans. For most, the tower of success built by American Jews is indistinguishable from the general American tower of white privileged success. That young woman was right in noticing that most white Americans, Jewish or WASP or otherwise, can't abstract from their experience to fully notice how people of color, and all others who don't fit the white privileged mold, are falling off that tower. They can't even identify how the social construct that is racism effuses all aspects of their lives, their choices, and their expectations of themselves and others, despite their good intentions.

At this point, you might think that I'm not being entirely fair. Yes, most of us and our children are a part of white America now. But we know plenty of young Jewish Americans who are very proudly Jewish. Many are devoted to Israel, devoted to good causes, and fight racism and other injustices. But if we are going to take our "Americanness" seriously, we must take a better look at, and better own all the ways that we have, and continue, to benefit from the worst elements of American racist culture. Whether we are comfortable with it or not, we American Jews *are* powerful. We are the power elite of this country. Some of the most powerful people in the world are seated here today.

I speak about racism and Jewish identity not because we are not good people. I speak of this because in owning race as central in American Jewish identity, we not only more effectively work with our success in this country, but we can return truly to the essence of what being Jewish in the world really means.

Our people have been known by many names over the centuries. Once, we were called Hebrews. In Hebrew, the word is *Ivri*, which translates "the other" or "from somewhere else." We were also called *Bnai Yisrael,* the Children of Israel. Israel, *Yisra'el,* literally means "struggling with God." In other words, we are to be the ones who struggle with ultimate issues of life, of values, of justice. Through the centuries, our moments of power in the world have been all too fleeting. Mostly, our greatest hope has been to be tolerated by the elites and powers that be. From our place of not living at the center of power, but at the periphery, we have responded always with the ability to critique injustice, to adopt the cause of the oppressed, and to envision a better and more just world. Even in times of acceptance by the non-Jewish authorities, at times when we participated fully in their societies, we always knew that we stand with one foot in the mainstream, and one foot outside that mainstream.

America is unique in Jewish history because the social construct of power and oppression in this society came to be based more on skin color than on religion or ethnic identity. Because of that, along with the best of American values and our own hard work, we now find ourselves among the authorities, among the power elite. Despite our only good intentions, we are—all of us—full participants and beneficiaries of the American evil known as racism.

For all these reasons, I call upon us all this year to reject our own self-labeling as white. I call upon all of us, the Jewish people—those of us who have skin that passes for white—to begin teaching our children that we are, nevertheless not white people. We are, and have always been—simply—Jewish people. Being Jewish is not about identifying as a race, or with any system that oppresses. The brilliance of being Jewish in all of human history is that we stubbornly refuse to fit into any social construct of power or oppression. We are simply *Ivri'im,* people from "somewhere else," people who struggle with God and justice, and who demand that the rest of the world does too, and see every human life as sacred because we are all in the image of God. And the truth is, we have never belonged to one race alone. The Torah tells us that we left Egypt with the *Erev Rav,* with a mixed multitude of peoples. Around the world there are Jews of color, Asian Jews, Jews of all kinds. The idea that Jews are white is not only ridiculous, it's offensive to who we really are! Yes, societies like America come along sometimes and give us privileges and even give the majority of us power labels like "white." In the American racist social construct, Jews are very much white people, but we must never again think of ourselves that way! It's time for us to opt out of the racist paradigm because we are Jews.

Imagine with me what we and our children could be like if we associate our Jewishness with an essential statement against all racism and discrimination in our society. Even as our children benefit from the best schools and jobs and housing that whiteness affords, we can be the ones to challenge the American racist system from within. We can be the ones who can change the business practices, the housing codes, the policing practices, the correctional facilities, the policies, the schools – motivated entirely by our values and our Jewish historical experience. Indeed, so many progressive leaders in this country have been Jews, including Jewish founders of the NAACP, motivated exactly by this vision. But so many more of us need to own our real power, which is not our whiteness, but our Jewishness. Our real power is our Torah, and our tradition that motivates us to remember the stranger for we were strangers in Egypt; that calls on us to lift up the cause of the stranger, the orphan, the widow, of all those who are oppressed. The greatest advancement of twenty-first century American society may be how the Jewish people consciously and unconsciously complete the sentence, "I am..." If we learn always to replace the word "white" with Jewish, a great future awaits us, and all peoples in this country and around the world.

I reassured that young woman not to feel bad that her years of Jewish education left her feeling uninspired. I told her that, in fact, she had a profoundly Jewish soul in her ability to question the white society that shaped her. I reminded her of Hillel's[2] famous teaching: What is hateful to you, do not do to others. All the rest is commentary. If she lives her life creating a world where Hillel's wisdom guides the way, then all the rest of Judaism will open to her on her path, and she, and all her peers can go live proudly as Jews, as a light to the nations. May we all be that light in this world that so badly needs us. *Amen.* ∎

---

2   Hillel (Hebrew: הלל) (110 BCE-10 AD), one of the most important figures in Jewish history, is associated with the development of the Mishnah and the Talmud. At the age of forty, Hillel went to the Land of Israel; forty years he spent in study; and the last third of his life he was the spiritual head of the Jewish people.

Daniel M. Jaffe

Reflections of a
White Maybe

ONE AFTERNOON IN 1984, as a young corporate lawyer in Boston's Back Bay, I was making small talk with my boss' secretary, and asked if she'd known any Jewish folks like me in her upstate New York hometown, a small city populated primarily by descendants of seventeenth century Dutch immigrants. Jenny, plump and pale-complexioned with freckles and very straight, light brown hair replied, "Jews in our town? No. We didn't have any blacks, Puerto Ricans, or Jews. We were all white."

I stared for a moment, uncertain whether I'd heard what I thought I'd heard: Jenny was categorizing me as non-white?

Had she defined me as a "minority," I wouldn't have noticed. Of course Jews were a minority in the U.S. But how could she say I wasn't white?

Stunned into silence, I retreated into my office and shut the door.

Wasn't whiteness defined by skin color? Had my complexion changed in the last few seconds? I looked down at the hand extending from my blue Oxford shirt cuff. My skin still vaguely resembled the Crayola flesh-colored crayon of my childhood as much as anyone's. In fact, if Jenny took a little sun, wouldn't her fair complexion pretty much match mine? If she hadn't known that I was Jewish, but had seen me on the street, would she still have regarded me as non-white?

Having grown up in a New Jersey suburb, I'd always thought of myself and most everyone around me as white. Ours was a community chock full of descendants of East European Jews, Sicilians, and Greeks, as well as Irishmen, Germans, and assorted other Northern Europeans. There were also some Hispanics in town – for example, our next door neighbors, Dr.

and Mrs. Enriquez from Guadalajara, Mexico—whom I always regarded as white, too. Sure, they spoke English with accents, but so did half of my Hebrew school teachers and all of the Holocaust-surviving Jewish grandparents I knew. What's more, my high school friend, Maria Rodriguez, had thinner, blonder hair and paler complexion than most everyone around. Hispanics were just a sub-group of whites, another variation of the rest of us, like olive-complected Tony Zappasodi, and wide-nosed and curly-haired Elena Sevastopoulos, and the Sephardic Jewish family from Morocco with tawnier complexion and thicker, blacker hair than us Ashkenazi Jews. Despite our variations, we all certainly more closely resembled one another than we did our high school's two black students or the waitresses in our favorite Chinese restaurant. We all were white.

My sense of racial identity was reinforced in the mid- and late-1970s in college and law school, during conversations with black, Puerto Rican, East Asian, and Native American friends, all of whom lumped me in the "white" category as opposed to them, "people of color" with their golden, brown, or black complexions. My friends were "people of color" and I was . . . what—colorless? No, just white. Back then, I pretty much thought of "white" as a neutral non-color.

This sense of self shifted in the early 1990s after I got to know Leo, a handsome young Puerto Rican scholar (thick wavy black hair, piercing brown eyes, tawny complexion) who would later become my life-partner and husband. During conversations about race, Leo enlightened me to awareness that "white" is just as much a color as any other. It's only "neutral" if one views the world from the perspective of whites who see themselves as the center of the racial universe, the traditional U.S. way of looking at things. All humanity is "of color," it's just a question of *which* color. By separating the world into "people of color" and "whites," my racially varied college and law school friends and I had all been perpetuating a white-dominant way of looking at the world. As soon as Leo made this should-have-been-obvious point to me, my whiteness blushed into redness.

The differences between Leo and me fascinated us both. Soon after we began dating in 1993, we reveled in learning about one another's cultural backgrounds: my ancestors had come to the U.S. from Eastern

Europe and Jerusalem; Leo's had arrived in Puerto Rico from Spain, Scotland, and Africa by way of Jamaica and Venezuela. My parents and I grew up in the U.S.; Leo and his parents grew up in Puerto Rico, then he moved to Boston in 1986 to attend graduate school. One day, we were engaged in some conversation about background when I made an offhand remark about "us white people."

Leo responded casually with, "You're not white, you're Jewish."

Again with this business of Jewish not equaling white!

Instantly, Jenny's earlier distinction sprang to mind. Having now had a good ten years to think about the notion of someone else defining me, I spoke up in irritation. "What do you mean, not white? Look at my skin color. Of course I'm white."

"No you're not."

"How can you say that? Just look at me."

"You just claim to be white because you want access to white privilege."

"Privilege? What are you talking about? I'm not trying to gain access to anything—I'm just talking about a physical trait. An objective physiological description. Look at my skin. I'm white."

"You're Jewish, not white. Just look at anti-Semitism."

Certainly, I knew that Jews suffered anti-Semitism in the U.S.—hadn't my grandmother had to mask her Jewishness during the Depression in order to secure employment in New York? Hadn't Jews been excluded from universities, law firms, country clubs, etc. in this country for decades? But I'd never conceptualized this as another form of racism. I'd always thought of anti-Semitism as a religious-cultural-based discrimination of us, a white sub-group. Apparently, for Leo the term "white" seemed more akin to WASP—White Anglo-Saxon Protestant—a notion that incorporates religious and even cultural background into racial classification. I certainly wasn't WASP, so, by that definition, I couldn't be "white." Maybe Jenny had had something like that in mind way back in 1984, too. Rather than regarding Jews as a sub-category of whites, they regarded us as a distinct category of our own.

Leo and I tangled and wrangled a bit, but didn't convince one another—not then, and not since. However, I've done a bit of thinking about this, and have reached at least one conclusion: "whiteness" in the U.S. is basically a euphemism for a certain "like-us-ness" by those who call the socio-economic shots, with the "us" depending on who's doing the looking and classifying.

And here we get to what really matters: what are the membership privileges of consequence that come with admission to the white club? We all know about historical exclusions that the law now tries to erase, exclusion from higher education, neighborhoods, jobs, and so forth. But what about other, social exclusions? Which other life aspects fill the basket of "white privilege" to which I might or might not have access depending on how I'm classified?

In 2001, after our coupleness had been solidified, Leo was interviewing for a job at Penn State University in State College, Pennsylvania. Our research revealed that, in the middle of the nineteenth century, the university had been established smack in the middle of the state in a purposely remote locale fairly equidistant from both Philadelphia and Pittsburgh, so that students would be kept as far as possible from sin. Amusing founding history.

After Leo's campus interview, his prospective department arranged for him to be shown around town by a local real estate agent. He told this woman with stiffly coiffured blond hair that if the job were offered to him and he accepted, he'd be bringing his male partner to live with him—"Are there any particular neighborhoods we should avoid?" Her broad smile froze: "You'll want to live as close to campus as possible." Then Leo contacted a spokesperson for the campus gay group, explaining that he, a gay professor, was interviewing for a job there. The spokesperson's first response told us all we needed to know: "You're interviewing for a job here? But...why?"

Nevertheless, so as to be sure we'd gathered all necessary information, I made my own trip to State College, driving the seven hours from Boston to scope things out for myself. Could we live there comfortably?

Beautiful campus with interesting architecture, varied landscaping, and a cute downtown full of quirky shops and cafés. When exploring a supermarket on the outskirts, I was delighted to discover all sorts of familiar products, even jars of Manishewitz gefilte fish and packages of frozen Goya-brand *frituras*—basic cultural sustenance. But as I walked down the aisles, I noticed that whenever I looked up, some blondie or other was staring at me. I touched my prominent nose—was I bleeding or something? I touched my dark brown wavy hair and curly beard—was the humidity causing them to frizz more than usual? No, nothing out of the ordinary. Perhaps these starers, men and women both, couldn't take their eyes off me because of my devastatingly handsome good looks? Not likely.

The whole experience made me very uncomfortable. I just couldn't fathom what was going on. That night, after I mentioned this to Leo on the telephone, he told me that a Bostonian colleague of his, a woman born in Sicily, had experienced something similar the previous summer when she and her equally swarthy, dark-haired husband and children were driving through Pennsylvania and spent the night here in State College. Wherever in town they went, people gawked.

My earlier feeling of discomfort was now intensified by aware-ness that I'd been gawked at because of perceived racial difference. I wondered what my black and Asian friends must feel like every day as they navigated a predominantly white world (that might or might not include me).

For better or worse, we decided that this purportedly sinless uni-versity town was not the best place for us. Rather, Leo accepted a job at the University of California, Santa Barbara. We moved. Southern California is where I have truly learned about white privilege, or, in its more regional form, Anglo privilege. In Santa Barbara, as in most of Southern California, the primary racial divide is not white-or-black or white-or-Asian, but Anglo-or-Latino: according to U.S. Census data for 2014, over 44 percent of Santa Barbara County is "Hispanic or Latino," and over 45 percent is "White alone, not Hispanic or Latino." (The numbers are over 38 percent for each group in California as a whole.) Whereas my "whiteness" is apparently debatable in the Northeast, my Angloness is indisputable here in Southern California. In Santa Barbara, statistically and in terms of how others regard us on the street, Leo is Latino and I am Anglo. So if there's any Anglo privilege to be had, it attaches to me.

Moving here, we rented an apartment for half a year so as to become situated, then we bought a house. Our first, very own house. With an enormous red bougainvillea blooming year-round in the back and palm trees out front and rose bushes and a yard and even an orange tree growing real-live oranges. Our very own slice of Santa Barbara, America's Riviera. California dreaming, indeed.

The property, small as it is, requires a good deal of maintenance; current drought aside, Santa Barbara's climate is so remarkable that a planted set of wooden teeth will sprout something or other if you water it right. We chose not to hire one of the hundreds of Latino gardeners in town because we prefer doing the work ourselves. So, weekends frequently see us mowing, raking, weeding, planting, watering, pruning, etc.

One Sunday soon after we moved in, while I was pruning an overgrown butterfly bush (gorgeous magenta grape-like flower clusters) in back, Leo was pruning the wall of white and pink oleander serving as fence along one side of our front yard. An older Anglo man walking his dog stopped on the front sidewalk and said to Leo, "You're doing a meticulous job. How much do you charge?"

Ever the quick wit, Leo responded with a smile, "I've got to charge a lot in order to cover the mortgage on the house."

This Anglo man scurried away, never to greet Leo again.

Annoying, but we laughed off the racial stereotyping. Later that week, after I related the incident to my Latino barber, he sighed and replied, "It happens to us all the time." He was not smiling.

Not long afterwards, Leo came home one day from a visit to Borders Bookstore (now defunct), which was having a 40 percent-off sale. He was visibly irritated.

"Didn't find anything?" I asked.

"I was buying a philosophy book and a poetry book, and the Anglo cashier says, 'You don't look like someone who'd be reading philosophy or poetry.'"

This was said to Leo, a university professor specializing in literary theory, a poet in his own right.

"Why do people feel comfortable saying things like that to me?" he asked. "It's so humiliating."

Burning inside, all I could do was reach my Anglo, maybe-white arms around him.

Another day, Leo returned home from downtown after lunchtime, and glumly fixed himself a sandwich.

"You didn't eat downtown?" I asked.

Reluctantly, he explained that he'd gone into a restaurant and had been seated by the hostess, but then he waited...for a menu that didn't come...for water that didn't come...while waiters served menus and water to other, Anglo customers who arrived after Leo. He waited and waited to see how long this would go on. After half an hour, he stood and left.

A few years after we arrived in town, new neighbors were moving in across the street one day so I went to welcome them—Judge Frank Ochoa and his wife, local TV news anchor Paula Lopez, whose family went so far back in Santa Barbara that some streets were named after her ancestors. In an effort to show cultural solidarity, I mentioned that Leo was from Puerto Rico. We got to talking about problems of racism in town. Judge Ochoa told me that once they were in a furniture store when an Anglo salesman approached and said, "This is the expensive section here. You want to look over there."

A few years ago, our nephew, my brother's young teenage son, Andrew, flew from New Jersey to Santa Barbara in order to spend a week with us. After showing him local sights, we took him for a few days to the big bad city of Los Angeles where we stayed in a hotel that offered guests an included breakfast buffet. Since we all went down to breakfast together, we took only one room key among the three of us; I kept it in my pocket. As we entered the dining room, none of the buffet staff checked our key, nor that of other guests. We grabbed a table, then Leo, Andrew, and I each perused the buffet at our own pace. As I was bringing a cup of coffee to the table where Andrew was already tucking into a waffle, I heard behind me a woman demanding in a loud voice:

"Where's your room key? Where's your room key?"

I turned. This Asian employee was not addressing me. She was yelling at Leo.

"Breakfast is for guests only! Where's your room key?"

Leo, a plate of breakfast sausages in hand, stood frozen, utterly flummoxed.

I strode over and said angrily, "He's with me."

The employee's face paled as she asked in a tone of incredulity, "With *you?*"

"Yes!" I said, adding, "How dare you! How dare you!"

"It's okay," mumbled Leo, turning and carrying his plate to the table where our nephew sat, watching.

I followed and said to Andrew, "Do you understand what just happened?" He nodded, avoiding my eyes and Leo's.

That racist employee never did ask to see my room key, nor that of any of the other Anglo guests. So as not to amplify Leo's embarrassment in front of Andrew, I turned the conversation to our day's plans. But, I had to hold back tears of rage, wondering how Leo managed to maintain composure. Apparently, he'd had more practice than I realized.

In the fourteen years we've lived in Southern California, no kitchen staff has ever accused me of sneaking into a hotel breakfast buffet or has otherwise humiliated me publicly. No passerby has ever inquired, while I was working in the front yard, how much I charge for gardening. No bookstore sales clerk has ever reacted with surprise at any purchase I made. No waiter has ignored me if I was alone in a restaurant. No salesman has ever re-directed me to the cheaper section of a furniture store. This, I have come to realize, is part of Anglo privilege: living free from race-based suspicion, humiliation, degradation.

And, living free from the burden of *expecting* mistreatment: repeatedly over the years, when I've answered the door for Latino workers coming to install cable TV, repair plumbing, prune our larger trees, I've seen these men initially dart their eyes about and mumble a nervous hello, as if bracing for an anticipated disrespectful interaction. Only after I thrust out my hand to shake theirs with, "Hi, I'm Dan," do they smile and appear to relax.

Yet another front yard experience comes to mind. For years, we were annoyed by neighbors (Anglo, by the way) who let their dogs wander onto our front lawn from the sidewalk and leave piles of dog dirt. We decided to put in a hedge as barrier between sidewalk and lawn. So, after buying ten small flowering drought-tolerant shrubs, I set out one morning to dig up a couple-foot wide trench of lawn, and plant. Coincidentally, that same day, the Ochoa's across the street were having a rail fence installed in their front yard by a crew of Latino landscapers. Late in the afternoon, absorbed in planting the eighth of the shrubs, I heard a honk and looked up: the Latino landscaping crew, having finished their job, were about to drive away, but before leaving they honked at me – so that each member of the crew could give me a thumbs-up gesture accompanied by broad smiles and nods. I waved back, not initially understanding their supportive reaction. Then it struck me – they were expressing solidarity: Anglo man working.

A few minutes later, at a point when I was head-to-toe sweaty and grimy, our Latino mailman, who'd been delivering mail for a couple years with barely a nod of the head, stopped his truck to give me a huge wave and smile. Ever since that day, he always waves and makes a point of engaging me in brief chitchat if our paths cross somewhere in the neighborhood. Unwittingly, by engaging in physical labor, I'd crossed a racial-social class divide, I'd broken a "like-us-ness/like-them-ness" barrier and thereby had elevated my status among local Latinos.

As delighted as I am to be regarded as one of the guys, I'm saddened because all this, too, is Anglo privilege – being appreciated for a respectful handshake and smile, for yard work, for basic human behaviors that shouldn't merit notice of any kind, let alone appreciation.

So here's what I've learned: Angloness/whiteness in the U.S. does not exist in and of itself, but only in opposition to some "other," a fluid and equally arbitrary concept. My own membership in this country's Anglo/white club shifts depending upon where I live, who the predominant "other" is, whose eye is doing the beholding, and whose lips are doing the designating. Yet what seems constant, is that membership in this club brings a host of dignity privileges whether or not one is aware of possessing or asserting them. However I regard myself, I must navigate the world with an awareness that I don't live surrounded by mirrors, but by the gaze of others. ■

Emily A. Klein

Quietly Being White

BEING WHITE FEELS LIKE I need to be quiet.
    I knew I was being raised racist before I had the words to describe it. Mostly, it felt like an uncomfortable shift in my chair at the kitchen table during one of my dad's dinner anecdotes. The only way I can begin to explain the way it felt is this. In the same way a child grows up and is taught to believe, beyond the shadow of a doubt, facts about their religion, that's the way I was taught about other races.

My dad was a court officer. Most of what he was exposed to in regards to other races was negative. I believe this shaped his beliefs to a certain degree. I don't know what his childhood was like and what he was taught about other races, and we have never discussed it.

I had very few encounters with people outside my race during my early childhood. I was raised in a strict Irish Catholic household and attended a very small traditional Catholic school up until the beginning of my senior year. It was then that I met my best friend who, just happened to be black.

Strangely, nothing about my early instruction seemed to match what I discovered about her as a person. She was smart, determined, funny, sweet and incredibly caring, and to top it all off, she was incredibly wealthy.

This was the first of many experiences I would encounter with people outside my race, who I later realized I identified with more than people of my own race and background. I started to question what I had been taught. I became angry with my family. Why didn't they accept other races? Why didn't they allow me to?

I don't know when the exact shift occurred. Maybe it was in some way a rebellion. Maybe I never felt accepted within my own race and prayed that I could fit in somewhere else.

The truth is, I don't remember what I was thinking when I was a kid. What I do know now is that today, there is a shortage on space for single white females with master's degrees on food stamps in society.

Society says being white is a privilege, but I have never felt that my skin was an advantage. I feel that in my experience, it has been less about skin and more about money. My financial situation—barely surviving—is what seems to define me. Where I live, very few kids receive free lunch. There is no need for it. Most times I am embarrassed for my kids. I don't want them to feel different. I went to college for ten years to ensure I would be able to support my family, and I can't find a job for the life of me. That makes being white quite a challenge.

I have heard that most of the people who receive government assistance are black or immigrants or just plain lazy. I can neither confirm nor deny any of these speculations. I've never had time to conduct a study, but I know I am none of these, yet every year I have no choice but to reapply for food stamps and make sure I stay up to date with my housing agent so I don't lose my assistance.

I get angry at the camaraderie within other races. I feel as if my own never looks out for me.

I get pissed when I see scholarships or exclusive opportunities only for other races because *goddammit*, I face a great deal of the same financial difficulties and economic disadvantage as they do, but my skin says otherwise. I have to hide my struggle to stay alive as a white person.

There is pressure all around me. Pressure to succeed. Pressure to measure up. What does your credit score look like? Your savings account? Your retirement? Wait you haven't started saving yet?

I feel sometimes I am missing one of the components of being white because I just don't have what it takes to "be."

My father used to tell me the system isn't set up for white people. And I didn't believe him but today, I know this to be true. The system wants its recipients to stay down. They make it damn near impossible to find your way out. If you are one of the few that gets lucky, it's most likely because you had some help from somewhere else. Sometimes I wonder if the system is like modern day slavery designed to mask itself in charity and good deeds to help the less fortunate out. I'm probably not supposed to think these things, let alone say them out loud.

Being poor means I am less accepted by my race. But at the same time, I am not accepted by other races that are in the same financial bracket as me because of the color of my skin. My daughter is half-Puerto Rican and my son is half-Jamaican. My daughter is beautiful, intelligent, witty, athletic and incredibly loyal. She will forever struggle to keep friends where we live because of her last name. My son hasn't reached that point yet, I don't know if he will, but I pray to God the kids don't pick up on his differences because I never want to see him struggle. I have thought about moving, maybe to a more culturally diverse district. But the truth is the kids there will still be the same. They will always be too much white or not white enough no matter where we go.

I feel like my skin color traps me. I feel being white means I have to hide my situation and alienate myself from everyone. I don't subscribe to society's expectations and that continually puts me in an uncomfortable situation.

I have also had to reprogram my brain. It is not easy. I have caught myself saying things so ugly I had to stop myself and try and figure out where the hell they came from. I think sometimes it comes from things I heard growing up. Other times I think it comes from resent from having to stay quiet, whether in a room full of white people down talking other races, or in a room where I am the only white person.

I don't consider my skin a privilege, but I also don't think explaining this to anyone in today's society really makes any difference. ■

Barbara Beckwith

"Aha" Moments

EARLY ONE WINTER MORNING, I realized that I needed money for my trip out of town. So I drove to the nearest bank outlet, used my card to get into the ATM area, grabbed my cash and rushed out. And then I realized that I'd failed to retrieve my card.

It was 5:00 a.m. But I was confident that I could hang around that deserted corner and ask the next person who showed up to let me in "to check if I left my card there." I loitered outside the ATM until a stranger gave me bank access: no problem.

I'd been reading about the concept of "white privilege," but not until that moment did the reality of everyday skin advantage sink in. Were I black, especially if I were also male, my request would most likely have been refused, albeit with a polite excuse, one of those aptly-named "little white lies."

Since then, I've begun to value these flashes of recognition: if unconscious prejudices can be revealed in a second, perhaps they can be undone just as quickly, in what I'm starting to call my "aha" moments.

For instance: I went to UPS to deliver a large package for a friend, but was told that sending a package of that size and weight required a credit card. I'd left my card at home but was allowed, despite posted regulations, to pay by check, without even a cursory look at the signature on my driver's license to be sure the handwriting matched the card's. I realized with a start: if my friend, who is African American, had delivered the package himself and had forgotten his credit card, the rules might not have been so blithely waived. My "trustworthy" skin color had trumped the rules.

I've also recognized how often my white privilege allows me to break social norms. At a lecture by a prominent historian who was speaking on historical and current discrimination against Asian Americans, I took a front row seat, as I usually do. The room was overheated, and my feet were starting to swell painfully inside my boots. So I took them off.

Sitting directly in front of the speaker, in my stocking feet, I realized in a flash: I could never afford to choose comfort over propriety if I were a person of color, whose behavior might be viewed as emblematic of her group rather than the bad manners of one individual, in this case, myself.

Over and over, I began to see how daily, my white skin gives me unearned credibility that I don't give others. At my first conference on white privilege, a woman spoke up from the audience to say that she was glad to be there, and grateful to be alive, because a truck had run her off the New Jersey Turnpike and driven off. The policemen who showed up did not believe her account and refused to write up a report.

Black members of the audience immediately responded with offers to back her up, saying they could track down the truck driver, report the police inaction, and insist that the Attorney General pursue the case.

Meanwhile, I sat there thinking: well, how do we know her story is true? What if no truck driver was involved? What if she had run her own car off the road? I did not bother to ask myself what would motivate her to make up such a story: I questioned her. And then I knew why: I was skeptical because she was black. Chagrined at catching myself thinking stereotypically, I nevertheless stayed in my seat and kept mum.

Over the next few years, I did start to speak up. And yet I continue to get flashes of insight into racist thinking and behavior of my own and of other white people, including family and friends.

"Aha" moments can also come from movies. Back in 1967, when I saw TV's first interracial kiss—*Star Trek's* Captain Kirk kissed Uhura, I was shocked. Yet now, viewing a re-run of *Ghost,* I'm shocked in reverse. The two main characters do not attempt a cross-racial kiss, although the plot required it. Even in 1990, when that movie came out, the film industry did not dare "go that far," which now dismays me.

I don't expect an end to my "aha" moments. My most recent recognition that racial associations are deep and unlikely to disappear completely, occurred while I was being prepped for an EKG by a doctor who was African American. As he applied electrode pads to my chest and my body, the words "This isn't right—this shouldn't be happening," rose up in my head.

Two of the doctors I visit regularly are black. One of my good friends is a doctor who is black. Where, then, did those "this is wrong" images come from? And what do I do about them?

Step back. Look my unconscious biases in the eye. Turn them around and try to understand them. And then let them go.

It can happen in an "aha" moment. ■

Meg J. Petersen

The White Notebooks

THESE NOTEBOOKS CHRONICLE AN ILLUSION, a fantasy, a massive deception. I relate here a personal history of a shared lie. Everything here is based on fantasy, but everything here is real.

The Question

I ADMIT TO HESITATING before answering. In fact, I admit to pausing so long I remember the wide curve and the dense forest along the stretch of I-93 we were navigating when she asked me the question.

"Would you give it all up?" she asked. We had been talking about white privilege. Not just a la Peggy McIntosh[1], but the real bone deep stuff I had noticed in my life, and which she had never experienced.

I was thinking about those things – the easy passage through the customs line at the airport, the way I am greeted by policemen, even when they want to ask me if I know how fast I was going. What would happen to my daily life without the veneer of normality and safety, the taken-for-granted ease with which I can move through the world without explanation, the power of being the kind of person people expect to see in certain places, like at the front of a college classroom. And the deeper things, the ancestral things, the ugly truths about whose money came from where, who might have been turned away because "they just didn't fit in" to the job or the apartment or the opportunity which was offered to me, complicity and profits from a not-at-all-distant past passed down.

---

1   Peggy McIntosh is an American feminist and anti-racism activist, who became known for her 1988 essay "White Privilege and Male Privilege: A Personal Account of Coming to See Correspondence Through Work in Women's Studies." She is the associate director of the Wellesley Center for Women, and a founder and co-director of the National S.E.E.D. Project on Inclusive Curriculum.

"Would you give up all that white privilege?" she asked again, perhaps thinking that I had not heard the question. "Would you give it up if you could?"

Finally, I answered her. "I would," I said, with what felt like a rock pressing on my chest. I was surprised at how deeply the hypothetical question had affected me. Would it have meant as much if a white friend had asked? But no white friend I could think of would ask that question. "I would," I answered, "if I could know that it meant everyone would be treated fairly. Otherwise, there would be no point."

She seemed unsatisfied with my answer. I could tell she would have preferred that I had not qualified it.

As I think about that answer now, part of me thinks it was correct, logical. To give up a power you might be able to use for good does seem futile and foolish, a needless surrender that only empowers the forces you are fighting. It's a very American answer—you keep every advantage you can use to get ahead. Does it matter if your motives are good?

On the other hand, the answer seems obscene. All the filth and blood and unimaginable suffering, unrecoverable loss that others have paid and continue to pay with their lives for my ill-gotten gain should make me want to vomit up my very existence, to snuff out my own life rather than live with that privilege. And it has, it has . . . How can I ever pay enough for that?

In thinking about it later, I realized the choice I gave was not the one I had, and that my whole life was just one long answer to that impossible question.

Whiteout

WHEN SNOWSTORMS GET TOO BAD in February in New Hampshire, we can have the kinds of blizzards that cause authorities to issue travel warnings. Things shut down. The snow can come so fast and hard that it almost seems to move horizontally, right at your windshield or your eyes, until, if you are walking or driving, it can eclipse the landscape in a whiteout, erasing the whole world. You can lose your way.

After the storm dies down, the whiteness of the newly-fallen snow buries the scenery, eliminating any landmarks. Whiteness can make things disappear. It can also blind you, as when the sun's ultraviolet rays reflect off its gleaming surface, damaging the corneas of your eyes.

I remember another whiteout, the milky liquid that came in little bottles with tiny brushes. Some of us in elementary school were obsessed with it. We used it to eliminate, not only the obvious errors, but any stray mark on the page. We could brush on whiteness and make things new. Sometimes we would use whiteout even on manila paper, as if it were the whiteness itself and not its capacity to blend with the background that gave it its magic power.

Like most people raised to be white, I grew up surrounded by whiteness, which I felt was normal. For as much as I knew, the whiteness of my small New Hampshire town had just happened naturally. It had always been that way. No black people or other people of color had ever lived there – this was because they would not want to. It was too cold, I assumed. There was nothing to be done about it. We might lament occasionally the lack of "diversity," but mostly such perfunctory regrets came later, when diversity was deemed to be important. When I was a child, I don't think anyone thought much about it. The people we knew were different enough from each other, and it wasn't something you could change after all. It would be like trying to change the weather (although we did talk a lot about that).

White erased everything so completely and effectively that I did not see it. Like snow blindness, like a blank wall. Not much to say about that.

Linguistics

IN LINGUISTIC TERMS, WHITE IS "unmarked." The unmarked category is the one which is anticipated. You don't have to mark it, or draw attention to it, because everyone assumes it anyway. When you hear the word "doctor," you might hear faint echoes of the unspoken: [white] [male] doctor. Power resides in being implicit, being unexpressed. You don't hear it. "The [white] boy ran down the road." It is what is understood, given, taken for granted, ordinary, normal. Everything else is defined in relation to what is not named. "The black boy ran down the road." The power of white derives from being unmarked, unremarked, unremarkable.

There is a way white people talk when they assume no people of color are present. In most of the kinds of white people spaces I find myself in, this doesn't manifest as outright racism, although sometimes it does. Most often I notice the pronouns, particularly the plural ones: us, them, they, we. Pronouns draw lines that include whites and exclude others. Pronouns are some of the most common words in the language. They are everywhere, as anyone who has ever tried to write a gender-neutral description of a person knows. They draw lines subtly, insidiously, and I find whites pulling me into their "we" or "us." Designating others who they rope away from me behind imaginary linguistic lines, as "they" or "them."

In these spaces, racists are also "them," never "us." Even when phrases loaded with racially-based assumptions are spoken, it is never by racists, because there are no racists here. Just us white folks.

In this white world, obliviousness is presumed to be endearing. "Well, I'm from New Hampshire," they say, by way of invoking a free pass to whatever ignorance will follow, "I don't have much experience with black people, or whatever they want to be called. Is black racist? Do I have to say African American?" "I know what it feels like to be a minority. One time I was a tourist in Bermuda and we stopped at a coffee shop, and I said to my sister, 'we are the only white people here.' And I wasn't even scared."

"Actually, we love black people—their music, their dance, their art…" Whiteness hits me with the force of a tsunami when I enter these spaces, knocking out everything but itself. It whispers enticingly in a conspiracy of comfort—"You are okay. You are one of us. You don't have to care. You are fine. Forget. Forget. Forget." Whiteness feels like negation—drawing attention to itself and eclipsing what it is not—making everything else "not," "un," "non," "other." Consuming whatever it can, devouring it and spitting it out in conveniently packaged chunks. Owning everything. It is the only thing that has value and your worth depends on accepting what you don't acknowledge. Erasure is the price of admission.

The Dream

WHITENESS IS SEDUCTIVELY SIMPLE when you settle into it because only *your* perspective, *your* discomfort, *your* inconvenience matters. This is what you are taught. Like the people of Omelas in Ursula Guin's[2] story, your happiness depends on the misery that you cannot allow yourself to see. Of course it is there, and of course it is terrible, but in your world people generally behave fairly, so you comfort yourself that "they" must have done something to deserve that, or it must be different somehow for them. We have to believe that on some level in order to keep on thinking of ourselves as good people. In order to maintain this dream, we become like the children who put their fingers in their ears and hum loudly to avoid being made responsible for hearing a direction.

But maintaining the dream actually requires far less effort. It helps that everyone in your world sees everything from your point of view, and that this is the view broadcasted across all media, packaged and sold to us, all from the standpoint of how it will affect white people. What do those black people want? How far will they go? The dream is facilitated by its collective nature. It reminds me of how we all would chant that we believed in fairies in order to save Tinkerbell. We believe in whiteness too, but part of believing in it is never speaking its name.

I once worked for a boss with a soporific honey-sweet voice. When she would speak to us about how well everything was going, how wonderful our place of work was, the amazing things that were going on there, she could lull even the most cantankerous of us into a momentary stupor. Leaving the meetings, you could almost see people shaking themselves awake as if to say "But wait a minute..." But it was too late. The effort did not come in believing her words, but in shaking them off and questioning why we had allowed ourselves to believe her when we knew the sky was falling down around us. Whiteness is like that. It is far easier to believe in it than to shake your head to free yourself.

Waking Up: A few vignettes

I HAD TO LEAVE WHITE SPACES in order to realize I had been living in them. It was like learning to see colors after living in a pallid, clouded universe.

---

2   Ursula Guin. *The Ones Who Walk Away from Omelas* (Creative Education, 1997).

Classwork

I ASKED A STUDENT, a young Jamaican girl, to make a poster about herself, including drawings of what she looked like and what she wanted to look like. The self-portrait on the left, which was supposed to represent what she looked like, was a fairly accurate rendition of her appearance. She had crayoned in the tight black curls of her close-cropped afro over a darkly shaded face. The girl she had drawn to represent what she wanted to look like had long blond hair that hung straight below her crayoned shoulders. The eyes were blue, framed with light brown eyelashes, a faint blush of light pink carefully shaded onto the cheeks. She had even added the frame of a little checked dress a la "Heidi" of the Alps.[3]

Struck dumb by its incredible horrible sadness, I could only mumble, "Are you sure this is what you want to look like?"

"Yes, Miss," she responded, smiling widely. "I want to look like you."

Lies

"I'VE BEEN LIED TO ALL MY LIFE!" I am at the harbor, and it is dusk, sitting with my boyfriend, staring at our arms where they lie next to each other on the edge of the railing. His arm is deep brown, and mine a lighter tanned shade. I hold up both of our arms together. "It's lies! It's all lies!"

"What are you talking about?" he asks me.

"Black people, white people, it's all lies. I have been being lied to all my life!" I am screaming now, partly in frustration that I don't have the words to express what I mean. The enormity of my discovery renders me completely inarticulate. I sputter back into silence. "Lies," I mutter, "lies."

He shakes his head.

Some years later, in a college classroom, my white-identified students will mutter with all the enthusiasm of potato bugs, that race is a social construction. I will wonder why they are not screaming about how they have been lied to all of their lives. How can they tell me that race is a fantasy and not have just felt their worlds fall down around them and be choking on the dust?

---

3   Refers to the character from the book of the same name, *Heidi,* a work of children's fiction published in 1881 by Swiss author, Johann Spyri.

Nice Tan

MY FIRST SON WAS BORN LIGHT, not at all what I expected. And his hair, when it came, was straight and fine and even lighter than mine. I couldn't think of him as black. Sure, his skin was darker than mine, but not all that much. People would see us together and not suspect that his father was black.

When I went shopping with him in the summer, salesclerks would remark on his "nice tan." One summer as we entered a children's museum, the clerk who stamped his hand with the pay stamp said, "I'm not going to forget him anyway, the little boy with the gorgeous tan!"

They all must think I totally ignore all those warnings about exposing your child to ultraviolet rays... or maybe they think he goes to the beach on his own. Anyway, I always have to explain, or choose not to explain, that it is his natural color. If I don't explain, am I trying to hide something or just trying to avoid a hassle? Or is that the same thing? Am I avoiding problems for me or for him? Are we required to explain the genetic make up of our children? How much information do we have to give?

Ready for School

WHEN SAM WAS ABOUT 4 YEARS OLD, we had an African American couple over for dinner. They were older than we were. Their children were grown. I remember the woman looking at Sam, who was drawing an elaborate castle complete with moat and a detailed fighting dragon. "He's *obviously* bright, that's good," she remarked. "Just make sure he is reading before you send him to school."

I looked at her curiously.

"They are going to think he is stupid. They are programmed to think that way about children of color. You have to be sure he's already reading because it makes it harder for them to think like that."

I nodded, realizing I had entered a whole new world.

Driver Education

IN DRIVER EDUCATION, you have to do your driving time in pairs. One sits in the back of the car while the other drives. My youngest son, Max, was paired with his best friend, blond-haired, blue-eyed Hans. The driver education teacher addressed Max in a loud voice, "Put your hands on the wheel." Max complied. The instructor turned to Hans in the back seat. "Oh phew," she said. "With a last name like Gonzalez, I was afraid he couldn't speak English."

For the rest of the driving time, she only talked to Hans.

Ferguson 2014

I'VE TRIED TO TRAIN MY SONS WELL. I have told them over and over again how to act with the police. I have shared with them the hard lessons I had to learn about impression management. When police ask for an ID, use your college ID; engage them in conversation, try to help them to see you as human. It's not unlike the advice given to kidnap victims, or people held hostage.

I know how to do this because I've been using these techniques with their teachers for years. When a teacher told me my son was doing well for a child of a single mother, I made sure she knew I was a college professor. I made sure they knew my child was smart and capable, resenting the necessity of helping them to see what every teacher should have seen, and thinking of all the parents who wouldn't be able to pull those particular cards out of the hands they had been dealt.

As I think about Ferguson, I pace around my kitchen muttering, "It's 2014. How could this still be happening in 2014?"

My son, twenty-one years old, stops me and says, "I don't know why you keep saying that. I don't know why you think it being 2014 should mean anything."

I ask him what he thinks the state of race relations will be in twenty years. He tells me, without having to miss a beat, that he doesn't think there will be any change. In the silence that follows, I want to scream at him, ask him how he can go on if he really believes that.

Checkboxes

I DON'T CHECK RACIAL BOXES. I can't seem to make myself define my identity by race. It seems like to check a box would mean to accept that race is something other than a fantasy. Does this really have to be the price of admission to serve on a jury? To get a driver's license? In order to drive a car on public roads, I have to accept racial illusions... When "decline to answer" is not an available choice and I have to check something, I check "two or more races" or "multiracial." Can anyone tell me that this is a lie? If race is a deception, am I obligated to participate in some collective delusion? If I don't check the "white" box, am I in denial about my whiteness, my privilege? If I do, am I trying to assert it? Does this resistance matter? Can I define my own identity? Or is that just more privilege?

Why I Don't Write About Being White

NAMING THINGS HAS A TENDENCY to make them real. A friend of mine asked me recently if I ever wanted to be black. It's not that simple. It's not like you can take whiteness off and shed it like you would a winter coat with the warmer weather, cast it aside when it is no longer useful. And I would be lying if I said it was no longer useful. Sometimes when I walk in the street or stand in an airport security line or walk through a store, I can feel my white skin protecting me, feel others reading it as safe, benign.

The security guard at the university lets me into the office without ID, without any kind of proof that I belong there. I am grateful to be let in. Yet I resent how much I sometimes welcome that protection. I want to believe I somehow deserve it. I am a good person, aren't I?

Unlearning Whiteness:

1. Know, first of all, that you don't know anything and much of what you have been taught serves only to keep you from questioning your place in the social order. It is all lies.

2. Know that while you may think that you never think about race, don't notice race, and that it doesn't matter to you, that some people have to think about race all the time. And just because you're not thinking about it, doesn't mean it isn't affecting you.

3. Know that laughing at racist references and racist jokes, even out of nervousness or politeness, is damaging.

4. Know that silence is the voice of complicity. (Yes, when you speak up, people will hassle you and not like you very much. They may even avoid your company. Get over it.)

5. Know that undoing your racist upbringing is hard work and this will demand everything in you.

6. Know that even if your parents were nice, well-intentioned people, you still had a racist upbringing.

7. Know that part of white privilege is never having to wonder if the bad things that happen to you are because of your race, and furthermore, know that it is exhausting to always have to wonder if the bad things that happen to you or your family are because of your race.

8. Know that things like the shooting of unarmed black teenagers feel really different to the mothers of unarmed, black teenagers.

9. Know and accept that you will never really "get there," and that there is no anti-racist certification badge. Be prepared to keep finding nasty racist residues in your subconscious. And don't expect people to congratulate you for your efforts to do what is right.

10. Know that despite all of this, and despite the fact that the work is eternal and that you cannot ever take a break from it (out of respect for those who don't have that option), know that despite all of this, the struggle will come to feel like the most meaningful thing in your life. Know you have to do this work, not for others, but for yourself. ■

Notes

1. The title was inspired by Toi Derricotte's *The Black Notebooks: An Interior Journey* (New York: W. W. Norton & Company, 1999).

2. The section "The Dream" was inspired by Ta-Nehisi Coates' use of the term in his book *Between the World and Me* (New York: Spiegel & Grau, 2015).

3. The idea of an anti-racist certification badge was inspired by Scott Woods's reference to "an anti-racist certification class."

Leah Mueller

The Illuminated Cross

SUMMER IN NEW ORLEANS LASTS A VERY LONG TIME, especially when you're nineteen and far from home. I lived alone, in a sparsely furnished apartment that was located in the posh Garden District. The view from my bay window was breathtaking. I could see banana trees through the ornate metal porch grating while I lay on my nineteen-dollar foam rubber mattress in front of the window and listened to music on my rented stereo. This gave my life a feeling of gentility that it sorely lacked in all other respects.

In the mornings, I took the streetcar to Tulane University. I couldn't afford tuition, but I worked in the cafeteria, filling the salad bar and bussing tables for privileged southern kids. Often, they screamed at me when a particular vegetable was gone from the salad bar, as though their lives would be ruined due to lack of tomatoes. I raced about the cafeteria in my polyester uniform, carrying plastic tubs filled with condiments, swiping my dirty rag across the surfaces of recently vacated tables, dumping half-eaten trays of food into the enormous trash bins. I was perpetually exhausted, and hungry as well.

In 1978, the population of New Orleans was 75 percent African American, which for the first time in my life, transformed me into a minority. I'd grown up in a liberal household, and my mother had taught me to be tolerant towards people of other races. Since most of my adolescence was spent in downstate Illinois, I had little contact with non-white folks, and my tolerance was mostly theoretical in nature. I was familiar with the legacies of powerful black women like Rosa Parks and Angela Davis. When I was twelve, I gave a dollar to the "Free Angela" campaign, in exchange for a black and white pin that bore her visage.

For several years, I wore the pin on my favorite denim hat, much to the derision of my all-white classmates in downstate Illinois. These kids hailed from solidly Republican farming families, and most of them were virulent racists. I sure as hell wasn't going to be like THEM.

The African Americans that I saw on the streets of New Orleans bore little resemblance to the heroes of my youth, and this discovery disturbed me greatly. Black women either ignored me or treated me with contempt. Black men paid a great deal of attention to me, but it wasn't the sort of attention I wanted. One afternoon, an exceptionally relentless fellow offered me thirty dollars so he could masturbate while he looked at my ankles. I was terrified by the prospect of such a thing, and he gradually upped his offer to seventy-five bucks. Seventy five dollars was a nice little chunk of cash for a few minutes of work, especially in 1978, but I still said no.

White men also hit on me all the time, but black guys were especially persistent, and their efforts to attract my attention were peculiarly aggressive and frightening. I was deeply saddened by this revelation, but that didn't stop them from pestering me. I wanted to say, "But I'm on your side!" but they wouldn't have cared. All they wanted was the chance to have sex with a white woman.

Life in New Orleans was both depressing and expensive. I couldn't afford my rent, and I contracted a stubborn urinary tract infection. After several days of cramping, I hauled myself from my mattress and took a bus to Charity Hospital. For nine hours, I filled out forms in front of the prostrate bodies of gunshot victims. I finally emerged from the building, clutching a jumbo-sized bottle of penicillin tablets. The pills cost me nothing, but the label on the bottle read "This patient is a resident of New Orleans Parish, and has proven that she does not have the funds to pay for medical treatment."

Charity Hospital had a psych ward on its top floor, and I certainly didn't want to end up there. I moved through my days like a person in the throes of walking pneumonia. I suffered from a sort of walking depression—I was miserable to the point of numbness, but still capable of minimal functioning. I had always been a voracious reader, and this helped a little. If I lay on my mattress with a library book or a free alternative newspaper, I could get lost in somebody else's reality for a few hours.

One evening after work, I stretched out on my bed with a new copy of *Figaro*, and opened the pages eagerly. It was an award-winning weekly newspaper with a decidedly liberal bent, and I always read the articles carefully, savoring the clever sentences. Its current cover featured a color photograph of David Duke, who had been recently appointed Grand Wizard of the Ku Klux Klan. Duke was a classic Aryan man, with pale skin, piercing blue eyes and expertly feathered blonde hair. His face wore a deceptively ingenuous expression, as if he had no idea why so many people considered him to be so loathsome.

The writer of the cover article was puzzled by Duke. He was the poster boy for racism, yet he held an advanced degree, and his IQ was rumored to be off the charts. It was convenient for liberals to believe that all racists were mouth breathers, but David did not adhere to the stereotype. The writer described the bookstore that Duke ran in nearby Metairie – a dark, cavernous establishment known only to insiders. Amongst other accoutrements, it contained an enormous cross that was bedecked with electric lights. Apparently, the cross was breathtaking in its immensity, especially when illuminated in an otherwise darkened room.

I was both repulsed and intrigued. I placed the newspaper on my mattress and stared thoughtfully at the banana trees. Obviously, David was a walking contradiction – a brilliant, charismatic fellow who held views that most sane people considered abhorrent. Perhaps if I spoke to him, he would say something that would resolve my own conundrum. I wondered whether he was in the telephone directory. He was secretive for reasons of personal safety, and most likely had an unlisted number.

I flipped open the phone book and ran my eyes through the column of names. In the midst of a slew of other Dukes, I managed to locate one person named David. It was hard for me to believe that he would be foolish enough to have his number in a public directory. Still, it was worth a try. If there was another man in the New Orleans metro area who bore the unfortunate name of David Duke, I could simply apologize to him and terminate the call.

I reached over to my phone and lifted the receiver. With one trembling finger, I dialed the number. A man answered on the second ring. "Hello" I said, in as nonchalant a tone as I could muster. "May I please speak to David Duke?"

There was a pause. "David's not here right now" the man replied. "If you give me your name and phone number, I'll make certain that he calls you back."

I felt a stab of disappointment, followed by an odd intuition that the fellow was lying, and that he was actually Duke. I persisted, "Oh, I'm sorry to hear that he isn't there. I wanted to congratulate him for the interview in *Figaro*. I thought that the columnist wrote a very even-handed, unbiased article. I'd like to talk to David about the Klan. I have some questions about it."

There was another pause. "Actually, this is David" the man said apologetically. "I have to be very careful about revealing my identity, even over the phone. I'm sure you understand."

"Of course I do" I assured him. "I imagine there are a lot of people who might harm you, but I'm not one of them. I'm curious about your bookstore, and would like to see it, and I'd also enjoy meeting you. If you have some time in your schedule, that is."

"Oh certainly!" Duke exclaimed. His voice was friendly and eager, as though he relished the idea of discussing white supremacy with an attentive young woman. "When would you like to come to the book-store? I can put you in my schedule as early as next week."

"Next week sounds fine" I assured him. "I'm free in the afternoons after two."

"Perfect" Duke said. "How about Tuesday?" He gave me his address in Metairie, emphasizing the importance of secrecy. "It's a plain white storefront with no windows" he explained. "Ring the doorbell, and I'll buzz you in. I'm sure you realize that I have to be very cautious."

As the days passed, I thought about my upcoming visit with Duke as little as possible. I went to my cafeteria job, and wandered around in a sort of focused daze, running my rag across the tables, dumping sliced cucumbers into gleaming steel pans. Finally, Tuesday afternoon arrived, and I hauled my weary body to the St. Charles streetcar. I rode downtown, disembarked on Canal Street, and wandered over to the nearby bus stop with my paper transfer.

Duke's bookstore was located near the boundary of Metairie and Kenner. The latter city existed as a hub for the nearby airport, but Metairie was a working class suburb, populated by an uneasy mix of blue-collar Republican white folks and African Americans. The bus ride was hot and interminable. I stared vacantly through the dirty window glass as the elegant buildings of the city gave way to mini-marts and gas stations. The bus rumbled and lurched through the streets, stopping every two blocks to disgorge passengers and pick up new ones. Everyone appeared to be sullen and exhausted.

As my stop neared, I grew anxious. What if I missed it? There was no way in hell that I was going to ask any of my fellow passengers for directions. Finally, tired of waiting, I pulled the cord, and disembarked from the bus. I stood for a moment on the sidewalk, blinking like a mole in the harsh mid-afternoon light. Then I squared my shoulders and strode down the street with a feigned sense of purpose, as if I was heading to a place where I really wanted to go.

Fortunately, my timing was perfect, and I was only two blocks from the bookstore. A grimy, two-story windowless building suddenly loomed in front of me. It looked exactly as David had described it, but I checked the address in my wallet to be sure. I wondered whether I should just hop on the next bus back to New Orleans. After a brief internal debate, I decided that I had come too far to change my mind.

Feeling slightly ill, I rang the doorbell, then stood on the threshold, fidgeting nervously. The door flew open, and Duke loomed above me. He was even taller than I had imagined, with a lean frame and long, gangling legs. His handsome face wore a friendly expression, as if he was sincerely glad to have the chance to meet me. Duke reached forward, grasped my hand, and gave it a firm shake. "Welcome to my store" he said expansively. "Are you thirsty? I can offer you a Pepsi."

I realized for the first time that I was extremely thirsty. Duke fished in one of his pockets, and finally located a key. He held the key aloft, squinted at it for a moment, and smiled. The two of us wandered into his shop, and he closed the door firmly. A commercial pop machine stood in one corner, next to the cash register. Duke strode briskly to the machine, unlocked it, and removed a bottle. "No charge, of course" he said. "That should quench your thirst. Let me know if you need another one." He fixed me with a beatific grin and watched approvingly as I took an appreciative gulp from the bottle. "How was your bus ride?" he asked. "Did you have any trouble finding my place?"

"None whatsoever" I assured him. The Pepsi had calmed my stomach somewhat, and I was finally able to focus on my surroundings. All of the walls were lined with pamphlets that bore such ominous titles as *The Negro Problem* and *Taking Back Our Heritage*. A glass shelf stood beside the cash register, filled to overflowing with souvenir coffee cups and glow-in-the-dark Klansman figurines. In its center stood a cheap plastic frame that contained a faded comic strip. The cartoon depicted a drooling black man with flabby lips and oversized feet. Its caption read, "He may be YOUR equal, but he sure as hell isn't mine!"

Feeling sick, I backed away from the counter. "What do you think of our inventory?" Duke asked. "Pretty impressive, huh?" "Well, there certainly is a lot of it" I said politely. "But really, what is the point of this bookstore? What are you trying to do here, exactly?"

For a moment, Duke appeared surprised, but he recovered quickly. "I started this bookstore with a mission" he explained. "I don't hate black people. They have their own heritage, and I respect that. You and I are white, however, and we have a different heritage. I'm proud of our heritage, and I want to preserve it."

Duke paused for a moment to allow his words to sink into my head. I stared at him, speechless. Convinced that he had a captive audience, Duke plunged on. "Now, one way that we ensure the continuance of our race is for white people to breed exclusively with other white people. If a person of Caucasian descent breeds with a person of African descent, this erodes the purity of our bloodline. Then, slowly but surely, our race begins to break down, to transform into something different and less pure."

It was obvious that Duke was convinced of the irrefutable truth of his words, that he deeply believed in the urgency of his mission, and felt compelled to defend it at all costs. He stared into my eyes like a trained hypnotist, while his long hands gestured in front of my face. I returned his gaze, nodded slowly, and found myself sinking into a kind of spell. Then I shook my head, as if I had returned to land after spending some time underwater, and opened my mouth to speak.

Undaunted, Duke continued his spiel. "Of course, the purity of the black race is also corrupted when the races mix, and they aren't happy about it either. So it would obviously be better for everyone concerned if they just stuck to breeding with people of their own kind."

I suddenly regained the power of speech. "What if a black person and a white person really want to start a family together?" I demanded. "Would you seek legislation that would make this impossible?"

Though my question struck me as one that any reasonable person might ask, Duke appeared surprised. After a long moment of consideration, he replied, "Well, probably not right away. I'd suggest my theory at first, and perhaps stricter measures would be necessary at a later time."

I was deeply chilled by the realization that Duke was willing to consider the enactment of laws designed to control human mating behavior. It was almost impossible for me to believe that any late-twentieth century adult would propose such an idea. Nevertheless, Duke stood in front of me, earnestly describing his vision of a Utopian future, one in which white people stayed white forever, with no interference from any other tribe. Transgressions from this norm would result in punishment, though he hadn't yet outlined exactly what form that punishment might take.

Feeling suddenly dizzy, I shifted my gaze to the walls of the shop. They seemed to revolve around me in a panoramic vista, as if I was viewing them from the center of a carousel. My eyes came to rest on the cartoon of the drooling black man, and nausea swept over me. When the vertigo finally lifted, I leveled my gaze at Duke. "I'm not interested in joining the Klan" I said. "I was just curious to find out how you operate over here. I'd only heard negative things, and I wanted to know your perspective. After hearing it, I'm more convinced than ever that it is best for all of us to work out our differences, and leave each other alone to live our lives as we see fit. Thanks for having me over, though."

I had been raised to be polite, even towards people whose ideas struck me as abhorrent. That obligatory politeness was part of my own white heritage, but it didn't run deep enough for me to allow myself to be manipulated by Duke's words. Duke stared at me with a puzzled expression on his face. He looked both disappointed and vaguely hostile, as if I had intentionally swindled him. Then he rearranged his face into a smile that was simultaneously chilling and radiant. "Well, I do hope you'll reconsider" he said.

"I need to get back to the city" I replied. I inched towards the door, placed my hand on the knob, and remembered that I had almost forgotten the illuminated cross. "I have one request," I said. "The *Figaro* reporter said that you have a huge cross that lights up in the dark. Can I see it?"

For a moment, Duke appeared pleased, but then he was seized by a recollection of his own. "The main bulb's burned out," he apologized. "The cross isn't working right now. Unfortunately, I can't illuminate it. But if you want to see it anyway, just follow me." He walked to the other side of the room, and threw open a door.

Tentatively, I followed him to the threshold and peered inside. The new room was larger than the shop area, and was obviously used for meetings. Duke's enormous cross hung majestically on one wall, and looked down upon folding chairs and cardboard boxes of Klan literature. Its bulbs gleamed ominously in the semi-darkness. "The effect is so much more dramatic when the bulbs are illuminated," Duke said sadly. "But you get the general idea." He reached inside one of the boxes and removed a handful of slightly yellowed newspapers. "Please take these, and read them if you get the chance."

Because I had been trained to be polite, I allowed Duke to place the newspapers into my left hand. My fingers reflexively clutched the pages before I could stop them, or think of an excuse. "If you don't mind, I'll be going now," I said. Duke stuck his hand out for me to shake, and I grasped it limply for a moment. Then I wandered towards the door and stepped outside.

I scurried away from Duke's bookstore–slowly at first, and then with increasing speed. I fervently hoped that the arrival of the bus would be swift, but I felt prepared to wait for as long as necessary. Finally, I collapsed into a bench at the bus stop and opened one of the newspapers. It was the most recent copy of the monthly Ku Klux Klan newsletter, filled with articles that described Klan events in the greater New Orleans metro area. In the corner of one page, a cartoon showed a line of Klansfolk striding down a city street, clad in their robes. All of them wore large shoes that pointed in the same direction. The accompanying caption read, "Keep on Ku-Kluxin'."

I could hear the rumble of the bus in the distance, so I closed the newspaper. For a moment, I considered abandoning the literature at the bus stop, but I had been taught that it was impolite to litter. Instead, I scooped up the parcel of papers from the bench and boarded the bus. As I fumbled in my purse for change, I accidentally dropped the clump of newspapers. They slid across the floor while I extracted the coins and dropped them hastily into the fare box.

The bus lurched forward and picked up momentum. An updraft caught one of the newspapers, and the pages tumbled through the aisle like autumn leaves. I stumbled down the center of the bus, and hastily gathered the papers while the passengers stared straight ahead, indifferent to my plight. One of the pages came to rest beside a middle-aged African American woman's foot. She lifted the paper from the floor and handed it to me. Finally, she re-directed her gaze towards the dirt-encrusted bus window and stared outside with an impassive expression on her face.

The woman, too, had been taught the dubious value of politeness, for reasons that were vastly different from mine. I had a choice, but she did not. "Thanks" I said, as I slid into the space behind her. Although I realized that my recent clumsiness had made subterfuge unnecessary, I folded the papers and stashed them safely in my purse. Then I settled into my seat and prepared myself for the ride downtown with my fellow humans—all of us exhausted, and just heading home for rest after a long, grueling day. ■

Roger Barbee

Useless

EACH DAY AFTER JUNIOR HIGH SCHOOL CLASSES, I would ride my bike to the *Daily Independent* on North Main Street and enter the lower back door that led to a large room full of big tables. Like all paperboys who had routes in town, I would go into the small, back circulation room and get my allotted papers from Mr. Harris, our manager. I would then return to the large room full of tables and roll my papers. But, we paperboys did not just roll papers, for that large room was a social center of sorts where we bragged loudly, kidded each other, talked about girls as only eighth grade boys can, and, if we had a nickel, bought a coke from the machine. Then, after the rolling of papers and social bantering was finished, we would stuff our papers in heavy canvas bags held to our bikes by the handle bars and front fender to go make our deliveries.

That large room, full of ink-stained tables with each holding its own center-piece of a white box overflowing with green rubber bands, was more than a room to roll papers. In that room I learned some lessons about life and myself that echo still like the smell of fresh newspaper ink. Because my parents were divorced, I lacked a male role model. I lived with my mother, four sisters, and younger brother. For me, positive male role models were rare, but Mr. Harris was one who filled that role early in my life. As I worked for him those three years, I learned how to manage money, work with my customers, and make good business decisions.

Since almost all of my customers worked in the cotton mill, some would be paid one week and some the next week. Thus, I had a "big" week when most of my eighty customers received their bi-monthly mill check and would pay for the paper, with a few paying a "little" a week. Sadly, some weeks a customer would ask me to come back since there was no money to pay for the paper, or worse, after a few weeks of not paying, a customer would skip out on me, leaving me with the bill. But, Mr. Harris was always there to guide me through those flush times and lean times. He would tell me how to set aside some of the "big" week money as a hedge against the "little" week. After all, he and I were in business, and I had to pay him for the papers I took out of that large room each day. So, as I would go through my route on collection day, I hoped that all my customers were at home and had money to pay for their two weeks of delivery.

He also taught me the importance of pleasing my customers. I learned that it mattered to be timely because people wanted the afternoon paper to find out what was going on in the area and the rest of the world, and that if someone wanted the paper "porched," I should learn to throw it on the porch from my bike, not in the yard and never on the roof. I also learned to be attentive to my customers and learned to chat with them, and listen to the older ones to learn what was on their minds. Mr. Harris taught me to know as much as I could about my customers and their families. I also learned how easy it was to make a mistake because one day I had about eight "extras" but could not figure out why I had so many papers remaining, and I owed for each paper I took out. As soon as Mr. Harris called telling me that Mrs. Reese had not received her paper, I knew: I had stopped to play a bit with Michael Tarleton, and had forgotten an entire side street off of Chestnut Avenue. So, on my bike I went in the dark to porch those late papers. Sometimes, people would move leaving me with a receipt book full of owed tickets.

However, Mr. Harris would make me pay part of the bill, but not all. "I'll split this with you, Roger," he would say, and went on to explain about not trusting people too much, and not extending too much credit. I soon learned that not delivering a paper could often encourage some customers to pay what they owed. I also learned that some customers would lie over a few dollars for a paper. Yet, Mr. Harris was always there guiding me through it all.

But there is one memory from that back room that Mr. Harris was not part of, and it is something that still ink-stains my life. And, like in all memories, I can't go back and change my actions to erase that stain. It is a memory that I carry, and it is one that I am ashamed of.

Each day in that back room, as we rolled papers and carried on, another employee of the paper would come through the room going to his duties. I don't know what his job was, but I think it was some type of delivery in circulation, for he was always there each afternoon. Each day when he walked through that room on his way upstairs he would greet us boys and chat in an open, honest way. I still see his clean, starched khaki pants, collared shirts, and proud carriage. He was polite, not overly friendly, but open to us boys. He would acknowledge us and our work, even ask how our routes were going. When one of us would see him arrive, we would greet him with, "Hey, Useless," or "Here comes Useless," because we never bothered to learn his name, or if we did, we soon stopped using it in favor of the awful nickname one of us had given him.

Sometimes a boy would kick him in the butt as he stood talking with us and leave a dirty foot print on the crisp, starched pants. However, no matter what happened in that room, he always maintained his poise and went on about his way in a purposeful, but unhurried manner. What haunts me is that I took part in this gang mentality to abuse a black man, someone as old as Mr. Harris, an adult. I used my white privilege in that ink-stained back room to degrade another person, and did not, until years later, take responsibility for my actions. Years later while reading *Native Son* and seeing Bigger's life in Richard Wright's novel, I remembered that gentleman and how I had treated him. As I read about Bigger and his struggles, I realized why I did it. Although poor and uneducated, I was white, and this whiteness gave me power over him or any other black man. And I used that power to a mean end. I now know, understand, and own why I did what I did, but I wonder how he did what he did? How did that man of poise and carriage enter that back room each afternoon knowing what awaited him— likely abuse by a bunch of white boys who knew nothing of life and its lessons, or of him and his circumstances? When he dressed each day for work, did he wonder if one of us would soil his starched pants by kicking him? Did he think of us as he entered the room and heard one of us announce his arrival?

I wish I knew his name so that his identity would be truly real to me. I wish I knew his name in order to know his story. I wish I knew his name so that I could try and find him, if he still lives. I wish I knew his name so that I could ask someone about him if he does not. I wish I knew his name so that I could see him as the man he was, not a scapegoat for my mean-spirited ignorance. I wish I knew his name so I could say it, to pronounce: "Mr. _____," and hear his given name come out of my mouth in a respectful way.

So, this ink-stain stays with me still. I have to admit my gang mentality, of taking the easy way, of doing what was convenient. I have to admit using my white privilege to abuse another person. I have to admit to acting without considering how my actions affected another person. I have to admit meanness to another person, of giving verbal and physical abuse to a gentleman who entered the room each day and treated me with civility. I returned his kindness with mean disrespect like all the others. That's a stain I hope never washes away for it reminds me to be vigilant. After all, Lucifer began as an angel. ■

Larry Montague

Fear of a White Rapper

"Yo, Flu Diddy! Spit some rhymes, yo."
"Yeah DJ Fluent, drop us a beat, son!"

CRINGE WHEN I THINK ABOUT THESE JOKES aimed at me by my "friends" back in high school, ten years ago now. It's not that the hallway ridicule has caused me some lasting trauma. I cringe because the authors of these insults are white, and I'm white, and our setting is a school that's 99.9 percent white in white collar suburbia. The lack of credibility—and respect—nearly makes me sick from embarrassment. To my sixteen-year-old buddies, being a white rapper was "trying to be black."

Trying to be black. It's not a new criticism in the world of music. I've read how Led Zeppelin borrowed from Leadbelly and that Mick Jagger emulated James Brown and about blue-eyed soul, and why Vanilla Ice enters your brain when you hear the word *poser*. I get it. Hip-hop is black culture. Period. But there are some legitimate white artists out there doing their thing, as they say. (Wait, who's "they?!")

It wasn't shame that caused me to take offense to these comments. I like black people like I like all people, I mean as long as they're good people. I wanted to be like Mike, too. (And Chuck D.) So why the hell am I still so embarrassed about the whole thing? It's not even rational. It's 2016; would this kind of pathetic banter even offend black people nowadays? It's evident they have a lot more pressing issues to deal with than to waste energy considering the thoughtless words of spoiled little punks. Well, I don't have bigger problems—being a white male and all—so let's talk about it.

I love hip-hop. My friends love hip-hop. We all loved it back then, too, including the friends under the bright light here. I was the only one in our circle that tried to *do* hip-hop, so naturally I became a target. Now, my school was almost entirely white—like a February blizzard—so I was a big target. Fresh meat for a bunch of privileged white kids who sat around bored on the top of Maslow's pyramid.

I can still remember the first time I wore a basketball jersey to school. It was such a big deal that even after I took it off, which was before lunch, people who hadn't seen me wearing it made a point to approach me in the cafeteria just so they could remind me of it and laugh in my face!

Is there any one thing more responsible for driving white people to commit cruel and regrettable acts than fear? Christopher Columbus commanded his men to enslave the Arawak people before he even knew whether they came in peace or in war. Thomas Jefferson penned the line, "...all men are created equal" while his slaves were kept under a tight watch. If Donald Trump becomes president of the United States, he vows to erect a wall on the border to keep Mexicans out of our country. I believe fear is the catalyst in all of these examples. Fear has afflicted white people—young and old—for far too long.

Nowadays, when I walk onto a stage, grab the microphone, and start spilling rap lyrics into the crowd I see the fear on the white faces in the audience. It usually manifests in that sadistic, insecure form of a shit-eating smirk, or sometimes even laughter. These people are cornered, up against the ropes of their small, square world. Here's a white guy that looks like he just walked out of an L.L. Bean catalog doing rap, doing something he doesn't look like he should be doing, doing... *what black people do.* I love it, not because I'm (trying to be) "Black and I'm Proud," but because I've forced these people to find a new category in which to pin me. I've flipped the script on 'em.

I also hate it because, although personally I feel as though I've transcended a stereotype, that's hardly a victory when prejudice is still apparent. What I mean is that, although I see the fear looking right at me, I don't believe it's a fear of me, per se. Instead I believe it's the terrifying realization that I would be following—and therefore admiring—black culture.

Since the dawn of oppression, hasn't the minority's influence on the public always signified danger to the oppressor? Think of slave uprisings and blacks that could read. Influence is power, and a shift in the balance of power is the majority's worst nightmare. I think this is still at play in modern day America. After all, this country is still three-quarters white.

I feel this reaction I get time and again boils down to a fear of the black man. (I say "man" because it's the relevant gender here and also because I believe rap still conjures up an image of a black male for most people.) Perhaps it's buried deep down in many of us and only perceptible in a relatively small percentage, such as those college classmates of mine who had Confederate flag decals on their trucks. I won't pretend to know the psychology or the statistics, but I believe this fear is there to some degree in all of us white people. I still get nervous whenever I tell a black person I rap. What if they don't want me to make hip-hop? Do they think I'm going to embarrass their culture?

This leads us to a good question: what if I'm really not as "real" of a rapper as I think I am, and my stage show comes off as a parody in the eyes and ears of the spectators? If that was the case, I'd be the perpetrator here. White people who are apt to judge me in the first place would feel comforted by someone mocking hip-hop style. Why? For one, if they thought I was doing it in jest, their own preconceptions about rap would be justifiable in their minds: "Rap is for black people; this white guy is definitely affirming that." Never mind the fact that they and their friends use Ebonics when they're drinking 40-ounces or driving around smoking blunts. *(Word.)* A foolish white rapper sits well with them, whether or not they sit well with themselves.

Secondly, these individuals would feel no threat from my performance because there would be no reason for them to take me seriously: "Oh, ok – he's joking. Good. I don't even have to judge him. Hey, black people can rap; that doesn't bother me. Let them have something, you know?"

Of course my intention is not to make a mockery of black culture or to relive that day in high school when I wore the jersey.

So, if people in the audience can't label me as a fraud because they see that I'm being authentically me on stage, then they have to accept what they're seeing and hearing as something legitimate. Then they're forced to deal with the situation. If someone's mind connects *rapper* with *black person,* then a conflict is going to arise the minute they hear me melodically rhyming words over a beat. Those people that quickly move past this initial conflict and proceed to listen with an open mind – thus judging me by the content of my character – are better off for it, and lend to a better world.

Those who get hung up on the issue of skin pigment alone (given they respect the message in my music) need to catch up to the rest of us in twenty-first century America. Is a white person looking up to a black figure really a cause for concern and judgment? From 2008 to infinity, every boy and girl aspiring to be president of the United States of America will be able to look up to a black man. I believe a country that can elect an African American man as its Commander-in-Chief for two consecutive terms and, at the same time, watch its black citizens stand up on every possible platform in order to uphold that their lives matter, is a country steeped in a stale fear that's serving as a dead weight on true progress. Obviously, this is a fear that has got to go, and soon.

Until that day, each time I get on stage to do hip-hop music I'm going to look into the eyes of every face in the crowd and prove to them I'm not afraid – to admit that skin color really doesn't matter; to admire a group of people because I appreciate what they do; to challenge the audience, even if they did just come to be entertained. That's why I always perform wearing my usual button-ups and khakis (the jersey has been in the closet since 2005) and talking how I normally talk. These work to jostle minds free from their borders. I figure if I stir the pot enough, these insecure white people will eventually smell how outdated their biases really are and start to avoid their old way of thinking like it's a rotting carcass. ■

Amy Nocton

A Story About Turbulence

THIS IS A STORY ABOUT TURBULENCE. I'd been thinking about its composition for weeks, but only found time to put pen to paper during a bumpy flight between Dublin and Rome one November morning. It is a story that became more complete during December's shortest days with the discovery of a speech written in 1968.

This is a story about friendship and memory. Jim was my father's best friend. They met while in the seminary, where their friendship developed over their shared love for expensive scotch and their mutual opposition to the Vietnam War and human rights abuses in the U.S. and abroad. Both men left the seminary around the same time over disagreements with their superiors. Both men went into business and married attractive blonds.

My father and mother had three children, of which I am the oldest. Jim and his wife never had kids. I don't know if it was by choice or not, and there is no one to ask now. Eileen died of pancreatic cancer years ago. Not too long thereafter, Jim died, too. And my father? He is now lost in the fog of Alzheimer's.

What I know and remember, though, is that Jim and Eileen doted on my siblings and me with the adoration of an aunt and uncle and were often recruited to care for us when my parents needed a getaway. I recall curious looks when the five of us would go out together. At the time, I thought nothing of it, but with adult hindsight I understand that people must have wondered who we belonged to. My brother and I are fair and blonde while my sister is a fair skinned beautiful blue eyed brunette. Certainly we could have been Eileen's children, but there is no way that any of us were mixed race. So, where did Jim fit into the picture?

My father tells me that Jim loved us so much (and had such a good appetite) that when I was still dining in a high chair I would offer Jim tidbits of whatever I had already drooled all over or had put in my mouth and Jim would happily accept. My father said it was absolutely disgusting. I now understand that it was an early form of communion. Jim was my father's chosen brother and, as such, my "gifted" uncle.

Though my father has never said as much, he has alluded to the fact that his friendship with Jim was what prompted him to get involved with Saul Alinsky as a community organizer in Chicago. I believe that my father met Alinsky when he visited Lawrence University, where my father was briefly a professor of philosophy. It was at Lawrence University that my father was also very involved in working with black student athletes and helping to organize them for better treatment within the athletic department at the time.

This is a story about heartbreak. Only recently, because of my father's forgetting, did I learn any of this. When packing up his Florida apartment to move him back to Connecticut, I found a newspaper clipping of an obituary for Saul Alinsky. I spoke with my father's sisters, who told me how their father was not pleased that his son was working so closely with this "subversive" man. Then I asked my father questions, and, when pressed, my father could still recall going into black neighborhoods to talk to and work with poor blacks in the projects of Chicago in the 1960s and how powerless he felt to do anything. My father told me that he shared this sentiment with Jim who, at the time, responded that there was one hope for elevating the status of blacks and that was the growing number of Hispanics, "because now the blacks had someone to look down on – someone with even lower status than they had."

While sorting through more of my father's things in December 2015, I also found the typescript of a speech my father wrote and delivered on April 7, 1968, at a Martin Luther King Memorial Service sponsored by the Students for Human Rights at Lawrence College. In it my father explained, "Since [Martin Luther King's] death, we have heard him hailed as the greatest American of his time. Not an American black man, but as a black American, deeply committed to saving not only black people from the disease of racism but white people also."

My father goes on to define and defend black power as something not to be feared by white people but as something essential for the liberation of both blacks and white. My father understood black power to encompass pride in being black; a redefinition of beauty according to black standards; economic, political, and social unity against whites who would prevent integration and force segregation and marginalization; and a condemnation of violence to attain change.

My father wrote and spoke these words during a time of social turbulence, political upheaval, and of people forgetting how to treat one another humanely. My father, whose best friend and chosen brother was Jim, a beloved black man, delivered this speech during a time not much unlike now.

This is a story about risk. When the Arno flooded its banks in 1966, before either Jim or my father had left the seminary, Jim went to help clean out the churches. When I was nineteen years old, I studied in Florence for the year. As I strolled the streets with my father during his visit just after Christmas, my father regaled me with stories Jim had shared of those days. My father and I would gaze up at the high water marks sprinkled throughout the city, and my father would instantly recall another tale about Jim cleaning muck in Florence. I have often wished I could have heard Jim's stories firsthand. I would have loved to have known what it was like for him to have been one of the few blacks in the city, as it is still a city with little racial integration.

Prior to my trip to Florence, I lived in Simsbury, Connecticut where ethnic diversity was limited to a handful of Indian and Chinese families, maybe a couple of black families, and enough Jewish families to close school in observance of the Jewish holy days. Although Jim was a part of my extended family, and while my interactions with him were carefree and loving, I never developed a similar comfort or familiarity with the African American kids who lived in our town or with the ABC (A Better Chance) students, or with those who were bussed in to attend school in Simsbury. Within the radius of my circle of friends there were a couple of black students, but in terms of long lasting friendships, they didn't really stick. I'm not sure if that is due to race or due to my being naturally introverted, technologically disengaged, and not having time to stay in touch with a lot of people who I liked or admired at one time. There is one African American acquaintance from childhood who has tried desperately to get me to make more of a commitment to a friendship, and, truth be told, I would love to be able to invest in such a friendship. He is brilliant and handsome and kind, but we never seem to find the time.

This is a story about loss. In later years, Jim and my father often ended up dressing alike without meaning to. One of the last images I have of them together before their tragic falling out is of the two of them walking away from me in Stuyvesant Town in Manhattan. They were planning their next motorcycle odyssey (they had swapped out Champ hunting on Lake Champlain for motorcycles when they entered their mid-fifties). They had both put on some weight, though Jim was far stouter, and they were laughing and chatting boisterously as they walked away, both wearing matching tan trench coats. They looked like a happy, paunchy interracial gay couple.

I still mourn Jim's death. I miss him, and I am sad that my father's dementia may have brought such a terrible end to their friendship. I'm sad that Jim died without ever having had the chance to understand that it was a disease that caused my father's seemingly mad, jealous behavior about a woman he had loved and Jim had befriended. I think my father's breaking ties with Jim was just another symptom of the beginnings of Alzheimer's insidious eating away at his brain, only none of us knew at the time.

This is an exercise in remembering. My father taught me early on to fight for social justice and to do everything I could to look beyond skin color. I took those lessons seriously. When studying in Florence, I ended up befriending people with similar beliefs to mine. We protested the racist treatment of African street vendors and watched as the vendors staged their own sit-ins and hunger strikes.

In recent years, I've wished I could talk to Jim or my father about how they see race relations now. When Obama was elected president, for one fleeting moment my father mused about how proud and amazed Jim would have been. I would love to have asked Jim what his impressions were of his place in our quirky Irish American family.

I would love to have pressed him or my father to know how, if ever, one sheds the worry about making a misstep when interacting with an unknown African American person. I would like to know more about my father's motivation for working in Chicago and whether or not my drive to do good and right wrongs, no matter how cliché that sounds, is rooted in the same knowledge of my own white privilege and my own white guilt. I can't visit these topics with them now though, so I will continue to grapple with my place and feelings and will likely never really figure it out. It is all far too nuanced and complicated for simple labels and explanations.

Still, I think that both Jim and my father would be pleased to see how both of my children are, for the moment, less preoccupied with race. My husband and I are fortunate that our children attend schools with quite a bit of ethnic and some racial diversity. I think that Jim and my father would be tickled to see their "granddaughter/great niece" make it her own mission to befriend every child at her school. Midway through last year she announced she had a new best friend, and they are in the same class this year. His skin is as opaque as hers is translucent, and they clearly adore one another. They are mischief-makers in the worst sense and have become fast friends. They show their affection for each other as many other eight-year-old boys and girls do, by rough housing and laughing while doing so.

This is a story about remembering in times of turbulence. It is knowing that the friendship that Jim and my father shared still defines much of who I am. When I told my father that I was writing about his relationship with Jim and how it influenced my experience with race, I was unsure of how he'd react. But at Jim's name, his eyes lit up and he said, "Gee, Amy, that's great. Wow. I can't wait to read your essay. Yeah, that's terrific." There was a pause. A few minutes passed, and then he asked, "So, is there any news? Did I already ask you that?" I nodded. He laughed, "Jesus, I'm beginning to sound like my mother!"

It is a story about turbulence. ■

Tereza Topferova Bottman

A Dispatch from the Margins in the Middle

THIS IS AN AMERICAN STORY. Pass the apple pie. Yet I am not American. Pass the strudel. This is your story and my story, intertwined. Shake up the sieve of whiteness and I, an immigrant "impostor" remain atop, a square peg jammed against a round hole. Flip the sieve and drop me. I will blend in with the rest of the white faces like grains of sand scattered all over this land.

My mother, sister and I came to this country in the late 1980s, escaping totalitarianism. I was a teenager, thrown for a loop. Everything about this culture confused me. Most of all, life felt lonely here.

Initially, what I could not understand were the invisible lines which seemed to divide people. In our daily interactions, white Americans often made it clear that I was not one of them. My family members were the odd ones out, the harmless, yet not-so-innocent strangers who ostensibly disrupted the harmonious, predictable existence of the status quo. This was in pre-grunge Pacific Northwest, mind you, not exactly a welcoming mecca of international influence back then. It was the small interactions that let us know our place, like when we'd tell Americans our names or I would open my mouth to utter a bit of small talk, out would come words carefully composed, but tainted with an odd way of thinking and a foreign accent about which I was – and still am – forever reminded. Immediately after introductions our conversations would come to an uncomfortable halt, the takeaway message being that we immigrants might as well be a different species.

Growing up in a family of political dissidents in the oppressive regime of 1970s and 1980s Czechoslovakia, I was taught to read between the lines, to look for the heart of the matter in the margins. New to this country, I could not yet read between the lines because I could hardly make out the words on the printed page. As a recent immigrant I gravitated toward those perceived as outsiders, as literally and figuratively un-American. I was mainly curious about those most obviously different from me. Europeans were old hat. Other immigrant kids from around the world whom I encountered in school were, in general, as inquiring about me as I was about them. Many of us bonded instantly as the outcasts in this society through jokes about not fitting in and during our favorite pastime of badmouthing Americans. It was harder for me, however, to get to know the African American students who were the majority at my high school. Something seemed to stand between us. I could not put my finger on what it was.

So I became a student of race relations. I listened to my multicultural friends' recounted experiences, I read, I continued to reach out to those with whom I longed to connect, sometimes messing up by saying something hurtful, then withdrawing into shame before poking my head out and trying to reach out again.

For instance, there was the time when I told my classmate in jest, or so I thought, to get his "black a**" outside if he was as bored as he had purported. Needless to say, this did not go over well coming from my unschooled white girl mouth. After the initial confrontation, we actually ended up having a deep, heartfelt talk which culminated in a joint crying session – one of those rare cathartic moments of candor and profound connection.

Despite being "othered" by many whites whose ancestors had settled in the U.S. generations before my family, I did make some white American friends. I now understand that the ideology of whiteness as status utterly envelops all of us Europeans in its poisonous embrace. It separates us from others as well as from ourselves. We cannot escape its cocoon. Rather, we carry whiteness with us like a charm that protects us from harm, shields us from impact as we dive from the known to the unknown, parachute from one spot on the globe to another as immigrants, tourists or do-gooders abroad. The poison of white supremacy we ingest with our mothers' milk lingers, sometimes intensifies when we start our lives as newcomers in this country with its charged racial history. It inoculates us with the notion that we are humans and the rest of humanity is inferior. As immigrants we do not immediately and adequately grasp the depth of that racialized history, let alone the present, and how it could possibly have created such rifts between people.

Reading about the sociology of class and White Anglo-Saxon Protestant (WASP) culture provided me with a key to unlock some of the mysteries that have colored my experience in this society but which I couldn't understand because my family comes from a Slavic stock, shaped by a mix of Jewish and Catholic influences, culturally different from the dominant U.S. WASP norm. But I still had questions. Gradually I came to find that I could credit much of my reality in this society to white supremacy culture. White supremacy's core tenets such as individualism and internalized white superiority outlined by a number of scholars I had encountered, manifest themselves everywhere. At first I was not able to see how they have impacted my perceptions or determined my own behavior because it is the water in which I have always swum.

At first glance, whiteness as status is all benefits, advantages, a shiny package of sparkly goodies. But the truth is that white people don't make it through unscathed. Clearly, maintaining this hegemonic system comes at a cost to us whites. Recent studies show that white middle-aged men, unlike other groups, have a mortality rate that is rising at a rapid pace. Obviously the set-up that positions white men at the top of society's chain is not working for them. On the contrary, they are dying from stress-related causes. There has also been a recent study which shows that white Americans are the biggest terror threat. According to this study, twice as many people have died in attacks by right-wing groups in America than by Muslim extremists since the attacks on 9/11. This is the deadly set-up that we are up against. And it is high time for us to attempt to break free from these narratives and redefine our place as white people in the society and the world.

How do I personally know that the system of white supremacy is hurting us all? White supremacy shows up in my life as fear, disconnectedness, fragility and an internalized sense of superiority. It can come off as guardedness and coldness. My partner who is black tells me that white people seem to always be holding back, scared to open up. This type of precious feedback has made an impact on me. Like so many white folks, I have been led to feel disconnected from the humanity of others as well as from my own. For example, as a school teacher, I am programmed not to feel empathy for my kids of color and to react punitively to keep them "in line" and quiet at all times. I am to go on with my agenda no matter what unsettling events happen in my students' lives or out in the world. I have to fight this socialization daily. As a white person, I constantly fear making mistakes, and breaking relationships with people of color before I even make them. This fear has lessened somewhat over time as I have befriended and deepened my ties with many friends of color and as I have become part of my partner's large African American family.

I recently had a conversation with a white activist about white supremacy culture. We both agreed that we guard ourselves around other white people too, because we fear being cast out from the only club to which we tentatively belong. I am highly mistrustful of other white people and perhaps this can ultimately be traced to my own fear of committing racist transgressions. It is as if my interactions with other whites hold up a mirror to how I may be seen by people of color. But I am also scared that the violence lurking beneath the mask of white supremacy, so closely tied with what bell hooks terms heteropatriarchy, will bubble out, targeting me as a woman, as someone with Jewish heritage, someone with a black partner and mixed race kids. This fear is real and visceral, but I organize despite it.

Two years ago, with several other white activists, we formed a regional chapter of Showing Up for Racial Justice in our city in the Pacific Northwest. As part of a nationwide effort, we "educate, organize and mobilize white people to work for racial justice." Our mission is to "act as part of a multi-racial majority for justice with passion and accountability." Our group raises funds for grassroots organizations led by people of color, we volunteer our time and skills, we bring food, we show up to and plan rallies, we phone-bank and door-knock to discuss issues pertinent to our community and to the #BlackLivesMatter movement, we educate ourselves as well as other white people in our circles, we practice interrupting racism. This is "heart" work for me. This is my antidote to violence, apathy and despair.

Deep down I am convinced that our capitalist system is closely tied with white supremacy and that one cannot be demolished without the other. That is the political ideology underpinning my activism.

In the context of the courageous #BlackLivesMatter fighters continuing to stand up for justice around the country, I try to embody what I long for other white people to do, which is to answer the call to acknowledge and renounce whiteness for its historical and current inseparability from racial violence and oppression. I want white people to organize and, en masse, divest ourselves from the narrow definition of success in this capitalistic society that forces us to subscribe to the deadly values of white supremacy. What is asked of us is nothing short of building a new world rooted in collective action, shaped by a narrative that strives to re-envision, co-create, collaborate, liberate across ingrained divisions of race, class, gender and all the rest. Many of us are already there, with our sleeves rolled up, weeding, tilling, preparing a new reality that we believe to be possible. This is your story and my story, intertwined. Pass the trowel, take the hoe, and let's keep working together. ■

Justine Cozell

Passing as a Person of Color

DON'T RECALL BEING ASKED ABOUT MY WHITENESS until I was eleven, when I moved from the suburbs of Chicago to the suburbs of Los Angeles. My two best, and virtually only, friends in Chicago were Indian American – one whose parents were from India and the other who was adopted from India as an infant by a white mother – which makes me think that while I wasn't aware of it, I may have been perceived as something other than white even then. My older sisters encountered more direct racism, ranging from being called "nigger" to "Jews who should go back to New York." This probably says more about the whiteness of the town we lived in than the darkness of our skin. When I started school in Southern California, "What are you?" became the question I encountered on an almost daily basis. In the beginning, I replied that I was white, but learned that to my peers, I didn't "look white." So I followed up more specifically: "My mother is Scottish American and WASP and my father is Italian American." (As time went on, I stopped replying with specifics. It was easier just to say, "My father's Italian," because that's what they were after – where did my brownness come from.) My fellow middle schoolers would often reply, "You're not white, you're Italian!" This confused me, even more so because I was only half Italian, but, in my school, the less white you were, the cooler you were. I was quick to jump on this bandwagon, and my style slowly evolved to a hybrid of *chola* and *guidette*. It began with the easier steps – liquid eyeliner, hoop earrings, and the standard chola uniform of a wife-beater and Dickies. But that only scratched the surface of my itch. I didn't just want to fit in. I wanted to feel this transformation from the inside. Bigger steps needed to be taken. Every aspect of my character had to deflect my whiteness. I combed over my life looking for opportunities that lent themselves to that shift and found one in religion.

Before this time, I never cared much for religion. I was the type who begged my parents to let me stay home on Sundays, and by this time, my family had stopped going altogether. I was raised Methodist on an agreement my parents made before my sisters and I were born that we'd take my father's last name (Americanized from Cucuzzella to Cozell when my father was a child, further confusing people as to my background) and my mother's religion. My father, coming from an Italian American family, was raised Catholic. So I had my connection. I'd convert to Catholicism. I dug up the cross my paternal grandparents gave me when I was born and started wearing it every day and transformed one of the shelves in my room into a shrine to Catholicism. Fortunately, I had saved a lot of mementos from family occasions. I arranged prayer cards with saints on the front from funerals on my dad's side and a Catholic prayer book my paternal grandmother had given me. I had postcards of angels I had originally bought because I thought the angels were pretty. And front and center was a beautiful, ornate gold cross that my father had bought for me at an exhibit at the Armand Hammer Museum called "Angels from the Vatican." No doubt my motivation for going was more about building my Catholic shrine than learning about Vatican artwork. I remember scouring the glass display case in the gift shop for a cross that would make a proper statement. I knew instantly when I saw it. It was bold and elaborate. It drew attention to itself. The only problem was that it was actually a replica of a Russian Orthodox cross. My dad tried to talk me out of it, believing I'd be happier with a replica of a Vatican cross. After all, I had begged him to take me because I was so eager to connect with Catholicism.

The dream of conversion was put on the back-burner when I discovered it would take a year of weekend classes before I was even close to becoming an official Catholic. I came to terms with a combination of procrastination ("I'm going to do it. Just not right now") and a certain "I'm Catholic at heart" kind of thinking. There was plenty of ground to cover besides religion, after all. I needed to know all about Italian American culture, for one, or rather Hollywood's version of Italian American culture. I started watching *Goodfellas* and *The Godfather* on a regular basis, reading the memoirs of Sammy "the Bull" Gravano, and taking a deeper interest in visiting my family in New York as regularly as I could convince my parents. (All much more enjoyable endeavors than studying religion.) I also became obsessed with lowrider oldies like The Delfonics and The Chi-Lites. Combining my Italian identity with aspects of Mexican American culture shared just how deeply confused I was. My identity felt empty, and I believed I just needed to push further into something real, something authentic. How I saw it, I was raised in the absence of culture, unlike my Mexican friends who grew up speaking Spanish and eating Oaxacan food. I resented it deeply and imagined that if I had been born into a family rooted in their culture, I would be at peace. My father was fully onboard with me discovering my roots. My mother, on the other hand, was disturbed. She hated the violence in the mafia movies we watched and, because she never identified with her own "roots," resented her history being washed over by the sudden surge of Italianness. My father and I became a sort of gang, and without Italian blood, she couldn't join. We picked on her for what we perceived as her non-Italian ways – anything from her casseroles to her non-confrontational nature. To be Italian was good. To be a WASP was bad. It became common during fights for her to shout desperately at me, "You know you're Scottish too!"

I would soon feel that sting that my mother felt of being cast as second-rate because she wasn't Italian. By eighth grade, I had developed a core group of friends. We were a mix of brown-haired girls – Jessica, Assyrian American; Deveena, Indian American; Vanessa, half-Mexican, half-white American; and me. All but me were first-generation Americans (with the exception of Vanessa's father, who was white). As a kid, my longing for a whole identity was amplified by my closeness with these three first generationers, their parents' cooking and their fluency in the language. To make matters worse, they easily picked up on my desire to identify with my Italian side, and running jokes about me being "authentic" arose. But what damaged my fragile ethnic ego more was when they made fun of me for being white. I was always on time, and they were always late. "It's because she's white!" they'd laugh. It stung, and I tried my hardest to be late, to eliminate whatever behavior might put me in the category of white. But then it would be something else–how I couldn't roll my r's or how I cried during *Titanic*, which was "such a white person movie." It seemed I could never cross the halfway mark to a complete identity.

Eventually, I grew exhausted of my evasions of whiteness. By junior year, I decided it was time to give up. I was just a dark white girl. One night, Jessica and I were driving. With my mission of cultural identity over, I finally felt safe telling her about my envy of her, Deveena, and Vanessa, and their relationship to their non-American cultures. I didn't have to protect my persona of the deeply rooted Italian American any-more. She responded, "Justine, my aunts and uncles always criticize how I speak Assyrian poorly, how I can't really dance Assyrian, how I dress like a white girl. They tell me I'm white-washed." This opened up a long conversation that would mark a turning point for me and how I perceived identity. My friends felt pulled too but in different ways than I did. Their families criticized them for rejecting their non-American culture, and beyond that, they felt a need to be perceived as American. It went beyond a desire to fit in to a fear of being perceived as "other." In the summertime, Deveena refused to lay out with us by the pool because she didn't want to get any darker. I had always thought she was crazy. Doesn't she realize what she has? She's not white! She's so lucky! Jessica agonized over her thick, curly hair and obsessed over removing her body hair because she didn't want to look like a "fobster," a term derived from "fresh off the boat." Vanessa expressed how lucky she was that her father was white, so that on job applications her last name wasn't Velasquez. I was naïve to the real-world implications of being a person of color, to how my friends' fight against perceived brownness carried much harsher consequences when they failed.

As an adult, I still have occasional pangs over being white, but it comes from a new place. In a community of mostly white, liberal, straight, cisgender academics, we benefit daily from the white hetero privilege we rail against. It takes an effort to recognize your own privilege, obviously one of the privileges of being white – we don't have to think about it. But realizing that you belong to the group of oppressors, that your whole life is built on the outcomes of that oppression, can lend itself to romanticizing life on the other side. Looking at America today, what liberally minded person wants to be white? Yet who wants to live without built-in privilege? I'm a white person who can pass as non-white. But because of the way I look, and my true cultural background, I enjoy a sort of low-risk ethnic identity. Although I am often perceived as non-white – mistaken for Hispanic, Middle Eastern, or Indian, among others – I look white enough to have never dealt with any consequences of being a person of color. More often than not, my ambiguous ethnicity works to my advantage.

When I lived in West Los Angeles, which has a large population of Persian Americans, I was often perceived as Persian. The majority of people who asked me if I was Persian were Persian themselves. The same thing happened when I lived near Glendale, which has a large population of Armenian Americans. Again, those who showed the most interest were Armenian themselves. This rule has held true in most communities I've lived in, or even on singular occasions, like attending an Indian wedding. As a result, when confronted with questions of my ethnicity, it's usually with warmth, and I've rarely felt "othered" in these situations, even after I reveal that I'm half-Italian and half-Scottish and WASP (I made a conscious decision after high school to always answer that question precisely, out of respect to my mother and accuracy). The only time I got a glimpse of what it was like to be a person of color was when I was traveling in the first couple of years after 9/11. I was almost always "randomly" searched at the airport. But it was never more than a minor irritation. I wasn't Muslim, and if matters escalated, they would be cleared up easily. I'm just a white girl. There's no reason to suspect me. That experience would of course be much different if I were actually Muslim, or even Middle Eastern of a different faith.

About six years ago, when I was twenty-six, my parents decided to change their name back from Cozell to Cucuzzella. My great uncle was the first to change the name sometime in the 1950s because job opportunities were fewer for Italian Americans. We always found the decision humorous, because Cozell isn't exactly an American-sounding name, unlike my paternal grandmother's family name, which went from Pisciotta to Prescott. People always had trouble gauging our background from our last name, and rightfully so. My great uncle just made it up. My father's father followed suit and changed his family's name in 1959 when my father was in elementary school. My father had always resented the change and toyed with the idea of changing it back. One day my uncle, his brother, sent him an old letter he'd found that my uncle had written about how much my father cried when it first happened. This inspired my dad to make the change, and my mother didn't mind going through with it for him. My dad asked me if I wanted to do it with them – he really wanted me to and thought I would too. Fifteen-year-old me would have rejoiced at the opportunity. One more element that would distinguish me as ethnic, and a major one at that. My name would announce it. But when presented with the chance, I said no. I had no desire to become a Cucuzzella. I was born Cozell, and identify with the name. But more than that, I love the name. Its ambiguity is its lure. ▪

Katherine Fishburn

Crossing the Color Line

FOR ME, BEING WHITE IN AMERICA is a daily struggle to fight not just the injustice but, I have to confess, the temptations of the ubiquitous – sometimes subtle; sometimes jarringly open – racism that surrounds me. Although I devoted my entire academic career to fighting racism, I am weary of the talking heads that seem to find racism in everything. And if I am also weary of the endless journey this country has taken in trying to rid itself of the poisonous legacy of slavery and racism, I cannot imagine how weary black Americans are of the continuing insidious racism they experience daily. As I hear in the news of yet another young black man being brutally gunned down by the police, I remind myself that these are our children being slaughtered in the streets. Blacks may be the victims but this isn't a *black* problem, it is an American problem and a national disgrace – a problem we are *all* faced with: one we all need to come together to address and to end.

I was raised in a small town in Maryland during the 1940s and 1950s by parents who were outsiders by virtue of origin, education and religion. My parents had been born and raised in the Midwest. Both went to college; my father earned a PhD in physical chemistry and became a college professor. My mother was raised as a Congrega-tionalist, my father an atheist. As a young married couple, they moved into a closely-knit community that was largely Lutheran and Catho-lic. My grandparents were unabashedly racist, one of them calling her dog "Nig." My mother led the way in our home toward raising two daughters who would resist and despise racist behavior and thinking. To this day I am not entirely clear why she made this break with my grandparents' attitudes.

As a child I knew no black children or adults. One black family I knew of sent their children to the Catholic schools. My sister and I attended the public school, which was entirely white. I remember quite vividly watching the images on television in the mid-1950s as white adults verbally and physically assaulted young blacks whose parents had the courage to send their offspring into the battle of desegregating southern schools. When I asked my mother why these adults and other authority figures were behaving so hatefully, she pretty much indicated that my question had no answer. Closer to home, although we ourselves could seldom afford to go to the movies, I somehow knew that in Frederick, Maryland, the blacks had to sit in the balcony at the movie theater. I did not know, however, that blacks had to sit at the back of the city buses. Riding in a bus was a rare treat for me, and once when we boarded, I begged my mother to let me sit in the rear so I could look out the window. I wasn't making a statement or taking a stand against segregation; on the contrary, I was being indulged. Looking back at the event, I now realize that three hard-working black adults had to stand because my mother, my sister and I were sitting in their place.

From 1967 to 1969, I was an English teacher (for grades seven through nine) at Governor Thomas Johnson High School in Frederick. When I was hired, the school was new (only in its second year), and enrolled very few black children. The rest of the city's black children were stuck in the old school across town. Segregation still ruled. During my tenure there, Washington D.C. became Resurrection City. This was the era of, "Burn, baby, burn!" When angry protests and riots began to destroy black neighborhoods in cities across the country in places like Los Angeles, Newark, Detroit, Chicago, and D.C., I wondered what was driving such violence. Coincidentally I happened to attend a book fair in Baltimore to which several publishing houses had sent vendors to promote sales of newly reissued black literature (all written by men) and of sociological studies of the black experience (mostly written by white men). The sales representatives loaded my arms with free copies, in the hopes that I would adopt them in my classroom. I staggered out of the conference center barely able to carry all the paperbacks I had been given.

Back home in my apartment I began to read. And read. And read. Reading Richard Wright's *Native Son* and *Black Boy* changed my life. Wright was so angry, his characters so warped by the racism that had blighted their lives I could hardly believe that the events he and others described had happened in my America. I clearly needed to know more about institutional and cultural racism in this country. So I read on, becoming enlightened about the grim reality and repercussions of this shameful history that had been kept hidden from me by my otherwise splendid education.

When I was given the opportunity to teach a course in a subject of my choosing to eighth-graders, I didn't hesitate to announce I would be offering a course in African American literature and history. The administrators at Thomas Johnson were as supportive as I could have wished, especially the associate principal J. Arthur Mott. While I was away on business, the history department's members, however, lodged a protest that I was trampling on their turf; I found their timing significant (i.e., cowardly), inasmuch as they waited until I was gone to complain. When I returned, with Mr. Mott's encouragement I called their bluff: telling them that they were free to teach black history themselves; I would even provide the material and lesson plans. They demurred.

One of my colleagues was married to a man who worked for *The Washington Post*. He generously provided me with poster-sized black and white photographs of the riots in D.C. Near the end of the course, I turned (as best I could, given my limited resources) a large lecture room into a riot scene. I hung the dozens of posters, played a mixed tape of screaming, shouts and sirens, darkened the room and gave my students the following assignment: if you're black, I said, write an essay in the first person describing what "you" as one of the white people in the photographs are thinking; if you're white, I continued, do the same as a black person. The students asked me if they could use swear words in their essays. I considered their request and said they could use "hell" and "damn" but nothing else.

This may very well have been the best assignment I have ever devised in my thirty years of teaching. The essays were stunning in their emotional rawness and budding awareness of what life on the other side of the color line might be like. A few of the white students, however, simply could not bring themselves to "become" black for even a fifty-minute class period. When I graded the papers these students had written, I gave them a very low grade (perhaps I failed them; I don't remember) and wrote on their essays "you were supposed to be black." One white family took umbrage at this reminder, claiming that I had called their son a "nigger." Initially, I pointed out that I would never call anyone, black or white, a "nigger" nor had I, in fact, referred to their son as a black person. When they persisted in attacking me, Mr. Mott stood up for me as I calmly spelled out what the assignment had been, adding as I felt I must, that although I had not called their son black I personally would not be offended if someone called me black. Whether I mollified them, I don't know, but that was the end of their protest.

In my second year of teaching, a local college was having trouble placing a black student-teacher with a mentor. When the coordinator told me this, I volunteered to supervise him. He was Fred ("Mad Dog") Carter, a local basketball star who was subsequently drafted by the Baltimore Bullets in 1969, where he played until he was traded to the Philadelphia 76ers who acquired him for what turned out to be the team's disastrous 1971-1972 season. (Carter, after serving twelve years as an assistant NBA coach, was hired as the 76ers' head coach in the early 1990s and later went on to become a commentator for ESPN.) As soon as he was assigned to me, I handed him the materials I had prepared for my course in black literature and history, telling him to read everything because he was going to be teaching the next section of this class. When the black students met him, they were thrilled (as were the whites): a famous black basketball star was going to be their new teacher! I was on my way to making a difference.

But I failed to do the right thing many times. In college I declined to participate in a sit-in at a diner near campus. I don't know why I refused to stand up and actually assist the budding civil rights movement. At least when Martin Luther King Jr., was assassinated on April 4, 1968, I literally stood up during a school assembly and protested the school's decision not to cancel classes for a day in his honor. I remember so vividly hearing the news that morning as I was getting ready to leave the house for work. It left a hole in my stomach. Yet when one of my impoverished young black students, Charles, was killed in a horrific house fire I didn't attend his funeral, although I'm sure it would have meant a lot to his surviving family members to have his teacher show her respects. By not attending, I disappointed the other black students who had come to trust me. One of those students I remember very well: Randi Hill, a smart pretty girl who wrote on the school picture she gave me: "To a nice and wonderful teacher." It broke her heart when I left for graduate school. Yet I had betrayed her and her black friends too. As I recall, there were six of us teaching English to the middle school students. When our department chair asked four of us to teach a different genre for one grading period, I chose poetry. The rule was, however, that we could not tell the students which genre we would be offering. The black students who had gravitated to me concluded that I probably would be teaching drama so they signed up for that course. Beforehand, they had begged me to tell them which one I would teach. But, always obedient, I was paralyzed by the dictum from above. They were crushed when they ended up with an inexperienced snotty young woman who was oblivious (or indifferent) to their need for attention and encouragement. I wouldn't learn to "misbehave" until I got to graduate school.

Braced by my success in teaching African American literature and my growing conviction that it was in this field alone that I could actually change the lives of my students, when I decided after two years as a secondary school teacher that I wanted to earn my PhD, I knew on the first day I arrived on campus that my dissertation was going to focus on the writings of Richard Wright. My major professor readily agreed to my plan. Yet I took no courses in black literature: there were none. I took no comprehensive exam in black literature: there was none. But, as has been my lifelong practice, I went to the library and I read. And read. And read.

Always a thorough researcher, I tried to read every single thing that had ever been written by and about Richard Wright, keeping the inter-library loan librarians busy ordering materials for me to borrow. For my language examination, I translated a book that had been written about Wright in French (Wright moved to France when he could no longer tolerate the indignities and oppression of his native country). Because Wright had known and read the French existentialists, I read Sartre and Camus, and everyone else who had influenced his thinking. One of the faculty, in learning of my thoroughness, told me it was a waste of time. I was shocked at his cavalier dismissal of the necessity of basic research. (I shall let him remain nameless, but how I scorned his laziness and privileged shallowness; to no one's surprise, he would move on to become a career administrator.) This would not be the first time my dedication to research would be mocked.

I defended my dissertation and published the manuscript as a book. Although it got me a job in the tenure track (as did the fact that I was a woman, no small irony as I would myself eventually become completely disenchanted with affirmative action hiring practices), it was received with considerable skepticism by the black male scholars who reviewed it. I had the distinct impression that I was now trampling on their turf. But I persevered, writing articles and books on African American (and later, African) literature. Additionally, I taught both undergraduate and graduate courses on the subject. Again to mixed reviews. One year, when I was responsible for scheduling graduate seminars in American literature, I scheduled five courses, two of which were in African American literature. Immediately one of my senior colleagues dashed off a note, complaining that I had only scheduled three courses in American literature. When I let him off the hook by writing that surely he had "overlooked" the two African American literature courses I would be teaching, he replied that, of course, he had not seen them. He was a self-professed "elite" educator and a drunk (now deceased), and I knew damned well his first note had revealed what he really felt. Others were less open about their scorn for the focus of my scholarship; none thought enough of it to reward my scholarly accomplishments with decent raises. When central administration sent out to the individual departments a form requiring each unit to account for its contributions to affirmative action, however, the chair turned to me. What I wrote and taught were very nearly the only contributions of my department for years.

Some black students were disappointed to sign up for my class and see a white woman walk in the first day. Some of them gave me credit for trying but in the end, felt I was unable to convey the full meaning and emotional impact of the literature we were studying. Others (black and white both) were delighted to be introduced to the field. Occasionally, I startled black students with my fairly intimate knowledge of black culture or slang (this was long before rap, which I find obscene and misogynistic especially in its attitudes toward black women). I remember, for example, using the term "high yellow" to blank stares. When I explained its meaning, they couldn't believe I knew something that they didn't. I chided them by remarking that I got paid to know things they didn't. During my career I had only a handful of doctoral students, but among them I mentored and served as the major professor for two black women who earned PhD's: the first in American studies, the other in African literature. Both women are successful professionals in their fields, the first a well-known artist in the D.C. area, the other a professor at Louisiana State University, I am very proud of them.

Near the end of my career I was given the opportunity to mentor at a distance a black man who was incarcerated in a maximum security prison in Georgia. He had asked one of my colleagues from a different department if she knew a poet he could correspond with. I agreed to write him. There is no doubt in my mind that this man taught me more than I could ever hope to teach him. He himself was an artist; his medium, colored pencils on paper. His drawings were some of the most powerful art I have ever encountered, encouraging me to resume my own interest in drawing and painting. He introduced me to the work of Jean-Michel Basquiat and the writings of Susan Sontag. I sent him limited amounts (as per prison regulations) of food, clothes, books and a subscription to *The New York Times.* He sent me contraband copies of prison forms that I transformed into poetry for him and his friends, who thought initially that I must be incarcerated myself because of the intimate knowledge of their lives my poems expressed. I learned as never before the utter inhumanity (and inanity) of our prison systems. During spring break that year, I flew to Georgia to meet him. Jeremy Bentham's concept of the panopticon and Michel Foucault's adaptation of it for his famous socio-philosophical study, *Discipline and Punish,* had never been more real to me. Nor have they been since.

Thus summarizes the first, largely successful, attempt on my part to educate both black and white students about the cultural contributions of African Americans to this country – and to conquer the demon of racism that surrounded me. But during the late 1970s and early 1980s, in order to meet its affirmative action goals, the provost's office (quite cynically, I felt) began hiring unqualified individuals to fill various administrative posts. These administrators became a joke among the faculty. Therein lies one of the unintended consequences of affirmative action: the growing suspicion among whites that black hires just didn't make the grade or have the necessary qualifications. How ironic that before affirmative action, we could expect that our black colleagues had superior qualifications in order to cross the color bar that would otherwise have kept them out.

Another unforeseen consequence was that instead of being evaluated on their individual merits, these hires were judged on the racial group they fell into. A third – more dire – consequence was the fate of so many ill-prepared black students who were just thrown into university life, and didn't have a chance because of the poor secondary education they had had, the disrupted home life they had experienced and the difficulty they encountered in trying to adjust to a competitive academic environment. I did what I could to help them, but I wasn't always successful – a failure that wasn't just personal but institutional. These young people were only statistics to the central administration. But in and out of the classroom, I felt I was making a solid contribution to the field and was, as I intended, changing the lives of my students for the better – evidence of the latter coming in positive evaluations at the end of the semester and, later, in grateful letters from former students.

A fourth consequence of affirmative action, additionally, is the fact that poor, underprivileged whites have not been included in this well-meaning outreach, while prosperous, privileged black children who did not need affirmative action – only equal opportunity – benefited from skewed admission policies. Here, I also think of an eighth-grader I taught: Lester Lookingbill, an impoverished neglected white child with what I now realize was a crippling undiagnosed learning disorder that I suspect was severe dyslexia. Even though he struggled to spell even the most simple words, such as "the," he was a remarkable poet. At the end of the course, in the literary pamphlet I distributed of the students' writing, Lester had three poems – he was that good. Lester was no more or less dismissed than the black children were by the other teachers in my middle school. Poverty and neglect (in addition to racism) doomed them to failure. Once I began teaching at the university level, I felt I had to do something to help students like them.

But after years of being ignored and often scorned by my colleagues for teaching and specializing in a field they only begrudgingly acknowledged as worthy of study, I began to grow bitter, especially as it was becoming increasing difficult for me to publish my deeply interdisciplinary scholarship, which was informed by my research in philosophy and the social sciences. From the very beginning, my work had been a precursor to cultural studies, an appreciation of which had not yet arrived in my department. When I asked and sought to answer the question of exactly how Western readers could succeed in understanding novels written by African writers, hindered as we were by our cultural and historical differences, one of my colleagues who had developed a cottage industry based on interpreting these very same novels, told me that I "couldn't write that book." I did anyway. But my problems were not limited to my immediate colleagues. In regards to my scholarship and writing, all too many black reviewers of my manuscripts claimed in their reports that I was (and I do quote) "part of the problem" because I had dared to use the Western philosophical tradition (in tandem with that of Africa) to formulate my questions and to help reveal the meaning and importance of black literature – as though Western culture had not marked this literature (for better or worse). It seemed particularly obtuse, narrow-minded and anti-intellectual, furthermore, to insist that there were no ideas or questions I could draw upon in my interpretations that did not originate in Africa. During this era I was, however, encouraged by none other than the influential and groundbreaking professors of black studies Dr. Nellie Y. McKay (University of Wisconsin) and Dr. Henry Louis Gates Jr. (W. E. B. Du Bois Professor of Humanities at

Harvard University). But still I felt I had been relegated to an academic ghetto: figuratively speaking I was too "black" for my department and too "white" for those functioning as gatekeepers to publishing success in the field of African and African American studies. Incidentally, for all the hostility my ideas generated, I did publish these books and most (but not all) of the essays I had written on African American literature. The rejected work hangs in my filing cabinet.

I was also too white, apparently, for my black colleagues. When one of them won a prestigious award from the University I threw her a catered party in my home, inviting dozens of her friends. But I was never invited to set foot in her house, nor did I ever learn where she lived. Moreover, when she invited Professor Gates to campus she failed to invite me to a dinner after one of his talks. During the question and answer period following this talk, I publicly defended the question a white student had asked him, which he had virtually laughed off. Gates was impressed by my intervention and said he looked forward to having dinner with me. When I told him I had not been invited, he himself issued an invitation overriding the decision of my own colleague. We had a splendid and productive conversation about the problems I was having convincing my department to take black studies seriously. At the same time, rather ironically, I felt, I was welcomed by the inter-departmental, interdisciplinary African Studies group on campus, the members of which invited me to join them on the basis of my teaching and research on South African and Nigerian literature.

During my tenure, the department recruited and hired a small number of African American faculty members, at least once offering a woman more money at an entry-level position than I was earning as an associate professor. Years later, on a one-time basis I received a compensatory raise, part of an effort of the elected advisory committee to the chair to correct a pattern of salary inequities.

Thus was born a bitter internal fight between the African American faculty members (joined by their white sympathizers) and the rest of the department. The blacks accused the whites of being jealous and of wanting to deny them the fruits of their success. Taking advantage of a weak and passive chair and with the insistence of the department's committee on diversity (one mandated by central administration), they demanded the entire department to sign a document by which we all would acknowledge our deep-seated, long-standing racism. I protested, arguing that the noble intentions of affirmative action had soured faculty relations and corrupted the system that determined faculty compensation; as I made these remarks, I was not unmindful of the fact that I, too, had been the beneficiary of affirmative action (for women). But obviously, not all affirmative action hires were equal – some were more equal than others. Referencing Richard Wright's "I Tried to Be a Communist," I prefaced my statement by stating that "I Tried to Be a Liberal." My response surprised everyone, most especially my black colleagues. When I asked to have my argument quoted in its entirety in the minutes of the meeting to ensure that my argument was clearly laid out, the dean through the chair (who tracked me down in Florida on spring break) put pressure on me to allow them to paraphrase what I had said to avoid making it look like my single, one-person statement spoke for the entire department – as though I had ever had any power at all to get the department to do my bidding.

So here I am, professor emeritus of English, sitting at my computer in another small city in Maryland, surrounded by many good people, some not so good – some of these so virulently racist they make me sick to my stomach. A neighbor a few doors down, who, as his massive vehicle proudly proclaims, served as a Marine in Iraq – decided to hang a Confederate flag in front of his house just days after the church massacre in Charleston, South Carolina. And today, I see that he has hung a Halloween skeleton from a tree. Am I not to see this as a lynching? My neighbors do. The dark irony haunts me. I want to say to this man and his wife, "You were proud to serve your country to save us from terrorists, yet you hang the flag of those who nearly destroyed the very country you fight for now. Does this make any sense?" And yet I say nothing. What's the point? I would change neither his mind nor his behavior. Plus he rather frightens me (an old woman) as he does many of my neighbors. Clearly, he doesn't want to "see" that the stars and bars are symbolic of racial prejudice and hatred. Either that or, more disturbingly, he is proud of his racism. The faux lynching makes me think the latter.

Moreover, I am weary of political correctness. (But don't for one minute put me in the camp of Donald Trump and Dr. Ben Carson. I live on facts not scare tactics and sloppy scientific claims such as Carson's inexplicable position on vaccines.) We are too quick to silence – or shout over – those with whom we disagree. Could I today, as I did in the 1960s, actually teach a book written by Dick Gregory that he provocatively entitled *Nigger: An Autobiography?* What about Harriet E. Wilson's nineteenth-century autobiographical novel *Our Nig: Sketches of the Life of a Free Black?*

That the language police have decreed we can't even use the word "nigger" to discuss the racism it conveys dispirits me. Gays have commandeered queer both informally and academically as is evident in the queer studies programs offered at progressive colleges and universities. By insisting that "nigger" cannot be spoken, the language police give those who would use the term more power to hurt and to harm the very people whom they claim to protect. They do nothing to improve the behavior or attitudes of those who employ it to convey the revulsion they hold toward our fellow citizens of African (and slavery's) descent. Clearly, as recent events keep reminding us, black males need to be protected from the police, but do black people really need to be protected from a word? Do they really think they can, in an Orwellian sense, actually prevent its use?

Those who would erase the word from the English language are (1) fighting a losing battle; in part because (2) their efforts increase the likelihood of it being used by racists who cannot resist the power of the word to hurt those it is used to describe or address. You can be sure the ex-Marine uses the term. It is far better to shrug it off and not give racists the satisfaction of seeing us becoming outraged by its use. And now in the popular press I hear outcries when whites use the (Hindi/ Sanskrit derived) word thug because it is an example of black male racial stereotyping. Or, whites are accused of co-opting this so-called black term for commercial reasons in a version of "cultural blackface," as have been a man and woman in Los Angeles who dared to name their vegan restaurant Thug Kitchen. When they were "outed" as white, all hell broke loose online and in the press.

All my life I have been a student of language and literature. Language drops and adds words; usage changes. I know from experience the fallacy in "sticks and stones can break my bones, but words can never hurt me." But let's stop arming the enemy.

Misrepresenting the origins of words is another issue altogether. I admit to cringing when I heard a black graduate student, who was studying with a prominent scholar of black English, repeat the linguistic myth that the word picnic is etymologically based on the racially derogatory word "pickaninny" (whether he learned this from his major professor I cannot say). This incorrect derivation is supposed to have originated in white usage based on the stereotype that all black people love to eat watermelons as they eat together informally by a stream or the edge of the woods. In reality, *picnic* (according to the Oxford English Dictionary, first used in English in 1748) comes from the French *pique-nique*. Why make up a slight when there have been so many real ones? Such a cavalier dismissal of truth undermines even the most impassioned pleas for racial justice and comity.

I am tired to death of the empty words diversity and empowerment (even more so because they are being co-opted by corporate interests). I am tired of slogans that remind whites to check your privilege and of those agitators who would cosset our feeble undergraduates by insisting (with more success than I like to acknowledge) that faculty must provide trigger warnings. Virtually everything I ever taught would require a trigger warning today, as I focused on the dangerous world we live in – including poverty, pain, racism, sexism, rape, beatings, and lynchings (there really is no end to this list). (Which brings me to the very real question: will this candid essay about my struggles to cross the color line ever see the light of day?) Have we raised a generation of cowardly brain-dead Americans who fear being exposed to new ideas? To difficult problems? Who cannot confront what frightens them but must run from it back to mommy and daddy? Does everybody on campus require a safe house? Such leveling of dangers – real, imagined, invented, experienced, anticipated – dismisses the real danger faced by abused women. And how is this generation ever going to survive the very real threat of terrorism now stalking the world? But I certainly don't like the company I seem to affiliate myself with when I express these opinions because I am equally tired of "birthers" and claims that our president is a Muslim. There is no doubt in my mind that much of the criticism directed at President Obama is driven by racism and possible resentment that a black man could achieve such power. I vividly remember *The Onion's* satirical headline after Obama's election: "Black Man Given Nation's Worst Job." Those on the right quickly saw to it that it would become the nation's worst job, with senate minority leader Mitch McConnell bluntly announcing in 2009 that: "The single most important thing we want to achieve is for President Obama to be a one-term president." Which, of course, leads to the question: having failed at that just what did the Republicans achieve?

There are many words, outside the realm of race relations, that I am tired of. Among those are military and governmental euphemisms such as the enemy has been *neutralized*, when the enemy (or the suspect) has been *killed*. Or the dehumanizing phrase *collateral damage* instead of *civilian deaths*. The right-wing's employment of scare tactics when its politicians refer to socialism, entitlements, welfare (leaving unmentioned as they do corporate welfare), and class warfare, when the disparity between the very wealthy 1 percent and the rest of us is so *staggeringly* huge we literally cannot imagine it. I am, however, not tired of the words justice, liberty, equality; or the phrases voting rights, good schools, integrated neighborhoods and living wage. I am tired of those who want to keep government out of our lives (the very government that, after all, builds and maintains our now underfunded and rotting infrastructure, and trains our underpaid military), but then turn around and support regulations to limit a woman's right and access to an abortion or gays' rights to be folded into the fabric of all society without fuss or complaint. I also continue to be horrified that, in a misguided effort to avoid condemning a suspect before trial, the media refer not to the *alleged perpetrator* but the alleged victim of a rape. For what other crimes do we *allege* a crime has been committed? Do we hear the *alleged corpse?* The *alleged robbed?*

Bah! I've lived too long some will think, but I have witnessed extraordinary change and real progress in racial relations in this country. I only wish that today's talking heads would show more respect for what their predecessors accomplished and stop alienating someone like me who has tried her damnedest not to fall into the shameful, inexcusable tar pit of racism.

I'm a scholar and an intellectual. If you want to make an argument stick, you better get your facts straight. Are large segments of society still racist? Absolutely. Are too many young black men imprisoned? Shamefully and tragically, yes. But what plagues this country is less black and white than the professional agitators would have us believe (I'm thinking in particular of that charlatan the Rev. Al Sharpton, who, to my horror, seems to have the ear of our president). Perhaps Ta-Nehisi Coates, a national correspondent for *The Atlantic,* can use his well deserved status as one of this year's MacArthur Fellows to improve the tenor of the conversation and help develop workable programs for change. If we're going to talk, let's talk about decent available housing, improving underfunded schools, reducing income inequality and ending widespread unemployment. Are police forces racist? Some are (too many); some aren't (not enough). But not all cops are bad; and not all blacks are innocent. Nor are the best-intentioned whites. In this country of haves and have-nots that we have created and successfully defended since its inception over 200 years ago, no one except the very young is innocent. But not all whites are guilty of racism just as not all blacks are victims. Being a victim, moreover, gives no one a monopoly on the truth. We can't solve our complex problems with slogans. Creating a climate where informed civil discourse is the norm is a prerequisite to overcoming that which separates us, that which encourages us to stereotype and vilify others. We need honest, thoughtful, fact-driven conversation, not sound bites and shouting matches. And, yes—all lives matter. We're in this together, folks. ▪

Ariane White

Beauty in Struggle

Being white means never having to think about it.

– James Baldwin

MY EXPERIENCE OF BEING WHITE in the United States of America is profoundly informed by James Baldwin's quote, which highlights how cultivating an awareness of injustice is a choice for those who occupy privileged positions and whose sense of the world is often bound up in not seeing or understanding the unearned benefits received over the course of a lifetime. For myself, as a white person seeking to challenge the systems behind the many ways in which privileges have been bestowed upon me, being white has become an ongoing process of unlearning all that I was socialized to accept as true, of learning to see with different eyes and to question my own perspective, as well as the origins of the many opportunities and comforts in my life that I have been taught to take for granted.

Although I recognize that being white is not the same for every white person – each individual's perspective is shaped by the intersections of many aspects of identity, along with our unique combination of life experiences – I also recognize the ways in which the common thread of whiteness throughout my life has conspired to privilege my needs and desires much more consistently than those of people of color in my life. That said, my experience of whiteness is very much informed by having been raised comfortably middle-class – with looming debts that provided access to opportunities generally reserved for social elites – and by my experiences being gendered female in a world that privileges and protects the well-being of men. Given the complexities of identity and the tendency for people to focus on the ways we have been excluded from opportunities or victimized by power structures, it has been a journey for me to begin to acknowledge the ways in which my privilege as a white person has so clearly impacted the trajectory of my life.

My first real sense that whiteness was something I needed to pay attention to came in middle school, when a classmate of mine – a black girl in the same grade as me – saw my name in the school paper for some reason. Perhaps it was misspelled or maybe she saw my name and equated its pronunciation with the word "Aryan," and she confronted me in the hallway: "Your name is Aryan White! Aryan White! Are your parents white supremacists or something?" As the tone of her voice escalated – accusatory, enraged – it became clear that she was edging this encounter toward a physical conflict. I began explaining, as quickly as I could: "It's Ar-i-ane, it's a French name. My parents are Jewish. There's no way they are white supremacists!" And somehow, the sincerity of my tone or some combination of other factors allowed her to back down from the impending conflict. This moment was my first direct encounter with a person of color's anger toward this system of white supremacy. At that age, I had only the vaguest understanding of such things, mostly informed by my family's history of having escaped from Europe before the Holocaust, and yet knowing that other branches of the family – unknown distant cousins or family friends – were erased by that particular manifestation of white supremacist thinking and action.

Carrying this name and the complex legacy of Eastern European Jewish history in the United States made me feel incredibly uncomfortable and confused: "I'm not a bad person. My family has faced injustices, *too*," I would say to myself. And yet I carry this name and this racial designation – white. No matter that our family name was changed from an unpronounceable (in English) Polish name when my grandfather came to this country. No matter that anti-Semitism continues to be a very real phenomenon. Entering this country from Eastern Europe allowed my family to become white, both in name and our experience. My grandfather was able to become a business owner and his children were able to attend college and become professionals. Virtually all barriers to access were eliminated for them as they claimed their place within this system, as part of middle-class, mainstream, white American society. Some cousins even belong to country clubs that a few generations ago were closed to Jewish people! This is the legacy I have inherited – one of close ties to the urban hubs in the United States that incubated the dreams of people who could assimilate into whiteness – dropping accents, religious and cultural norms, even names – in order to reach for all that this country promises to (some of) those who arrive.

And yet, it wasn't until college that I began to fully see around the edges of this system to understand the depth of my middle school classmate's anger or to investigate the low-grade discomfort I felt as I carried this evolving self-consciousness about my name and the history contained within it. My family sacrificed a lot to make sure that I had access to the best possible college education, imploring me to not allow money to be the basis of my decision about where to attend school. And so, after thirteen years of attending only public schools in a west coast, suburban area, I found myself cocooned inside a bubble of privilege and entitlement of a variety I had never encountered before: a small, private, liberal arts college in New England. Upon arriving at this campus, all my worldly possessions trailing behind me, or on their way in a few UPS shipping boxes, I encountered on a visceral level what it meant to be privileged. And it became clear to me that it was no accident that the vast majority of my classmates were white. Their realities included having been acculturated into whiteness and privilege at the best boarding schools in the country. Their presence on this campus was one they carried as if it were a divinely granted right; they felt at home on campus to the extent that there was not one proverbial table they wouldn't kick their feet up onto, and no mess so big that their parents wouldn't pay to have cleaned up, no questions asked. Of course, this depiction of my classmates is somewhat hyperbolic and overgeneralized. I also met some amazingly thoughtful, compassionate, intelligent people who make the world a better place on a daily basis. Yet those are the people who already had some awareness of their own advantages and felt a genuine sense of gratitude for the opportunities afforded to them, even if most of us had yet to develop a deeper systemic analysis about the factors that contributed to them. The part that troubled me most was witnessing for the first time the monolithic unconsciousness of white supremacist culture and thinking–the culture that acts as if the world is ours for the taking and blames individuals, not systems, for any barriers to access to idyllic learning environments such as the one we occupied–and feeling profoundly unsettled by finding myself to some extent embraced and included in such an environment.

As much as my middle school classmate's anger propelled me to confront the discomfort of being inextricably linked to white supremacy (even though my family's history is not one of unquestioned privilege throughout generations), I found myself grappling with a similar ambivalence in this college environment. I felt very separate from and outside of this mainstream experience of unchecked privilege and yet I had been granted access to this space, as well. There was no doubt that, on some level, I "belonged" in this environment, that my credentials were considered valid and I could participate in this shared experience–even if I didn't have a brand new Hummer to park on the lawn, unfazed by the consequences of daily parking tickets; nor could I avoid the dining hall food by eating at fancy restaurants in town whenever I wanted. At the same time, I still benefited incalculably from the privilege of learning with some of the best scholars in my field, people who would mentor me through every academic challenge, and continue to support me in life to this day. I benefited from access to internships, travel opportunities, and free lectures offered by some of the most inspiring minds of our time. And I had this school's name to add to my other names that opened doors and forged connections like nothing else could.

This truth became undeniable when my studies took me to China and even there, people had heard of the reputation of the school I attended as being one of the strongest in foreign language instruction in the U.S., if not the world. As a white person learning Chinese for just a few years, I had more jobs open to me than most Chinese people in that era who had desperately been learning English all of their lives, hoping for a glimpse of some of the goodies I did not even question. Such was the white supremacist system operating within the structures of global capitalism. At the same time, I did not have the clarity to name it as such. I simply found myself feeling quite often that same unsettling ambivalence, a questioning discomfort about what I sensed happening around me, constantly wondering what my place was in all of it. My discomfort deepened as I noticed that the behavior of some of my peers did not improve when they were no longer ensconced within the bubble of our idyllic campus. Instead, they inflicted their bad behavior – irresponsible drinking, condescending attitudes, cultural supremacy – everywhere we went, with a whole new country full of people to clean up the messes they left behind. It was embarrassing. Thus, my experience of developing my consciousness as a white person was characterized in this era by nearly constant embarrassment by my peers' behavior while, at the same time, beginning to acknowledge that my presence in these shared spaces with them was made possible by some of the same systemic forces that shaped their behavior. Despite the subconscious awareness of the need to claim partial responsibility for my own privilege and to begin to call out what I found to be so unacceptable, at the time, I mostly only knew how to distance myself from those whose actions continually made me feel that particular brand of shame that was nearly intolerable.

I am incredibly grateful to have had the chance to travel to China as I did, even as I am aware that it was, in and of itself, a function of white privilege that afforded me this opportunity. I learned so much about what it means to be white and how the white supremacist system operates on a global scale by witnessing myself and other white people act out our privilege in China. I also learned from witnessing the internalized white supremacy I encountered among the Chinese people, as well as through conversations with Chinese people about the versions of cultural supremacy that exist among distinct ethnic and linguistic groups in China. As an outsider to this dynamic, I could more clearly detect the ways in which certain ethnic and linguistic groups were systemically marginalized and could see how the experience of privilege prevented the dominant group from having a structural analysis of those dynamics. Finally, upon returning to the U.S., it became blatantly clear how these same dynamics of cultural supremacy and the normativity of whiteness function to preserve a particular social order in the United States.

Nowhere were these dynamics more glaringly obvious to me than when I began my teaching career at a large public high school in the Los Angeles area – the one that I had graduated from. I had benefited, as a white student, from a magnet program that had been funded in the 1970s as a half-hearted attempt to equalize educational opportunities for students of diverse backgrounds. In reality, these programs kept students just as segregated as they had been, tracked into different levels of classes with incredible disparities in terms of the quality and type of educational experiences they offered. My track as a student had been one that set me to a path of success that granted me access to an elite college experience. As a student, I only focused on my own experience, thinking that I earned these opportunities by virtue of my hard work; I could not see the systemic barriers that many of my peers faced. I did not go so far as to judge my less conventionally successful peers outright; I simply ignored them. This form of indifference was, in and of itself, a form of complicity and collusion with the existing system. As a young, white person, I played my part in preserving the status quo by focusing solely on my own success, as if my achievements were somehow indicators of what was possible for all other people as well.

As a teacher, however, I came into the profession wanting the very best for all of my students, and was horrified when I began to understand the intricacies of the educational system with all its deeply entrenched inequities. Teaching both within the magnet program I had come through as a student and in classes open to the broader school population, I witnessed how corresponding attitudes of entitlement and constraint were bred into students in these different programs. In the magnet program, the predominantly white and Asian students were repeatedly told in both subtle and overt ways that they were successful and college-bound. They were treated as if they were special by teachers as well as administrators, and were trained to believe that their views and opinions mattered, that they deserved to be treated with respect. Their teachers knew them well and followed up on them, supporting them in producing quality work. At the same time, students in the regular school received little guidance at all. There was one counselor for every 1,000 students, so most students did not even know who the counselor was. Classes were much larger and teachers had fuller teaching schedules. There was also little collaboration between teachers, so there was little connection between the various subjects, furthering the sense among students that school was comprised of arbitrary and disconnected subjects determined by the whims of each individual teacher and irrelevant to their lives beyond the classroom. Students in this school were lucky if their teachers knew their names and lucky, too, if their teachers showed up to class most days of the week. Such was the environment I entered into as a new teacher.

Compounding the complexities of my new position, in my non-magnet classes, I was often the only white person in the room. Taking on the role of teacher was the first time in my life that I had so much responsibility and authority over other people in a professional environment. It was unnerving to all of a sudden have so much institutional authority over my students and to see how they saw me—as another white woman they had to deal with who didn't know anything about them or their lives. In these early moments of my teaching career, I had to confront the many assumptions I had subconsciously made about what it takes to be a good student and the tremendous disconnect between my idealistic notions of learning and what my students' lives were like. I had to humble myself to realize that I truly didn't know very much about my students or their families and to put myself back in the mindset of a learner in order to begin to try to meet their needs in the classroom. This journey led me to AWARE-LA[1], where I encountered other white people, many of whom also worked in educational settings and with communities of color, who were similarly grappling with how to show up effectively in these spaces and seeking to learn how to interrupt the prevailing narratives that perpetuate white supremacy. It was in this space that I developed the capacity to reflect on my individual experiences and to begin to place them within a more systemic analysis of dynamics connected to race. My time in AWARE-LA meetings helped give me the courage to be transparent with my students about what I was beginning to understand as institutional racism and to be able to reflect with them

---

1   AWARE-LA (The Alliance of White Anti-Racists Everywhere, Los Angeles) is an all-volunteer alliance of white anti-racist people organizing to challenge racism and work for racial justice in transformative alliance with people of color.

on my role as a teacher and as a white person within this system. Once they saw that I was willing to engage in these conversations, my classes began to come alive and students began to step into the challenge of bravely engaging in dialogue about complicated and controversial issues. My students and I learned together what it takes to create a space where everyone can be supported to speak up, and is challenged to thoughtfully reflect. In order for this to happen, I had to be willing to model this and engage with them, using myself as an example. Through this process, they too became more adept at systemic analysis and were better able to find the capacity to critically reflect on their experiences beyond the particularities of their own struggles and to be able to more effectively speak out against the systems that stifle their rights to be fully themselves and to thrive in their personal and professional lives.

Thus, for me, being white in the U.S. at this critical juncture in human history mandates that I face the uncomfortable tension that characterizes my position within this system. I need to find ways to speak up about the injustices that I see, even if it means giving up some of my own personal security, some of the short-term benefits that unconsciously embrace a privileged existence. With my eyes opened as they have been by these experiences and many more, this choice becomes an imperative: By leveraging my privilege to dismantle unjust systems, there is a chance that I can reclaim my full humanity and cultivate equitable, humane relationships with white people and people of color. Together, there is a chance to implement just and sustainable systems that honor each individual's gifts and that function harmoniously within the natural environment. To shy away from my role in this—for myself as a white person to fail to see how working for racial justice benefits everyone, myself included—would be to condemn humanity to a short tenure on this planet and to ensure that our final years are characterized by ever-increasing violence and fragmentation. Since I refuse to succumb to the negativity of this bleak image, I am committed to being vigilant, that whenever I am seduced to close my eyes and to retreat into the comforts afforded by privilege, I must remember to blink and open my eyes again. Through this continual effort, and through seeing the beauty inherent within this struggle, I aim to do all that I can to bring into existence a healthier world for all of us. ■

Shireen Day

Unexpectedly White and Privileged

RECENTLY MET A FRIEND AT A LUXURY HOTEL in Boulder, Colorado. We needed the bellman. I glanced into the dimly lit lobby and saw a young black man wearing a white shirt and navy slacks. *There's the bellman*, I thought. But as he walked toward us, I realized he was just another hotel guest (and much better dressed than me).

My inner critic immediately asked, *What's the matter with you? How could you think this man is the hired help?*

I wondered – if I had met this young man outside on a trail, would I have seen him as a tourist? Or if he had been wearing running clothes, would I have imagined him to be a visiting athlete? Or perhaps if I had seen him in a bar, would I have leapt to the idea that he was a musician from some other part of the country?

As these stereotypes of African Americans flashed through my mind, I realized that all of my thinking centered on one idea – that a young black man couldn't be a resident of Boulder. My thirty years of living in this overwhelmingly white city has allowed certain reductive images to take root in my psyche.

Boulder is a wealthy, liberal, extremely well-educated community. We worry about our carbon footprint. We do yoga. We meditate. Age, our athletic endeavors, our focus on healthy eating, and the high cost of housing are factors that define and perhaps divide us. We believe in social justice. Yet, I never discussed race with my white friends and neighbors until I started writing this essay.

In this homogeneous community, race isn't a defining issue. In some ways it's a hypothetical construct shaped by politically correct thinking and limited by a lack of real experiences. It's common to confuse any discussion of race with racism and to think that racist behavior happens somewhere else.

I always assumed that several powerful experiences in my childhood and as an adult had inoculated me from being able to internalize implicitly racist stereotypes, but my reaction in the hotel shows me otherwise. And it's truly distressing to admit that the invisible tentacles of racism have become part of my inner stream of thoughts. I'm now forced to ask myself, *How did I become part of the system of white privilege when my childhood trained me to think of myself, a white girl, as "other"?*

Looking Back

IN 1968, NOT LONG AFTER Martin Luther King Jr. was assassinated, I moved from a wealthy white neighborhood in Short Hills, New Jersey to the small island of St. Thomas in the United States Virgin Islands. I was suddenly transformed from a privileged white child surrounded by people who looked more or less like me into a nameless eight-year-old whom my new schoolmates called "White Cheese." This moniker meant outsider or tourist.

For the first time in my life, I was acutely aware of my white skin and I didn't like it. Within a year I learned to speak the local Calypso dialect. My skin bronzed to a shade that, combined with my dark eyes and hair, allowed me to pass for Puerto Rican. While this moved me up a notch on the racial hierarchy, I found even more acceptance when I joined my classmates in disparaging new white kids or teachers. In my new home, white meant less than, vulnerable, other. "White Cheese" was something that could be eaten. I didn't want to be those things, and yet, ultimately, I couldn't hide that I was both white and a girl.

In the late 1960s, St. Thomas was transitioning away from a more traditional society in which the local fishing boats brought the night's catch into the harbor each day and vendors sold local produce in the market, to a tourist-based economy. In those days, the racial divide expressed itself in a very distinct manner. White adults ran the tourist businesses and bars. They had sailboats, powerboats, and money to take airplanes to a different places, but they were not as respectable as the black elders in our tiny community. They were definitely not part of the island's social and political structure. They didn't go to church.

It was a time of upheaval in my own life, and many of my best experiences with adults happened with black authority figures that touched my life. Judge Gordon kindly rescued me from a tension filled courtroom during my parents' high conflict day in divorce court. In my Anglican church school, Father Clark made daily trips to the chapel so much more interesting than our white priest. Mrs. Brady and Mrs. Jarvis were the two teachers who demanded we all work hard and stand tall. They were tough and we knew it. And Dr. Heath, my family physician, could give an injection that didn't hurt very much.

I remember the first time I saw a white police officer. I was ten years old. He was sitting across from me at a soda fountain. I stared at him so intensely that he asked me what was wrong with me. Until that moment, it hadn't occurred to me that whites could join the police force—a force whose behavior toward whites was known to range from nonchalant to aggressive.

My internal stereotypes regarding race were very different from those on the mainland. When I first heard the slogans "Black Power" and "Black is Beautiful," they seemed to be shouting the obvious. I had grown up with the idea that everything about being white was less desirable, and in my initial efforts to fit in, I most decidedly benefited from devaluing myself and other whites.

After a series of family disasters, I moved to Tehran, Iran, where I spent my teen years. The Shah was still in power. I attended an international school. Nationality, not race, was the defining issue, but I still embodied the lessons I learned in St. Thomas and I felt very much like an outsider. This theme followed me back to America and eventually to Colorado, where I attended Colorado College. It followed me to Boulder, where I have lived since 1984.

Taking a Different Perspective in Graduate School

IN 1987, I WAS STUDYING FOR MY MASTER's degree in social work. My clinical internship was at the University of Colorado's Center for Multicultural Counseling. I had looked forward to being part of a diverse group of mental health professionals and students. I was sure that I would learn a lot and that I could also make my own contributions.

During the first three days, the white students attended a training where we were asked, *Who are the oppressors?* The answer was simple—if you had white skin you were part of the system that oppressed people of color, and were inherently racist. Because people of color weren't part of the power structure, they couldn't be racist.

Our discussions of race were an emotional minefield. I struggled with what seemed too narrow a definition of racism because it made no allowances for me, for what I experienced. The child who had found great joy in passing for Puerto Rican didn't fully identify as white. To add to my own complex narrative, I was also the daughter of a white American mother and a Jewish Iranian father. No matter how I looked at race and ethnicity, I felt like forces larger than myself were shaping my identity.

I fought against the center's definition of racism. I argued that anyone could harbor negative thoughts and feelings about another race, whether or not they had political power. I told them, yes, I was white, but once they got to know me, they would know that I had lived most of my life as someone who wasn't part of the majority and that I understood political and social oppression on a personal level. I quickly learned that the counseling staff didn't want to hear about my experiences. They couldn't see beyond my skin. Eventually, an African American psychologist invited me into her office and said, "You know, Shireen, I've been thinking about you. You're not white like most whites. Your story is different."

I smiled, hoping she could really see me for who I was, but she continued, "You have to recognize that your skin allows you to pass unnoticed in white culture. If your skin were darker, that's what people would react to. You can blend in. You have opportunities and options that I don't."

From where I stand today, I know she was undeniably right. I live within the framework of white privilege. My skin insulates me from the oppression that people of color face in white America. My experiences would be very different if I were black, or Latina, or Arab, or Asian. But at that time in my life, I insisted that I was not part of the privilege paradigm.

Learning to Acknowledge, Reflect, and Process

AS A MENTAL HEALTH PROFESSIONAL, I am also well aware that unconscious thoughts and feelings limit how accurately we see ourselves. Although I believed that my childhood experiences as "the other race" would prevent me from becoming one of those white people that see racial differences through the prism of stereotype I have learned that living in a monoculture has resulted in me perceiving my own white race as the norm. If that young man in the hotel lobby had been white, I'm sure that I would have started my sorting process with an image of a twenty-something white man I already knew. My mind would likely have traversed the continuum from known to unknown. *Is that Alex? Does he go to the University of Colorado? Is he a guest? Is he the bellman?*

This makes me wonder. How do people who have always lived inside the liberal white bubble, where politically correct thinking is heavily enforced, ever notice the racism lodged in their own minds?

Being a white woman in Boulder is different than being a white child in St. Thomas, I am clearly part of the majority now. I am an adult. I have options. I could excuse myself and say that my offense is not a big deal because in that moment at the hotel my mind didn't call up the negative stereotypes of a drug lord, crack addict, or gangster. But stereotypical thinking–whether positive or negative–is one of the tools of dehumanization. It's a one-dimensional picture that occludes the rich and complex reality of what makes us human. That's why I'm horrified that I have become someone who thinks in stereotypes, even if it's only that first thought. I'm horrified that I have unknowingly internalized our covert cultural coding system and began applying limiting stereotypes to individuals with black skin.

As I think about this part of my adult cognition, I realize that my world has become much smaller, monochromatic, and limited than the world of my childhood. I miss having discussions that include race and ethnicity. There is an upside to someone asking where I'm from and understanding my history. And yet, within the confines of my predominantly white community, it seems any traces of my own ethnicity have vanished.

In St. Thomas, skin color was part of our human landscape. Talking about race wasn't unequivocally racist; it was often descriptive and essential to everyday conversation. But in white culture, this skill doesn't exist. There really is no language to discuss what it means to be white. Our own race becomes invisible to us.

In the United States, I never have to fight for acceptance. No one pulls away when they see me walking down the sidewalk. No one tightens the grip on his or her bag. Although I've given my children instructions about how to behave toward the police, I did so without the terror that these instructions might eventually save their lives.

The psychologist at the multicultural center predicted that I would experience the world of white privilege in a way that she wouldn't. She was absolutely right.

While our American culture offers many undeniable opportunities and freedoms, the truth is that our original economic and political systems were based on privileging a few and oppressing the many. The legacy of the slave trade and the dehumanization of black people is still part of our economic, social, and political history. It's the elephant in the living room. It's not something we can erase.

How could such a powerful history of racism just suddenly disappear? How could it not metastasize into institutional racism such as Jim Crow laws, racial barriers to voting, education inequities in far too many communities where the majority of students are persons of color, and in egregiously discriminatory police behavior?

I understand white people's fear of answering these questions. I don't think anyone wants to believe they could be part of such a heinous system or risk being called racist, but maybe we need to stop worrying about the labels and realize that we can't avoid missteps as we build the skills to recognize and discuss race in America.

What if we taught that there aren't just racist and non-racist people? What if we explored the issue that we live in a country with invisible messages about race that stem from our history and get re-enacted both in obvious and not so obvious ways? What if we said that doing the work to understand our white selves is not about defending the possibility that we might have racist thoughts and feelings, but acknowledging that everybody is likely to have some racist thoughts instinctively and immediately?

What if we reinforced in one another the ability to slow down, to take the time to notice if we grip our child's hand more tightly as we walk past a black person? To notice if we become vigilant when a black person gets in line next to us at the grocery store, or if we sing the praises of a black professional but never actually refer anyone to that person's medical or legal practice?

To me, being white in America requires more than a belief that all people are equal, or concluding that having elected an African American president means we have become a post-racial society. It requires noticing how my thoughts and behavior change when I see someone who doesn't look like me. It means taking the time to imagine what would be different in my own life if my skin were a different color. It means reflecting on my own specific behaviors that translate as aggressions toward people of color.

Overt white privilege can be defined as benefitting from a system that gives me countless advantages simply by virtue of my skin color. But a less obvious form of white privilege is the ability to remain ignorant about another race or ethnicity because what happens to them doesn't directly affect me. It's the reliance on stereotypes rather than reality.

When I acknowledge that I live in a racist culture, I am forced to consider my place in that continuum from the subtlest practices of white privilege to the most obvious behaviors of a white supremacist. The question is not whether or not I am racist. The question is what do I do about it?

When #BlackLivesMatter became part of our cultural conversation and African Americans began sharing their experiences, their trauma, their stories, and their personal views, I knew enough not to say "all lives matter." I knew that black lives were under siege in a way that white lives were not. But I learned that I still need to listen, to reflect, and let the words of African Americans build my understanding of how both overt and covert racism affect me, affect all of us. My job is to ask my white community and myself how we can do better. ■

Keith Kohnhorst

"Scared"

I N 1992, MY NEW GIRLFRIEND gave me an ultimatum to get off welfare and get a job. "You have disabilities, but you're not disabled," she said. At thirty-one, I wasn't getting any younger, and if I wouldn't buck up for her, I'd never buck up for any woman. A week later, I got lucky and found a sinecure, which helped make the scary transition to the world of work a little easier.

Get this: I gave up seven hundred free dollars a month to work 140 hours a month for just one thousand dollars. It meant I was essentially toiling away for two dollars an hour for the Association for Retarded Citizens (ARC), who paid me to take a group of older DD's out to lunch every day. Since "retarded" was pejorative, we called them "developmentally disabled," or "DD's" for short.

Filling out a welfare form to let the government know I was now gainfully employed with full benefits to disqualify me from all government assistance, was not so simple. I'd been addicted to the dole and the easy lifestyle it afforded me for over a decade. It was money for nothing but it came with a price: I'd felt emasculated as though I were moving around the swimming pool of life by holding on to the sides, afraid to go into the deep end, afraid I'd flail and drown.

Now I was swimming, albeit with a dog-paddle stroke, damn lucky to find this sinecure and become a tax-paying, thirty-five hours a week, fifty weeks per year working stiff. Besides health insurance and paid vacations, one of the fringe benefits of a job was that for the first time in my life I had a routine: I got up at 7:00 a.m. five days a week and joined the rat race. Every morning, I walked a block up to Haight Street to catch the 71 Noriega bus; it was always full of financial district workers, movers and shakers. I felt a sense of pride and freedom as though the shackles of dependency on Uncle Sam had been broken.

I fantasized about going on *The Rush Limbaugh Show* as a liberal admitting that the conservatives were right about the dole being addictive, sharing my struggle to man-up, and challenging others to follow suit, becoming a darling of right-wing radio. I would tell Rush that 80 percent of welfare recipients could work (look at me!), but were gaming the system and becoming dependent on Uncle Sam—welfare mothers and lazy people like me—and were getting fat checks from anonymous hard-working Americans. I'd steer clear of playing the race card, but the black color of the card would be implied.

My girlfriend Lisa and I celebrated my new job at a Thai restaurant on Geary Street. We were in a great mood slurping up Pad Thai, and sneaking a smooch for dessert. We hopped on the 24 bus for a ride up Divisadero to my flat just past Oak Street. I was renting a three-room flat (one room was full of old prosthetic parts), complete with fourteen-foot ceilings, for $300 a month from my prosthetist's father, who owned the building, and enjoyed helping out a man in need.

Several African Americans got on the bus as we passed through the Western Addition, a neighborhood known as a mecca for drug dealers. I smiled at the new passengers, empathizing with their plight, feeling akin to them as a one-legged man, a former welfare recipient, struggling to get by in this cruel world. I thought about those Sunday nights when I would leave my artificial leg behind, and go dancing at the Kennel Club. Boogying down the sidewalk on crutches and one leg to the club, I would pass by Popeyes Chicken, and inhale the addictive odor of chicken grease, and nod at the curious onlookers, all of them black, their smiles as warm as the chicken they were taking home. I rarely felt afraid, as if my missing limb made me an honorary member of the black race—just like Bill Clinton, our new president—and immune to the threat of violence. I felt that blacks and I were both handicapped in trying to navigate a world doling out privileges and perks to able-bodied white America.

Lisa gave me a kiss on the cheek and smiled broadly at me as the electric bus sizzled up Divisadero Street. Two older black women got on the bus. The women reminded me of the ladies who took care of my developmentally disabled seniors and me when we would file into the nearby Third Baptist Church's senior center for our dollar lunch and coffee. We were the only white people in the church, but the black seniors there were always kind and generous to us.

The women on the bus nodded at us as they sat down, both burdened with heavy loads on their laps. One woman carried a bag of groceries and the other a little girl, her hair braided beautifully. Lisa commented on the girl's hair. "It's nothing but trouble," the woman laughed and honked the little girl's nose. "And so is she!"

We all laughed, the little girl reaching up to honk the old lady's nose. The world was in order. The races were getting along. The truth was we all had our burden, be it physical, economic or racial. I sat smiling, musing about everyone's struggle – white, yellow, and brown – when I noticed for the first time a young, black teenager, maybe sixteen, sitting across from us. He was staring at me – not Lisa – with pure hatred. His small frame was buried in oversized pants and a big, gray flannel shirt. Bloodshot black eyes of hatred glared at me from under a baseball cap. He met my nervous smile with a frown and, gripping both sides of his seat, jerked forward towards me as if ready to attack. I flinched, looked away, and squirmed. I was 100 percent sure he wanted to kill me. An angry young white man would have frightened me too, but this dark-skinned young man pierced me to the core. Why?

Evidently, the white man's burden was see-through, for I felt transparent and the young man was sneering at my visceral discomfort. Couldn't he see the bionic leg extending out from my shorts? Couldn't he see that I was a colorblind liberal? Why didn't he give me the benefit of the doubt? Was he jealous seeing and not feeling the vibe of two lovers? I felt victimized. Maybe he had read my mind and violently entered one of my fantasies about appearing on Rush Limbaugh's show. What was clear was that I was really too frightened to contemplate his existence – who he was, where he came from, what he felt in his daily life, his struggles, his anger. What was he doing that night? Where were his parents? I would never come close to standing in this teen's shoes. He personified the "angry young black man hating whitey," and I was scared of him. Deep down, truth be told, I was scared of all of them. Luckily, when Lisa and I got off the bus, the boy didn't follow us.

Metaphorically, this teen has stalked me for the past twenty-three years. I'm still running from him. First, I stopped frequenting the Fillmore and Western Addition neighborhoods down the street, where I might have run into the angry teen. A year later, after a shooting in the *taquería* up the block, Lisa and I moved to the safety of the Santa Cruz Mountains to start a family. Over the years, I have periodically visualized the angry teen on the bus beating the hell out of me for some unknown, but deserving reason. I can still feel his perceived hatred of me. I still look away.

Now, even with the races "getting along better" and the election of a black president in a "post-racial society," I'd still lurch across the street to avoid that young black man coming my way. I sometimes wonder whether he's still coming and going. Chances are he was arrested before age twenty-three. Was he in prison? Is he employed? How about married? Maybe he beat the odds, and found a mentor and now coaches kids at Roosevelt Middle School.

I taught some beautiful African men at De Anza College. They were tall and black as night with dazzling smiles – Eritreans, Somalis, Ethiopians – all trying to learn English and get ahead. They were vulnerable, many of them having seen famine and horrible atrocities committed. I had extraordinary powers, and sometimes felt like an impostor just imparting the white man's burden.

In 2015, from the safety of my warm living room high in the Santa Cruz Mountains, I empathized with Ferguson's African Americans on TV, but I wouldn't venture down from my ivory tower to join a peaceful, integrated protest against police brutality in the black community. It all looked too hardcore. A part of me feels that I too shot Michael Brown. I sympathize with blacks at universities like the one in Missouri where, even at institutions of higher learning, taunts and racial epithets are still slung at people of color, and structural racism keeps rearing its ugly head. If I had tenure at Ithaca University, I would march with empowered, educated blacks and enlightened white liberals, and silently take up the Zulu chant: "*Amandla Awethu* – Power is ours!"

Ours? Not by a long shot. However hard this handicapped, white liberal, former welfare recipient has had it and might like to deceive himself that he's an honorary member of the black community, truth be told, the answer is an emphatic no. I'm scared of "angry" black teens and men from the ghetto or the projects, and will never know them, can never know them, don't want to know them. Do you? I'm fifty-six now and have never spoken to an African American teenager. Please be nice to me and leave me alone. ▪

Linda M. Crate

We're All Connected

'VE NEVER CARED ABOUT THE COLOR of a person's skin. To me
it never mattered as much as the true character of a person. I wasn't
taught to hate and so I loved everyone regardless of their skin tone.
I couldn't control what color my skin was when I was born and neither
could they. I never held it against anyone.

Yet it seems that some people hold my skin color against me. I don't
know why this is, but I feel that it's something that is taught. Because
I've met friendly people of different races and people who simply stare
me down for no good reason aside from the fact that I happen to be
at work and they see me.

I have heard plenty stories of racism on both sides of the spectrum,
but it seems that the white person is always the racist one and it doesn't
matter if someone of a different race insults them. That's not racism,
that's what they deserve. It really annoys me because the actions of a few
people's ancestors shouldn't affect the way everyone is treated. Simply
because slavery existed at one point in our history doesn't mean that
everyone approved of it.

It's like saying because one is German that simply makes you a
Nazi regardless of your beliefs. I have always found that rather stupid.

Some people argue white privilege. I know it does exist and I know
it's an issue. However, this is nothing I decided. Hating me because
of my race accomplishes nothing. It does not make white privilege go
away. It does not solve that issue. All hate does is cause more issues
and complications.

I never asked to be born white just like they didn't ask to be born
into whatever race they were born into. While I don't judge people

because of their race, I have seen people judge me for mine. It always hurts me because I'm not the type of person that cares about those sorts of things. I am aware, of course, but it does not bother me what a person's skin tone is, merely the fiber of their being and their hearts.

Once whilst at work, a woman of a different race tried to start a fight with me simply because I was white. I was so ashamed for her. I don't understand the thought process behind that one. You're going to punish me for something that was out of my control? It is all nauseating to me.

There was nothing I could really do as I was at work, but I tried to be civil and remain calm, although I wanted to run. She was making me feel bad for something I had no control over. Maybe she was having a bad day or I reminded her of someone she didn't like, but either way that was a terrifying experience for me, since I already suffered from some social anxiety.

A person is a person and should be judged for the way they treat others and how hard they work and what they value, not because of their skin tone.

Together we can change the world. I can imagine a much better world if we focus on the things we can change instead of those that we cannot. ■

Dance

WHEN I WAS FIFTEEN, an African boy invited me, a white girl, to a dance at the private boys' school in Hartford, Connecticut where he was a newly arrived foreign student. His school, the Watkinson School, was established in 1881, eighty years earlier. It was originally the Watkinson Juvenile Asylum and Farm School, named after David Watkinson (1778-1857), a successful Hartford businessman, whose will included a bequest to establish a school for troubled boys.

I don't know if the school's mission in the 1960s was still to educate and rehabilitate "troubled boys," but something of that remained in its local reputation. I met the boy at the home of a neighbor whose older son also attended Watkinson. The son, whom I'll call "David Barton," was in my grade, though he was a year older. He had had a hard time at his previous schools, and his parents hoped that the Watkinson faculty and staff would give him the help he needed. These days he'd undoubtedly be diagnosed with dyslexia or another learning disability, but at that time he struggled in an ill-defined way. Awkward, vaguely inappropriate in conversation, he was clearly an outsider who appeared not to have friends. In his twenties he would become a fervent anti-Communist, and when he was home from college, he would stop by to see my parents, leaving off pamphlets from the John Birch Society.

But I am getting ahead of my story about a dance invitation, an incident that still haunts me to this day.

■ ■ ■

UNTIL THE EVENING WHEN I MET the boy from Africa, the only black people I had ever known were the African American women who cleaned for middle-class white families like mine. The women would take the bus from Hartford out to the suburbs, usually going to a different house each day of the week. Every Wednesday a woman named Florence came to our house. Florence's husband had died of a heart attack as he was having a tooth pulled, and after that she had to raise her ten children on just what she made cleaning. She was hard-working and warm, and my brother, sister and I liked her, but it never occurred to us to ask who was taking care of all her children while she worked, or to imagine how we'd feel if our mother left us every morning to take care of other families' homes.

Even the death of Florence's husband, sad as we knew it to be, seemed different from the deaths of other fathers, somehow not as tragic. We were told that he'd never been to the dentist before and died of fright. (Perhaps this was Florence's explanation to our mother.) We didn't speculate about this situation, as if not going to the dentist earlier was an actual choice he'd made, unaffected by race and finances. To us there was something vaguely comical about his lack of experience, hence comical about his death. These were undercurrents, perhaps affected by our father's attitudes toward race, but nothing anyone ever said aloud.

Our mother, who had lost her own father when she was nine, and whose sympathies ran deeper than those of our father, was concerned about Florence and made lunch for her on the days she cleaned for us, gave her extra food and clothes, and was careful that her Social Security was paid. Florence's difficulties also galvanized our mother into political action. In those years, Connecticut's population was predominantly Roman Catholic, and state politics were influenced by church doctrine. In fact, it was not until 1965 that the state's law banning contraception was declared unconstitutional by the U.S. Supreme Court *(Griswold v. Connecticut)*. A decade before that decision, our mother considered it criminal that a poor woman like Florence had no access to birth control and so kept having children. Racism undoubtedly tinged my mother's concern, though I believe she would have been equally distressed had Florence been poor and white. In any event, my mother joined Planned Parenthood and wrote letters to the Connecticut legislature demanding change.

Florence would often talk to our mother, who was a good listener, but we children knew little about her life and nothing about the lives of the African Americans who lived in Hartford, only a few miles from our neighborhood. We knew that "colored people" (this was the phrase of my childhood) lived in certain areas of the city. We would see them, with their dark, straightened hair and pronounced features, when our grandmother took us on the bus downtown each fall to buy school clothes. Sometimes they rode the bus with us (in the north seating wasn't segregated), or we'd glimpse them walking along the sidewalk, or they'd wait on us in the department stores. We knew that they lived in run-down neighborhoods, but these were not places we ever went to or asked to go, just as it didn't occur to us to question why they didn't live in our community. They were as remote as the families in our picture books about foreign countries. We knew, in fact, even less about them, since we had no children's books about the experiences of African Americans. The women who cleaned and traveled back and forth between these two worlds were like messengers whose stories were never deciphered, at least not by us.

An aura of the forbidden shadowed this remoteness, a boundary we couldn't cross. Several years ago when I was in New York City and spent an afternoon at an exhibit of Roy DeCarava's photographs of Harlem in the 1950s and 1960s, I felt drawn back into my childhood and adolescent perceptions, glimpsing in the photographs moments that were intimate and mysterious, in a world where there was, disturbingly – this was the feeling that arose in me – no place for me. This sense of being excluded, of being forbidden to enter, was so surprisingly familiar and so deep, that I imagine I must have felt it even as a small child, unaware that these boundaries had been erected by those with white skin like my own.

The boundaries appeared even sharper every April during our school vacation, when we would drive from Connecticut to Newport News, Virginia to spend a week with my father's parents. My father was raised in a section of Newport News that now has very few white people, but when my father and his brother and sisters were growing up there, it was one of the areas of town where "quality white folks" lived. (The phrase was used by my relatives with a shade of irony as if to suggest they were quoting, rather than bragging, although they certainly considered themselves respectable middle-class.) This was before the interstate highway system connected the country, and as we traveled the back roads of Maryland and Virginia, we were aware that there were many more African Americans living in these states than in New England. We passed their shacks and glimpsed at the men collecting on porches and street corners, and small children playing in the dirt while their mothers walked together along the road or worked the fields.

Throughout my father's childhood, my grandparents employed a black woman who cooked and cleaned for them named Charity, whom everyone liked, though we were told she couldn't be trusted. There were stories about Charity hiding food (a bag of carrots, a roast) in the trashcan out by the back gate, then taking it with her when she left. These were not grounds for firing her. It was taken for granted in my father's family that "totin'" – the dialect term – was what black people did, almost as if it were in the genes, which was why you had to keep a watchful, if benevolent eye on their movements. If you asked about the stealing, you could expect them to create some fabulous tale as an excuse. This was just an accepted practice, and the lies and excuses made for a good story later.

My grandfather was a good storyteller, and he used to retell these stories about Charity to underscore his point that "the colored" were different from us, a lesser kind of human being, closer to the animals, and that was how God had made the world and wanted it to be. My father and his brother and sisters accepted this view as well; it was part of their heritage, and the air they breathed. Sometimes my grandfather would put on a record of "Negro dialect" sermons full of mispronun-ciations, his favorite being "The Psaltree," in which the psaltery was misunderstood to be a kind of tree, pronounced "peasletree," and all the grownups would have a good laugh. Sometimes too, my father and his brother listened to jazz recordings by black performers, and when he was in high school, my father would sometimes sneak out of the house at night to hear Fats Waller and other well-known jazz musicians perform in Newport News and in Virginia Beach. Later he told us that the black performers whose music he loved were not permitted to stay in the same hotels as the white musicians – a situation whose patent unfairness he saw as unfortunate but unavoidable.

On several of these family visits, our grandmother accompanied us on excursions to the historical sites of Jamestown and Williamsburg. It was in Jamestown that I first became aware of the signs "White" and "Colored" above drinking fountains and the doors to restrooms. I watched uneasily as a group of black schoolchildren drank from a rusty fountain attached to the peeling back wall of one building – clearly less well tended than the white fountain, if tended at all. I was eight years old and didn't know then about segregated schools, hotels and lunch counters. I asked my grandmother why there were two different fountains, and she looked startled, as if she'd never anticipated such a question. She hesitated, then explained that "colored people" weren't as clean as we were. She may even have indicated that African Americans in the north were cleaner than those from the south. In her own Christian Science church, a pew at the very back of the sanctuary was marked with a purple ribbon to show that it was reserved for the one or two African American parishioners. Even as a child, this struck me as wrong, especially in a church.

Still, if I note now the painfully unquestioning racism of my father's family, I must also say that my grandmother was kind to everyone, regardless of race, and my grandfather had a reputation for treating the African American men who worked under him well. At the Newport News Shipbuilding and Dry Dock Company, where he worked his entire life, most of it as a superintendent, he helped institute the first apprenticeship program for young black men. Perhaps as a result of this, perhaps because of his position, he was invited to give the sermon one Sunday in an African American church, which he described as "one of the proudest moments of my life," and I have no reason to doubt the genuineness of those sentiments. He felt, profoundly, that northerners like me didn't know anything about race, and later, when I became involved in radical student politics and began talking to him about the civil rights movement, he was disappointed, even angry with me. We angered each other, and it is only as an adult that I understood that my grandfather, despite his rampant prejudices, was acquainted with more black people than I have ever known and, in a practical sense, did more to improve their individual lives than my attendance at rallies and the signing of petitions ever achieved.

As confusing as I found segregation in the South, however, my experiences on these April vacations never led me to notice the privileges I had as a middle-class white child growing up in New England, or to question the absence of anyone who wasn't white among my own friends and in my community. It wasn't until the evening at our neighbors', where I met the boy from Africa, that I came up sharply against the ways my family's legacy of racial prejudice had defined me.

■ ■ ■

THE NEIGHBORS, WHOM I'VE CALLED "THE BARTONS," lived directly behind us, their back yard separated from ours by a row of hemlocks and a tall oak tree. Our families had been friends for many years. When my parents fenced in the yard for our dog, they put in a back gate so the two families could go back and forth. Mr. Barton was a conservative businessman who worked in insurance, like so many fathers in Hartford. In addition to their older son, David, there was a younger son who played with my brother and sister. Our mothers were close.

The evening began with a telephone call from Mrs. Barton, asking if my brother and I could come over after supper. The family had invited a boy from David's class for dinner, a foreign student from Africa, and Mrs. Barton thought it would be nice for this boy to meet some other young people.

I didn't want to go. David and I had attended each other's birthday parties as small children, but our different school experiences had since separated us and we had little in common beyond our mothers' friendship and the proximity of our houses. My mother, however, saw the evening as a way to repay a debt to the Barton family, who were particularly generous about sharing their large and open backyard with us. So after supper, as requested, my brother and I made our way through the gate to the Barton's well-lit house, where Mrs. Barton introduced us to their guest.

I don't remember his name, nor the name of the country he was from. For a long time, working on this essay, I did not give him a name.

In my memory, he was "the African boy"—an impression, a role, a place setter in a story that centered on me and my troubling confusion about race. I believed I was being more honest that way until it occurred to me that not naming him might well be a form of racism, for I had had no qualms fictionalizing the names of our neighbors. The student from Africa deserved the respect of a name whether or not I recalled his real one. And not surprisingly, once I settled on "James," he became more real to me, and I could sense his humanity in a way I hadn't quite before. Until then, it was as if he'd stepped out of one of the oldest story plots and into my life—the stranger who comes to town and disturbs the complacency of its inhabitants. I considered giving him an African name—I'm still uncertain about this—but not knowing his country made this problematic. And because he spoke such perfect English, and because, at least in my experience, foreign students in the 1960s would often assume an English name as a way of fitting in, or to make it easier for us to remember their names, despite my hesitation, I've stayed with "James."

He was extraordinarily polite, smiling warmly and shaking my hand and my brother's as we were introduced. We talked a bit, and then the five of us—David, James, the two younger boys, and I—trooped downstairs to a large finished room in the Bartons' basement, where there was a Ping-Pong table and refreshments. David soon disappeared upstairs, and the rest of us played Ping-Pong, drank Cokes, and ate popcorn. Then the two younger boys took out a board game while James and I continued playing Ping-Pong.

James was tall, well-dressed, and very dark skinned. He spoke with a lilting English accent, as if he had attended British schools in Africa before coming to the States, which perhaps he had. I'd never met anyone from Africa before. My knowledge of the continent had come from whatever scraps of history we learned in seventh grade geography class and from the *National Geographic*, which my brother and I occasionally skimmed, looking for pictures of tribal women with naked drooping breasts. My impressions were also derived in a haphazard, unconscious way from the *Little Black Sambo* books in the attic of my grandparents' house in Newport News.

When my mother told me of Mrs. Barton's invitation, I'd assumed that this boy had been magically plucked from a tribe to go to school in Connecticut. And so he surprised me. He was urbane and witty, and we joked back and forth as the Ping-Pong ball ricocheted across the table. The unease I usually felt around boys my age had mysteriously disappeared in the kitchen, and I suddenly saw myself as a girl whom it might be fun to be around. As the evening wore on and David remained upstairs, I suspected that my brother and I had been invited to make up for David's deficiencies as a host, but I didn't mind. What I'd reluctantly agreed to as a family obligation had turned into a lively evening, and I was glad I had gone.

At the time, I was struggling with my own social difficulties. I was in my second year at a private day school for girls in a nearby town, and finding a boy to invite to school dances was a terrifying endeavor, complicated by the fact that I was attracted to the sorts of popular, athletic, confident boys who never noticed me. The dances – there were three or four each year – might have appeared even more challenging for the one African American girl at the school, who was a class ahead of me. But she was vivacious and well-liked and always brought a boy from her neighborhood in Hartford to the dances. It didn't occur to me until years later to wonder what it must have been like for her to be the only black girl in a school of 120 privileged white girls, or to consider all the ways in which her experience would have been quite different from ours.

■ ■ ■

I DID NOT EXPECT TO SEE JAMES AGAIN. As much as I'd enjoyed talking with him, it didn't occur to me to regret this. He had appeared to me like a stranger with whom you fall into an engaging conversation on a train, and then you disembark, returning to your separate life. So I was unprepared when the telephone rang a few nights later and I heard his lilting voice on the other end. There was a dance at his school in a couple of weeks, the Christmas formal: would I go with him?

I stood in my father's study, rigid, feeling a coldness descend through my body as if something terrible had happened, a disaster I'd carelessly brought on myself. I was polite, but brief. I told him I'd have to ask my parents, and he said he'd call me back in a couple of days.

When I told my mother, she was upset. She'd thought it was nice our neighbors had invited the African boy for dinner ("so far from his home and family") and had been pleased that my brother and I agreed to go over to their house that evening, but now she saw him as taking advantage of the hospitality he'd been offered. Her face looked stricken, as if I'd just announced a death: "Mrs. Barton told me you'd been so nice, so friendly. He must have misunderstood!" She also blamed the school; she felt the school officials had a responsibility to the African boy to explain to him about American culture, and they had failed.

We stood in the kitchen, where we had been doing the dishes. She told me not to worry, she'd take care of it, and a day or so later she told me that Mrs. Barton had been distressed and apologetic, and had either called the boy, or the school, to decline for me. In any event, he never called back.

It would have been, for my parents, out of the question that I attend the dance, even if I'd begged to go. But my own feelings were more complicated. Despite the scarcity of invitations from boys, I loved dancing—the music, the swirl of bodies, the dimmed lights. And I liked James and remembered how at ease I had felt with him. I imagined myself at the dance, an idealized me, laughing, talking a lot, as, in fact, I'd been when we played Ping-Pong. I remembered my openness, and I understood that what had happened was my fault, not his.

Yet the thought of going to the dance terrified me. I feared that I would be jeopardizing something fragile if I were seen with James, even if it was at a school event where I knew no one but David. Word would get around, and I'd get labeled as the sort of girl who went out with dark-skinned boys. I'd acquire a bad reputation, as bad as a girl who was "fast," and no respectable boy would ask me out again. My parents didn't need to spell this out for me: in a thousand ways I'd absorbed the warning. Then again, I thought, my hopes careening perversely in the opposite direction, maybe I was wrong, and if I went to the dance with James—he was, after all, a foreign student, and wasn't that a little different?—this might lead to other invitations.

These days, when interracial dating has become common, it's hard to convey how fraught such relationships once were, evoking disapproval and opprobrium, often violence. It was not until 1967 that the U.S. Supreme Court, in *Loving v. Virginia,* declared the last of the anti-miscegenation laws unconstitutional. Just three years before that decision, a girl in my class invited a boy from Ohio to our Senior Prom, and we were all thrown by a flurry of rumors that he was one-eighth black. Someone knew someone back in Shaker Heights, where this boy lived, who said that he had an African American great-grandparent, and my classmate, who heard these rumors after the boy accepted her invitation, was uncertain what to do. But this was just a rumor; she couldn't disinvite him, and by then, perhaps sensing the winds of rebellion that were about to change everything, we found the boy's forbidden ethnicity exciting.

When I was fifteen, however, I wouldn't have risked challenging social strictures – it wasn't something I could imagine doing. Still, I worried about James, and I shared these worries with my mother. If I didn't go with him to the dance, whom would he invite? "He needs to find a girl of his own race," my mother said firmly. "But he's a boarding student," I argued. "Where will he ever meet anyone?" "What about that girl in your school?" she countered. "What does she do? She always goes to the dances." I explained what I thought should be obvious: the girl from my school grew up in Hartford, so of course she knew boys from her neighborhood. It wasn't the same.

But here I hit a wall in my mother's sympathy. The boy had transgressed, whether or not he knew the border was there. I persisted in my worries, perhaps to expiate my own guilt and confusion. James had been so nice. I knew he hadn't been wrong to call me, in that we'd had a good time talking at the Bartons'. What sense did it make that I wouldn't go to the dance?

And yet, my parents' disapproval of this boy whom they'd never met undermined my confidence in my perceptions. I'd liked James, but we'd only played Ping-Pong together. Perhaps my parents were right; perhaps he was not to be trusted.

■ ■ ■

I NEVER LEARNED WHAT HAPPENED TO JAMES, if he graduated from the school in Hartford, if he went on to college in the States or returned to his family in Africa. Our neighbors never mentioned him again, nor did my parents. I never told any of my friends. By the time I was in college and became involved in the civil rights movement, I feared my family history betrayed an inherited racism it was best to deny, even to myself. I worried that I still harbored deep inside, in a primitive and unwelcomed form, the racist beliefs I'd grown up with. They'd rise up when I'd see two black men walking toward me on the street and I'd feel nervous and wonder if I should cross to the other side. And again years later, when I confused one of my African American colleagues with another. I thought the only way to banish these racist responses was to pretend that they didn't exist.

When I finally allowed James back into my memory a few years ago, I found myself wondering what had been said to him, how it was explained that he was not to call me back. What did he make of this white girl, so friendly in an American home – then turned distant and frightened on the telephone – who lacked the moral courage to accept his invitation or decline it herself? I wonder if he was made to feel he'd misjudged the warmth of the evening. I wonder if he became more wary. My own participation in his learning of the sad lessons of race in America still shames me today.

And I'm also aware that the dance represented a lost opportunity for me. I loved my family, but I was beginning to feel confined by the narrowness of their dreams for me, and by the relentlessly middle-class expectations of the community in which we lived. As childhood receded, I sensed that doors were closing rather than opening in my life. Spending an evening talking with a boy from a different culture was an unexpected gift, but I was too entangled in my family's racism to imagine spending more time with him. This was a door that opened, but I did not allow myself to walk through it. ■

Gregory Mengel

Swimming with the Current

I N THE FALL OF 1981, MY SENIOR YEAR IN HIGH SCHOOL, I thought it would be hilarious if my friends and I arrived at a class-mate's Halloween party dressed as Klansmen. To us, the Ku Klux Klan was ancient history like racism itself, with no enduring relevance to our lives. It seemed like innocent mischief. We wanted to make a dramatic entrance, so we parked a few blocks away and arrived on foot, wearing sheets and makeshift hoods and carrying torches. Our entrance was pretty dramatic, even though our torches wouldn't stay lit, and we were tripping over our costumes. We were initially met with shock, but every-one seemed to get the joke. The moment passed, and the party went on.

At this point, you may be disappointed to read that this story does not have an afterschool special ending, in which we experienced some deep learning about our foolishness. Indeed, nothing happened. We were never called out. No one even hinted that what we'd done was racist. No one told anyone's parents or the school about it. There were no negative consequences for us, and the episode was soon forgotten. We did not learn anything. And that really is the point of the story. In 1981, the overwhelming whiteness of my community inoculated us against even knowing our own history.

I attended public school in Boardman, Ohio, one of several sub-urban towns that formed a ring around the city of Youngstown. These suburbs were virtually all white. In fact, I did not have a single non-white classmate for the entire thirteen years I was a student in that school system. And this was no accident. I have since come to understand that white suburbia was the outcome of deliberate social engineering. It is a product of institutional policies and practices backed by state violence and white racial terrorism. Because none of this history was included in what we learned in school, we felt free to see ourselves as simply "raceless." We were just normal Americans, living normal lives in a normal town. Racism, as we understood it, was something that existed elsewhere. For some of my friends, this meant it was okay to refer to black people as "niggers," as long as you only meant *certain* black people.

My parents taught me that racial prejudice is wrong, but I think that was more of a critique of our extended family than an encouragement to make black friends. The racism of my community as a whole was defined by a combination of racial homogeneity and reflexive anti-blackness, which is why we could think dressing up as Klansmen would be funny in the first place. It is the reason we didn't know that the Klan in Youngstown had targeted not only black people, but also Italian immigrants, who in the early twentieth century, were not yet seen as white. It's possible that their victims included some of my classmates' parents and grandparents. This racism also meant that everyone was keenly aware of the borders that divided middle-class Boardman from the mostly black and low-income South Side of Youngstown. When people I knew mentioned the South Side, it was primarily to remind each other of the danger and chaos that lurked there. We treated it the way one treats quicksand or a thicket; we learned both to avoid the place, and not to ask why it existed.

Racial isolation is never absolute, of course, which is part of how it works on the psyche. Before I was born, my family began making a yearly pilgrimage from Ohio to Florida, where my grandparents lived. Ironically, despite growing up a couple of miles from Youngstown's South Side, those trips to the South are my earliest memories of seeing black people in person. My parents offered no guidance on what to make of the difference. They were probably trying to be colorblind, but their "good intentions" only left me confused. My parents, of course, were not the only source of my racial conditioning.

On a family picnic during one of our Florida vacations, I had an experience that perfectly epitomizes my early racial conditioning. It was the late 1960s. Jim Crow was technically deceased, but his body was still warm. We were at a public park with my grandparents and some cousins. Folks were fishing in the lake, many of them black. I was no older than five, and I did what came naturally; I wandered down to the lake and threw a rock in the water. Suddenly, a black girl of maybe twelve leapt up from the grass and came chasing after me, yelling about how I had scared the fish away. Terrified, I ran as fast as I could back to the safety of my family. The girl stopped a little ways away, derided me some more, and then went back to her folks. I was feeling relieved to have survived the encounter, but embarrassed about my foolishness. Then my grandmother, who had witnessed the episode, and found it hilarious, said something like, "Y'all scared of that nigger girl?" With that one quip, she managed to simultaneously double-down on my humiliation, and teach me an unforgettable lesson about both gender and race. My well-founded embarrassment about the fishing incident was surpassed by a deep shame of running away from a girl, while my grandmother's mocking tone and use of the n-word let me know that black people are fundamentally underserving of our consideration.

I had already internalized plenty of racist training when, at age nine or ten, I joined the YMCA to take swimming lessons. The YMCA was in downtown Youngstown, and thus not racially segregated like my daily life. Going there could have been a world-expanding experience, but it was too late. The discomfort I felt from being around those black boys revealed that a deep racial schism had already formed in my consciousness. The experience brought up vague feelings of fear, aversion, and shame, none of which I would have been able to name. At the time, I understood only that if I braved those Saturday mornings for a couple of months, I would no longer have to endure that particular discomfort. And, sadly, I was right about that. I remained adrift in whiteness for the next three decades, until I began to make a concerted effort to expand my racial comfort zone.

I lived in the Youngstown area until I was almost thirty years old, and I spent a good deal of that time paddling madly to escape the sinking ship that was the local economy. The steel industry, which had been the economic backbone of the Mahoning Valley for a century, had disappeared practically overnight, leaving social (and environmental) devastation in its wake. Somehow, though, in the midst of this economic collapse, I managed to get a decent part-time job in a supermarket, which helped pay for my tuition to the local state university. After completing my bachelor's in computer science, I landed an entry-level programmer job at a drugstore chain headquartered in downtown Youngstown. This startup, launched by the parent company of the supermarket where I was working, was a rare bright spot in a bleak job market. I took advantage of the many opportunities for training and career development the job offered, and eventually gained enough experience to make a cross-country, cross-industry leap to the Bay Area, where I now work in the software industry.

I used to recount my career path as a story of my determination to escape the dismal fate of the post-industrial working class. I thought of myself as smart and clear-sighted for having chosen a promising field of study, working hard, and staying out of trouble. While not a total fabrication, this story was far from complete. Leaving aside the fact that "staying out of trouble" is easier for people who look like me; my upward trajectory began before I could walk. It was my family's whiteness that allowed us to live in a neighborhood relatively free of both crime and police, and gave me access to an excellent school system. As I said, housing policies and practices had all but completely excluded non-white families from Boardman, and the surrounding suburbs. Needless to say, I received a quality education, socially as well as academically. And the middle-class norms I was immersed in there made college seem attainable if not inevitable, despite my high-school educated parents.

Meanwhile, I was able to land the supermarket job that helped pay my college tuition because a parent in my all-white Boy Scout troop happened to be an executive with the company. And when I was seeking a programmer job after college, I was able to get an interview in the IT department of that startup drugstore chain in large part by using connections I had from working for the parent company. I may also have gotten a boost from that same executive. Once in that job, it was easy to form relationships with my coworkers and managers, almost all of whom had similar race and class backgrounds. We regularly went to happy hour where we engaged in shoptalk, gossip, and general bonding.

There is no question that these connections helped open opportunities for advancement.

Given the racial realities of my life, I really ought to change my metaphor. I haven't been swimming so much as being swept along by a current of white privilege. While it is hard to imagine anything epitomizing my privilege more starkly than making light of the terrorism that helped cement it, the privileges that have truly mattered are those that flowed from the structural advantages of whiteness. These are the privileges that buoyed my existence like an unsinkable life-raft. They have been working for me since before I was born, securing my safety, my education, my employment and my social mobility, ensuring that I would never have to notice that life is a lot harder for people who don't look like me.

Perhaps, it's a sign of progress that kids can no longer get away with dressing up as Klansmen for Halloween, and overtly racist language is no longer acceptable. Yet I wonder how much of our outrage over blatant racism is driven by a need to identify as the "good white people." I do know that rejecting explicitly racist speech and behavior has done little to address the structural aspects of inequality. Genuine progress will have occurred I think when enough of us white people are willing to look at how racism benefits and implicates each of us. Only then will we be able to begin to repair the harm and build a society that works for everyone. ■

Brett Biebel

Erasures

I F MY HIGH SCHOOL WAS AT ALL DIVERSE, it was only because
of a group of sixty or so international students, most of them from
China, Taiwan, Korea, and Japan.[1] They boarded at the small, Catholic, Minnesota campus during the academic year, paying college-level
prices to stay in an old university dormitory and take classes designed to
give them the English background that would guarantee admission to a
strong, American university. They also brought with them a whole host
of political and social complexities stemming from their necessary role
as part of the school's economic engine and their status as a clear, though
significant, minority. We needed their money. But whether or not we
ever considered them to be fully part of the culture is an open question.

My most direct experience with the precarious status of international
students came on the basketball court. I remember one student, let's
call him "Frank," in particular.[2] He was an outgoing kid with a huge
smile and a hyper-kinetic personality. He was always nodding, running
or jumping, making us laugh and generally upping the fun quotient
of any classroom. He taught us Mandarin curse words and chuckled
when we had to pronounce them ten times to get them even close to

---

1   And, in fact, it's unfair of me to present them as a group. There were the same splits
and cliques among them as there were among us white kids, though theirs were often about
history and geopolitics. The Chinese would not approve of my listing Taiwan as a separate entity. The Koreans and the Japanese would spar over historical wrongs. There were gender role
debates too. Of course, I should point out that all of this is clearer to me in retrospect than
it was at the time. For the most part, the "dorm kids," as we called them, kept to themselves,
forming sub-cliques as part of a larger grouping. The white kids (and nearly all of us were
white) had our own sub-cliques, and rare were the students who could fluently cross over.

2   In what I can only assume was an attempt to assimilate, most of the international students took Americanized names. Perhaps it was a compassionate nod to Anglo pronunciation.

correct. More than that, he was one of those few high school students who didn't seem to care at all about cliques or social status. He was nice to everyone, and if the novelty of difference was what first caught our attention, I'm happy to say I got to know him well enough to call him a legitimate friend. I don't know where Frank is today, but he was an important, joyful part of my high school experience.

That he was my freshman-year teammate solidified the bond even further. And it was the deepening relationship that helped me to see some of the hypocrisy, some of the privilege, inherent in our situation.

Frank was a Carlos Gomez kind of basketball player. He was quick and possessed legitimate athleticism. He was, in fact, also an important member of the track team. What he lacked, however, was coordination and skill with the ball. He wasn't the worst player on our team, but he also didn't earn much playing time. Mostly, though, Frank was ignored, if not in a social sense then certainly in a basketball one. I remember him receiving the least one-to-one instructional time of any of us. There was never a real effort to develop Frank as a player.[3] We welcomed him, but it was almost like our primary goal was making sure he didn't slow us down. We were sociable. Polite, but not friendly. Human, but only to the point where it began to cost us something. I don't know how Frank felt about this. I never asked. I also never did anything except to notice it. I was bothered. Honestly frustrated. Though I was also totally unaware of how to fix it. It was one of those odd moments when the importance of cohesion and teamwork obscured a destructive attitude. In order to avoid disruption, I just went with the flow. I accepted something I didn't like and stayed quiet during practice. It was easier that way.

The feeling stuck with me, though. After each season, we were asked, as players, to fill out a yearly evaluation form, offering feedback on the coaching staff and the program. On mine, I talked about the dorm kids. I talked about Frank. Instead of the usual, pro forma check marks and okays, I wrote an extensive critique of our handling of the

---

3   I think this is directly attributable to his difference. Though Frank spoke English well enough to communicate, the nuance of teaching basketball presented a challenge. I don't think anyone was being actively mean. We were, though, aware of the difficulties of encountering difference. We were aware of an increased demand on our time. We may have been, above all, too lazy to be genuinely open.

international students. I wrote anonymously and for a page and a half about exclusion and the team concept and our halfway treatment of the internationals. Come out for the team, we told them. Only to ignore them when they arrived. I wrote the word "racist," and I used the form to vent all of my real feelings in the most sanctioned and bureaucratic way.[4] I honestly remember feeling no hostility toward the coaching staff or the existing authority structures while writing. I do remember being disappointed. I remember it as one of those adults-don't-have-all-the-answers moments of realization, and I recall being struck by some version of a revelation involving the ability to separate malicious intent from negative outcomes.[5] It was my first real awareness of white privilege. It was knowing that I was implicated, understanding that it was wrong, and being part of it nonetheless. The way we treated the international students was abhorrent. For a Catholic, it was sinful. And blame lay with no one and everyone all at once.

No part of this story is designed to excuse me or impart any sense of nobility. If I spoke up at the end, it was too little, too late. More than that, I wasn't any different from my white teammates. I acted the same, and I felt the same sense of foreboding, the same fear of imminent defeat, when we saw black players warming up and stretching on the opposite sideline. Even now, as an adult teaching in diverse college classrooms, I, like many of my friends and acquaintances, struggle to know how candidly race should be addressed. I struggle to understand my position and my role in leading discussions that could revolve around my power and privilege. What I'm trying to communicate is that white privilege isn't invisible. It's camouflaged. Actively hidden. It's one of those hard truths that we're more comfortable denying. One of those things that's easier to face when we can apply it to someone else, a coach, maybe, or some other member of a more elite class. Even speaking out, that's

---

4   I think people knew I wrote it. Later, my dad, who was involved in the basketball community from the high school through college levels, mentioned that someone had written about my school's treatment of international students on a year-end evaluation form. I don't know if he was asking me if I did it. I don't recall if I told him.

5   When I learned the difference between *de facto* and *de jure* segregation, this was the scenario I pictured.

what a small part of me was trying to do. I wanted to make it someone else's problem.

■ ■ ■

AS ILLUSTRATED BY MY high school basketball experience, sport occupies a unique place in the cultural debate about race. Arguably the most important football-related news of 2015 had nothing at all to do with a score. In early November, a group of University of Missouri football players announced their intention to boycott all football-related activities in order to protest what activists have called a hostile racial environment on campus.[6] The entire story is an instructive example of why race lies lurking within so many of our discussions about athletics. As Dave Zirin wrote, "There is no football team without black labor. That means there aren't million-dollar coaching salaries without black labor. There isn't a nucleus of campus social life without black labor. There isn't the weekly economic boon to Columbia, Missouri, bringing in millions in revenue to hotels, restaurants, and other assorted businesses without black labor. The power brokers of Columbia need these games to be played."[7] Black athletes are often our most visible black citizens, and the power dynamics of the games themselves mimic the power dynamics of the culture.

There is a large divide between the people who play the games and those who run them. In the wake of the Donald Sterling scandal last year, *FiveThirtyEight* gathered some important data on athletic diversity. They found that, on the whole, the majority of players in the three major professional leagues, the NBA, NFL, and MLB, were minorities. The head coaches, owners, and league office staff, however, were mostly white.

6   A larger protest movement had been well underway before the football announcement. One student was already a week into a hunger strike. That the football team contributed to an increase in both coverage and administrative pressure says something about the power of athletics, but it also poses questions about our cultural priorities. Why does the willingness of student athletes to miss a football game generate more concern than another student's conscious decision to starve himself? It's worth considering whether the strike is a laudable flexing of muscles, an unfortunate prerequisite for action, or some combination of both.

7   Dave Zirin. "Black Mizzou Football Players Are Going on Strike Over Campus Racism," *The Nation,* November 8, 2015. Accessed January 15, 2016, http://www.thenation.com/article/black-mizzou-football-players-are-going-on-strike-over-campus-racism/.

FiveThirtyEight's data illustrate Zirin's point. Our major college and professional sports create significant revenue for a largely white power structure, and minority labor is the generative engine. The University of Missouri scandal had been brewing for months before the threatened strike, but the school's eventual decision to capitulate to protesters' demands came only in the wake of renewed public and financial pressure directly related to the power of football. The game raised the stakes of the conflict, and it helped bring about a solution desired by many of the protesters. The question I'm left with is: *What happens next?* On Tuesday, November 10, 2015, after a strike of less than seventy-two hours, Missouri football players were back at practice. In one sense, this is a resolution, though my concern is that it might be a hollow one. Part of me wants to laud the student athletes for their political engagement. Another part, however, is concerned that the controversy is now about the easy narrative of victory and defeat. I'm worried that the football team's victory will come to stand in for the broader victory desired by the protesters. I'm afraid that the game is over. And that, when games end, there's no reason, no real desire, to keep talking.

My dilemma as a former athlete and a devout fan is that I want sports to have a prominent role in important cultural conversations while also recognizing the destructive impact they can have on our attitudes about each other. Sports are fantastic at setting the stakes of a conflict. They excel at driving a conversation, but that conversation is often centered on, even obsessed with, wins and losses.[8] A complex issue like American race relations demands so much more than a narrative of victory and defeat. It demands a dynamic narrative of change. It demands constant engagement and a constant willingness to question assumptions. It demands an openness to different perspectives that seems to run directly counter to the competitive spirit. Sport may be able to open our eyes, it may be able to add discursive juice, but can it really help create a new culture? Can it spawn action

---

8   Perhaps this has something to do with my reluctance to stand up for Frank in practice. I feel ashamed to admit that I might have actually believed he was slowing us down. I might have actually thought that drawing attention to any part of the situation in practice would have impacted our ability to function as a team. I might have chosen what I thought was a better chance at victory over the dignity of another person.

that goes beyond the removal of an embattled university president or the scrawling of a cathartic essay on the back of an official form? Can it foster substantive change?

The paradox at the heart of the University of Missouri story is that sport helped to bring about a change that we cannot really evaluate. It accomplished a concrete goal without really addressing the heart of the myriad moments that caused the crisis in the first place. Is the resignation of a president really enough to turn a tide largely made up of institutionalized moments? Will a new president prevent drunk white students from confronting their black peers with the n-word? How much control does one individual, even one very powerful individual, have on the attitudes of hundreds, even thousands of people? Even more, how much ability does one person have when it comes to changing an entire culture? What if Missouri is just image-managing, fulfilling pressurized demands in order to turn down the heat without really committing to meeting the issue head-on? Maybe the whole situation is a "win" for justice. Maybe it's a win for equality. But when racial injustice is insidiously institutional, when it's the result of so many different individuals acting with abstract motives, how can we gauge what's really a win for inclusion? What's really a win for diversity and citizenship and the human power of getting along, and what happens if the leaders aren't the problem? How do you fix a pernicious climate that isn't always the result of direct intent?

■ ■ ■

SOME VERSION OF THESE QUESTIONS was what troubled me at the end of the high school basketball season, sitting in a drafty room with a dull pencil, poised over a choppily Xeroxed form. Along with that gnawing sense of Catholic guilt, they were the cause of all my internal second-guessing in the days after submitting my evaluation. I had criticized good people. Used some pretty aggressive language to describe men that I admired and respected. There's nothing special about this internal conflict. It's a universal experience and the basis of "hate the sin; love the sinner" maxims. It's also, though, the exact feeling that sits at the foundation of my experience as a white male who also cares about diversity and inclusion. I want to acknowledge privilege without sacrificing credibility. I want, somehow, for the relationship between power and racism, exclusion and virtue, to be nuanced and complex. And I don't want "racist" to become the kind of trump word that eclipses the potential for conversation and change.

To accuse someone of racism is to imply that that person is unchangeable. It brands him, loads him or her up with a set of images that recalls fire hoses and hoods and crosses on fire. And the pejorative connotation rooted in the term "political correctness" has something to do with the fact that the fear of being called racist changes the way we talk without having any real impact on our actions. As a white male, I feel that fear even now, trying to type my way into a definition that I can own while not coming across as an asshole.[9] It's a balancing act, and the sheer amount of effort it takes to move through a series of rhetorical constructs is the basis for all those rants against the "PC Police." Because of the difficulty of talking about race as a white person, I often remain quiet, hoping to let others lead. Because of the pressure involved when race is brought up, I also often enter these conversations hyper-aware of myself and simply try to leave with my reputation intact. My fear of the racist label dictates my contribution to the conversation.[10] This isn't the right approach. It's bad for me as an individual, and it's bad for us as a diverse people. You cannot learn if your biggest concern is image management. You cannot share if you're afraid to risk your audience's approval. You cannot engage with difference if you aren't also willing to be open about yourself.

To me, the best conversations about race involve the most honest possible sharing of perspectives. They involve a grappling with history

---

9   I'm afraid of "losing" the conversation. Coming out on the wrong side of the reader-writer transaction.

10   Unscientifically, I think this fear lies at the heart of the philosophy of being "color-blind." If race doesn't differentiate us, then we can let go of some of the fear associated with it. Of course, this papering over of difference often serves to alleviate discomfort in a way that's anesthetizing. It numbs us, keeping the conversation on polite, socially approved grounds. The trouble with this is that it also cuts off possibilities for regenerative discomfort. It is itself numb to the necessity of having to have difficult discussions, having to actually and occasionally feel uncomfortable, in order to actively change anyone's perspective and, perhaps even more importantly, in order to alter one's own.

and a willingness to admit one's own biases. More than anything, they involve being open to nuanced distinctions and paying detailed attention to what our discursive partners say, as opposed to what we want to hear.[11] As a white male, I have to acknowledge my position of privilege. And that privileged position, I think, requires that I listen first. It requires that I ask genuine, clarifying questions rather than argumentative ones. It requires that I gain some semblance of true understanding before I respond.

When I do respond, though, it has to be both compassionate and unafraid. I can't self-effacingly undercut my own perspective with reference to my privileged status. I have to admit the privilege without for one second believing that it negates my ability to speak. And I think my own listeners have to believe that too. White privilege is real. But it can't be all we see. Because these conversations have to show us the possibilities for change. They cannot become competitions. They must help us understand that institutional racism was created by billions of choices, small and large, and the only way it ends is through one-by-one reversals. Through discussion and understanding and interaction. There is no magic wand. No perfect firing or fix-it hire. Racism and prejudice and white privilege[12] will continue to exist, and the key to ending them lies in knowing which kinds to condemn and rightfully vilify and which to approach as "teaching moments." Dynamic possibilities for change. Opportunities to "unerase," to "uncamouflage," to "unhide" the subtly racist, and the privileged parts of ourselves. To acknowledge they exist without granting them approval. Indeed, to recognize them in order to embrace the process of rooting them out. This is the lesson I draw from the #BlackLivesMatter movement. We really do have to change. And we have to talk, and keep talking, about how we'll do it. We can't be looking to win. We can't be afraid to lose.

---

11   Or, in some cases, what we hope to hear so that we can experience the powerful rush of getting angry.

12   I think these terms are related. They overlap. Perhaps they represent the same attitude and are only distinguished by a matter of degree. Part of what I'm talking about is understanding what those degrees are and how to amplify our indignation when it comes to genuine racism and prejudice and how to more gently nudge people away from ignorant attitudes that result from their, from our, privileged positions.

The role of sport is crucial in all of this. It's an incredible engine for conversation and a testament to the power of visibility. It's also not a very good framework for discussion. In untangling sport and race, part of my own challenge is grasping the importance of teamwork removed from the context of competition. Sport helped me see Frank's ostracism. It helped me notice more instances of exclusion out in the world. I saw him as a teammate, and I eventually understood that when it happened to him it was also happening to me. It's the acknowledgment of another's unique humanity that makes teamwork so powerful. The challenge is extending this attitude to those we usually think of as opponents. The challenge is including the "other" in our definition of team. We may all have a distinct role. But we can't forget that we're in it together. ■

Perry Brass

Whiteness Is Only "Sin-Deep"

MOST OF WHAT WE UNDERSTAND and see as "whiteness" that is, as a particular ethnicity and physical type that can be deemed as "normal," acceptable, or passible in American society is actually a reaction to "sin," guilt, or unworthiness. Growing up as a Jew in the Deep South (specifically Savannah, Georgia) in the 1950s and into the 1960s, I was constantly made aware of this. In many ways, this was an act of beneficence bestowed on me. The fact that I did not and *could* not fit in meant that, even as a child, I was able to see things in ways that other more "acceptable" people (i.e. "genuinely" white Christians and even some of the Jews who consciously imitated them) could not.

I questioned them.

This in itself came from a Jewish point of view: Jews admire questioners. To be able to question means not to take things at face value, and the whole history of Judaism has been a questionable situation. As an alien people (the classic English author W. Somerset Maugham referred to us as "the alien corn") that for centuries were held responsible for so many of the "crimes" and punishments of the world – from the death of Jesus to the Black Death in the Middle Ages, to wars and bank failures in modern times – Jews had to look askance at the "accepted wisdom" and question it.

And so I did. At seven years old holding my mother's hand at the Sears and Roebuck's in Savannah in the early 1950s, I passed a pair of segregated water fountains: one labeled "White," the other "Colored."

"Is the water that comes out of that fountain *colored?*" I asked.

My mother's hand stiffened. Even as a Jew you were not supposed to question this. It was a given in the South that black people could do "unspeakable" things to a water fountain.

"No," she whispered. "The water that comes out of that fountain is not colored. The people who use it are."

"Well, if the water's the same, why can't the same people use it?"

My mother, who had been born in the South and was very acclimatized to southern prejudices, told me there were certain things that should not be questioned. "They just *are.*"

I shook my head and brought it up to my father, who was also born in the South but having been a soldier in Europe during World War II, had learned to think for himself.

"The *goyim* do that," he explained – meaning the non-Jews. "It's disgusting. It has nothing to do with real humans. There are some wonderful colored people. Remember that."

My father, who died in 1958 of colon-rectal cancer, did not believe in integration. He believed in friendship, and that whites and blacks should be friends, just the same way that Jews and Christians should. They should live in their own world, but be given respect. As for the idea that black people were lower than whites, or more prone to sinfulness and the diseases permeating from it (a constant fixation in the South where public restrooms were segregated out of the genteel belief that one could easily catch certain diseases of the nether regions from toilet seats – thus keeping many a southerner safe from finger-pointing: "Yep! Must'a been that ol' toilet seat. Jus' don't know how they let one o' *them* sit on it!") . . . my father thought that was simply garbage.

"I fought in the War not to think that way. If Hitler had won, they would have wiped out all the Jews – and the colored."

Being a Jew, you were never considered totally white, and I went through that accusation constantly as a kid. Whiteness in its most "pure" form was virginal, without sin, or disease. It was part of a pristine, white-glove realm into which white, uprightly-Protestant ladies were supposed to be born, and which Southern gentlemen were supposed to protect. It was never loud, or obnoxious. And one never showed anger or feelings in an open way there. This was clamped down on me strenuously and even Jews, famous from Abraham through Freud for investigating their feelings, had to neurotically buy into it. It peppered the way Jewish men behaved publicly while growing up, and I became used to understanding that there was a public manner of behaving and also a "Jewish" one.

That is, for Jews to *be* Jews they had to do it behind closed doors.

This lead to a strange, touching intimacy, often veering on homoerotic, that I quickly picked up on. Southern Jews had to be schizoid to survive: something could easily be seen as "too Jewish." Too pronounced, loud, or *overt*. I was told that you had to be cautious and discreet about your Jewishness; there were things you had to keep to yourself, like hand gestures, or your voice or facial expressions. There was a definite "Jewish" accent. You didn't want to be accused of having one. Or in ordinary conversation drop Yiddish words to *goyim*, thereby telling them that you were not one of them. At the synagogue men could shake hands and touch each other's shoulders or even hug each other—you could not do this outside, anymore than you might wear an item of ceremonial clothing, like a long *tallis* (a prayer shawl) on the street. Jews who violated this code were pejoratively labeled "Yankees," or (far worse) "pushy."

Because as an Ashkenazic (Eastern European) Jew I had blue eyes and fair skin, I might not ordinarily be pegged as "Jewish," although I did not look like an Anglo-Saxon or Anglo-Scottish Southerner either. Jews who looked obviously Mediterranean or even North African were made to feel extremely self-conscious. There was something too "black" or *schwartzeish* about them. This was especially true if your hair was kinky enough to create a "Jew-fro," a white variation of an Afro. You might feel at that point extremely ghettoized, as if your very existence were under threat or suspicion.

This was also true if your profession involved handling money—*real* money. If you were a WASP banker who never actually handled the filthy stuff, it was OK. But if you actually handled it, as in being a pawnbroker, a retailer, or a bookkeeper behind a back window actually counting the *gelt*, you had to be careful because people were watching not only how you made money, but also how you spent it. You could not be ostentatious about it, splurging, or impulsive.

To do so put you in that most revolting southern category: "Nigger Rich."

Decent white people never did such things. It was almost logical to assume that this kind of free spending could easily end up in drinking, or worse, sexual license, or (even *lower*) drug use. There was also the threat of you descending into bankruptcy and a public exposure of either your own poverty, or... the public revelation of (uh-oh!) the questionable sources of your own wealth.

My mother, being automatically southern in her thinking, thought that all black people got their money in this manner, through gambling, prostitution, or loan sharking. The idea that they might work hard for it was beyond her. Jewish wealth, however, was simply a given: it went with the Jewish place in the scheme of things – that Jewish men would become professionals (doctors, lawyers, or certified accountants) and would have a Jewish head, or *kopf*, for business.

That my father died absolutely bankrupt throwing us into a situation of poverty acknowledged by the rest of the community was doubly humiliating to her: it was not only very *un*-Jewish, but worse, we had to resort to a public charity just to have him buried.

"Even *schwartzes*," she told me, "have burial insurance. He had *nothing*."

This made me understand that white people, living on their green plateau of superiority, never had to think about things like burial. It was simply a given. There was definitely a "white" family structure into which you were born, without having to prove your own worthiness.

Jews, like blacks, did not have this.

On the good side, being a Jew in the South put me in a position of accepting an "otherness" that *other* white people as a birthright did not have. My father, having been, as I said, in the War, made me feel proud of my Jewishness. "Don't let anyone ever make you feel otherwise." This was a beautiful legacy from him, although a difficult one to hold onto. By the age of eleven, I was living as a Jew in a segregated public housing project where we were the only Jewish family; I felt alien both from the white people there and other Jews. But as I later learned, to my satisfaction, there was nothing to hold me to the South: I had no privileges or real ties there. I realized that just being white, or a shallow approximation of it, was not enough.

This was driven back to me in my senior year of high school when I joined a Jewish youth group from my synagogue. We would get together in the prosperous homes of other kids and talk about the "issues" of the day. Of course integration came up. There were a lot of feelings against it. If blacks wanted equality, why didn't they just "buy it like we did?" I heard about how Miami had once been restricted to Jews, then Jews came in and bought big hotels there. I just listened. Being an impoverished Jew, I wasn't going to buy my way into anything. Then the slightly older son of a local rabbi got up. He said that no matter what, integration was the movement of the future and we, as Jews, needed to do something about it.

He looked seriously at us. "So, what can we do?"

There was no answer. Then he answered his own question:

"We could be nicer to our *schwartzes*," he stated flatly. "That would be the Jewish contribution to integration."

I never wanted to return to the group again.

Schwartzes? That was all black people were, just maids and handymen working for you? I couldn't believe that he'd said that—I was sure that these smart Jewish kids from wealthy homes would be more... anyway, I'd been called a "nigger" in the projects before, because I still seriously just didn't look white enough.

I knew how that felt.

By seventeen I was openly queer, at least to myself and a few of my friends. Even in the most guarded acknowledgment of this, I had fallen into one of those "sin cracks" that still terrifies white southerners. These were the cracks they could never talk about, except in the most negative or violent ways. Here virginity ended, and raw embarrassment and revulsion rushed in. I had become very much a part of that revulsion; but at least I found that I was no longer alone in it.

This became evident to me later, when on visits back I discovered that the only integrated bars in Savannah were gay ones, just as the only social cliques open to anyone were queer ones. Southern cities of a moderate size like Savannah had a roving nighttime underground—what the author John Rechy referred to as "the City of Night" – and it became easy for me to become a member of that. What happened during the daytime, except for certain guarded eye movements, was different. But in the solace of night, when most citizens were either watching sports on TV or were safe in bed, those sin-boundaries protecting whiteness in all of its tight-lipped primness could be lowered; or at least afforded some kind of truce.

By nineteen, I was living in New York, a city at that point almost as segregated as Savannah. There were upper-class whites and working class whites, and both groups tried to keep those famously grasping *sins* of money as far from them as possible. This left the Jews and, of course, Italians, especially those of a more outsider-ethnic orientation, the ones usually whispered about as "Mafiosi." I often heard that Jews and Italians got along well because they were both Mediterranean and open about their feelings. Many of my friends were Italians and I liked being in their presence. I also became enthralled with Jewish New Yorkers; they were so much more out of the "Jewish closet" than Southern ones.

They could be blatantly sexy and indulge in their own hungers and desires. In short, they had an appetite toward life itself. In the South, Jews couldn't even talk openly about food: a roaring, sexy kind of appetite was simply not a *white* thing to have. Gluttony was definitely *not* a pardonable sin. To talk about food meant that you didn't have enough of it, as your friends and neighbors might assume. After its invasion by the North following the Civil War and the Depression of 1929 that lingered for decades below the Mason-Dixon line, the South developed a habitual, stiff-necked pride that refused any kind of spontaneous joy at the table, or in the bedroom.

Jews, to survive at all, had to fall behind that.

In New York, people conversed openly about food, sex, and money. They were raucous in their discussions about them, insane with the craziness of material hungers. It was intoxicatingly juicy to me; down right liberating.

Still there were always places where that horse blanket of white shame operated.

One day in my early twenties I was listening to the radio. A man who was a local New York public health official was boasting that *venereal disease* – as it was called then, we had not yet cut a path into the more candid jargon of STDs, "sexually transmitted diseases" – had been almost wiped out.

"The only places you see it now are among homosexuals and blacks."

I felt enraged. What a stupid, public health lie! I had several straight friends who'd caught gonorrhea, or "the clap" as they called it. But they'd had enough money to go to a private doctor who kept everything hushed up. Richer gay men did the same thing, but poor street queens, the "vernacular" queers who stormed the Stonewall Inn and made the police take notice, had to go to a public health clinic where they used a fictitious name, and I'm sure that black men and women did the same thing.

So, in effect, white people could still stay "free of sin," certainly as long as popular beliefs stood behind it. And that would stay part of the real definition of *whiteness,* for the longest time. ■

Betsy Reeder

Bastion

I NEVER THOUGHT MUCH ABOUT what it means to be white because when I was growing up, I was too busy fuming over what it means to be female in a society still intent on keeping "women in their place." It was the sixties, and women still wore dresses in public most of the time, taught their daughters to "sit like a lady," and typically worked as housewives. It felt all wrong to me, a tomboy, who wanted to ride horses, climb trees, and basically run as wild as the pack of boys roaming our rural landscape.

It wasn't until the assassination of Martin Luther King Jr., that I began to grasp the racial divide in our nation. I remember how shaken my mother was, and how she wept as she watched the funeral on our little black-and-white TV. Suddenly being white felt vaguely shameful, as if I had played an unwitting role in this national tragedy. A new self-consciousness lurked in my awareness when I was around my African American classmates, as if I feared they saw me as one of "them," a monstrous racist.

Still, I didn't know what it means to be white. It was the default position in my country, my community. Something I didn't have to question or contemplate.

Until one day, many years later, I did.

I was shopping at the local grocery store when I stepped up to the fish counter. Ahead of me was a middle-aged African American man. Moments after I lined up behind him, a Caucasian man in a stained white apron appeared behind the counter. He looked directly at me and asked if he could take my order. I gaped at him. Obviously, I was *behind* someone, which meant I was *second* in line.

"This man is ahead of me," I said.

The man in question turned his head and said, quietly, "It's okay."

I froze. Clearly, this African American man did not want me to make a scene, which is exactly what I felt like doing. I'd never been in such a situation and was aghast at such a flagrant display of racist bile.

But I bit my tongue and placed my order, glaring at the clerk as he sliced and weighed my salmon fillet. My fish packet secured, I made a hasty retreat, feeling angry and deeply embarrassed. I could only imagine how much more so the recipient of the insult felt.

It was a little later, when I stood in the checkout line, that a blind eye opened, and I had my first real understanding of what it means to be white.

Let's suppose the cashier – a white teen – is in a foul mood today and won't make eye contact. She doesn't smile or speak to me. I thank her as I leave, and she doesn't respond. How does this affect me?

Scarcely at all. For a few moments, I may think the young lady is rude and unprofessional. I may berate her whole generation as self-centered and lacking in civility. Then I may or may not decide to be more charitable and tell myself the clerk has a tedious, minimum-wage job, may have just broken up with her boyfriend, could be having horrendous menstrual cramps but couldn't afford to stay home…and decide to give her a break and forget the whole thing.

The very *last thing* I would think is that this grocery-store worker dislikes me. How could she; she doesn't know me!

But suppose I am a woman with dark skin. My first thought is very likely to be, "This person dislikes me. She is being passively aggressive because she dislikes me."

It would be so easy to conclude she finds me somehow reprehensible, unworthy of respect because of my race. Her behavior is triggered not by her bad day, but by me; it is an unspoken monologue of hostility, the bedfellow of hatred. It's ugly and it's *personal*.

Now even if my rational mind is telling me not to jump to such a conclusion, how could I possibly avoid feeling the chill of its shadow? And what would it be like, even if one could somehow avoid overt racial insults, to feel that chill again and again and again across an entire lifetime?

That's when I got it, what white privilege has been for me. It's living without that shadow. It's the freedom to go through life without those constant little knife blades poking at my confidence and self-esteem. Every encounter I have with a rude or thoughtless or distracted stranger is entirely impersonal and leaves no wound. I wear a shield of armor I was never aware of or grateful for.

Now, I am, and I am deeply sorry that shield doesn't exist for all. White privilege is a bastion that will stand longer than the dreary Confederate flag, largely because most of us who enjoy its benefits are utterly unaware of it. ■

Jason Courtmanche

Race Adrift

WHEN I WAS TWENTY-ONE, I attended a workshop on combating racism, and the speaker said to a roomful of white undergraduates, "If you have a black friend and have never discussed racism, you don't have a friend. You have an acquaintance."

Friend or Acquaintance?

I GREW UP CONSIDERING myself not racist. My mother had black colleagues at the school where she taught. My father had several black acquaintances from his childhood. Both of my grandparents worked with lots of black people. We had a black family in our neighborhood, and all three kids came to our birthday parties and we went to theirs. We played whiffle ball in the summer, and had snowball fights in the winter. Race did not seem to matter.

I know now that I am racist and that I benefit daily from racism. In saying this, I don't mean to be hyperbolic, nor do I mean to lessen the significance of racism by suggesting it is so ubiquitous that it's moot. I say this because I believe that our fears about acknowledging our own racism or the institutionalized racism we benefit from prevent us from making any actual progress toward racial understanding or racial justice. We need to acknowledge racism and we need to talk about it.

I think about race all the time, but I was thinking about it acutely this semester, in part because I was thinking about writing this essay, but also because something came up in a class that made me think about that workshop I attended twenty-five years ago. For a couple years I have been teaching a first-year course on the importance of reading, and in our discussions my students and I found ourselves talking about the role stories have in shaping relationships. Ultimately, we came to the subject of race, which remains an incredibly taboo subject, and a student made the observation that racism breeds whenever and wherever we fail to share stories about it. The students and I discussed the protests that had been occurring at the University of Missouri and at Yale, and I shared that it seemed to me that too few people (mostly whites in positions of power) were really listening to the stories the mostly black students were trying to tell. Too many would-be listeners were reducing the situations to issues of privilege and Halloween costumes, when in reality the students were talking about institutionalized racism and the many microaggressions that kill by a thousand cuts.

This discussion made me think about Lisa Delpit's *Other People's Children,* a book I often require teachers to read in graduate courses on the teaching of writing. Delpit addresses the overwhelmingly white corps of teachers who teach all these children who are not white, and her main argument centers around a chapter called "The Silenced Dialogue" in which she argues, quite simply, that white teachers need to listen to black teachers, students, and members of the school community they serve. White teachers like myself need to hear black people's stories—need to learn about their values, their cultures, their customs, and their histories—in order to be effective teachers of their children. Many white teachers reading this book for the first time react defensively, but I only have to recall a trip to the UConn African American Community Center during my teacher education program to remind myself of the validity of Delpit's argument. There were nine of us, and we were all white. There was a mural on one wall with silhouettes of prominent African Americans throughout history, and I was the only one of the nine of us who could identify more than Martin Luther King Jr.'s profile.

I was impressed by my students that day, and they made me think about the process of my own re-education about race, which was catalyzed during a four year period between sophomore year of high school and sophomore year of college, when I was about the age my current students are. My re-education, however, did not take place in school but was the result of one particular friendship.

Not All Prejudice is Alike

WE HAD MANY BLACK STUDENTS AT NOTRE DAME. About a fifth of the 265 guys in my freshman class were black, and all the athletic teams (except the hockey team) were well-integrated. But integration didn't mean that the white guys and the black guys hung out with each other much. The school was still pretty segregated internally, and at lunch, although there were a handful of individual black guys who sat here and there at tables full of white guys, most of the black guys sat together at one table with Alex Campbell, who all the white guys called a "wigger."

My lunch table, for whatever reason, was the only one where black and white guys sat together in numbers that reflected the demographics of the school. About four of the twelve guys at our table were black. I'm sure I wasn't alone in taking pride in this fact. However, the fact that our social circle was more integrated than others was not necessarily an indication that the white guys in our group were any less racist than our other white classmates. Racist jokes were common fare at the lunch table. And although there were plenty of jokes about being Irish or Italian, and we probably all thought this was an indication that we were enlightened because we were equal opportunity ball-breakers, what we didn't understand was that not all race prejudice is equal. As Chris Rock has observed, jokes about Asians being good at math and Jews being good at making money are not quite as insidious as jokes about blacks being subhuman.

Generally speaking, I was not above laughing at the racist jokes of others, though I tried to avoid telling them. But I remember one notable exception that pains me to admit. We were talking at the lunch table about surnames and what they meant. We were all pretty much just a generation or two removed from immigration (honestly, the black guys probably had families that had been here longer than ours), and we often talked about ethnicity and identity. On this particular day, we were trying to determine the meanings of our names, and one of the guys who was perhaps the biggest blow-hard among us was saying that in Gaelic his surname meant "excellence." Now, most of the black guys had European surnames like Tyson or Russell, and many of them had Irish surnames like Boykin or McDaniel. One of the black guys in our group–Tchad Moore–shared my paternal grandmother's maiden name. One theory about where the Irish surname Moore comes from is that it was given to those Irish who intermarried with the Moors who came to Ireland from Spain and North Africa in the seventeenth century. In our family, we used to joke that we were the Black Irish. So when one of the guys said to Tchad Moore, "I wonder what your name means?", I just blurted out, "nigger." The table exploded in laughter, except for Tchad. Tchad, who was perhaps the most dignified of all my friends, who was always dressed so stylishly and was so much more mature than most if not all of us, looked at me not like he was angry but like he was betrayed. Over the next several days, I apologized several times, and Tchad graciously accepted both my apology and my explanation about the family joke, but our friendship was never the same. He was from then on distant with me, and at the end of sophomore year left Notre Dame to return to his local high school. I don't assume my insult was the cause. Lots of guys left Notre Dame after freshman or sophomore year, and a disproportionate number of them were the black guys, but we generally stayed friendly with them, since we saw them around or played against them in sports, but Tchad and I never spoke again.

Proximity

IN HIGH SCHOOL, everything was alphabetized: locker assignments, seating in homeroom, tryouts in football. Everything. Alphabetically, Maceo Cleaver and I were separated by five guys. Our lockers were in the same hallway block. Our homeroom seats were diagonally across from each other, arranged in just such a way that Maceo could flick me in the back of the head while the teacher wasn't looking. Only one guy stood between us on the football field during try-outs and later, after we both made the team, that same guy was the only one standing between us during warm-ups. Proximity had as much to do with making us friends as anything else.

Maceo was not my first or closest black friend during the first year of high school. At first I was closer to Joe Tyson and Xavier Russell, because they were both on the football team's taxi squad with me–meaning we were three of the last four guys to make the team. But during the spring of sophomore year, I got my license and a 1973 Chevelle. I started spending a lot of time with a few of the guys in particular – Tony, Kenny, and Maceo. We called ourselves, "The Four Horsemen."

We had a lot in common, especially our home lives. All of us had recently experienced different disruptions to our families, and all of us had landed in tough spots, mostly living with our mothers. After my parents divorced, I moved into a two family home owned by my stepfather in a section of Hamden near the Tilcon-Tomasso gravel pit. Tony and his sister had just moved with their mother to a small cape in a wooded section of Hamden after their father had left them. Kenny's father had lost his job, so he and his brother shared a room in a section of the basement of their grandmother's house, in a neighborhood right by the New Haven dump. Maceo and his sister lived with their mother in an apartment on Chapel Street in a seedy part of New Haven, right by St. Raphael's Hospital. We saw ourselves as unified by family dysfunction and sub-standard living arrangements, and often joked about the gravel pit, the dump and the hospital. As with the multicultural ball-breaking at the lunch table, I think Kenny, Tony, and I saw this shared hardship as something that trumped racial difference.

Because I had the car, I used to drive us around everywhere, and in that first summer of freedom, Tony, Maceo and I all got jobs in the dish room of St. Raphael's hospital. (Kenny got a job there the following summer.) I used to park my car on Day Street by Maceo's apartment building, to avoid having to pay for the parking garage, and after work we'd all hang out. Soon, however, Tony got a car of his own, and a girlfriend, so I began spending a lot of time at Maceo's.

I liked hanging out at Maceo's. His mom was cool and smart and attractive. She was tall and thin and light-skinned like him, with the same green eyes. She was studying law at Yale. His sister Joju was also cool, smart and attractive, though Maceo did not like me to acknowledge any of those things.

Maceo's mom kept odd hours because she was in law school, and practiced a sort of free-range parenting that was atypical even for the mid-1980s. Maceo and I often found ourselves sitting with her at the kitchen table after a late night of gallivanting around the city, having deep conversations about life. It was during these conversations that I learned that Maceo was the son of Eldridge Cleaver, the Black Panther Minister of Information who ran for president in 1968, and who fled to Cuba to avoid capture after he was charged with trying to kill a police officer in a shootout, and that his mother was Kathleen Neal Cleaver, Eldridge's wife and one of the most prominent and influential women in the Black Panther Party. Maceo had been born in exile in Algeria, and his sister had been born in North Korea.

I don't want to cast Maceo into the role of Bagger Vance or Red from *The Shawshank Redemption*. I don't want to tell a puerile story about race or a conversion narrative about prejudice. But my friend-ship with Maceo—which was as flawed and complicated, and fraught with misunderstandings and disagreements as possible—was perhaps the most important friendship of my life. My friendship with Maceo brought me into a world that was largely hidden from me, or at best misrepresented.

One of the first things I did after learning who Maceo's parents were was to read *Soul On Ice*. Then I went on a reading binge, absorbing as much literature by and about African Americans as I could. I recall vividly the impressions made by *Malcolm X Speaks* and *Cry Freedom*. I also asked Maceo and his mom lots of questions. At the time, I had tremendous difficulty accepting what I saw as the angry messages of the Black Panthers, Malcolm X, and Stokely Carmichael. I was much more comfortable with the more peaceful writings of Martin Luther King Jr. or Stephen Biko. I wanted progress and change but I wanted it to come without disruptions. I wanted to not be made uncomfortable.

Once we began college, Maceo majored in African studies and would send me his reading lists. I would read as much as I could so we could talk and argue during the summer and winter breaks. Meanwhile, as an English major and sociology minor at UConn, I took sociology courses on race and English courses like Black Writers I and II, with the professor who would later be my honors thesis advisor, Rufus Blanshard. Rufus had created those courses after having been active in the civil rights movement and adopting two African American children. For my honors thesis, I wrote about Toni Morrison and John Edgar Wideman.

My friendship with Maceo was not easy. I did not always like what I heard or agree with what Maceo had to say, and we often argued. At times we even avoided each other for days after a particularly heated discussion. But we respected each other enough – loved each other, even, though we would have never said so – that we never quit the friendship and we never avoided returning to our difficult conversations.

I remember there were times when I wanted so badly to defend myself and my ancestors against any racist charges. I learned in a course I took that at one point in Mexican history a group of Irish conscripts had defected from the English army and joined up with the Mexicans, seeing in their fight a common enemy. I shared this proudly with Maceo, who countered with stories of Irish violence upon African Americans in New York and elsewhere during the Civil War, because Irish men resented the idea of fighting to free slaves who would simply become competitors for scarce employment opportunities.

Maceo never let me win these arguments, which was exasperating, but in hindsight he was right, even though he was infuriating. In fact, over time, Maceo's relentless nature caused all our other white friends to cut ties with him, and they would even ask me why I put up with him. Honestly, I can't explain why I maintained our friendship. Perhaps it was because I got to see my familiar world through a different set of eyes, though that seems to sell the friendship short. Nonetheless, with Maceo I witnessed microaggressions and police profiling, and workplace discrimination that I had heard about and read about but never would have experienced firsthand.

One time Maceo and I were walking down Quinnipiac Avenue, and a white woman entering the street from a retail parking lot, seeing our approach, quickly locked her car door. (Remember, we were Catholic school boys and were thus pretty clean cut in appearance.)

Another time, a fight broke out between a bunch of guys from our high school, and some guys from another high school in front of Naples Pizza, right in the heart of Yale's campus. There were at least a dozen guys throwing punches when the police arrived, and we all ran. After we thought it was safe, we all returned on foot to retrieve our cars. The police were waiting to ambush us, but Maceo, who was the only black guy in the fight, was the only one of us the police arrested and took away in their cruiser.

The hospital where we all worked liked to hire boys from Catholic high schools. We mostly worked twenty hours a week, but Maceo could only get twelve hours, no matter how hard he worked or how reliable he proved to be. The really odd thing was that this occurred despite the fact that our immediate supervisors were black. But this internalized racism was also becoming increasingly revealed to me, as well. Like the time Maceo and George attempted to crash a party at a black fraternity but the brothers wouldn't let George in because he was too dark.

I also witnessed the latent hostility many black people had for whites but which was typically held in check in the workplace and in public. One time I was emerging from Maceo's apartment, which was not in the best of neighborhoods, and a man sitting on the stoop of the apartment building next door began to verbally attack me because he thought I was there to buy drugs or hire a prostitute. I was terrified when he stood up and began to approach me, but fortunately for me his voice drew the attention of the neighbors, and the woman who lived below Maceo's family came to the window and shouted down to her neighbor that I was friends with the boy upstairs, and not there to buy drugs or a prostitute. The man stopped on a dime, apologized, and returned to his stoop.

When I related this story to Maceo later, he said to me something he often said—"It's a whole other world."

The Drift

I THINK BACK TO THOSE YEARS, and to that friendship in particular, and I realize that I had an unusual and privileged experience. Unfortunately, Maceo and I did not remain close. At first it was just normal circumstances that drew us apart. Both of us chose to remain at college for the summer between our junior and senior years. Although we wrote letters now and then, since email and social media were not part of anyone's world yet, our correspondence became less frequent. Then I moved to California for graduate school, and we just fell out of touch. Last I heard, Maceo had moved to the Middle East, converted to Islam, married, opened a dojo, and wrote a book titled *Soul on Islam,* riffing upon the title of his father's book.

In one sense, it's not so unusual that Maceo and I drifted apart. In fact, I have very little contact with any of my high school friends. But somehow my life seems like it has become more racially segregated than it was in high school. I guess I assumed that since I had so many black friends in high school and in college – including a roommate and a housemate, which is remarkable considering how white UConn was in the late 1980s – that my adult life would be more integrated. But the reverse seems to have happened.

I'm Facebook friends with a few of the black guys I knew in high school, as well as with a former girlfriend. I exchange Christmas cards with George Logan, and Mark Bigard lives near my uncle and always says to say hello. But I have no contact with any of my black friends from college, except one guy from grad school who lives in the D.C. area. Otherwise, in general I see very few black people in my personal or my professional life at all. There is one black couple in our circle of friends. I have a black colleague across the hall I get along with. But I still don't understand how or why there are not more black people in my life.

Maybe it's a silly example, but whenever I chat on Facebook with my friend in D.C., I peek at his friends and notice that they're over-whelmingly black. Mine are not. Why are our social circles these horribly skewed Venn diagrams of race? It feels like high school all over again, with that one table of black guys eating by themselves.

I wish I knew. I wish I knew why a disproportionate number of the sixty-one guys who entered high school with me but dropped out by senior year were black. I wish I knew why schools of education strug-gle to recruit black people into the profession. I wish I knew why my incredibly diverse circle of friends includes more Africans from Africa than it does African Americans descended from slaves. I assume the causes are institutional, but I can't see the mechanisms.

I'm happy that when my son came home from school and told me how much he liked his funny social studies teacher that I didn't learn until parent-teacher conferences that he was black. I'm glad that when my son told me how much he disliked his bus driver because he was such a jerk that he never mentioned that he was black. My son seems relatively blind to the significance of skin color, as does his sister. But I know from my own life that this is likely just superficial, that without friendships and shared stories, my son's and daughter's understandings of race are limited, at best.

I don't have good answers to my questions or my confusions. I don't know if anyone does. I do know that we need to talk and tell each other our stories, and that we can't let fear make us shy away when those conversations get uncomfortable or heated. But truly, that's the easy part. The hard part is putting people in position to even have those conversations. Where do we begin? ▪

Beth Lyon Barnett

Liza Pearl

THE SUMMER BEFORE MY PARENTS sent me away to camp, my aunt's maid Hazel walked her daughter Liza Pearl across the street to play. It was a busy thoroughfare, and like me, Liza Pearl was only eight years old. She had tight black braids and a shy, sweet smile. She said she liked to play house and paper dolls and jacks. I liked to play Buck Rogers and kickball. We compromised with hopscotch, a game drawn with chalk on the sidewalk. Once in awhile, she won.

Liza Pearl wore hand-me-down clothes. I could tell because her shirt had my school's name on it, and I knew she didn't go there.

Sometimes we crawled under the lilac bushes out of the hot sun and told stories. Hers were filled with castles, magic and faraway lands. She got a distant look in her eyes and stopped at the most exciting part. She giggled when I poked her to continue, and I could see the pink of her mouth and her big white teeth.

My best friend Caroline and Liza Pearl didn't know each other. Caroline loved to climb trees. One day, she and I decided to try to reach the top of the twin poplar trees in the empty lot behind my house. We each weighed about eighty pounds, and the slender limbs of the trees held us as we shimmied to the tops. I waved at Caroline from my treetop. Just as she started to wave back, the limb on which she stood broke. I watched in horror as she crashed to the ground and landed with a thud.

Before I could climb down my tree, I saw Liza Pearl, arms swinging, dash across the street. She rushed to Caroline who lay flat on her back gasping for breath. Liza Pearl quickly rolled Caroline to her side and patted her on the back.

I slid down the tree taking all the branches with me, and watched, paralyzed with fear. "I think she's turning blue," I cried.

Liza Pearl hit her again, harder. Caroline took a deep breath and coughed. Her color returned, and after a few moments, she sat up.

"Anything broke?" Liza Pearl asked.

Caroline gingerly felt her arms and legs.

"Shouldn't be climbing no spindly trees," Liza Pearl said.

Caroline stood up and brushed herself off.

Liza Pearl grinned. "My mother just baked some cookies. Bet she'd give us some."

Caroline shook her head. "I'm not allowed to play with niggers," she said.

I stared at her, too stunned to speak.

Liza Pearl's smile faded, replaced by hurt and anger. Then, eyes lowered, she dodged the heavy traffic and ran back across the street.

I watched her go, an ache in my heart. "Why did you say that?"

"Because it's true. My father says we can't associate with them."

I ran to the curb, calling after Liza Pearl. She and her mother stood in the doorway of my aunt's house. Hazel looked at me and shook her head before she and Liza Pearl, both with their heads held high, walked to the bus stop. The bus came and they climbed aboard.

I never saw Liza Pearl again.

But I've always remembered her, never more poignantly than the day I stepped off a train in Texas, a seventeen-year-old girl bound for college. I went to a cab parked at the curb and asked the Negro driver if he would take me to my school. "I'm not allowed to carry whites," he replied, his tone defiant and resentful. Then he drove away. I felt the same rejection and hurt I'd seen in Liza Pearl's eyes.

■ ■ ■

IN MY THIRTIES, I worked for a volunteer child advocate agency, and found myself assigned to a case in the dingy, mostly black settlements where teenage boys clustered in the streets. The sight of them scared me. I thought maybe I should have carried pepper spray, but then I saw laughing children playing hopscotch like Liza Pearl and I used to do. They smiled and waved as I walked by, and I decided I didn't need pepper spray.

Florence had come to live with us when I was very small. She had her own room with a bath next to the kitchen. A heavyset black woman with an infectious laugh and two thumbs on her right hand, she cooked and cleaned every day except Thursdays and Sundays.

Florence worked for us for many years, and became a much-loved member of our family. I never knew or wondered where she went on her days off, but she always returned the next day wearing her freshly pressed white uniform and her polished white shoes.

When Florence passed away, I attended her funeral. I realized she'd had a life apart from mine—a daughter who worked in the mayor's office and grandchildren older than I.

Stylishly dressed women who wore matching hats adorned with flowers and ribbons sat quietly during church speeches and announcements. Had my Florence looked like them on her days off?

I was the only white person in the church. The ushers seated me with the family. I felt uncomfortable and under dressed in my simple, dark blue pantsuit. Florence's great-granddaughter, a pretty, chocolate-colored child of eight, leaned forward and said, "Don't worry. The funeral service will begin soon." Her kindness reminded me of Liza Pearl.

At fifty, I lived in suburbia, a nice house in an all white area. One day, a woman and her black husband moved in next door. The man drove a new car, but with windows so dark no one could tell who was behind the wheel. I asked him about that and he said, "Otherwise, the police stop me. They say black men don't belong here." I remembered Caroline didn't think Liza Pearl belonged either.

I'm older now—yet there are still people who must be reminded that black lives matter. Law enforcement officers kill African Americans on the street. Racial slurs occur with frequency on university campuses.

I fume at prejudice and write stories and books about it, and send letters to the editor. I know in my heart that Liza Pearl and I would agree—things are better. But not enough has changed since our hopscotch days. There is still much to do. ■

Ann Chandonnet

A White Mother Speaks

WHEN MY FIRST SON WAS A YEAR OLD, still small enough to ride in a baby backpack, the Anchorage supermarket checker kept giving me a hard time: "He's so dark. Your husband must be dark."

Slapping my pound of carrots on the conveyor belt, I tried to ignore the curious bitch. Eventually my husband accompanied us to the supermarket, and the checker kept her trap shut from then on. I'm pretty sure she thought I slept around.

Our first son was adopted from Costa Rica. We were living in Oakland, California at the time, and applied through the County Adoption Agency. Oakland was then 50 percent black. At an orientation meeting, we stated we would like a baby of any color. "You need to be extra special to adopt a black baby," we were told.

Prospects did not look good. This was not long after the People's Park[1] era, and many single mothers were giving their babies up at one or two years old. But most were hanging onto the infants I craved. And, worst of all, there were three qualified couples for every one available child. I really disliked the thought of "competition" with other couples yearning as we were for parenthood.

A couple of months later, I met a friend of my boss, a kindly man who had served with the Peace Corps in Costa Rica. I blurted out my poor baby prospects. Lo and behold, he knew several people in San Jose, and soon my husband and I were hiring a lawyer there to apply for an infant who had not yet been born.

---

1   A park created during the radical political activism of the late 1960s. near the University of California, Berkeley.

After a good deal of paperwork and translating said paperwork, a home study and fingerprinting, we found ourselves winging south to sign papers to adopt a ten-day-old male. On the one hand, the baby had a big head of black hair – which everyone declared would fall out. On the other hand, he was non-thriving, but I felt more positive when the San Francisco-trained pediatrician who examined his reflexes said, "He just needs TLC (tender loving care)."

Summoning all my stubbornness, I made an appointment with the local consulate. I managed to wangle our five-pound-two-ounce-brown-eyed child a ninety day tourist visa. I whisked Baby home to Oakland and fed him every two hours for two weeks. By then our twenty-one incher started to look less like a concentration camp victim. In a couple of months, he was able to stay awake for more than an hour at a time. His cheeks were plump! Success at last! [With the exception of lookie-loos like the supermarket checker.]

(BTW, his big head of hair never did fall out. It just got adorably curly.)

When Baby was ten months old, we moved to Anchorage, Alaska. (In the meantime, I had taken our son to Vancouver to re-enter the country as a registered alien.) When he turned two, we decided to apply for a second child – a girl this time. There was a small monkey wrench in the works; shortly after our home study was completed, I became pregnant. So when the State Adoption Agency called with news of a healthy boy, I was squirming in an emotional stew. A hundred other qualified couples had turned this baby down because he was African American. To my husband and me, health was more important than gender or race.

Then, as had happened previously, I showed signs of miscarriage. I told our social worker that I needed time to consider. After my gyne-cologist gave me a fifty-fifty chance of carrying to term, he said, "My wife had three miscarriages before she gave birth." But he modified that positive statement with a negative, "Don't turn down any babies."

My breasts grew. My belly swelled. I began to hope.

But, at ten weeks gestation, although my blood work still showed pregnant, palpating proved I was no longer carrying. After tears and hugs, we phoned our patient social worker and blurted something like, "We'll take him." Our second son was five weeks old on the day he was flown to Anchorage, and our first son couldn't wait to hold him. And neither could I.

At age thirty-one, I now have two wonderful sons. Two gorgeous boys who match neither each other nor me. And that is how it came about one summer afternoon when they were three and one respectively, sitting in my grocery cart, a man approached me for sex. Of course, I must sleep with anyone. This supermarket stocked condoms next to the bubble gum at the registers, so I suppose I should have expected this scene. (I'd already had a door slammed in my face when a neighbor got a glimpse of my new son's hue.)

At four, our older son, equipped with character references from two people who had known him for more than two years, became an American citizen. He liked the little flag; he thought the ceremony was way too long.

Instead of learning what it is to be "white in America," I have learned as an adult what it is to be black or Hispanic. When my older son was about to begin kindergarten, I received letters from the school district instructing me to register him for English as a Second Language. Well, he had picked up a few words from the television program *Villa Alegre*. But I had spoken (and sung) English to him since he was ten days old. Eventually I was able to get my five-year-old mono-linguist dismissed from attending the ESL class. (Eventually I met the ESL instructor. She was Chinese; English was her second language.)

When I drove my sons to hobby shops to buy stickers for their skateboards, I was ignored. But their shopping was followed in big, shiny mirrors hanging in the corners near the ceiling. Obviously they were potential shoplifters. "Their kind" was like that.

When my teenaged black son bought a Swatch at Nordstrom's, the clerk gave him the wrong change. I was window shopping on the opposite side of the jewelry counter, and saw his quizzical look. He wasn't sure what to do. However, I knew instantly what had happened, charged over, identified "my son" and told the clerk to get with it. I should have reported the bitch, but I was too angry. I just wanted to exit ASAP.

When he was twenty or so, he and his non-black best friend went riding on their motor bikes in a thousand-acre park near downtown Anchorage. They were shot at. The police never found that white van.

We fed these kids well. They swam, skated, skied, biked, hiked, picked berries, played ice hockey, learned chess, and built "forts." They're both over forty now. One is six feet; the other, five ten. If one of these linebackers spontaneously hugs me in public, the concealed carriers start to reach inside their car coats.

Americans are damned rude. If your group sports a variety of skin tones, irrepressible Americans are sure that gives them the right *and* the permission to ask impolite questions: "Who's this?" "Was he illegitimate?" "Was that his name when you got him?" "Do they call you 'Mom'?" "How is the experiment going?" "Is your daughter-in-law black?" Or they make assumptions: "I see you have the baseball team with you today."

The oldest of five, I grew up in rural Massachusetts as a consummate WASP, weighed down by the big thumbs of bigoted parents and their ancestors. When my paternal grandfather was selling property in the 1950s, he refused to sell it to the "damned Greeks or the damned Irish." My blue-eyed, blonde mother didn't like to admit that her great-grandparents on her mother's side were MicMac Indians. My farmer father was concerned that all my high school BFF's were Catholic. I did not encounter mixed-race couples until I attended graduate school in Madison, Wisconsin.

As a mother, I've learned how whites see themselves: as the golden monarchs perched on top of the heap; as the hasty administrators of justice; as the smug definers of good manners; and as the year-round, prelapsarian scrooges found everywhere. If you're white and live in Alaska, you lower your voice when discussing the "others." If you're white and live in Missouri, you assume all other whites think as you do about those dreaded welfare recipients. If you're white and live in North Carolina, you assume everyone likes dead Obama jokes. If you're white and live almost anywhere in these fifty states, all those "others" are ugly, irresponsible, shiftless, dirty, stupid and very, very different. And they lunch on weird food like spicy soup with worms.

Perhaps I should mention that I married a Shiftless French-Cana-
dian Catholic. And I'm still in touch with two of those Catholic BFF's.

Retired, I live thirty miles from Ferguson. I consider myself a
lapsed Protestant, a lapsed Yankee, a lapsed white. I admit to being the
extremely proud mother of two sons as well as the proud grandmother
of three beautiful girls under nine. Those precious, talented girls must
now make their way in the world – and it's downright thrilling that the
United States is becoming the land of Hispanics.

P.S. We have never told our son about those hundred couples. ▪

Barbara Kellam-Scott

New to New Jersey, 1967

W**E WEREN'T ENTIRELY THE RUBES** our neighbors thought we were, though as the daughter of this man from Ohio, I'd been very carefully sheltered. Only a couple of years earlier, in sixth grade, I wasn't allowed to serve on safety patrol, because Dad found it inappropriate for a girl to stand on a street corner in Ohio's capital city, even in the nearly suburban North End, even to help her younger neighbors get home from school safely, even though she walked seven blocks to and from school herself, right down High Street.

Now, newly turned fourteen, I had moved to New Jersey and was living in real suburbia, close enough to New York City for day trips, or for Mother and Dad to go to actual Broadway plays, but out in the world of wide lawns where wild rabbits might nest and multiple-car garages. Many of our neighbors drove into the city each day for work, or parked at Ridgewood and rode the train. Dad drove what was still our only car, a couple of close-packed towns away, to the job that had brought us here. He told us the front lawn of the building was carefully manicured as a croquet court, and only the super-privileged members of the staff were invited out to play on it at lunchtime.

I'd gotten through the eighth grade here, and mourned the loss of my violin teacher and my seat in the orchestra that always won the citywide competition. The spring concert of the little six-piece effort in my new school, where Mark and I took turns being "concert master," had left Dad in tears, and not in a good way. After Mother took me to the high school we shared with half of the next town to register for my freshman year, we decided not to tell Dad more than that there was no program at all for strings. We would keep to ourselves the grudging suggestion that I might be able to play oboe parts in the stage band, as long as I sat behind the risers where nobody would see my bow moving.

My older brother, Jeff, was still angry, not so much for anything specific that he'd left behind in Columbus as for the way he was treated by the rich kids at this high school, just when he should have been enjoying the privileges of an upperclassman. He had no great strengths to fall back on, and that must have added to Dad's grief at what he'd dragged us into. He'd had no idea, when he accepted the transfer to the home office of his magazine, of the cost of living near New York. We were renting a barely adequate house. We couldn't afford a second car. Everything was just so much harder.

And then the news of riots.

They would demand we become aware that there were people with harder lives yet. And they would threaten even what we were struggling to accept; or at least what Dad was aware of. It must have been on the New York news reports when it started on Thursday, but the first I knew about anything would be after the weekend. I didn't see Thursday's evening paper, from Newark itself, with the headline on page one and above the fold, as Dad would say, but still below a photo of the crowning of Miss Tall ("White") America, when the Mayor assured us the "Trouble in Central Ward [was an] Isolated Incident."

By the next day's paper, it was *the* headline, most of the front page, with words like "riots" and "mobs," and even "battleground." The State Troopers and the National Guard had already been called in. A few people were dead, hundreds hurt, even more arrested. I was oblivious. I couldn't tell you what I was doing that day, or on Saturday as a police detective was killed by a sniper and stones were thrown in Plainfield, a town just in our direction and still 30 percent "Negro." By Sunday the headline was a little quieter, and the riot news was less than half the page, but there had been the whole weekend for Dad to worry and look at the maps.

Monday morning, July 17, he stopped shielding us, or at least me and my ten-year-old brother, Charley. Mother got us all up before Dad was to leave for work. He assembled us in the kitchen, at the back of the house. "Newark's been burning all weekend." I had no idea where Newark was. "If it starts in Paterson this week, they'll be coming over the hill for honky." As much as I struggled, I couldn't make anything of what he was saying. Mother had her fists on her hips, so it was clearly serious. I wanted to cry, but I didn't know why. Jeff had his arms folded on his chest and was nodding knowingly. He was dressed already, and not protesting about being up. The men must have already been talking about it.

"I have to go to work now, but I'll have the radio on all day. Your Mother will have the radio on here too. She or Jeff will be here in the kitchen the whole time to listen for news." I didn't like being one of the children, left out of this whole crisis. *"Listen!"* Dad shouted, grabbing Charley's arm that was reaching out toward the dog, *"This is serious!"*

When he was sure he had our full attention, he gave us more detailed instructions. "You are to stay in the back of the house. Go through the living room only to go upstairs, and stay as far away from the front window as you can, or get down out of sight. You can play outside, but only in the back yard, and that means your bikes too. Only as far as the back of the house. Keep the dog on her leash, and keep her inside as much as you can. *Do you hear?"* We nodded yes. I was starting to be frightened, though I still had no idea just what the threat was.

"If your Mother hears one word about Paterson, she'll call me, and you will have to come in and help her pack up what will fit in the car." His words weren't from any scenario I could recognize. "Barbara, you'll need to get your cat into her carrier. If you don't, we will leave her here. I'm sorry, but we have to be ready to go." Mother moved over to me and put her hand on my shoulder. "If I hear anything," Dad continued, "I will come home immediately. We'll load the car, and we'll go back to Ohio... We'll have to go by back roads." Well, that at least explained where he meant for us to go, but I still had no idea why. And who was "honky"?

Dad finally picked up his briefcase, and he and Mother kissed in that wistful way they did when they hadn't had enough sleep and something had gone or was about to go very wrong. She obeyed him and stayed in the kitchen while he drove out the driveway and off to work. She dutifully turned on the radio to WCBS AM, an all-news station. Then she sent Charley and me back upstairs to get dressed while she made our breakfast. I tried not to look at the window as I passed it. Jeff sat down at the table and turned a worried face to the back yard, chewing his thumbnail and looking very responsible.

I wish I could remember more about how that day of waiting went. Between Mother and the radio, I must have learned something about what had happened in Newark, how close Paterson was, and why there was a risk that it would catch fire. I must have learned who "honky" was, though my parents never said a word of either fear or dislike of colored people, as I think we called them. They were mostly a mystery to me, people who showed up on TV sometimes. I knew there was a lot going on for them, but Mother and I were usually busy with dinner while Dad watched Walter Cronkite.

I must have mostly stayed inside that day, to keep an eye on Susie, my cat, and help Mother, who I think was getting all of our clothes washed and ironed and ready to pack if we needed to. I might have crept upstairs to read on my bed, but my desk was in a front window, and I wouldn't have dared sat there, though I couldn't help envisioning gangs sweeping over the hill where Paterson lurked.

I do know that Dad came home from work at the normal time. Nobody watched Walter Cronkite, because the TV was in the living room with the big dangerous window facing the street. We left the lights off in there. Things stayed pretty subdued. We might have eaten out on the screened back porch, because it would have been hot. And the summer unfolded without further terror. High school began, and the next year we moved to Ramsey, to our own house, but I don't remember safety from riots figuring into the move. Ramsey High had one black physical education teacher, and she seemed to fit in like all the other physical education teachers, and I never thought much more about how she was different.

In fact, I don't remember that race ever came up again in our lives until I fell in love with a Pakistani man the summer I turned twenty. And somehow Dad was more upset about the places I wanted to go with Zeb than he had been with the couple of other guys I'd actually dated, and I didn't understand why until after I married a white man the following year. But again, when I got it, I was more than a little disappointed to know how much of Dad's sheltering me had always been based on fear. ∎

Bonnie Schell

Being White in Atlanta During Desegregation

THE SUPREME COURT'S ORDER to desegregate schools was made on May 17, 1954 when I was ten years old, but nothing happened when I was in fifth grade except that Miss Milam, our teacher, slipped on some milk the boys had spilled on purpose, broke her hip and had to leave teaching. I stayed home for four days with asthma because I had known what was going to happen to Miss Milam and said nothing. I missed long division completely. The other thing that happened was that adults began to have bad tempers and cluster in whispers.

I had never seen any ten year olds whose skin was different from mine in Southwest Atlanta except for Julie Mae who was an albino with pink eyes, a hat and long sleeves to protect her from light. I had only seen little black children because on Sundays after church my stepfather would drive us by the big AME Zion Church so we could see all the decorated little children, who were called "pickaninnies," getting out of church. They had short pigtails with bows and multicolored barrettes sticking out like the rays of rainbows. They were allowed to skip down the sidewalk by themselves without holding their mothers' hands, something I longed to do. The boys would run around wildly on the grass, sometimes in the street, with their fathers yanking their arms back to the curb. Their mamas wore beautiful big hats and gloves to match. My mama wore a small navy hat and white gloves.

I did know one colored girl who lived at the end of Morrow Road in a tiny house rented from my grandpa. Her name was Geneva and she didn't go to school because there wasn't a colored school in Clayton

County. When my mother was little during the depression, she went to a one-room school house in Stockbridge, Georgia where black children who wanted to learn to read could sit in the back row if there was room. The women of Geneva's family took in heavy washing from both white and black farm families. The women used huge iron pots in the front yard for washing in well water. The blankets and towels were laid out on granite stones to dry. My mama had a Bendix washing machine.

One day when grandpa went down there and was chewing the fat with Geneva's daddy, I walked casually behind the house and found Geneva with a bottle of red fingernail polish. She painted mine and I painted hers. Up close the skin across her wide nose, cheeks and forehead looked like polished mahogany. She had big black eyes, long lashes, and a faded dress made out of feed sack cotton. Her elbows, knees and ankle bones were too big for her legs and arms. When we came back out front, grandpa already had the hickory switches in his right hand. I stood dead still. I thought he was coming after Geneva.

"Bonnie Jo, git yourself over here, now."

Me? Geneva stood behind her daddy. My grandpa had fire in his eyes. I had been allowed to play with Geneva since we were both toddlers and dug in the dirt to find roly-poly bugs.

"It is written," boomed my grandpa without his teeth, "behold a great red dragon having seven heads and ten horns and seven crowns upon his heads. And the great red dragon was cast out, that old serpent, called the Devil and Satan, which deceiveth the whole world." My grandpa fell in a well for seven days when he was twenty-seven and had no mind when he was rescued except for the Book of Revelations upon which on special Sundays, he exhorted sinners at Noah's Art Methodist Church.

I tucked my nails into the palms of my hands and Geneva hid her hands behind her back. "But the red comes off with polish remover," I pleaded.

"Woe upon you," cried my grandpa as he leveled the switches across my legs, over and over, until I could feel the welts swelling and saw my own blood on the ends of the hickory switches. Then he grabbed my hands and laid the switches across my fingers.

"Marks of the Devil," shouted Grandpa.

I was mortified to be punished in front of colored people.

"Have mercy," said Geneva's daddy softly.

Grandpa paid no attention to Geneva's daddy who stepped forward to block Grandpa's rage. Grandpa grabbed my dress, then by the neck and marched me back up the road to his farm house where my grandmother rung out warm cloths for my legs, but said nothing to him.

My mother and her sisters wore glossy natural pink nail polish. They had been allowed to leave the farm and go to business school in Atlanta while the brothers stayed out of even high school to help their father with the farm. Then they left to become truck drivers but built their homes on grandpa's land. Mama went to live with Captain and Mrs. Robbins of the Salvation Army, and she learned to play a horn. While she was going to business college she worked in the Salvation Army's shelter that fed the poor. The preaching came after the eating, and then the black men had to go back on the streets mama said. They couldn't sleep on cots in the shelter alongside white men.

Black women who got on the Lynhurst bus smelled like fried fat back, boiled collards, and bleach. The inside of their hands was a beautiful rosy pink like the center of watermelon. Hattie, who came to iron for mama (except for my stepfather's handkerchiefs which I had to do myself) never spoke of children or had any pictures to show. She was quiet except for humming most of the time. My mother had an ironing machine for sheets and pillowcases. Once Hattie burned her hand on it and her dark skin came off. Her blood was red, not black as I had been told, and the skin underneath was the same color as mine. Hattie took care of it and made a bandage out of a strip of her apron, because the hospital near us wouldn't bandage the hands of a colored woman. I got her some ice cubes because I had learned in Girl Scouts that ice was better for a burn than Vaseline petroleum jelly. That day Hattie ironed until six o'clock and got on the bus in the dark after my mama came home from work, so I don't think Hattie had any children at her house to cook for. Maybe she didn't have a husband either.

Black men didn't come to our neighborhood unless they were hired to dig a trench for rain water or to work on a roof. They could not even come into the house or onto a porch, but black women even helped with births and burials out in the country. When my grandmother had twins, a black woman wet-nursed one of the babies. I had seen a lot of black men on chain gangs up and down highways. If you saw one downtown coming toward you on the side walk, you were supposed to cross over to the other side of the street because they had knives in their pockets. Little black boys were clever like Little Black Sambo and Brer Rabbit. They could trick you into doing what they wanted. My Uncle Hollis was killed at a bar by a black man who shot him in the back due to mistaken identity. My mother's family never talked about the incident because Uncle Hollis was in a bar, and they were Methodists.

Nothing happened in sixth grade except clusters of parents at my Presbyterian church raised their voices about "state's rights" and "separate but equal" in the Fellowship Hall. Before that, the men would kid the girls about having boyfriends or ask us if we liked school. Now they stared at us with worried brows, but said nothing to us anymore as if we had done something wrong.

Public water fountains and restrooms were marked for whites and "Colored Only." If you put your mouth on the white's faucet, you would get trench mouth. If you put your mouth on the colored fountain's spout, you would get pregnant with a black baby. I had permission to check out books in the adult section of the Carnegie Library so I drank from the colored water fountain to prove that warning was a lie. Once I opened the door of the black women's bathroom in the Woolworth's five and dime store. The toilet spaces didn't have doors; there was no mirror on the wall.

In seventh grade my parents said I might not be able to go to Southwest High School. They wanted me to go to a better school like Arlington in northeast Atlanta. They talked about driving me there and getting to work on time and somehow getting money out of our house. I remember having to wear my best plaid skirt, white blouse and polished shoes to go for an interview. I don't think the private school liked me, because in eighth grade I started Southwest High as a sub-freshman. Some of us were separated into an advanced Ford Foundation scholars program. He was a rich man intent on helping the South catch up. Classes were hard.

One by one, the boys left Southwest High to go to Georgia Military Academy (GMA), which was owned by the wife of the movie star, Paul Newman. Only four boys were left in advanced classes: Richie, tiny, pimpled and according to the teachers, a genius at math; Will, a giant with pale skin and pink cheeks; Ted with beautiful eyes, but sloping shoulders whose mother wore a hairnet all the time like a waitress; and Jack with curly blonde hair who wanted to be a war correspondent in Vietnam. Jack and I became an award-winning debate team that beat Arlington School when we were debating whether or not the English school system was better than the American. Ted was my boyfriend. He was in ROTC and wore a uniform on Fridays when we had to eat fish sticks because of the Catholics even though Southwest Atlanta didn't even have a Catholic church. In history we studied the Constitution except for the fourteenth and fifteenth amendments, which the teacher said might be taken out.

Before the boys left for GMA, the girls had to sit on the back row in math class because the smart boys were expected to go to Georgia Tech. Now that most of the boys were gone, the girls had the same little green Fisher & Zeeber math book Georgia Tech used for freshmen even though girls couldn't go there or become engineers. In social studies we were assigned to read the front page of *The Atlanta Constitution* which "Covers Dixie like the Dew" and also to watch the six o'clock news. All the black children trying to go to white schools seemed to be in Alabama, Arkansas and Mississippi. I saw the National Guard in Arkansas shield nine black students from entering a white school. Who could learn anything if people had been jeering and throwing rocks at you before you got inside? My stepfather said they would close the school and they did. On TV I saw police use electric cattle prods to break up college student demonstrations. The news made me sick because I thought all people were born basically good and followed The Golden Rule. My stepfather said the National Guard and the police had no choice; when I was older and had bills to pay, I would understand.

In the summer Atlanta closed the Adams Park public swimming pool so colored kids wouldn't pee in it. My parents got a letter from the school saying the Cotillion Club was being canceled for the tenth graders. That club taught girls to walk with a book on their head, how to accept compliments, how to waltz and jitterbug. My father said there wouldn't be any school dances or proms even though we had no black students. My mother said that if blacks and whites got married, their children would be multicolored and have a hard time. My stepfather said Martin Luther King Jr. was smart and could speak well because everyone knew he was part white. Malcolm X had red hair.

Parents didn't talk about what was happening, and Reverend Griggs who began every sermon with "When you walk down the road of life," didn't talk about it either. Some mothers and the elders wanted the church to open a private elementary school. They said it was because young children needed a Christian education they weren't getting in public schools anymore.

One Wednesday night, two well-dressed black people, a soprano and tenor, showed up at our choir practice to ask if they could join. The choir director and organist said they didn't think the petitioning singers would like Presbyterian music which stuck to the notes on the page. The choir director closed the door. I didn't understand the decision because our popular quartet had lost its tenor due to divorce.

My best friend Carolyn and I always went to the corner drugstore where black people came to the back door to get their prescriptions. We sat on red stools at the counter, and had Cherry Cokes or root beer floats. We talked from 3:30 p.m. to 5:00 p.m. because we weren't allowed to tie up the phone at home. One Friday we came as usual to the drugstore and the stools had been taken out, and across the counter were displays of greeting cards. The pharmacist said they were "modernizing."

My sister and I weren't allowed to go to the mailbox at the end of the driveway because neighbors were saying that black men might drive their fast cars up on the curb and grab us. My stepfather put an extra bolt lock and sliding chain lock on the front, side and back doors and a heavy plant stand in front of the porch door to the yard. He painted all the windows shut. There were going to be crimes in our neighborhood so that white people would put their houses on the market and move. There was a rumor that Hank Aaron, a black baseball player, had looked at a house with a swimming pool and tennis court on the nicest street in Southwest Atlanta. He was able to pay cash for it. There was a rumor that an executive at the Chevrolet plant in Marietta was being transferred back to Detroit. The family might sell to the first buyer because they weren't southerners. Then the Klan would take care of them, my grandma said.

At night I had three flashlights under my pillow. I listened for strange sounds. I watched for headlight beams pulling into our driveway. On the city bus, black women began to shove against me when they moved down the aisle to the back. Men who used to look at their laps glared at me. It seemed to me that the boogie man who hid under beds, in closets and behind doors might be real. I was always afraid and jumpy, day and night, of an unknown thing. It seemed to me that the adults were creating a monster and now we were all afraid of it.

In 1962 I went to a private all girls' college to be a teacher, even though I wanted to be a writer and politician. If you became a teacher in Georgia for five years, you got a scholarship that paid part of the tuition and books. The college had a black student from Africa who spoke French and perfect English and a blind student who ate with her hands. I rode two buses back and forth as a day student. Once coming home, when my books were heavy, I went to the back of the bus where the colored people sat behind a line on the floor. I took a seat. The woman next to me said "You best get up because you're going to cause us trouble."

In the summer of 1963, Hattie asked for time off to go by bus to the March on Washington for jobs and freedom. My stepfather said it was silly for Hattie to go since she had six jobs ironing and cleaning. When Hattie came back, all she told me was that all the speakers were men. I asked her what Martin Luther King Jr. said and she replied, "Wait means never."

That same August I went to church camp at Camp Calvin where the counselors were student pastors from the Presbyterian seminary. We read Dr. King's "Letter from a Birmingham Jail" in the tradition of Paul writing to the early Christian churches. I came home to educate my parents.

"The founding fathers said that all men are created equal," I started, "and Jesus said we are to love one another as He loved us."

"We have to be realistic," retorted my stepfather.

"Remember when I got in trouble with Mrs. Hitchcock for asking in Sunday School how Cain and Abel got wives to make children? Did they marry their sisters?"

"You were a smarty pants and still are."

"Well Cain wasn't marked with dark skin because he killed his brother. Every continent and people have creation stories, even Africa."

"Look here, Bonnie Jo, we have to believe the Bible. It's the Word of God."

"No it isn't. Parts of it are just recordings of what people believed at the time, and we have interpreted the words to suit ourselves about race. The Bible says Cain was a tiller of the soil. That didn't mean that Negroes had to work the fields for plantation owners, and not rise to do other more skilled work."

"Look here, I have many black friends," my stepfather then asserted.

"Then why don't they come to see us and have supper? You're a bigot."

My stepfather slammed his fist down on the dining table and got purple in the face. "You are grounded for a month and I'll see that Rev. Griggs talks to the Presbytery about these so called counselors you had at camp, and you won't ever go back. Do you hear me?" I heard.

At my college we were served supper by black women dressed in black dresses with starched white aprons. I heard from two girls that some of those women lived in the basement of one of the administration buildings. The housing was free and the school funded the women's children, who lived with their grandmothers or aunts, to go on to a black college. My English professor said if the women were paid a living wage, they could live where they chose to. Why would they want to live in Decatur slums or in Atlanta's Buttermilk Bottom, my piano teacher asked, instead of a perfectly restored nineteenth century brick building with gardens and antique furniture?

On November 22, 1963, I was in a botany class walking the campus to identify different leaves by their Latin names when a runner came to tell us that President Kennedy had been shot and was dead. The professor said those who wanted to leave class could, but he was going to continue to cover material that would be on a test. I left and rode the bus home early. Hattie was crying. My mother was mute. My stepfather said Kennedy sympathized with communists and that he had sent his brother, the Attorney General, into the South to disturb voting and community schools, which had operated just fine without his Yankee intervention. The president got what he deserved.

How could this be? Did a black man really shoot the president I had voted for?

I watched the funeral procession on TV. It was sad, serious, and calm. I felt like screaming. I cried that week for no reason and couldn't talk. Sometimes I felt sick to my stomach, but I didn't want to eat. Every morning I slammed doors and screamed at my mother and sister who seemed to be from another planet. I couldn't sleep or pay attention to words in a book.

Ted took me to a production of *Othello*. The Moor was played by the white director of the small downtown Academy Theater. I was incensed and raised my voice so loud about denying black people a chance that Ted said I embarrassed him. The following week we broke up because I was "moody and unpredictable." Sometimes I waited after classes until dark and trudged up the hill to the observatory to see glimpses of other planets revolving around our sun. I wondered if in other universes space beings might not look like humans. I didn't want to go home to the questions on what I had been doing and the pontificating opinions about race, disparaging remarks about downtown where people had begun to shop where they pleased. In my bedroom, I struggled with John Milton and his descriptions of celestial light and dark obstinate angels. Where had light as good and dark as evil come from? In Classics, I could not focus and confused one God's deed with another's.

The college told my parents I needed to be evaluated by a psychiatrist. Dr. Yochem, with buffed fingernails and a bust of Freud on his desk, asked me about fears of sex and seduction in the dark. He didn't comment on my ideas about social justice or an understanding between colored and white people, or how separate could never be equal when both parties didn't have the same power. I could tell that he didn't like me. He didn't know how afraid I was of him and my own mind, which he had already cemented with Thorazine.

The dean let me stay in school. She said I could take an "Incomplete" in some courses and write my term papers over the summer. I wondered, when black students were allowed to attend my college, would they be given the same accommodation?

In summer of 1965 I went to see my grandparents. I walked down the road to find Geneva. She had taken over her dead mother's washing business. When I saw her, there were three stair-step children running around behind her. Although she smiled at me, the sparkle was gone from her unfathomable eyes. I wanted to talk to Geneva about her life and mine, but she was too busy to chat. I turned around and went back up the road crying and mad at her. Were we far more different than I could ever understand? ∎

Ray DiZazzo
_____

Am I A Racist?

'M SIXTY-NINE YEARS OLD, I consider myself a progressive Democrat, and for me, one of the most challenging aspects of being white in America is living with the possibility that I may be racist.

I tell myself I'm not, of course, but sometimes I'm not sure. I understand the horrors and injustices African Americans have endured at the hands of whites, and I empathize with their painful journey, but the uncomfortable truth is that sometimes I find myself harboring feelings of resentment toward them—or, rather, toward *some* of them.

My internal conflict goes something like this:

I have met many African Americans that I honestly consider not so much black or white, but just everyday good people. They are typically educated (not necessarily highly educated), responsible individuals who look and act, not exactly, but more or less like the people I associate with. They seem to fit comfortably into what I would consider a typical American way of life.

But there are also African Americans who stir those feelings of resentment in me. Many seem to project an image of arrogance. Some strut as if ready for a fight, and others talk loudly and angrily about how whites don't value black lives. Sometimes they try to take over public events to demand respect. These African Americans *don't* seem to fit in comfortably—at least not into my world. And it seems to me they foster a negative perception of African Americans in general.

So, am I a racist or not? Frankly, I'm not sure. But I am sure that the indecision and self-doubt are, for me, significant aspects of being a white man in America.

The Michael Brown and Tamir Rice tragedies offer good examples. Following those terrible incidents, loud, angry groups of African Americans blamed the police for brutality, and not valuing black lives. I believe that to a significant degree their accusations were warranted. But I don't believe Michael Brown's and Tamir Rice's families and supporters acknowledged that in both those tragic cases their sons also bore significant responsibility. Michael Brown had just robbed a liquor store, and he chose to wrestle with an armed police officer. Tamir Rice was aiming what appeared to be a loaded firearm at passersby in a Cleveland park.

On one hand, it seems logical to me that because the families were reluctant to accept at least some measure of responsibility, many white people felt resentful toward those families and their supporters. I've imagined that they might have verbalized their feelings something like this: "Wait a minute! We're supposed to take *all* the blame for this when none of it would have happened if these two young men hadn't prompted the police action in the first place?"

On the other hand, regardless of what these two individuals did, can there be any justification for, in Michael's case, shooting an unarmed man multiple times? And in Tamir's case, opening fire at a young boy with virtually no time to size up the situation? Would the same things have happened if the boys had been white?

Again, I'm just not sure, and for me, that's the problem.

Whatever the case, this line of thinking raises yet another difficult question— *"Why?"* Why did these two African American individuals act out these deadly events? I believe we as a predominately white society have prevented many African Americans from gaining the tools needed to earn respect. In too many cases we have not provided quality education, equal opportunities or fair treatment. And, yes, we have certainly been bigots. We persecute some blacks because we say they "cause trouble," but we've created the situations and environments that *made* some of them "troublesome." So, we continue to persecute them, they continue to cause trouble, and all this leads to a self-perpetuating cycle of violence, harassment, resentment and mistrust.

At the risk of belaboring this idea, here's one more "why" question: Why have we whites treated African Americans this way? Because of the color of their skin? Because of their history as slaves? Because our grandfathers "taught" us that "nigger" lives are not as valuable as white lives? That "Negroes" are not as smart as whites? That they are lazy? If you are middle-aged or a senior (as I said, I'm closing in on seventy) there's a good chance you were "taught" some or all of these things in your youth. And they are a perfectly legitimate reason why some blacks feel persecuted and undervalued in our society.

But then again . . .

As I've said, I'm honestly not sure about any of this. All of which takes me back to my original dilemma – am I, or am I not a racist? And a lack of that answer, an uncomfortable sense of indecision hovering just below the surface, encapsulates what it's like for me to be white in America. ■

David B. Axelrod

Cop Story

'VE BEEN DRIVING ON THE HIGHWAY for about twelve hours but when I get off, it's too soon. My motel is on the east side of the city, and I've exited on the west. It's about midnight on a cold, rainy night, and I find a wide boulevard that runs crosstown. I'm not thinking about my speed until I see the flashing lights of the cop car behind me, pulling me over.

I figure maybe I can save the cop some trouble if I get out of my car and walk over to him. Maybe I can talk my way out of the ticket. But as I approach, he jumps out of the car and hollers at me, "What are you doing? Get back in the car. I want your license and registration."

I walk to the rear of my car to open my trunk. I've got my brief-case in it and I need to retrieve the information for him. As the trunk lid pops open and I reach down to get what I need, I hear him shout something. I turn with my briefcase in my hand to find him standing in full firing position–feet spread, hands stretched out toward me with his gun aimed straight at me.

"I said 'freeze,'" he shouts at me. "What are you doing?"

"I had to get my license out," I tell him.

"Put the briefcase on the ground," he orders me, adding, "slowly."

I do, and he tells me to, "Take the license out, slowly."

I do, and he tells me, "Get back in your car and wait for me," just beginning to lower the gun.

I scurry into the car with my wallet and briefcase. He follows me to my window and takes my papers back to the cop car. I wait a while until he returns to hand my papers back together with a speeding ticket.

As I watch him drive away, I think to myself, "If I were black, I would probably be dead. He wouldn't have waited to see what I was doing when I turned. I'd be lying in the gutter with however many bullets in me. He gave me the benefit of the doubt."

I can't help thinking, it's America. It shouldn't be this way but life is dangerous – much more dangerous for some people than others. I can't help but ask myself, "Should I be grateful that I'm white or feel guilty?" ■

Alexander Jones

Being White in America

WHEN I READ THAT SOMEONE WAS LOOKING for personal narratives about what it means to be white in America a wave of confidence that I would have an easy time sitting down and writing an easy piece about it surged through me. I turned it over in my mind, sure that the meaning of being white in America would flow onto the page quickly and easily.

But it hasn't.

I figured that I have a few advantages. First I'm Jewish, which I've always thought gave me a perspective about white Christian America that others lacked; it's made me a fly on the wall for conversations that have made me uncomfortable, from time to time. Second, I've been the only white person, or one of a minority of white people on more than one occasion—I grew up in a town of minorities, I've worked a few jobs where I was the only white person. Lastly, I've dated black women; my current girlfriend is black, and we just had the preliminary marriage-house-kids discussion, and both our races didn't really make a difference in the talk.

But now, actually trying to transmute my lofty ideas into words, it's a snail's pace at best, and I keep referring back to the description page for further clarification that it's just not going to give me. I had some tasty anecdotes lined up, and some thoughtful commentary to share, but none of it feels quite right, none of it seems to quite get at what I think I'm thinking.

Because race in America is a slippery subject.

We all know racism when we see it, but it's not as easy to define as we like to believe. There's the basic idea that racism is discriminating against someone because they're black. Hiring an unqualified white guy when there's a qualified black guy. Going out of your way to ask a white guy for directions when there are plenty of black people on the same street, both of which I've seen other white people do. There's also the more controversial academic idea that racism is an institutionalized power structure that whites benefit from, so only whites can be racist. I originally balked at this definition because it seemed to discount people's thoughts and feelings, until a black coworker put it into perspective for me. I've never had a black boss. I've never rented an apartment from someone black, only had a handful of black teachers, none at the college level, and I've made more money than black people doing the same job. I thought it was unfair but didn't complain. I definitely didn't tell my coworkers.

Some truths:

Racism exists. Institutional racism exists. I don't know if that's because of the actual laws and policies that are written or because racists are the ones enforcing them, but I don't think it matters.

White privilege also exists.

Whether most white people will call it that doesn't matter. We know it's true. White people will discuss race and racial issues, just not with anyone who can be perceived as a minority, and certainly not with someone black. Sometimes this is just ingrained habit. Some white people worry about saying the wrong thing, and being branded racist. For me it's because I know I'm on the winning team even if I didn't ask to play—it's kind of like beating a buddy at a game of cards and trying not to rub it in that you just walked away with his cash—either out of a desire to keep the peace or guilt.

Most white people won't admit that they're racist, even though we all are. But that goes for everyone. Some of the most derogatory things I've ever heard came out of the mouths of other minorities. One time, I was hanging out with some coworkers and a black guy jogged past us. He was in great shape, muscles on top of muscles, jogging at a quick pace with barely a drop of sweat coming off him. A Portuguese Brazilian coworker watched him go by and said, "Damn! Imagine what he could do in a field of cotton." I've seen Indian store owners actively watch and then hassle black or Hispanic people who are lighter skinned than they are and then look at me for sly approval. I hope I'm not trying to explain away racism by saying that it's okay because everyone is doing it, but everyone is. So the problem goes deeper than just white people.

Most white people are also good people. I'm an optimist, so I like to think that most people are good people. Sometimes myopic, selfish, small minded or petty, but not usually malicious. And willing to delude ourselves. Currently I have a white coworker who was outraged and disgusted after he watched the video of the South Carolina police officer shooting Walter Scott in the back while he was running away. This same white coworker also gets along well with our black coworkers but will use the word "nigger" in casual conversation when he knows there aren't any black people around. This hypocrisy always frustrates but rarely baffles me. I just hope that if the chips are down he'll prove to be the good guy I hope he is. I would guess that the Germans and Poles who sheltered Jews during the Holocaust used occasional anti-Semitic slurs, here and there. And black people can and will turn around and hate on gays.

The root of white privilege is simple: the best thing to be is a rich American. And being white in America is American. People come to America from all over the world to pursue the idealized American Dream where you start with nothing but ambition and make your fortune with hard work and smarts. This is vastly over exaggerated silliness, but I've met crippled pipe-fitters with their homes in foreclosure who believe it. Pursuing money in America is to pursue a dream of whiteness. It's why black cops will give black citizens a harder time than they deserve and Indians will look at me for approval when a black kid takes too long in the candy aisle. Because once you've made the money, you'll be accepted by the white American society. Supposedly. The subliminal message is that white Americanness is yours when you've made the money to put on a suit and tie, drive an expensive car and have a house with a pool. The fact that things don't work out that way for many people is considered their personal failing, not white America's.

As an optimist I think things will improve. A lot of people point to Barack Obama as a symbol of post-racial America, and while I think he couldn't have been elected twenty or thirty years ago, I don't think that means we're close to done dealing with racism as an issue. But maybe, just maybe we're at the top of the fifth inning and Jackie Robinson is up at bat. Personally, as I contemplate a future that might include a half-black kid, I wonder what I'll have to tell him about teachers and cops and coworkers' gazes lingering on him (or her) for no reason. But on the other hand, I hope my potential child looks like the both of us. ∎

Culley Holderfield

What We Talk About When We Talk About Racism

[SPOILER ALERT: This post contains plot points from "Go Set a Watchman" (to the extent that the book had a plot)]

HAVE ROOTS THAT EXTEND TO THE DEEP SOUTH. My father was born in Mississippi, though he left as a young man. Growing up, when we visited my grandmother in Jackson we learned propriety and manners. We also watched her hang onto her house for too long out of concern that if she were to sell it, a black family might buy it. The worst thing for her would be that a sale she profited from would lead to racial contamination of the white neighborhood she'd lived in for fifty years. If you were to have asked her if she was racist, she would have said of course not. Black people were fine in her mind as long as they knew their place.

My uncle, her brother-in-law, was an unrepentant bigot and white supremacist. Integration was ruining the city of Jackson in his mind, and he didn't mind saying so. Sitting in his wood-paneled den with burled bookcases containing a VHS collection consisting solely of John Wayne movies, he would hold forth. He bragged about chasing the niggers off his lawn with his Remington shotgun. And we just sat there, shocked that such language was emanating from someone so related to us.

I just read *Go Set a Watchman* immediately after reading *To Kill a Mockingbird,* and I'm pondering the controversy surrounding Atticus Finch's "sudden" onset of racism in the "sequel." The big reveal in *Go Set a Watchman* is that Scout discovers that her father, the Atticus Finch known for his unimpeachable moral character, is in fact racist. It turns out that he is the head of Maycomb's Citizens' Council, organized after *Brown v. Board of Education* to oppose integration of the schools. This is the same Atticus Finch who, in *To Kill a Mockingbird,* stalwartly defends Tom Robinson, a black man accused of raping a white woman. The reveal shocks Scout and the reader. Scout comes to realize that no one is perfect, and her father is simply responding to Federal overreach not out of hate, but out of principle. Nonetheless, the damage is done.

This shift has spawned some controversy, as people devoted to *To Kill a Mockingbird* struggle to square this new version of Atticus with his kind and courageous iteration in the first book. This very controversy gets at what white people don't get about racism. We think that it is about how we treat other people, how accepting we are, how many black friends we have. Maybe we like hip-hop and Spike Lee, and think that because of that we aren't racist. In fact, Atticus Finch is a consistent racist. He was racist in the first book, and he is racist in its sequel. One of the oddities of Harper Lee's most recent book is that it was the first book she wrote. *Go Set a Watchman* was the initial manuscript her agent shopped around to editors. *To Kill a Mockingbird* resulted from Tay Hohoff's adroit editing of the original. In fact, they are simply two drafts of the same book. Atticus in the "sequel" was Atticus before he defended Tom Robinson.

In both books, Atticus treats everyone, regardless of skin color, with kindness and respect. That makes him a kind person. Maybe he's not a bigot. Maybe he's not even prejudiced. But, he's racist. Just like my grandmother was racist, just like my uncle was racist. Atticus is racist because he labors to maintain the social constructs that keep men like Tom in their place. Even while he is devoted to the rule of law and to the precept that all people are entitled to equal measures of justice, he harbors the same notion that my grandmother did that people's places in the world depend on the color of their skin.

It boils down to what we talk about when we talk about racism. People want to characterize racist people as prejudiced bigots, as small-minded, in-bred rednecks. Doing so makes righteous condemnation possible. Doing so puts as much distance between us and racists as our skin tone does to distinguish us from people of color. Donald Trump is no Atticus Finch, after all. The thing is that bigotry and prejudice are not racism. They are racism's cohorts. Its ugly little friends. Racism is about structural inequity. Racism is systemic oppression. An individual's racism stems from his or her position in the structural hierarchy and has little to do with how one feels about the "other."

We have a black president now, which is great. But that doesn't mean that racism is over and done with. We live in a country where all things being equal, Emily and Greg are still more employable than Lakisha and Jamal. We live in a country where being born black or brown increases your chances of being pulled over by police, limits financing for homes and small businesses, and increases your probability of contracting expensive diseases such as diabetes and heart disease.

Those of us with ties to the Deep South have all had moments similar to Scout's when she realizes that people she loves and who love her harbor allegiances to a past, and to a present in which some people are more equal than others. With *Go Set a Watchman*, we all have that now. Atticus Finch, indelibly etched in our minds with the righteous bearing of Gregory Peck, now embarrasses us. We want to disassociate ourselves from him. But the answer to racism isn't distancing ourselves from him.

White people have to acknowledge our past and our present. Simply being born white in this country gives us a head start. To paraphrase Ann Richards in regards to George W. Bush, we were born on third base but grew up thinking we hit a triple. Cottoning to our advantage isn't enough, of course. We have to then do something about it. By all means, treat everyone with compassion and kindness. By all means, have friends who look different from you. But, in the context of racism, it doesn't matter whether you have black friends or whether you have a bigoted bone in your body. What matters is what you are doing to address a system that would rather incarcerate young black men than educate them, or what you are doing to address an economic system in which the average net worth of white families is more than ten times that of black families, or what you are doing to provide other paths to success than selling drugs or shooting hoops.

Until we realize that we can be kind and good people at heart and still be racist, our conversations about race will never lead to real change. My grandmother did sell her house, and the neighborhood is now racially diverse. It gives me perverse pleasure to think that she may have been on the cutting edge of racial integration in that neighborhood. My uncle never changed, because he was a bigot through and through. He has passed on now, and the world is probably a better place for it. Atticus Finch never changed either, as he was a man of his time and place. We are all people of our time and our place. Maybe now is the time and place that we start talking about what we're talking about when we talk about racism. ■

Carter M. Douglass

Shore to Shore

loaded like spoons
into the belly of Jesus
where we lay for weeks for months

– from Lucille Clifton's poem, "Slaveships," in which
the ships were named Jesus, Angel, Grace of God.

To EXTEND OUR TRIP, a two-week Serengeti safari, and to make the transition from wearing khaki and living in tents, we chose Zanzibar: exotic spice island of teeming bazaars, ancient saffron-masted Arabian boats, and white sand beaches. We traded endless grassy plains for the Indian Ocean, and the soulfulness of elephants for a wariness of humanity. We left the broad smiles of spear-wielding Maasai and the joyous cries of *"Jambo!"* from every dirt-poor gathering. Then, as Stone Town watched us, we began to hug our hidden money pouches closer.

One day's guided tour took us to the underground holding pen of those sold as slaves. Chains are still rooted in the concrete troughs, which served as beds, where a high tide could wash through – or over. They were brought to this den from distant homelands. They were crammed onto these slabs so efficiently that there was no space between them. Yet, in their terrible shared fate, they were parted by their many mother tongues and could not communicate.

Above the cave was the slave market. It was here that wives were torn from husbands and children from mothers. All were lined up according to size, tied to a tree, and whipped. Those who did not cry or faint brought the highest prices.

The Anglican Cathedral Church of Christ now occupies the market site. Where the whipping tree once grew, an altar sits in a circle of white marble. The circle has an edge of red stone, in remembrance of the blood shed there. Former slaves who were hired to build the church erected twelve of the pillars upside down. The bishop, understanding their testament, declared that the columns would forever remain inverted.

Standing on that common ground, I whispered, weeping, "Oh, Lucille – I am learning!"

But how am I to truly learn this? The lesson came in the grip and grit of Zanzibar, so far from our farm in Virginia, where generations have dusted the communion set that sits on the table in the old hall. It's lovely – but not sterling. (That's how we know this wasn't the set used for the regular congregation of the chapel that once stood on the land.) Imprinted on the bottom are the words, "Hard – White – Metal." This is the pitcher and cup from which the slaves of our place were served the blood of Jesus. ■

John Railey

I Want to Be Black, a Dispatch from the Southern River

TO BE WHITE IN AMERICA, at least for some Southern liberals like me, is to be on a never-ending, paradoxical quest to be black.

You want to somehow absolve your guilt by somehow absorbing black identity and generational pain: the vomit and crap of packed holds in slave ships, the nakedness of slave auctions, slavery, Jim Crow and today's conservative flashback to the Crow in the form of voter suppression and police brutality.

You want to be black but you don't. You know deep down the costs and you don't want to pay them now anymore than you would have wanted your ancestors to have paid the costs then, if you're honest and like your inheritance, whether it's money or simply white privilege.

You just want to be cool and knowing and guilt-free, like you suppose blacks are now.

You proclaim that you understand blacks, but you know you never will. Even though you know that many a forgotten or hidden Southern family tree contains significant amounts of blood shared with blacks, both through bloodlines and bloodshed.

It all flows together, an endless river of rapids that sweeps us along, black and white, crashing us against countless boulders of violence and hate, drowning many of us or at least killing our souls. We can't save each other because we can't save ourselves.

But every once in a great while, some of us get a chance to surface from the froth and grab at something better, together.

For me, that happened when I fell into the fight for compensation for the victims of my state's forced sterilization program. When North Carolina's program started in the late 1920s, around the same time that about thirty other states were establishing these programs, the white, black and American Indian targets were proportionate to the general population. But toward the end of North Carolina's program, it zeroed in on black women and girls on public assistance. It was, I would reluctantly come to realize, American genocide.

I grew up haunted by race in Southampton County, Virginia, the site of America's only sustained slave revolt, which was led by the slave preacher Nat Turner in the dog days of August 1831. The Reverend Turner led in the killing of almost sixty white men, women and children before he and the rest of his rebels were captured, and for the most part, hung within a mile of the house in which I was raised.

My Quaker-rooted father told me all about it, explaining that we should never condone violence, but we should understand its wellspring. My father was a lawyer who lost business for standing up for integration. He was a friend of Terry Sanford, the progressive North Carolina governor who stood up for integration in the early 1960s in a way no other Southern governors did.

Sanford also led the state when North Carolina's sterilization program shifted its focus to black women and girls, a fact of which he was seemingly oblivious.

I grappled with that in the early 2000s. As part of an investigative team at the *Winston-Salem Journal,* I tracked down victims of North Carolina's sterilization program. I met several of the victims, most of all, Nial Rameriz, who grew up as black and poor as I grew up white and privileged.

I thought I knew all about blacks. My father had stood up for African Americans. I had gone to school with blacks through the first strange years of integration, before I followed my warped adolescent heart to join white church friends at the local private school. And like so many other Southern children, a wonderful black housekeeper helped to raise me, in my case, the late, great Della Evans. I loved her and just assumed that she loved me. I thought I knew all about her world, just because I had made some modest inquires about her and her life, and visited her home.

As I started to work the sterilization compensation story, I realized just how little I knew about Della, or any blacks, for that matter.

My newspaper, which had supported forced sterilization back in the day, started the fight for compensation.

As the editorial-page editor of my paper, I would join with black allies in winning the fight, making North Carolina the first state in the nation to compensate victims of a forced sterilization program.

At first, I didn't trust my future allies anymore than they trusted me.

Nial Ramirez, as she's acknowledged to me since, thought of me as a naïve, if well-meaning white boy. Larry Womble, a black legislator from Winston-Salem, might have thought the same.

Over the years of this fight, we've slowly gotten to know each other. After Larry was almost killed in a car wreck in a pivotal point in the fight, I sat by his hospital bed for hours, seeking advice on the fight for reparations.

Nial, sterilized in North Carolina but now living in Georgia, talked to me often on the phone, pushing me on. When I'd whine about the friends I was losing over my obsession on the compensation fight, she'd chastise that as too much white-boy whining compared to what she'd been through, being betrayed by a white doctor and other whites she'd trusted.

I'd thought of government as basically good, out to help you. She thought of government as basically bad, out to hurt you.

I talked to other black sterilization victims who felt the same way.

Gradually, through this compensation fight, and hanging out with Nial and other victims, I began to get a feel, albeit a nascent one, of what it's like to be black. Not in any physical sense, of course. No white from my background is ever going to get that. We're never going to really feel what it's like to catch the hard stares, to worry about whether a policeman means you good or bad, to know what it's like to go to a second-hand school with second-hand books and toys when your parents' tax dollars were supporting better schools for white folk.

But through shared fights with blacks, we whites can at least get some cerebral sense of what it might mean to be black. What that's meant for me is to radicalize my thinking, at least by the tame but oppressive terms of the South in which I was raised, to call out still-segregated schools, renewal of voter oppression, police abuses, continued discomfort with interracial marriage, and the ubiquitous history deniers and their rebel flags.

Along the way, the South's most lethal weapon is her hugs and kisses. She smothers you with her kindness, she kills you with her love. She is your family friend who brought you ham biscuits when you were sick and nurtured you. Even as that friend supported segregation.

How do you stand up to that culture?

You have to be prepared to lose the love of friends as you stand up for the rights of underdogs, whether they're black, brown or white. That takes a special kind of courage, one I'm not sure I have, but one for which I keep striving.

I often say I'd love to be black. But I bet my newfound friends wouldn't want to put me through the pain of being black.

Our river flows on. ■

Ben Johnston

Train Ride

I T'S BECAUSE I'M BLACK, ISN'T IT?"

"No, it's because you're a piece of shit! Get the fuck off my train!"

The train attendant walked back into the conductor's compartment and his voice boomed over the loudspeaker, crackling through the car, "If there are any off-duty police officers onboard the train, please, move up to the first car."

I'm sitting about half a car back, peering between the headrests in front of me. A young black man, who looks to be about my age, is flailing his arms around, and pacing back and forth in the handicap section of the train.

"You're a racist piece of shit! The only reason you don't want me on this train is because I'm a black man. It's because we're all black!"

The two young girls with him are nodding in approval. The white attendant is shaking his head, his eyes bulging out of his head.

"I'm kicking you off this train because you personally threatened me, not because you're black. Don't play that fucking card, man!"

"I'm not getting off this train! I have a ticket, we all have tickets! Get out of my face, or I'm going to fuck you up!"

The attendant's laugh bellows through the car. He is easily a foot and a half taller than the young man threatening him. There has been no physical contact, but the threat of it is already making passengers uncomfortable. I watch as they squirm uneasily in their seats. After holding up the train for more than fifteen minutes, they are eventually ushered off onto a platform. The train continues to roll.

As the attendant starts to collect tickets from my car, he sheepishly apologizes to the curious commuters. I show him my ticket and then bluntly ask, "So what happened?"

"Oh, nothing. He threatened me, and I don't find that acceptable on my train. So I asked him to depart at the next platform. Then he started screaming that it was because he was black..." he purposely raises his voice and looks around at the other passengers, "...which it most certainly was not. He was just an asshole."

He hole punches my ticket voucher and clips it to my headrest. Silently, he proceeds down the aisle noisily clicking his hole puncher. A couple behind me thanks him as he passes.

"You know, people like that aren't usually on this train. It's because of that drunken conductor that derailed that SEPTA in Philly. Now all of those people have to ride this train instead. I hope there are no more problems."

"It's alright honey, I'm sure there won't be. It's sad, could you imagine riding on the SEPTA everyday with that kind of noise and bullshit? How they stay on schedule is above me."

"I know dear. SEPTA should have their lines all working fine, so we won't have to deal with that situation again. I hate how they jump to the conclusion that it's always about race. It wasn't because he was black; it was because he made a threat. You heard the man."

"Yes, definitely not because he was black."

They nuzzle into each other over an armrest and stare at the passing scenery through the oblong window.

Walking to my girlfriend's apartment in West Harlem, I relate the incident on the train to her. I mimic the young man, "It's because I'm black, isn't it?"

She squeezes my arm, "Don't say that too loud around here. You're liable to get your ass kicked just talking about it, especially with everything in Ferguson and Baltimore. Not to mention here, with so many protesters outside my building yesterday, I could barely get into City Hall."

"Sorry, I didn't mean to say that so loud, plus I was just telling you a story."

"That doesn't matter. You're a young white male, and when it comes to discussing race, you have a target painted on your back. Just don't say anything like that too loud, people may get the wrong idea."

"Gotcha. I know baby, sorry."

We walk into a bar and order a round. For a few hours, we're the only white people there. No one else seems to notice. ▪

Beth Kwiatek

My White American Self

Bus driver, bus driver, king of the Jews.
Walking in the jungle in tennis shoes.
Looked up a tree. What did I see?
A God-damn nigger going pee on me!

MY COUSINS TAUGHT ME THIS SONG when I was in third grade. At the playground I decided to share it with my friend Doris. I stopped right before I got to the word "nigger." Doris was black. I was not. I told her I forgot the rest.

I remember learning about slavery in seventh grade. It was 1977, and the history teacher referred to it as "an economic institution." I had a pit in my stomach. I looked over at Tahmina. She was black. I felt bad. My ancestors were not slaves.

In eighth grade, I invited Tahmina to my house. I don't remember what we played, did, or said. I felt so good about myself for having a black friend. I don't think she stayed for dinner. I know I did not invite her back.

The first time I realized I was white was when I was a Peace Corps Volunteer in Niger, Africa. It was 1989 and I was twenty-four years old. I was the perfect candidate. I had a degree in English. I came from a large second-generation Italian and Polish Catholic family. All my letters of reference stated I was "color-blind."

Training was in-country for three months. I was taught basic French. My first lesson, *"Je suis Americain"* was followed by, *"Je suis corps de la paix."* We sat under huts in small groups for our cultural lessons. This is what I remember: "Dark-skinned Hausa tribe members were slaves to light-skinned Hausa members"; "Women are second class citizens";

and "It is okay for American women to wear shorts." I also remember being taken to the capital: to the U.S. Ambassador's pool to swim, to the French grocery store to buy apples and chocolates, and to the Grand Marché to buy West African fabric and cloth.

I was assigned as a physical education teacher in the only all-girls École Normal. It was in the village of Tillaberi. (It did not matter to the Peace Corps that the girls did not play sports, or run, or jump.) I worked for the Ministry of Youth and Culture. I lived "at the local level"; Peace Corps volunteers were not given the perks of other aid workers. I lived on the school grounds and pumped my water at the well along with the students.

In Peace Corps, I knew I was American. In Peace Corps, I knew I was white. I felt the power of my passport and Peace Corps I.D. I felt the power of my real employer – the U.S. government. And most importantly I felt the power of my white skin. Let me give you an example: The president of Niger was Ali Saibou, a military dictator. He was coming to our village and school. It was a big deal. Attendance was mandatory. But not for me. I skipped town. I did not want the president to see my white face in a sea of black faces. I went to visit a fellow volunteer in a neighboring village. I did not get into trouble. *"Je suis Americain."*

As a child I did not think of myself as white. But I knew I was not black. In 1969 my father moved our family to a small farming community one hour south of Buffalo, New York. Names like Bernhoft, Feldman, Ahrens, and Ehman spoke of its German heritage, except I never heard any classmates refer to themselves as German American. Outside of town "on the hill," there was a small African American Muslim community. My parents were descendants of Polish and Italian immigrants who worked in the Lackawanna steel plants. My parents grew up, worked side-by-side, and were comfortable with just about anybody and everybody. We were expected to be like them.

My parents and grandparents had an awareness of all things political and unjust.

I took pride in their stories. My grandpa Tony taught two black women how to drive because their husbands would not. My mother's childhood house was next to a "black whore house." Her mother, my grandmother, taught the kids that lived there how to knit. My mother carpooled rides to work and school with Tahmina's mom. My favorite stories involved my father. He was a New York State Trooper. Once he was called to settle a dispute. Abdullah Amir shot at Mr. Sullivan's tires. Mr. Sullivan asked my father to do something about it. My father asked Abdullah why he shot at Mr. Sullivan's tires. Abdullah said, "Because I told him if he drove that fast down the street again when my kids are playing I am going to shoot his tires out." My father looked at Mr. Sullivan and said, "He told you he was going to shoot your tires out if you drove too fast."

My parents were fair, respectful, and honest. I noticed though that they didn't have any black friends. And when O.J. Simpson played for the Buffalo Bills my father yelled at the TV, "run, nigger, run."

In college my best friend was black. We bonded because we were both uncool, did not drink, and were a bit chubby from eating too many donuts late at night. Our friendship grew after college. When she called me on the phone, my gay roommate (who I now realize was more honest than I was) would purposely irritate her and say, "It's your black friend who sounds like a white girl." When she graduated with a PhD I was so happy and proud. I took her out to dinner and got her a designer watch. As a joke, I bought her a vintage ceramic jet-black, black mammy-face tchotchke. She wrote me a letter to tell me she was hurt by the black mammy-face. I wrote her back. I told her I didn't think of her as black. She wrote me again. I had hurt her. Again.

What was I seeing? What was I not seeing?

Seeing and calling out my whiteness has been almost impossible. Not just the invisibility of it all in the imaginary backpack kind of way. I know that "flesh" covered Band-Aids are for me. I know that I probably won't be followed around a store by a security guard. I know that I can see my "race" represented on TV. And I know that if the police stop me, I will be given the benefit of doubt. I am a feminist. I know all about privilege – male, class, and white.

But the real truth of the matter is that I never saw myself as white except when I was in the presence of non-whiteness. Do white people even exist without a non-white person around? Even now, with all my consciousness raising and activism, the words slip out of my mouth: black dentist, black politician, black friend. Black. Black. Black.

My grandparents and parents were more than progressive or just politically correct. They taught me to see, really see, the arrogance and ugliness of white people. I always knew that as a white person my life would be easier and without a certain kind of pain. With their World War II sensibilities, their civil rights experiences, their actions of common sense and decency, and (especially) my mother's letter writing campaigns, my parents taught me to speak up.

I did speak up. I still do. I have a keen sense for injustice, racism, arrogance, entitlement thanks to college, Peace Corps, graduate and PhD programs, and fifteen years of work as a social worker in one of the most segregated cities in the country. You name it; I see it. I can academic-speak with the best of any faculty member or social scientist about privilege, power, oppression theory, racialized policies, the school-to-prison pipeline, trickle-down economics, modes of containment, post-colonial theory, blah, blah, blah. I even started a dissertation: "White Out: Transcending the Colonizing Eye" . . . blah, blah, blah.

I have also learned that academic-speak means nothing. I didn't need to read Patricia Williams' book about how her white colleagues and law students dissed her because she is black. In graduate school, my social work professor told his black colleague that her braids bordered on unprofessional. I say his comment bordered on racism. This is what I heard from my white PhD professors whose disciplines were race, power, and privilege: "I would love to take down Cornell West." "bell hooks and Angela Davis sold out." And, my personal favorite, "I adopted a black child from South Africa." I can just hear my father, "You couldn't find a black child in the States? I hear they're cheaper."

Needless to say, those professors were clearly uncritical of their own shit and superiority. But what about me? I was missing something. Looking at my own whiteness is like looking at a negative space. I didn't see it. I didn't feel it. I didn't know it was there. Kind of like putting up a #BlackLivesMatter sign and then doing nothing about it. I was my mom and my dad. Doing good work. Instead of yelling, "Run, nigger, run," I was drooling over nigger-go-home clothes from J. Crew and chatting about nigger-digger fingernails.

I have learned that for me, my whiteness is a space – a historical and relational one. Whiteness and blackness is about what happens in the in-between. It is a historical space because when I see, greet, or meet a non-white person, I feel the centuries of history bubbled up between us: slavery, Jim Crow, genocide, citizenship, favor, advantages, anger and rage, and ease and dis-ease. My visual reference is Charlie Brown talking about "Pig Pen": "Don't think of it as dust. Just think of it as the dirt and dust of far-off lands blowing over here and settling. It staggers the imagination!"

It is a relational space because one cannot exist without the "other." We name each other white or black. And because of history, any inter-action for me is deeply personal, whether I am conscious of it or not. Therefore all my interactions are relational.

Most, most, most, importantly, I could not and cannot truly see and even get beyond my whiteness without experiencing the relational in the pig pen of the historical. And by relational, I mean relationships. Relationships as in best friends, breaking bread, talking about lovers and sex, witnessing and sharing pain and grief, making fun, laughing, eating and drinking, talking about God, going to God, refusing God, sometimes singing and sometimes dancing, but always, always, always full of honesty and love. And, always, always, always owning up to racial slights, hurts and outright wounds, most of which fall on my side, the white side.

My best friends are black. I write this not to validate an arrival to a non-existing post-racial place. I write this to make the point that without these fully and at times brutally honest relationships, both grown and nurtured within that historical space called race relations, both grown and nurtured from the ordinary dailiness of our lives, I am able to see my white self.

The original sin of being white is the inherent world of ease, ben-efits, claim, comfort, and mirrored-images that come with being born white. I cannot dis-own my whiteness. I cannot reject my whiteness. I cannot refuse my whiteness. Not one white person can. Saying so is no more effective than the "Imagine Peace" bumper sticker. As Chandra Mohanty would say, "nothing but a meaningless, empty, gesture."

My white sins are sins of omission—my sins of failing to do something I can and ought to do. Inactions are a breach of moral law. When I fail to have relationships with my black brothers and sisters that are intimate and honest, when I hesitate in gesture or response – pleasant and unpleasant—or, when I allow my knee jerk, culturally learned hostilities and insults to surface and stay, how then can I see and know my whiteness? And ultimately see what it means for me to be white in America.

Claudia Rankine writes in her book *Citizen*, her ode for white people about how it feels to be black in America, "Though you can retire from an injury, you can't walk away because you feel bad." I would say, therein lies the difference. This is what it means for me to be white in America. I can walk away. I see my whiteness. I own my whiteness. I work against my whiteness. But at times I commit my sin of omission: I get tired of witnessing the pain and suffering. I get tired from the energy I expend to fight. I get tired of always examining my life and my community for evidence of privilege and power. I can walk away. I can turn it off. I can commit the sin of omission. Sometimes, I knowingly do nothing.

The other night I was reading the book *Follow the Drinking Gourd* to my child. I purchased the book thinking it was an illustrated text to the lyrics. I was wrong. It was the story of the Underground Railroad. When I got to the picture of a slave on an auction block I stopped reading. I hadn't expected that. It was honest. But how do I explain to my white child about slavery and its enduring legacy: that his black and brown brothers and sisters will find the world less inviting, less responsive, and less sincere? Something black children his age have probably already experienced. You can do what I did. You can commit the sin of omission. You close the book and say, "Mama doesn't like this book. Let's pick another." ▪

Maria Lisella

Shades, Color, and Internal Dialogues in White America

WHEN THE ELEVATOR DOORS OPENED one morning in a Sheraton Hotel, I took a survey of its occupants: One solitary black man; well-built, handsome, positioned in the left corner. He must have been coming down from the Club Floor, exclusively accessed with a card he had to have had in his hand, or...maybe not.

I made eye contact, and smiled. He does not return the smile. Has he divined that my smile is not genuine but instead a nervous tic intended to take the hint of danger out of the moment? Is there any danger here? Would I have smiled at a white man?

Now I have a well-built, unsmiling black man standing in a corner of the elevator. I shift my position and place myself smack in front of the control panel. Without moving my head, my eyes locate the alarm button.

We reach the lobby in seconds, so this internal dialogue now seems unnecessary, and in hindsight, even shame-inducing, yet it is as common as the tar on the street.

I grew up in a black neighborhood in New York City. I was not taught to be afraid of black people; yet, as a young woman, I learned how to profile. Did I need to react that strongly in the elevator? Probably not. Were some of my reactions to sharing space with a black man over the top and exaggerated? Likely. Is it better to be safe than sorry? Of course.

This elevator moment had a thousand layers: As a feminist, I have been taught to be on guard in a space when alone with any strange man. As a travel writer, I often find myself in foreign environments, so I do take safety precautions, but I usually do not feel as self-conscious as I was during this incident.

My automatic responses are part of a skill set that has been customized to increase my mobility in the world—as a small, now middle-aged white woman who travels alone for business.

This series of safety-net reflexes has served me well in the urban environment in which I live. For instance, when a man stalked me on the subway, I talked to another passenger to create a witness. But when the person is black, I am left with my own sense of guilt. I question myself: Was all of that angst necessary? I brush it away, knowing how incredibly complex a simple or potential transaction with a person of a different skin color presents to me.

I have visited sixty countries, including a few in Africa and the Caribbean. Places where black people reside and run the show, who are in charge. I am aware of the distinctions among black people: ethnic black versus American black.

And I have learned to listen to my gut, no matter who is in the elevator; to be safe rather than sorry; to not let dogma obfuscate good sense, even at the cost of not looking politically correct.

For many years, my cousin drove a cab to support his daytime political activism for affordable housing in Cambridge, Massachusetts. He consciously tried not to profile his customers. Today, he is still haunted by the half-dozen stick-ups he was a victim of, particularly because most of the perpetrators were young black men. After being robbed repeatedly at knifepoint, he had had enough. This time he chased the black teenager into the heart of a black neighborhood, and once my cousin came to his senses, he realized how the situation must have looked—a tall white guy chasing a black kid in Roxbury. Needless to say, he hightailed it back to the cab, rattled. As a result, he no longer picks up young black male passengers blindly, and has become more discreet in developing distinctions among them.

One occasion that highlights the false pitch of political correctness comes to mind. Two liberal New Yorkers told me about the night someone knocked on their apartment door in Greenwich Village. Rather than look through the peephole, they opened the door. There stood a young black man they had never seen before. Within moments, he had talked his way into the middle of their living room. Once inside, he held them up at gunpoint. When retelling the incident, they explained why they had refused to report it to the police. Their defense was "He didn't look the type."

I remember thinking this incident was ridiculous. First of all, these people ignored basic safety, and secondly, even though a crime had been committed, no one was held accountable. I wondered if, behind it all, the two victims felt a pang of shame for blindly opening their door to a total stranger, while at the same time letting a criminal go free because he was black.

I am the granddaughter of Italian immigrants who fled poverty in Southern Italy at the turn of the century. My grandparents were nearly illiterate; my siblings all have PhDs. I speak Italian and I study it, and I am the only one in my family who frequently visits cousins and friends in Italy, the "old country."

I grew up in South Jamaica, Queens, New York. My cousins did too, but their take on our lives in Jamaica diverge vastly from mine. As adults, they joined the "white flight" and fled to Long Island.

One member of my family is very freewheeling with the n-word, so much so that my mother, who is ninety-six years old, has to remind him before he begins one of his rants that he is not allowed to utter that word in her house.

His discussions are circular: A younger, black junior executive in his office had been promoted over him. His story went like this: "They GAVE him a degree from Harvard; all these n's, they get Harvard degrees for free ..."

Interrupting his angry blast, I took a chance: "The person you need to be pissed off at is the guy you see in the mirror every morning. You could have gotten a degree for free on the G.I. Bill, but because you're white, you thought you wouldn't have to." A jaw-dropping silence followed.

I didn't do this to be a heroine; I did it because, to my ears, he sounded outrageous. I did it because I understood the hurt behind his rant: It was inconceivable to him that, under any circumstances, a dark-skinned person could pass him by. I did it to jolt him, to redirect his anger.

To be fair, I have never been in that particular situation. I have not been in nose-to-nose competition with a black person for the same position.

My cousin's rant is not without ground. The world changed and he did not. During the civil rights movement, his consciousness slipped through the cracks.

While his rant is without merit on so many levels, his anger is real and raw. To me, its source is a relatively invisible enemy: A capitalist system that is neither democratic nor fair but pits one race against the other for the same prize.

Not exactly a parallel scenario, but I have sometimes felt that the literary world pays more attention to black authors than to Italian American writers; for instance, that their work is taken more seriously and they are perceived to have more profound messages. I suspect that black authors fight tooth and nail for every line of attention they get too, and feel they are short-changed.

This calls up another dilemma. When the stakes are small – from poetry prizes to book reviews – things get ugly. We compete against one another across color and class lines. We chase the same jobs, the same prizes, just as my cousin was chasing that promotion; we are pitted against one another for a few crumbs. When a black person does get that job, how long does it take before you hear the suspicious comments: How did she or he get it? Was it merited? Is it patronizing? Is it worthy of discussion? Is it another attempt to level an eternally imbalanced playing field? How many generations does it take to clear the decks, to be on equal footing?

It is not my style to rant and rave about any of this – I would consider it politically incorrect – but I have indeed felt it. Is this irrational? At times.

I find the Mafia image hurtful and limiting. Yet, I see Italian Americans who glorify the Mafia do so for much the same reason young black kids imitate the biggest and most successful drug dealers – because they feel impotent. Criminals are power-grabbers in a society that these people have yet to figure out how to navigate.

My political activism has focused predominantly on childcare and reproductive rights. I have found few Italian American women in the trenches, and even fewer black women, yet these are issues common to all of us.

One very still afternoon on 116th Drive in South Jamaica, a pickup truck filled with dark-skinned men stopped in front to repair the street. They all spoke Italian. My grandmother explained that they were Ethiopian or Eritrean. She left out the fact that Mussolini had taken control of parts of North Africa during World War II with dire results. At six, I knew enough about politics – familial and global – to not question what she said. Back then, everyone was Italian – Jesus, Mary, Joseph, and the next-door neighbors, even if they were black.

She observed: We were all southerners. As uneducated as she was, she made me understand that mainstream America never ran through South Jamaica. We were safe in this dreamland of black Americans from the same classes – working to middle-class – living side by side; as long as we did not reach too far, we could occupy the same space.

That distance from white middle-class America gave us the freedom to retain our ethnic identity without being stigmatized as foreigners. It was a non-issue among our black neighbors. Hanging back in Jamaica allowed me to be who I am.

Had my parents moved to a lily-white middle-class neighborhood when I was younger, I would not have developed such a strong ethnic identity. In our pursuit of upward mobility, we would likely have dropped the second language. I may have identified with the most powerful people in the big room of society: whites. But I would have been disappointed, because in that room, I am a marginal white person, often mistaken for Latina, Jewish, or Greek.

Eventually, we moved from our three-room apartment to a house of three generations. Bellerose, which literally means "beautiful rose" and is located on the border between Queens and Nassau, was predominantly Irish Catholic, and far from paradise.

There, we met racism for the first time. We were the "niggers and spics." Many of our new neighbors had never met a black person. Most were also pro-Vietnam war, and anti-feminist, yet pro-labor.

Our family lost touch with our old neighbors. They didn't feel comfortable coming to a white neighborhood; we could be accused of block-busting; or, worse, either we or our old neighbors might get attacked. That is how volatile that moment was in 1961. Black people were speaking up for the first time. Their anger was no longer a secret. White people were running scared.

It made me wonder if I'd only imagined those early years of peace and love in South Jamaica. In hindsight, once we moved, we did not act heroically. We did not visit our old neighbors. We did not stand up for them nor did we protect them when they visited us. Confusion set in. The public conversations of the 1960s seemed to disregard the old ways of getting along with each other: As neighbors, as best friends living on the same street. Protest marches and demonstrations featuring black people made me feel that I would never again find a place at their table. Would our whiteness erase our ordinary humanity? Would black people ever believe us?

When my grandmother was hospitalized, our former neighbor visited her. On the way to her room, a white nurse directed Thelma to the black lady in the bed next to my grandmother. On the way, Thelma saw my grandmother, hugged her, and called her "Mamma." Could that happen again in the new consciousness of an ever more stratified America?

When attending Queensborough Community College, I had been studying European art, history, and dance, but shifted my focus to American culture. I opted for American modern dance, jazz—and what could be more American than black literature?

I was the only white girl in the class, and when the white, Scottish-accented Professor Sheena Gillespie walked in, the other students were miffed and challenged her. Gillespie responded that, not being an American, she carried less baggage. I admired her pluck and her willingness to put the course on the map. Because she was white, I felt less like an interloper and that it was okay for me to be there, although my fellow students were less than welcoming. Upon closer examination, I identified with the most powerful person in the room, and that gave me a sense of belonging.

But that didn't change the hostile atmosphere. It was the 1970s, the first years of Open Admission when it cost $45 a semester to attend community college. I shared a classroom with my peers. We may have had similar academic backgrounds, came from similar social classes, and for certain, we were reading the same books. None of them spoke to me. I was barely tolerated. Why was it so hard for the black students to accept my presence? Was it my fault that a black professor was not teaching the course? Why was I receiving the brunt of their frustration over a system that I had nothing to do with creating? I was studying their literature. Would it have been different if they knew that my Southern Italian relatives had been sharecroppers in Italy? Or, that they were considered the N's of Italy? Would it have been different if they knew my grandparents were called *terrone*, a derogatory term used by Northern Italians to signify laziness and ignorance? Or, did they feel the burden of discrimination was theirs alone to bear? We shared none of this. We learned about the Harlem Renaissance and nothing about each other.

This is not to equate the racism in America with that in Italy. My father recalled want ads in the 1940s that specifically outlined who the candidates should be: Wanted Anglo-Saxon boy; Italians need not apply. But when asked how he felt about it, he said, "It was prejudice, I didn't like it, but I got over it... it was nothing like what the blacks faced."

I learned neither hate nor fear at my parents' dinner table. I learned empathy but sometimes confusion. I learned that hardly anyone in America is not an outsider.

As a journalist, I am a spectator, a witness. I have met people in positions of great power and great wealth, but I always feel like an impostor. A veteran reporter advised me about this: "The minute you stop feeling like an impostor, you can no longer do your job—you're not supposed to be 'one of them.'"

I am an olive-skinned American. I am neither fearless nor infallible.

Will I stand in front of the control panel in the next elevator I enter? Will I surreptitiously locate the alarm button? And will I do this with more alacrity if the other passenger is male and black? When I see a gang of teenage boys, I cross the street, whether they are white or black, but is my fear deepened by the color of their skin?

Being a white woman in America carries a burden and a pass.

As a woman, I receive lower wages than my male counterparts. I am considered white, and the advantages of that happenstance are incalculable.

Until America's darker-skinned citizens are no longer subjected to capricious standards of behavior, or grilled over the coals of institutional discrimination, we are all hobbled by a chaotic environment that disavows trust.

For now, I act on good faith, respond to my gut, and listen to my very inquisitive inner voice. ■

John Amen

America in Black and White

1.

LAUDED AS THE FOUNDATIONAL ELEMENTS of a democratic society, neither agreement nor disagreement necessarily indicates an engaged consideration of pertinent issues; in fact, either can serve as a formidable shield, insulating one from destabilizing emotions, thoughts, and information. In addition, many issues, including "white privilege" and the broader dynamics of racism, are complex and paradoxical, matters that may not lend themselves to consummate resolution but instead demand to be explored in their indeterminacy, a process often truncated by the terminal nature of agreement or disagreement.

At different points in his National Book Award-winning title, *Between the World and Me,* Ta-Nehisi Coates[1] discusses his undergraduate experiences at Howard, including how his professors encouraged him to observe and mine psychological discomfort, rather than deflect or prematurely dissipate it through reliance on default positions: "I began to see discord, argument, chaos, perhaps even fear, as a kind of power. I was learning to live in the disquiet... The gnawing discomfort, the chaos, the intellectual vertigo was not an alarm. It was a beacon" (52). Coates' primary intent, with this passage and the book as a whole, is not necessarily to craft incontrovertible arguments, but rather to discuss entrenched paradigms in such a way that a reader may *suspend* agreement or disagreement; more importantly, come to recognize defense mechanisms that surface as symptoms of a fundamental and multigenerational conditioning. It's not so much our positions, Coates suggests, but rather our reactions and habituation that warrant review.

Forty or so pages later in the same text, Coates addresses his son (as he does in much of the book; in fact, the work is ostensibly an epistolary manifesto authored for his son's benefit): "The entire narrative of this country argues against the truth of who you are"(99), to which one might respond, "Yes, this is true for all of us," a universalization of Coates' passage that some readers might dub an egregious misappropriation. Each of us, though, has been to some degree entranced by educational, religious, familial, and socio-cultural conditioning. Our positions, thoughts, and feelings are frequently not our own, so to speak, but rather contemporary iterations of a mostly unexamined body of content – emotional, mental, and somatic – passed down from generation to generation. We react, as if hypnotized, predictably agreeing or disagreeing; history (or karma) is our master. We're each lost in our own version of what Coates describes as a "dream that thrives on generalization," a dream that "is the enemy of all art, courageous thinking, and honest writing"(50).

2.

THREE STORIES COME TO MIND, the first involving an incident that occurred when I was fourteen and living in a rural North Carolina town. I was playing basketball with five other white kids, three or four of whom kept using the word "nigger." Finally I said, "Why don't you guys quit using that word?" Two or three of the boys immediately took offense. I almost ended up in a fistfight with one of the boys, all of whom stormed off in a group following an exchange of threats and insults. I felt gratified that I had adhered to my position on a matter that seemed important but was also aware that a sacrifice had been involved. Those boys, who lived in the same valley as me, would no longer be my friends. I can't say that I grieved the loss of these specific relationships; however, the incident had an impact. I now realize that I concluded, on some level, and carried this conclusion with me into my adult years, that one can keep silent and remain a member of a community of sorts or speak one's mind and accept the consequences of isolation; in other words, that inclusion necessitates self-betrayal (quite an interpretive leap, granted). A corollary to that was: party lines and prescribed stances are typically what bond people rather than an authentic sense of connection or relational intimacy (also an interpretive leap, but, unfortunately, one that seems to have substantial merit).

The second story involves a more recent experience. I was at a coffee shop with three black friends. The conversation came around to the recent (at that time) events in Ferguson, Missouri. I recall thinking to myself: if someone asks you a question, fine, address it as succinctly as possible. But don't elaborate, explore, or ad lib on this subject! Was I concerned that I might inadvertently say something inappropriate? I have to admit that I was quite uncomfortable (not with my friends, per se, but with the conversation and my awkwardness in the face of it), and couldn't help projecting that these guys were starting to regard me as the proverbial villain. It wouldn't be long, I silently fretted, before I, the lone white guy in the mix, became the scapegoat. This wasn't an accurate perception of the situation, though I was reminded–attempting to navigate my malaise in real time–how it feels to be the "outsider," to encounter the anxiety, shame, and compensatory self-righteousness that often arise in the face of even imagined disenfranchisement or what I'd call disempowerment-by-numbers. I now reflect on that situation as a missed opportunity for explorative conversation. I ran into one of the guys a week or two later and mumbled, "I'm sorry I didn't say more when we were talking at the coffee shop." I found myself adding, "I mean, I pretty much agreed with everything you guys said." Ugh, my own knee-jerk attempt to come across as being "on the right side" or ensure that I was perceived in a desirable way; i.e., desirable to me (even if I *did* pretty much agree with everything they said), but more glaringly illustrative of the internal experiences that are so rarely vocalized, those opportune confusions that, if honestly expressed rather than censored or euphemized, might serve to forge connection rather than preserving distance.

The third story: I was invited to give a reading and conduct a writing workshop in a maximum security prison. After going through multiple security points, two white guards ushered my contact, Hugh (a black man in his fifties), and me into a drab room, in the corner of which were twenty or so chairs and a couple of rusty tables. A few minutes later, the inmates made their entrance. They were all black. I'm guessing that their ages ranged from early twenties to late sixties. The guards and I were the only white people in the room. This glaring imbalance and possible socio-cultural metaphor struck me immediately. I was self-conscious of my skin color and what it potentially represented, specifically for the black inmates who were now taking their seats. I shared a few poems, and the guys seemed to appreciate the pieces; however, the conversation between poems was particularly fertile, touching on the possible causes of violence and addiction as well as the redemptive nature of art. A couple of times I saw the guards glance disapprovingly in our direction. All in all, this was one of those experiences during which I remained mostly engaged and curious (with and about the tumultuousness of my own internal experience as well as what others were communicating) despite a relatively high level of discomfort. This takes practice. I need to keep practicing.

3.

LEGISLATION, AS MANY HAVE POINTED OUT, doesn't transform the recalcitrant heart, though it can "restrain the heartless," as Martin Luther King Jr. said in 1963. "It may be true," he added, "that the law cannot make a man love me but it can keep him from lynching me and I think that is pretty important, also."[2] Fifty plus years later we have indeed eliminated lynching, at least overtly, though it occurs now in more surreptitious ways, including discriminatory treatment by law-enforcement officials, gerrymandering, and state laws that discouragingly complicate or egregiously impede a citizen's right to participate in the constitutional process.[3]

The election of Barack Obama as U.S. president in 2008 brought to the social surface polarized notions regarding the country's so-called core values. It also highlighted the shadow of capitalism; specifically, the appetite for power, and revealed the numerous ways in which prejudicial norms can be politically, economically, and governmentally camouflaged. Whoever wins the 2016 presidential election may be female but will most certainly be white (apologies to Ben Carson, but I don't think he can capture the Republican ticket; or, if he somehow did, the general election), and I'll venture that the political or two-party polarization, as we've come to describe it, will subside within a year of the new Chief Executive's inauguration. Discord, disagreement, even vitriol will persist, but the current level of automatic polarization will lessen. What's worse is that this transition will occur without being sufficiently acknowledged. We'll witness a glaring lack of collective speculation as to what role race may have played during the Obama years or, furthermore, the role of race; i.e., whiteness restored, in the subsequent détente. The pervasive role of race in the U.S. will be swept into the social and political margins once again.

4.

My wife and i are spending a week at an exquisite retreat center in North Carolina. I can't help but notice that everyone here is white. In an integrated society or a society without a history of deep and reinforced divisions; or at least a society that had sincerely addressed or was sincerely addressing that history, if indeed any of these scenarios are imaginable, one would observe a more pronounced racial, ethnic, and even political diversity within any group of people. Segregation is, of course, primarily psychological and secondarily literal, in either case stoked by media and the gatekeeper of unhealed history. In terms of the U.S., many assert that this segregative bent is more pronounced in the southern states, though I notice similar dynamics in northern cities and on the West Coast. That said, in the northeast and Pacific Coast cities, the general hype and party line are more ostensibly progressive. I'm pretty certain, however, that progressive politics are insufficient to dismantle decades of reinforced conditioning; in fact, it's likely that progressive politics simply mask that conditioning more effectively.

Recently someone on Facebook asked "friends" to list ten writers who had influenced them the most. The six whites whose lists I saw each listed 9-10 white writers. The five blacks whose lists I saw each listed 9-10 black writers. There's nothing inherently pathological in this pattern, but again, in an integrated culture, one would expect to observe people alluding to a wider variety of influences. Black writers, white writers, Asian writers. Simply people who write. Integration isn't a reality in the U.S., and may not be for the foreseeable future, but it's worth conjuring, if for no other reason than to create a contrast that more boldly illustrates the current and longstanding sociological climate.

If you're wondering, I didn't post a list. If I had, I would've proba-bly compiled one that included John Ashbery and Audre Lorde. Doris

Lessing and James McBride. Osip Mandelstamm and Octavia Butler. Though in many ways representative of my story, such a list, if I'm rigororously self-evaluative, would've also been tweaked a bit for what I'd call PC-value. The truth is, my early and fundamental influences were almost entirely white writers. This reflects the impact of immediate sources, the texts that were made available at school and at home; in other words, what existed within immediate educational and familial parameters. What's most intriguing is that I often harbored, and still can harbor, "contempt prior to investigation"[4] when it came to "other" sources, many of which ended up being substantial influences. The proclivity for unfounded bias is certainly not one that originated with me – I can't rightly say it was "mine" – but rather an energetic transmission that I received, that most of us receive, if not prior to birth at least soon after it, upon which I in turn, over a course of years, put my individual stamp. I'm not certain whether this ubiquitous and contagious germ has a traceable origin; perhaps it's inherent to human DNA, even inseparable from the essence of life itself. Occasionally, perhaps as a result of a particular psychological upheaval or rearrangement, perhaps the result of what might be called grace, an individual peers through that much referenced veil of illusion, if only for a moment breaking the trance of separateness, shedding those prejudices, egoistic proclivities, and dismissive attitudes that accompany it. I'm not sure whether this can happen on a macro or collective level, at least in any sustained fashion, though of course a society's policies evolve over time, reflecting paradigmatic shifts, and these changes do represent a certain progress.

5.

I DON'T HAVE CHILDREN, but many of my friends now have grandchildren. I wonder what transpires in these children's hearts, regardless of their skin tone. How do they balance and reconcile notions of humility, as so commonly espoused in schools, churches, and families with simultaneous messages that promote, prescribe, and practically sanctify competition and success? Are they informed or buffered by their beliefs? Are their bearings oriented towards separateness? When they encounter themselves regarding someone as "other," or when they perceive that they themselves are being labeled in that fashion, what is their response, relationally and psychologically? Are they equipped to examine themselves and their thinking? Do they have the capacity to observe their own fears and reactions without being consumed by them? The "dream" to which Coates repeatedly refers is seductive. To live in its numbing auspices is to know the soporific of self-righteousness. The price of waking is high. One doesn't wake once. Waking is an ongoing choice, a commitment practiced moment by moment; often punctuated, unfortunately, by long periods of slumber.

Yes, reparations[5] are probably in order, would constitute a legislative and fiscal statement, a gestural compensation for the systematic exploitation of flesh and muscle, the long decades of deprived wealth. Such a policy would represent an important collective statement that the U.S. was accepting on some collective level the need to be roused from a destructive dream, a legacy of blindness and willful denial. In fact, it would be a major accomplishment if we managed, as a society, to even discuss the matter *hypothetically*. That said, such an exploration – nevermind actually agreeing to move forward, then formulizing and implementing a just and pragmatic protocol – has very little chance of occurring in this country. The historical, economic and psychological stakes are too high.

I recall leaving that maximum security prison where I read poems and led a workshop. It was a sunny day. I climbed into my rental car and started driving back towards the hotel where I was staying. I soon realized that I didn't have my phone, which meant I was without a GPS. After driving for about twenty minutes, I accepted that I was utterly lost and pulled off the highway. I remember a street protected by a red, white, and blue gate. I pulled up to a guard station. The guard stepped suspiciously to my window and asked me if I needed help. I told him generally where I was going, and he pointed me in the right direction. As I resumed driving, I saw the blue sky, McMansions all around me, sun pouring down in curtains of shimmering light. Chemical-green grass. Towering trees. Bleached driveways and sidewalks. Somewhere, in one of those yards, the sound of laughing children and a barking dog.

Remembering that scene reminds me of how I often feel when I approach my own neighborhood and home. "Home," a beautiful and dangerous word, one that evokes for me associations of freedom and safety, but also complacency. So many times I've come off the main road, turned into the neighborhood, seen that manicured street unfurling before me, a few impeccably dressed neighbors walking a dog, the gas lamps flickering, oaks and elms and Japanese maples swaying in the breeze. There are times when I'm so fatigued and desperate that I feel, for a moment, that I've made it back to the Garden, my own private Eden, a sanctuary out of evil's reach, where I can convince myself that I'm a man who's worked hard for and deserves what he has. Sometimes I can almost believe that my mind and heart are my own, and that there's no blood on my hands. ∎

Notes

1. Ta-Neshi Coates. *Between the World and Me.* (New York: Spiegel & Grau, 2014). Coates writes, "race is the child of racism, not the father" (7), reminding us that many ethnic groups now regarded as "white" were not always regarded as such (Irish and Italians, among others), that the tendency to operate divisively precedes the criteria by which divisions are implemented. Identity, individual or collective, is inevitably a construct, both unstable and random, including when that identity is based on race. Coates' work is inspired in great part by James Baldwin, the following lines from whom comprise the epigraph from the third section of *Between the World and Me:* "And have brought humanity to the edge of oblivion: because they think they are white."

2. Both quotes are excerpted from Martin Luther King Jr.'s address at Western Michigan University, December 18, 1963.

3. It should also be noted that debt, strategically created and sustained, established as a U.S. norm especially over the past sixty years or so, has served to alienate a majority of people from the political process, as well as other empowering processes, perhaps more than any other single factor. The cultivated myopia that accompanies financial burden serves to deprioritize any matters other than immediate survival. In this way, the U.S. has been transformed from a democracy to a plutocracy, a process that culminated in 2010 with the Supreme Court's ruling in *Citizens United vs. Federal Election Commission,* No. 08-205, 558 U.S. 310.

4. Herbert Spencer (1820-1903) was an English philosopher, biologist, anthropologist, sociologist, and prominent political theorist of the Victorian era. The full quote from Spencer is: "There is a principle which is a bar against all information, which is proof against all arguments, and which cannot fail to keep a man in everlasting ignorance – that principle is contempt prior to investigation."

5. Cf. various articles arguing for or against reparations, including Coates' "The Case for Reparations," published in the June 2014 issue of *The Atlantic.*

June Elizabeth Dunn

What It Means to Be White-Bred and Not From the Upper Crust

I F YOU DRIVE FROM THE EAST SIDE of the city of Stamford, Connecticut, along West Avenue into the town of Darien, you may see a sign, weathered and barely legible, on the right side of the road just as you cross the border. The sign reads, "Welcome to arien," the "D" missing for as long as I can recall, since the early 1970s at least, when I first learned how to read, and when my family moved into the town. I asked my parents why no one would fix the sign and replace the "D." My father just shrugged my question off, and replied that someone must like it that way. Years passed and the sign weathered on unchanged. Then when I was in Mrs. Goldstein's fifth grade class I made the connection as we studied World War II history—"Aryan" rhymes with "Darien" I chimed to my classmates, and the mystery of the missing "D" was solved for me. Someone must have wanted the sign that way, as my father said, someone who thought the moniker appropriate for some reason, just like the moniker for the Metro-North New Haven line into Manhattan—the "Aryan Express." As a pre-teen, I was confused as to why anyone would want to be associated with the term "Aryan," given Hitler's motivation for the Holocaust. But the more I observed as I aged and became conscious of just how "white" Darien was, and in relation to it how white I was, the more I realized how appropriate the sign was, its black lettering fading into a dingy white background.

What I first intuited about being white was that there just wasn't one shade of it, that whiteness was mutable, and based upon such things as the kind of job your father had, what part of the town you lived in, the church you went to, the places you vacationed (if at all), and your physical attractiveness. It wasn't until years later that I understood why this was so, but at seven years old, having moved with my family into Darien from a neighboring city in 1971, I only considered being white as a matter of fact. The people who lived in Darien, my friends, my family, were all white; people who were non-white worked in Darien as domestics, custodians, or as shop-help, and lived in cities. I knew nothing about Darien being a "Sundown Town" (an all-white community that had laws that required non-whites to be out of the town by sundown), until my teens, and even though "bussing" was being passionately debated in the surrounding cities and across the country during the 1970s, and was probably discussed among adults, we children were ignorant of what it was and meant. All I knew at seven was that there was no need to question my whiteness or others' non-whiteness and qualify it, just as I felt no need to question why the sun rose in the east or set in the west. It was just the order of things.

Yet within my snow-blinded reflection upon the communal whiteness of Darien, I slowly began to discern the distinct shading that stratified it. For one, my family lived in Noroton Heights, a section of Darien that was home to many European immigrant families who worked on the estates in town, or in the surrounding communities, or whose fathers, like mine, were in the trades—construction workers, masons, plumbers, and the like Albero, Lyons, Orawsky, Ursone, Guarino, Ryan, and Vitucci were some of the family surnames in our neighborhood, peppered with Mason, Pleasant, Handler, and Miller. Most of our families attended St. John's, the Catholic church, and very few, if any, of our parents were educated beyond high school. I wondered, when I started second grade that year, if any of this had to do with why I was placed in "Special Education" classes, because the majority of my peers in those classes were also from working class families, and I had been in "normal" classes at my previous school. I questioned my parents about this just as I questioned the missing "D" from the sign, and just as my father answered that question, he similarly replied to my latter one, "The teachers know what they're doing," someone must want it this way. Both of my parents held the working class belief that one should never question a teacher's authority, and so I remained in Special Education, where both my sister and brother tracked along with me, until I was "accidentally" placed in a regular (college prep) English class in ninth grade, and the teacher allowed me to stay in it.

If the stigma of being in the "dummy class" was difficult for me to negotiate, being excluded from the rites of upper-middle-class girlhood passage was more trying as I approached my teen years. Lessons in skiing, sailing, music, horseback riding, dance were not part of my childhood, nor were family vacations, home or abroad, or trips into Manhattan to see "The Nutcracker" or to skate at Rockefeller Center during the Christmas holidays, things that were standard for my peers whose fathers commuted into the city for work. I may have resembled these peers in being white, but I knew that there was more to whiteness than that – that the lessons, the clothing, the travel, even the type of food eaten – all enhanced that whiteness, all things that I did not have because of my family's social background. I recall, on more than one occasion, my family being referred to as "white trash" by the town's "mean girls" and seething at the insult. It wasn't just because of my family fitting into the working class stereotype, my father literally having a "redneck" from working outside, and attending NASCAR races as opposed to Formula One events, and my mother fronting a country music band. I was insulted by the word itself and what they thought about us – that we weren't really white, simply white trash. Yet I did not know who I resented more at that time: my family who couldn't provide me with the entree into a society I desired, or a society that made the rules that prevented me from becoming a part of it. Thus, I worked hard at both, trying to pass at being "whiter" than I was by doing such things as purposefully not introducing my parents to my peers and their families if I encountered them in public, or saving up my babysitting money to buy "preppy" trappings like Lacoste shirts and espadrilles. At the same time, in a way to hedge my bets I later realized, I cultivated the pose of an iconoclast, challenging the societal norms I found elitist and hypocritical, as if those norms were never ones I personally desired for myself. Darien's open secret in regard to its racist and anti-Semitic policies was something I felt compelled to expose at every opportunity that presented itself, but in my rage at being slighted, I wound up exposing my own racism, and unintentionally hurting another person in the process.

It was in ninth grade that I learned that race mattered in ways that I never before needed to confront. The only interactions I had in school with anyone who was non-white was with the custodians and cafeteria workers, people with whom I felt comfortable conversing because they reminded me of my own family. My father's father had been a school custodian in Darien, and my mother's mother was a school cafeteria worker at the same school, so my grandparents' narratives and values were familiar to me in the conversations that I had with our middle school's custodians and cafeteria workers. Since I had learned about slavery and the Civil War in elementary school, as well as the history of the civil rights movement, I thought about how that history may have affected the lives of custodians like Laverne, who had told me that she had grown up down south. It was only after I learned in a class discussion that Darien had unwritten policies of not permitting non-white and non-Christian people to move into town, along with its "Sundown Town" practice of putting non-whites in the back of patrol cars after 8:00 p.m., and dropping them off at the neighboring cities' borders, did I think that Darien itself was also affecting their lives negatively. So I decided that I was going to "make a statement" about Darien's racist policies for one of my English class assignments.

Our teacher had separated our class into small groups to choose scenes from *Romeo and Juliet* to perform and make relevant to American society. I convinced my group that it would be a great idea to show the evils of racism and the division between the Capulets and the Montagues by having Missy be a white Juliet, and Richard, a black Romeo, and that I would play a black Nurse. I modeled my Nurse on Hattie McDaniel's "Mammy" in *Gone with the Wind,* replete with "black face" and the "dees and dems" of minstrelsy dialogue that I had seen in movies on television. While I knew people who were black and conversed with them on a nearly daily basis at school, my fourteen-year-old self decided that the way to correctly perform as a black person would be to model it on the way black characters were presented on television. The day of our performance, after Richard and I had put on our black face, and I my kerchief, gold hoop earrings, and pillow-stuffed breasts and belly, we made our way down the hall to our classroom. Laverne happened to be heading in our direction. She stopped walking immediately when she saw us. We both smiled at her and told her we were doing an assignment for our English class, but instead of smiling and asking us more about it as she usually did about our classwork, she stared hard at us for a moment, said nothing, and walked passed us. I knew I had done something wrong and offended her somehow, yet couldn't figure it out, especially after we performed our scene to the great amusement of all, including the teacher, and earned an "A" for our interpretation. When I next saw Laverne she was polite but distant with me, and that is how she behaved towards me until the end of the school year. I never asked her what I did wrong, nor did she mention the incident. It wasn't until a year or so later in high school, when learning about Jim Crow laws and minstrel shows that I thought back to that day and realized that instead of exposing society's racism, I was unwittingly revealing my own. The Nurse in Shakespeare's play may have been intended to be a figure of fun, but by my directing it as a Minstrel act, I was making a caricature of black culture, a joke about racism in the context of a play meant to be a tragedy. Race mattered in a different way to me with that realization. My whiteness, by being so invested in itself and its cultural references to the exclusion of knowing anything else, could actually – and did – hurt another person.

From that moment on I made it a point to consciously think about whiteness and myself as white, and how my motivations to take action on issues might be influenced by it. However, it wasn't until college that my newfound consciousness of being white was challenged on more than one occasion. I went to Norwalk Community College right after graduating from high school, and after that, the Stamford branch of the University of Connecticut (UCONN), thus my daily interactions and friendships with my fellow students weren't with those from privileged backgrounds, since those individuals had the means to attend more selective colleges. Many of my new peers were not white, and more than a few were from the housing projects in the south and west sides of Stamford. Growing up in Darien, one learned that certain topics weren't meant to be discussed in polite conversation, or could be discussed in the context of history and current events only, and race was one of those topics. Conversely, race was a topic I began to discuss regularly at college. If we weren't examining the subject in our classes, we were talking about it at lunch or during our breaks between classes, and not just in an "academic" context. We were very personal and frank with each other, and rarely if ever got offended by each other's assumptions.

One friend, Pat, who lived in a housing project on the South Side, was especially direct with those of us she commonly lumped together as "you white people" when she wanted to get a discussion on race going. She'd point out the ways we "acted white," from how we spoke, dressed, ate, walked, and assumed our place in society in general. And then we'd ask her if the same held true with "acting black." Within the back-and-forth we all began to think more critically of our racial classifications, and in the process learned that there were so many other factors that went into race, like one's socio-economic class status that I had intuited early on had somehow affected my whiteness. I pointed this out to Pat the first time she invited me to her apartment, and told me beforehand that I had to wear a suit jacket, carry a briefcase and walk, as she put it, "as if you had a stick up your behind" so her neighbors would think I was a social worker and not break into my car or rob me. I didn't own a suit jacket or a briefcase, for one, and when she tried to teach me how to "walk white" by modeling it for me, and I kept either tripping over my feet or looking like I was about to pass gas, she gave up, saying, after she stopped laughing through her tears, that I definitely wasn't "white enough." So I went as I was and visited her throughout our years together at UCONN, and my car was never broken into, nor was I ever robbed.

This was long before 2005, long before I learned that I would one day become "white enough," and that I would like it, *a lot*. In August 2005, I started teaching at Southeastern Louisiana University in Hammond, about an hour's drive north of New Orleans. I had been invited by a friend who was chair of the English department to teach at the university, since my temporary non-tenure-track position in Connecticut had ended that year, and she thought it would be a good experience for me and my future students to work together. As a typical northerner, I was anticipating that southern whites would be by-and-large racist, and that I, who had been a residential tutor for A Better Chance Program, a teacher and administrator for an Upward Bound Program, a program coordinator for Girls, Inc., a former employee of a radical lesbian separatist collective, a professor of feminist theory and a scholar of literature by "marginalized" writers, would have a great deal to teach my southern counterparts about their racism. I wasn't initially disproved of my assumptions, and within my first week of living in Louisiana, believed them to be true. For instance, within a day or so after my arrival, I went shopping at the local supermarket, and when I was at the end of one line waiting to be checked out, a manager from the courtesy desk called me over to an empty lane to ring up my purchases. I let the couple in front of me know that a new line was opening, but the manager said, "No, no, ma'am. I'm just taking your order." Okay, I thought, perhaps this was an example of southern hospitality, so I thanked him for his kindness and went over to him, though I suspected that my being white, and the couple in front of me being black may have had something to do with his offer.

A similar incident happened a couple of days later at another store when I was again at the back of a line, and a young woman who was bagging called me over to an open register. Yes, there were black customers before me; there were white ones as well, though by their mannerisms and dress, they were decidedly not from the middle-class white neighborhood, "Villa West," where I was living (otherwise referred to by the locals as "Vanilla West"). I thanked her and noted that those in front of me should probably go first. She stared at me, and the few people in front of me turned around and stared at me also, none making a move to go over to the young woman's lane. I had a brief impulse to launch into a lecture on civil rights at the checkout line in a grocery store when the middle-aged black woman who was immediately in front of me said, "You go on, ma'am. She's waiting for you..." So I went to the open lane and made my purchases, knowing that my taking a stand at that moment might cause more harm than good, especially because I was unsure of what I felt or who was in "the wrong," or whether anything was wrong at all because no one but me seemed to indicate that anything was amiss. But something was unsettled within me by these two incidents; it revealed who I really was, rather than who I thought myself to be. As I left the store, before I had even crossed the parking lot to get to my car, I realized what troubled me – I had finally become "white."

Perhaps it took my leaving the North to recognize that I had become what I wanted to be yet also despised because of how rejected I felt growing up. I may be white, I always told myself, but I'll never be white like that, I smugly thought. But here I was in Louisiana, removed from familiar people and places that kept my self-perception siloed into thinking I was still the same shade of white at forty-one that I was at seven. Somewhere along those years I acquired the suit jacket, the briefcase, the "stick up the behind" walk and attitude that my friend Pat said conveyed the right type of whiteness. And to my chagrin, I found myself in another situation in which I believed myself to be in a morally superior position to others, only to realize that I was the one who needed to learn the lesson. However, instead of thinking deeply upon my newfound whiteness and its implications for me and what it said about society, I began to revel in it and work it like a bright, shiny toy that I alone possessed. I strode into stores and establishments with the confidence in knowing that even if I didn't have the money to afford the baubles inside them, no one would deny me the right to have them. Always polite and friendly, I interacted with everyone, like a *marotte* being bandied about society by a jester, without the self-irony, or the audience finding anything about my performance in the least absurd. I may have been a northerner, but my whiteness nonetheless aligned me with entitlement despite my outsider status in Louisiana.

In late August 2005, I cashed in some of my "privilege chips" without the slightest hesitation or question that those chips may have been ill-gotten, or that they may have prevented others from their fair share of basic necessities. You've seen the pictures, read the stories about Hurricanes Katrina and Rita and their aftermath in Louisiana and Mississippi – people were left homeless, possession-less – where the flooding and tornadoes decimated homes and lives. Hammond was the next largest city north of New Orleans and west of Slidell, where many of those displaced, both black and white, headed for refuge. FEMA's reputation for ineptitude at that time was well-earned, and when relief trucks headed into the city, the only time people were aware of the trucks' imminent arrivals were when large crowds congregated in open parking lots, and there were no tents or speakers put up to indicate that a religious revival was about to occur. I found myself on one of those lots one day waiting with the others, and when the trailer truck arrived and the back of it opened, the rules were posted and called out by the emergency workers distributing the supplies: "One bag of ice per person; no more than two MREs[1] and two bottles of water per person." Like most in the crowd, I was sweaty, covered in mosquito bites, dressed in casual attire, and wearing a large-brimmed hat for protection from the sun. But unlike most, my sunburned whiteness shone through and eventually drew the attention of two of the emergency workers who called me up to the tailgate and off to the side. One stated, "Ma'am, I bet you could use a couple of bags of ice at your home…" I agreed and thanked him. He continued, "And a case of water and MREs too, I bet…" "Oh, yes, sir! That would be so very kind of you – thank you!" Then he and his colleague jumped off the tailgate and carried my supplies to my car for me, and I gushed my appreciation to them again. Perhaps others also received as equal a bounty, and perhaps the rules were never enforced at all, or done so haphazardly. What I do know is that those rules did not apply to me, and that through my whiteness I had denied others. This was just the order of things.

I wish I could say that there is a clear lesson I learned through my experiences with whiteness I could share with you. I find it both troubling and revelatory that I have never written a personal narrative that flowed as easily as this one until I came to this paragraph, the conclusion, the part where I am expected to summarize an argument, and offer new ways of thinking about the subject. All I can offer is this: I could write about my experiences about whiteness with such ease because I never really had to think about them as they occurred. Now that I've

---

1   MRE is military slang for "Meals, Ready to Eat."

shared them with you, when it's necessary for me to shape meaning of these experiences, and what it ultimately means to be white for me, I am at a loss. Writing this narrative has opened an avenue of personal inquiry for me that I had only previously examined piecemeal. Maybe what's preventing me from reaching a conclusion is due to fear, or confusion, or resistance to take actions I'm not ready to take. I do not know. What I am sure of however, is just like this essay, coming to terms with whiteness is an unfinished business, which despite how hard I try, I may never find a resolution. ■

Sara Sherr

Nothing Will Show You Your Own Racism Like Tinder: On Being White in America

WHAT DOES IT MEAN to be white in America? Imagine me, in fifth grade. Imagine me rummaging around in a hat held out by my teacher. Imagine this activity: our teacher is splitting us up by fake race to teach us what it was like for black kids in the 1960s. Imagine me drawing the piece of paper that puts me on the white side.

Imagine the only black kid in the class, Wilkins Hatton. Wilkins picks right after me, and Wilkins lands on the black side.

Imagine the silence for a second, will you? It wasn't a pregnant pause. It was a car crash pause. I walked over to the side with white students and sat down.

Nothing, and I mean nothing, will show you your own racism like Tinder will. A face pops up on your screen. Tinder wants to know, would you fuck this girl?

If the girl is black, the answer is no. It's an automatic no.

If the girl is white, I'll look at her. I'll consider. I'll imagine the writhing, the moaning, I'll wonder whether we could fall in love. Most of the time, I click the little green check mark that means, "Yes Tinder, I would fuck this girl."

I'm gay but it doesn't matter. I'm a girl. but it doesn't matter. You can wax poetic about intersectionality all you want but when it comes down to it, my parents both have six figure incomes. I don't have any college debt. I grew up spending weekends in a fucking country club for God's sake, a country club of which my father later became president.

If I get published for this story, it'll be one more example of standing on people's heads, on people's shoulders, on their windpipes, all because my ancestors came to America from Europe on a boat and they passed through Ellis Island and they looked like the people in charge.

Am I excused for acknowledging my shimmering cloak of white privilege? Yes and no.

I went to see the movie *Selma* by myself. It felt important. Plus, a girl I was in love with told me it was the best movie she ever saw.

There's a moment in that movie where Coretta Scott King is about to meet with Malcolm X, and she's nervous. She's speaking to Amelia Boynton.

This is what Amelia Boynton says:

> "We are descendants of people who innovated, created, and loved despite pressures and tortures unimaginable. They are in our bloodstream, pumping our hearts every second. They've prepared you. You are already prepared."

When Amelia Boynton said that, or I mean, when Lorraine Toussaint said it while playing Amelia Boynton, it felt like praying. It felt like those words were the lock that clicked everything into place, like stars had been shot through my bloodstream.

I felt jealous when I heard Amelia Boynton's character say that. I felt jealous I wasn't black.

After I saw *Selma*, I sat down in a room full of white people to take part in an organized discussion. I said the things I was supposed to say to impress people. I said, "We can talk about race all we want, but the women in that movie hardly had any agency." I said, "I read that black women felt alienated from the feminist movement." I said, "That movement was for white women." I said, "We need to talk about intersectionality."

I said all this to the white male moderator, this asshole Clark I worked with at peace camp in Maine. Clark nodded, like he was really impressed with what I said.

I didn't believe any of it. What I should have said is, "I'm devastated they killed Jimmy Lee Jackson." What I should have said is, "Emmett Till breathes in my blood."

Maybe I should have said, "I read *Citizen* by Claudia Rankine. There was an empty seat next to a black man on the subway, and because of Claudia Rankine, I took it. I sat next to him."

Am I not racist for wanting to fuck Samira Wiley? For loving Beyoncé? Because I completely jived with Chimamanda Ngozi Adichie's *Americanah*? Because I read *What Is The What* by Dave Eggers, so I've essentially placed myself psychically in the position of a Sudanese refugee?

Of course that doesn't make me not racist. As Claire Vaye Watkins says in her *Tin House* essay "On Pandering,": "After all, it's so much gentler to be presented with an ugliness of which you'd been completely and honestly oblivious than one you were trying to pretend didn't exist."

That I have institutionalized, embedded, implicit racism doesn't exempt me from human moments. I wasn't exempted from loving the black director of my summer camp violently, from being hurled into a dark pit of depression when he died.

I wasn't ever exempted from love. That's my point. When Obama was elected president, I felt the very ground under my feet shift, I felt a bounce in the earth; the white, bright light of hope.

There was a little black boy at that camp named Samatar and I loved him as much as I imagine a mother might love a son. We played basketball every day fifteen minutes before lunch. I just believe in Samatar, that's all. When I think about Samatar I also think about the sun.

Still, I'm more afraid of black men than white ones when I'm on the street alone at night. Still, I censor myself in conversations with black people to make sure race doesn't come up. Still, I have that whole Tinder problem.

But I'm awake. I'm aware. I get mad when I see a black person as the villain in a 1990s film, a Mexican as the thug, and the black girl always as the best friend but never the lead.

Here's the real question; how can I go back to the 1990s, and wrench these associations from my subconscious?

I have a friend Quin, and she is white. When she was growing up, her mom only let her play with black dolls. Quin is probably the only white person I know without institutionalized racism.

There was one black girl I tried to fuck. Her name was Toni, and she was on my basketball team. I think I tried to fuck her to prove to myself I'm not racist. Or maybe I tried to fuck her because I thought she was hot.

Or maybe it's possible for both seemingly contradictory truths to be true at once.

What did I do to try and fuck Toni? I flirted, cracked jokes, chatted with the friend she brought to our games.

When none of these seemed to work, I just sent her a text telling her I thought she was hot. I asked if she wanted to get drinks.

Toni responded saying, "I'm sorry but I don't think of you that way. I think you're great but I don't want it to be awkward."

She added, "I just got out of a relationship. I think you met my ex-girlfriend? You were chatting with her on the sideline at our game."

■ ■ ■

I'VE FUCKED BLACK GUYS. This black guy Matt fingered me on a basketball court under shoo ting stars, he gave me an earthquake orgasm and the next day brought me a yellow flower at breakfast.

I went to junior prom with a black guy named Evan, but we stopped off before prom to hook up in a bank parking lot. I remember he turned me over and put his penis above my butt crack. Not in my butt crack, but in the space before ass cheeks break off to form ass cheeks.

I had sex with a black guy named Michael. Michael told me he wanted to hook up consistently while his penis was inside me. I never texted him back after that.

■ ■ ■

WHAT WAS IT LIKE TO GROW UP white in America? Does being Jewish count as being white?

If you grew up with the kind of privilege I did, you'd be sure that Jewish is the same as white. I don't want to negate the Holocaust. The Holocaust is a bright ache I carry at the core of all my interactions with my family. Would I go to the gas chamber for my sister? Of course I would.

But I mean, I'm tan. I'm tanner than most people. I've been asked whether I was half black a handful of times in my life. I was mortified every time.

Growing up white in America meant whispering "They all look the same," to my sister during the National Ballet performance and then responding, "Shh," after she said, "Yeah, except the black one."

It means remembering that moment now, at age twenty-four, and that moment took place when I was seven.

It meant a constant stream of black housekeepers, and resenting those black housekeepers for hiding my sports jerseys during my frantic searches before games.

It meant that there was a grand total of one black kid in my elementary school and his name was Wilkins. Remember Wilkins?

Wilkins was very good at soccer and still, "Wilkins means ball hog," we taunted. Or maybe that was just me. I thought I was very clever for coming up with that.

No one else was named Wilkins. Wilkins did not come to middle school with us.

■ ■ ■

SINCE WE'RE BRINGING PEOPLE BACK UP, let's go back to Toni. That girl from my basketball team I told you about. You know, full circle and all of that.

Toni is fucking cool, and she's fucking hot. She's got a slamming body, and she writes all these really excellent Facebook statuses. Toni made a status on her birthday, and it read:

> "Man I love y'all. Your resistance, strength, resilience,
> courage, and beautiful brown existence that refuses to
> be caged, belittled, or silenced. Y'all give me so much

life. And as I bring in another rotation around the sun and year on this earth I am continuously grateful for having been born into this body and to such amazing ppl. I continuously feel held and I know I wouldn't have made it this far without you. Our bodies in existence are forced to endure so much and we fight so much bs, but I wouldn't trade this skin or queerness for the world."

When I read Toni's status, I was struck by the same lightness that wracked me after Amelia Boynton's words in *Selma*. Reading those words felt like praying. And I felt jealous again. Again, I felt jealous I wasn't black.

I felt like I had enough agency to comment. I was gay too, so that had to count for something, didn't it? I commented: "You're amazing happy birthday."

An hour later, Toni had changed her status. She'd edited it; it's a new function you can do on Facebook. You can also see a post's edit history. She changed the last sentence. It now read, *I wouldn't trade this skin for the world.*

She'd taken out the queerness.

It's true that the sentence is more beautiful as I wouldn't trade this skin for the world than I wouldn't trade this skin or queerness for the world. The part of me that loves aesthetics roots for that version of the ending. But in my narcissistic, egotistical, humiliation-projecting bubble of the world, I felt shamed out of the conversation. ▪

Deborah Mashibini-Prior

"Good" Hair

MY GRANDMOTHER ONCE SAID, as she gazed at my daughter's hair, "too bad she didn't take more from your side of the family Debby."

As a white person I have always had "good" hair. My daughter, whose biological father is African, does not. If my daughter wasn't biracial I would likely be clueless or at best only partially aware of the amount of time, attention, concern, and money many black women – including my daughter – spend on their hair. My own hair has caused only minor annoyances, and only two passing periods of consternation I can remember: the first, my teenage longing to have my hair grow past the middle of my shoulder blades; and the second, my brief existential crisis in the 1970s when I was involved with a small feminist organization and became obsessed with whether it was okay to have long hair both on my head and my legs; or whether growing one necessitated cutting the other. It was a tug of war between my vain desire to keep my male-attracting decoration and wanting to be "politically correct." I kept the long hair.

In my twenties as that hair finally found its way past my shoulder blades and on towards my waist, we were living in a predominantly black neighborhood. I became obsessed with the determination to not exemplify the stereotype of a white mother who doesn't know how to care for her child's hair. I was extremely conscious of trying to keep her hair in check. Properly. With grease and neat parts and braids. She hated having me do it.

By the time my daughter was three, we had met and made family with a man who proudly wore dreads the entire thirty years we were together. By the time she was five, she began to beg for freedom from the combs, hours and bother she noticed was applied only to her head.

We finally allowed her to dread. It was the summer between first and second grade. She liked it. It was easy and she was unselfconscious. I was proud of how we looked together. My daughter's hair exemplified my desire to be politically correct among the artists and nonprofit workers where I spent most of my time, and my own long straight hair continued to make me feel attractive.

By the time she was in middle school, my daughter became self-conscious about her locks and wanted something different. Truly, she wanted my hair. Long, straight, flowing in the breeze; both quickly and easily washed and combed. None of her teen idols had hair that looked like hers. It didn't help that the majority of children of color in our neighborhood were Hispanic or Native American. Their hair so much more easily mimicked the Eurocentric styles that were popular then.

I will never forget one very awkward period when my daughter tried every hair product and heat straightening tool she could get her hands on (this was before I became willing to invest money in a "real" straightening treatment) to mimic the young Hispanic girls who were fashioning their bangs to stand upright like the crest of a wave above their faces. My daughter's hair could achieve that look after extended periods in the bathroom for about as long as it took her to get to school before it would kink back up.

When she entered high school I finally gave in, and my daughter and I made our first trip to one of Albuquerque, New Mexico's two black hair salons. She had it straightened and felt beautiful. No matter how I tried to reinforce the fact that she was beautiful and perfect with her natural hair, those reassurances always felt at least a little inauthentic even to me since I had the hair texture she wanted to achieve.

Through my daughter's high school and college years, we experimented with chemical straightening products, tried braided extensions, then went back to dreadlocks, back to chemicals, back to braided extensions, and back to dreadlocks again. She is in her mid-thirties now with hair that has been straightened with some version of chemicals since her sophomore year in college.

As my daughter makes one of her now routine every six-month appointments for the $300 "natural" keratin treatments that she (thankfully) and I (hopefully) understand are not quite as damaging to her hair as traditional chemical relaxers, I wonder if the hair that my daughter was born with will ever be "good" enough. "Good" enough for her to feel like she can attain and maintain a professional job, to feel and be attractive to the men she would love to attract, and to feel good about the self that looks back from her mirror.

My hair has always been an easy decoration, a magnet for what feels like positive sexual attention, and as an older woman it helps me maintain a sense of youthfulness. Yes, other aspects of who I am, what I do, and how I conduct myself contribute to my self-image, and most in much more meaningful ways. But I certainly do have "good" hair – an attribute I would likely never have been so aware of without the contrast of my daughter's experience.

And so it is, with my daughter and I: our mostly happy (for me) and happy only when it's tamed and conquered (for her) relationship with our hair. ■

Julie Parson Nesbitt

"A Cool Baby, and a Good One Too:" Reflections of a White Mom

IN ORDER TO BETTER UNDERSTAND my own assumptions as the white mother of a black child, I decided to interview my ten-year-old son and find out what our family feels like to him. Here is an edited version of that interview:

J. This is an interview with Daniel Nesbitt on November 20, 2015 by his mom, Julie Nesbitt. Daniel, are you there?

D. Yep!

J. Thank you for helping me with my paper. My first question for you is, what does it feel like to have a white mom?

D. Not normal, but I like it.

J. So, why is it not normal?

D. Because, I think that it's sorta not the way it is. White people should be with white people and black people should be with black people.

J. One thing I was wondering Daniel, is, if you remember some of the first times you realized you were a black kid?

D. I always knew since I was first born.

J. Oh, since you were first born you knew?

D. Yep!

J. OK. Was there any special way you knew?

D. Yep! Because I looked at my SKIN!

J. OK, that makes sense!... So if there's a white mom and she has a black kid, what would you tell her so that she could do a good job to be a mom to that kid?

D. Don't push your kid that hard.

J. That's a good one! Anything else?

D. I know how it feels!

J. ...Let's say it was a newborn baby, what would you tell him to expect?

D. That you are gonna be a cool baby, and a good one, too. [starts humming and singing] *Black and yellow, black and yellow mmm mmm mmm ...*

J. What if you didn't have a white mom, what if you had a black mom and a black dad, what do you think it would feel like?

D. [singing the words] *It feels very good, cuz you're not the only one... mmm mmm mmm*

J. Because you're the only black one in the family, and that's hard?

D. Yep! [singing words] *I'm the only one, only one, mmm mmm mmm*

J. I can understand that... So, what could a white mom do to help her understand her black child?

D. Go to the DICK-tionary!

J. OK, we're gonna stop now!

D. DICK DICK DICK!!!

In this brief interview, I hear my son's loneliness at being the only black person in our nuclear family of two: "I'm the only one, only one," a sadness he can only reveal by singing. I hear his empathy with other children in the same situation: "I know how it feels!" Being black is foundational to him, something he's known "since I was first born." He was excited to do the interview, yet also felt uncomfortable at times, resorting to silly words and cursing when he wasn't sure what to say. When Daniel says, "black people should be with black people, and white people should be with white people," I hear his longing for and identification with his late black father; his black pride and identity; and his rebellion against me, his white mom. I hear his concrete thinking, a product in part of Fetal Alcohol Syndrome. To Daniel, having a white mom is "not normal;" I'm relieved when he adds, "but I like it."

Single Mom

My son, DANIEL, NOW TEN YEARS OLD, is hilarious, mixed up, angry and bright, engaging and sometimes aggressive. Newly long-legged and lanky, his long arms stretch out to snatch a Frisbee from the air while he zooms down the soccer field. His tightly-napped hair is shaved on the sides and tall on top, to emulate David Accam, his favorite soccer player. In kindergarten, my son could not sit still for three minutes on his mat (the teacher kept a detailed chart); when upset, he threw pencils and chairs across the room, locked himself in the bathroom, or ran into the street. He felt valued and loved at that (mostly white middle-class) school, but could not adapt. They sent him to a school for children with special needs (mostly black and brown kids). There, when he had tantrums half the school went on lock-down, and I was called to come pick him up. By the end of second grade, he had been pushed out of that school, too, and I no longer had a job. The last straw for me was when the principal called the police on my child. He was seven years old.

Like many others, my husband and I entered the world of parenting via adoption with joy, anticipation, and confidence. Since Rod was black, and I am white, it felt right for us to add a black or perhaps biracial child to our life. Rod and I had been married for fifteen years; living in a cross-racial family already, I felt comfortable with a trans-racial adoption. There were many children in need of homes in our city, and most of them were black. Our child would have a black parent for guidance; we lived in an unusually diverse neighborhood; our friends, relatives, and community circles were filled with people of many races, ethnicities and backgrounds. Since college, I had sought to educate myself about racial issues, and immerse myself in cross-cultural communities and anti-racism work. We passed the adoption agency's extensive counseling process with flying colors; our family and friends were thrilled; and we were ready to be loving and capable parents raising a child to successful adulthood.

Nothing could have prepared me for what happened next.

On a quiet Saturday morning, five years after we brought home our son, my husband and Daniel were watching cartoons when Rod suffered a massive heart attack. He died almost before reaching the hospital. I went to sleep with a much-loved husband of nineteen years and a child with a million-dollar smile. I woke up a widow with a grief-stricken, traumatized five year old who had just watched his father die. With no warning, I was a single mom.

White (Widowed, Adoptive) Mom

THE COMPLEX PROCESS OF ADOPTION is not only about love – it's also economic. The assumption of white privilege and the ability to bestow white middle-class values are a hidden agenda underlying the narrative of the heroic adoption. Although I haven't researched this, I would bet that lack of financial resources is a leading reason why birth mothers, facing a crisis, make an adoption plan. And because in our country economic inequality and racism are intertwined, structural racism must be an element in the process of white adults adopting black children. Not because white parents who adopt are racist individuals, but because white people, for historical and political reasons, are more likely to have the financial resources needed to adopt a child. White privilege is based on the systemic, historic and ongoing oppression of black people and communities. As a white, middle-class parent, I am using my privileges to adopt a child from a less-privileged family.

In 1972, the National Association of Black Social Workers issued a statement strongly opposing trans-racial adoption:

> "The National Association of Black Social Workers has taken a vehement stand against the placement of black children in white homes for any reason. We affirm the inviolable position of black children in black families where they belong physically, psychologically and culturally... Only a black family can transmit the emotional and sensitive subtleties of perception and reaction essential for a black child's survival in a racist society."

I did not intend to be a single white mom of a black son, but I am. This statement, issued more than forty years ago, still holds true in many respects. Parenting is a huge responsibility; trans-racial parenting exponentially more so. And the most tense, complex, and fraught relationships in our country are between black and white people – however you define those terms. It's built into our national DNA; breaking up black families has been an ongoing process since slavery. For a complex set of reasons, my son's birth mother chose not to raise this child, and I chose to raise him. I'm now a part of that process.

The Black Male Body

IN HIS INCISIVE BOOK, *Between the World and Me,* Ta-Nahesi Coates' focus on the black male body as the site and target of racist violence speaks directly to my life as the mother of a black son. My son delights in his body. He dances when he is happy. His long thin arms stretch and twine. His skinny boy-legs twist and spin imitating hip-hop dancers. My too-cool-for-school son excitedly calls "Look, Mom, look!" as he invents moves so graceful and astounding they take my breath away. Inspired by reading both of Coates' books, I try giving Daniel "the talk" about police racism. But he's just not ready to hear it. Like a much younger child, he still thinks he's invincible, the Hulk, a superhero. Being black is his pride and sometimes his armor against me, the white mother. He says: "Daddy understood me because he was black. Only blacks understand blacks." Yes, my son, I hear you. Better than you suspect. I agree with you more than you know. But he doesn't want my agreement; he wants his blackness, his maleness, his own unique and powerful self. Yet this very self he rejoices in makes him vulnerable. As Coates chillingly says: "In America, it is tradition to destroy the black body—it is heritage."

Being black in America is a form of trauma every day. Poet Claudia Rankine confronts racism and unexamined white privilege in her searing poetry indictment, *Citizen:* "You take in things you don't want all the time. The second you hear or see some ordinary moment, all its intended targets, all the meanings behind the retreating seconds, as far as you are able to see, come into focus..."

In this essay, I've chosen not to define the terms white and black because I'm considering how the world Daniel and I live in impose those definitions on us. However you define white, white is how I'm seen as Daniel and I walk down the street, meet with a teacher, play on the playground. I don't hear or see "all the meanings behind the retreating seconds" that Daniel sees in those moments. But I notice other children wondering who that white lady is shooting hoops; I catch the white teacher's infinitesimal sigh of relief when I walk into the conference room; I feel the slight scowl of disapproval from older black women when Daniel melts down at Target.

Am I imposing my white, middle-class standards on my black son? Of course I am. This question confronted me while reading *Between the World and Me.* By pointedly and repeatedly using the phrase, "People who believe they are white," Coates issues a challenge like a thumb in the eye to examine my own white identity. I've examined race in terms of blackness, and conscientiously learned about racism. But have I ever explored where my ideas of whiteness come from, or dug into the roots of my white identity? What makes me believe I am white? What are the assumptions underlying my own white privilege? How did I come to my beliefs?

Bad Hair

I WAS BORN TO JEWISH PARENTS at a time when being Jewish in this country was equated with being white. My hard-working father parlayed the traits of an immigrant's child and the advantages of his era into a white middle-class adulthood, laying the foundations of privilege for us. My parents chose to move to an all-white suburb of Chicago that was (and still is) a bastion of WASP privilege. Upper income, with beautiful old oak trees, it contained a small neighborhood of Catholic families and the town's two Jewish families—ours and my friend Carol's.

I never faced outward discrimination growing up (my older sister did), but, in a way I could never quite surface, I always felt like an outsider there. I assumed I was white because everyone I knew was white, and I was considered the same. But I felt somehow different. Maybe it was my hair? In that era the height of feminine teenage beauty was dish-water blonde, stick-straight hair parted in the middle. Frizz was not acceptable, and my dark brown, untamably curly hair exploded into frizz at the slightest sign of moisture. My older sister and I spent hours sitting under giant puffy hair dryers punishing our unruly hair by wrapping it in huge prickly curlers, only to have our falsely straight hair betray us at the first sign of rain.

When I read black women poets Nikki Giovanni and Gwendolyn Brooks, I immediately identified with the term "bad hair." Finally something made sense. I wasn't black, but my hair wasn't white! Strange as it sounds, that made sense to me. I think that early, confusing feeling of being different created an opening for me to later understand and accept the concept of racism.

Our family discourse on race was open and liberal. My mother told us: "you can marry anyone you want, as long as they're not Republican." We discussed the civil rights movement, the Vietnam War, and other issues of the day. But we lived in the suburbs. When Dr. King was shot and the West Side (where my future husband's family lived) burned, we watched it on TV, safe in our leafy suburb. We would have described ourselves as "not prejudiced." But the realities of race were distant from us.

Soccer, China, and Chicago: A Political Awakening

I LEARNED ABOUT POLITICS in college by playing soccer. The men's team at the large, state university was made up of agriculture students from Libya, Argentina, Ethiopia, India, Chile, Saudi Arabia, Mexico, Iran, and even Tibet. After the games, everyone went to a bar and argued politics while getting plastered on cheap Wisconsin beer. I learned about imperialism, colonialism, the struggles between Arabs and Jews, the overthrow of Salvador Allende. I read Freire, Neruda, and Marx. My boyfriend was Ethiopian and my roommate was a gay Latino man. I hung out with lesbian poets and became a life-long feminist.

But not one of my college friends, male or female, was African American. If there was a black student group, I was unaware of it. My world view had exploded, but racism and whiteness still did not touch me personally. In that international, many-cultured, and multi-class group, I understood myself as a Jewish girl, a privileged American, and uncomplicatedly white.

In Western China, where I taught English after college in the early 1980s, I stood out. In a city of four million, I was one of fifteen people who was neither Han Chinese nor Tibetan. Crowds gathered around to gape at me in the market. Because they didn't guess I was fluent in Chinese (it was my college major), I could easily eavesdrop on their conversations. They liked my "proletarian" jeans, but were shocked at how I boldly exposed my waist by tucking in my shirt! At that time in China, people still wore "Mao" suits and called each other "comrade," a title I found refreshingly non-sexist. My students were warned not to mix with the "Capitalist." I was said to be on the look-out for a Chinese husband, and my Clash tapes could cause spontaneous orgies to erupt. While I was relentlessly watched and monitored, I also had rare privileges, such as my own apartment and delicious wood-ear fungus soup for breakfast every morning. But despite my high status as a "foreign expert," the isolation and constant awareness of being different wore me down. My experience living in China gave me my first taste of how it feels to be explicitly, unavoidably "other," and later helped me empathize with how my black son might feel in an all-white group of people.

After college, I fulfilled the goal of my suburban childhood – I moved to the city. Chicago is a city that takes its politics personally. Race and racism permeate everything from the narrowest alley up to the mayor's office. I was in my early twenties when the fight to elect our first black mayor, Harold Washington, opened my eyes. It was an overtly racist brawl where anti-Washington voters wore buttons showing a watermelon with a slash mark. I can still hear Harold Washington's deep, booming voice scathingly describe one politician as "a racist from the top of his head to the tips of his toes!" Campaign efforts were often divided by neighborhood, and because of Chicago's severe segregation, also by race. I was fortunate to help found and be part of "Artists for Washington," a group that included black, white, Asian American and Latino artists. Despite anti-Washington viciousness and racism, it felt like an idealistic time: I was part of a multicultural movement of people working together to achieve social justice in our city.

During that time, I worked at Guild Bookstore, an independent bookstore with a left-wing political bent. The manager, Richard Bray, along with artist-activist Sue Ying, decided to start a cross-cultural artist's event series. I've heard people remember those events as if somehow "naturally" artists from across the segregated city came together, but it was an intentional effort. We had fun and mixed it up, for example, featuring Puerto Rican poet David Hernandez with African American blues poet Reggie Young, white septuagenarian Elizabeth Eddy, and me. We hosted book parties for Gwendolyn Brooks and Haki Madhubuti, Nigerian Nobel Prize winner Wole Soyinka, Peter Matthiesen after the banning of his book *In the Spirit of Crazy Horse* about the stand-off on Pine Ridge, and the great James Baldwin, who drank Scotch with us in the back of the store. It was a unique and exciting time that indelibly shaped my life – in many ways. Among life-long friendships I built during those days was anti-apartheid activist, Prexy Nesbitt, who introduced me to his cousin, Rod.

Consent

UNTIL THE PRINCIPAL CALLED the police on my son, I had worked hard to cooperate with the public school system. I believed strongly in public education, and I wanted the system to work for us. We had many skilled and dedicated teachers and caring principals. When, in kindergarten, "Hurricane Daniel" turned the teacher's lounge into a FEMA-worthy disaster, the floor ankle-deep in ripped-up paper, chairs overturned and the heavy sofa on its side, the principal waded right in to calm him down.

But as Daniel's Individual Educational Plan (IEP) lengthened with an alphabet soup of diagnoses and detailed remedial strategies, I struggled with suggestions to put him on psychotropic drugs and even to have him hospitalized. The turning point came with a new principal as he began second grade. With ADHD and learning disabilities, Daniel had trouble sitting in a chair and couldn't read. To keep him compliant and prevent outbursts, my peer-oriented son was placed alone in a study carrel all day playing video games on a school iPad. When he acted out, the new principal showily ordered increasingly isolating, threatening and punitive measures – from the study carrel to the "Quiet Room" to placing the whole wing of his school on lock-down.

Research has shown that exclusionary discipline is "highly correlated with high school dropout, arrest, and incarceration" (Losen, 2015, p. 31). Daniel thoroughly internalized the shame of being separated from other kids and not worthy of being taught. He insisted that he was a "bad kid." He showed his shame in daily physical uncontrollable rages, earning "aggressive" on his ever-lengthening IEP (although he never tried to hurt another person). The principal called several times a week threatening to have Daniel taken away by social services "in an ambulance" if I did not come immediately to pick him up. These threats terrified me; I would rush out to get Daniel, and eventually lost my job.

However, unlike many Chicago Public School (CPS) parents in my situation, I had the financial resources to hire a lawyer. Suing CPS empowered me. They backed down and agreed to place him in a therapeutic school. And when they chose a school for autistic children (because we lived on that bus line), I fought back. I also became active in community groups working for an elected school board, supporting the teacher's union, and protesting the proliferation of charter schools. Finally, I decided to return to school myself for a master's in educational policy. As I told my supportive lawyer, I wasn't through fighting yet.

The principal was a bully, but how best to understand her actions? Was she an insensitive monster? A stone-cold racist? Did she just not understand my son's needs? Although I eventually used every means to discredit this abhorrent woman, it's important to put her actions into a larger framework. Black kids from pre-school and up are disproportionately targeted for disciplinary punishment (Losen, 2015). And this is not simply because black students have bad behavior; a black student's chance of being punitively excluded is almost double the rate of a white student—for the same behavior. In addition, students with disability status are almost twice as likely to be suspended from school. I won't forgive Daniel's principal, but she is also part of a larger structure that systemically, disproportionately and often lethally punishes students for being black, male, and having emotional and behavioral disabilities.

"That They Teach Me"

MY RESOURCES AND PRIVILEGES allowed me to enroll Daniel in a private residential therapeutic school. This school uses an approach based on neurological studies of brain development in children who have suffered trauma (including early neglect, violence, and prenatal drug exposure). Initially, I held my breath as I watched Daniel slowly change. Now when I ask him what he wants to be when he grows up, instead of "I'll be in jail," he says "soccer coach." Over two years, his reading has climbed from kindergarten to fourth grade level. Recently I asked Daniel what he wants in a school; instead of saying "Play video games," he said: "That they teach me." And I felt, at least for the moment, we had disrupted the school-to-prison pipeline.

Consent or Opt-Out?

MY SON WILL LEAVE his therapeutic school at the end of this year, and I search desperately for a school that will fulfill all my requirements, hopes and longings for him. Educator Mike Rose says, "A good education helps us make sense of the world and find our way in it" (Rose, 2009, p. 33). I critique my white middle-class values, which may or may not actually be white and middle-class. I could care less about test scores. Much more important is whether a school has both recess and physical education. I'm no longer interested in special admission schools that are mostly white. My son needs a school that will help him shape a positive self-image as a black boy and later a black man. He needs a stable, consistent learning environment with support for his special needs: anger, frustration, aggression, ADHD, and a host of other learning disabilities. He needs teachers who will not just see his problems but will appreciate his strengths: he is smart, funny, thoughtful, caring; he wants to learn, be loved, and be good. The school must also be close to home. Obviously, this school does not exist.

I would like to stay in the public school system and fight to change it; at the same time, I have to do what's best for my child. Should I be one of those parents who pulls her child out of the public school system because she can? Or, should I stay and fight in the public school war zone, with its massive cuts of special education services and huge classroom sizes, despite potential consequences for my child? Or, can I ethically do both?

Your Ass On The Line

AS I TRY TO UNDERSTAND where I come from as a white parent of a black child, my son is my best and hardest teacher. How should I respond when he tells me "whites don't understand blacks"? How do I explain when a child on the playground wonders aloud if I am his social worker? What will happen when he asks to meet his birth mother, who lives across the city? I listen to the wisdom of bell hooks who says "We have nothing in this culture that prepares young black boys to love themselves," and Kevin Powell when he urges a new masculinity for black men that includes respect for women and feminist consciousness (hooks and Powell, 2015). I often feel I'm fighting to save my son's life, but I also have to ask: at what cost to him? What, anyway, are "white middle-class values"? That I want my son to go to college? That I expect him not to curse in public? Not to sag his pants? To grow up feeling physically safe and financially secure? None of these strikes me as anything different from what a black mother might want. I constantly ask myself: What else do I need to understand? I know that, alone, I can't provide a generations-laden culture that makes a family "black." My son has the memory of the deeply comforting timbre of his late father's voice, the buttery warmth of his Aunt Karen's mac 'n cheese casserole, Uncle Prexy reminding him "make it easy on yourself!" and older cousins who generously hang out with him. Yet, I know it's not the same or enough. How will he learn the split-second instinct for survival he will need in a racist world?

I haven't fooled myself. I know that even the proverbial village can not overcome the contradictions inherent in our lives. But, finally, I disagree with the 1972 statement by the Association of Black Social Workers, because I don't believe it works to create the world I want for my black son, or for all our children. My husband and I agreed on one goal to raise our child: that he or she grow up to be, in the Yiddish phrase, a *mensch*. A good and caring person in the world. I believe I can raise my son to be a healthy, successful, and loving black man. I believe this, not because I'm the greatest, most racially conscious white person or the best parent; I'm not and never will be. But because I'm Daniel's mother; I love him and this is my job, the only one I cannot fail.

Poet and writer Alice Walker said that her mother, who had no opportunity herself to travel or to write, provided Alice the two things she needed for her future: a suitcase and a typewriter. I need to similarly provide my son for a life beyond the one I know.

I have to provide my son with the foundational tools he will need as a black boy and man in a global city and complex world that includes everything from systemic lethal racism to transformative creativity and unfathomable beauty. We are lucky. We have an incredibly loving family, neighbors, friends, and caregivers. They are white, black, and biracial, Jewish and Muslim. Daniel has multiple role models in sports and music, the books we read, the movies we see, and the events we attend. If, as our lives develop, we need to join a black church, even though our family is Jewish, to have more immersion in black culture, then we will. Or, maybe he'll have a bar mitzvah.

I hope and have to believe that white supremacy will not solely define my son's future. Of course, I could be wrong.

In her brilliant and deeply moving book, *Being Bad: My Baby Brother and the School-to-Prison Pipeline*, Crystal T. Laura writes, "love is the action a person takes to enhance, protect, or alter another's life on his or her terms... to fearlessly put your ass on the line to help somebody meet a fuller measure of his or her own humanity." (70) That is one of the best descriptions of parenting I've heard.

I watch my friends who are black mothers of black children, and I learn from their extra efforts to be protective by being strict. I am terrified every day of the risks my son faces. I take the school-to-prison pipeline very personally. I wrench myself away from being the mother I dreamed I would be: like my own mom, the parent who just wants her child to be "happy." Because, as difficult as it is for me to accept, being that mother will not help Daniel. In fact, being that mother could endanger him. That's one privilege I don't have.

As a parent, it is terrifying and bitter to accept that you cannot physically protect your child. I think this is a reality for parents of black children in a way it is not for most white middle-class parents. This week we grieve for and protest the murder of seventeen-year-old Laquan MacDonald. As he walked away holding a three-inch knife, he was shot sixteen times by a white police officer and left to bleed out in the street while eight police officers watched. Just stood and watched. In this virulently racist society, I may not always be able to keep my son safe. But one thing I know: he will never grow up to heartlessly watch someone die in the street. That is our job as parents.

When Daniel says that a black baby with a white mom is "a cool baby, and a good one, too" I hear him affirming his "cool" black identity. And I hear the *mensch* in him adding that having a white mom can make him "a good one, too." And I proudly think, *Yes, that's my son.* ■

Bibliography

Ta-Nahesi Coates. *Between the World and Me.* (New York: Speigel & Grau (Penguin Random House, 2015).

Ta-Nahesi Coates. *The Beautiful Struggle: A Father, Two Sons, and an Unlikely Road to Manhood.* (New York: Penguin Random House, 2009).

bell hooks and Powell, Kevin. Conversation: "Black Masculinity, Threat or Threatened / The New School." (2015). Found online at https://www.youtube.com/watch?v=FoXNzyK70Bk.

Crystal T. Laura. *Being Bad: My Baby Brother and the School-to-Prison Pipeline.* (New York, NY: Teachers College Press, 2014).

Daniel J. Losen, ed. *Closing the School Discipline Gap: Equitable Remedies for Ex-cessive Exclusion.* (New York, NY: Teachers College Press, 2015).

National Association of Black Social Workers, "Position Statement on Trans-Racial Adoption," September 1972, found online at http://pages.uoregon.edu/adoption/archive/NabswTRA.htm

Daniel Nesbitt. Interview by Julie Nesbitt in Albuquerque, New Mexico, 2015.

Claudia Rankine. *Citizen, An American Lyric.* (Minnesota: Graywolf Press, 2014).

Rose, Mike. *Why School? Reclaiming Education for All of Us.* (New York and London: The New Press, 2009).

Kristina Quynn

My Brother, My ~~Nigger~~

I DO NOT REMEMBER THE BRICK through the living room window or the cross burning on the front lawn. I've been told those events happened when we were infants. Or that's what I think I have been told about 1968, the year my liberal humanist and visibly WASPY parents adopted my brother, Eric–a mixed-race baby whose paternal half of the gene pool marked him "black" in the 1970s, and "African American" in the 1980s. I do not know what his label is today. I cannot tell you if his race is recorded on his birth certificate or adoption paperwork. I do know his adoption would have been one of 730 interracial adoptions that took place that year across the United States and the first to take place in Southern Colorado.

Now, more than forty years later, I suspect the brick through the window and the burnt cross may be part of a collective–but not personal–memory. A memory projected through PBS documentaries featuring black and white images of black men in pressed trousers marching through southern streets alongside black women in fitted shirt-dresses. A memory *juxtaposed* with photographs of white men festooned in white-coned sheets with crosses flaming at their backs. This is the mutable and collective quality of a black and white past I remember vaguely and, in all likelihood, inaccurately. It is a collective past my brother and I do not talk about, even though we were inseparable for much of our childhood and we still talk about a great many topics openly and with mutual interest. It is a past with all of its silences, inaccuracies, and wondrous unconventionality that gave an initial shape to my understanding of what it means to be white in America in the later-twentieth and early-twenty-first centuries. It takes an "other" of color to make a white woman, and there's been many a Hollywood movie starring such mega-celebrities like Sandra Bullock and Michelle Pfeiffer to prove it.

I do not know how my brother understands his racial classification, his being adopted, or his memories of us growing up. Nor will I speak for him, for those are his stories to tell if he chooses. I do know that I understand my classification of "white" only in relation to "other" that began with my relationship with my brother.

My parents adopted Eric in the waning years of a turbulent decade in 1968, one of the most turbulent years of the 1960s. Change was in the air and America's new racial landscapes beckoned my peace-loving, religiously-oriented, and civically-minded parents. Eric was nine months old, and I was fifteen months old. Eric's adoption was the first interracial adoption in Pueblo County, a steelmill town in Colorado where the local influences of the mafia and the Klu Klux Klan had only just started to decline and the primary labor force was an expansive and expanding Mexican American community. But, once again, I don't remember any of that.

I do remember my mother revealing, years later, that my father's side of the family had secretly held a spark of hope that Eric might resemble his birth mother, but when seeing him for the first time, my grandmother could not help but mumble repeatedly under her breath, "He's so dark. I didn't think he would be so dark." Such is family lore, my mother's memory, and a glimpse into how a desire for whiteness can surface in the remarks of an otherwise well-mannered grandmother.

I stress what I don't remember only because, like my encounter with movies, television shows, and the astounding array of characters who give shape to my life (whether living persons or cultural constructions), such indirect memories create a backdrop, a collective historical and familial context upon which I arrange and make meaning out of my immediate experiences.

It took years before I could gather enough information through television and schoolyard play so that I might begin articulating the differences between Eric and I. The skin color was obvious. Eric's adoption was never a secret. And my resemblance (and eventually my brother, Forrest's) to our biological parents was a similarity that only heightened

Eric's dissimilarity. When we were in kindergarten, I told Eric that he was darker because he ate more chocolate than I did. Again, I knew he was adopted, but that didn't account for a difference in skin color, and in a five-year-old's logic eating too much chocolate made more sense than intricacies of paperwork, biological and adoptive parents. Never mind a discourse of racial difference and history of racial categories at work in America that my parents did their best to escape and shield us from. Our parents were stalwart. Eric was their son. Eric was my brother. Blood ties did not matter. Thus, why should categories of race not matter either?

Eric didn't eat chocolate for years.

I remember this conversation. We were lying in the back of the VW Squareback in our pajamas and with blankets on our way to the drive-in to see a movie that I cannot recall. I know I saw the contrast between his color and mine early on or I would have never been able to keep him from eating chocolate. As an adult, I can now look back and note that my power to make him alter his candy preferences had little to do with the intelligence of my theory, or with my being the older sister, or with any other number of explanations. My power rested in my looking like our parents, having blonde hair, blue eyes, and paler skin. My power rested in being part of the majority.

My majority status also provided me the power in the fourth grade to chase my brother around the living room and call him "~~nigger~~." The rules of the game are no longer clear to me – if they were even clear back then – but this game of chase was a repetition of a game played on the playground at school. A version of tag at recess. I did not yet have images of black men and women running through southern woods or midwestern city streets in terror. I had not seen cinematic depictions of whites lynching blacks and immigrants in late-nineteenth and early-twentieth-century America. I had not yet read W. E. B. Du Bois' *The Souls of Black Folk,* nor had I wept at the picture postcards of lynched blacks and immigrants archived in *Without Sanctuary.* As one of the white majority, I had without knowledge or clarity, mimicked what Du Bois and the NAACP had called the "Shame of America."

This chase took place in 1976, a decade after the Civil Rights Acts made segregation illegal and provided equal access to jobs, schools and voting booths for people of color. That one label became the indelible mark and maker of our difference. Whiteness is most visible when deployed overtly. And so often it accompanies shame. I remember my mother's fear as well as her tears. "What did you call him?" stopped me in my tracks. As I look back, I think that I must have known my relationship with Eric would never be the same because the connection between power and race my parents had worked so hard to erase, to make invisible in our home would inevitably come home with me from school.

It was only a nickname. It was. It was...and, yet, I was the one doing the chasing. Perhaps that seemed my natural place because of my skin color, to be doing both the chasing and the name-calling. There must have been a part of me even then which understood, in some small way, the power I had.

I suspect I was jealous of Eric having a nickname, of his getting so much attention. Of the two of us, he was the extroverted one, the quick-witted and friendly one, and I was the shy, socially awkward sister who followed along. Since first grade, he had made our friends for us. He was, to my introvert's eyes, the lucky one to get chased on the playground and the one to have a nickname. In retrospect, I question: could I really have been so naïve or so innocent as a child? Probably not, but my understanding of the playground gets confused with my memory of defending my own actions to my mother in light of her shaking me and her tears. There's a tone of disappointment and pain that a child recognizes in her parent's voice that carries the weight of world-weariness, and that tells the child she has fucked up beyond measure. I remember that tone.

For years I have tried to understand the hows and whys of Eric being chased both on the playground and at home in a post-civil rights America. Depending on where I am mentally and emotionally and on the particular day, the lessons I take from my memories vary. In general, my memories of understanding race as a site of difference between my brother and I surface as a constellation of "holy shit, I never thought of that before" moments—for which I owe him an immense debt of gratitude. Until talking with Eric, I never considered the privilege that

I have to give lip to a Kansas police officer for issuing me a speeding ticket that Eric could never speak the same way to power. His inner monologue keeps him silent and safe:

"Keep your hands in sight."

"Make no sudden moves."

"No lip. Say, 'Yes, sir' and 'No, sir.'"

Right now, at this moment, I see that my whiteness (as all whiteness in America), depends on a colored "other" to define itself. I also recognize that my ability to write about my experiences about whiteness relies on my ability to recollect black and white images of my brother in black ink on these white pages. Being white in America means that I can write a tale like this and title it "My Brother, My ~~Nigger~~" and it strikes a chord. It is a provocative title that requires a strike through. Whereas if my brother were to write a story of our childhood and call it "My Sister, My Cracker" ... No strike through necessary. That word, "~~nigger~~," resonates across familiar landscapes of American history and popular culture. It carries the pejorative residues of oppression and the complex textures of cultural re-appropriation. We can hear both the voice of the slave master and the voice of Richard Pryor if we listen closely enough. "~~Nigger~~" is also part of my experiential landscape, part of my childhood memories, and part of a shared social consciousness that constructs who I am—for better or worse. On these pages, I use the strike through strategically both to maintain the accuracy of my voice as a young girl at a time when I cavalierly engaged in a racist play and to mark my prolonged shame in so easily imitating the slave master (rather than Richard Pryor). Maybe I became "white" when my brother became "~~nigger~~." I do not remember having a sense of race or of the socially constructed meanings of "white" and "black" before the chase. I suspect I am not alone in experiencing such moments of racial becoming and that many of these memories carry forth feelings of shame for many white Americans. My shame compels a strike through to maintain a sense of integrity while refusing to let overt language of oppression continue to be unmarked. The strike through signifies my desire for the past to be the past; for my memories to remain difficult, accurate, and even shameful (neither sanitized nor politically correct);

and for the language of racial difference to surface as a trace rather than the force of continued oppression of an America of brothers and sisters.

Being white in America means that I can still profit—albeit via cultural capital—through my association with my black brother. I'm pretty sure he doesn't think of me the same way.

I benefit from the invisibility of my own privilege and, yet, because I have grown up in a racially aware family. To pretend I don't see color means ignoring the way stereotypes, misinformation, misrepresentation, and mistakes about race continue to shape our institutions and personal interactions. I also see that social equality—when it means equal treatment on the playgrounds of politics, big businesses, material wealth and, once again, personal relationships—is an ideal to be worked towards, for it did not miraculously take place with the enactment of mid-1960s civil rights legislation. Because I was lucky enough to grow up in an interracial family (I will have to tell you about my parents' divorce and my mother's remarriage to a black man with six children another time—a black and white *Brady Bunch* 1980's style), I see a continuation of America's civil rights movement as a necessary exercise that would shift the balance of power in this country without attempting to erase the visibility of skin color. But that is a memory waiting to be made. ■

Christopher M. Rzigalinski

I Have a Confession to Make: My Struggle with Whiteness

A FEW YEARS AGO, the woman I was dating said to me, "You don't know how to utilize your white male privilege." I was confused by her comment. I never considered my life in the metrics of skin color before. Perhaps that was because I was never forced to confront my whiteness in any real way. A friend and colleague at the university where I was teaching at the time gave me the same piece of constructive criticism a few months later. The question of my racial identity was extending into my professional life. I was teaching courses on popular music and multimedia composition, while finishing my master's degree. Until that point, I approached my research and courses as case studies, trying to understand everything I was not. I wanted to know everything about life outside of being white, being straight, and being male. I was always more interested in examining the people and communities I identified with the least. But I was not sophisticated enough to make connections between my personal experiences and my intellectual interests in civil rights, cultural and social liminality, and queer politics to better understand my own identity. All of that changed during my last semester of coursework.

That semester I took seminars in postmodernism, queer theory, and slavery's lasting impact on American race relations into the twenty-first century. I devoted my life up to that point to the idea that there were real world implications to my studies, but it was not until that moment that I saw the connections to my life. It was a tumultuous period. In

2012 and 2013, the United States was reeling from the murder of Trayvon Martin and awaiting George Zimmerman's prosecution. The national conversation on how to respond to the growing immigrant population, as well as the campaign for undocumented students' rights, was reaching a fever pitch. And the foundation was being constructed for a historic Supreme Court decision to ban state-level restrictions on same-sex marriage. One prevalent thread through those seminars and the media coverage of current events that barraged me every day was the notion that various communities were identifying themselves in direct opposition to white heterosexual maleness. I began to wonder, then, what was my place as someone that identified as a straight white man? Who was I, and how could I help ameliorate these social, cultural, and political divides? Moreover, how could I take part in a contemporary conversation about race in which white perspectives seemed unwelcome? Had power relations shifted so much in the early twenty-first century that the backlash against white heterosexual male dominance had forever rendered white men mute and impotent?

My scholarly, artistic, and personal goals developed when I began to recognize and harness white male privilege so it could be dismantled, thereby creating a communicative network with women, people of color, the economically disadvantaged, and other oppressed communities from whose oppression whites, specifically men, have benefited. I started with a confession, both to myself and the world around me: "I am a white heterosexual male." Strangely, it was the first time I ever said it aloud. I was compelled to do so after reading Peggy McIntosh's revelation in "White Privilege: Unpacking the Invisible Knapsack":

> "I think whites are carefully taught not to recognize white privilege, as males are taught not to recognize male privilege. So I have begun in an untutored way to ask what it is like to have white privilege. I have come to see white privilege as an invisible package of unearned assets that I can count on cashing in each day, but about which I was "meant" to remain oblivious. White privilege is like an invisible weightless knapsack

of special provisions, maps, passports, codebooks, visas, clothes, tools, and blank checks.[1]"

For McIntosh, white privilege needs to be discovered, named, and examined because it is ingrained in the institutional fabric of life in the United States. But how did this function in *my life?*

I was disturbed to realize the everyday practices I engaged in that illustrated my protected position. It was in the money that I inherited to pay my own way through undergraduate and graduate schools. It was in the university system that enabled me to maintain a part time lecturer line in two academic departments. It was in the schedule that afforded me the time to consistently get eight hours of sleep and still have enough time to stay in shape by exercising for two hours each morning. It was in my ability to live at my parents' house while finishing my master's degree without paying for rent, utilities, or groceries. It was in my disposable income that allowed me to amass a collection of over 10,000 CDs, vinyl records, and books. I knew this list was a work in progress, but I couldn't help falling victim to feelings of guilt. For the first time I noticed some of the benefits coming from my skin color, and I thought it was unfair. I did not know how to look in the mirror the same way again. I did not know how to engage my graduate seminar cohort and adequately discuss their research grounded in the history of oppressed communities.

The worst part was that any time I tried to discuss my feelings and how they were informing my approach to scholarship, I was shut down. My feelings were dismissed as "white guilt." I was not disturbed by the criticism as much as the way it destroyed a chance for constructive dialogue. But I found hope in Michael S. Kimmel's "Toward a Pedagogy of the Oppressor":

> "Guilt may be appropriate, even a necessary feeling—for a while. It does not freeze us in abjection but can motivate us to transform the circumstances that made us feel guilty in the first place, to make connections between our experiences and others' and to become and remain

---

1   Peggy McIntosh, "White Privilege: Unpacking the Invisible Knapsack," http://www.cirtl.net/files/PartI_CreatingAwareness_WhitePrivilegeUnpackingtheInvisibleKnapsack.pdf.

accountable to the struggles for equality and justice around the world. Guilt can politicize us.[2]"

Those of us that identify as white can capitalize on these negative emotions, overcoming discomfort with education and community building. I knew that an open dialogue would help me learn even more about my status so I could move further from it. I saw this project as a real world intervention I could begin facilitating with the next generation of young American women and men I worked with in undergraduate classes.

I was eager to engage my students about how they viewed their own whiteness and whether they had grown up cognizant of experiencing mechanisms of privilege in their own lives. I structured my fall 2014 and spring 2015 courses around the subject at an especially crucial time. The students in my class—mostly eighteen to twenty-two-year olds—were being confronted every day with violence between black communities and police. The tension was exemplified by the deaths of Michael Brown in Ferguson, Missouri; Eric Garner in Staten Island, New York; and a history of tension in our adopted hometown of New Brunswick, New Jersey. I wanted students to be aware that the events portrayed in the news and social media could happen to them. I encouraged them to think about how white people should develop strategic responses to national movements like #BlackLivesMatter and effective methods to combat the harmful white supremacist ideologies that led to the shooting of nine African Americans at the Emanuel AME Church in Charleston, South Carolina by twenty-one-year-old Dylann Roof. We created what Mark Chou and Roland Bleiker call a conversation of "prefigurative politics" that capitalized on that uncomfortable silence too often prevalent in classrooms between white students and their peers of color. Chou and Bleiker define the term as "a genre of activism that is small in scale and limited in impact but nevertheless can show the way toward a more democratic political community."[3] The white

---

2   Michael S. Kimmel, "Toward a Pedagogy of the Oppressor," *Privilege: A Reader,* ed. Michael S. Kimmel and Abby L. Ferber (Boulder, CO: Westview Press, 2003), 9.

3   Mark Chou and Roland Bleiker, "Betrayed by Politics: Verbatim Theater as Prefigurative Politics," *Doing Democracy: Activist Art and Cultural Politics,* ed. Nancy S. Love and Mark Mattern (Albany, NY: SUNY Press, 2013), 232.

students and I negotiated social and political tensions by recognizing ourselves as *performers* of whiteness. Performative doubleness is a notion that Marvin Carlson revisits in discussing Richard Bauman's interpretation of "performance": "all performance involves a consciousness of doubleness, through which the actual execution of an action is placed in mental comparison with the potential, an ideal, or a remembered original model of that action. Normally this comparison is made by an observer of the action – the theatre public, the school's teacher, the scientist – but the double consciousness, not the external observation, is what is most central.[4]" Bauman's idea of double consciousness is the ability to be aware of the self as both subject and object, something many students recognized in the much graver struggle outlined in W. E. B. Du Bois' *The Souls of Black Folk*. Those with white privilege considered the implicit motivations and circumstances that enabled that behavior and, in turn, started to gain more understanding into a civil rights struggle haunting African Americans to this day. At no point did we equate the experience of racism against African Americans with the task to unpack white privilege; but we did illuminate the common need for mutual compassion. We wanted to establish a space of participatory democracy in the classroom through the exchange of ideas and emotions, where implicit white privilege was interrogated so white students and their peers of color could see a little better how it impacted their everyday interactions at school and beyond campus lines. It was a small step forward.

Given the realities of American life in the twenty-first century, this kind of open mindedness must translate into everyday life in the United States, not just in the safer space of academia. National demographics are shifting even more towards diversity. The United States Census projects that whites will be outnumbered for the first time in United States history by 2060[5]. It makes political and social sense to embrace, rather than fight, this change in order to understand how everyone

---

4   Marvin Carlson, "What is Performance," *The Performance Studies Reader,* ed. Henry Bial (New York: Routledge, 2004), 71.

5   Sandra L. Colby and Jennifer M. Ortman, "Projections and the Size and Composition of the U.S. Population: 2014 to 2060," March 2015, http://www.census.gov/content/dam/Census/library/publications/2015/demo/p25-1143.pdf.

fits into our shared future. It is our patriotic duty to define a common vision of progress. We must also confront the reality that the present age of terrorism has ties to white supremacy. It is the residual effect of Western colonization, globalization, and many other exercises in dominance. But every day, Americans are not helpless. By recognizing the white chauvinism ingrained into the history of our country that has long maligned people of different races, ethnicities, religions, and sexual orientations on a personal level we can ameliorate the hate that enables such destruction.

It is equally as dangerous to assume that there is a uniform experience of whiteness. Being white in America varies according to economic standing, geographic location, and several other factors. And there are times when the United States' much-needed affirmative action policies may overlook struggling lower class whites. But that circumstance is an unfortunate reaction to the oppressive white power structure that was generated the moment Europeans commandeered land in the New World from indigenous populations. Generating a more egalitarian country for people of all colors means untangling white privilege. Surrendering to white guilt, fear, and anger will only create a larger divide. I realize that this essay seems idealistic. But it is a developing collection of thoughts about how I am trying to approach my own life. By no means do I intend to preach or proselytize. I am still struggling to find my place in this country that I care about very deeply. This essay is my early attempt to do that. I might never know how to utilize my white male privilege, but I'm beginning to learn from it. I also want to learn from communities other than those with which I identify to be a better human being and a better citizen. ∎

Wendy Zagray Warren

Choosing to See: What's a White Person Like Me Doing in a Reflective Place Like This?

We sometimes don't see what is right in front of us – there are things we seem only to be able to see in our peripheral vision. Perhaps they are too painful to look at straight on.

– my journal note after reading Tiffany Midge's poem
"After Viewing the Holocaust Museum's Room of Shoes and
a Gallery of Plains' Indian Moccasins: Washington, D.C."

First Steps

I DROVE OVER THE MOUNTAINS to Browning, Montana, with my stomach churning. I had agreed to facilitate at a Montana Writing Project Summer Institute at the Blackfeet Nation, and I was headed there to meet my co-directors, both Blackfeet, at one of their homes. It had only been a month or two since I had been asked to fill this role, a quick replacement for the previous director who was Lakota. I am white. During the course of the institute, we would be working with practicing teachers (indigenous and non-indigenous), writing about cultural reconciliation in the heart of Blackfeet Country. This was intense work, involving people's hearts as well as their minds, and conversations are often difficult to navigate. A facilitation team often works closely together before embarking on such an endeavor, yet I only had brief contact with the co-facilitators with whom I would spend the next three weeks. I had been working in my school district and in the state on an educational mandate passed in Montana called Indian

Education for All. Most of that work, however, had taken place in familiar surroundings. Familiar meaning mostly with white colleagues in the Flathead Valley where I lived.

Now I was headed into what for me was a new world. After cresting the Backbone of the Earth, which I had only known as the continental divide, I found myself careening down its east side, my emotions somersaulting until I reached the driveway of the home of a co-facilitator and her husband. Respecting their privacy, I'll call them Karen and Jack. It was 5:00 p.m., and the institute was to begin the following day. The plan was for the third member of our team, who I'll call Wade, to join us so we could finalize the agenda I had painstakingly drawn out. Because my colleagues were Blackfeet and I was not, I thought this was a contribution I could make to our collective work. I had met Wade only briefly, but I had read his book, and I was awed by his relative fame. Karen and I had exchanged only brief emails. As much as I wanted to engage in this work on so many levels, I was just plain scared. Unsure of every move, I drove down the long driveway and over the cattle guard, down a steep hill and into a river valley. There, I saw a barn, a house, and some horses out in the field.

Dogs greeted my car and accompanied me to the door of the house. In that moment, I realized I had never been in a Native person's home. Hands shaking, I knocked. Someone yelled, "Come in," and I desperately hoped I was at the right house. I pushed open the door to see a man, a woman, a teenage girl who was Jack and Karen's daughter, and Wade, just sitting down to a dinner of salmon and potatoes. "Supper time," Karen says. We hadn't talked about a meal. I worried that I was intruding, yet I was sure this was the time we had arranged. I thought we would get right to work—there was so much to do. But I sat down and ate, my stomach unclenching just enough to take in a piece of salmon. I listened to the scattered conversation around me, afraid to speak. I watched as dishes were cleared.

I felt relief when it appeared time for our work together to begin. From my bag, I retrieved copies of an agenda I had carefully worked up and handed them around the table. I hoped this would provide an entry-point for a conversation about plans for our institute. I would have preferred that we had written this together, but we hadn't found a time our schedules would mesh, and no one but me seemed to feel that need. Jack stayed at the table as we talked. Jack, Karen and Wade began to tease each other and then me about this document I had laid out, a schedule for three weeks, pre-planned. This type of planning was the only way I had ever seen a Summer Institute operate; I clung tightly to the familiar. I didn't understand the teasing, and I could feel panic begin to rise. I knew cross-cultural work wouldn't be easy, but I thought surely no one expected to run a three-week institute without planning. I later came to recognize that a point of discomfort like this is exactly where learning can begin, if I stay open enough to allow it. In that moment, however, all I cared about was deciding how we would begin the next day when our seminar participants walked through the door.

Instead, the three briefly looked over the plan, exchanging amused looks, and the conversation turned to the encampment planned for our second week. The institute would begin within the four walls of a room at Blackfeet Community College and would then move outdoors, to a tipi encampment to be set up in a meadow at Karen and Jack's ranch. During that time, Jack would put on a sweat, as I learned he had during the previous year's institute. I only had a vague idea what a sweat even was, and I had no idea how it would work into a summer institute. I was already so uncomfortable, however, I didn't want to ask any stupid questions. I decided all I could do was listen and watch as carefully as I tried not to misstep. I tried to talk myself into thinking of it as an adventure, rather than acknowledging my fear.

The institute unfolded with the writing and sharing that is a part of every National Writing Project Summer Institute, but I felt myself quickly drawn into a spiral of learning that went far beyond anything I could have planned. I heard personal stories, from both leaders and participants, of things I had never known: Indian Boarding Schools, allotment, starvation, massacres—Federal Indian policies intended to erase a people. For the first time, I understood this process as genocide. I was saddened, sickened, and guilt-ridden. I clung to every word, trying to absorb the experiences of the people in the room. Why hadn't I heard these stories before—about the lives of these people who live next door, yet I rarely see? They were telling me the history of this land now labeled a reservation, yet it is also the history of the United States, a history I thought I knew.

Gradually, I relaxed into the flow of our days in the classroom. At the beginning of the second week, as we entered the period of encampment, I was once again thrown into dissonance. I had no idea what to expect, but I looked forward to being on the land. The group worked together to set up tipis and prepare meals. We spent much of our time together sitting in a circle, listening to the stories of Jack's friend and mentor, a Blood elder, who had driven down from Canada. I kept wondering when he would begin his presentation. It took a day before I realized he was teaching; it was the form I didn't recognize. There were messages in the stories meant just for me at that moment in time, if I listened with care and was open to receive them. This is individualized learning at its finest. No one was going to interpret the story for me or give me the "right" answers. The learning was up to me. I allowed myself to be wrapped in the beauty of the land and this form of education far removed from any lecture hall. As I continued to feel my way into this learning journey, the impact of what had happened on this land pushed its way past my head straight to my heart. I felt anger rising to meet the shame I felt. My skin is the color of the perpetrators. And I had been mis-educated, lied to, about what had happened here. I thought I lived in a democracy, and I had bought the myth of meritocracy I'd been sold. Here before me now was a whole new way of being in the world I had never been exposed to, filled with people's stories that had been concealed from my view.

When the sweat lodge was ready, other members of the Blackfeet community joined our group. Dressed in the way Karen had advised, with most of my skin covered, I entered the small opening of the sweat lodge to find the women's side full. Without thinking, I began to crawl in front of other women to the only open space I could see, opposite the door. "No," a woman whispered to me kindly, motioning me back toward the entrance. I returned and squeezed myself into as small a space as possible, pulling my legs tight against my chest. When Karen entered and moved into her spot to the right of Jack, the sweat's leader, the door closed. That was the spot I had been moving toward, I realized, and I covered my face with my hands. At some point during the three rounds of the sweat, I forgot my embarrassment as I traveled to a place I had not visited before. It was a journey inward – into the core of the earth, into the center of myself. I emerged feeling refreshed; renewed.

Jack, Wade and Karen had spoken of Niitsitapi (Blackfoot) ways of knowing, which cannot be divorced from spirituality. I felt overwhelmed with the beauty of a sense of connection to the land and community that I had missed all my life – without ever knowing it was missing. I had been welcomed here. I found myself drawn to this world, not yet recognizing that my thinking had re-entered the realm of stereotype. This new conception was of "the noble warrior," an image of a proud people, able to overcome any adversity and to live in the beauty of centuries-old traditions. This was different from the stereotype I had arrived with, which was closer to that of "the poor, downtrodden Indian." These stereotypes have been carefully taught, through the media and in textbooks. Most of us don't even recognize they have become a part of our thinking.

Of course, both of these stereotypes get in the way of learning to know people or interpreting what I see. While it's certainly true that the people I met had forged a good path for themselves, their lives were certainly not easy. The obstacles created by the U.S. government were not immediately obvious. The people who have survived them carry a kind of resilience I had only previously recognized in Holocaust survivors. I was in awe. At this stage, I was not yet aware of my ongoing generalizations, of how influenced I was by a white norm. Bound up in binary thinking, the collective terms "us" and "them" still acted as a guide. All I wanted was to immerse myself fully in this new world. "They" have it so right, I thought, and I've lived so wrong. Aware of small shifts in my attitudes, I made symbolic adjustments. I removed my watch and took off my wedding ring, thinking this would help me try on a new way of perceiving the world.

Because I was well-steeped in the white supremacist thinking we've all been taught, my stereotypes held tight as I continued to think of "the Indians" in general terms and of "the Blackfeet" as if they were unified in their thinking. It would take a few more years of summer institutes on the Blackfeet Nation before I could see the vast diversity among Blackfeet peoples. This change in perception came through direct experience over time. One year, for example, a number of Blackfeet participants fought against the "looseness" of the institute and clamored for an agenda, wanting to stay on schedule. Another year, a Blackfeet participant declined the invitation to participate in the sweat lodge. I learned that some Blackfeet do their best to practice spiritual traditions handed down from their ancestors, but because these practices were almost lost during the time they were outlawed by the U.S. Government, it's difficult to know what "traditional" actually means. Others practice Catholicism or belong to the Baptist church. Considering the great diversity I know exists among people from European backgrounds, even if they are from the same country, I wonder why I would have expected uniformity within any tribal group. Such is the power of stereotypes. Clearly, for me this was the beginning of a learning journey that will never end.

What It Means to be White in America

HERE'S THE THING: I didn't *have* to do any of this. And THIS is what it means to be white in America: I can look away. I can say I don't see color, that I treat everyone respectfully. I can say because I'm not impacted by any bias in the system, it must not exist. I don't have to seek out the stories of others who might disrupt my perception of reality.

Nowhere in my education have I been asked to look closely at the social and economic hierarchy of this country. Never in the courses I took to become a certified teacher was I ever asked to address the racism and classism upon which this country was built. It took forty years of living before someone asked me to think about whose land I walked upon each day and suggested that someone's gain is almost always someone else's loss. I hadn't learned to see the systems that perpetuate these ongoing cycles. In fact, if you are white in America, you are encouraged to look away. Surrounded by a white norm that matched my reality, I have been socialized to think of it as simply THE norm. I couldn't see anything else. America's institutions are carefully arranged to allow this illusion to continue. When people or textbooks refer to Americans, they don't mean all Americans. They mean the people who operate within these cultural norms. Therefore, I assumed everyone operated under these value systems. More harmful yet, I was led to believe that this is what everyone should strive for. These are, after all, the value systems of what is called the "developed" world. The narrative is that all other countries should strive to develop a system like "ours." I therefore assumed that the lifestyle and cultural norms of a white, middle-class culture is what everyone else wants. From this vantage point, our institutions seemed to be set up in a way that was intended to help them get it. Adopting this lifestyle was the definition of "making it." I now know that for people raised with a different set of cultural norms, this often requires renouncing any other ways of knowing or being in the world. Giving up your identity is a high price to pay. And THIS is where we can begin to talk about loss.

The multiple interconnected losses among people oppressed by the systems that keep our country's norm in place are overwhelming. Certainly, throughout the history of this country, the damage has compounded. One might think that, conversely, white people from the middle- and upper-classes have only to gain from these systems set up to privilege them. I have come to realize, however, that as long as inequitable social and economic hierarchies are maintained, everyone loses.

Racism and classism operate on two levels: individual and systemic. The damage, then, occurs on these two levels as well. As an individual, if I am not aware that there are ways of being in the world beyond the range of my narrow experience, my choices are limited. Because we live in a segregated society, chances are I am in contact with people who move through the world in much the same way I do. Therefore, my life will likely follow a similar pattern. After spending even a relatively short time with the Blackfeet Nation, those patterns began to be disrupted. For the first time, I became aware of ways of knowing and being in the world I hadn't known existed, which opened a range of possibilities for how I might choose to live my life. As I began to notice what I had and hadn't been taught, or the misinformation I had received, I felt a sense of betrayal. There is no excuse for lies and omission within our system of public education. Yet the stories that exist to uphold the myths of our nation, which Lee Anne Bell calls "stock stories," continue to be passed down from generation to generation[1].

Because I am white in America, these dominant narratives allow me, as an individual, to easily avoid feelings of guilt, shame, and fear of retribution that come from knowing that the wealth accumulated in white society has come at the expense of everyone else. It is no coincidence that the economic breakdown is along racial lines. This has occurred as a result of systematized racism. Think, for a moment, about who was allowed to own land in colonial America, and who later owned plantations and factories. Think about the subsequent ongoing lines of inherited wealth. Think about who has and has not been allowed to vote as systems became institutionalized in this nation, and that the votes of these white men were magnified according to the number of slaves he owned. Think about how those votes affected who was elected to create the laws and enact the policies of this country, the impact of which reverberates throughout our lives today. Think, most of all, about the violent means used to enforce this hierarchy.

Despite the color of my skin, I'm not directly responsible for the country's historic choices. Yet I have clearly benefited from these policies, even if I haven't recognized that fact. Because people who have been oppressed by these laws and systems must be quite aware of their existence, my ignorance just makes me look like a fool. And while my schooling and life experiences have permitted me to remain oblivious to how these systems operate and the cruelty that maintains them, at some level I've known something is out of adjustment. I can look around and see the inequities. Yet any time this nagging feeling arises, it's always been easier just to push it back down. As authors Björn Krondorfer[2]

---

1   Lee Anne Bell, the Barbara Silver Horowitz Director of Education at Barnard College/Columbia University, teaches urban education, social justice education and teaching through storytelling and the arts.

2   Björn Krondorfer is Director of the Martin-Springer Institute at Northern Arizona University and Endowed Professor of Religious Studies in the Department of Comparative Cultural Studies.

and john a. powell[3] remind us, however, repression comes at a price. Denial is not an escape. The agony of losses we have not yet mourned brings about psychological, intellectual and physical pain for all of us. Further, the unresolved pain of each generation will continue to resurface until it damages the entire society, damage which is becoming increasingly evident. Even if we are not direct perpetrators, ongoing white resistance only deepens the wounds. The resulting injury is to our own humanity.

Some countries have tried to directly confront the oppression brought about by colonization through the establishment of Truth and Reconciliation tribunals. But not ours. There seems to be a misconception that avoiding *truth* will somehow allow us to evade the accompanying pain and shame. In addition, because the nation operates in a value system hyper-focused on economic gain, there is a fear of the need for financial retribution. Yet without truth, there can be no reconciliation. As the divides between perceived races and classes continue to grow ever wider due to systems of institutional apartheid that remain solidly in place, I fear the consequences will be dire. Yet being white in America means I may not even see them coming.

We Don't Know What We Don't Know

A COUPLE OF YEARS INTO MY WORK with the Blackfeet Nation, I had a phone conversation with an indigenous colleague about white privilege. During the course of the discussion I said, "I don't think most white people know there is such a thing as white privilege. I'm just beginning to learn about it, myself…" A profound silence greeted me. Perhaps my colleague was trying to conjure a vision of the forty-year-old white woman who was on the other end of the line, wondering how someone could be so blind for so long. Finally, she found a way to communicate her shock. "They don't know? How is that even possible?"

I understand better now how hard that must be to imagine. A person experiencing them would, of course, assume that the daily micro-aggressions and the acceptance of systems that privilege some and oppress

---

3   An internationally recognized expert in the areas of civil rights and civil liberties, john a. powell is a Professor of Law, holds the Robert D. Haas Chancellor's Chair in Equity, and is Director of the Institute for a Fair and Inclusive Society at Berkeley Law, University of California.

others must be intentional. How can anyone believe that a person could live in this country and remain unaware of these things? It really is possible, however, and I am living proof of this. Until I heard the stories of people who had been oppressed by these systems, I honestly didn't know inherent inequities were still a part of them. These stories helped me be able to see with new eyes—from a different perspective.

Reflecting back on my colleague's shock during that "white privilege" conversation, I wonder if there was any way for her to believe that my ignorance was real. My next thought slices to my core. Could it be that people oppressed by these systems think that almost all white people conscientiously support them? I get a sick feeling as I realize of course they do. I try to find evidence that might cause anyone to think otherwise, and I emerge empty-handed. I guess I've just assumed that people would automatically think the best of me and "my people," trusting in the good intentions of my motives. This now seems utterly ridiculous when all evidence points to the contrary. Why would I think such a thing? I have no answer except that I have bought into the narrative about the purity of America's mission, even though the nation's history certainly exemplifies little that seems pure.

I face this thought with horror. I try to imagine how painful it must be to believe that most white people know exactly what's happening, and nonetheless support systems and institutions set up to benefit them and disadvantage others. It would then be easy to assume that the many comments, which offend because they are rooted in white supremacist thinking, are also intentional. Yet why would anyone make a different assumption? I become viscerally aware of the anger that would result from thinking that these things are intended to hurt. Of course, there is no doubt that in some cases they are. Yet based on my own experience, I sincerely believe that in many cases, the action or inaction on the part of white people is because, as hard as it must be to believe, we *just don't know*.

If we can entertain the thought, even just for a moment, that at least some white people operate from a place of ignorance when it comes to issues of systemic racial oppression, then perhaps we might also imagine that *awareness* could lead them to want to do better. Efforts toward equity could then cross the imaginary lines of race. Working together, we just might be able to tap the root of the problem. Indeed, there are examples of some organizations in this country where this is already occurring. And while some white people will still desperately cling to the "truth" of Manifest Destiny, I am hopeful that many truly do want an inclusive society. The problem is they think they are living in one.

Maya Angelou says when you know better, you can do better, and I certainly agree. At the moment, our nation has yet to begin to address even the first part of that equation. How will we address this, and perhaps more importantly, how will we ensure the next generation doesn't bask in our ignorance?

My Responsibility: To Know Better and to Do Better

I've COME TO UNDERSTAND that if I'm white in America and I'm not actively working against systems of racism and classism, they will continue. Doing nothing is a default stance that maintains the status quo. If I remain dormant, a bystander, I am part of the problem. I am supporting racism. Instead, I want to work to change the legacy of what it means to be white in America.

For anyone joining me, our paths will likely be different. No worries; there is plenty to do. After my experience in Blackfeet Country, I knew I had a lot to learn. And if I have stereotypes about Native peoples, I most certainly have them about other folks as well. Once I figured out that I didn't even know the stereotypes I carried until something caused them to shatter, I knew I needed to find plenty of hammers. In Blackfeet Country, I was fortunate that people generously shared their stories. But like many, I was mostly around people whose stories sounded a lot like mine. I need to find ways to unlearn the "stock stories" I've been taught and re-educate myself. So I started to read, seeking out authors who have had life experiences quite different from my own. I seek out websites that help me see the news from different perspectives.

Then I can believe the stories I hear. This seems obvious, but it is so important, because much of what I learn counteracts what I thought I knew. Many people's realities have been hidden from my view. Through my reading, I'm coming to see how "whiteness" was invented and used as a powerful weapon, and how many of the prevailing stereotypes are rooted in the eugenics movement that took hold in this country at the turn of the century. Indeed, much of the racism that remains institutionalized in the laws and policies of this country are a legacy from the time eugenics was practiced as a science.

And while I can't hold myself accountable for the past, I am responsible for inequities that remain entrenched in systems, especially in public education where I've spent my career. My own research, for example, has convinced me that recent policy decisions to attach high stakes to standardized test results absolutely result in racialized outcomes. The impact of this policy will reverberate for generations to come.

As an educator, I have a responsibility to work toward an equitable future for each of my students. What might happen if we collectively demanded that our schools teach the truth about the history of our nation? What if topics of race and class were purposefully raised in schools, and educators learned to carefully facilitate such conversations? What if students were taught to communicate with people they perceive to be different from them? These are the only ways students can begin to understand the inequities of our present reality and take the first steps toward leading our country to a different future. Rather than the riots and rebellion some fear, it seems to me that if these steps were carefully taken, we might actually end up engaging students through a curriculum that is actually relevant to their lives. It is much more likely that repressing these truths, which are the lived realities of some and yet invisible to others, can only lead to increasing levels of frustration and anger. How much better would it be to face the truth of the past and the present head-on, and imagine together what a truly multicultural society might look like? This process could begin by refusing to accept a curriculum based solely on a European perspective, and the perpetuation of "stock stories" that model the ideals of a white middle-class value system. An inclusive, multicultural curriculum is the only thing that will truly ensure that students are college, career, and more importantly, *community*-ready. I am devoting myself to writing for change.

These are just a few examples of a course I can chart for myself. My hope is that somewhere within my story, you might catch a glimpse of your own. Being white in America means that I have important choices to make at this critical historic juncture. I am choosing to see. Once my eyes are open, I can actively work against ongoing systems of racism and classism, or I can continue to participate in them, simply by living my life. Continuing to ignore the pain of others comes at great cost to my own humanity and to our nation as a whole. I am just not willing to take that risk. ■

Note: I have changed people's names in this narrative, out of respect for them and knowing that the events portrayed reveal only my personal perspective.

Jamie Utt

Legacies and Lessons: Learning to be White and to Divest from Whiteness

WHEN I WAS A KID, my grandfather was my hero. There was no one in the world that I looked up to more than him, and he taught me a lot of incredible things.

He taught me the value of service, as he volunteered nearly every day of his retirement to help people with disabilities access the beauty of the great outdoors. He taught me the importance of laughter and play, always the one to make jokes and to get down on his hands and knees to play with the kids in his older age. He taught me to love and value nature, taking me often into the wilderness. Some of my favorite memories with him are simply sitting in silence on a cold, crisp morning on the eastern plains of Colorado.

Among all of my memories with my grandfather, there is one more deeply seated in my subconscious than perhaps any other. It's not a particularly happy memory, but it's an important one.

I grew up in Grand Junction, Colorado, a town where almost everyone I interacted with was white despite approximately twenty percent of the population being Latino. I don't know that I had ever met a black person when, at three or four years old, I was visiting Grandpa in the suburbs of Denver. One day we went for a ride together in his truck and drove down through the capital of my home state.

I remember the drive vividly. We were making our way through a neighborhood where everyone I could see outside the truck was black. I distinctly remember holding up my hands, turning them from front to back, comparing them to the skin tones I saw outside of the cab of the truck. Curiously, I thought to myself, "Wow, why does everyone here look so different from me?"

It was in that moment that my grandfather taught me another lesson. In a serious tone he said, "Jamie, this neighborhood is dangerous. Put your head down and don't pick it up until I tell you."

I obeyed, terrified.

He never said a word about race, but he made his point clear. I realize now, as I turn this memory over and over in my mind, that he was teaching me two clear lessons. One was about fear. The other was about what it means to be White in a society that has been built by and for people who look like me.

For most of the twenty-seven-odd years since my grandfather taught me those lessons, I didn't think much about them, though they've guided my behavior and my thoughts, resulting in fear, mistrust, and anxiety about those who are not like me. As is the case with many young white people in the United States, I developed a fascination with black, indigenous, and Latino cultures, often appropriating parts of them in my search for identity in a society that long-ago demanded light-skinned European immigrants to give up our ethnic identities for access to whiteness. My fascination, though, was always trivial, wanting the "coolness" but still fearing and even, when I am honest with myself, loathing people of color.

The second lesson my grandfather taught me that day was about more than fear, and it has had an even more formative influence on my identity. My grandfather was teaching me to be white. He was teaching me that whiteness is something set in opposition to blackness that should be protected. He taught me that I'd find safety in my whiteness.

I feel fortunate that in my teenage years, two mentors called on me to think deeper and more critically about these lessons and about my search for meaning in a society that overtly told me race no longer mattered while covertly showing me that racial identity and oppression is central to everything.

Both mentors introduced me to the importance of choice, of agency, in my relationship to my own racial identity. The first, a white camp counselor, helped me to understand that whether or not I wanted to reckon with my race and the race of others, U.S. society is built fundamentally upon institutional racism. Further, the U.S. will always be a nation of racial oppression unless individuals choose to change the world around us. He taught me that my supposedly progressive values demand a tenuous balance between self-reflection about my own complicity in racism and action toward realizing change—what Paulo Freire calls "praxis."

The second mentor, a black professor, must have seen in me what is all too common in young, white activists: a fervent desire to act for change that can often do more harm than good. My actions were driven by a self-loathing attitude toward my white identity and by a paternalistic desire to "help" people of color. With an incredible patience that amazes me to this day, he pushed me to understand my own stake in working for racial justice, to explore what it would mean for me as a White person to change my relationship to whiteness. He lovingly held me accountable (which often hurt) to the ways that my paternalism was enacted through harmful microaggressions, and he pushed me to redefine my relationship to the whiteness in which I'd been taught to invest in by my grandfather, and nearly every white person in my life. Finally, he taught me the value of trusting the leadership of people of Color in racial justice movements, reminding me that my role is not to lead but to "call in" other white people to change.

To this day, I'm not sure why these mentors invested such incredible emotional energy in me, but I'm thankful they did. They helped me realize that the lesson my grandfather taught me about whiteness is actually reflective of a choice that every single white person faces.

Dr. Zeus Leonardo articulates this choice well when he stresses that white people must decide between investing in and enacting our identities through "the perspective of a white racial paradigm" or "through non-white discourses or strategies of anti-whiteness." In this way of thinking about race, "'whiteness' is a racial discourse, whereas the category 'white people' represents a socially constructed identity, usually based on skin color."

Put simply, white people can choose to invest in whiteness, the path of least resistance, and to reap its benefits, or we can seek to divest from whiteness, articulating our white identity through perspectives of racial justice. If white people are not whiteness, then we have agency in choosing our relationship to whiteness.

For me, realizing that I have a choice in how I relate to whiteness is incredibly empowering! Though I know he never meant to communicate this message, my grandfather used the same emotion he'd been taught to draw from when investing in whiteness—fear—to present a false choice: one between whiteness and insecurity. He clearly communicated I was safe in my all-white environment, but that I was inherently unsafe when I was surrounded by blackness, by the "other."

Now, though, I understand the falsehood inherent in this way of thinking about whiteness. I realize now that I can surely invest in whiteness and, in doing so, maintain the status quo, one that privileges me in countless ways. However, the alternative is not insecurity and fear. The alternative is in realizing that, as David Roediger once noted, "Whiteness is nothing but oppressive and false," which opens the door to exploration of new and different ways of understanding ourselves.

The alternative is something I've experienced most powerfully when I am in diverse communities of people who are all working for racial justice, characterized by healthier relationships forged through struggle to realize new ways of being and acting in a racialized world while striving to dismantle systems of oppression. But I have also experienced this alternative in the struggle with those who share my identity, wading through difficult conversations, even when we seem diametrically opposed in our opinions on racial and other forms of oppression.

These new ways of being do not mean that we ought to run and hide from our whiteness, to avoid accountability for our enactments of privilege. Quite to the contrary, we must confront whiteness through our relationship to it and, in doing so, seek ways to divest from whiteness, even as that seems so very abstract, confusing, and scary.

It is in this liminality that I find hope, as liminal space, for me, is imaginative space. And how do we even begin to engender just societies without imagination? As I explore new ways of being white and of divesting from whiteness, I hope to explore what Leonardo calls "third space...neither enemy nor ally but a concrete subject of struggle."

Notably, this struggle cannot take place in isolation. We as white people must remember that our privilege demands ignorance about the lived realities of those who experience racial oppression, and as such, we must listen to and trust in the leadership and perspective of people of color. One of the lessons about whiteness inherent in my grandfather's words was that whiteness should isolate me from the lived truths of people of color, forever constricting the beautiful diversity of what can be known. Divestment, on the other hand, demands that we as white people allow in and trust the perspectives of people of color who strive for liberation. This listening is most definitely the root of justice.

We must also choose to invest in one another, in calling upon those we love to divest. And this work in community in and of itself is an act of resistance to a whiteness rooted in capitalism that demands isolation, rugged individualism, and competition. To take the hands of those around us in multiracial struggle is to fundamentally resist the demands of whiteness, an act that opens the door to realization of those new, racially just ways of being.

In my own journey, I'm not yet sure what divestment can and should look like, and to explore this space is scary! It means that I make a lot of mistakes and that I am often unsure of what is to come. But I feel most confident in my identity when I am investing in accountable relationships across differences, when I reflect on how I can live more fully into my racial justice values, and when I see my identity as one of action against whiteness (in all of the messiness and mistakes) rather than passively being white, coasting along with the inherent privileges and benefits of whiteness.

The more I reflect upon the lessons my grandfather taught me, both the good and the ugly, the more I wish he were alive today. I wish that we could sit in his truck, breathing in the crisp air of a fall day on the eastern plains of Colorado, and I wish that I could talk to him about what I learned that day, oh so many years ago. I'd want to ask him what he thinks it means to be white. I'd want to ask him what he thinks of the idea that white people can turn their backs on whiteness and ask him about how he thinks we can choose to divest from whiteness. Most of all, I'd want to ask him what hope he sees for our future in a society that increasingly relies on coded racial oppressions while trying to convince white people that race is irrelevant.

Knowing, though, that I can't have that conversation with him, instead I must choose to think differently about the messages I teach the children in my life—my nieces and nephew, my godchildren, and my someday children. It gives me hope to think now about how I can engage them differently in thinking about whiteness than how Grandpa did. And it makes it much easier to imagine also passing along the lessons of service, love for the outdoors, and playfulness that Grandpa also taught me. ▪

Works Cited

Paulo Freire, *Pedagogy of the Oppressed: 30th Anniversary Edition* (New York: Continuum International, 2005).

Zeus Leonardo, *Race, Whiteness, and Education* (New York: Routledge, 2009).

David R. Roediger, *The Wages of Whiteness: Race and the Making of the American Working Class.* (New York: Verso, 1999).

Derald Wing Sue, *Microaggressions in Everyday Life: Race, Gender, and Sexual Orientation* (Hoboken: John Wiley, 2010).

Julie Dreyer Wang

What Does It Mean to Be "White" in America?

AS A "WHITE" WOMAN BORN IN ENGLAND, living in the U.S. since my early twenties, and now, age sixty-eight, dividing my time between Maine and Benin, West Africa, where I live with a "black" Beninese man I offer, perhaps, a slightly different viewpoint on race, and what it means to be white in America.

To start, let's acknowledge that the idea of race is an artificial construct. Most biologists and anthropologists don't recognize race as a biologically valid classification because there is more genetic variation within ethnic groups than between them. So simply having a discussion about race assumes that I accept race as a valid way to sort human beings into different categories. I do not. I believe we have more in common as human beings than the superficial differences created by our skin color, the shape of our faces or eyes and the way our hair grows. We are far more divided by income, education and upbringing than by skin color.

In Africa, having black skin is the norm. The sun is hot. Black skin is a protective advantage. A black African man knows who he is and where he belongs. He has a tribal, linguistic and cultural identity, as well as a country which is "home." Black Americans have no such privileges. They did not come to America of their own volition and have never truly been treated as equals, despite what the laws on the books say. For the first 350 years they were not even acknowledged as full citizens of the United States. For many, they have no "home" to go back to in Africa because the ties have long since been severed. Black

Americans do not feel truly at "home" in the United States and never have, if James Baldwin and Richard Wright are to be believed. Certainly, they do not feel safe, according to Ta-Nehisi Coates.

Americans may feel proud to have elected a black president, who, ironically, could just as easily be seen as half white. But that is quite different from living in a post-racial society. On the contrary, racism in America has never been more overt. Republicans, to their shame, have done everything in their power to thwart Barack Obama by playing the race card, primarily with middle- and working class white men, to whom it appeals.

So with that as background, what does it mean to me to be white in America? It means that I am ashamed of my country of adoption. A country that maintains that a single drop of black blood entitles people who think they are white to feel superior and to treat those they categorize as black with undeserved suspicion and harshness. Do differences in skin color really signify something meaningful? Or is it simply that for centuries black Americans have been deprived of equal rights, equal education and equal opportunity, encaged in the inner city and treated with disrespect? This has inevitably taken a toll on their ability to succeed and integrate into white society, in short, to become like "us."

To be white for me means that many of the white people I know in the U.S. indulge in soft bigotry without being aware of it. For example, a white friend, who lives in Charleston, South Carolina in winter and Maine in summer, sincerely believes that the black people who are worth anything have already escaped to the suburbs. In her words, "only the trash are left in the inner city." She doubts that places like Baltimore are worth saving.

It means that I am embarrassed to tell people in West Africa that I am American. The people there have long understood that Americans are racist, but because they are genuinely good and open-hearted human beings they try to give the white Americans they meet the benefit of the doubt. I suspect that is their first mistake. America has gone out of its way to ensure that corrupt and self-serving politicians remain in charge of the majority of African countries, so long as they are compliant with the political and economic needs of the U.S.

But it is not only America that shames me. It is also all those white European countries that are currently ignoring the disgraceful plight of immigrants in Calais, and refusing to give visas to those trying to gain entry to Europe in order to survive. To its shame, the U.S. has done precisely nothing to welcome black immigrants into its midst in this current crisis. Even getting a three-week travel visa for my black boyfriend is an impossibility because white Americans don't want any more black Africans in their country, fearful that they will outstay their visa. As we all know, the streets in America are paved with gold, so why would anyone willingly leave?

Every year, I leave the country for six months because I find deeply distressing the pervasive use of guns and subsequent violence, particularly against black Americans. I am dismayed by the pervasive level of ignorance about the rest of the world and our obligations towards our fellow human beings. I return every six months to stay in touch with my family, especially my grandchildren.

As to my role in helping to dismantle old myths, I am currently writing a memoir about my experiences in West Africa. In it I acknowledge my own evolution from growing up in a bigoted environment in England, to my gradual acceptance of all black people, be they in America or in Africa, as fellow human beings of equal worth.

It is a journey we each need to take. First we must acknowledge our own personal racist attitudes and prejudices, most of which lie hidden just below the surface. Then we need to understand that the police brutality towards black Americans, which many of us condemn, is actually a reflection of the way we encourage our police forces to operate. We put them in place; they are simply carrying out our orders.

We have met the enemy and he is us. ■

Carol Ehrlich

The White Privilege Question

WE ROCKED IN THE HOSTEL that Saturday night. A bunch of singles on retreat, we attempted valiantly to sing in harmony. Someone said, "Let's sing 'The Night They Drove Old Dixie Down.'"

Most of us agreed readily, including me. That old hit was perfect for a sing-along – or so I thought.

But Sam turned to Troy, the one African American in a crowd of thirty white faces. "Would you be offended if we sang this song?" asked Sam.

Everyone was quiet. Finally, Troy said, "I'm okay with it."

Sam's question stunned me. I knew that song mourned the confederacy, a racist system with a slave-based economy. Why had I failed to think that Troy might feel offended? A nascent answer mumbled deep within my psyche. I listened. But I couldn't make sense of the answer.

Then everyone's singing drowned out that muffled reply. I sang by reflex. I don't know if Sam or Troy sang.

A week later, Troy, Sam, and I attended a board meeting of the singles group that had organized that retreat. First on our agenda was a go-around, in which the meeting attendees each briefly stated their thoughts and feelings.

Troy said, "I think I need to be around other black men more."

The rest of us, all white people, nodded. Of course we understood. We were reasonable.

That meeting, in 2000, was the last I saw of Troy. At our next monthly meeting, Sam announced that Troy had resigned because his schedule left him with no more time for our board.

Yet in Troy's absence, that question from the retreat echoed within me. Why had I failed to think that Troy, an African American, might be offended by that song? Somewhere beneath that question, the nascent answer responded incoherently.

But memories and insights arose. "The Night They Drove Old Dixie Down" had been part of my personal landscape. I sang and danced to it in 1969, when it first hit the charts. In 1972, I heard Joan Baez sing it in concert. She led us all in a rousing sing-along. Only twenty-eight years later, I noticed that no black people had appeared at that concert.

All those years later, I recognized other parts of my personal landscape—lessons and memories of American history. I knew about white people capturing black Africans, locking them in chains, bringing them to America, selling them as slaves. I knew that the descendants of those slaves had suffered segregation and lynchings. I remembered turning on the television to watch the 1963 March on Washington for Jobs and Freedom, where Rev. Martin Luther King Jr. delivered his speech, "I have a dream…" I remembered watching newscasts of white supremacists battering demonstrators on the Edmund Pettis Bridge, where they marched in response to the killing of civil rights activist Jimmie Lee Jackson. So why did I fail to consider how a song that mourned a slave-based economy would affect African Americans? The answer to that question was struggling to speak.

Gradually, that emerging answer grew into an articulate understanding of something insidious. This something pollutes our American culture. It seeps into the unconsciousness of so many white people. Today we call this something "white privilege."

Like the air we breathe, many of us never think about white privilege. It saturates the deepest part of our psyches. And who wants to delve into one's psyche while attending a concert, or singing at a retreat? Having fun is so much easier if we avoid thinking about how our white privilege affects black people. Assuming that the white viewpoint is the same as everyone else's frees us of any challenges, and raises our fun quotient.

What was the harm? The civil rights movement had brought about integration, the Voting Rights Act, equal opportunity.

But then, other events entered my personal landscape. In 2012, white George Zimmerman killed Trayvon Martin, a seventeen-year-old African American who was wearing a hoodie and carrying candy. In 2013, the Supreme Court struck down a significant portion of the Voting Rights Act. In 2015, white supremacist Dylann Roof killed nine African Americans at Mother Emanuel African Methodist Episcopal Church in Charleston, South Carolina. A morass of other racially charged injustices crowded the media.

During that time, other questions about Troy and that singles retreat arose for me. Was Troy really okay with us singing that song? Did he just say he was okay because he was afraid that others might accuse him of being "politically correct" and ruining their fun? These questions are unanswerable.

But a broad look at my personal landscape raised questions that focused beyond that retreat. Why do so many white Americans fail to think about whether African Americans share our viewpoint? Do we create situations in which many African Americans feel they must protect themselves by being dishonest with us? These questions bring me back to that singles' retreat when Sam asked Troy, "Would you be offended if we sang this song?" That interchange provoked so many questions for me–questions that challenge white privilege.

Today, the ultimate answer to all these questions resounds within. As a white American, my job is to pose questions that challenge white privilege. These questions delve into my psychic recesses, where white privilege resides. The first step for all white Americans who want to challenge white privilege in our culture is to begin within our own psyches. ■

Josh Couvares

Just White Noise

TENSED UP A LITTLE WHEN I HEARD IT, this distant thump of
drums and synth like a warning shot in the night. It was dark out,
and my girlfriend and I were walking along the Hudson. We'd just
eaten dinner at some restaurant in a town I didn't know and the boardwalk was quiet, just a few couples and families strolling along, my
arm around Kristen's waist in the warmth of an August night. As we
moved past yachts idling in the water, my stomach full of cheap food
and beer, everything around me felt safe – then I made out the music:
it came from the only car in the parking lot ahead of us, the muffled
voice of a rapper I recognized, a song I liked, but as I looked ahead it
only put me on edge.

There were a few guys leaning against the car, its doors open, the
metal frame a moaning buzz of subwoofer and bass. They were black,
probably high schoolers, and their faces were half-hidden by the hoods
of their sweatshirts as they passed around a Poland Springs bottle filled
with something other than water, I figured.

It occurred to me we were the only white people I'd seen walking
on the boardwalk and I was beginning to feel like we were somewhere
we didn't belong. The kids talked too loud, laughed even louder – a kind
of audio-marking of their territory that went hand in hand with the
volume of their music, like they were saying they were exactly where
they were supposed to be, were you?

"Let's turn around before the parking lot," I said.

"Why? Because of them?"

"Let's just turn around."

But she was right—it was because of them, even if I wouldn't admit it. Something about their movements made me nervous, their slow-bodied gestures like they had no purpose to be there but were happy to wait for one.

If I were alone I wouldn't have cared, but I didn't like the idea of Kristen walking past them; I imagined the worst, the things they'd say or do, and even though I knew these knee jerk scenarios had almost no chance of happening. I wanted to play it safe. So we turned around. Crisis averted, I thought.

What this means is that not only am I racist; I'm also sexist.

I should know better. I grew up in Manchester, Connecticut where you were a minority in high school if you were white. You'd think I'd be used to these kinds of situations. But there on that boardwalk I felt like I didn't belong. And why? Those kids could just have been trying to find something to do for the night, and maybe there was vodka in that water bottle but that didn't mean they wanted to cause any trouble, didn't I do the same thing when I was their age? Didn't I play the music in my car even louder?

Maybe growing up in Manchester wasn't enough. Even though my high school was diverse, you wouldn't have known this from my classes; by senior year I took all honors and AP classes, which looked more like an episode of *Friends* than a multiracial school. We may have been diverse, but the only thing I knew about diversity was that it was what my sister wrote her college essay on so she could get into Boston College; and the only time I thought about race was when I had to fill out my CMT Scantron in elementary school, and I didn't know what Caucasian meant.

Race was never something I had to deal with until I was a senior in high school and I drove my friend Tyler Broome to see his probation officer. He was on the track team with me and we were going before practice. I started up my beat-up car and my CD started blaring as soon as the ignition caught, Dave Matthews singing about his tripping billies over his acoustic guitar. I turned it off as we pulled out of the school parking lot and put the radio on instead.

We talked less than usual on the ride over—only about the events we'd be doing at the next track meet, but not what he was doing here in my car, not about why he had to see a parole officer in the first place. I knew his brother dealt drugs and was probably responsible for whatever trouble Tyler had gotten into, but I didn't bring it up.

I waited in the car while Tyler was at his appointment and I imagined what he'd done. Sold weed? Fucked someone up? This is what I was thinking, and I wanted to ask him but I didn't want to be intrusive. And I knew what it would have sounded like, it would've been like saying, *a black teenager—exactly what you'd expect.*

He got back in, said thanks and I told him no problem; I never asked him and we never talked about it again. Truth is, I only wanted to ask him because these were the things I could've been caught doing.

But if I got caught doing them, would I have had the same consequences? I wasn't sure.

■ ■ ■

WHEN I TURNED BACK AWAY from the parking lot that night in August, I was doing it because I was a white guy in boat shoes and a button-down, and to be white in America is to see yourself as seen by a black man—and do they see me as a human being, or just another entitled racist prick? And are they right?

"If those kids felt any anger towards white people, didn't I look like the perfect receptacle for it, like I was another white guy with money that I got because of the advantages that came along with my skin color, even though those shoes were the same beat up pair I'd worn since high school, and that shirt was bought from a thrift store for a few bucks?" How could they know that the way they might look at me is the way I look at others who have more advantages than I'd ever been given, that there are people out there with stable families who are cushioned from the sharp edges of life by their parents' money, who have more than I could ever hope for? I wanted them to know that I saw that the system was stacked against them and, to a lesser extent, against me, that whatever you are in America you're carrying around empty promises, that none of us are as free as we want.

But I never said any of this. I placed it with the rest of the things they say you're supposed to leave unspoken. I was thinking about them, these black kids who stood before me, but who's to say they even noticed my girlfriend and me? As we turned and left the same way we came, I felt like we were just white noise lost in the blare of their music, and all I could hear was the silence of a conversation left unsounded. ■

Pam Nath

Saving Myself

I AM STANDING IN THE SECURITY LINE at the airport, in a five-a.m.-induced-haze. I am making my way through the rat maze formed by movable dividers; the mass of humanity around me is about ten rows thick. One full turn behind me is a white woman with a young child, maybe two years old. For a minute, I imagine I am her, surrounded by *big* strangers, and wonder why she is not crying. This maze makes no sense and is *so* scary. I consider letting the young girl and her mother go ahead of me, but wonder about others in the line. Will they think I am just "privileging" another white person? I wonder myself if I would be similarly attuned to a child of another race. I also realize that I can't know what others in the line are navigating: could there be others who are late for their planes? "We all have to make our own way through the lane," I sigh.

It is a complex package of identities I bear – white, woman, separated by just one generation from poor Pittsburgh mill workers. Both of my parents were the first people in their families to go to college. But my father eventually held the position of city manager of a majority black town – Farrell, Pennsylvania. We lived in an adjoining majority white town which had fewer problems in terms of economic challenges, crime, etc. When people in Farrell organized to change the law so that the city manager actually had to live *in the city*, we moved to a house that was on *the very edge* of Farrell's city limits, and I mean the very edge. The house right next to us was in Hermitage.

My thoughts at the airport are interrupted by the sight of a man moving through the "first-class" line, bypassing all of us. In her book *Shock Doctrine: The Rise of Disaster Capitalism,* Naomi Klein describes how, in Iraq and in cities across the United States, we are creating "green zones" and gated communities where the elite are kept comfortably safe from the growing and increasingly oppressed population, as well as the violence and environmental devastation outside "the gates".[1] This privilege to fly first class, to bypass this mass of humanity, with all its varied hurts and needs, to not have to engage it or be troubled by it, is very much on my mind as I finish making my way through the long security line and eventually navigate past the cushy seats at the front of the airplane—where he is sitting reading *The Wall Street Journal*. I struggle past him, carrying my suitcase onboard because I don't want to pay the fee to check my bags, but I know I am not all that different from him. How is his decision to fly first-class different from my own family's choices on where to live?

Since 2007, I have been living in New Orleans, where the city elite exploited the "opportunity" of Katrina to rid itself of its poor black residents, envisioning the creation of a new and "better" city. Four large public housing developments that formed the core of a number of Black neighborhoods in the city were demolished;[2] rising rents in gentrifying neighborhoods are rapidly displacing long-term residents of the city.[3] All the city's teachers—most of them middle-class black women were fired in the aftermath of the storm[4], and a good percentage of the teachers now are young white folks from Teach For America and similar organizations, with limited teaching experience, and no

---

1   Naomi Klein, *The Shock Doctrine: The Rise of Disaster Capitalism* (Toronto: Alfred A. Knopf Canada, 2007).

2   See these two articles, which clarifies my point: Katy Reckdahl, "10 Years After Katrina, New Orleans Public Housing Still in Limbo," *Next City,* June 15, 2015. https://nextcity. org/features/view/10-years-after-katrina-new-orleans-public-housing-still-in-limbo-iberville; and Dani McClain, "Former Residents of New Orleans's Demolished Housing Projects Tell Their Stories," *The Nation,* August 28, 2015. http://www.thenation.com/article/former-residents-of-new-orleans-demolished-housing-projects-tell-their-stories/.

3   Robert McClendon, "Where will working poor live in future New Orleans, if gentrification continues?" *NOLA.com, The Times-Picayune,* July 30, 2015, http://www.nola.com/futureofneworleans/2015/07/where_will_the_working_poor_li.html.

4   Corey Mitchell, "Death of My Career: What happened to New Orleans' veteran black teachers?" *New Orleans, Education Week,* August 19, 2015, http://neworleans.edweek.org/veteran-black-female-teachers-fired/.

ties with the communities from where their students come. Similarly, the development boom has not brought jobs for people from the city to the degree that was hoped or promised; the unemployment rate for black folks far exceeds the overall employment rate in the city.[5]

I could go on and on. It is not easy to live in this place, to have the friends I have, and to hear of their deep grief and pain as a result of the remaking of the place they called home, especially as one bearing the burden of ancestors who have purged other lands in other times, many times over. Horrid things happen every day, and to people who I know well, to people I love. I don't want to close my eyes to the pain of others whose lives are bruised and battered by the structures of our society, what bell hooks refers to as imperialist capitalist, white supremacist heteropatriarchy, but sometimes I feel like I am drowning in misery. The choice to flee into "elite status" is at least to some extent available to me, through no merit of my own. It's a small consolation to those who might covet the privilege that I don't want it, with the constant temptation to escape in any number of ways, coupled with the lure of false self-congratulation and praise from others for the "sacrifice" I have chosen to make.

My relationship with New Orleans began in the late 1990s when I spent a summer here; when I finally moved to the city in 2007, what I was aware of was that I was interested in doing work related to racism, and doing so felt impossible in the majority white town in northwest Ohio in which I had been living for the previous ten years. In the first conversation I ever remember having with my mother about race, occasioned by my work in New Orleans, she shared with me that she and my father had agreed that he'd take the job in Farrell because they had been made aware during the civil rights movements of racial inequities and they wanted to "help black people." My parents and I had good intentions, of course, but there were so many unexamined assumptions in the choices my parents made, and then those I made, following in their footsteps. We saw ourselves as people who could and should help black people. We didn't question whether they needed or wanted our help, or what it was that made us "qualified" or capable to provide it.

---

5   Julianne Malveaux, "Black unemployment has not improved," *The New Orleans Tribune*, http://www.theneworleanstribune.com/main/black-unemployment-has-not-improved.

And perhaps most basically, my parents and I (and the organization for which I work) assumed that it is people of color who need help as a result of racism.

My brilliant and sensitive mother was well conditioned, both by family norms and her position as a white, working class woman to care for her own battered soul indirectly through caring for the needs of others. I am the first generation to open my eyes to the structural privileges that my whiteness brings (not just the disadvantages that people of color face as a result of racism), the first to aspire to "solidarity" rather than "help," although just like my mother, I have had to work to distinguish my own needs from those of others. Even now, I still struggle all the time with uncertainty about the right balance of caring for others and for myself.

I took a pay cut to take a position with a faith-based organization that made it possible for me to move to the city, obscuring the fact that like many of the white people who moved to New Orleans in Katrina's aftermath, I lacked much of the knowledge and skills that I would need to carry out the tasks that were assigned to me. I wasn't aware of how much my understanding of race, racism, and myself was shaped by my socialization as a white person, and an unarticulated belief that "working at racism" meant "helping" black people. The community that I came "to help" would have to teach and train me, to prevent me from doing harm, let alone to make it possible for me to do any effective work. I didn't know that it was me who needed saving.

■ ■ ■

WITHIN SIX MONTHS OF MY ARRIVAL in New Orleans, on December 20, 2007, I was one of a number of people arrested both outside and inside City Hall in New Orleans. At the time, I was attempting to get into a City Council meeting where a vote was scheduled on whether four large public housing developments would be demolished. This was happening in the midst of a housing crisis and continued displacement of former residents of New Orleans who were unable to find affordable housing. The homelessness rate had doubled since Katrina. Police had locked the gates and blocked the hallway into the Council Chambers from many public housing residents and other persons concerned about the loss of usable housing stock. The official explanation was that the Chambers were full, and allowing our entry would violate fire codes, but the claims of our friends inside were later validated by video documentation that clearly revealed empty seats. In addition, a City Council meeting two weeks prior had been very well attended, with folks lined up against the walls, and people had not been shut out of that meeting.

I was charged with disturbing the police and resisting arrest. What was even more dramatic to me than my own arrest was the brutal police response to unarmed and nonviolent protesters, both to those within the chambers chanting that people should be allowed in, and to those outside shaking the locked gates and demanding to be admitted. Protesters, many of whom were my friends were tased (in many cases repeatedly and in one case, resulting in a woman going into a seizure), pepper-sprayed, pulled by their hair, and otherwise brutally treated by the police. Both tasers and pepper-spray, a chemical weapon, have sometimes resulted in deaths when used against protesters.

A couple of months later, I witnessed a young black colleague being arrested and charged with battery of a police officer and resisting arrest simply for asking why he was being asked to give the police officer his license when I was the one driving the car. I began to hear stories of daily police harassment, police brutality, and false arrests that explained why so many of my black friends don't share my shock at any of these events. The #BlackLivesMatter movement has now brought popular attention to the extent of police brutality toward black folks, but back then, it was a shock to me.

Similarly, protest was new to me. My education at majority white schools in majority white towns had taught me very little of the history of the civil and human rights protests in this country, and nothing of state oppression of protest movements (including killing leaders of these movements), like the Black Panthers, the American Indian Movement, Students for a Democratic Society, or the Weather Underground. I am embarrassed to admit that it was naiveté, enabled by my lack of historical knowledge, and not optimism that led me to believe that there was a real chance that the police response outside the New Orleans City Hall would provoke national outrage and the beginning of a movement for justice in the country.

Learning that there has always been a movement of people working for a more just world, made possible a choice that I previously didn't know existed. I used to think "I wish I had been alive in the 1960's," unaware of the possibilities for getting involved in social change that exist right now. It also taught me something about the intractability of oppressive structural power, the difficulty of change, which has led to many hours of reflection and conversation about what it is that blocks social change.

When I look back on my writing during those first several years in New Orleans, I am struck by how much I used to worry about my white identity and the privilege it afforded me. For example, I was living in a black city for the first time in my life and functioning as part of a multiracial community. Everyday encounters, like standing in line at the airport, brought up questions of identity, privilege, and oppression for me. In a sense, I was playing catch-up; the first four decades of my life shielded me from these questions. "I never really thought about myself as white," is a reflection often heard from participants in anti-racism trainings that I've been a part of.

On one of my visits to my mother, I asked her about her experiences of race growing up. From visiting my grandparents, I knew that there were black people in their neighborhood. When she confirmed that there were both black and white students at her school, I asked her how they got along. Did she have black friends? Did the black kids and the white kids hang out together or were they in different groups? Now that my life involves thinking and talking about race on a daily basis, I saw these questions as basically neutral, not about my mother's character and not invoking blame or guilt, but my mom seemed immobilized by them. "It makes her nervous when you ask her those questions around me," a black friend from New Orleans who was visiting with me suggested, but I suspect that my mother would have been nervous regardless of his presence. I think there's a lot of white people who never talk about race, and so we aren't sure how, and we're worried about being labeled as racist if we say something that could reveal some unintentional racism lurking inside us or be misunderstood as doing so. As a result, it's not uncommon for white people to avoid thinking or talking about race and racism.

White people are more likely to graduate from college, be employed, get paid higher wages. We are more likely to be in upper management positions or other positions of power in institutions and in society, get arrested less often, and live longer. Blind to my own whiteness and the everyday benefits it brings, including the ways that white people collectively benefit as a result of resources rooted in stolen land and uncompensated labor, I was vulnerable to seeing my achievements as the result of my own hard work and good character, even if these assumptions operated in largely unconscious ways in my psyche.

I was socialized in seeing myself as an individual, not as a member of a group, and that also left me longing for a sense of community. As a young child, I often articulated a wish to be from a big family. I think *The Brady Bunch* and other popular media gave me the sense that big families were close, and that spoke to the longing inside of me for more connection. My family wasn't close, and although I appreciate the sense of independence with which I was raised, I realize how much I longed to feel a part of a whole that was bigger than myself. Without realizing it, I think I became a community organizer because I myself so badly needed community. As I've increasingly defined the work that I need to do as being about organizing other white people for racial justice as part of a multiracial movement for collective liberation, I have sensed a similar longing in many other white people.

As one part of building that sense of community, I have learned more about white people, like Anne Braden, Sara and Angelina Grimke, Viola Liuzzo, James Reeb and others who I now count as my ancestors, people who have gone before me in the work of dismantling white supremacy. I can follow in their footsteps, and having that sense of rootedness has meant the world to me. I am not alone.

Another part of the community culture that I and others are working to build includes a desire to call other white people in instead of calling them out, and to create a more loving humane culture as the basis for our relationships with one another. In her description of white supremacy culture, Tema Okun writes of the perfectionism that too often plagues white community.[6] Early on in my anti-racism journey, I heard people of color articulate that there are "no throw away people." I've witnessed people of color being a lot gentler toward white people than we are towards ourselves. I see in myself a tendency to see things in dualistic ways, to judge people or institutions as good or bad. Many of the people of color with whom I work with are very aware of the flaws in white institutions and white people (myself included). A black woman I worked closely with often responded "of course it is" whenever I questioned whether racism was shaping my reactions. At first, her response was jarring and disconcerting, and as I fought back a desire to justify myself, it was really freeing to accept that I am a product of the culture in which I was raised. As psychologist Beverly Daniel Tatum has said, racism is in the air we all breathe.[7] Now I can go about the business of being part of a multiracial movement working at changing that, rather than investing so much energy in evaluating my own performance. This does not mean that I don't need to keep working at self-assessment, both in terms of my individual behavior and the strategies that I am a part of in my community work, but I don't have to worry about being "thrown away" because of the mistakes I make, and can more easily grow and thrive in the work that I do.

I share the fear with many white people that something I do or say might hurt a person of color I care about. But it has changed how I see things to know that white supremacy is *killing* people of color. A thoughtless comment I might make or something I do might trigger feelings associated with this reality, but the bigger issue is the overall institutional structures. I think the more I am aware of just how radical a change our world needs, the less I feel that I, as one individual, can make a big difference simply by cleaning myself up, improving my own behavior. But I can be part of a bigger whole that is working on making things better on a much larger scale.

■ ■ ■

6   Tema Okun, "White Supremacy Culture," dRworks, http://collectiveliberation.org/wp-content/uploads/2013/01/White_Supremacy_Culture_Okun.pdf.

7   Beverly Daniel Tatum, *Why Are All the Black Kids Sitting Together in the Cafeteria: And Other Conversations About Race* (New York: Basic Books, 1997).

AT THE MENNONITE CHURCH USA ASSEMBLY in Pittsburgh in 2011, I was part of a discussion about how white people who want to address racism are eager to take service trips to communities of color. One man at my table said "Well it makes sense because you want to go to where the problem is!" I cringed, but I knew it was close to what I had believed as well. Think about the words "you want to go to where the problem is." My upbringing taught me to care about the harm that racism does to black people, but it did very little to help me identify how structural racism has played a role in shaping our society in ways that are harmful to me and my people as well. In a speech he gave in 1966, Stokely Carmichael, one of the leaders of the Student Nonviolent Coordinating Committee (SNCC), addressed the lie that says that people of color and communities of color are where the problem lies, and we white people can work to solve the problem by helping people of color:

> "I maintain that every civil rights bill in this country was passed for white people, not for Black people. For example, I am Black.... [W]hile I am Black I am a human being, and therefore I have the right to go into any public place. White people didn't know that. Every time I tried to go into a place they stopped me. So some boys had to write a bill to tell that white man, "He's a human being; don't stop him." That bill was for that white man, not for me.... *I knew that I could vote and that that wasn't a privilege; it was my right. Every time I tried I was shot, killed or jailed, beaten or economically deprived. So somebody had to write a bill for white people to tell them, When a black man comes to vote, don't bother him."* That bill, again, was for white people, not for black people;... *I know I can live anyplace I want to live. It is white people across this country who are incapable of allowing me to live where I want to live. You need a civil rights bill, not me.*[8]" [Emphasis added]

---

8   Stokely Carmichael, "Black Power Address at University of California, Berkeley," delivered on October 29, 1966.

I have come to believe that if we do not untangle the lie inside of us that racism doesn't affect white communities, it will pollute all our efforts to work towards social justice. It's one of the ways that white supremacy maintains and reinforces itself even as we try to undo it. Systemic inequalities result in communities of color being seen as a "problem." Institutions—often white run—control resources devoted to addressing these "problems," and we as individual white folks get the high of being helpers, those who "serve." We get to continue to see ourselves in control and as people who have agency and efficacy, while our tendency to see people of color as victims, as those to whom things are done, and people who need help, is reinforced.

This lie also keeps us from seeing the ways that white communities are broken by racism, from seeing how much work there is to do there, and so it leaves people who live in white communities without the understanding that there are plenty of reasons why it is to their own benefit to dismantle imperialist capitalist white supremacist heteropatriarchy, and that there is plenty that they can do to dismantle it right where they are.

■ ■ ■

I'M CALMER THESE DAYS. And on most days, I no longer feel like I'm drowning. I have more of a sense of my own limitations, more of a sense of being part of a whole, and thus no longer feel individually responsible for making it all better. I am gentler with my mistakes. Talk of race doesn't scare me. I see myself as someone who needs and deserves to be taken care of, and I work to nurture myself through spiritual practices that range from daily journaling to spending time outside by bodies of water, something we have in abundance here in New Orleans. I have a sense of purpose, without feeling like everything depends on me. I work at loving myself just for being, not for what I do. I work at loving others for the same thing.

■ ■ ■

SEATED ON THE PLANE, I watched the flight attendant escort to her seat a young black girl, maybe ten years old. She is timid. It is her first time flying, she tells the flight attendant, who in an attempt to provide care gives the young girl her own private lesson on how to put the air mask on her face should it drop because she needs to maintain a flow of oxygen. Again for a moment, I imagine I am that little girl, and how this talk of oxygen masks must sound so scary to this young girl, alone among strangers, flying for the first time. It is the second time that day when I've wondered why a young child is not crying. The flight attendant tells the girl how to push the button to get her attention, if she should need it. Hearing a thirty-something white man suggest that maybe this little girl would feel safer up front, closer to the flight attendant who takes this idea into consideration and goes to check it out, makes me hopeful. When the attendant actually escorts the girl to first-class, I am taken by the image of this little black girl sitting in a big comfy seat, aided partly by the care and concern of a white man.

This seems to be a different world from one where it was once commonplace for angry white men and women to hatefully demand that black people remain in their place: at the backs of buses and separate drinking fountains, underfunded schools, or imprisoned for political activities, false charges or minor offenses that are not applied to white people. While it is some improvement that it's now possible to find people of color in first-class seats—an equal playing field does not exist. More and more, I am beginning to realize that's not even the dream I want to pour my passion and gifts into. Instead, when all is said and done, *I don't want there to be green zones surrounded by growing misery.*

Throughout centuries, men and women of conscience, with varied skin colors, different levels of class, privilege, and many other diverse identities, have taken risks (some big, some small) to fight for a more just world for all of us. I want to continue to be a part of that movement, and my vision of this just world I'm working toward is one where we struggle together in a beloved community, caring for our souls, and never forgetting the lessons that none of us are free until all of us are free. ■

Sam Shain

The Reality of White Privilege

I HAVE LIVED MOST OF MY LIFE IN MAINE, a place with few black people. This did not stop my parents from teaching me at a very young age that when judging the value of a fellow human being, color is not important. I am lucky I was not tainted by bigotry. I am not excusing those who have been poisoned by ignorant influences, but I do feel sorry for them. Unfortunately, it's those individuals who often grow up to become the most vocal, and in the age of the Internet, a meme or anecdote, whether it is true or not, can spread like wildfire and shape opinion.

Quite frankly, the worst part of being white in America is the loud crowd that acts as though it is a terrible gig being white in America. I am talking about white people who feel they are being discriminated against when minorities ask for equality, and the Fox News crowd that perpetuates these ideas. Those groups of people who believe Christmas is under attack, or that a "gay agenda" goes further than one's desire to marry, have a family and live in peace. The only thing these people do is embarrass themselves as Americans with their childish "What about me?" attitude that does not justify complaint. As an American, I am literally ashamed of people who think this way.

What they fail to recognize is a history of oppression that has always excluded rich, Christian, straight white men – the same group who now claim they are being persecuted. They look at a few black people who have risen to power, particularly our president, and act as if this alone is an indication that racism has been extinguished. They are unapologetic when a white "gunman" goes off the deep end, yet expect every

Muslim to condemn radical Islamic terrorists—as though any major media outlet in America would ever present the Muslim community with such an opportunity. I personally believe that there are powerful people in this world who have an interest in the division of different groups, and couldn't be happier about Islamophobia in America.

I have met plenty of outward racists in my life. One day as I pumped my gas, I was wearing a shirt that said "Atlanta Black Crackers," a team from the old Negro baseball league. When I went in to pay, a white person looked at my white skin, misinterpreted my shirt, and thought it would be appropriate to say, "Nice shirt. I wish a nigger would come in here and try to rob us so I could fuck him up!" Speechless, I glanced back at the other worker behind him, an older white man, dressed in fancier clothes, who was more-than-likely the manager on duty, waiting for him to reprimand his employee. Not only did he not say anything, he chuckled. Although I think the disgusted expression on my face said enough, I do regret not actually telling them I would never patronize their business again. Ever since that moment, I have tried to be more proactive when someone spouts racist nonsense. I don't think it is productive to be tolerant of intolerance.

I work as a musician playing in all sorts of different bars, so I end up talking to all kinds of people. Recently, I was in a discussion with an acquaintance, a former basketball player, who said he generally didn't like black people because he felt as though they excluded him on the court when he had spent time in the Southern states. In his conversation, he wasn't afraid to toss around the offensive n-word. My brother, who is the drummer in my band, and I let this guy have it. We pointed out how rude, ignorant, and foolish he sounded. By giving this guy some real feedback and letting him know we would not tolerate his race bashing, he toned down his attitude considerably. In fact, at a recent pickup basketball game, he guarded a black acquaintance of mine. Despite my worries and concerns, the two of them were joking around, even conversing on a more personal level on the sidelines by the time the pickup game ended. Was I able to change his viewpoint completely? I don't know, but what I do know is that our conversation had some impact on his behavior.

Having real conversations about race and trying to make a positive impact can make a difference. For so many people, diversity is such a terrifying proposition. If someone has grown up with negative stereotypes regarding an entire race, ethnicity, or religion, it is far easier for them to steer clear of different types of people rather than try to connect with people individually. This deeply rooted distrust seeps its way into stressful situations, such as the recent confrontations with the police and the black community. I believe that subliminal racism, which inevitably exists, is possibly just as harmful as out-and-out bigotry.

For example, my father was living in Florida (before I was born) when one day his car broke down in a predominantly black section of town. He told me a guy spat at him as he walked by. Or when I vacationed in Jamaica, as I rode in my nice little shuttle on my way to a nice little resort with a bunch of other white people, I saw graffiti on walls that said things like "NO WHITEY" or "DIE WHITEY." It creeped me out, no question, but I at least understand why. I understand that their animosity was created by white people who have and continue to hold a sense of superiority over what they see as the "inferior" black race. On the other hand, some white people actually believe that they experience more discrimination than black people. It's a silly idea, but it's easy to delude ourselves into thinking that inequality is a result of cultural failures, racial pathology and a convoluted narrative involving black-on-black crime, hoodies, rap music and people wearing their pants too low that ignores a history of slavery and oppression. I simply cannot understand, absent any historical evidence of blanket white oppression, why a white person would think they are being persecuted because of the color of their skin.

What does it mean to be white in America? Fortunate. Being white, statistically I am in a better position to succeed than a black person. I come from a lower- to middle-class household, and as I think about starting a family, I am on my way to the same class level. Straight out of the womb, I have had less to worry about than any minority, and I defy anyone who rejects that statement. Not only am I statistically in a better position, but as evident through the media, I am able to whine and complain as though I am the persecuted one, and millions would actually believe me. If I were to do something terrible and kill someone, I would never be labeled a "terrorist," I would be a lone-wolf "gunman" or "shooter." People would use me as a reason to support the Second Amendment, and in the same breath, condemn the mental health system. Can the same be said of a Muslim? If I decided to set fire to a vehicle after the Red Sox won the World Series, I would not be labeled a "thug," I would be labeled a drunken frat boy. Can the same be said of a black person? If I was walking away from a cop, possibly even making the poor decision of attacking said cop, I am confident of the likelihood that I would be stunned with a Taser as opposed to being shot in the back thanks to my light skin and the preconceived notions regarding my race.

To be clear, as I have many friends who are police officers and I acknowledge the difficulty of their profession, I believe this often comes from the subliminal racism I discussed previously. Most police officers clearly do their jobs to protect and serve the community. I would suspect a very microscopic percentage is outwardly hateful and racist. I think more than police officers, people in general have tainted perceptions of minorities, which become magnified in stressful situations that can translate into a more lethal mistake if you are a police officer. There is evidence to support this claim.

Let me be incredibly clear – this is not to say all white people are racist. I would never make such a blanket assumption about an entire group of people. However, there are some who think terrible, ignorant things about other races. There are even more who believe that when someone asks for or demands equality they are in fact seeking special privileges. We have a media that often fuels these thoughts. We must be vigilant in identifying this hate and ignorance, and do our best as individuals; especially white people like myself, to shame and condemn this kind of attitude. Most people are good. Most white people are not racist – but we must change the minds of those who are. Is there white privilege in America? Absolutely. Anyone systematically fighting to keep white privilege alive is embarrassing a large group of white people such as myself. Anyone spreading this agenda and fanning these flames for political or financial gain should be ashamed of themselves. As a white person, I reject the notion and reality of white privilege. Until everyone else does, however, I'm sure I will continue to inherently enjoy it. That is the true problem.

I am proud to point out that historically racial equality has improved. I am hopeful more people will acknowledge race-relations has not, and that respect, tolerance, and equality clearly has room for improvement as we move forward together as Americans. ▪

Chivvis Moore

White Man's Burden

WHITE? WHAT'S WHITE?
When I was in grammar school, we were taught there were four races and that they were called red, black, yellow and white.

"Red" was "Indians" or "redskins," and "black" was fairly clear, since, despite all the variations on black, anyone who had dark brown skin was considered black. No capital letter in those days. And "yellow" covered all Asians. No special category for anyone from Latin America or anywhere in the Middle East; these populations were never mentioned.

Then there was white. That was us, in the schools I went to as a child in St. Louis, Missouri in the 1950s. The lucky ones. No color. White. Sounded nice. So did the colors, actually, but they weren't mentioned much. They were the backdrop, setting off a contrast to our whiteness.

When I was seven years old, my father's company moved him to Brazil, where we lived for three years. I remember loving both Rio de Janeiro and Sao Paulo – the ocean, the mountains, the trees, the shoes made of straw, the streetcar, the people we met who were so warm to us and vibrant in a way I had never experienced. But something very different also impressed itself on my child's brain – the *favelas*, the vast impoverished areas where the poor lived along the hills outside the city. I was lucky to live in Brazil during those years as a child. The older I've become, the more gratitude I have for the chance to live outside the U.S. It is the greatest gift my parents could have given me.

Why then, on our return to the U.S., did an older friend and I, at nine, come up with the idea that it would be fun and funny to call Lucybelle, the African American woman who came once a week to help my mother with housework: "Nigger! Nigger!" I have never forgotten it and I have never forgiven myself for it. I never will. And I have never understood why we did it. I have no memory of planning it. We were living in Birmingham, Michigan, a suburb of Detroit, white and wealthy, but I don't recall ever having encountered such overt expression of racism in the community, and certainly never at home. My parents did not intend to raise us to be either racist or cruel. When my mother came home that afternoon and found Lucybelle lying on my parents' bed crying, she was appalled. I was paddled, and my mouth washed out with soap. We were both made to apologize, of course – for all the good that could have done – and we were made to understand that we had done a terrible thing.

That is my sordid beginning. I was also a thief at the time – I stole a friend's bracelet, returning it only when I was caught, and regularly stole money from my father's pants pocket. My parents feared I was amoral, that I simply could not be taught the reasons for choosing right over wrong.

What changed? I wish I could remember how change came. The next thing I remember associated with race was when I was twelve or thirteen years old, writing a letter to President Eisenhower demanding justice, after I read in the newspaper that a black man in a southern U.S. state had been lynched for stealing a loaf of bread.

From that time on, I was very aware of my whiteness and the privilege it gave me in contrast to black Americans. In junior high and high school in another wealthy suburb, this time outside New York City, I would sneak into Harlem on the train, attracted by the energy and life lived on the streets, by the way people expressed their feelings in voice and gesture, in contrast to the drab, staid, inhibited aura of a suburbia I was growing to hate. I was becoming ashamed to have so much more than the African Americans I worked with on the few volunteer projects I was able to participate in, until I was forbidden by my overprotective parents to go into Harlem at all.

In high school, I had a great social studies teacher, a woman who opened my eyes to worlds outside my own, outside the U.S. – to Ghana, and China, and Egypt. Yet I was too susceptible to my parents' liberal-Democrat-type views, too influenced by a Kissinger-taught conservative college roommate, and too immersed in my own emotional problems to pay real attention to the Vietnam War. The U.S. Government must know what is right.

When the Freedom Rides for black voting rights in the South were organized, I wanted very much to participate. Once again, I allowed my behavior to be curtailed by my parents' wishes: they begged me not to go to the South, for their sakes, they said, and promised that when I was eighteen, I could do whatever I wanted. That summer I went to Europe instead. The only thing I did that showed the faintest concern for the racism on which our nation was built, was to volunteer one summer and then return years later to the Gila River Indian Community in Arizona, training teenage members of the Pima and Maricopa tribes to publish their own newspaper, and help establish a community newspaper and radio station. In the late 1960s, I briefly taught civil rights news coverage at then California State College, Hayward, where I got an intensive education in racism, including my own, from the head of the Black Students Union on campus. I worked with black youth putting out a newspaper in a housing project and with a Chicano group who were initiating newspapers for their own community. Other than these small efforts, I did nothing at all.

So, if I were to allow it, I could spend a lot of time steeping in regret. I woke up so late, so much later than so many of my peers. I regret my inattention, my ignorance, my unwillingness to look, to learn what was really going on and what populations were being destroyed with my tacit consent. I was unaware of U.S. policies in any part of the rest of the world.

In 1978, I read a book. I was working as a carpenter in the San Francisco Bay Area and was intrigued when a friend lent me *Architecture for the Poor,* [1] about building low-cost mud brick housing. Three months after reading the book, I was in Egypt, offering to volunteer on the building project. That was the action that has determined the course of my life ever since. I lived a year in Egypt, and knew upon leaving that I would return to the Middle East and live much of my life in the Arab and Muslim worlds.

---

1   Hassan Fathy, *Architecture for the Poor: An Experiment in Rural Egypt* (University of Chicago Press, 1973).

And I did—moving to Syria for two years as the U.S. bombed Iraqis fleeing along the highway from Kuwait in the First Gulf War, returning to Egypt for another two years on a teaching fellowship while I studied for a master's in teaching English as a foreign language, moving after that to Israel, where I taught both Palestinian and Jewish citizens of Israel, and finally, making my home for eleven years in the West Bank, teaching at Birzeit University.

It was during these years that I finally learned in depth about the racist basis of U.S. history and current undertakings. Working in the Institute of Women's Studies at the University, preparing courses for my students in the Institute's Master's Program in Gender, Law and Development, listening to people and paying attention to the world around me, I came the closest I've yet to come to understanding what it means to be a white citizen of the United States of America.

Since that time, my life has been connected with the lives of Arabs, both Muslim and Christian. I was lucky when I returned to the U.S. after sixteen years in the Middle East to find a Palestinian American dynamo of a woman with enough projects for volunteers and paid staff. I have worked with and for her from that time on.

I am inspired by the efforts on the part of Arabs I know to take pride in their identities in a country that is increasingly distrustful of and abusive to them. I am encouraged as they work to awaken American understanding of who they are and to integrate and enrich our multiethnic population. I am joyful as I listen to their music, speak Arabic, admire the calligraphy, painting, ceramics, and clothing that are their heritage.

Increasingly informed and heartened by the presence of people of color in our midst, I turn my own efforts toward my fellow white Americans who are as ignorant, as unaware, as I have been much of my life.

■ ■ ■

IT'S BEEN A GRADUAL AND DRASTIC awakening to realize that I was born into a category of people in the world who are distinguished by the fact that we have and still do colonize, invade and exploit the rest of the world, and—even more important—by the fact that we whites living now are reaping the benefits that these criminal acts have supplied and continue to supply us.

Oh, we can ask—which white? Poor white, rich white; urban white, rural white? Working class, or poor white trash white? George W. Bush white? Trump white? Hilary Clinton white? Arab white? Latino white? The 99 percent white, or the 1 percent white? Old white? Young white? White living in the mines of Kentucky or in the plains of Nebraska? Jewish white? Muslim white? Christian white? And within all these categories—which kind of Jewish Muslim Christian white? The more you consider them, the more the differences proliferate.

I look at my skin. I am not white. Pinkish, maybe? Pig-colored?

And yet—despite all these differences—the category "white" has always meant something very particular in the Americas, from the Northwest Passages in the Arctic to the Tierra del Fuego in South America, and throughout the world. Those who are called and who call themselves white are marked by two qualities. One of these qualities is ethnic: we who are called white are of European descent, and within that category, of primarily Anglo-Saxon ancestry. Maybe the term "Euro-ethnic" would be more appropriate.

A corollary is that color trumps whiteness in defining who is white and who is not. So the population of Latin America that came originally from Europe, by merging with the Native populations, is no longer counted as white, just as the child of a slave raped by her master, however light her skin color, was counted not white, but black.

Geographically, whites mostly inhabit northern areas—historically the northern states in the U.S.; Canada and the United States in North America; and the northernmost European countries—with countries in the south of Europe—Spain, Italy, Greece—sliding down the economic scale. Hence the concept of the Global North and Global South.

These ethnic and geographical factors cut fairly neatly through all the messy categories in the above list of whites if you add one more: whites have almost always been and still are the colonizers.

This fact results in another quality, the most important one: privilege.

Awareness of reality makes it a fraught history that a white person carries today in the United States of America.

How can I rest easy as I walk the ghetto wastelands of our cities and know the limitations on education, jobs and other opportunities that their residents, if they survive, must deal with all their lives? How can I watch the seemingly endless videos of black men and women being gunned down by police, see Arab and Muslim Americans hounded, regulated, surveilled and mapped, without being aware that in some ways the poorest white will always have more privilege in this country than any person of color?

Each day I feel a physical pain in my chest. Our CIA operatives, soldiers, drone operators, our war department personnel kill across the planet. Those in the countries we destroy wash up corpses on Mediterranean shores and die in prisons in Israel and Guantanamo Bay. More and more, I feel that we on this planet are one. So how can I live carefree as populations of color across the planet starve to death or worse, due to our wars and our actions around trade, the environment, economics and politics, domestic and foreign, while we back home reap the profits?

This is what being white in America means to me: it means that I belong to a race of oppressors, past and present. I am ashamed to be white, in my own country and in relation to the Global South.

In 1899, as the United States was initiating the war that placed the people of Cuba, the Philippine Islands, Puerto Rico and Guam under U.S. control, the British poet Rudyard Kipling wrote a poem encouraging white Americans in their imperialistic ventures: Civilizing "Your new-caught, sullen peoples / Half devil and half child" would be a thankless job, he warned, even as he urged the whites to "Take up the White Man's burden – / And reap his old reward: / The blame of those ye better / The hate of those ye guard...."

Thus a poem written more than a century ago predicted the role whites would play in U.S. history, and how we would justify our role in precisely the hypocritical terms we use today when we crow about providing "aid" to "developing" countries. And it was predicted that we would complain, as we do now, when the exploited populations turned against us.

Being white in America today requires that we take Kipling's idea of the white man's burden and turn it on its head. It means we have the job – it would hardly be fair to call it a burden – to stop our government from invading, killing, oppressing and bossing other people. It means recognizing how we whites profit from our so-called "humanitarian" ventures, and civilizing ourselves to become citizens of the world.

Being white in America means we have an obligation, not to lean on useless guilt, but to pay attention to what is being done in our name. It means we are charged to work, in any way we can – *by any means necessary* – to stop the injustices we are perpetrating against the peoples of color inside this country and outside of it, and not to become discouraged knowing we will always come up short. It means we must listen to and learn from the people whose lives we are destroying. Our lives and our souls require that we respect their humanity, and that we begin to retrieve our own. ▪

Elena Murphy

White-Handed Compliments

THE YOUNG MAN SAT NEXT TO ME in the passenger seat, sharing his wit and enthusiasm with a stream of commentary. The drive was long – an hour and a half – and draped with a backdrop of velvet hills and straggly trees. It was the second time I had given him a ride since starting my job as a mental health counselor for foster youth. He wasn't my client, but since I had a low caseload, I had volunteered to pick him up and drive him to a recently formed advisory board run by foster youth. He was a young man of color who had spent most of his childhood in foster care. Despite the hardship of growing up in the system, he graduated high school and was in his second year of college, earning a 4.0. On our long drives together, it was clear why he had been asked to join the youth run board. He was enthusiastic, smart and confident. Not only was he open to conversation, he carried the majority of it. This was rare with the youth I worked with.

At the time of our drive I had been in my position for a few months. I only had a couple of clients and was still learning the details of the work. During my orientation to the agency, trainers encouraged the room full of newly hired, predominantly white staff to welcome conversations on race with clients and their families. They spoke of honesty and vulnerability and I felt encouraged. I envisioned myself engaging in fiercely real conversations about race and privilege with young people and their parents. The racial disparities between workers and clients was glaring. It made me uncomfortable, but I used the promise of meaningful discourse as validation for my role in a system I knew to be oppressive.

By the time I started driving the young man to his meetings, I had yet to have a conversation about race. In fact, in my entire time at the agency I never spoke genuinely about race with any of my clients. My feelings and understandings about racism and white supremacy stayed theoretical. I spoke at length about race to my coworkers, friends and family, but didn't say a word – did not acknowledge it at all – while speaking with the children, youth and adults of color I worked for. The young man in my car didn't speak directly about race either. He spoke of his experience in foster care, his accomplishments at school and work, his failed romantic relationships and economics and politics. I let him lead the conversation and hardly said more than a few words at a time. Periodically, he teased me with controversial statements, urging me to challenge him. I had plenty of feelings about the subjects he discussed, but I have always had a habit of losing my words. Despite his age, he was confident and knowledgeable and spoke with authority, which intimidated me. I limited my responses to a handful of clumsy words at a time.

In our second drive together, the young man continued to share pieces of his life with me. I made a point of not prodding him with too many questions, letting him steer the conversation. Halfway through our drive, he described his first experience with public speaking. A couple of years earlier the director of my agency asked him to speak at a national event addressing the needs of foster youth. As a teenager he stood before policymakers and agency directors to advocate for himself and the nation's foster youth.

The young man observed, "It's funny, all these people keep asking me to talk about my opinions."

In an attempt to assure him that he deserved the honors I said, "Well, it's no surprise to me. You speak very well. You really convey your thoughts effectively."

As the words tumbled out of my mouth I already felt the stirrings of regret. Regret turned to panic when the young man slumped in his seat and brought his arms forward in exaggerated gesture, "yo, yo, yo, sup? I'm speakin' good, homies."

My horror took the form of a smile as I laughed frigidly, "oh, well, I didn't mean it like that."

The young man smirked and skillfully steered the conversation in a new direction. But I was far away from him as my mind attempted to contradict the weight in my stomach. My comment had nothing to do with the color of this young man's skin. I had genuine respect and appreciation for people who spoke with eloquence, especially as someone who fumbled over words so easily. I would have said it to anybody. I only sounded like a condescending white person, but I was misunderstood. I wasn't that person.

I told myself everything I could to feel less guilty for my remark. But I couldn't stop hearing the lines from Jamila Lyiscott's poem, "3 Ways to Speak English," "Today a baffled lady observed the shell where my soul dwells/And announced that I'm 'articulate.'" As desperately as I tried to distance myself from that baffled lady – to list the ways we were different – the similarities of our features were undeniable. I resented the lady, and all the other white people, whose ignorance created circumstances that placed false meaning on my good intention. I was sensitive to articulation, making me generous with compliments. The only reason I couldn't dole out such compliments without regard for race was because of these other white people who didn't know, didn't care, didn't try. I was trapped by my whiteness – wasn't free to express admiration or reveal insecurity. I was confined by the ignorance of another.

I try now to be gentle with myself as I reflect on my frantic attempts to preserve my self-image. It seems natural to explain away behaviors to protect one's feelings of goodness – I see it all the time in myself and other white people. I am also not the first white person to draw a line dividing my racial community and separating myself from those I deem as problematic. My defensiveness was instinctual and commonplace, however, it also put up a wall between the young man and me. It prevented me from seeing the truth behind the words I had spoken.

Those words continued to nag at me, revealing the shallowness of my defenses. It took me a long time to drop the excuses. Now that I'm far away from that drive in the car, I can acknowledge that even though there was some truth to my justifications, my intentions were beside the point. When the young man reacted the way he did, he was sending me a message about the implications of my words. I live in a different reality than him and other people of color, and my reality limited my understanding of the violence of language. Language is heavy with meaning. It has been used to strip away culture, identity and history. It plays a key role in advancing white supremacy. When I, as a white person, make a comment about somebody's speech, I am making a judgment grounded in my whiteness and Eurocentricity. Each time I defend myself by justifying my intentions, I inadvertently demand that anyone outside of my identity puts aside their own truths to meet me in mine. As a member of the white community, this is an easy thing to do. I have been socialized to believe mine are the only truths and anyone who can't adapt to them is ignorant, wrong, bad or unfair.

Whenever I think about the comment I made to the young man in my car, my biggest regret is not what I said, but what I didn't say. With humor, this young man skillfully confronted me about my biases and racism and instead of showing respect and vulnerability, I self-consciously brushed away his efforts. This young man was smart, focused and resilient and, because of my defensiveness, I not only missed an opportunity to hear him, but I denied him an opportunity to speak. This is what pains me the most when I think about my white defenses. There have been so many missed opportunities for me to listen and so many moments when I unknowingly silenced another. The more I observe myself, the more I understand how isolating it is to protect my white identity.

That ride in the car was one of the first moments in my job when, out of fear and discomfort, I dodged an opportunity to acknowledge the divide between my world and the world of people of color. It was one of the first moments when I neglected to enter another person's reality and provide space for them to be heard and seen. It was one of the first moments I blindly promoted white supremacy. There were many more moments to come. While I waited for my clients to approach me on issues of race in the formal, measured style of communication I was used to, I ignored, dismissed and deflected every attempt they made to express their experiences. Despite my theoretical willingness to explore racism, I was still too entrenched in my white reality to acknowledge the deeper truths behind race, power and privilege. Ten months into my time at the agency, when I could no longer ignore the weight in my stomach, I began to pick apart my role in the system. I saw how ill equipped I was to discuss race with youth of color. They understood the topic far better than I did and my education was coming at their expense. I examined my motivations and found that my desperate need to feel like the "good" kind of white person influenced almost every decision I made. I looked critically at my position in the agency and discovered that I was just another white person working in an oppressive system targeting people of color.

These realizations blanketed me in guilt and shame, but they also opened my world. I left my job a couple of months later; it was my first step in addressing my personal expressions of racism. It seemed worthwhile to self-isolate and explore my biases and ignorance, but I also can't escape an ever persistent feeling of uncertainty. If there's a privilege in choice, what does my decision to leave my job mean? When so many people of color are forced into a system that dehumanizes, demonizes and exposes them to trauma, what roles do power and privilege play in my entering and leaving that system at will? I don't have answers to these questions, but they tumble around in my head as I continue to distance myself from what I used to do. It's hard to know the difference between fighting racism and running from it. I try to observe my biases and expand my awareness, but I can't help doubting. The only solace I find is in the reminder that this has very little to do with me as an individual. I will never be a "good" white person. There's no room for ego in addressing racism. All I can do is remind myself of the young man who once sat next to me in the car. That young man deserves safety in using his voice, walking down the street and existing in this country. My doubts, defenses and biases may rise up from inside of me, but I find it's much easier to forgive them when I remember that my work is just as much for me as it is for the local, national and global communities of which I'm a part. Self-examination may be the strongest tool I have in the fight against racism, but it is only when I let go of my ego that I can truly learn to heal. ▪

Karen Johnson

What Does It Mean to Be White in America?

BEING WHITE IN AMERICA means that I feel out of place even as I am writing this essay. It is rude, disrespectful, and I am speaking out of turn, in an arena where I may not be welcome. Being white in America means that for those of us who do believe that racial issues continue to plague our society, we are also at a loss of what to do with that belief. For those of us who want to improve the future for our children, by helping to create a world with less racial tension, more understanding and an open dialogue, being white in America means attempting to do so without offending anyone. It means fearing, in an attempt to prove ourselves not racist, we will come across as just that.

I grew up in a very typical suburbia, where I was surrounded with varying shades of white. All of my friends were white. All of my neighbors were white. All of my parents' friends were white. Like many suburban schools in the 1980s and 1990s and even today, only a handful of children of color attended my school. I remember, in elementary school, that there was one black boy and one black girl. I recall their faces and names very clearly, because they were different from the rest of us.

Although I was oblivious to it, in retrospect, I enjoyed the privilege of not being memorable or different. I enjoyed the gift of anonymity as one in a sea of white, brown-haired, regular-looking kids in my suburban, almost all-white town.

I continued to benefit from this invisible, yet pervasive privilege bestowed upon me at birth as I entered college: a predominantly white liberal arts school in the Northeast. My oblivion of "race" as anything worth thinking about continued, as did my ability to blend in. During spring break of my freshman year, however, I had my first glimpse into my "whiteness."

I spent my spring break building houses for Habitat for Humanity in rural Mississippi. A twenty-four-hour drive took me to, what seemed to be, a different world. Or at least a different century. As we drove into the town where our assignment was, we saw row after row of dilapidated houses with no windows or doors. Yet people lived in these homes. Newspapers and sheets covered holes in the walls. We would later learn that many did not have electricity. Some did not have plumbing. The normal suburban necessities I had always enjoyed were nowhere. It was 1999. I stared out the window in silent awe. Where had I traveled to?

The week I spent building houses in rural Mississippi changed my life. I had never spent time with so many black people. I had never sat next to, or spoke with, so many people living in poverty. I returned to my prestigious college on the hill, to my air-conditioned dorm room, with a new sense of awareness, but I did not know what to do with it. I enrolled in African American history the next semester—one of only two white students in the class. A typically outspoken participant, I found myself silenced in this course. Not by my peers. Not by my professor. I silenced myself. What could I possibly have to offer as a white student? I had one experience in black America, and it hardly qualified me to offer up opinions and comments in class.

Despite or maybe because of my obvious and often uncomfortable whiteness, my interest in racial relations continued as I became a teacher. Four years after that trip to Mississippi, I found myself teaching high school English in Omaha, Nebraska. I taught at a semi-suburban high school, where the percentage of students of color was far higher than in the schools I had attended growing up. I was earning my master's degree in secondary education, and as I pondered thesis topics, my advisor asked what I was interested in, with regards to education. What did I want to research and analyze? I wanted to delve into why so many more of my black students were failing than my white students, and why so many more of my black students were in detention and getting suspended. Why so few of the parents of my black students attended parent-teacher conferences while the white parents were lined up twenty people deep. But again, I was faced with a dilemma. What would be the repercussions of asking these questions, of doing this research? What right did I have to delve into the home life, and the history of the families of these students who were failing and in trouble? Did my curiosity, my desire to learn about the causes of these disparaging percentages at my school make me racist? What role does a white teacher, a white person, have in performing this research? Although often uncomfortable, I did, in the end, write my thesis about white privilege. I interviewed my own students of color and was able to deepen my understanding of my whiteness as I heard their personal stories of racism.

This awkwardness, this fear of saying too much, not saying enough, saying something racist, quiets white Americans. Some of us are so damn scared of being perceived as racist, that we become silent participants in the racism that continues to seep through generations in this country. Our floundering, our confusion about what we are supposed to do, our fear of getting it wrong, makes us complicit in the problem.

Sixteen years after that life-changing trip to rural Mississippi, I am a thirty-five-year-old mother of three very white children. We live in predominantly white suburbia. And my children are growing up with the same oblivion I did. They are enjoying the same privileges I did, and they don't know it. My son has one black student in his class, so does my daughter. Everyone knows the names of these children. Not for any other reason than they are different from the rest, and that which stands out, becomes memorable–for good or bad. Not everyone knows my children's names – the regular white, brown-haired kids. They blend into the stark white background, as I have done throughout my life.

Being white in America, to me, means not knowing what to do about being white in America. Ignoring a black person at the grocery store because she is black makes you racist. But what about finding yourself as that over-the-top chatty white lady in the checkout line desperate to make small talk with the black mom? Even if the black mom is clearly not interested? But what if that white mom wants to show her kids (kids who have limited interactions with people of color) that all moms can be friends? What if that mom is on the brink of saying, "But talk to me, black mom! I'm like you! And I like black people!

And I'm trying to raise non-racist kids!" Does that make her racist? I suspect it does.

Being white in America means knowing you are privileged. It means knowing you were given a gift that you didn't ask for, and maybe don't deserve. Being white in America means being confused about how to conduct oneself, feeling fearful of speaking out of turn, and wanting to help enact change, but having no idea where one's place is in that journey. It means writing a thesis that maybe you shouldn't have. It means creating an essay like this, that maybe you don't have the right to create. But it also means fearing if you stay silent that you are an even bigger part of the problem. ■

Al Ormsby

Ramblings of a
White Liberal

WHAT DOES IT MEAN to be white in America? This is an unusual question for a white person. We don't normally think about race from a first person perspective. This is because in American culture racial definitions are anything but neutral. By this I mean that race is seen from the standpoint of just one particular group, mine. What we see is assumed to be "universal" and not just a white interpretation. It is a reality that is hidden from everyone's view, even ours. Yet, this blind spot doesn't change the fact that we write the rules. Therefore before discussing the experiential side of being white it would be helpful to digress for a moment to clarify who we are. This requires addressing a more literal interpretation of the central question; namely-in America, what do we mean when we say that an individual is white?

Our society's method of racial categorizing requires that all "others" be defined first, what's left is understood to be "white." Therefore the question "is this person white" is almost never asked by my fellow Caucasians. "Is this person black" (or in similar instances another category of non-white) is what we are most accustomed to inquire about. As such black is defined as having any physical characteristics that indicates the presence of even the most minimally observable black lineage. In some cases, that can be so slight that it serves to create enough doubt to generate considerable discussion. In our culture it is virtually impossible for a white person to have never encountered a query about whether or not a particular individual is black. Making "whiteness" an elimination game places "otherness" at the core of one's thinking. You are pointed away from the central theme, purity; for only a person of pure (Caucasian) blood can be white. Yet, what's most important here is that white is assumed if there isn't any noticeable "stain." It's the stain that's crucial because it and not the whiteness is what we see. While spectrums are most common in the real world being white in America requires that you have no noticeable "impurities."

Since our race is dependent on purity, just a smattering of non-white inheritance in our children means that the genes that make us white are lost when passed on to the next generation. Therefore our identity is not only more precarious than that of non-whites but potentially endangered by them. This explains why our focus is on the stain rather than the whiteness. Being the group that is most attentive to the impurities of others means that we see ourselves as being located at the center of the "universe;" everyone else views things from a peripheral position. Needless to say this affects how I as well as most of my white brethren experience "race."

The definition of whiteness itself is what makes us unaware that there is even such a thing as the unique "experience" of being white. While the protective bubble that we create is for the most part invisible to us, evidence of its existence frequently emerges when we are in "mixed company." It turns out that viewing white culture as the unquestionable "normal" makes it all too easy for us to say something inappropriate when we stroll outside our comfort zone. You tend to forget that language isn't non-biased, but instead devised to accommodate the thinking of the dominant culture. The fact that I think of myself as a tolerant and non-racist person has not always prevented me from falling into this trap. The last time this happened was just a few years ago when my wife Lisa and I visited a friend in the city I grew up in. The friend was African American, and his wife was Caucasian. Their grown daughter is of mixed race, but as is to be expected in our society, she identified herself as black. When I got to my friend's house, to my surprise I found that there were a number of people there. All of them were white except for their daughter who was in town visiting them. Lisa and I had just visited her mentally ill brother in Detroit. He was living in the same house that they both had grown-up in. For some forgotten reason, the topic of her brother and our visit to Detroit came up. It was when my friend and his wife were out of the room (possibly in the kitchen). This meant that except for their visiting daughter the only people remaining in the living room were (pure) white. Lisa explained that she was very upset by the poor conditions that her brother was living in. She was referring to the dilapidated state of her old family house. Without even thinking, I added that he lived in a changing inner-city neighborhood that was even more rundown than the house. I then proceeded to elaborate in detail on its ugliness. With some intensity, I noted that he was oblivious to the rising crime rate.

A rundown inner-city eye sore with rampant crime in the nation's rust belt is polite "white speak" for a "black ghetto." Or, in other words, her white brother was in such bad shape he couldn't even get up the wherewithal to move out of what had become an African American slum. While the facts of what I added were all true, I was also subtlety painting the above picture as a way of conveying what bad shape her brother was in. For underneath all these facts, true or not, the hidden message being broadcast was that since a crime ridden urban neighborhood is synonymous with a black ghetto, any normal white person no matter how bad his economic situation wouldn't be living there. Of course it was understood without saying that the same standard wouldn't apply to a normal black person in similar financial circumstances.

Almost everyone including myself was consciously focused on only the factual aspects of what I had just said, and not on any subliminal code that was inadvertently hiding behind cleverly constructed language. I say almost, because based on her facial expression and body language my friend's daughter appeared to quickly pick up the hidden meaning. Maybe not immediately, but soon I would pick up her uneasiness. Her relaxed persona changed quite abruptly because my comments had suddenly made her aware that she was in mixed company and must be watchful of what she says. My awareness of her reaction made me feel terrible. My knee jerk white speak had made my friend's daughter feel uncomfortable in her own family home. Such a painful insight quieted me for the rest of the evening. Yet this incident made me realize that even I, an open-minded "universal person," underneath it all still thought like a parochial white man. My whiteness was not as I had thought only in my complexion.

On that day I came to understand why cultural diversity is so important. All white people, even the most progressive of the lot, can't help being defined by the absence of any visible non-white linage. This means that to some extent all of us experience a racially secluded existence that makes it impossible to completely understand the black perspective in all its nuances. Thinking about it now, the evidence of this truism was there long before I became aware of it. My parents had the habit of immediately locking the car doors when they saw a black face. They did this without saying a word; it was automatic. I must have picked up the habit from them. I have always instinctively, without fore or after thought locked the driver's side door when traveling through an African American neighborhood. Such happenings have made me aware of the influence my parents along with the white world I grew up in have had on me. For someone like me, this is a real revelation. I say this because from an early age I have seen myself as an objective observer of the wrongs perpetrated by racism. I now understand that I can't help from being a subjective observer as well.

Despite what most of my fellow whites believe, when it pertains to race there is no favored position; everyone views events from their own particular periphery. And yes, whether we know it or not there is a unique experience in being white. While it is true that this reality also includes me, it doesn't change the fact that from where I stand I see the opinions of most whites as not only highly subjective but self-servingly so. Maybe its human nature, but when you see your group's culture, history, values, and even the biases inherent in language as being the unquestionable starting point, you cannot help but tilt "reality" to best serve what you think is beneficial to you.

During my years as a civil servant I witnessed firsthand how quickly a group's subjective judgment can be transformed into a mindset that protects its perceived interests. The most prevalent white view of affirmative action is a striking example of a dominant culture's self-serving opinions presenting themselves as just being the common norm. Affirmative action is an area where we whites have the most strongly held misperceptions. This is because no other controversy is as good a lightning rod in bringing the multi-headed nature of racism to the surface. Therefore, you can't talk about what it means to be white in America without facing the Caucasian understanding of affirmative action head on. When a white person says that an African American was appointed to a particular position because of her race, it is clearly understood to mean that she isn't really qualified for it and wouldn't have gotten the job if she had to compete on a fair playing field against qualified whites. Note, that the subtleties of language don't allow one to make such a statement without the above assumption automatically kicking in. Yet, if you look at the words themselves there is nothing there that precludes the possibility that the exact opposite may be true. In fact, my civil service experience has showed me that the opposite is indeed more common.

Before taking it any further, you need to know a few things about civil service promotions at my former place of employment. They were made by a combination of two factors. One was a formal exam (usually written), and the other was the in-house interview. The exam narrowed the field to a specific list of potential appointees, and the interview decided among them. The last step in the process was subjective allowing for a good deal of management discretion. In the case where the exam was just oral such discretion played an even larger role. With this background I now proceed to the specific circumstances that underscore what's wrong with the typical Caucasian view of affirmative action. During my tenure at the agency there was an opening for a relatively high position, Assistant Regional Administrator (ARA). The Civil Service list included just one African American candidate. He was an individual of considerable integrity and anything but a sycophant. He was known for his even handed treatment of staff even when those above him were less interested in fairness and more concerned with self-serving arbitrariness. Because he hadn't sufficiently cultivated the favor of upper management, he would have normally been passed over without a thought. Yet in this situation, the candidate was not only highly principled but had a proven track record that made him by leaps and bounds the most qualified individual for the position at hand.

This is where affirmative action was determinative. Affirmative action mandated that management justify in writing why a member of a protected group was not selected. This justification wasn't perfunctory and required solid objective evidence as well as a good deal of work (something that wasn't very welcomed). Yet despite the work, if he had been arguably less qualified than the other candidates he still would have been rejected. It would have just meant more annoying paper work. However, in this case any attempt to justify not appointing him would have been noticeably weak and therefore act as a red flag that would likely trigger a more in-depth investigation of promotional practices (something even less welcomed). In effect, since the risk was too high and the downside too steep they had to appoint him. It meant that in this situation their subjective discretion was stripped away. Unlike with a white candidate who was clearly at the top of the heap, they couldn't safely pass over this exceptional African American. It also meant that unlike the situation that existed before affirmative action, the candidate most objectively qualified was actually selected. As you might have guessed, prior to affirmative action this wasn't usually the case.

Unfortunately this last point is never mentioned. While it is true that the candidate who made it through that final step was almost always white, what's conveniently forgotten is that he was rarely the most qualified white candidate (let alone the most qualified person) for the position. In fact, being the most qualified was never a top priority; being in with management was. And this entailed a history of making the proper alliances, befriending the right people, adhering to a kind of organizational political correctness and of course being good at telling those above you what they wished to hear. No matter how qualified you were or how well you did on the written tests, being too outspoken or stepping on the wrong toes was a sure way of being passed over for promotion. In the above mentioned case, affirmative action opened the door to this very highly qualified candidate that without it would not have normally moved up the ladder. And this is where race was crucial. If having to justify before an independent review why you aren't selecting the most qualified candidate has any substantive meaning, being African American was definitely an advantage.

This fact was clear to management. When no blacks were present, white aspirants were repeatedly told (by white managers) that they better toe the line since being white meant that they could easily be cast aside. There was no independent review to protect us. Of course this helped to make whites see affirmative action as unjust and discriminatory. And this too is where I saw things differently. When I was given the spiel about the vulnerability of being white I took it to mean that in regards to promotions nothing had changed for me. I had been there long enough to know that the same situation (arbitrary favoritism) had existed for me before affirmative action and therefore this new policy didn't affect my chances at all. In the past, management had no need to defend their arbitrary discretion by resorting to racial fears. In more recent times management's use of inappropriate threats against white employees was a reflection of their anger over losing some of their unrestrained power. It had nothing to do with any concern for white workers since they had no intention of abandoning any of the long standing prerogatives they held over us. Sadly, I wasn't very successful in convincing my white cohorts of this. The appeal to racial fears (and prejudices) was just too formidable. What most whites failed to see was that affirmative action tossed the outer cover aside and revealed the implacable truth underneath it. When an authoritarian administration made up of mostly Caucasians sees an action or policy as serving their interests, they can be just as arbitrary and oppressive with whites as they have historically been with non-whites. Affirmative action didn't cause the problem; it exposed it.

I would be remiss if I didn't acknowledge an additional truth. During my years in civil service, the African Americans who were promoted were as a group better qualified than their white counterparts. Not surprising since most of the time objective evidence is a better measuring stick than subjective favoritism. Remember, no objective justification was required for not promoting a white person. A crucial result of affirmative action, that dares not tell its name, was that the quality and competence of the managers in charge were significantly elevated. This is where attempting to undue the harmful effects of racism improved everyone's general lot. Both white and black workers benefited from having top notch people in management that would not have been there otherwise. In addition, the fairer playing field at the top trickled down to the bottom. The African American that was appointed Assistant Regional Administrator (ARA) set such a positive tone throughout the agency that if a year later an election for his position had been held he would have received 90 percent of both the black and white vote. In my thirty years at the agency, there wasn't a white ARA that had such a favorable impact. What's important to remember is that this isn't a comparison between black and white managers but just another way of saying that there wasn't an ARA appointed the old fashion way (i.e., subjective favoritism) that was as impressive.

Despite what's implied, to say that an African American was promoted because of her race does not mean that she was not qualified for her position; in fact, in most cases the reverse is true. If we take it a step further, we see how everyday language speaks to the way the dominant culture sees the world. By allowing a good deal of unsaid baggage to automatically attach itself to what is said, it makes this add-on appear to be an integral part of the original statement rather than what it is, a biased and irrelevant appendage. While remaining unseen and unquestioned, the truth about affirmative action is prevented from being verbalized. What should be a positive is thereby transformed into a negative. Although it is unfortunate that most of my fellow whites fail to decipher this, you have to remember that when two very powerful co-conspirators, biased language and fear (the bedrock of racism) join forces they are exceedingly good at covering up the truth. To reiterate, the truth is that affirmative action replaced a policy of subjective favoritism and not, as our language subliminally implies, one of objective fairness. The fact that it doesn't benefit exceptional white talent in the same manner as it does exceptional black talent doesn't mean that it bears any responsibility for this failing. If any measurable harm has been done to whites, it has been the result of attempts to preserve preexisting hierarchical arrangements and not affirmative action policies.

Unfortunately the reverse isn't true. While affirmative action hasn't harmed anyone, the long-standing and routine practices that make it necessary enable a particularly potent brand of racism. This fact takes us back to what's behind all the misconceptions and racial divisions, the notion of blood purity. White people don't realize the monsters they must enable to maintain this charade. We can't advance as human beings let alone understand anyone's experience of race without first confronting the evils of pure blood racism; the most prevalent and lethal form of the disease. It is what separated Nazi style anti-Semitism from the older more traditional types. It didn't matter how many generations ago your genetic Jewish relative converted to Christianity; if you had any documentable Jewish lineage you could never be as welcomed as a full member of the community. Contrast this with Malcolm X being asked about his brown skin tone. He readily acknowledged that there were whites in his family tree; but he made it a point to denounce them as rapists. The story spoke for itself; his standing in black America was unaffected. Does anyone really think that this situation would be so easily dismissed by a pure blood racist? Does anyone really think that the Nazis would have accepted an individual with Jewish heritage even if her Hebrew relatives were rapists? No matter the circumstances does anyone really think that the KKK would see a person with noticeable black ancestry as white?

These rhetorical questions supply good evidence that Anglo American racism is fundamentally a white problem, and in the case of its most insidious aspects, this is even truer. For the most part, black and other non-white communities have no real equivalent of pure blood racism. While African Americans and other people of non-pure white lineage can have preconceived negative notions about individuals based solely on their physical appearance, it is much more difficult for them to be pure blood racist. This fact is important because it is pure blood racism that is at the core of the worst of our racial injustices. Preconceived notions are not normally carved in stone, and with positive experiences, are usually amenable to correction. On the other hand, the finality and irrationality of the pure blood variety has historically proven to be exceedingly resistant to change; no matter one's interactions. What's more, unlike traditional antisemitism and historical Hebrew-Greek-Roman-African on African slavery, pure blood racism has been responsible, for history's worst holocausts. Some fifteen million African victims of the trans-Atlantic slave trade and the six and half million Jewish/Roma victims of the Nazi death camps are two good examples. Yet, it doesn't end there. It's no accident that most brutal and lethal system of human slavery ever; the one lasting in the America's for more than a quarter of a millennium, was the only model of its type rooted in racial purity.

Yet, what's most disturbing to me as a white person is that the Nazis and the KKK are just a small part of the problem. Strip away all the subtlety, and you see that polite society's standard for racial classification is based on essentially the same principle as theirs: i.e.: white equals no known non-whites in your family tree. Such definitions are not only arbitrary but exceedingly dangerous. History tells us that they have allowed for the enslavement, rape and in some cases even murder of one's own children and siblings. This is powerful stuff that should never be forgotten. When even good people unwittingly adopt the criteria of groups like the Nazis and the KKK, it leaves the door open for the devils of our nature to sneak through. Since whites have created the problem, we have a moral obligation to prevent this from occurring and this entails that we be pro-actively part of the solution.

In this pursuit, we white liberals mustn't forget that because of our skin color we are under the same protective cover as most of society's reactive forces. This places us in an extremely advantageous position to challenge those of our race who in order to resist positive change, attempt to turn the truth upside down by conjuring up a faux counter narrative. Like what we have seen with opposition to affirmative action, when you have no moral ground to stand on, you confuse the issue by wearing the victim's garb. As you proudly resist, you scream at the top of your lungs about the oppressiveness of "political correctness." And you do it loudly and so often that no one even thinks to ask the most obvious question; what in the world is "political" about political correctness (PC)? Where is the list of people who have been arrested, awaiting trial, had their property seized or have been imprisoned? That list is from the drug war, and that is "politically incorrect." Apparently the anti-government "right" needs to associate anything they don't like using political authority; even if it is completely unwarranted.

Being perfectly situated to expose such lies places the burden on us to ask those who spread them, what's your problem with civil society? After all what's referred to as PC is clearly more of a cultural than political phenomenon. Evolving cultural norms are the flip side of an evolving civil society, not an oppressive government. Aren't the self-identified opponents of PC repeatedly telling us that civil society (not government) should be the entity that's responsible for solving all problems? When state authority is for the most part dormant and it's the culture, i.e., the civil society that is attempting to tackle the problem of racism, why is it necessary to falsely insinuate that the government is oppressing you? The answer to this question is all too obvious. This is why we white liberals must be at the forefront of those who demand that they answer it, and not let up until they shut up.

Seeing to it that we whites are part of the solution means that we are part of a larger work in progress, a more humane world and a better existence for everyone. I would like to think that this speaks to the best of what it means to be white in America today. ■

Rebel Sowell

White Privilege

"WHITE PRIVILEGE" IS A PUZZLING TERM TO ME. Growing up, I never once thought I was privileged, whether from my skin color or from my birth family. Being female, I always thought men had the better deal. My parents never mentioned anything about me going to college, only that I needed to find a rich man, or at least one who made a decent living, marry and raise a family.

My middle-class family struggled and worked hard for everything. We considered ourselves fortunate to have oatmeal for breakfast, a bologna sandwich for lunch, and hamburger goulash for dinner. We had a roof over our heads, clothes on our backs, and food in our bellies. We couldn't ask for more.

I grew up in a time of neighborhood schools. I have to admit that I did not meet or get to know a person of color until I reached junior high. My first black friend was a sweet girl who hung out occasionally with me during lunch and stood beside me during gym. We never talked about the difference of our skin color. She never once mentioned that my name offended her; in fact, she thought "Rebel" was cool. We spoke on the phone often, but never arranged a get together at each other's houses. I do not know why that was, I can only guess, but we lost contact when I moved away, though we wrote back and forth for a short time. I ran into her years later and discovered we had both become school teachers.

I guess what I am trying to say is that neither one of us was privileged, but managed our lives just fine. While I was a single mother, I struggled to pay the bills like everyone else in my neighborhood: black, Hispanic, Asian, and white. I was able to attend college through a Pell

Grant and worked several part-time jobs. I did what I had to do to survive and worked toward my dreams. There were no privileges because of my white skin.

If there were any privileges I noticed, it was those of males and people who came from wealthy families. And I don't begrudge them. I wish I had come from wealth; it would have made my life easier. I often wished I had been born male, because I saw males, no matter their race, getting jobs that I could not. Now I am proud to be a woman. I've learned there is no point in wishing to be something I'm not. I have no idea what it is like to be anyone other than myself. What I do know is that our skin color does not and should not matter. Not all people of color have had it bad, and not all white people have had it good. We all have our individual stories to tell. We've all seen pain and sadness, and at times felt discriminated against. We can sit around and whine about it, but it will not change a thing. All we can do is follow our own paths. I'm in this game of life, and I have to do my best no matter what uniform I was born into.

Today, I do not know if white privilege still exists. I have not experienced it, only heard of it by people who are unhappy with their lot in life and are looking for someone to blame, or who want to cause division. I have to admit I am troubled when I hear the word "racism" applied strictly to white people, as if only they can be racist. We have all races in positions of power and privilege, all of whom made it through their own merits. I think it is time we reconsider the term "white privilege" and shelve it where it belongs: with the history books. Once we start thinking of all races as the "human race," we can move forward. By dividing citizens into categories, we only create more unrest and hatred in this world. It is time to connect with each other and acknowledge our similarities and differences. As J. Allen Boone explained in a passage from *Passion for Life: Psychology and the Human Spirit* by Muriel James and John James, "All living things are individual instruments...We are members of a vast cosmic orchestra, in which each living instrument is essential to the complementary and harmonious playing of the whole." ■

Carol Weliky

Just Beneath White

WHAT IS YOUR ETHNICITY?

Here we go again:

- ☐ Hispanic or Latino
- ☐ Not Hispanic or Latino
- ☐ American Indian or Alaska Native
- ☐ Asian
- ☐ Black or African American
- ☐ Native Hawaiian or Other Pacific Islander
- ☐ White
- ■ Jew

I'm filling out a class registration form, and here is my invisible bullet point, just beneath "white." I am white, with olive skin notwithstanding. (An aunt called me *little sabra*[1] growing up because of my darker skin and curly black hair.) It would be an absurd presumption, a kind of oppression chic, to not call myself "white." And yet, just beneath my white skin, there is so much troubled history, resentment, fear.

Thirty years ago, back in Brooklyn, momma warned me not to cross the Hudson. *There be dragons,* she might just as well have said, *and they are anti-Semites.* I hopped on a bus and traveled as far as I could, away from all things Jewish, from grime, crime and cramped living. I wasn't

---

1   *Sabra* is an informal slang term that refers to any Israeli Jew born in Israel.

oblivious. In Jewish summer camp upstate, local kids threw stones and slurs at us at the county fair; I learned that "kike" meant me. In my twenties, I spent a summer living in the Adirondacks and going to and from town meant passing the house with the full-size Nazi flag hanging from the window. There was always that bit of uncertainty: would they attack us one night? A friend of my sister's who moved upstate for the small town life returned within the year. "Not a good place for Jews." The worst types seemed to have staked out the best places. But *shtetl* life was not for me.

It was 1980, and I landed in Oregon, where then-Governor Tom McCall had advised folks to come and visit but not stay. I stayed. Duly deputized, a friend of my new housemates let me know I was sort of trespassing. Jews, she added, sure liked to go everywhere. In random conversations with bus drivers, store owners, in a book group, at a party, someone would pull out the phrase, "you New York-types." Or ask, with a disarming smile, "What is your ethnicity?" You could hear the question coming long before it was spoken, a chess move you knew in your bones. The eager wish to catalogue, to know: "Ah, a Jew. Thought so." I was no longer with my people, and I felt it.

White in America overwhelmingly means Christian, even if you abandoned your faith or had never had it to begin with, the way Jews are Jewish whether secular or religious. It doesn't matter if I believe Jewish is a race, religion, or ethnicity. Jew-haters believe fervently in the Jewish race. Whether I agree or not is inconsequential to my existential status. The world wants to know if I am Jewish. It keeps its options open, and so must I. I don't want to put my "X" on white because I feel somewhat alienated from the party, unsure exactly who is friend or foe. Jews are well-accepted in America, and I do not want to overstate the case. My whiteness protects me, privileges me, and hides me as well.

Twenty years ago I worked in county government as a secretary. All but one of the other women in support positions was black. All were Christian, and most were extremely devout, with strong church affiliations. One day I rang up one of my coworkers to ask a question. She was away from her desk and her voice mail kicked in; her message, intended for the public, signed off with "God bless you." I covered another coworker at the reception desk during her lunch break every day, squaring off with a "Jesus Loves You" sign just above the telephone. Religion was bleeding into our government office. This seemed so clearly inappropriate to me. I hoped others would see it wasn't simply Jewish self-interest on my part, or anti-Christian, to object.

I suppose if I'd been a more skilled or diplomatic person, it might not have come to this, but we ended up in a mediation session to hash it out. "I can't separate my religion from who I am," one of the women flatly stated. She was middle-aged and had grown up in segregated Portland, in pre-civil rights era America. Clearly she'd experienced a world of prejudice my relative privilege knew nothing of. "Christians are persecuted all over the world!" another shouted at me. Here I was, a white woman, trying to tell black women what they shouldn't do. There was too much history at that table, too little meeting of the minds. I was oppressor, oppressed, and entirely at sea. It was bad enough my black coworkers, as devout Christians, believed that I, as a Jew, would end up going to Hell. In so many words, they pretty much told me I could go there.

The Brooklyn neighborhood my sister and I grew up in was largely black and Jewish. The first boy I kissed was black; so was the girl who taught me to peck out a boogie woogie on the black keys of her family piano. I felt comfortable in that mixed world, the world I'd known up until then. When our third grade teacher ushered in a new girl one day, we sat momentarily silent as she introduced her. "Class, this is Elizabeth Smith." Elizabeth Smith had bright blonde hair and blue eyes. Television and Dick & Jane aside, she was for many of us our first up-close White Anglo-Saxon Protestant. She may as well have been from the moon.

As the neighborhood became more black, whites who could afford it moved to the suburbs, the familiar pattern. The women my mother played mah jongg with, the men my father played handball with at the Jewish Community Center, disappeared. My sister was beaten up by black girls at school. In memory it was the end of, if not color blindness, then a kind of color unselfconsciousness. We moved to a whiter neighborhood of Italians, Irish, Greeks, Jews. People like ourselves. (Years later my parents, secular first-generation Jews with a strong Jewish identity, saw their neighborhood change again. But this time the new demographic was other Jews – religious Jews who kept the Sabbath, who opened stores largely irrelevant to my parents' needs. My parents were not happy. In the aggregate, the neighborhood was full of pious hypocrites, people who shunned them for being the wrong kind of Jews. And yet, my mother's close friend on the block was an observant woman. What they found in common trumped what they didn't.

I'm a writer and daydreamer, happiest in the closed world of kitchen, yard, desk, or out in nature, walking trails. I'm tired, I'm lazy, I want ease. My whiteness confers the luxury of willful oblivion, but it goes only so far. For instance: every week, if not every day, come new stories of police violence against black men and women –unarmed, armed, guilty, innocent– the crisis of black demolition remains a constant. It's a crisis of forest, not just trees. I am obligated to witness this. Here's the other aspect of my whiteness: every week, if not day, synagogues are vandalized, Jewish gravestones kicked over, Jews spat upon and called names (to their faces, behind closed doors), diminished proportionate to the visibility as Jews. It doesn't matter if I'm a reform or orthodox Jew; whether I marry a Christian, or eat bacon; stroll the streets in caftan or velvet *shtreiml*, carry on *Shabbos* or *daven* in *shul*. The world always wants to know: beneath the white, are you a Jew?

My whiteness is a passport whose benefits I enjoy; it gives access. But I was born with dual citizenship, and that dualism sometimes chafes. Just beneath white, I want to write "Jew" because to assert Jew is to raise a defiant middle finger to history – the history of my dear people's destruction and permanent unease within the dark side of European Christianity, the progenitors of whom we talk about when we talk about being white in America. This class I'm registering for, a community college math course, is filled with young people, and they are Vietnamese, Chinese, Thai, Mexican, Arab, Jamaican, and African American, with a smattering of working class whites. I check "White," sit up, get ready to learn. ∎

Becky Swanberg

What it's Like (For Me) to Be White in America

'VE STARTED TO WRITE THIS ESSAY SEVERAL TIMES over several months. I've pieced it together in my head, stringing along sentences as I do the dishes or bathe my kids or navigate traffic. I thought time would let the ideas brew, thought I'd sit down eventually and it would all spill out with clarity. But several months later and two days from the deadline, I realize that while time can improve ideas, it cannot create a new vocabulary. And when it comes to matters of my own race, I barely have feelings. I might have opinions. But I certainly don't have words.

I'm white.

I didn't grow up talking about my race. There was no pride about what it means to be white or any defining qualities that I would have attributed to my race. I only knew that kids in middle school seemed to naturally sort by skin color, and that continued into high school. Certain groups seemed to be more defined by their race, but the rest of us just...were.

We were what you are when you don't have a race; we were white. That was the extent of my own racial awareness.

At twenty-three, my husband and I opened a home for teenage boys, helping teens transition from the justice system and prepare for life on their own. Suddenly, our family, our kitchen table, our Christmas letter had different races represented. I was amazed at how honestly our teens could talk about race, and how openly they resented white people. Our guys would say things like, "Ya'll pretty cool...for white people."

I was confused. What did being white have to do with anything? Why would we be judged based on their interactions with others? And what was so white about us anyways?

The conversations evolved as my own awareness and ability to talk about race evolved. Our teens had grown up in the same country as us, but their experiences of that country were radically different. In their minds, being white was the epitome of the "system," the upper hand, the accusing parties, the ins and outs of a way of life that didn't quite give them enough to succeed. From where they stood, white America was judgmental, oppressive and unforgiving. The whole system, the story of their childhoods, was unforgiving. And most of their experiences had left them with a negative view of white people.

In the middle of that conversation, among the every day life where we played Madden on the X-box, shot hoops on the driveway, and loaded the van to get movies at Blockbuster, walls began to come down. We did homework and set the table, and broke up fights in the living room, all with the racial conversation playing or, sometimes, simply happening in the background. We stuck through the craziness that is life with teens, and tried to speak hope and cast a vision of what their lives might be. Slowly, I came to understand a bigger picture of life, a more complex idea about the nature of race, and the unique experiences of others.

During those crazy years, our own babies came into the world, and these little white infants were rocked, read to, and celebrated by a multiracial community. As we waited for our third to be born, her four-year-old brother was crossing his fingers, hoping that the baby would "be brown" like his older brothers. At four years old, he wasn't color blind; he was something better, not blind to color but appreciative of it.

As I left that community, an unexpected thing happened to me: I found a new awareness of my race but still lacked an adequate vocabulary or confidence to talk about it. I knew I was white and privileged, and I felt a deep desire to do something constructive with that knowledge. But even now, years later, I struggle to find a place in the conversation.

How do I talk about race with my own race, people who mostly resent the conversation altogether? How can we, as white people, address the wounds of society when we minimize the damages of years past? Can we do something besides offer pat answers or middle-class solutions to deep systemic issues? Can we even agree that something is terribly wrong, and that we have a responsibility to be a part of the solution?

How do I talk about race with other races? What level of responsibility do I take for the slaughter of Native Americans, the institution of slavery, and the countless other ways that my own race has acted in inhumane ways toward others? How do I enter the conversation and admit that I'm uncomfortable with this topic, that I have prejudices that linger even though I don't want to believe in them? How do I say that I am, at best, willing to work toward unity, and I am, at worst, hoping it will come without me and at little cost?

In my weakest moments, in the dark corners of my cowardly heart, I want to hide from the race discussion. I want to believe that bigger minds and better hearts are at work on this, and that the world will be fine if I do nothing. Because when it comes to issues of race, this is what I'm good at: doing nothing.

When I walked into Payless Shoes and heard the salesgirl talking on the phone, rudely mocking a job applicant who came "straight from the ghetto," I said nothing.

When I see people rant on my Facebook feed, people that I know and love and respect... until they say ridiculous and hurtful things in regards to race, I bang my head on the kitchen counter and say nothing.

When we tried to leave Walmart and my friend was stopped for no reason other than the color of his skin, my jaw dropped and words escaped me. He read the angry questions in my eyes: Should we report this? Who do we talk to? How can this still be happening? "Not worth it," he shrugged, and continued out of the store. So I said nothing.

And all my outraged nothings will never change anything.

So for me, to be white in America is to feel useless in matters of race, to feel that I have contributed to the pain of others, to understand just enough to know that I don't understand much, and to recognize that I feel impotent to affect change. I have a voice with no words, a place at the table without the stomach to really be present. I feel as though my eyes have been opened but my mouth can't quite articulate what I see.

For me, it has been a slow journey from racial cluelessness to increasing awareness. The friendships that I have made across racial lines have truly been the changing point, the place of discovery and insight that I needed to help me begin seeing the world for what it really is. I hope to continue to grow, to move from awareness to empowerment, to come to a place where I am less worried about what I bring to the discussion, and more focused on how the issues are affecting people every day.

Wondering what to say and who to say it to...that's what it's like (for me) to be white in America. ∎

Elena Harap

So Tactlessly Thwarted

AUTHOR'S NOTE: Some names and identifying details in this essay have been changed to protect the privacy of individuals.

IN 1954 I WAS A SIXTEEN-YEAR-OLD middle-class college-bound white girl in segregated Nashville, Tennessee. I was a junior, and a square. I was myopic and wore round glasses in plastic frames tapered like bat wings at the temples, white shirts with Peter Pan collars, pleated skirts, cinch belts, white socks, and penny loafers. It would be six years before a Fisk University undergraduate, Diane Nash[1] , would stand on the steps of the courthouse in Nashville, and confront Mayor Ben West on the issue of whites-only lunch counters in the city's department stores. "Do *you* feel it is wrong to discriminate against a person solely on the basis of their race or color?" Mayor West would answer 'yes' in full view of the media and the public. He later explained, "It was a moral question—one that a *man* had to answer, not a politician.[2]" Nashville merchants were somewhat relieved by West's answer and a few weeks later in May, six Nashville lunch counters began serving blacks. The students in Nashville had won an important victory.

During the 1950s, segregation was the only system I knew. Nashville's residential neighborhoods, schools, churches, eating places, restrooms, waiting rooms, buses, and movie theaters were segregated. There were, however, some exceptions. In junior high I had a friend

---

1   Diane Nash is a civil rights activist and was the leader and strategist of the student wing of the 1960s civil rights movement. In 1960, while a student at Fisk University, Nash led the Nashville sit-ins, which lasted from February-May.

2   Juan Williams, *Eyes on the Prize: America's Civil Rights Years, 1954-1965* (New York: Viking Penguin Inc., 1987), 138-140.

whose Quaker parents worked at Fisk; they were white administrators at a university founded for young black men and women. Located in North Nashville, Fisk University was half-an-hour's drive from my neighborhood south of downtown – an expanse of green lawns and brick classroom buildings where at the faculty level blacks and whites lived and worked side-by-side. My friend's father assisted the college president, Charles Johnson, while her mother ran the International Student Center. They lived in a comfortable frame house at the edge of campus, driving their children across town to attend all-white schools.

While visiting my friend's house on the Fisk campus, I met peers of any color. In addition, I belonged to a girls' club organized by another Quaker, Marian Fuson, whose husband taught chemistry at Fisk. A natural activist, Marian, a young mother, resisted Nashville's rigid color barrier by creating the "World Interest Club" in her home – a simple but quietly revolutionary project in which black and white girls planned and prepared meals from various countries, and ate together. Otherwise my world was separate and unequal.

Nashville was divided into "colored" and "white," and race meant some unalterable set of rules we were expected to know without question. A 1964 *Webster's New World Dictionary* defines *race* (from Latin *generatio,* a begetting) as anything from "major biological divisions of mankind," to "a group of plants or animals with distinguishing traits that are passed on to the offspring; breed." My friend Lynda Patton – a black studies teacher who looks for the biological truth within popular beliefs – observed that since human beings can reproduce with one another, and have fertile offspring we must all be the same race. On the matter of "biological divisions" the dictionary notes that "the term has acquired so many unscientific connotations that in this sense it is often replaced. . . by ethnic stock or group." This distinction makes sense to me; colors, ethnicities, and cultures differ, not race. In Nashville, colored and white were considered two distinct cultures, one privileged, one denied; a legacy of Southern slavery held in place by Jim Crow laws.

I speak from a white perspective about a particular moment in my adolescence when the South's system of segregation was challenged. A crack wedged open this wall of segregation when the Nashville Youth

Orchestra, where I played flute, attempted to desegregate itself, and managed to hold one rehearsal with both black and white performers before our decision was reversed. For a few hours, a group of hitherto estranged teenagers from both cultures experienced collegiality based on ability and a shared interest in classical music—after which the wedge was withdrawn, the crack closed, the experiment terminated. The young people went their separate ways, and I continued to live by the privileges that accrued to my complexion. It was only after decades spent away from the South that I confronted a deeply submerged sense of having failed my sisters, my brothers, and myself.

■ ■ ■

Now in my sixties and having lived for many years in Massachusetts and Vermont, I am a founding member of The Streetfeet Women—a tenacious little group of writers and performers in Boston representing a wide variety of cultural backgrounds. In 2000, I had to contribute to a Streefeet program for teenagers about formative moments in adolescence. I decided to revisit my own adolescent moment and pulled out a file of materials I'd kept for forty-six years, labeled "Nashville Youth Orchestra." It would be the first time in decades that I had looked at this file.

A mass of documents and images jostled inside a worn brown folder. The Constitution of the Nashville Youth Orchestra. Notes on meetings with the Nashville Symphony Board. Letters from public leaders supporting me, as an officer of the organization, in our effort to desegregate the orchestra and open it to Negro musicians. Clippings from the *New York Herald Tribune* reporting a Forum in which two anonymous girls, one colored and one white, from a southern town explained why they couldn't play their flutes together in the same orchestra. A photo booth strip taken at the airport capturing the girls themselves: my bat wing glasses, red lipstick smile, and houndstooth-checkered wool jacket, Grace Williams' luminous eyes, straightened hair, and velvet-collared tweed coat.

The story knitted up and unraveled very quickly in early 1954. The all-white high school orchestra, formed under the aegis of the (equally white) Nashville Symphony, was developing its first Constitution and By-laws, under the guidance of conductor Ralph Hall:

> Article III, Section I: Membership is open to qualified students between grades seven and sixteen...
> Section III: Playing ability and personal qualifications shall be the determining factors in the selection of members.

It happened that Robert Armer, the assistant conductor of the Youth Orchestra, was also my flute teacher. Mr. Armer was a graduate student in education at Peabody College for Teachers. Originally from Los Angeles, he was seen as an outsider who taught students from both sides of Nashville's color line. An intense, dark-haired, wiry man of enormous energy, he urged the members of the orchestra to consider the absurdity of barring students from Pearl High, Nashville's black public high school—which had a superb marching and concert band—from auditioning and playing with us. If we agreed, he would ask the Pearl High's band leader to recommend players for the Youth Orchestra.

I remember we voted in favor of desegregation, or, a term heard more and more at that time, *integration*. Then on Saturday, January 16th, the day of the auditions, we rehearsed for an hour at Peabody Demonstration School, a white school affiliated with Peabody College for Teachers, with both black and white applicants sitting in to fill vacant chairs. Then the judges (four first-chair players) and the applicants took their places, backs to each other, and the auditions began. Everyone had to play a scale and sight-read. Players were rated on intonation, rhythm, and tone quality. When a candidate tried out for a section that was already full, the entire section had to re-audition. Grace Williams, a flutist from Pearl High, placed second in my section, with her clear, lyrical sound. At the end of three hours, five black and two white students were accepted and invited to the next rehearsal. As a result of these auditions, two white students lost their chairs in the orchestra.

In the week between auditions and the first rehearsal, phones were ringing off the hook and complaints flowed to the Symphony Board. I was told later that music teachers whose students lost their places, were outraged and demanded restitution. There was talk of major donors withdrawing their support from the Symphony. On the following Friday, Mr. Armer brought the Youth Orchestra officers the shocking news that the Board had ordered us to disinvite the new players. As far as the Board was concerned, permission had never been granted, as it was claimed, to integrate the membership. The next morning, before our afternoon orchestra rehearsal, I had a flute lesson. "What will you tell the Pearl students?" Mr. Armer asked. As I saw it, the students and its officers were going to be the mouthpiece for the establishment, and be forced to enact Symphony Board's segregation policies. It was a crash course in bigotry.

Not long after this happened, I sat down at my typewriter and began writing about the incident. I wanted to create a record, something I could come back to if I wished. I also wanted as complete a picture of the situation as I could get, just for the sake of getting things straight in my head. I tried to sort out who did or did not give permission for the tryouts and auditions to proceed, why we were allowed to go ahead, and then told it hadn't been cleared. After a Youth Orchestra officers' meeting with the president and secretary of the Symphony Board, the conductors, and a member of the Ladies Guild, I came to this astonishing conclusion: No one who was present was actually at fault. No one was actually against integrating the Youth Orchestra.

If I can trust my own record-keeping, it appears that the president of the Symphony Board knowingly neglected to inform his Board of the auditions: *Mr. Mason [the President] knew that the board had disapproved the same question in regard to the Big Symphony, but he told Mr. Hall [the conductor] to go ahead. The Symphony Board as [a] whole knew nothing about the matter. . . I believe that Mr. Mason had an idea that if the whole thing were done quietly, it wouldn't raise a fuss. Exactly what he expected to be done I do not know... The Youth Orchestra, believing itself to have the authority, proceeded with auditions and accepted five Negro players and two whites.*

A power vacuum was created. "Let the kids try it," Mr. Mason could have reasoned, "If it works out, fine; if it doesn't, we'll tell them it's not time yet. I won't announce this to the whole Board; then if there is trouble I'll be able to say that the integration took place without proper authority. As for this man Armer, who is so chummy with the band leader over at Pearl High, he'll be leaving Nashville after he gets his degree, so why not let him invite some kids to this audition." Or perhaps he said something oblique to Ralph Hall which any southerner would have known meant NO; but Mr. Hall, not from the South, interpreted it as YES. Is this how change begins, an illusion of power that breaks some social taboo while a greater power allows the change so long as its own position remains secure? Did we fail? Did we contribute towards a movement for change? It was not a time when high school students were becoming part of a larger movement; this would happen a few years later. In the meantime, when the cards were put on the table, we ended up playing according to the old rules.

My record went on: *We said, should we kick out the white students who were new, if we were going to kick out the Negroes? The Board members there said that that was dodging the issue, which, as they saw it, was a racial one.*

We figured, although we didn't ask outright, that if we did not do what Mr. Mason said, the Board would be against it anyway, and if we didn't do what they said the Youth Orchestra probably wouldn't be, which wouldn't help anybody. There didn't seem to be anything else to do. My reasoning at sixteen years old didn't include dismantling an organization in order to rebuild it based on a more equitable model. This is why the very act of putting the facts on record is a measure of the turmoil I experienced during this time. Paralyzed, I felt there was no conceivable action except, as faithfully as possible, to witness.

And so, according to my notes, the outcome: *At the end of the rehearsal, we called in the Negro students... We said that the Board had not approved the auditions we had held and even though we wanted and desperately needed them in the orchestra, we couldn't keep them in or hold any more open auditions. It was horrible, but those students reacted with truly adult maturity. They said that they understood, and knew it was hard to do [a] thing like this. We told them that we, the Youth Orchestra Executive Committee, would present the matter before the Symphony Board and we all ended by saying that perhaps, somehow, it would work toward progress in the long run.*

My mind refuses to recapture the details of this scene. We had been rehearsing at the War Memorial Auditorium, the city's downtown concert hall. Did we call the black students into a side room? Did we wait until everyone had left to set up our meeting on the stage? According to my notes, adults from the Symphony organization were present; did they say anything? I can only remember that I stood up and carried out my responsibility by telling the black students they had to leave the orchestra. On a January afternoon, after a couple of hours of playing Mozart and Vaughan-Williams, I cooperated in an act destructive of music making and human dignity.

I have likewise repressed images of Mr. Mason and the other Board members who listened to the Youth Orchestra officers present our case after the damage had been done. These were ordinary white Southern patrons of the arts, some liberal, many of them conservative. On March 29th the Youth Orchestra officers met with them, still hoping we could get them to reverse their decision about the black musicians. I must have felt important, sitting down with representatives of wealth and power at the heavy oblong table in the Board's meeting room at the Third National Bank. In my record, I sketched a seating plan of where everyone sat at the table, and a second row behind them. There must have been about thirty people at this meeting.

What are the things we save, and why? I wonder about this folder of evidence I put together so carefully, wanting to believe that someone in authority would listen and take the right action. The file contains a carefully typed outline on a half sheet of recycled paper from my father's office, for our March 29th meeting–reviewing and assessing the situation, persuading the Board to act otherwise. In this way I organized my speech to the Symphony Board:

    I.   Getting Permission
        a.   Before orch. vote, asked Mr. Hall
        b.   Were told had Board's backing
        c.   Acted with that belief

   II. Week after
        a.   Told not to keep Negro players

    b. Met with Pres. of board
    c. Kicked out 5 members, held no more auditions
    d. All over now, but-

III. What did it mean?
    a. Individuals hurt
    b. Failure of democratic process
    c. Bad example; many people interested

IV. What could it mean?
    a. Wreck Symphony Association? No
    b. Support from unused sources
       1. 7 yrs. ago, more Negro ticket holders than now
       2. Other citizens who hadn't supported
    c. Would big Symphony have to follow?
       1. Leave it to youth
       2. In this case, not trouble with youth
       3. Youth Orch. vibrant–Louisville deal
       4. Better to have it in one organization than not at all
    d. If it were an actuality, many people wouldn't actively object
    e. Precedent set

V. What next?
    a. Accept first 5 in fall
    b. Hold open auditions then
    c. Know we have backing of Board.
    d. Must know decision soon.

As I review this material, the sixteen-year-old invites the sixty-six-year-old to go back, as if she might be more clear-eyed, "just for the sake of getting things straight." But things are more crooked than ever. I don't know whether to marvel at this honest, linear exposition of racism, ideals, compromises, and adjustments to keep the status quo, or to turn away in grief and humiliation from what happened, what could not be changed.

I also kept a note of the questions we were asked by the Board: *Have any other Southern Youth Orchestras admitted Negroes? There were some questions on how we held the auditions, how we got permission, etc. Mr. Hall and Mr. M. told just what they'd said to each other when Mr. H. called the Board Pres. to ask him what he thought of the idea. (This was right after the 1st vote.) One man asked us if we had ever tried to raise any money for the Symphony.* On April 14th we got our answer. On a sheet of legal-sized paper, a letter in the form of a resolution adopted by the Symphony Board and signed by a lawyer and Board member who had been appointed liaison with the Youth Orchestra stated the following:

"TO THE MEMBERS OF THE YOUTH ORCHESTRA OF NASHVILLE.

RESOLVED... That opportunities [to play and perform symphonic music] be provided in the same manner and by the same methods used by the public school system... that the Board... institute plans for the establishment of a Youth Orchestra for all of the negro youth of Nashville and Davidson County.

We... will faithfully endeavor to carry out this resolution... We offer you our continued sponsorship on this basis, and, with an honest apology for the misunderstanding, which existed too long, we urge your continued devotion to good music..."

That was the end. Nothing in my files suggests that the proposed Negro orchestra ever came about. In May of 1954 I wrote: *I recently learned (from talking to Grace and also from Mr. Armer) that... [Two Symphony Board members] visited all the students who were ousted from the Youth Orch, at their homes, and talked with them. Grace didn't say too much about what they said—I guess it was something similar to what was in the letter. She did say that they mentioned the idea of a Negro orchestra. I gathered that her reaction was one of disgust. She said she thought it was sort of "going backwards," and that the other kids felt the same way.*

Considering our world at that time, this ultimatum was driven by fear from our elders. During the controversy – I learned later from a friend – my mother was desperately fearful for my father's job as a professor of Curriculum Development at Nashville's Peabody College. Grace's parents might have known terror from the onset at possible reprisals by the Klan. We did not resist, as Diane Nash and her colleagues did six years later. We didn't hold hands and sing. No one taught us to analyze the socio-political issues in the context of a larger struggle. No whites quit the Youth Orchestra, except Assistant Conductor Bob Armer, who offered his resignation in protest, and bass clarinetist Dan Collins, who later went on to Juilliard and a professional career in New York. Grace and I, however, were invited to speak and perform a Baroque duet at a *New York Herald Tribune* Forum on "The Progress of Freedom in the United States," October 18, 1954.

We were flown to New York, my first air travel, and put up at the Waldorf-Astoria. I remember the dishes room service brought to our room, the lamb chop Grace had ordered revealed in solitary splendor under its silver cover. We posed in the airport for a strip of instant photographs and I wrote to my older sister on Waldorf letterhead: *This is just to prove that I actually did stay at the Waldorf... We told our story of the Youth Orchestra – I, from my point of view, and Grace as one of the Negro students who had to withdraw from the orchestra. Afterwards we tooted our flutes for the audience, which they loved. They liked the novelty, I suppose; whether they will remember what we said, I don't know. The thing was held at the Hunter College auditorium, a big, beautiful hall; we sat in the audience and only came up to speak, since we were both supposed to be kept completely anonymous, including the city we came from.*

Our segment of the program that evening was titled "Contrasting Approaches," with the subheading "In a Southern City: Two High School Girls." Governor Thomas E. Dewey opened the Forum; Margaret Just Butcher of the Board of Education in Washington spoke on "The Washington D.C. Story," Charles Johnson of Fisk, a sociologist as well as president of the University, on "How Soon Will Southern Schools be Integrated?," and Thurgood Marshall delivered the remarks, "Steps Ahead." At the reception, we were introduced to the tall and courtly future Supreme Court Justice; we stood around as New York newspaper folk chatted over cocktails. I heard a guest asking the *Tribune* music critic, "How were they?" and he replied, "They were all right; a little out of tune."

At seventeen, I'd written of the Forum experience almost as a lark rather than as the result of conflict, anguish, and deprivation, unaware that while my parents supported the action I had taken, they were also at risk. I never learned how the *Tribune* got wind of Nashville's Youth Orchestra crisis or who decided to send us to New York. We flew home, back to flute lessons with Mr. Armer, and occasional chamber music performances at the Fisk University Chapel. Resilient, we went on with our lives because that was what you did. I eventually lost contact with Grace, although I heard she was playing first chair in the Oak Ridge Symphony in East Tennessee, and later on became a chairman of the National Parent-Teachers Organization. I remained an amateur flutist. I remained a mind bent and shaped by the events of spring 1954.

Recently, I phoned my high school classmate Dan Collins, the lanky, laid-back, abundantly talented bass clarinet player who chose to quit the Youth Orchestra when it became clear that segregation was the order of the day. "I haven't thought about it for years," he said, "but I remember those Pearl High students—there was a bassoonist, a clarinetist, and a flutist, who came to my house in the country when we were trying to get them into the orchestra."

"They went to your house?" I was incredulous. White kids in Nashville didn't invite black kids to rehearse in their homes. "I could never have done that," I exclaimed. "I didn't even ask my parents," Dan went on. "Nothing was said—at least I don't remember anything." He lived in a rural town and commuted into Nashville to attend our high school.

"Did Mr. Armer arrange that rehearsal?" I asked. "I know he taught and coached at Pearl High and he knew the band director, Mr. Gunther."

"I guess he did. You know, Bob Armer persuaded me to go to Interlochen in Michigan in 1953, and in 1954 he helped me get a scholarship. There were a few black students there, not very many, but at least I had some exposure. But I didn't see the Pearl kids after I left the Youth Orchestra."

"So you knew these students before they auditioned, and then they were told they couldn't stay. You had a personal connection. Maybe that had to do with your dropping out. I never even thought of quitting."

"Yes, it just seemed like we weren't getting anywhere, so that was the right thing to do. I remember another Symphony member trying to convince me that it wasn't a good idea."

"Maybe that's why you didn't think about it a lot afterwards. I was left with a feeling of failure and guilt that haunts me to this day." Maybe, I thought, there's an inverse ratio between the degree of resistance to evil, and the emotional fallout afterwards.

We exchanged email addresses and hung up, Dan promising to record further recollections of 1954. Two different stories, two different levels of maturity. I reflected that even in high school Dan had grasped the loss for the black students from the point of view of a professional musician. Their schools weren't funded for orchestra, only band. Some of these players, who were approaching college and possible music careers with no experience in orchestral playing, would be competing with students like myself who had been playing in a school orchestra since the fourth grade. As I was planning on becoming an English teacher, I had no interest in being a professional musician. Preoccupied with maintenance of the orchestra as an organization, I never considered that its demise might not be such a disaster, that it was already compromised.

■ ■ ■

My state of mind as time went on—a muddle of disappointment, anger, and self-blame—was brilliantly and presciently presented by a black parent who wrote to the president of the Nashville Symphony Board, in February 1954. He was John Hope II, Director of Industrial Relations in the Division of Race Relations at Fisk University, a researcher, respected sociologist, and a man familiar with the insanities of racism. His letter still awes and comforts me. With the utmost civility and dignity, Mr. Hope laid out both the black and white issues and differing perspectives, unsparingly indicting the system of segregation. I quote most of this letter because it affirms that when moral violence is done, the privileged person is degraded as well as the one abused; and that the sense of responsibility and the urgency with which I continue to explore this story and its sequels, are natural and predictable.

FROM A LETTER BY JOHN HOPE II
TO THE PRESIDENT, CIVIC MUSIC
ASSOCIATION, NASHVILLE, TENNESSEE,
FEBRUARY 17, 1954

Dear Sir:

I am advised that in recent weeks your Association has countermanded the decision of the Youth Orchestra as a whole to open its competition for membership to all qualified students on the basis of their musical skill and ability without regard to race. If this is true, I wish to register my sincere regret as a parent of children whose aspirations for the full development of their musical talents are restricted by such a policy of exclusion and whose motivation to reach their full musical potentialities has already been seriously weakened by this incident although neither has suffered the indignity of having this door to opportunity opened to them and then quickly closed. *The psychological and social impact of your action, however, upon the white youth who thus sought to implement their belief in democratic living and were apparently so tactlessly thwarted may be much more serious over the coming months and years.* [Emphasis added]

It is difficult for me to comprehend how young people with the sensitivity and intelligence to interpret and execute the music of Bach and Beethoven can be rationally convinced that their action was inappropriate. Knowing the critical independence of my own children, I cannot help being happy that I do not have to present a justification for this action. Many of the young people who saw fit to take the action which has apparently been repudiated by the Association will find it difficult to understand or accept the verdict in the light of the immediate futures many of them face. Some of them will be going into other sections of the country as students or to work under unsegregated conditions, others will be joining various branches of the armed forces where they will work, play, and fight under unsegregated conditions whether they are in the North or South; Europe or Asia. They will be taking arms to protect and preserve the democratic way of life which this action appears to deny. I ask that you search your own conscience closely... before taking the responsibility for an action which runs counter to the more progressive trend in the South as well as in the nation and the world at large. I view this unfortunate incident as an opportunity for the elite of our community to rise to the full stature implied by our boast that Nashville is the "Athens of the South" and the center of music and culture of this area. We can affirm and strengthen our city's right to such titles or prove them false in the eyes of our children and our nation.

Sincerely yours,
John Hope II
Director of Industrial Relations

■ ■ ■

Coda

ON MAY 17, 1954, the Supreme Court's decision in *Brown v. Board of Education* declared school segregation unconstitutional, saying in summary that legally-sanctioned segregation of white and Negro children in public schools purely on the basis of color was illegal because separate facilities are inherently unequal. Nashville began a grade-a-year process of desegregation that worked its way to the high school level sometime in the 1970s. The Symphony, of course, was released from its excuse for starting an all-black orchestra, and at some point abandoned its segregationist position. By the early 1960s, a Nashville jazz player and successful studio musician named Bob Holmes taught string classes for black children who still had no orchestra training at school, and created an all-black youth orchestra in Nashville called Cremona Strings. One of Holmes' students, Kay George Roberts, became a conductor and returned to lead a Nashville Symphony outdoor park concert the summer after she received her PhD from Yale.

In March 1967, thirty years old and pregnant with my first child, I was still wrestling with memories of 1954. I wrote from my home in Boston to Dr. C. B. Hunt of the Peabody College Music faculty to see how the Youth Orchestra was doing. *I think my own life was deeply affected by that Youth Orchestra incident. At any rate I now find myself working for a settlement house in a Negro neighborhood and participating in an exciting inter-racial theatre in Cambridge. With perspective of time and the things I've learned through our theatre group, I wonder why it did not seriously occur to me to resign from the Youth Orchestra when the Negro players were dismissed; why I accepted the Symphony Board's decision so passively. I hope you will be able to tell me that the situation has changed for the better!*

Hunt replied: *I remember quite well your efforts in the Youth Orchestra and mine as a member of the Board of Directors of the Symphony. Although it seemed to both of us at the time that we had failed, it seems apparent now that something happened during the middle 50's. . .The proposal to develop an All-Negro youth symphony never went through . . . At the present time, students compete for and receive places in the Youth Symphony regardless of any factors other than musicianship. . . there are always several, sometimes as many as 15 or 20, Negroes in the Youth Symphony. The situation is the same with the Nashville Symphony Orchestra though not in such great numbers. Annual auditions are held and the best players are selected regardless of any other factors.*

Having gone through my Nashville Youth Orchestra file with its yellowed documents, I wrote my theatre piece for Streetfeet; it was read by the group at Brattleboro High School in Vermont in the spring of 2000. I am still myopic, still an amateur musician, and more or less square. This story is never complete. And the conversations continue. "What you felt wasn't guilt," my friend Lynda tells me with sisterly authority, "it was *motivation*." ■

Amie Heasley

From a White Mother to Her Black Daughter

DEAR AVA:

Your mother has never felt the sound of the doors of an idling minivan locking. She doesn't know the sting of a cashier who winces at brushing fingertips during a routine shopping transaction. She won't experience the shun of another pedestrian crossing the street to avoid passing her by.

On July 13, 2013, your mother spent much of the day reflecting on the verdict. You probably are (and definitely were) too young to remember that day or that verdict. Nevertheless, your mother ached for the family of Trayvon Martin. If she's honest, she ached for you, too.

Your mother cannot imagine what it would be like to lose you. She cannot imagine what it would be like to lose you to gun violence. She cannot imagine what it would be like to lose you to gun violence because you wore a hoodie, because you decided to walk through a gated community, because of the color of your skin.

How should your mother, a white, middle-aged woman, explain this fear to you?

It's the one that scares her most. The conversation about black and white that's miles from black and white. It will be harder than the birds and the bees. Tougher still than the heart-to-heart about your spending nine months in another woman's tummy. The color of your skin is not the same color as your mother's. There is no gray in this truth. Your mom wishes this discussion was as silly and carefree as that *Saturday Night Live* skit imitating Frank Sinatra and Stevie Wonder: "You are black. I am white. Life's an Eskimo Pie, let's take a bite."

Your blackness versus her whiteness. This wasn't a topic your mom ever dreamt she would've had to explore. Her path to having a child scarred her to the point where she doubted becoming, being anybody's mom. Flash forward to now, and wham, she is your mother—the suburban, white forty-year-old woman with an adopted, black twenty-three-month-old daughter. When you are older, you'll realize that succinctness doesn't come easy to your mom. So here's her way of saying it plain: it's less complicated to say only that you're her daughter. Because that's how she feels. You are hers and she is yours. Your mother understands that might not always be enough for you or the world around you.

Like many white kids, your mom grew up on a standard mantra: "This is the United States of Colorblind. If you work hard enough, play by the rules, pull up the bootstraps, blah-blah-blah, the American dream will become your American way of life." Yet Jennifer Harvey, associate professor of religion at Drake University, wrote: "These statements are so abstract they're mostly meaningless when handed to a seven- (or even seventeen) year-old. That's at best. At worst, they're empty filler—stand-ins for the actual conversations about race, racial difference and racism we need to be having with our kids. Sugar when our kids need protein."

(Sorry for quoting somebody else's words, but if you haven't noticed, your mom needs all the help she can get. How else is she going to fill your head—your heart—with the protein Ms. Harvey recommends?)

Ava, we are living in an unprecedented time. Some have said it's a post-racial time. After all, Americans elected a black president. Twice. Americans, however, also acquitted a white man who stalked and killed an unarmed black boy. Yes, a boy. Seventeen years old should be defined as a boy in any parent or non-parent's book.

The death of Trayvon Martin left your white mother wondering if justice for blacks in America will ever, in the words of Martin Luther King Jr., "roll down like water." Whether people think George Zimmerman stood his ground or acted in self-defense is a mere bruise on a rotten apple. Black president or not, racism continues to fester. There are lingering scabs to dig and disinfect. White people must stand up and open their mouths. They must take an active role in the digging and disinfecting, no matter their embarrassment, discomfort or flat out inadequacy. Yes, sweet girl, in your home, too. Your mother must summon the courage to spark the dialogue. Scratch that. Your mother must splay the dialogue. Splay the wound. Your mother must attempt to put into words what the outcome of George's trial and Trayvon's death will mean for you, a black girl raised in a white household in an America that whitewashes racism.

Forgive her again, Ava, but your mom has another citation to share: Studies have shown that parents of children of color are much more likely to talk to their kids about race and racism than white parents. Parents of color must teach their children how to survive in a racially inequitable society, while still maintaining racial pride and positive self-esteem (Hale-Benson, 1990; Hughes et al., 2006; Lesane-Brown, 2006).

How can your mother, who has thrived within a system stacked in her favor, begin to skew this research, at least in her own home?

Because you are black, you will confront a lifetime of discrimination. If you become a mother, you might also learn that having a black daughter is not the same as having a black son. Though it's troubling to admit, this detail played a role in your mom and dad's decision to adopt you. Your parents were open to all races, but did state a preference for a girl. (They had a choice, unlike black parents of black sons.)

Your mother (in particular) had reservations about raising a black son. In America. In 2011. The year the one and only amazing you arrived. This was well before headlines carried the names Trayvon Martin and George Zimmerman.

When you are in high school, will these two names appear in our nation's history books? Will you read about the #BlackLivesMatter movement? Speaking of reading, you hand deliver the same book to your mom or dad night after night at your bedtime. It's an alphabet book, and when the story reaches the letter "u," the animal "u" represents is a unicorn. Your mother has a confession: she has often made fun of the fact that the animal "u" represents a unicorn. Aren't there any real animals that begin with "u"? She doesn't know. What she does know is true equality remains a unicorn in this country, especially for black men. As your mom, the mother of an adopted child, which will yield similar and different challenges than a biological child, she couldn't stomach that truth. Your mother couldn't handle the risk of her black little boy being shot for, let's say, playing with a Nerf gun.

Before your adoption, your parents went through various "training" classes, including a class on interracial adoption. Most of what your mom and dad gleaned at that class was beyond duh, beyond cliché, but it did shed some worthwhile light. A black woman adopted by a white family came to the class, told stories of her upbringing and allowed the group to ask her anything. Every question was safe.

Can I straighten my black daughter's hair by giving her a home perm?

Did you play with white kids?

Did you date white guys?

Why don't black people like casseroles?

Plenty of the questions and answers brought laughter. Plenty of the questions and answers brought surprising information, too.

White parents teach their white kids not to talk to strangers, to wash their hands after going to the bathroom and before eating, to say please and thank you, to drink from a cup and ride a bicycle, to put away their markers and Legos, to use their words, not their fists. Your mother is oversimplifying. Generalizing. It isn't her intention to patronize these responsibilities, but black parents have to, as John Metta wrote, give their kids "'The Talk.' When they are sat down at the age of five or so and told that their best friend's father is not sick, and not in a bad mood—he just doesn't want his son playing with you." Black parents shoulder the added burden of having to teach their black sons things like, "NEVER run alone in public." If a young black man is seen running down the street, the immediate perception is he's done something wrong. He's running from something or somebody. He's a punk. He "looks like he's up to no good." He's one of "these assholes" who "always gets away" (George Zimmerman).

Your mom walked out of that interracial training session more concerned than ever about the prospect of adopting a black son. While she doesn't regret the decision to state a preference for adopting a girl (it gave your mom and dad you), she does regret past prejudicial thoughts she's had about black men. Yes, the suburban, white forty-year-old woman with an adopted, black twenty-three-month-old daughter has had racist thoughts. She has also directly and routinely benefited from institutionalized racism. Not a single white person is immune, but owning the disease, Ava, is the first step toward redemption.

Not long after the ruling, the president said: "You know, when Trayvon Martin was first shot, I said that this could have been my son. Another way of saying that is Trayvon Martin could have been me thirty-five years ago. And when you think about why, in the African American community at least, there's a lot of pain around what happened here, I think it's important to recognize that the African American community is looking at this issue through a set of experiences and a history that doesn't go away."

Your white mother can and should do her best to prepare you, her black daughter, but she must also brace herself for your reality. Your mom is afraid for you. It doesn't paralyze her from living or stop her from mothering, but the anxiety is palpable. Your mother wants to spare you from prejudice, a pain she will never know. (Can anybody prevent pain they cannot know?) She wants to shield you from profiling, violence, her own internalized racism, ignorance, media distortion and bias, injustice, political agendas, adults who gun down kids for wearing baggy sweatshirts with hoods—just about anything and everything besides catching fireflies in July and eating ice cream sandwiches for breakfast.

It is quite possible you could one day have a boyfriend who resembles Trayvon. You could take a shortcut through a nearby neighborhood with him on your way home from school. You could be followed by somebody who thinks your boyfriend who resembles Trayvon looks suspicious.

You could hear the doors of a minivan lock as you cross its path. You could feel the disgust of a sales clerk who evades sprinkling your change into your palm. You could watch another fellow human being retreat to the opposite side of the road. All and only because you are black.

You will look to your mom for answers to why well after your "Why Phase." She will search and struggle for the perfect response when there's no such thing. Another unicorn.

Someday, maybe an unseasonably warm and bright evening after daycare or school, you will ask your mother if you are black and what being black means. In America. In 20__? She promises she will give you an answer. Please bear with her, she might blurt something flimsy or blubber something sentimental. She might put her arms around you, even though the last thing you want to do is hug your mother. She might ask you more questions than you'll ask her.

Your mom might mumble, she might stutter or falter, but she will speak. She will offer you a space and a place to respond. She won't rush or pressure or judge. She will wait and trust the words to come.

All her hope and love,

Your Mother. ■

Benjamin V. Marshall

How I Became White

I DID NOT USE A BLEACHING CREAM or any other lightening techniques or whatever it was that the late Michael Jackson used to whiten his face. I have neither the patience nor money to undergo elective, cosmetic surgery. In fact, I did not realize that I was being treated as white until after it had happened. White, in this case, has almost become the synonym for middle-class, reliable and credit worthy. I have been in the same job and house for a while but the circumstances around me have shifted. Like a giant kaleidoscope where the pieces of glass twist into a different pattern or a fun house mirror that reflects not me but the others around me, I stayed the same, but how others saw me, more specifically how the banking industry perceived me, altered my racial designation.

It was not always as such. I am frequently mistaken for something other than what I am, sometimes different races within the same week. I have been dissed at Denny's just like others, and like other blacks, I did the happy dance when that branch where the incident happened closed and the property sold and was made into a parking lot. Another time, in a Sears, a black woman complained that the white man in front of her, meaning me, was being treated better than she was. In a Neiman Marcus a few years later, when I tried to make a purchase of some cologne, a white sales clerk informed me that the store did not take credit cards, assuming that since I was black—she perceived me as black which possibly meant I was poor or a thief. Who needs this crap when you are just picking out a leaf blower or cologne? Lately, I've been shopping online a lot.

There's an old *Saturday Night Live* sketch of Eddie Murphy, who with help of elaborate make up is disguised as white and middle-class.

He passes as such. When he and the proprietor of the newsstand are alone, Eddie tries to pay for a newspaper, and the proprietor reminds him to just take it. "Take it" says the proprietor. "Come on. You know the rules." And Eddie Murphy, reluctant to conform, takes the newspaper and leaves no money, realizing that white skin has quite a bit of privilege with everyday items.

I went through something similar, whose pleasing outcome also left me confused.

The recent economic downturn took its toll on a great many households, though not mine and not my brother's or sister's. This is a post-*Raisin in the Sun* story. It's post-Jeffersons, too. It's not about moving into the neighborhood where the others run screaming from you. It's not about moving on up. We tightened our belts and scrimped but none of us lost our houses or were forced into real deprivation. It's just the opposite. It's about refinancing a mortgage. A honky problem. A first world, honky problem. A problem that turned me white.

A few years ago, I applied to refinance my mortgage through my credit union in order to take advantage of the lower interest rates. I never anticipated any real difficulty. After all, my primary mortgage was with them. I once had a home equity loan to refurbish the bathroom. The bathroom is completed, and that loan was paid off. I had a good credit history with no delinquencies. The credit union was now my primary bank with direct deposit and a savings account. The real bona fides of middle-class credit worthiness. The first world identity and concerns. And the first world identity still means white, no matter how attractive the TV commercials are cast, with tall, caramel and mocha colored actors, shaved heads and controlled 'fros. Still I know what I had to go through in order to apply for a lower credit rate. I've gone through enough paperwork to know the application process. So I was more than surprised when the credit union turned me down. Yet not turned down, directly. The most apt phrase is intentionally discouraged.

With this application, I was told that the mortgage and refinancing people that used to be in the local branch were now ensconced in some central office where there was no direct contact with the public. All the mortgages had to go through one man, a man whose last name sounded like a woman's secondary sex organs. He must have been teased mercilessly throughout his school years. Evidently, he took out his frustrations on so many around him. I sent in the application, and after two weeks, I called to make sure the paperwork was received.

The mortgage man did not contact me directly, but he sent word through one harried woman or another that I was to contact him. And that I should send in the secondary paperwork – pay stubs and W2 forms – again.

After sending the paperwork to him a second time, he insisted, through an intermediary, to fax the paperwork. I did. I had a fax machine at home. I asked that they contact me to let me know if they received the forms. They said that they did not. A few weeks went by and I contacted them, yet again. I managed to speak to the Mortgage Man, Mr. Women's-Secondary-Sex-Organs. He asked for a photo copy of my driver's license to be faxed. I did so. They asked which phone number to contact me: the landline, office or cell. I said landline. They always called the office. Two weeks after our last conversation, I called to find out the status, and nothing had been done with the application. Again he asked for yet another copy of my driver's license. This was the third copy, and the fact that faxes of my driver's license number were now being used for either wall paper or toilet paper did not thrill me.

Mr. Women's-Secondary-Sex-Organs said they would call with their decision. I reminded him again to call my landline number.

A couple of months later, my application was denied. The given reason was that the applicant apparently did not care anymore. Angry at being rejected but somewhat relieved that I did not have to deal with the rigmarole anymore, I looked at my paperwork and wondered what was awry – pay check stubs, proof of ownership and driver's license. I scanned until I saw one thing I marked. On the application is a place for demographic information. Where they asked for race, I was honest and checked the box marked "Black" for African American. As I have always done. My zip code is often designated as "ghetto," although there are sections of my neighborhood with magnificent houses, some even featured in the *The New York Times*. My house is not one of them. It's just average. This apparently meant less than ideal. And it was all determined by numbers and a man who refused to believe the credit worthiness no matter how many times I supplied proof.

After about a year, a local commercial bank offered a new program to refinance. Cautiously, I made the inquiry and was sent the application. At home, I came to the demographic question again. Black, White, Native American, Asian. I agonized a little. This bank doesn't know me. They'll look at this and throw the application right out. Rates were lower, but the restrictions were tighter. There were news stories of people being rejected, right, left and center. Then I saw the little box at the end of the list of racial identities. "Choose not to respond." "Cool," I thought. That's the box I marked. Choose not to respond. I set-up an appointment to meet with the loan officer.

I entered the bank. I met the loan officer whom I'm calling Sarah. This is not her real name. Sarah was clearly from an Asian country, and since I have taught English to foreign students for a few years, I am not deterred by accents, nor confused by immigrants as gatekeepers. Also, being a little old school, I wore a jacket and carried my school brief case into the bank. I was a sharp contrast to another man, a tall white guy in jeans and flip-flops, who was also applying for a loan.

Sarah quietly gave the side-eye to the other man sitting at her coworker's station. Sarah's coworker was also Asian. I assumed that the man had issues being screened for a loan. Everything that the neighboring loan officer said, the man said "no" with almost undisguised hostility. This other man seemed to torture the loan officer with his stubborn refusal to provide information. Sarah turned her eyes to me and saw a quiet, softly spoken man in a jacket, a college professor, with a brief case, armed with extra copies of pay stubs and W2 forms. I handed Sarah the application form. I froze for a moment as she scanned the page with the demographic. She paused on that page. Now, I am fair skinned. And as I stated before, I have been mistaken for any number of ethnicities and races. I assumed that Sarah would reject me then and there, but she told me only that I had neglected to sign one line. I signed. She happily took the application, remarking how I was so prepared, and said that I would have to wait up to four weeks to be approved.

It took less than two.

She arranged for a building inspector as part of the application process. The building inspector came and appraised my house for more than I thought and even cut me a deal on the flood insurance because of the designation on the flood zone. My house is just on the edge of a flood zone – and miles from the nearest thing that could be construed as a navigable body of water. The inspector, who was independent and not a bank employee, also seemed happy with a cooperative client and made the decision that flood insurance was not necessary. Thus I was saved a great yearly expense. But this was just another example of how I was now not considered a risk therefore more things were given to me. I received the reduced rate. Sarah could not have been more pleased if she had received the check herself. I celebrated with friends.

What am I to get from all this? The perceptions of Mr. Female-Secondary-Sex-Organs and Sarah the Asian immigrant could be seen as emblematic of two business styles. The one, impersonal, dismissing the statistics and scores, and considering only the box marked "Black." And there is the other who sat down and saw me eye to eye and saw someone with proper business attire, a professional demeanor and the income level to back it up. And let's face it, I really don't know if Mr. Female-Secondary-Sex-Organs was actually white, or if he focused only on race, All I heard was a voice full of condescension, boredom and disdain. My prejudging him is just as bad as his misjudging me.

I felt a cringe of remorse for not admitting my heritage, and for keeping it secret just for the sake of something as mercantile as a better mortgage rate. If I had to deny my heritage, I hoped it would have to be for a far more noble cause, like keeping secrets from the Nazis, infiltrating the KKK, or defeating ISIS.

The title of this article is misleading, as I have not become white. Rather, I chose not to choose and was presumed to be more reliable and therefore, white by default. Is this what it means to be white, to be secure in your place in the world? Is the disguise the reality? Is the omission of racial identity a practical way to get what you want? Is the disguise the way to thrive when one's authentic self can cost you? ∎

"It is precisely this black-white experience which may prove of indispensable value to us in the world we face today. The world is no longer white, and it will never be white again."

— James Baldwin, "Stranger in the Village"
James Baldwin: Collected Essays by Toni Morrison (1998)

AFTERWORD

■ ■ ■

Tara Betts

Humidity Clinging to All of Us

AS I WAS READING THROUGH *What Does it Mean to be White in America?*, a range of thoughts I've had about race over the years swept over me in waves. At times, the thoughts I had felt like a film clinging to my skin on a sticky July afternoon without air conditioning, a palpable and inescapable feeling in the air. Many poets of color used to go where Taylor Mali (a teacher and slam poet) once had an upscale Manhattan penthouse apartment. It was there he asked "What does it mean to be white? What's good about being white?" Many of them were befuddled about coming up with a thoughtful response, but I think among these eighty-two personal essays, there are some possible answers to that question.

As a way of linking this text to a host of writers and thinkers who have grappled with race, and whiteness in particular, I wanted to mention some other texts that underscore the importance of discussing whiteness and why this book is furthering that conversation. One of the remarkable things about this collection is how much critical self-examination and concrete actions individuals can undertake. These more personal takes could be discussed and taught in tandem with a range of other books that address ways of thinking across disciplines of academic study and public debate. The truth is some of the voices allow some people to speak frankly for the first time. The writings here address how the idea of whiteness impacts how people relate to other people and larger cultural phenomena, and it is based on them being identified as white. Tim Wise, a publicly vocal ally, even as he reiterates what critical race theorists of color have already said, has written some useful texts. Patricia J. Williams' *The Alchemy of Race and Rights* is another possibility. One of the other texts that the contributors mentioned included Toni Morrison's *Playing in the Dark,* which discusses how whiteness is often defined by the barometer of blackness, and definitely appears in a few of the essays. Thandeka's *Learning to Be White* considers the trauma of being separated from other human beings and realizing that this behavior is how learning to be white impacts the humanity of everyone touched by it. Dr. Joy DeGruy's work is a helpful resource too. Thoughtful essays by Eula Biss, Claudia Rankine's *Citizen,* Ta-Nehesi Coates, Richard Wright, bell hooks, W. E. B. DuBois are all names that make an impact on the thinking of writers here, but so do white radicals and activists of color. There is even a nod to poets in spoken word, like Scott Woods and Jamila Lyiscott, two out of many within a tradition of poetry that has created a remarkable entry into identity politics conversations for communities across the U.S. and online. So, in many ways, this book is expanding a conversation that educators, organizers, and book clubs can continue.

In furthering conversations about whiteness, *What Does it Mean to be White in America?* elaborates on not just voices and representations, it acts as a sort of handbook. Some people will ask: How do I start to talk about whiteness? How can I be a better ally? How can I actively address racism? A great many of these writings are not just defining what it means to be white in social situations, but offer concrete steps to challenge racism and misconceptions about whiteness. How do some people begin to challenge dilemmas that they never had to deal with, or the challenges that foment hostility between races? This collection features people who ask these sorts of questions by acknowledging that other people experience them, inquire about how they can change these circumstances, see a parallel with their own experiences, or offer concrete steps for that change.

This book is not a dismissal of the hard conversations or a series of evasive moves. I have recalled how white people have told me that they are one-sixteenth Choctaw or Cherokee, when they have never set foot on a reservation, or how they would be terrified to be on the West or South Sides of Chicago, even if a bullet never rang its call. What does it mean to be white in a predominantly black neighborhood, a restaurant, a retail store, or a bank waiting to hear back about a loan application? And more importantly, some of the contributors ask what role should I take in addressing whiteness honestly without being patronizing or resentful. Everyone brings their experiences with whiteness to the table, even if one is not white. Lately, I have been thinking of W. E. B. DuBois' idea of double-consciousness, the notion that people of color have been keenly aware of what white people think, yet the reverse is often not clear because we are living in a time where whiteness is changing and becoming more complex. It is not just about power or the standard of beauty. It is also about figuring out how the rankings of whiteness by class, color, and relationships are becoming more complicated.

I would be remiss if I did not discuss my own relationship to whiteness as a mixed woman who identifies as black. My white mother affirmed my identity(ies) in ways that people I hold near and dear did not always experience. It is particularly telling that white parents raising children of color are teaching their children lessons about race that my mother taught my brothers and me. I know that sometimes I could slip by unnoticed if I kept my mouth shut, but if I spoke up or if people looked closely, they wondered about my nose, the bass in my voice, my frames of reference. I am the same color as my white mother, but I was often the one who spoke up when my friends were harassed in college. Usually, I have only been followed in stores when I have been thought to be Latina, but I know and I watch how people respond to other black people, even when I am not the recipient of racial profiling. Sometimes, I have literally seen people look confused until the moment of realization dawns upon them. *She's one of them,* and I don't flinch. Benjamin V. Marshall's essay touches upon this awareness of being seen as white and not identifying as white. After one loan application is denied, Marshall declines to check the box that defines him as "black," he goes to another bank. He is aware that his appearance as white confers benefits. However, it is not always possible to pick and choose when racial identity is disclosed, and some people will not ever deny the family members that look "less white" than other people. Those moments of being seen as white, especially when you've been called racial epithets or experienced discrimination, can be discombobulating and infuriating.

Moments in my own life compel me to consider what does it mean to deal with Latino people, Asian people, and Native American/First Nation people? What does it mean to have people view a mixed race child as somehow less than their mother or father? When someone wonders what it means to be the mother of a black child, someone might be able to look toward Amie Heasley's letter to her daughter and Julie Parson-Nesbitt's essay. What does it mean to have a black sibling via trans-racial adoption or marriage? So, the visual representations of race and families are going to force that conversation, even our soon-to-be-outgoing President Obama had a mother very much like my own, and his presence has opened up a reactionary racist response that seems to be magnified by some of the xenophobic attacks by Trump supporters. Several articles have said Obama has received more death threats than any other president of the United States. Many of them have been racially motivated. Sadly, it speaks to the reality that many people still experience what Public Enemy called "Fear of a Black Planet," but this book is tackling other fears too.

How terrifying can it be to think you may be racist or benefit from racism, much like the interracial couple in a Buzzfeed video sketch. In it, the couple visits an ancestry.com-like website company and the white partner discovers her ancestors owned her fiancé's ancestors. Who would want to claim that? On the other hand, if you're a person of color, there are days when you might wish for whiteness, not because it is the standard of beauty and success, but because it would be liberating. Imagine not thinking about discrimination or racial profiling for a day, a week, a month, or a year. What could you accomplish with the time and no need to decompress from the daily stress of being non-white? So, of course there is talk of white guilt, white privilege, and intersectionality on these pages. It's an inevitable conversation that is becoming more impossible to avoid.

This anthology is a step toward complicating language around racial identity and negotiating what white people must consider as their families become less white, as the United States looks more like a global reality, and people of all sorts engage in dismantling white privilege. As I was writing, one of my friends said "Being white means never having to answer what 'being white' means." The statement was reminiscent of one of the early scenes in the 1992 film *Deep Cover* when Laurence Fishburne is asked, "What is the difference between a black man and a nigger?" Fishburne responds with "The nigger is the one who would answer that question." In a falsely-named post-racial era, black people never would have to consider such a question if the era was really post-racial, and white people would have already interrogated whiteness as many of the contributors in this book have begun doing, so this is a good beginning, no matter how uncomfortable.

Some of the notable essays make the multiplicities of the white experience artful and evident. Poet Martha Collins' extended metaphor of snowfall and representations of whiteness that are gradually melting away (and need to melt) struck me. Jan Priddy's cataloging of white objects connects those objects to memories of her own experiences. Christina Berchini itemizes and challenges many of the common responses that are evident of a lot more work that needs to be done. Although I see "white privilege" as a systematic presence that affects how individuals have been conditioned to respond in particular situations, I want to know more about the full story of why some of the women Darci Halstead Garcia worked with were unhappy. Even Garcia makes a point in favor of looking at individual people and the multiple sides of a story. Sidney Kidd's essay is conversational and anecdotal in a way that makes poverty and discrimination based on class compelling, and reveals some of the honest talks that happen between individuals. When Carole Gozansky Garrison says "goodness wasn't the province of white people," the shift may be as simple as noticing that people, including people of color are helpful and kind, not in a "magical Negro" or subservient context, but as human beings, much like the specific acts that allied do according to Janie Starr. Abe Lateiner reflects in his poetic hybrid essay on the ominous presence of blood oozing and spilling over the simple joys of every life that are tainted by knowing the violence perpetrated on people of color who may not experience some of the same joys.

Even when I cringed as I read a couple of the preceding essays, I considered that some things need to be said, yet I also found myself thinking of Meg J. Petersen saying "Whiteness is seductively simple when you settle into it because only *your* perspective, *your* discomfort, *your* inconvenience matters."

To me, these sorts of "inconveniences" make a story like J. Kates' "August 1965" even more compelling. Kates considers how race and class are paired in the organizing of black steam-laundry workers stymied by children of the KKK, which leads to his fleeing Mississippi before sundown and continuing to work with SNCC in Harlem. Anne Mavor's essay on embracing the histories of her white ancestors also looks at what it means to have hindsight and know your origins, but also being thoughtful about acting more conscientious with people of color in the present. Historical context from essays by Sara Estes, Gil Fagiani, Kates, Mavor, and Bonnie Schell make the need for examining whiteness here even more salient.

When a rabbi addresses how Jews can confront their own non-white identity and racism, when a young white emcee talks about appropriation and who influenced him, when a white professor of African American literature must face the privileges described in the literature that she loves, when an athlete realizes what his teammates encounter daily as they awe fans and put money in team owners' pockets, when a person wonders how an interaction with a police officer might have been like if they were black, when a person visits an underground holding pen for slaves in Africa, what are the next steps for a more inclusive world that acknowledges racism and seeks to make communities less racist? As the contributors address some of these situations, they ask some of the questions that people of color often negotiate daily, and are discussing them in a way that creates a platform where it is not just people of color negotiating intersectionality and race. These essays and anecdotes are moments of self-reflection and growth where change and making connections become more tangible.

This book explores how people inextricably carry memories of race with memories of class, gender, regional particularities, degrees of ability and disability, family, history, education, and work. John Amen says legislation "doesn't transform the recalcitrant heart" but it does "restrain the heartless," I would gather that it does not transform the mind either. As more people undam the fount of conversations and thoughts like these welling up beneath the surfaces of skin and social constructs that assemble whiteness, the flow will devastate some and saturate others with ideas in discomfort, outrage, alienation, and confusion. Hopefully, some people will read these stories and find themselves liberated from old perspectives that don't serve anyone. *What Does it Mean to be White in America?* is working toward drenching everyone in the humidity of race in the air, clinging to all of us.■

"It is an extraordinary achievement to be trapped in the dungeon of color and to dare shake down its walls and to step out of it, leaving the jailhouse keeper in the rubble."

—James Baldwin, "Dark Days"
James Baldwin: Collected Essays by Toni Morrison (1998)

APPENDIX 1

Ten Things Everyone Should Know About Race

OUR EYES TELL US that people look different. No one has trouble distinguishing a Czech from a Chinese. But what do those differences mean? Are they biological? Has race always been with us? How does race affect people today? There's less – and more – to race than meets the eye:

1. *Race is a modern idea.* Ancient societies, like the Greeks, did not divide people according to physical distinctions, but according to religion, status, class, even language. The English language didn't even have the word 'race' until it turns up in 1508 in a poem by William Dunbar referring to a line of kings.

2. *Race has no genetic basis.* Not one characteristic, trait or even gene distinguishes all the members of one so-called race from all the members of another so-called race.

3. *Human subspecies don't exist.* Unlike many animals, modern humans simply haven't been around long enough or isolated enough to evolve into separate subspecies or races. Despite surface appearances, we are one of the most similar of all species.

4. *Skin color really is only skin deep.* Most traits are inherited independently from one another. The genes influencing skin color have nothing to do with the genes influencing hair form, eye shape, blood type, musical talent, athletic ability or forms of

intelligence. Knowing someone's skin color doesn't necessarily tell you anything else about him or her.

5. *Most variation is within, not between, "races."* Of the small amount of total human variation, 85 percent exists within any local population, be they Italians, Kurds, Koreans or Cherokees. About 94 percent can be found within any continent. That means two random Koreans may be as genetically different as a Korean and an Italian.

6. *Slavery predates race.* Throughout much of human history, societies have enslaved others, often as a result of conquest or war, even debt, but not because of physical characteristics or a belief in natural inferiority. Due to a unique set of historical circumstances, ours was the first slave system where all the slaves shared similar physical characteristics.

7. *Race and freedom evolved together.* The U.S. was founded on the radical new principle that "All men are created equal." But our early economy was based largely on slavery. How could this anomaly be rationalized? The new idea of race helped explain why some people could be denied the rights and freedoms that others took for granted.

8. *Race justified social inequalities as natural.* As the race idea evolved, white superiority became "common sense" in America. It justified not only slavery but also the extermination of Indians, exclusion of Asian immigrants, and the taking of Mexican lands by a nation that professed a belief in democracy. Racial practices were institutionalized within American government, laws, and society.

9. *Race isn't biological, but racism is still real.* Race is a powerful social idea that gives people different access to opportunities and resources. Our government and social institutions have created advantages that disproportionately channel wealth, power,

and resources to white people. This affects everyone, whether we are aware of it or not.

10. *Colorblindness will not end racism.* Pretending race doesn't exist is not the same as creating equality. Race is more than stereotypes and individual prejudice. To combat racism, we need to identify and remedy social policies and institutional practices that advantage some groups at the expense of others. ■

"RACE - The Power of an Illusion" was produced by California Newsreel in association with the Independent Television Service (ITVS). Major funding provided by the Ford Foundation and the Corporation for Public Broadcasting Diversity Fund. © 2003 California Newsreel. All rights reserved. Reprinted with permission.

Glossary

Words Matter—Some Definitions to Consider

AFRICAN AMERICAN: A racial classification specifier that was advanced in the 1980s to give Americans of African descent a title equivalent to Euro-Americans. While the term peaked in popularity during the 1990s and 2000s, today it is often perceived as carrying a self-conscious political correctness that is unnecessary in an informal context, yet is rarely considered offensive. Nevertheless, many blacks do not embrace the term "African American" because it denotes a connection to a country far removed from their American ancestry. Interestingly and according to a recent study in the *Journal of Experimental Social Psychology*,[1] it found that among white Americans, the term "black" elicits a more negative association than "African American." Immigrants from some African, Caribbean, Central American, and South American nations and their descendants may or may not identify with this term because land and resources were not stolen from them in this space, and their ancestors were not brought to America as slaves. (See "black.")

AFFIRMATIVE ACTION: Created during the 1960s, affirmative action is a policy that an institution or organization actively engages to improve opportunities for historically excluded or underrepresented groups (such as women and minorities) to overcome the effects of segregation and other forms of past discrimination in American society. The controversy surrounding the constitutionality of affirmative action programs has made the topic one of heated debate. The use of racial quotas as part of affirmative action led to charges of reverse discrimination in the late 1970s. During the 1980s, the federal

---

1   Erika V. Hall, Katherine W. Phillips, Sarah S.M. Townsend, "A rose by any other name? The consequences of subtyping 'African-Americans' from 'Blacks'" *Journal of Experimental Social Psychology* 56 (2015), 183-190.

government's role in affirmative action had become considerably diluted, and in 1989, the Supreme Court gave greater standing to claims of reverse discrimination. The Civil Rights Act of 1991 reaffirmed the government's commitment to affirmative action, but the Supreme Court placed limits on the use of race in awarding government contracts and in achieving educational diversity. By the late 1990s, California, and other states banned the use of preferential treatment based on race and sex. Many white people believe that affirmative action is a form of reverse discrimination.

ANTI-RACISM: Refers to an agenda that calls for an end to condoning and promoting racism by advocating for accountability in relationships irrespective of race, color, or ethnicity.

ANTI-RACIST: A person who identifies and challenges the values, structures and behaviors that perpetuate systemic racism.

ANTI-SEMITISM: Prejudice against, hatred of, or discrimination against Jews as an ethnic, religious, or racial group. A person who holds such a position is called an "anti-Semite." Anti-Semitism is widely considered to be a form of racism.

BIAS: A subjective opinion, preference or prejudice without basis in fact that influences an individual's or group's ability to evaluate a particular situation objectively or accurately.

BIGOTRY: Being closed-minded and having a systematic intolerance of any race, creed, belief, or opinion that differs from one's own.

BLACK: A racial classification specifier of Americans with total or partial ancestry from Africa. "Black" replaced the derogatory terminology applied to African Americans such as "negro" or "nigger" because it was turned into a positive designation during the Black Power movement. (See "African American" and "Black Power Movement.")

BLACK POWER MOVEMENT: A popular slogan in the late 1960s, it was first used by Stokely Carmichael in June 1966 during a civil rights march in Mississippi. The Black Power movement, ignited by the 1965 assassination of Malcolm X coupled with the urban uprisings of 1964 and 1965, evolved to maximize political and economic power to achieve self-determination in the United States. One of the most misunderstood and understudied protest movements in American history (Jeffries 2006), many whites believed that Black Power was synonymous with violence and black racism, but it was, in fact, a logical extension of the struggle waged by the civil rights movement.[2] Some black leaders viewed the movement as separatist; some blacks believed that by closing ranks, they could challenge and rectify white-dominated institutions that would bring them closer to a fully integrated society; others had grown weary of Martin Luther King Jr.'s "dream" and non-violent tactics and adopted a more nationalistic approach; while many saw Black Power as a way of emphasizing Black Pride and African American culture. While the differences between these currents were explicit—and hotly debated—the idea of Black Power exerted significant influence in black communities. It helped organize community self-help groups and institutions that did not depend on white people. It was used to create black and other ethnic studies programs at colleges, mobilize black people to vote, and encouraged greater racial pride and self-esteem. However, by the mid-1970s, the movement was for all intents and purposes over. Government repression, which included the assassinations of Black Panthers Bobby Hutton in Oakland, Mark Clark and Fred Hampton in Chicago, and Carl Hampton of Houston; compounded by raids, arrests, and harassment of many of the movement's members, receives much of the credit for the Black Power movement's demise. By 1973, activists began to concentrate their efforts on getting blacks and progressive whites elected to public office as a significantly less dangerous enterprise.

CIVIL RIGHTS MOVEMENT: The civil rights movement (which was initiated in the nineteenth century and peaked during the late-1960s) was a nonviolent series of events to secure full civil rights to African Americans in the United States of America. Black men and women along with whites, organized and led the movement at national and local levels, which marked a sea-change in American social, political, economic and civic life. They pursued their goals through boycotts, sit-ins, negotiations, petitions, marches and nonviolent protest demonstrations. It brought with it court battles, bombings, and other violence; prompted worldwide media coverage and intense public debate; forged enduring civic, economic and religious alliances; and disrupted and realigned the nation's two major political parties. It also influenced the American Indian and Asian American movements of the 1960s, as well as launched the gay and modern women's rights movements of the 1970s.

---

2   *International Encyclopedia of the Social Sciences* (Thomson Gale, 2008). http://www.encyclopedia.com/topic/Black_power_movement.aspx.

COLOR BLINDNESS: A sociological term that is a powerful and appealing liberal discourse in which white people insist that they do not notice a person's skin color. What it is, in fact, is the refusal to recognize that race is the baggage people of color carry with them, and that racism is part of their everyday lives.

CULTURE: Refers to the cumulative deposit of knowledge, experience, beliefs, values, attitudes, meanings, hierarchies, religion, notions of time, roles, concepts of the universe, and material objects and possessions acquired by a group of people in the course of generations through individual and group striving. Culture guides people how to perceive, feel, think, act, and discern what is acceptable or unacceptable, important or unimportant, and right or wrong.

DESEGREGATION: The elimination of laws, customs, or practices that people from different religions, ancestries, and ethnic groups are restricted to specific or separate public facilities, neighborhoods, schools, organizations, or the like.

DIASPORA: A Greek term that means "to scatter," diaspora was used exclusively to describe the dispersion of the Jewish people following their expulsion from the Holy Land. Today it is used to describe a community of people who live outside their shared country of origin or ancestry, but maintain active connections with it. Whether one is aware of his or her heritage, nearly every American is part of at least one diaspora. Many of us come from mixed heritages, and, therefore, claim multiple diaspora communities.

DISCRIMINATION: The practice of unfairly treating a person or group of people differently based on specific characteristics such as race, nationality, religion, ethnic affiliation, age, sexual orientation, marital or family status, and physical or mental disability. Discrimination usually leads to the denial of cultural, economic, educational, political or social rights of members of a specific non-dominant group.

DIVERSITY: A term used to describe a variation between people using a range of factors such as ethnicity, national origin, gender, ability, age, physical characteristics, religion, values, sexual orientation, disability, socio-economic class, or life experiences. In many cases, the term diversity also implies an appreciation of these differences.

ETHNICITY: A shared cultural heritage that includes beliefs, behaviors and traditions held in common by a group of people bound by linguistic, historical, geographical, religious or racial homogeneity.

ETHNOCENTRISM: The tendency to view others using one's own group and customs as the standard for judgment, and seeing one's group and customs as the best.

EQUALITY: It means that every person enjoys the same status, and should be treated the same way so that everyone can realize their full potential. Often the discourse of equality is used to perpetuate discriminatory practices because there is a focus on same or equal treatment, which is perceived as fair by the dominant culture. If the focus remains on the treatment (which is a form of denial that ignores how dominant institutions do not meet the needs of racialized people) and not the result, then equality will never be achieved.

HERITAGE: The full range of our inherited traditions, monuments, objects, and culture that also influences our behavioral activities. Heritage includes, but is much more than preserving, excavating, displaying, or restoring a collection of old things. It is both tangible and intangible, in the sense that ideas and memories – of songs, recipes, language, dances, and many other elements of who we are and how we identify ourselves – are as important as historical buildings and archaeological sites.

IMMIGRANT: A person who moves from his or her native country to another with the intention of resettlement.

INSTITUTIONAL OPPRESSION: Occurs when established laws, customs, and practices systematically reflect and produce inequities based on one's membership in targeted social identity groups. If oppressive consequences accrue to institutional laws, customs, or practices, the institution is oppressive whether or not the individuals maintaining those practices have oppressive intentions.

INSTITUTIONAL RACISM: A form of racism that occurs when institutions, including corporations, governments, colleges and universities discriminate either deliberately or indirectly, against certain groups of people and limits their rights. Race-based discrimination in housing, education, employment and health are also forms of institutional racism. Institutional racism is more subtle, less visible, and, therefore, more difficult to identify than individual acts of racism, but no less destructive to human life and human dignity. For example, the people who manage or work in these institutions may not be racists, but by simply carrying out their job, many are unaware that their role contributes to a discriminatory outcome.

INTEGRATION: Integration is the process of ending systematic racial segregation. On May 17, 1954, the Supreme Court declared in its landmark unanimous decision, *Brown v. Board of Education,* that separate schooling of black and white children was inherently unequal, marking the beginning of the modern civil rights movement. Over the next twenty years, the civil rights revolution put in place laws that attempted to guarantee (essentially for the first time since our nation's founding), that no one should be restricted in their access to education, jobs, voting, travel, public accommodations, or housing because of race. For most people, this was what integration meant. Although a number of blacks and other people of color have achieved success as a result of integration, race remains one of the most intractable problems in America, in large part due to personal biases and racial stereotyping (by and of all races), which cannot be altered by legislation or lawsuits. Desegregation is largely a legal matter, integration largely a social one.

JIM CROW: Named after a character in a plantation song from the American South, Jim Crow refers to a series of racist laws and measures against African Americans and other people of color that enforced racial segregation in the South between the end of Reconstruction in 1877, and the beginning of the civil rights movement in the 1950s. It was codified on local and state levels and most famously with the "separate but equal" decision of the U.S. Supreme Court in *Plessy v. Ferguson* (1896). The effects of Jim Crow are relevant today.

MANIFEST DESTINY: A term for the attitude prevalent during American expansion of the West in the nineteenth-century. It expressed the belief that it was White Anglo-Saxon Americans' providential mission to expand their civilization and institutions across North America, from coast to coast. This expansion involved not merely territorial aggrandizement, but the progress of liberty and individual economic opportunity as well. It fueled western settlement, Native American removal, war with Mexico and extended beyond America's continental boundaries into the Pacific and Caribbean islands. The phrase was first employed by John L. O'Sullivan in an article on the annexation of Texas published in the July-August 1845 edition of the *United States Magazine and Democratic Review.*[3]

MAJORITY: When we're talking about race, ethnicity, gender, religion, or any other socially meaningful group of people, the majority refers to the social

---

3   Eric Foner and John A. Garraty, eds. *The Reader's Companion to American History* (NY: Houghton Mifflin Harcourt, 1991).

group considered to have the most power. In the United States, white people are considered the majority.

MELTING POT: A term used to refer to an American monocultural society in which there is a conscious attempt to assimilate diverse peoples into a homogeneous culture, rather than to participate as equals in the society while maintaining various cultural or ethnic identities used to describe the assimilation of immigrants to the United States. The exact term "melting pot" came into general usage in 1908, after the premiere of the play, *The Melting Pot,* by Israel Zangwill.[4] This term is often challenged, however, by those who assert that cultural differences within a society are valuable and should be preserved. (See "Multiculturalism.")

MICROAGGRESSION: The everyday verbal, nonverbal, and environmental slights, snubs, or insults, whether intentional or unintentional, which communicate hostile, derogatory, or negative messages to target persons based solely upon their marginalized group membership.[5]

MINORITY: A minority is any category of people distinguished by either a physical or cultural difference that society has subordinated. The differentiation can be based on one or more observable human characteristics, including ethnicity, race, religion, caste, gender, wealth, health or sexual orientation. In the social sciences, the term "minority" is used to refer to categories of persons (such as African Americans, Native Americans, Asian Americans, and Latinos) who hold fewer positions of social power. Most people of color detest being referred to as a "minority" because it implies the not so hidden connotation of being labeled as insignificant.

MULTICULTURALISM: A philosophy that became a significant force in American society in the 1970s and 1980s, to appreciate ethnic diversity and encourage people to learn about and respect diverse ethnic backgrounds.

OPPRESSION: The socially supported mistreatment and exploitation of a group, category, or group of people or individuals. Oppression is built into institutions like government and education systems. It gives power and

---

4   Israel Zangwill, *The Melting Pot,* Wikipedia, accessed February 29, 2016, https://en.wikipedia.org/wiki/The_Melting_Pot_(play).

5   Derald Wing Sue, "Microaggressions: More than Just Race," *Psychology Today,* November 17, 2010 https://www.psychologytoday.com/blog/microaggressions-in-every-day-life/201011/microaggressions-more-just-race.

positions of dominance to some groups of people over other groups of people. (See "Institutional Oppression.")

PEOPLE OF COLOR: The term is an attempt to describe people with a more positive term than "non-white" or "minority" because it frames them in the context of the dominant group. Identifying as a person of color in solidarity with other people of color acknowledges similar or shared oppressions by white people, a willingness to work together against racism and perhaps, a deeper commitment to allyship.

POLITICAL CORRECTNESS: (Also known as "politically correct.") Conforming to a particular socio-political ideology or point of view, especially to a liberal point of view concerned with promoting tolerance and avoiding offense in matters of race, class, gender, and sexual orientation. Commonly abbreviated to "PC."

POWER: Basically, all power is relational, but the concept of power to anti-racism is clear: racism cannot be understood without understanding that power is not only an individual relationship but a cultural one, and that power relationships are shifting constantly. Power can be used malignantly and intentionally, but need not be, and individuals within a culture may benefit from a power that they are unaware of.

PREJUDICE: A pre-judgment or unjustifiable, and usually negative, attitude of one type of individual or groups toward another group and its members. Such negative attitudes are typically based on unsupported generalizations (or stereotypes) that deny the right of individual members of certain groups to be recognized and treated as individuals with individual characteristics.[6]

RACE: Race is a socially meaningful category of people who share biologically transmitted traits that are obvious and considered important, such as facial features, stature and hair texture. But for most cultures, skin color seems to be the most important trait when it comes to race. Although humans are sometimes divided into races, the morphological variation between races is not indicative of major differences in DNA, which has led some scientists to describe all humans as belonging to the same race—the human race. Race is associated with biology, whereas ethnicity is associated with culture.

---

6   *Institute for Democratic Renewal and Project Change Anti-Racism Initiative. A Community Builder's Tool Kit* (Claremont, CA: Claremont Graduate University). http://www.racialequitytools.org/resourcefiles/idr.pdf.

RACIAL PROFILING: The act of suspecting or targeting a person of a certain race based on a stereotype about their race.

RACIST: A person who believes that a particular race is superior to another.

RACISM: Oppression against individuals or groups based on their actual or perceived racial identity. The use of race to establish and justify a social hierarchy and system of power that privileges, preferences or advances certain individuals or groups of people usually at the expense of others. Racism is perpetuated through both interpersonal and institutional practices.

REVERSE DISCRIMINATION: It is defined as engaging in actions that have a negative impact or that disfavor someone who was traditionally in a majority position. Often, reverse discrimination cases involve programs meant to advance or promote minorities and address inequality, such as affirmative action.[7]

REVERSE RACISM: A phenomenon in which discrimination against a dominant or formerly dominant racial group of the majority takes place. It has been described as "preferential treatment, discriminating in favor of members of under-represented groups, which have been treated unjustly in the past, against innocent people."[8] Many racial justice activists argue that reverse racism and reverse discrimination is just misinterpreted racial prejudice. Such activists argue the definition of racism isn't just one individual's belief that a certain race is superior to others, but also includes institutional oppression.

SEGREGATION: A system that keeps different groups separate from each other, either through physical dividers or using social pressures and laws. Segregation may also be a mutually voluntary arrangement but more frequently it is enforced by the majority group and its institutions. Exclusive neighborhoods and gated communities that are predominantly white are examples of economic segregation and demonstrate how whiteness and middle- to upper-class ideologies are mutually reinforcing.

SOCIAL CLASS: A status hierarchy in which individuals and groups are classified on the basis of esteem and prestige acquired mainly through economic success and accumulation of wealth. Social class may also refer to any

---

7   "Find Law" (Thomson Reuters, 2016) http://employment.findlaw.com/employ-ment-discrimination/reverse-discrimination.html#sthash.qOE5dPpb.dpuf.

8   Louis P. Pojman,"The Case Against Affirmative Action" http://www.csus.edu/indiv/g/gaskilld/business_computer_ethics/the%20case%20against%20affirmative%20action.htm.

particular level in such a hierarchy. Four common social classes informally recognized in many societies are: (1) upper-class, (2) middle-class, (3) working-class, and (4) lower-class (poor).

SOCIAL JUSTICE: It is defined as "promoting a just society by challenging injustice and valuing diversity." It exists when "all people share a common humanity and therefore have a right to equitable treatment, support for their human rights, and a fair allocation of community resources." In conditions of social justice, people are "not be discriminated against, nor their welfare and well-being constrained or prejudiced on the basis of gender, sexuality, religion, political affiliations, age, race, belief, disability, location, social class, socioeconomic circumstances, or other characteristic of background or group membership" (Toowoomba Catholic Education, 2006). Social justice involves activists who have a sense of their own agency as well as a sense of social responsibility toward and with others and the society as a whole.

STEREOTYPE: It is used to categorize a group of people with attitudes, beliefs, and feelings that are widespread and socially sanctioned. These assumptions can be positive and negative, but all have damaging effects. Stereotypes support the maintenance of institutionalized oppression by seemingly validating misinformation or beliefs.

WHITE: A racial classification specifier used for people of European ancestry. The contemporary usage of "white people" as a group contrasts with the terms "black," "colored," or "non-white," which originates in the seventeenth century. Today it is used as a racial classifier in multiracial societies, such as the United States (White American), the United Kingdom (White British), Brazil (White Brazilian), and South Africa (White South African). Various social constructs of whiteness have been significant to national identity, public policy, religion, population statistics, racial segregation, affirmative action, white privilege, eugenics, racial marginalization and racial quotas.

WHITENESS: A social construct that has created a racial hierarchy that has shaped all the social, cultural, educational, political, and economic institutions of society, whiteness is linked to domination and is a form of race privilege that is often invisible to white people who are not conscious of its power.

WHITE PRIVILEGE: It implies that being born with white skin in America affords people certain unearned privileges in life that people of another skin color simple are not afforded. There are many different types of privilege, not just skin color privilege, which impacts the way people can move through the world or are discriminated against. It is not something you earned, it is something you are born into that afford you opportunities others may not have.

WHITE SUPREMACY: White supremacy—the belief in the superiority of the white race, especially in matters of intelligence and culture—achieved the height of its popularity during the period of European colonial expansion to the Western Hemisphere, Africa, and Asia stretching from the late 1800s to the first half of the twentieth-century. White supremacists have based their ideas on a variety of theories and supposedly proven facts; the most prominent of these include the claims of pseudo-scientific racist academic research that attempted to correlate inferiority and pathological behavior with categories of racial phenotypes, especially head size in the case of eugenics. There is a direct correlation between the rise of imperialism and colonialism, and the expansion of white supremacist ideology justifying the changing international order, which increasingly saw Europeans assuming political control over peoples of darker skin color through military force and ideological means, such as religion and education. It is important to note that the range of those considered "white" expanded considerably in the twentieth century. For example, in the United States, not all ethnic groups with white skin were initially considered white. It was not until well into the twentieth century that the Irish and Italians, for example, were considered white. By the end of that century, the United States federal government had also expanded its definition of whites to include Arabs. ■

APPENDIX 3

Suggested Reading

Alexander, Michelle. *The New Jim Crow: Mass Incarceration in the Age of Colorblindness*. New York: The New Press, 2012.

Aronson, Marc. *Race: A History Beyond Black and White*. New York: Atheneum Books for Young Readers, 2007.

Baldwin, James. *The Price of the Ticket. Collected Nonfiction 1948-1985*. New York: St. Martin's Press, 1985.

Barndt, Joseph. *Understanding and Dismantling Racism: The Twenty-First Century Challenge to White America*. Minneapolis: Fortress Press, 2007.

Barnes, Annie S. *Say It Loud: Middle-Class Blacks Talk about Racism and What to Do about It*. Cleveland, OH: Pilgrim Press, 2000.

Battalora, Jacqueline. *Birth of a White Nation: The Invention of White People and Its Relevance Today*. Durham, CT: Strategic Book Publishing, 2013.

Benjamin, Rich. *Searching for Whitopia: An Improbable Journey to the Heart of White America*. New York: Hyperion, 2009.

Bonilla-Silva, Eduardo. *Racism without Racists: Color-Blind Racism and the Persistence of Racial Inequality in America*. New York: Rowman & Littlefield Publishers, 2013.

Brown, Michael K. and Martin Carnoy, et. al. *Whitewashing Race: The Myth of a Color-Blind Society*. Berkeley, CA: Univ. of California Press, 2005.

Chang, Jeff. *Who We Be: A Cultural History of Race in Post-Civil Rights America.* New York: Picador, 2016.

Colby, Tanner. *Some of My Best Friends Are Black: The Strange Story of Integration in America.* New York: Penguin Books, 2012.

Du Bois, W. E. B. *The Souls of Black Folk.* Dover Publications, 1994.

Frankenberg, Ruth. *White Women, Race Matters: The Social Construction of Whiteness.* Minneapolis: Univ. of Minnesota Press, 1993.

Fredrickson, George M. *Racism: A Short History.* New Jersey: Princeton Univ. Press, 2003.

Glaude Jr., Eddie S. *Democracy in Black: How Race Still Enslaves the American Soul.* New York: Crown, 2016.

Goad, Jim. *The Redneck Manifesto: How Hillbillies, Hicks, and White Trash Became America's Scapegoats.* New York: Simon & Schuster, 1998.

Gonzalez, Juan and Joseph Torres. *News For All The People: The Epic Story of Race and the American Media.* New York: Verso, 2012.

Goodman, Alan H. Race: *Are We So Different.* Hoboken, NJ: Wiley-Blackwell, 2012.

Goodman, Alan H., Yolanda T. Moses and Joseph L. Jones. *Race: Are We So Different.* Hoboken, NJ: Wiley-Blackwell, 2012.

Hartigan, John. *Odd Tribes: Toward a Cultural Analysis of White People.* Durham, NC: Duke Univ. Press, 2005.

Hill, Jane H. *The Everyday Language of White Racism.* Hoboken, NJ: Wiley-Blackwell, 2008.

Ignatiev, Noel and John Garvey. *Race Traitor.* London: Routledge, 1996.

Ioanide, Paula. *The Emotional Politics of Racism: How Feelings Trump Facts in an Era of Colorblindness.* Palo Alto, CA: Stanford University Press, 2015.

Irving, Debby. *Waking Up White, and Finding Myself in the Story of Race.* Elephant Room Press, 2014.

Isaac, Benjamin. *The Invention of Racism in Classical Antiquity.* New Jersey: Princeton University Press, 2006.

Jacobson, Matthew Frye. *Roots Too: White Ethnic Revival in Post-Civil Rights America.* Boston: Harvard University Press, 2008.

Jensen, Robert. *The Heart of Whiteness: Confronting Race, Racism and White Privilege.* San Francisco: City Lights Publishers, 2005.

Joseph, Peniel E. *Waiting 'Til the Midnight Hour: A Narrative History of Black Power in America.* New York: Holt, 2007.

Katznelson, Ira. *When Affirmative Action Was White: An Untold History of Racial Inequality in Twentieth-Century America.* New York: W. W. Norton & Company, 2006.

Kendall, Frances. *Understanding White Privilege: Creating Pathways to Authentic Relationships Across Race.* London: Routledge, 2012.

Kennedy, Randall. *The Persistence of the Color Line: Racial Politics and the Obama Presidency.* New York: Vintage, 2012.

Kivel, Paul. *Uprooting Racism: How White People Can Work for Racial Justice.* British Columbia: New Society Publishers, 2011.

Lebron, Christopher J. *The Color of Our Shame: Race and Justice in Our Time.* New York: Oxford University Press, 2015.

Linker, Maureen. *Intellectual Empathy: Critical Thinking for Social Justice.* Ann Arbor, MI: Univ. of Michigan Press, 2014.

Lipsitz, George. *The Possessive Investment in Whiteness: How White People Profit from Identity Politics.* Philadelphia: Temple Univ. Press, 2006.

López, Ian Haney. *Dog Whistle Politics: How Coded Racial Appeals Have Reinvented Racism and Wrecked the Middle Class.* New York: Oxford Univ. Press, 2015.

Mills, Charles W. *The Racial Contract.* New York: Cornell Univ. Press, 1999.

Morrison, Toni. *Playing in the Dark: Whiteness and the Literary Imagination*. New York: Vintage, 1993.

Oliver, Melvin and Thomas M. Shapiro. *Black Wealth / White Wealth: A New Perspective on Racial Inequality*. London: Routledge, 2006.

Olson, Joel. *Abolition Of White Democracy*. Minneapolis: Univ. of Minnesota Press, 1994.

Painter, Nell Irvin. *The History of White People*. New York: W. W. Norton & Company, 2011.

Pierce, Jennifer. *Racing for Innocence: Whiteness, Gender, and the Backlash Against Affirmative Action*. Palo Alto, CA: Stanford Univ. Press, 2012.

Roediger, David R. *Black on White: Black Writers on What It Means to Be White*. New York: Schocken, 1999.

Roediger, David R. *Working Toward Whiteness: How America's Immigrants Became White: The Strange Journey from Ellis Island to the Suburbs*. New York: Basic Books, 2006.

Román, Ediberto and Michael A. Olivas. *Those Damned Immigrants: America's Hysteria over Undocumented Immigration*. New York: New York Univ. Press, 2013.

Rothenberg, Paula S. *White Privilege: Essential Readings on the Other Side of Racism*. New York: Worth Publishers, 2015.

Sue, Derald Wing. *Race Talk and the Conspiracy of Silence: Understanding and Facilitating Difficult Dialogues on Race*. Hoboken, NJ: Wiley-Blackwell, 2016.

Tatum, Beverly Daniel. *Why Are All the Black Kids Sitting Together in the Cafeteria: And Other Conversations About Race*. New York: Basic Books, 2003.

Terkel, Studs. *Race: How Blacks and Whites Think and Feel About the American Obsession*. New York: The New Press, 2012

Thandeka. *Learning to Be White: Money, Race and God in America.* New York: Bloomsbury Academic, 2000.

Tochluk, Shelly. *Witnessing Whiteness: The Need to Talk About Race and How to Do It.* Lanham, MD: R&L Education, 2010.

Vilson, Jose. *This Is Not A Test: A New Narrative on Race, Class, and Education.* Chicago: Haymarket Books, 2014.

Walker, Rebecca. *Black Cool: One Thousand Streams of Blackness.* Berkeley, CA: Soft Skull Press, 2012.

Wallis, Jim. *America's Original Sin: Racism, White Privilege, and the Bridge to a New America.* Ada, MI: Brazos Press, 2016.

Waters, Mary C. *Ethnic Options: Choosing Identities in America.* Berkeley, CA: Univ. of California Press, 1990.

Wise, Tim. *Colorblind: The Rise of Post-Racial Politics and the Retreat from Racial Equity.* San Francisco, CA: City Lights Publishers, 2010.

Womack, Ytasha L. *Post Black: How a New Generation Is Redefining African American Identity.* Chicago: Chicago Review Press, 2010.

Woodson, Carter Godwin. *The Mis-Education of the Negro.* Lindenhurst, NY: Tribeca Books, 2013.

Wray, Matt. *Not Quite White: White Trash and the Boundaries of Whiteness.* Durham, NC: Duke Univ. Press, 2006.

Yancy, George. *Look, A White!: Philosophical Essays on Whiteness.* Philadelphia: Temple Univ. Press, 2012.

Zack, Naomi. *White Privilege and Black Rights: The Injustice of U.S. Police Racial Profiling and Homicide.* Lanham, MD: R&L Education, 2015. ∎

ABOUT THE CONTRIBUTORS

JOHN AMEN is the author of five poetry collections, including his most recent release, *strange theater* (New York Quarterly Books, 2015). His work has been translated into Spanish, French, Hungarian, Korean, and Hebrew, and has appeared in journals nationally and internationally. A frequent music reviewer for *No Depression*, he founded and continues to edit *The Pedestal Magazine*.

DAVID B. AXELROD has published twenty-one books of poetry, and his work has appeared in hundreds of magazines and anthologies. He holds an MA from The Johns Hopkins University, an MFA from the University of Iowa Writers' Workshop; and a PhD in non-profit program design and adminis-tration from Union Institute. He is the recipient of the 2014 Florida Book Award Gold Medal; the 2015 Coalition of Visionary Resources Award for non-fiction as co-author and editor of the critical biography, *Merlin Stone Remembered: Her Life and Works* (Llewellyn Publications, 2015); and three Fulbright Awards, including his being the first official Fulbright Poet-in-Resi-dence in the People's Republic of China. Axelrod's poetry has been translated into and published in fifteen languages, and is a student of nine languages. He serves as a vice president for the Florida division of Writers Unlimited Agency, Inc., a not-for-profit, educational service for writers which he founded in 1976, and as president of the Creative Happiness Institute, Inc. He resides in Daytona Beach. www.poetrydoctor.org.

ROGER BARBEE earned his MA from George Mason University. He is a retired educator with over forty years' experience teaching literature and composition from the sixth grade through college. Having grown up in Kannapolis, North

Carolina, he now lives in the Shenandoah Valley in Virginia where he writes regularly for *The Mountain Courier*.

BETH LYON BARNETT has published two novels, *Adam's Needle* (2015), and *Jazz Town* (2012). A Thorpe-Menn nominee, her work has appeared in numerous magazines and periodicals including *The Kansas City Star, Parents,* and *Kansas!* Born and raised in Kansas City, she is a graduate of Mills College. www.BethLyonBarnett.com.

BARBARA BECKWITH is a journalist and essayist whose writing has been published in more than forty newspapers and magazines, including *The New York Times, Washington Post, Boston Globe, Smithsonian, Columbia Journalism Review, Ms.,* and *Essence.* Her work has also appeared in the anthologies *Inside the Ropes: Sportswriters Get Their Game On* (Bison Books, 2008), and *Season of Adventure* (Seal Press, 1996); as well as in the *White Privilege Conference Journal,* and NPR's *Cognoscenti.* She is the author of the personal essay series, *What Was I Thinking?* including her latest volume, *Everyday Racism: Questions and Quandaries* (Crandall, Dostie & Douglass Books, 2015). Beckwith received her BA from Wellesley College, an MA from Tufts University, and an MA from Boston University. She has been a National Writers Union (UAW Local 1981) activist and Boston Chapter Steering Committee member since the 1980s, and served three terms on the NWU's national executive board. She lives in Cambridge, Massachusetts. www.barbarabeckwith.net.

CHRISTINA BERCHINI, a native New Yorker from Brooklyn, received her PhD in curriculum, instruction, and teacher education from Michigan State University. She teaches teacher education courses at the University of Wisconsin Eau Claire, and has published scholarship on whiteness in the International Journal of Qualitative Studies, the Journal of Adolescent and Adult Literacy, and other scholarly forums. Her mainstream work has appeared in outlets such as *Education Week Teacher, The Huffington Post,* and *Inside Higher Education.* Berchini's research on whiteness has won the Association of Teacher Educator's Distinguished Dissertation in Teacher Education award.

BRETT BIEBEL is a writer and teacher living in Iowa. He has an MFA from Minnesota State University, and his fiction has appeared in several literary journals, including *Bartleby Snopes, The Writing Disorder, Line Zero, The White Whale Review,* and *Great River Review.* Biebel has published essays on football, popular television, and the 1919 World Series. He is the winner of the Robert C. Wright Award for fiction, has presented his work as part of Minnesota State University's Good Thunder Reading Series, and is polishing the manuscripts of two novels. He blogs about sports and culture at http://seasonwithout.wordpress.com.

LYNN Z. BLOOM launched her literary career as a writer of creative nonfiction (before the label was invented) with *Doctor Spock: Biography of a Conservative Radical* (Bobbs-Merril,1972), and has since published twenty-one books. Her most recent books are *The Seven Deadly Virtues and Other Lively Essays* (Univ. of South Carolina Press, 2008), and *Writers Without Borders: Writing and Teaching Writing in Troubled Times* (Parlor Press, 2008). Among her 175 plus shorter works, "(Im)Patient," (Prose Studies, 2005), was named a Notable American Essay. Her food and travel writings include "Consuming Prose: The Delectable Rhetoric of Food Writing" (College English, 2008), and "Why the Worst Trips Make the Best Stories" (Assay, 2015). Bloom, who received her PhD from the University of Michigan, serves as the Aetna Chair of Writing and Board of Trustees Distinguished Professor at the University of Connecticut Storrs, and Honorary Professor at the University of Waikato, Hamilton New Zealand. She has received awards from the Fulbright Program, the National Institute of the Humanities, and the U.S. Department of Agriculture, among others.

TEREZA TOPFEROVA BOTTMAN emigrated as a teenager to the U.S. from Prague, Czech Republic. She holds a certificate in documentary studies from Lewis & Clark College, an MEd from Portland State University, and a BA in drama from Bard College. She is a public school teacher in Portland, Oregon, and her writing has appeared on several blogs, including *Love Isn't Enough* (formerly *Anti-Racist Parent*), and *Cultural Detective*. This is her first publication in a book.

PERRY BRASS, born in Savannah, Georgia, has published nineteen books of poetry, novels, short fiction, science fiction, plays, and the bestselling advice books, his most recent *The Manly Pursuit of Desire and Love* (Belhue Press, 2015). He is a six-time finalist for the Lambda Literary Awards, has won four IPPY Awards from the Independent Publishers Group (IPG), and was a finalist for a prestigious Ferro-Grumley Fiction Award from the Ferro-Grumley Foundation for his novel, *King of Angels* (Belhue Press, 2012). An activist in the LGBT movement since 1969, he is one of the co-founders of the Gay Men's Health Project Clinic, the first clinic specifically for gay men on the

East Coast. Brass blogs regularly for the *The Huffington Post,* and the *Good Men Project.* www.perrybrass.com.

ANN CHANDONNET is a journalist, book reviewer, culinary historian and poet. She received an MS in English literature from the University of Wisconsin in Madison. During her thirty-four years in Alaska, she won awards from Alaska Press Women, an award for her series about Fetal Alcohol Syndrome from the Alaska Press Club, and a national poetry award in wilderness writing. Her poems have appeared in anthologies, including *Last New Land: Stories of Alaska Past and Present, In the Dreamlight, Hunger and Dreams: The Alaskan Womens Anthology, Black Sun, New Moon,* and *A Long Line of Joy.* Chandonnet's latest poetry collections is *Canoeing in the Rain: Poems for My Aleut-Athabascan Son* (Meredith Bliss, 1990). Her book, *Gold Rush Grub: From Turpentine Stew to Hoochinoo* (University of Alaska Press, 2005), won an Outstanding Book Award from the American Association of School Librarians. Currently a resident of Lake St. Louis, Missouri, Chandonnet demonstrates open hearth cooking at the Daniel Boone Historic Site in Defiance.

MARTHA COLLINS has published eight books of poetry, including *Admit One: An American Scrapbook* (Univ. of Pittsburgh, 2016), *White Papers* (Univ. of Pittsburgh, 2012), and the book-length poem *Blue Front* (Graywolf Press, 2006), which won an Anisfield-Wolf Award and was chosen as one of 25 Books to Remember by the New York Public Library. Her other awards include fellowships from the NEA, the Bunting Institute, the Witter Bynner Foundation, and the Ingram Merrill Foundation, as well as three Pushcart Prizes and a Lannan Foundation residency fellowship. Founder of the creative writing program at UMass-Boston, Collins taught at Oberlin College for ten years, and is now editor-at-large for Oberlin's *FIELD* magazine. She has also published four collections of co-translated Vietnamese poetry.

SEAN CONROY was born in McCook, Nebraska and currently resides in Hays, Kansas. He has a BS in human biology from Chadron State College, a BS from the University of Nebraska Medical Center, and an MPAS from Union College, Lincoln, Nebraska. His first book, *Through the Eyes of a Young Physician Assistant Non-Fiction* (Open Books Press, 2016), is forthcoming. https://seanconroypac.wordpress.com.

MARLA PRESLEY COOPER earned a BAAS from Stephen F. Austin State University in Nacogdoches, Texas, with an emphasis on hospital laboratory medicine. When she was diagnosed in 1980 with multiple sclerosis and retired on disability, she began writing. Subsequently, her essays and articles have appeared in *The Dallas Times Herald, The Dallas Morning News, The Odessa American, Good Old Days, Accent on Living, Strides, Beyond Boundaries,* and *Good Times.* Her personal-experience essay won the Ethel Harvey Award for Nonfiction, and was published in the *The Chapbook* (1992). Her work has also been published in *The Old Sorehead Gazette, High Lonesome–An Anthology of Works by West Texas Writers,* and *West Texas Christmas Stories.* Cooper's fiction has appeared in *Texas Short Fiction, A World In Itself* and *Texas Short Fiction, A World In Itself II.* She is the author of *From Basic to Bastogne: W.G. Presley's War Stories as Told to Marla Presley Cooper* (IUniverse, 2007), and is currently working on her memoir.

JASON COURTMANCHE earned his MA in rhetoric and composition from Humboldt State University and subsequently taught high school English for twelve years prior to earning his PhD at the University of Connecticut in 2006, where he is currently the director of the Connecticut Writing Project and a lecturer in English. His work has appeared in *What Is "College-Level" Writing,* Volume 2, *California Quarterly; Re: Verse, Kimera, Rockhurst Review, The Leaflet, UConn Magazine, The Hartford Courant,* and *CT News Junkie.* Forthcoming publications include chapters in *Nathaniel Hawthorne in the College Classroom* (AMS Press, 2016), and *Writing Teachers Teaching Reading* (NCTE, 2016). He was awarded a fellowship from Teachers For a New Era in 2011, a University Teaching Scholar award from the Institute for Teaching and Learning in 2012, and an award for Excellence in the Promotion of Literacy on behalf of the Connecticut Writing Project from the New England Reading Association in 2013. Since 2014, Courtmanche has served as the president of the Nathaniel Hawthorne Society and is the author of *How Nathaniel Hawthorne's Narratives Are Shaped By Sin* (Edwin Mellen Press, 2008). His blog on education, *The Write Space,* can be accessed at http://jasoncourtmanche.blogspot.com.

JOSH COUVARES was raised in Manchester, Connecticut and studied English and Economics at the University of Connecticut. His work has appeared in *Long River Review* and *The Hartford Courant.* He currently works and lives in New York City.

JUSTINE COZELL received an MFA in poetry from Warren Wilson College in 2012. She currently teaches first-year writing at the University of Connecticut.

LINDA M. CRATE, a Pennsylvanian native born in Pittsburgh yet raised in the rural town of Conneautville, is a graduate of Edinboro University of Pennsylvania. Her poetry, short stories, articles, and reviews have been published in a myriad of online and print magazines. She is the author of two chapbooks, *Mermaid Crashing into Dawn* (Fowlpox Press, 2013) and *Less Than a Man* (The Camel Saloon, 2014), and the fantasy novels, *Blood & Magic* (2015), and *Dragons & Magic* (2015), part of her "Magic" series.

SHIREEN DAY grew up in four distinctly different cultures: New Jersey, the U.S. Virgin Islands, Iran and Iowa. She earned her BA in sociology from Colorado College, and an MS in social work from the University of Denver. She currently resides in Boulder, Colorado. www.shireenday.com.

RAY DIZAZZO, an author of fiction, non-fiction, poetry and criticism, received an associate in arts degree in business management from Orange Coast College in Costa Mesa, California. His work has appeared in numerous publications, notably, *Westways, The Berkeley Poetry Review, Beyond Baroque, East River Review, Painted Bride Quarterly, Invisible City, California Quarterly* and others. He is a Pushcart Prize nominee and the recipient of the Percival Roberts Book Award, and as a recipient of the Rhysling Award, his work was anthologized in their annual publication, *The Alchemy of Stars: Burning with a Vision and Contemporary Literary Criticism.* DiZazzo has written twelve books, including *The Clarity Factor* (Sourcebooks, 2009) and three poetry collections. His recent collection is *The Water Bulls* (Granite-Collen, 2009). www.raydizazzo.com.

CARTER H. DOUGLASS is the seventh generation to live on the family farm in Virginia's Shenandoah Valley, from which ancestors left to fight on both sides of the Civil War. She published a chapbook, *Somebody's Child* (Little Steps Press, 2000), and her work has been published in the *Potomac Review.* She is a member of the Squaw Valley Community of Writers and serves on the board of Furious Flower Poetry Center at James Madison University, the only academic center in the nation devoted to African American poetry. Her mentorship and friendship with Lucille Clifton continues to open doors.

JUNE ELIZABETH DUNN is assistant dean of the Office of Continuing Studies and Enhanced Learning at Eastern Connecticut State University. Her work has appeared in *Virginia Woolf: Turning the Centuries* (Pace Univ. Press, 2000) and *The Journal of the Sylvia Townsend Warner Society* (2012). She received the Paul Monette Dissertation Prize in 2005 for *Troubled Houses: Irish Women Writing the Great War* (Graduate Center, CUNY).

CAROL B. EHRLICH is a freelance writer. She received an MA in communication from The Johns Hopkins University, and attended the Jubilee Anti-Racism Training, sponsored by the Unitarian Universalist Association. She lives in Kensington, Maryland.

SARA ESTES is a Nashville-based author and journalist. She is the lead art writer at *The Tennessean,* a weekly columnist at *BURNAWAY,* and an editor and member of the Board of Directors at the art journal *Number.* Her writing has been featured in *The Bitter Southerner, Oxford American, Chapter 16, BURNAWAY, Nashville Scene, Nashville Arts Magazine, ArtsNash,* and elsewhere. Estes is a 2015 recipient of a Bonnaroo Works Fund Grant for fiction writing.

GIL FAGIANI is a translator, essayist, short-story writer, and poet. A graduate of Hunter School of Social Work, his work has been translated into French, Greek, Italian, and Spanish. He has published five poetry collections, recently *Logos* (Guernica Editions, 2015), *Stone Walls,* (Bordighera Press, 2014), and *Chianti in Connecticut,* (Bordighera Press, 2010), as well as three chapbooks. Fagiani's poetry has appeared in eighteen anthologies and publications such as *The New York Times, Descant, Skidrow Penthouse, Bitter Oleander, Mudfish, Maintenant, The Paterson Literary Review,* and *The Journal of Italian Translation.* A social worker by profession, Fagiani directed a residential treatment program for recovering alcoholics and drug addicts in downtown Brooklyn for twenty-one years. He currently co-curates the Italian American Writers' Association's monthly reading series in Manhattan, and is an associate editor of *Feile-Festa: A Literary Arts Journal.*

KATHERINE FISHBURN is Professor Emeritus, Michigan State University where she taught in the English Department for thirty years. Her essays have appeared in various journals such as *Studies in the Novel* and *Research in African Literatures.* She is author of six scholarly books, including *Richard Wright's Hero: The Faces of a Rebel-Victim, The Unexpected Universe of Doris Lessing: A Study in Narrative Technique, Reading Buchi Emecheta: Cross-Cultural Conversations* and *The Problem of Embodiment in Early African American Narrative.* She is also author of one book of poetry, *The Dead Are So Disappointing* (Michigan State Univ. Press, 2000). Her poems have been published in *Snowy Egret, Enizagam, Quarter After Eight* and *The Florida Review,* where in 2001 she won the Editors' Award in Poetry. Before earning her PhD, she taught English for two years at Governor Thomas Johnson High School in Frederick, Maryland. Also a visual artist, in retirement Fishburn has had three one-woman shows at galleries in Michigan. In 2013, three of her paintings appeared on the covers of the *Mid-American Review,* Volume 34.

KURT MICHAEL FRIESE received his BA at Coe College in Cedar Rapids, Iowa before graduating from the New England Culinary Institute, where he later was a chef-instructor. With thirty-five years of professional foodservice experience, for nineteen years he has been chef and owner of Devotay, a restaurant and bar in Iowa City, a community leader of sustainable cuisine that supports local farmers and food artisans. He has served on the boards of Slow Food USA, the Iowa Food Systems Council, and the NewBo City Market. His columns and photos on food, wine and travel have appeared regularly in local, regional and national newspapers and magazines. In 2006, Friese founded *Edible Iowa* magazine, a member of the James Beard Award-winning Edible Communities family of publications. He is the author of the cookbooks, *Chasing Chiles: Hot Spots Along the Pepper Trail* (Chelsea Green, 2011, and *A Cook's Journey: Slow Food in the Heartland* (Ice Cube Books, 2008).

DARCI HALSTEAD GARCIA is a full-time student at Eastern Florida State College working on her BS in health services with a minor in literature. She began writing as a teenager, but only recently professionally. *What Does it Mean to Be White in America?* is her first publication. She currently resides in Palm Bay, Florida.

CAROLE GOZANSKY GARRISON in a former life was an Atlanta police officer and UN supervisor in Cambodia. After completing her PhD at Ohio State University, she spent over thirty years as a professor of criminal justice and women's studies. Recently retired from higher education, she has turned her focus from academic writings to non-fiction short stories. Her most current work appears in *VietNow National Magazine* and the *Sacrifice: What Would You Give?: An Anthology of Inspirational Essays.*

ELENA HARAP co-edited and contributed to the anthologies, *Laughing in the Kitchen,* and *The Bones We Carry.* Her poems and essays have appeared in *Bayou, Amoskeag, Spare Change News* and *Out of Line,* as well as NPR. She received an honorable mention for poetry in *Anthropology and Humanism* and, as a member of the Streetfeet Women, a 1998 Gustavus Myers Award. Harap holds an MFA in creative nonfiction from Vermont College of Fine Arts, and lives in Putney, Vermont.

AMIE HEASLEY has worked as a freelance writer for the marketing and advertising industry for over a decade. She earned a BA in journalism from Michigan State University and an MFA in creative writing from Western Michigan University. Her work has been featured in the *Stoneboat Literary Journal*. Some of her work can also be found online at *Monkeybicycle, Juked, Prick of The Spindle, Corium,* and *The Boiler Journal.* Heasley resides in Kalamazoo, Michigan and she blogs at chopperchronicles.blogspot.com and aheasley.wordpress.com.

CULLEY HOLDERFIELD is a graduate of the University of North Carolina at Chapel Hill. He writes fiction, poetry, and nonfiction, and his work has appeared in a variety of publications, notably *Wildfire Magazine and Earth and Soul: An Anthology of North Carolina Poetry* with poetry forthcoming from Damfino Press. He works in community development finance in Durham, North Carolina.

DANIEL M. JAFFE received an AB from Princeton University, a JD from Harvard Law School, and an MFA from Vermont College. He has published three books of fiction, recently *The Genealogy of Understanding* (Lethe Press, 2014), as well as the chapbook, *One-Foot Lover* (Seven Kitchens Press, 2009), and dozens of short stories and personal essays in various literary journals and anthologies. He compiled and edited *With Signs and Wonders: An International Anthology of Jewish Fabulist Fiction* (Invisible Cities Press, 2001). He also translated Dina Rubina's Russian-Israeli novels, *Here Comes the Messiah!* (Zephyr Press, 2000); and *The White Dove of Córdoba* (2010), currently being developed into a feature film. Jaffe won the 2003 John E. Profant Foundation for the Arts Literature Competition, and has been a finalist for numerous literary awards such as the 2014 Rainbow Awards, the 2009 American Fiction Prize, and *ForeWord Magazine's* 2002 Book of the Year Awards. He currently resides in Santa Barbara, California. http://danieljaffe.tripod.com.

KAREN R. JOHNSON, a former English teacher, now a freelance writer and mother of three, earned her BA degree at the College of the Holy Cross in Worcester, Massachusetts and an MA at The University of Nebraska, Omaha.

Her MA was earned upon her completion of her thesis: "The Dynamics of Racism and White Privilege in an Urban Public School." Johnson is a contributor in the anthology, *Lose the Cape: Never Will I Ever (and then I had kids!)* (Kat Biggie Press, 2015), and her work has also been featured in *The Good Men Project, Scary Mommy,* and *Good Housekeeping,* and elsewhere. She resides in the Kansas City area and blogs at *The 21st Century SAHM.* http://www.the21stcenturysahm.com.

BEN JOHNSTON is a graduate of the York College of Pennsylvania. He was awarded third place in the creative nonfiction category of the Bob Hoffman Writing Contest. This is his first time appearing in a widely published work. He currently resides in Pennsylvania.

ALEXANDER JONES has published several works of short fiction and poetry. His short stories have been published widely, notably in *FarCryZine, Bastion Magazine, DenimSkin, Carrot Bean Magazine, Babbling of the Irrational, Hopper Review, Squawk Back,* and *Crack the Spine.* His fiction, "Driving Out in the Woods One Night" was featured in Akashic Book's Wilderness Wednesday series. He won the 2012 GoRail Freight Railroad Essay Contest, and one of his short stories received an honorable mention in Writer's Digest 2015 Annual Short Story Contest. Jones has a BA in English with a creative writing concentration from State University of New York, New Paltz, an AAS in plumbing and heating technology from NEIT, and a welding certificate from Apex Technical School. He is both a metal fabricator and freelance writer, and lives in Jersey City.

J. KATES is a poet and literary translator who lives in Fitzwilliam, New Hampshire. He serves as the president and co-director of Zephyr Press, a non-profit press that focuses on contemporary works in translation from Russia, Eastern Europe and Asia. He has been awarded a National Endowment for the Arts Creative Writing Fellowship in Poetry, a Translation Project Fellowship, an Individual Artist Fellowship from the New Hampshire State Council on the Arts, and the Cliff Becker Book Prize in Translation for the *Selected Poems of Mikhail Yeryomin* (White Pine Press, 2014). A former president of the American Literary Translators Association, he is the translation editor of *Contemporary Russian Poetry,* the editor of *In the Grip of Strange Thoughts: Russian Poetry in a New Era* (Zephyr Press, 2000), and co-translator of four books of Latin American poetry. Kates has published three poetry chapbooks, recently *Metes and Bounds* (Accents Publishing, 2010), and *The Old*

Testament (Cold Hub Press, 2010); and the poetry collection, *The Briar Patch: Selected Poems & Translations* (Hobblebush Books, 2012). His latest translation, *Muddy River: Selected Poems by Sergey Stratanovsky* (Carcanet Press, 2016), is forthcoming.

BARBARA KELLAM-SCOTT has been a published writer for almost thirty-five years, building a career writing features for local newspapers, trade magazines and regional papers, and corporate ghostwriting in telecommunications. She earned a BA in intercultural studies at Ramapo College of New Jersey, completed graduate work in sociology at Princeton University, received a certificate in Christian theology from Newark School of Theology, and studied Hebrew at Princeton Theological Seminary. Her work on the Bellcore EXCHANGE was repeatedly recognized by her peers in the Society for Technical Communications. She is an advocate for social justice issues on local, regional, and national levels as an Elder in the Presbyterian Church (USA), and writes feminist biblical interpretations and other topics in a lay ministry as Writer-in-Residence of the Presbytery of the Palisades. She is currently working on a collection of short stories on race under the working title, *Those People Over There.*

SIDNEY KIDD, born in Dillon, South Carolina, received a BS from Francis Marion University. His work has appeared in *Play Girl Magazine, McSweeney's, Projected Letters, The Atticus Review, Crab Fat Literary Magazine, The Snow Island Review* and *The River Walk Journal.*

LAUREN KINNARD is originally from Columbia, Tennessee and studied at the University of Tennessee. She currently works as a Spanish teacher and diversity practitioner in Atlanta, Georgia. She is pursuing a MS in Social Foundations of Education at Georgia State University. www.lauren-kinnard.blogspot.com.

EMILY A. KLEIN was born and raised in Long Island, New York, and received a BA in language and literature from State University of New York, Old Westbury, and an MA in psychotherapy and social work from Stonybrook University. She recently published her debut poetry collection, *Ember Belly* (2014), and her work has appeared in various publications, including *The Long Island Quarterly* and *The Mighty.* http://spectrumawesome.blogspot.com.

KEITH KOHNHORST has worked as a reporter for KPFA radio (Pacifica), and taught ESL and developmental writing for seventeen years at several Silicon Valley colleges. A prize-winning short-story writer ("Thoroughbred Times"), he is the author of several books, including the popular grammar text, *A*

Phrasal Verb Affair (Pro Lingua Associates). He lives with his family in the Santa Cruz Mountains.

BETH KWIATEK has a graduate degree in social work from the University of Buffalo. When she was a PhD candidate in the women's studies department, she worked as an adjunct instructor and taught a feminist theory and practice course, as well as developed and taught a consciousness-raising and anti-racism course. When Kwiatek left the university after the long-standing women's studies department folded, she has since worked for over fifteen years as a social and social justice worker in the city of Buffalo. She is currently focusing on her blog *iiswhite* at https://iiswhite.wordpress.com.

ABE LATEINER taught low-income children in public schools for ten years, when burnout offered him the opportunity to look in the mirror and begin to understand whiteness. He now works as a racial justice activist, educator, and organizer of white people in support of black lives. He also organizes young progressive people with wealth via Resource Generation and other donor networks. Lateiner is a co-founder of the Port Cafe, a pay-what-you-can pop-up community cafe in Cambridge, Massachusetts. He documents his journey to collaboratively deprogram his supremacist mentalities at www.risksomething.org.

MARIA LISELLA is the sixth winner in the competition for Queens Poet Laureate 2015-2018, and the first Italian American. She is the author of the collection, *Thieves in the Family,*(NYQ Books, 2014), and two chapbooks, *Amore on Hope Street* and *Two Naked Feet.* Her work will appear in the forthcoming anthology, *The Travelers a Vade Mecum,* published by Red Hen Press. A charter member of the online poetry circle brevitas, she co-curates the Italian American Writers Association readings, and is a co-founder of the Vito Marcantonio Forum. Lisella is an award-winning travel writer and currently a New York Expert for *USA Today.*

BENJAMIN V. MARSHALL is an associate professor of English at Middlesex County College, New Jersey. He received an MFA in creative writing from the University of Massachusetts in Amherst, and was awarded fellowships from the National Endowment for the Humanities, New Jersey State Council on the Arts, the Virginia Center for the Creative Arts, the Helene Wurlitzer Foundation and the Geraldine R. Dodge Foundation. His full-length plays include *The Red Train Café* at Interact Theatre (Philadelphia), *Pride Film and*

Plays (Chicago), *One Legged Race* at Playwrights Theatre of New Jersey, *Henry's Bridge* at Theatre for a New City (NYC), and *Carlos and LaVonne*, second prize in the Theodore Ward Playwriting Contest (Chicago). Marshall has had short plays produced by HBO's New Writers Workshop, WBEZ's *Off the Air* program and Australia's Short and Sweet Festival, and his poetry and short fiction have appeared in several literary magazines, notably *Art and Understanding, Jonathon* and *phati'tude*. He is a member of the Dramatists Guild.

DEBORAH MASHIBINI-PRIOR is a poet and teaches as an adjunct instructor from her home in Enfield, New Hampshire. She completed an MA in poetry from Southern Illinois University Edwardsville and received the William Carlin Slattery Award for Poetry. Her work has appeared in online and print journals, notably *The Harwood Anthology, American Society: What Poets See, Untamed Ink, Drum Voices Revue, The St. Louis Black Pages, HEArtOnline*, and *Postcard Poems & Prose*.

ANNE MAVOR is a visual artist who grew up in Woods Hole, Massachusetts and currently lives in Portland, Oregon. She has a BA in art from Kirkland College, and an MFA in creative writing from Antioch University, Los Angeles. She also attended the Feminist Studio Workshop at the Woman's Building in Los Angeles where she developed an interest in using personal and social content in her artwork. Another influence has been Reevaluation Counseling, an international peer counseling organization that emphasizes the elimination of all oppressions. She is the author of *Strong Hearts, Inspired Minds: 21 Artists Who Are Mothers Tell Their Stories* (Rowanberry Books, 1996). Her work has appeared in *Yes!, Mothering, Hemispheres, Interweave Knits*, and *The Spirit of Pregnancy: An Interactive Anthology for Your Journey to Motherhood*, www.annemavor.com.

PATRIK MCDADE is the founder and program director at People-Places-Things, Intercultural Communication Services. He has published several articles on language teaching, social justice, and intercultural communication in *Clamor Magazine*, as well as industry specific journals and newsletters. A graduate of the University of Arizona, he received a Teaching English as a Second Language Certificate from Portland State University, where he bases his intercultural work. www.pptpdx.com.

GREGORY MENGEL is a social justice writer and educator whose work focuses on racial and ecological healing. He received his PhD in philosophy and religion from the California Institute of Integral Studies in San Francisco. Mengel's work has appeared in *The Evolutionary Epic: Science's Story and Humanity's Response* and *A Legacy for Living Systems: Gregory Bateson as Precursor to Biosemiotics*, as well as online at AllThingsHealing.com, Pachamama.org, and SensingPlace.com. He is cofounder of Beyond Separation, an organization offering transformational experiences for white-identified people committed to the collective healing of white supremacy. Mengel also teaches in the Untraining White Liberal Racism program offered by The UNtraining. He resides in Oakland, California and blogs at CosmologyOfWhiteness.blogspot.com.

LARRY MONTAGUE grew up in the Adirondack Mountains of New York, and studied at Paul Smith's College. He is a hip-hop artist and stay-at-home dad. He currently resides in Huntington, Vermont. This is his first publication. https://fluentmusic.bandcamp.com.

CHIVVIS MOORE is the author of *First Tie Your Camel, Then Trust in God: An American Feminist in the Arab World* (North Loop Books, 2016), based on sixteen years living in Syria, Egypt and the West Bank. She has worked as a journalist for *The Courier-Journal* in Louisville, Kentucky, and *The Daily Review* in Hayward, California. She currently works for Zawaya, a non-profit organization that seeks to contribute to the multicultural discourse of the San Francisco Bay Area with the Arab arts. She received a BA with honors from Harvard University, and an MA in TOEFL from the American University in Cairo. She lives in Oakland, California.

LEAH MUELLER, an independent writer from Tacoma, Washington is a graduate of Evergreen State College in Olympia. She is the author of the chapbook, *Queen of Dorksville* (Crisis Chronicles Press, 2012), and two full-length books, *Allergic to Everything* (Writing Knights Press, 2015) and *The Underside of the Snake* (Red Ferret Press, 2015). Mueller's work has appeared in *Origins Journal, Talking Soup, Silver Birch Press, Semaphore, MaDCap, Cultured Vultures*, and many other publications. She is a regular contributor to *Quail Bell* magazine, and was a featured poet at the 2015 New York Poetry Festival.

ELENA MURPHY was born and raised in the San Francisco Bay Area. She earned her BA in social work at San Francisco State University and currently lives in Oakland, California. *What Does It Mean to Be White in America?* is her first publication.

PAMELA NATH has a PhD in counseling and developmental psychology from the University of Notre Dame. She currently lives and works in New Orleans as a community organizer for Mennonite Central Committee. Nath is also a member of European Dissent, a group of white people affiliated with the People's Institute for Survival and Beyond who are organizing for racial justice and collective liberation. Her work has been published in *The Mennonite* and *Bridge the Gulf,* a blog.

HARMONY NEAL has a BA from Knox College, and an MFA from the University of Illinois, and was the 2011-2013 Fiction Fellow at Emory University. Her essays and stories have been published in *Eleven Eleven, Psychopomp, Gulf Coast, Nashville Review, The Gettysburg Review, Alaska Quarterly Review, New Letters, Grist, Paper Darts, storySouth,* and *The Toast,* among others. She currently resides in Northfield, Minnesota.

JULIE PARSON NESBITT received an MFA in creative writing at University of Pittsburgh, and is currently working towards an MA in social and cultural foundations of education at DePaul University. She is the author of the poetry collection *Finders* (West End Press, 1996), and co-editor with Michael Warr and Luis J. Rodriguez of *Power Lines: A Decade of Poetry from Chicago's Guild Complex* (Tia Chucha Press, 1999). A recipient of the Gwendolyn Brooks Significant Illinois Poet Award, Nesbitt is a contributing editor to West End Press. She lives and works in Chicago.

AMY NOCTON was born in Iowa but has lived most of her life in Connecticut. She holds an MA in international affairs with a specialization in Latin American Studies from the University of Connecticut, an MA in education from the University of Hartford, and an MA in Spanish from Middlebury College. She also studied at the Università di Firenze and has traveled extensively throughout the Spanish-speaking world. Nocton published a Spanish-language short story in *Inti: Revista Literatura Hispánica,* poetry in the Connecticut Writing Project's *Teacher-Writer,* and recently published two co-authored conference proceedings with the International Conference ICT for Language Learning, She is an adjunct professor of English at the University of Connecticut and teaches Spanish and Italian at RHAM High School, where upper-level Spanish students receive Early College Experience (ECE) credit from the UConn where she won the UConn Institute for Teaching and Learning's ECE Teacher of the Year Award in 2012. Her high school students publish a bilingual blog during the academic year called *Perdidos en sus pensamientos,* which can be found at https://theunnamedspanishblog. wordpress.com.

AL ORMSBY, a retired civil servant and long-time activist, has been involved in numerous political as well as social justice campaigns for many years, with his efforts focused primarily on media communications. He has an undergraduate degree in political science from the State University of New York at Buffalo, and has done graduate work at NYU and the New School of Social Research. He is the author of *Justice For All: Liberalism in its Finest Hour* (Shires Press, 2015), and lives in Saratoga Springs, New York.

MEG J. PETERSEN is the director of the National Writing Project in New Hampshire, and a professor of English at Plymouth State University. Her work has appeared in *Sargasso Quisqueya: La Republica Extended, phati'tude, Concrete Wolf, English Journal, Regrets Only, The Why and Later, The International Journal for Teaching Writing,* and other publications. Petersen is a former New England Teachers of English Association poet of the year, and a featured poet on the NH Poets Showcase. She was the recipient of a Fulbright fellowship to the Dominican Republic to work with teachers on teaching writing.

JAN PRIDDY received an MFA in writing from Pacific University, and completed her undergraduate work in the visual arts at the University of Washington. Her poetry, fiction, and nonfiction have earned her an Oregon Literary Arts Fellowship, Arts & Letters Fellowship, Soapstone residency, and a Pushcart nomination. Her work has been published in journals such as *The MacGuffin, CALYX, Work Magazine, Raven Chronicles, The Humanist,* and *North American Review,* as well as in *Women Runners.* Priddy lives, teaches, and writes in the northwest corner of her home state of Oregon, and blogs at *Quiet Minds,* http://janpriddyoregon.blogspot.com.

KRISTINA QUYNN was raised in an interracial family in Colorado. After earning a PhD at Michigan State University, she returned to Colorado to teach contemporary literature and argumentative writing at Colorado State University, Fort Collins. Her research focuses on topics of gender, self-representation, and experimentations with form in modern and contemporary literature and criticism. Her work has appeared in *The Journal of the Midwest Modern Language Association, Drama and Dismemberment/Dismemberment of Drama,* and *The Encyclopedia of Sex and Gender.* She is currently co-editor of *Critical Innovations: Reading and Writing Experimental Texts,* a collection of experimental, enacted literary criticism.

JOHN RAILEY is the editorial page editor of the *Winston-Salem Journal* and the author of the memoir *Rage to Redemption in the Sterilization Age: A Confrontation with American Genocide* (Cascade Books, 2015). A native of Tidewater, Virginia and graduate of the University of North Carolina at Chapel Hill, Railey has won numerous state and national awards for his work.

BETSY REEDER, raised in rural Maryland, studied writing at Towson University and ecology at the University of California at Davis, and currently works as a biologist. Her poetry appeared in the *Maryland Poetry Review*, and she has published articles, editorials, and poems in a variety of non-profit publications. Academic works have been published by Harcourt, as well as in-house by Loyola University Maryland.

GENNA RIVIECCIO received her BA in screenwriting from Loyola Marymount University. She has received a number of festival recognitions for her screenplays from The Indie Gathering, Austin Film Festival and writemovies.com. She later transitioned to literature after moving to New York and published her first novel, *She's Lost Control* (Lulu, 2011), and started a literary quarterly called, *The Opiate*. Rivieccio's work has also appeared on *thosethatthis*, *The Toast* and *Pop-Matters*. She runs the pop culture blog, *Culled Culture*, www.culledculture.com.

CHRISTOPHER M. RZIGALINSKI was raised in South River, New Jersey. He received an MA in American studies from Rutgers University-Newark. His sound collages appear as companions to *With Regard To: Light and Dark* (2015). Rzigalinski is planning to relocate to Los Angeles to further his career pursuits. www.cmrzigalinski.com.

LORRAINE SAINT PIERRE has an MFA from Sarah Lawrence College, Bronxville, New York. She is a seeress, a spiritual counselor in private practice, professional name, LuhrenLoup. She has written the novels *COMICS, 53, Alice in the World;* and *Converting Hull 1042;* a memoir, *Manhattan Seeress;* and a poetry chapbook, *The Arcanum.* Her novel *COMICS* was staged at the University of Maine, Orono, she performed in *Waste & Void,* a theatrical one-act film; and she has worked on *The Spirit of John Lennon,* a filmed ritual with artist Gianni Motti at Metro Pictures Art Gallery in New York City, and *In The Cards,* a documentary about her life and work. "On Moving To Harlem" is part of an ongoing larger work, as yet untitled. www.luhrenloup.com.

BONNIE SCHELL has a BA from Agnes Scott College and an MA from Arizona State University. Her poetry and short stories have appeared in *Quarry West 35/36, Poets & Writers of the Monterey Bay, Cream City Review, WNC Woman, Chinquapin 9 & 15, Knut House: Insanity Edition, Coast Lines: Eight Santa Cruz Poets* (Small Poetry Press, 1996) and *Flash Fiction: When Genres Collide* (Peak Output Unlimited, 1990). Schell, who was raised in Atlanta, Georgia, and spent thirty years living in California, retired from mental health advocacy work and now lives in Asheville, North Carolina.

SAM SHAIN resides in Hallowell, Maine. He is a former journalist, aspiring novelist, a dreamer, and a bullshit detector.

SARA SHERR recently graduated with an MFA in poetry from Adelphi University. She studied literature at Ursinus College in Pennsylvania, where she was co-president of the Literary Society. Her poems have been published in *Metazen, Corvus,* and *The Lantern.* She currently lives in New York City, and is the lead writer for spoilednyc.com.

REBEL SOWELL earned her MFA in creative writing from Southern New Hampshire University. She has published short stories and poetry in literary magazines: *The Tableau, The Sandstorm,* and *Chaos West of the Pecos.* Her short story "Lonely People" in the *Riding Light Review* was recently nominated for the Pushcart Prize. She has written two novels and is currently writing a third. Raised in West Texas, she now resides in Norman, Oklahoma.

JANIE STARR is a writer and activist, living on an island in Washington State, where she leads anti-racism ally workshops, and works for environmental and social justice. She earned an MPH in women's sexuality from the University of North Carolina, Chapel Hill, and an MA in psychology from Antioch University, Seattle. The author of the memoir, *Bone Marrow Boogie, the Dance of a Lifetime* (Kota Press, 2002), her essays have appeared in *RN Journal for Nurses, Applied Radiology, Ducts.org, Wanderlustandlipstick.com,* and the anthologies, *Cup of Comfort for Women,* and *Female Nomad And Friends.*

RABBI GIL STEINLAUF joined Adas Israel Congregation in Washington D.C. as senior rabbi in 2008. In 2014, Steinlauf is the first senior rabbi of a large, historic, conservative congregation to come out as openly gay. He is a summa cum laude graduate of Princeton University, studied at the Pardes Institute in Jerusalem, earned an MHL from the University of Judaism, and received rabbinic ordination and an MA at the Jewish Theological Seminary in New York. Steinlauf has pioneered three nationally recognized projects now operating out of Adas Israel: YP@AI for Jewish Young Professionals, MakomDC for twenty-first century experiential learning, and the Jewish Mindfulness Center of Washington for meditation, yoga, and contemplative Jewish practices. As a result, he has bridged the congregation's traditional and less-traditional gaps, and fostered intelligent, authentic dialogue about LBGT issues, as well as many other cutting-edge issues, in twenty-first century Judaism and Jewish culture.

SUSAN STERLING received a PhD in comparative literature from the University of California at Berkeley and an MFA from Warren Wilson College. Her essays and stories have appeared in *The New York Times, The North American Review, The Christian Science Monitor, Crab Orchard Review, Witness, cream city review, Under the Sun, Down East, The Marlboro Review,* and *The Examined Life,* among other journals. Her works have been anthologized in *The Best American Sports Writing 1998, The Berkeley Women's Literary Revolution, The Way Life Should Be: Stories by Contemporary Maine Writers,* and *A Healing Touch: True Stories of Life, Death,* and *Hospice.* Her essay "Radiation Blooms" was awarded the John Guyon Prize in Literary Nonfiction by *Crab Orchard Review* and was listed as a notable essay in *The Best American Essays 2007.* Sterling is also the author of the novel, *Dancing in the Kitchen* (Publerati, 2012). She currently resides in Falmouth, Maine.

BECKY SWANBERG graduated from Grace University with a BA in elementary education and the Bible. After working with teens for seven years, she is currently a stay-at-home mom in Omaha, Nebraska.

SAM TANNER received his PhD in critical literacy and English education from the University of Minnesota. He taught high school English and drama in the Twin Cities for twelve years prior to accepting a job as an assistant professor of literacy education in the Pennsylvania State University system. His academic work has appeared in such publications as *English Journal* and *Research in Drama Education.* He recently published, *Shot Across the River Styx* (The Daily Publishing Press, 2015), an amalgam of magical realism and memoir. He lives in State College Pennsylvania. http://www.samjtanner.com.

JAMIE UTT is a diversity and consultant and sexual violence prevention educator who works with schools to create more equitable, safer, and more justice-centered educational environments. He is currently pursuing his PhD in Teaching, Learning, and Sociocultural studies at the University of Arizona where he is studying the role that white educators' racial identity plays in their teaching practice. He lives in Tucson, Arizona. http://jamieutt.com.

JULIE DREYER WANG received her BA from McGill University, an MA in landscape design from Radcliffe College, and attended the Harvard Business School Owner President Management Program. She is the co-author, with Neil Olshan of *Everything You Wanted to Know About Phobias But Were Afraid to Ask* (Beaufort Books, 1981). Her work has been published in *New York Magazine, Psychology Today, Harper's Bazaar, Vogue, Pharmaceutical Executive,* and online in *Mused—the Bella Online Literary Review.* Born in England, Wang was educated in Canada, and currently divides her time between coastal Maine and Benin, West Africa.

WENDY ZAGRAY WARREN, an educator and teacher-educator for over twenty-five years, recently earned her EdD, and currently works as an independent writer and scholar, and as a consultant for the Memorial Library/Olga Lengyel Institute for Holocaust Studies and Human Rights. Her work has appeared in *The Poverty and Education Reader: A Call for Equity in Many Voices, Phi Delta Kappan,* where she served as guest-editor for a special section on Montana's Indian Education for All, the *Journal of the Montana Writing Project,* and *Full Circle: A Journal for Teachers Implementing Indian Education for All,* where, as co-founder, she also served as director of publications. Warren currently lives near Berea, Kentucky.

CAROL WELIKY grew up in Brooklyn, New York and attended Brooklyn College. She later received a BA in English from Portland State University. She has written songs, poetry and short fiction, and has collaborated on several projects with other writers and artists. A line of her poetry, stamped in concrete, can be found along Portland's newest light rail line. Weliky retired from public service in 2014, and is currently at work on a novel.

ARIANE WHITE earned an MEd from the Institute for Humane Education, and a BA in Chinese language and literature with a minor in Spanish language and literature from Middlebury College. She earned a single-subject teaching credential in English from UCLA and has been an educator in the Los Angeles area for more than a decade. Her work has appeared in the *Harvard Educational Review.*

ADAM WIER was born in Indianapolis, moved to New York City at seventeen. He earned a BA in Spanish-English Translation from Hunter College (CUNY), where he graduated summa cum laude and valedictorian. He served as the head translator for *¡Hey Yo! ¡Yo Soy! 40 Years of Nuyorican Street Poetry* (2Leaf Press, 2012) and *¿What's in a Nombre? (phati'tude,* 2012). He has also translated articles for the online magazine *Warscapes* (2013) and was one of several translators to bring Roberto Echavarren's book, *The Russian Nights* (forthcoming) to English. Wier has penned three original plays produced by Haberdash Theatre, *The Asexual Revolution* (2007), *Remember Me* (2006), and *Tom's Dilemma* (2008). He won a Fulbright Fellowship and relocated to Cali, Colombia to teach. He currently lives in Le Mans, France where he teaches English and translates Spanish and French to English. ∎

ABOUT GABRIELLE DAVID

PHOTO: Samuel LaHoz

GABRIELLE DAVID is a multidisciplinary artist who is a musician, photographer, digital designer (epub, print and web), poet and writer. She attended LaGuardia Community College (CUNY) and New School University.

For twenty-four years, she worked as a desktop publisher and word processing specialist at Fortune 500 firms, and through her former company, Chimeara Communications, Inc., designed promotional materials for a wide range of clients. David managed and performed in bands during the 1970s and early 1980s; and was a partner of hotshots unlimited photography (1982-1986). She became involved in the New York poetry scene during the 1990s and served as literature coordinator at the Langston Hughes Community Library and Cultural Center in Queens throughout most of that decade. Her work with the library prompted the creation of *phati'tude Literary Magazine*, which eventually became a programming incentive under the Intercultural Alliance of Artists & Scholars, Inc. (IAAS), a NY-based nonprofit organization which she founded in 2000 and has served as executive director since its inception. Other program initiatives include phatLiterature, A Literary TV Program, and 2Leaf Press, of which she currently serves as publisher. David has participated in panel discussions and workshops, published articles and essays in numerous publications, and is the editor of *Branches of the Tree of Life,* (2014), and co-editor of *¡Hey Yo! Yo Soy, 40 Years of Nuyorican Street Poetry* (2012). She is the author of the chapbooks, *Spring Has Returned and I Am Renewed* (1996), and *This is Me: A Collection of Poems and Things* (1994). Her collection of essays, *Beyond Identity: Exploring Multicultural Literature in the 21st Century,* is forthcoming. www.gabrielle-david.com. ▪

ABOUT SEAN FREDERICK FORBES

SEAN FREDERICK FORBES is a professor, scholar and the author of the poetry collection, *Providencia: A Book of Poems* (2013). His work has appeared in various journals including *Chagrin River Review, Crab Orchard Review, Long River Review, Midwest Quarterly,* and *Sargasso: A Journal of Caribbean Literature, Language and Culture.*

Forbes has appeared on radio and television programs, and his work was featured online on Poem-a-Day, sponsored by the Academy of American Poets in 2014. He studied English and Africana Studies at Queens College (CUNY), where he was an Andrew W. Mellon Fellow, and went on to receive his MA and PhD in English from the University of Connecticut. In 2009, Forbes received a Woodrow Wilson Mellon Mays University Fellows Travel and Research Grant for travel to Providencia, Colombia.

He currently serves as a board member of the Intercultural Alliance of Artists & Scholars, Inc. (IAAS), is the series editor of 2Leaf Press' series, 2LP EXPLORATIONS IN DIVERSITY, and is the poetry and nonfiction reader for the journal *WESTVIEW* published by Southwestern Oklahoma State University. Forbes teaches creative writing and poetry, and is the director of the creative writing program at the University of Connecticut. He leads professional learning and growth workshops for elementary and secondary school teachers who seek to advance creative writing to the language arts curriculum. He was the associate director of Humanities House, a living and learning community, at the University of Connecticut during the 2013-2014 academic year. www.seanfrederickforbes.com. ∎

ABOUT DEBBY IRVING

PHOTO: Emily Irving

DEBBY IRVING is a racial justice educator, consultant, trainer, and public speaker, and the author of the acclaimed book, *Waking Up White* (2012). Having worked as a community organizer and classroom teacher for twenty-five years, Irving is devoted to working with white people to raise awareness of the differential impacts that interactions, communities, and institutions can have on people along racial lines. She strives to equip and motivate white people to engage in racial justice initiatives with resilience, skill, courage and humility. Irving's early career included serving as General Manager of Boston's Dance Umbrella and later First Night Boston, where she developed outreach programs connecting Boston youth with artists. Both organizations sparked her interest in building community and her awareness of the complexities inherent in working across difference. Her professional focus eventually shifted to K-12 education, which ultimately led her to the graduate school course, "Racial and Cultural Identities," which influenced and changed the trajectory of her life to become a racial justice educator.

A graduate of the Winsor School in Boston, she holds a BA from Kenyon College and an MBA from Simmons College. She has trained with The People's Institute for Survival and Beyond, Crossroads Anti-Racism, VISIONS, Lee Mun Wah's Mindful Facilitation, and has appeared at The White Privilege Conference, NCORE, National Summit for Courageous Conversation, National Race Amity Conference, the People of Color Conference, and Facing Race. An enthusiastic lifelong learner, Irving works regularly with her coach Dr. Eddie Moore Jr. to stay focused on growing beyond white patterns of thought and behavior. She has appeared on numerous television and radio programs, notably MSNBC and Tedx Talk. www.debbyirving.com. ■

ABOUT TARA BETTS

PHOTO: Tony Smith/DesignSmith

TARA BETTS is an award-winning poet, author and scholar. She holds a PhD in English from Binghamton University, and an MFA in creative writing from New England College. She was a lecturer in creative writing at Rutgers University in New Brunswick, New Jersey and is currently a professor at University of Illinois. A Cave Canem graduate, she held residencies from the Ragdale Foundation, Centrum and Caldera, and was awarded an Illinois Arts Council Artist fellowship. Her work has appeared in numerous journals and anthologies, including *POETRY, Ninth Letter, Crab Orchard Review, Essence, Gathering Ground, Bum Rush the Page, Villanelles,* both *Spoken Word Revolution* anthologies, *The Break Beat Poets, Octavia's Brood: Science Fiction Stories from Social Justice Movements,* and *GHOST FISHING: An Eco-Justice Poetry Anthology.*

Betts serves as the poetry editor for *Blackberry: a magazine* and is a contributing editor for *Radius.* An activist, she co-founded GirlSpeak, a weekly writing/leadership workshop for young women, and over the years has worked with numerous organizations by conducting short-term workshops in schools, community centers, jail, and detention centers. She appeared on HBO's "Def Poetry Jam" and the Black Family Channel series "SPOKEN" with Jessica Care Moore, and has performed in Cuba, London, New York, the West Coast, and the Midwest at venues such as The New School, The Museum of Contemporary Art, and Studio Museum of Harlem, with appearances at festivals throughout the country. Betts is the author of *Arc and Hue* (2009) and the libretto, *The Greatest: An Homage to Muhammad Ali* (2010). Her book, *Break the Habit* (Trio House Press), is forthcoming. www.tarabetts.net ∎

OTHER BOOKS BY 2LEAF PRESS

2Leaf Press challenges the status quo by publishing alternative fiction, nonfiction, poetry and bilingual works by activists, academics, poets and authors dedicated to diversity and social justice with scholarship that is accessible to the general public. 2Leaf Press produces high quality and beautifully produced hardcover, paperback and ebook formats through our series: 2LP Translations, 2LP Classics, Nuyorican World Series, and 2LP Explorations in Diversity.

NOVELS
The Morning Side of the Hill
A Novella by Ezra E. Fitz, with an Introduction by Ernesto Quiñonez

LITERARY NONFICTION
Our Nuyorican Thing, The Birth of a Self-Made Identity
by Samuel Carrion Diaz, with an Introduction by Urayoán Noel
(NUYORICAN WORLD SERIES)

YOUNG ADULT
Puerto Rican Folktales/Cuentos folclóricos puertorriqueños
by Lisa Sánchez González
(NUYORICAN WORLD SERIES)
(Available in Hard Cover only)

ANTHOLOGIES

What Does it Mean to be White in America? Breaking the White Code of Silence, A Collection of Personal Narratives
Edited by Gabrielle David and Sean Frederick Forbes
Introduciton by Debby Irving and Afterword by Tara Betts
(2LP EXPLORATIONS IN DIVERSITY)
For more information about the contributors,
visit our website at www.whiteinamerica.org

WHEREABOUTS: Stepping Out of Place,
An Outside in Literary & Travel Magazine Anthology
Edited by Brandi Dawn Henderson

PLAYS

Rivers of Women, The Play
by Shirley Bradley LeFlore, with photographs by Michael J. Bracey
(Available in Paperback only)

POETRY

Tartessos and Other Cities, Poems by Claire Millikin
by Claire Millikin, with an Introduction by Fred Marchant

Off Course: Roundabouts & Deviations
by A. Robert Lee

The Death of the Goddess, A Poem in Twelve Cantos
by Patrick Colm Hogan,
with an Introduction by Rachel Fell McDermott

Branches of the Tree of Life, The Collected Poems of Abiodun Oyewole 1969-2013
by Abiodun Oyewole, edited by Gabrielle David,
with an Introduction by Betty J. Dopson

After Houses, Poetry for the Homeless
by Claire Millikin, with an Introduction by Tara Betts

Birds on the Kiswar Tree
by Odi Gonzales, Translated by Lynn Levin
(2LP TRANSLATIONS)

Boricua Passport
by J.L. Torres
(NUYORICAN WORLD SERIES)

Incessant Beauty, A Bilingual Anthology
by Ana Rossetti, Edited and Translated by Carmela Ferradáns
(2LP TRANSLATIONS)

The Last of the Po'Ricans y Otros Afro-artifacts
Poems by Not4Prophet, Graphics by Vagabond
with an Introduction by Tony Medina
(NUYORICAN WORLD SERIES)

Providencia, A Book of Poems
by Sean Frederick Forbes, with an Introduction by V. Penelope Pelizzon

Broke Baroque
by Tony Medina, with an Introduction by Ishmael Reed

Brassbones & Rainbows, The Collected Works of Shirley Bradley LeFlore
by Shirley Bradley LeFlore, Preface by Amina Baraka,
with an Introduction by Gabrielle David

Imaginarium: Sightings, Galleries, Sightlines
by A. Robert Lee

Hey Yo! Yo Soy!, 40 Years of Nuyorican Street Poetry
The Collected Works of Jesús Papoleto Meléndez

by Jesús Papoleto Meléndez
Edited by Gabrielle David and Kevin E. Tobar Pesántez
Translations by Adam Wier, Carolina Fung Feng, Marjorie González
Foreword by Samuel Diaz and Carmen M. Pietri-Diaz,
Introduction by Sandra Maria Esteves,
Afterword by Jaime "Shaggy" Flores
(NUYORICAN WORLD SERIES)

All eBook editions are available on Amazon/Kindle, Barnes & Noble/
Nook, Kobo, iTunes/iBooks, Google Play, and other online outlets.
Check out our catalogs and book previews at 2Leaf Press' website.

2Leaf Press is an imprint owned and operated by the Intercultural
Alliance of Artists & Scholars, Inc. (IAAS), a NY-based nonprofit organization that publishes and promotes multicultural literature.

NEW YORK
www.2leafpress.org

CPSIA information can be obtained
at www.ICGtesting.com
Printed in the USA
FSOW03n1958250716
23111FS